····· STRUNG OUT ON ARCHAEOLOGY ·····

STRUNG OUT ON
ARCHAEOLOGY

AN INTRODUCTION TO ARCHAEOLOGICAL RESEARCH

· · · · ·

LAURIE A. WILKIE

WITH ILLUSTRATIONS BY
ALEXANDRA WILKIE FARNSWORTH

Routledge
Taylor & Francis Group

LONDON AND NEW YORK

First published 2014 by Left Coast Press, Inc.

Published 2016 by Routledge
2 Park Square, Milton Park, Abingdon, Oxon OX14 4RN
52 Vanderbilt Avenue, New York, NY 10017

Routledge is an imprint of the Taylor & Francis Group, an informa business

Library of Congress Cataloging-in-Publication Data

Wilkie, Laurie A., 1968-
Strung out on archaeology:an introduction to archaeological research/Laurie A. Wilkie; with illustrations by Alexandra Wilkie Farnsworth.
     pages cm
Includes bibliographical references and index.
ISBN 978-1-61132-267-5 (pbk. : alk. paper)—ISBN 978-1-61132-269-9 (consumer ebook)
 1. Archaeology—Methodology. 2. Archaeology and history. 3. Carnival—Louisiana—New Orleans. 4. Beads—Louisiana—New Orleans. 5. New Orleans (La.)—Antiquities. I. Title. II. Title: Introduction to archaeological research.
 CC75.W464 2014
 930.1028—dc23

                    2013049058

ISBN 13: 978-1-61132-267-5 (pbk)

First published 2014 by Left Coast Press, Inc.

Published 2016 by Routledge
2 Park Square, Milton Park, Abingdon, Oxon OX14 4RN
52 Vanderbilt Avenue, New York, NY 10017

Routledge is an imprint of the Taylor & Francis Group, an informa business

Library of Congress Cataloging-in-Publication Data

Wilkie, Laurie A., 1968-
Strung out on archaeology:an introduction to archaeological research/Laurie A. Wilkie; with illustrations by Alexandra Wilkie Farnsworth.
    pages cm
Includes bibliographical references and index.
ISBN 978-1-61132-267-5 (pbk. : alk. paper)—ISBN 978-1-61132-269-9 (consumer ebook)
  1. Archaeology—Methodology. 2. Archaeology and history. 3. Carnival—Louisiana—New Orleans. 4. Beads—Louisiana—New Orleans. 5. New Orleans (La.)—Antiquities. I. Title. II. Title: Introduction to archaeological research.
  CC75.W464 2014
  930.1028—dc23

                            2013049058

ISBN 13: 978-1-61132-267-5 (pbk)

To my daughter Alex:
Let's hope we sell enough of
these to pay for your college education;
if not, it's still really flattering to have a book dedicated to you,
right?

CONTENTS

· · · CONTENTS · · ·

ILLUSTRATIONS

Figures

Tables.

PREFACE:
WHAT IS THIS BOOK ABOUT?

This book is about two of my greatest passions: archaeology and Mardi Gras, and the ways they can inform one another. In the United States, most citizens holding a high school diploma have heard of archaeology and the celebrations of New Orleans Mardi Gras, but are likely to have misconceptions about each. Archaeologists are often conflated with the characters of Indiana Jones, Lara Croft, or some other treasure-hunting adventurer who has been labeled as an archaeologist in popular culture. Likewise, when people hear "Mardi Gras," they are more likely than not to think simply of girls-gone-wild-spring-break-type debauchery without having any sense of the traditions and heritage associated with these centuries-old traditions. A text book revolving around these topics gives me the opportunity to illuminate understandings of one of these topics through the other and vice versa. While this book is primarily an introduction to Archaeology, I will use a contemporary archaeology project focusing on the bead throwing culture of Louisiana Mardi Gras to explain and illustrate archaeological thought and methodology.

You might think, Mardi Gras and Archaeology? Together? That seems like a cynical mash-up imagined by a publisher to sell a less-than-solid introductory textbook, doesn't it? But no, the idea originated with me and for some particular personal and intellectual reasons. To explain why this book exists as it does requires some background information, or what we will later learn the post-processualist archaeologists called "historical context".

A few years ago, the *New York Times* ran an article profiling a local man who was a retired public servant (a fire-fighter, I believe) who liked to dig up local bottle pits throughout the city. The article portrayed the gentleman, who was very enthusiastic about what he did, as a local hero who was bringing to light the city's unknown history. Local archaeologists were appalled—here was a man who was destroying archaeological sites to build a personal collection of artifacts to display at his house.

Archaeologists, as you will see if you read beyond the preface, are very conscious of the fact that every time they excavate a site, that site is destroyed. Excavation is a process through which we dismantle the spatial relationships between things in the ground that have been created by people, the elements, and time. Archaeologists excavate not to find things, but to understand how things got where they are, what that may tell us about how they were used, and what they meant to the people who either intentionally or unintentionally left them there. We use detailed record keeping to ensure that the spatial relationships between things found in the earth are documented for others to access and that the materials we find are kept in a facility that allows future scholars access to those materials.

Archaeologists do not sell things, and they do not keep things. They do not build vast private collections of the things they have found. Because our field methods are time consuming, we take a lot longer to dig a site than a retired guy with a shovel. In fact, it was the recognition that the retired guy with the shovel was destroying more sites than the combined excavation power of New York's archaeological community could scientifically excavate in the same block of time that led to an archaeological backlash against the bottle-hunting local hero on the New York Times' website.

At the time, I read through the postings to see what this whole blow-up had to say about the relationship between archaeologists and the general public, and I noticed several disturbing trends. First, the archaeologists tended to come off as self-righteous pinheads—and secondly, and more importantly, the non-archaeological respondents were greatly in favor of the local hero and condemned the archaeologists as, well, self-righteous pinheads.

Being an archaeologist myself, I recognized that my colleagues' earnestness and passion were being misunderstood and misinterpreted by other readers. However, I also realized that unlike the local hero, who enthusiastically talked about the visceral thrill of finding old objects in the ground, the archaeologists had universally failed to communicate equal enthusiasm for their subject in a way that was accessible. They only managed to look like they were selfishly hogging all the archaeological fun for themselves.

The general public is generally receptive to and interested in archaeology. What we do is pretty cool. We find stuff in the ground and then come up with feasible stories about how it got there and what it means. It's sort of magical or at least, very Sherlock Holmes-like. Our bottle-hunting friend had managed to capture the coolness-of-finding-stuff part of archaeology; the archaeologists failed to convey "why- it's-the-finding-out-how-it-got-there-and-what-it means-that-is-the-more important-part" of the argument.

The chances are, if you are reading this book, it is because you are taking an introductory course in archaeology, and you've chosen to take this class because it seems like a more interesting way to fulfill a social sciences breadth requirement than say, sociology or political science. You would, incidentally, be quite right. You are then, not only a potential anthropology major or future archaeologist, you are also a potential supporter of archaeology long after you leave the university and do something lucrative like practice law or plumbing. It is not merely benevolence to my discipline that I want to instill in you, however. I sincerely believe that thinking like an archaeologist, or learning to see the social world as also a physical one, is a valuable tool for anyone. An introductory course can either solidify your interest in this subject or send you screaming to Sociology 101.

I entered university as a very practical dual major in marketing and advertising (my parents still wonder where they failed). I took my first archaeology class because I had an elective open and the human evolution course that I really wanted to take wasn't being offered until spring. Archaeology was my second choice. An energetic, freshly hired young historical archaeologist taught the course, and was really able to communicate how much he loved his field. His enthusiasm was infectious, and led me to pay attention in lecture and motivated me to read the course materials. I remember not only the lectures from that class but also the two books.

I remember the first book for its dreadful and tedious presentation of the field. It was a textbook that managed to make the fascinating field of archaeology seem boring and pinheaded. The second book, however, was a treasure called *In Small Things Forgotten,* by the historical archaeologist, James Deetz.

I picked up the book to start reading it on a Sunday morning after a hard night of under-aged drinking (okay, maybe it was actually Sunday afternoon). I was still in bed and hadn't managed to raise the blinds in the dorm. I figured reading would be a good way to delay the inevitable departure from bed and the equally inevitable wave of nausea that would greet me. My intention was to read the portion assigned for our discussion section: the first couple of chapters. Instead, I read the book from cover to cover in one reading, and upon finally getting out of bed, found myself excited and invigorated by the possibilities for future research presented in that short, lovely, pithy book. Deetz was able to make a pile of colonial pottery, a bunch of tombstones, postholes, and trash pits enthralling and meaningful. I am not alone when I say that Deetz's book almost single-handedly inspired me to become an archaeologist.

What made Deetz's book so engaging? The recipe is hard to reconstruct exactly. But, it included interesting interpretations connecting materials that didn't seem intuitively to be related until Deetz brought them together; discussions relating material culture to topics of identity, culture and ethnicity that were resonant with contemporary society, and a healthy dollop of good-natured Southern wit.

Further, Deetz did not just give you his interpretations, but he laid out the ideas that influenced him and the thought processes that led to his understanding of the arch-aeological materials. He conveyed the discovery of meaning was just as exciting as the discovery of the things in the first place. If you only read one archaeology book this semester, I would recommend you read the first edition of *In Small Things Forgotten.* If you read two books, however, I would suggest you read this one as well; for the goal of this book is to provide a broader context for the breadth and depth of archaeological thinking than Deetz was able to in his short work and to do it in a more interesting way than the traditional archaeological textbook. Now that the historical context is fleshed out, we can return finally to the point of this preface, what the hell is this book about?

When I sat down to write this book, I hoped to create the anti-text-book textbook. An un-textbook, if you will. I have rarely used textbooks in my 20 plus years of teaching intro-ductory archaeology because frankly, most of them are incredibly boring and annoying. Have you ever wondered what motivates someone to write a textbook?

For the best-selling textbook authors, there are substantial royalties to be made from selling endless new editions of an over-priced text. But there is also a political motivation for writing textbooks—it is a way of defining the discipline to both outsiders and to those who want to become insiders. Textbooks are a way to indoctrinate a generation of new scholars to your vision of what the discipline is or should be. Textbook authors disguise their agenda through such tricks as writing in the third person (this renders the author and his/or her motives invisible) and presenting a single, authoritative narrative about "THE WAY THINGS ARE."

There are a few notable exceptions to this, and to protect myself from insulting too many people by not talking about their books, I will limit myself to mentioning Matthew Johnson's wonderful textbook on archaeological theory, in which he constantly reminds the reader of his authorial presence and his opinions on what he is presenting.

In this book, you will rarely have the opportunity to forget that I am here as your narrator, so hopefully we'll get along all right. My agenda is this: to present an introduction to archaeology that celebrates the intellectual, methodological, and topical diversity of archaeology. Diversity in archaeological practice is a result of diversity in archaeological thinking. There is no one right answer to be had from archaeological remains, despite what many textbooks may lead you to believe.

I get very frustrated by scholars who think there is only one way to think about archaeological materials, and there are only particular kinds of questions worth asking of them. I believe that archaeology is most vibrant and healthy as a field when we have as wide a range of questions and topics being studied through as many different approaches as possible. From any archaeological site, there is the possibility of asking and addressing a multitude of different, and even sometimes, contradictory-seeming questions.

And this is where the Mardi Gras study comes in. Mardi Gras is a well-known American celebration that is usually understood in the popular imagination as a drunken celebration with parades, nudity, and plastic beads. The beads themselves are a ubiquitous and often unremarked upon part of the celebrations. They are, for the most part, rather generic and unremarkable. Most of the beads, if you took them away from the Mardi Gras celebrations, do not possess any characteristics that would distinguish them as Mardi Gras beads from any other generic plastic strand of beads. Yet, when we collect and analyze these artifacts in an archaeological way and subject them to archaeological ways of thinking and interpretation, these mundane objects can be used to understand changing gender roles, world economic relationships, redistribution and exchange relationships between urban and rural communities, group formation, social stratification, population movements, and even expressions of sexual and racial inequality.

While the subjects we can get at through our analysis of the beads are sometimes quite serious, the beads themselves and the process through which they are acquired are quite absurd and ridiculous. Working with such a seemingly trivial sort of artifact helped me to keep a sense of humor, and hopefully kept me from getting too self-righteous or pinheaded in my discussions. Likewise, it is my hope that at times during this book you will alternate between thinking, "this is ludicrous to be spending so much time considering plastic beads" and "oh, wow, archaeology actually works."

Archaeology is a hands-on discipline. We learn by doing, by getting dirty, and by putting our hands on things to figure them out; it requires methodology. But archaeology is also a head-game—the evidence we work with is the material traces left by past peoples, residues of their social lives, and to sort out what these remnants represent requires mental agility; it requires theory. Because we enter into our studies of human life through materials, archaeologists have the ability to bring to light aspects and understandings of the human experience not available through any other means. The chaos that is Mardi Gras is physically experienced in a richly constructed material world, a world best understood through an archaeological perspective. Carnival is about inverting and asserting social order and social relations, and in doing so, making more visible the economic, social, racial, and gender hierarchies that shape contemporary American society. Archaeology is also about rendering things visible. First, through the discovery and recovery of objects from the ground (or the water, such as in shipwreck archaeology, or the air, as in this study), we make objects discarded in the past visible in the present. Through our analysis and interpretation of those objects, we make past human lives observable for our contemporary consideration as well.

The archaeology of Mardi Gras therefore provides a unique opportunity to render visible not only our contemporary society, but also the tools through which we study that society. In other words, by studying Carnival archaeologically, we ultimately will come to learn more about archaeology itself. Or at least, that is my intent in dragging you along in this exercise of mine.

Part of what makes this book unique is that I will draw upon different analyses, tools, or theories in each chapter to create different understandings (or interpretations) of the Mardi Gras beads "excavated" for this project. Typically, textbook authors draw upon a range of different case studies to illustrate different kinds of archaeological methods or areas of study. That approach creates the false impression that to do different kinds of archaeologies requires different kinds of sites or evidence. The point of looking at the Mardi Gras beads over and over again is to demonstrate how asking different research questions of the exact same materials can lead to wildly different (yet all equally valid) interpretations. I will also introduce more traditional case studies from archaeological sites that span a broader chronological and geographical span so that you develop an understanding of how these ideas and methods are used to study more distant human pasts.

Now that I've introduced the why and how of the book, let me briefly tell you what to expect from the structure of the book. I understand that not every reader will have a full understanding of Mardi Gras and its traditions as observed in Louisiana, and have probably never been to a Mardi Gras parade. Therefore, the first chapter recounts what it is like to attend a Mardi Gras parade and begins to introduce my methods and the Mardi Gras Bead contemporary archaeology project that I first developed in 1997. Chapter two provides a fuller introduction to the hows and whats of basic archaeological concepts and introduces the field of contemporary archaeology, of which the Mardi Gras project is part.

Chapters three, four, and five will introduce the trends in thinking that shaped archaeological practice in the past and the methods those ways of thinking introduced to the discipline. When writing the history of archaeological thought, many authors try to suggest an evolutionary sequence, in which one school of thought neatly replaces the previous one. I refute this by illustrating how it was necessary in the study of Mardi Gras beads to draw on the entirety of archaeology's intellectual and methodological history, not just its most recent practices. After completing these chapters, you will have a solid understanding of basic archaeological theorizing and methodological tools and practices, as well as be introduced to some of the well-known characters of archaeology's past.

The second part of the book will be looking at how we can apply different theoretical orientations, methodologies and research questions to the same archaeological assemblage to create multiple, yet all equally valid, interpretations of the human experience of Carnival. Each chapter will highlight a research topic that has been widely studied in archaeology. Chapter six will focus on "technology", chapter seven on economics and trade systems, and chapter eight covers group identity. We will shift to discussing archaeological studies of sex and gender in chapter nine and consider Marxist-influenced studies of power in chapter 10. Environmental disasters, depopulation, sustainability, revitalization movements, and cultural change and diffusion will be explored in chapter 11, and in the final chapter, I will discuss archaeologies of religion, the politics and ethics of archaeological practice, and make final observations on the relationships between archaeology and Mardi Gras. And because this is a textbook, you will find a handy glossary in the back of the book. If you encounter words that are italicized and bold-faced in the text, that term has a glossary entry for your learning pleasure.

My intention is that when we reach the end of this journey together, you will: 1) have a better understanding of what I mean when I say archaeology is both a mindset (or dare I say it, a kind of theoretical position) and a set of techniques that allow us to study the human experience of a material world; and 2) you will have learned a great deal about the uniquely American festival that is Mardi Gras.

Archaeologists are known as a fairly friendly and casual bunch of folks, and nothing is really more open and honest than Mardi Gras where the good, bad, and ugly of people's personalities emerge for all to see. Keeping in the spirit of both Mardi Gras and Archaeology, at the onset of this journey, let's agree that we're going to envision ourselves sitting on a screened porch during a warm Louisiana night. The lights are dim to keep the bugs down, the frogs are chirping outside, we've got a couple of rocking chairs, and more than a few cold beers—unless you're underage, in which case, there are some cokes (the generic term for "soda" in Louisiana), sweet tea, and Abita root beers for you. I warn you, there will be times when I get a little preachy, or seem to be using technical terms, but just be patient and humor an aging archaeologist. We're going to settle in for a nice chat about two of the most fascinating subjects I can imagine—archaeology and Mardi Gras beads.

Acknowledgements

First, I would like to thank the people of Louisiana, particularly New Orleans, who every year, welcome millions of visitors to enjoy the cultural wealth and beauty of their homes. They suffer traffic, a certain number of unforgivably loutish visitors, trash, street closures, crowded restaurants and politely and warmly give directions and guidance. The krewes and other parading organizations put on the greatest free show in the world, and give generously of their time and throws to strangers. I hope that I have done them justice in these pages and have captured their complex and interesting histories and present. As an outsider, I have only presented the face they present to the public, and in no way want to suggest that I understand much about the inner workings of any of these secret societies—that is for others to do. My work here is inspired with great love and affection for what they give to the world in hosting Mardi Gras each year.

Thanks go to many people who have helped with this project over the years. For a project that seems as low-tech as this one was, I have managed to accrue many debts. I would like to thank the many Louisianans who helped me over the years, but particularly Ralph, Diane, and Meredith Chesson, the Krewe of Orpheus, the Pointe Coupe Animal Shelter, and the faculty and graduate students of Lousiana State University's (LSU) department of Geography and Anthropology (be they still there or moved on) for teaching me about and learning about Mardi Gras with me, especially Anne Mosher, Dydia DeLyser, Helen Regis, Bill Davidson, Andrew Curtiss, Sherry Wagoner Toups, and Erica Roberts. David Palmer, Kira Blaisdell-Sloan, Jen Abraham, Jeremy Cramer, and Jude LaGarde were among the folks who caught beads for me at different venues.

Paul Farnsworth was immensely helpful throughout the course of this research, attending parades, providing lab and storage space for way too many beads, and tolerating the screaming females who descended upon him from California at Carnival time. I hope he has as many good memories of Carnival together as Alex and I do.

The staffs of Hill Memorial Library at LSU, Tulane's library, and the New Orleans Historical Collection were all very helpful, as were staff at LSU's periodical room.

In the lab, Danielle Holliman, Leah Grant, and Edward De Harrow have been particularly helpful with sorting through beads; and Danielle, in particular, did a great deal of work with the glass beads. Gloria Keng and Juvenal D. Quiñónes helped during the final stages of the project. Gloria quickly ran across the lab whenever I made a loud gurgling noise while working on Photoshop trying to finalize the figures. She was of the greatest help. When I realized we really had to have a picture of a typical undergraduate toolkit, Juvenal good-naturedly unpacked everything he owned and put it on display for the camera.

I've discussed this project with many people over the years, and I have benefitted particularly from discussions with Rosemary Joyce, Sabrina Agarwal, Junko Habu, Jun Sunseri, Lisa Maher, Kent Lightfoot, Pat Kirch, Margaret Conkey, Ruth Tringham, Steve Shackley, Russell Sheptek, Nico Tripcevich, Mary Beaudry, Doug Armstrong, Rodney Harrison, Dan Hicks, Carolyn White, Sarah Tarlow, Roberta Gilchrist, Kim Christensen, Teresa Bulger, Barb Voss, Heather Law, Bonnie Clark, David Palmer, Kira Blaisdell-Sloan, Anne Mosher, Bernie Brittingham, Annelise Morris, Katrina Eichner, Christopher Lowman, Amy Moreland, David Watson, and Jerry Howard. I apologize to anyone I've forgotten! This project has extended for many years! Some of these same folks have looked at versions of the manuscript or papers that preceded the manuscript, as have Mike Way, Frances Bright, and Christopher Lowman. After reading the manuscript, Mike decided to attend Lundi Gras and was able to collect 2013 assemblages from Orpheus and Proteus for me, ensuring that this book will not be the last word on this subject for me. Annelise Morris gets a special shout-out for coming in for the 9th inning and helping me with editing, formatting, creating the glossary, and other manuscript organizational tasks that allowed her to use her considerable powers of OCD for the benefit of humankind. She is a scholar and a superwoman. Oh, and I should add, she is most definitely a rock star.

I want to thank Amy Moreland and David Watson for helping me find economic and demographic statistics that I used in parts of the study. Mitch Allen has been encouraging throughout this process, and it is a special joy to work with such a gifted professional in the publishing world and an accomplished professional archaeologist. Even in the earliest stages of this work, his input was invaluable, and in the later stages he forced me to expand the work in necessary ways that ultimately have made it a better-rounded work. I am pretty sure that I hated him at times, however. Other people associated with Left Coast Press, Inc. also deserve shout-outs. Ryan Harris helped me work through the electronic files for the figures for the book and with great kindness pointed out that power point doesn't really produce print quality figures and helped with remounting and laying out figures with multiple images from my photograph files. In 1989, I had the great pleasure of working in the Turks and Caicos with a great fellow young UCLA archaeology student … imagine my pleasure when in 2013 I received an email from that same person telling me she was going to help shepherd the book through the copyediting and production process! Jerryll Moreno is easily the best copyeditor I have ever worked with. It makes such a difference when you work with someone who is also a professional archaeologist! I've greatly enjoyed her professionalism as well as catching up after so many years (though despite the passage of years, we're both still really young, just to be clear). I would also like to thank Margery Cantor who designed this work, and all of the other folks who helped shepherd the book through publication and distribution.

I would like to acknowledge (or pay homage, since each has retired to the celestial Carnival) to three authors who have served as inspiration for me through the legacy of their works: James Deetz, Lyle Saxon, and Robert Tallant. I think every student who studies historical archaeology wants to grow up to be Jim Deetz after reading *In Small Things Forgotten*. I have no such delusions, but rereading his wonderful prose inspires me to at least *attempt* to be a better, more charming, and accessible Laurie Wilkie. Lyle Saxon and Robert Tallant were writers and chroniclers of Louisiana's folk culture, and through their lyrical prose they were able to capture the joy, frustration, humor, and absurdity that is Louisiana's festival life. If I have managed to at least channel their great warmth and affection for Louisiana in writing this book, I'll be very satisfied.

I want to give particular love and thanks to Alexandra Wilkie Farnsworth and Mark Cooper Emerson, my two Muses. Alex has accompanied me to every field season and has become an expert on Mardi Gras in her own right. I could always count on her being ready to add an additional site to our season and to work hard to collect the biggest sample. She helped sort, catalog, and analyze plastic beads, cups, doubloons, stuffed animals, and other silliness we collected as part of this work. She has grown up surrounded by the colors purple, green, and gold and never lost her enthusiasm for the project. As my illustrator, she has created lovely renditions of the medallions and captured something of the essence of classic archaeological field reports in her inked drawings. Mardi Gras beads are not as exciting in the lab as they are in the field, but as a photographer, Alex has tried to make the beads pop with life, as well as capture some of the chaos and excitement of the contexts from which they were excavated. Mark came into my life after the research for this project was nearly complete. Mardi Gras is the last place I can imagine my husband Mark, a man who prefers open spaces to large crowds, but he has helped me search through west Texas thrift shops for beads, and kindly shared his office at Sul Ross State University during the fall of 2012 so I had a place to write. He went as far as to marry me to ensure I could have library privileges during my sabbatical. His patience (his great, great patience) and good humor helped me through times when chapters weren't working and a new computer seemed to eat my table files daily. Any errors, strangeness or offensiveness that you encounter in this text are to be credited to the author alone!

CHAPTER 1:
THE PARADE, 2009

My daughter and I are sitting on a grungy street curb. In the gutter by our feet is a mass of discarded crawfish shells, wadded-up napkins, stepped-on Louisiana hot links, candy wrappers, broken strands of beads, and who knows what else. Fortunately for us, the stale-beer smell emanating from this clotted mass is currently stronger than the competing aromatic hint of piss. As I watch my daughter violently flick "popper" firecrackers at the street in front of her, I think of the sacrifices I have made in the name of archaeology. We've been sitting here for what seems like a day, but in reality, it has been about 45 minutes. We are not-so-patiently awaiting the arrival of the Krewe of Bacchus and its annual Carnival parade.

I am not good at waiting, and my bored eleven-year-old is not making the wait any easier. She should have been a pro at Mardi Gras by now—she attended her first parade at six months of age. Yet, every year, she manages to forget how long she has to wait for the parade to arrive, that it smells bad, that people push and shove, and that if she wants to pee, she just has to wait until we walk back over by the Amtrak station—the only place with a reasonably clean public toilet.

"What time is it?" she asks, for the fifth time in as many minutes. I tell her an earlier time than I did previously to see if she is even listening to my answers. She's not.

"When is the parade supposed to start?"

"At five o'clock," I answer, again.

"You just said it is after seven. Where's the parade? It's late."

She doesn't pause for any answers, and she has a routine of complaints she'll spin through, ending with the inevitable, "I'm bored."

I say nothing in response. I've already reminded her that the parade starts miles away, so of course, it won't reach us at the advertised start time. I have also already reminded her that the parades at Mardi Gras are always late. In the street in front of us, children are playing catch with footballs and other toys caught at earlier parades. Music is blasting. There are certain songs that are always played at Mardi Gras: "Mardi Gras Mambo," "When You go to Mardi Gras," "On the Bayou," and so on. It is festive and nostalgic the first eight times you hear each of these songs in a Carnival season, but the next 48 times are a little grating on the psyche. People are drinking canned American beer pulled from coolers that double as seats.

Figure 1.1. Bead ladders lining St. Charles. Photograph by Alexandra Wilkie Farnsworth.

We are awaiting the parade in an area known as the no man's land, the grassy median that divides the two sides of the street. We are on St. Charles Street, just to the southwest of Lee Circle and the freeway, an area not popular with tourists who cling closer to the circle itself and to Canal Street. In the residential areas of the route, property owners rope off their front yards and set up yard furniture and tables to prevent others from standing on their property. The most passive aggressive piece of parade furniture is the children's viewing ladder. Imagine a tall ladder with a booster seat attached to the top, as well as some sort of container for holding beads (Figure 1.1). Some are decorated with purple, green, and gold ribbons and other Mardi Gras themes. They line the parade routes in the residential neighborhoods like sentries, protecting properties from the invasion of uninvited parade spectators. Perched at the top of these contraptions, small children hold nets and signs and invite floats to throw them as many favors as possible.

And that is why we are here: to collect the stuff thrown at the parades. This is not just some greed-fueled quest; we are on a nobler quest than the hoards that surround us. We are here as scientists, *social* scientists, archaeologists to be exact. Alex is here as my able assistant; she is actually quite infected with the greed of bead lust, a trait that makes her a very useful fieldworker. We have a bag labeled "Bacchus 2009" that will contain all samples we will "excavate" from this parade. Later, the beads contained in this bag will be meticulously cataloged, with their colors, finishes, lengths, diameters, and shapes all measured, noted, and recorded in a standardized format that will allow me to compare this set of beads with those gathered at other parades at other times. It is this basic data drawn from material culture that will allow me to construct interpretations about subjects as varied as the economics, politics, and gender relations of Mardi Gras (see chapters six, eight, and nine). But I get ahead of myself. The parade isn't here yet.

Vendors with pushcarts meander by with their wheeled bazaars offering a wide array of appalling crap like firework snaps, goofy hats, lighted necklaces, giant cigars, inflatable hammers, and any other number of goods that can be obtained at your local dollar store. I've already been suckered into buying the kid some of this expensive crap—anything to buy a few minutes of pre-parade peace. I lean forward to peer down the street and grumpily adjust the flashing rabbit ears that inexplicably adorn my own head (Figure 1.2). I think briefly about how I should have thought to dress as Indiana Jones or Lara Croft.

There are several ways to determine the proximity of an approaching parade. Night parades, like Bacchus, often have large spotlights mounted on a truck in the beginning of the parade. By watching the skyline for their methodical arcing, you can see, first, if the parade is even moving yet and, second, its approach. Sometimes, shortly before a parade, an electric company's cherry picker, mounted at the same height as the tallest float in the parade, will slowly drive along the route checking that no utility lines will be hit and pulled down by a float. Mass electrocutions taking place at a Mardi Gras parade would be bad for New Orleans' reputation, after all.

The best indicator that the parade nears is when you see the street vendors start to flee in the opposite direction. The sprinting vendors are closely followed by New Orleans' Finest driving en mass down the parade route. With their sirens bleating and chirping, motorcycle cops slowly drive along the parade route at the curb edge to force the crowd up on the sidewalk. For the remainder of the parade, horse-mounted officers provide the same service—driving the crowd back from the street. There is good reason for doing this. People mob the floats, and it is common for these papier-mâché titans to hit parade goers. The parades feature numerous marching bands, whose lines stretch the full width of the street. I pity the high school students—especially the barely clad baton twirlers—marching on the outside lanes of their bands, walking along the curb, and facing the drunken crowds.

Many tourists think that the city of New Orleans puts on Mardi Gras. It doesn't. The city pays for the police and the clean up. The city rents porta-potties. The city advertises Mardi Gras. Mardi Gras is hosted by social organizations called krewes. The first New Orleans krewe, the Mystick Krewe of Comus, was founded in 1858. It was a secret society of American society men who wanted to reinvigorate Carnival celebrations in the city. Although the French brought Mardi Gras to New Orleans, supposedly as early as 1699 when the d'Iberville brothers first camped on the site that would become the city, by the 1850s, the yearly festival was marked more for its increased murder rate than anything else. A group of American businessmen reacted against proposals to outlaw Carnival by organizing a public procession that featured torch-lit floats and an exclusive masked ball. This uniquely American take on Mardi Gras became popular in the old French city, and other krewes were organized. It is the membership dues and fund-raising activities of krewe members and these organizations that pay for the beautiful parades. Even after the devastation of Katrina, New Orleans' Mardi Gras has managed to avoid corporate sponsorship.

Figure 1.2. Laurie and Alex attending a 2009 Mardi Gras parade in New Orleans. Photograph by Paul Farnsworth.

The throws so coveted by parade goers—the plastic cups, the doubloons, stuffed animals, party favors, and beads—are all bought by individual krewe members. The throws are everywhere at Mardi Gras, but no one has seriously studied them—until now. As an archaeologist who studies the recent and, sometimes, contemporary past, I realized that the material culture of Mardi Gras deserved archaeological study. My sites are the parades themselves. My physical tools are my ability to beg, catch, and jump; my mental tools are the intellectual and methodological tools of archaeological thinking and doing. While I don't use a trowel or shovel, I am still conducting a kind of excavation; I control for the variables of time and space in my collection strategy just as an archaeologist digging in the ground does. Instead of being surrounded in soil, my artifacts are held in place ever momentarily by air as they travel to the place where they are deposited—my hand. Most things archaeologists find have been discarded by their users and left to accumulate and be covered over long periods of time. You might say by collecting the objects directly at the time of discard, I'm merely simplifying the archaeological process.

As the police approach, the crowd rises. Those who have been sitting on curbs or lawn chairs get to their feet. Children are put on top of coolers, ladders, or shoulders so they can see, and everyone jostles toward the front. My daughter and I are short; we absolutely have to be in the front if we are going to catch many throws. The first part of the parade consists of black cars with dark tinted windows carrying miscellaneous and mysterious dignitaries associated with the Krewe of Bacchus. A large black SUV emblazoned with the logo of Blaine Kern Studios eases by us. Some people clap golf-tournament-style. Blaine Kern is synonymous with Mardi Gras for many. His studio creates most of the magnificent floats that characterize Mardi Gras celebrations in New Orleans. Each parade starts differently; some feature stilt walkers, Shriners in little cars, and masked and robed horseback riders. There is typically an American flag and banner honoring veterans of the military branches. These marchers receive boisterous applause.

At night parades, there are flambeaux carriers holding flaming torches who walk with gas tanks filled with naphtha strapped to their backs. The first torch carriers were enslaved people, and it is reputed that many of the modern carriers come from long family lines of flambeaux carriers. Flambeaux carrying has a performative aesthetic associated with it, and many carriers twirl, throw, and swirl the torches creating another-worldly light spectacle as they parade. The tradition was once to toss pennies at the feet of the torch carriers. The nice interpretation of this practice was that it was a means of thanking or tipping the carriers; but, I suspect there was no small element of racist intent to the practice—white men tossing pennies to watch a black man with a torch bend over to retrieve a few cents. Today, if pennies, or even quarters, are thrown, the flambeaux carriers pointedly ignore them or glare in the direction of the tosser. The better sort of New Orleanian will discretely approach a flambeaux carrier whose work they've enjoyed and slip them a folded bill or two.

The early part of the parade features few throws. The riding lieutenants on horseback may throw some aluminum doubloons featuring the krewe logo and parade theme, and the Shriners toss some handfuls of candy. Some parade goers covet the doubloons and maintain collections that date back to the 1960s, the heyday of this throw; but most people are here for the beads: shiny plastic beads. The bigger and longer, the better; and if they are beads specific to the parade of Bacchus, well, that's the best!

We will collect and catalog these throws as well, but they are not the main focus of our study. Still, by recording this information, it will be available to other interested scholars to use. This is standard archaeological practice—an ethically responsible archaeologist will record all materials encountered. Many sites include multiple periods of occupation, so an archaeologist interested in a British Roman period site, for instance, will still record and collect evidence from the Anglo Saxon and Medieval sites that overlay the Roman-era occupations.

The royal float approaches, and Alex and I strain to see the top of the float where the king sits. Since its founding in 1968, the Krewe of Bacchus has featured a celebrity king. In most krewes, the king is a member of the organization who has high standing in the city. Bacchus is different. One doesn't need to be of old New Orleans blood and good breeding to join Bacchus; one only needs to be nominated by a member and be able to pay the annual dues. The krewe generally includes from 1,000 to 1,300 members, and the parade is one of the largest of the season. This year, the newspapers have told us to expect 33 floats, including the ever-favorites Bacchagator, Bacchasaurus, Bacchawhoppa, and King Kong family floats.

This year's celebrity king is Val Kilmer. Alex has never heard of him. "I think he played Batman and Tarzan at some point," I explain. With the king's float, the throws begin. Each float can be seen as a microcosm of the parade. The king's float is multi-tiered, with only the king perched on top of a throne surrounded by large purple grapes. Grapes are a theme that reoccurs on other floats, and which creates a sense of aesthetic unity to the parade. Later, I will discuss ways that different parade organizations also use material symbols and color schemes to signal their organization's identity to parade goers. Behind the king is a large representation of Bacchus himself, the god's hand outstretched in a pose that could be seen as either a wave or a tossing gesture. At the human king's feet are bags of the finest beads and doubloons with his image. He wears a large crown and a kingly beaded and fur-decorated cape over white satin leggings and knee-high silver boots. When so moved, the king waves and throws gifts to his admirers; other times, he drinks from a giant chalice and allows others on the float to throw on his behalf.

The grapes and chalice may be symbols of the Greek God, and his gifts are a fore-shadowing of the generosity of the floats to follow. King Bacchus in his costume is dressed more like a king from a Medieval-themed dinner theater. While every parade season features a new King Bacchus, each wears the same costume, ritually ceding their identity to that of the Roman god of wine. The men attending to the king are dressed in formal wear. Their black suits and white shirts demarcate them as important but not to be confused with the king. On the bottom level of the float are small children bedecked in smaller versions of the royal garb. They are the most enthusiastic throwers of the king's treasure, and they represent the future of the parade. The most generous of the parades are also the ones with the most ornate and structured floats. The most elite organizations have floats that are only used in their parades, while smaller groups share floats with other parades by simply labeling them with different names. This self-conscious use of materials to convey understanding is what makes Mardi Gras so rich for archaeological study.

Even before the float is before us, the crowd has assumed the begging pose—our hands have flown up beseechingly in unison, and our voices call out for gifts in a whining buzz. In the roar, a few words can be made out. "Throw me something." "Here! Here!" "BEADS!" We see the rain of beads cascading off the float as it approaches: perfect glittering circles arcing through the air. The crowd surges upward, jumping and grasping, hands hoping to clench around this plastic piece of wonder. We join the crowd, expressing our hunger, trying to make eye contact with a sympathetic rider who will throw something gently to the short girls in front. We are swallowed by a thicket of arms and hands. We hear beads being caught around us, the distinctive clicking of flesh and plastic. It only incites our fervor.

We do not get a clear look at the costumed figure who is Kilmer, even though King Bacchus defies the New Orleans city ordinance that requires all float riders remain masked at all times. Riders also must be tethered to the float by a harness. Lots of drinking takes place on floats, and before the harnesses were required, riders had a habit of flopping off of floats when they hit potholes. No maskers fall off this float, and it speeds out of our reach. We are now in the street, and we find ourselves pushed back on the curb by the mounted police clearing the road for the first marching band. The crowd retreats backward. The lucky few who have caught favors are inspecting their treasure and reliving their success. "Did you see how I caught that? I must have jumped five feet straight up!" The lootless look on enviously.

It is hard to explain bead lust to the uninitiated. There are psychology studies that demonstrate that humans are hardwired to be attracted to shiny things. That is certainly the case with the beads. It is the rare individual who can watch the distribution of beads at Mardi Gras and not want some for themselves.

Despite our pleas and upward springs into the air, we come away from the king's float empty-handed and regroup while the first marching band performs. Alex is despondent. "I'm not going to get anything!" she wails. I remind her that the beginning of the parade is always roughest, and that when the tall people get their fill, we'll be able to catch things as well. This is little consolation. "And don't forget the viewing standings after Lee circle. Once the floats hit the viewing stands, the parade stops so each float can be viewed and each band perform." Where we are on the route, the parade will come to a halt every few moments, which will allow us to approach the float and beg more personally for throws. As a child, Alex was cherub-faced and always did well obtaining stuffed animals and beads. She is still reasonably cute, even at the awkward front-edge of adolescence.

As we wait, I scan the crowd. There are a bunch of students from a local university behind us. They are quite inebriated, and several of the girls are wearing sweatshirts that have been cut-down flash-dance-style—with neckline lowered and sleeves removed. They clearly intend to bargain for beads with assets other than words. The displays of nudity in exchange for beads generated a great deal of attention for Mardi Gras in the

1980s and 1990s. The practice began in the French Quarter among people standing on balconies and people on the street, and it involved shows of both male and female nudity—women flashing their breasts or butts, men pulling out their penises. From the French Quarter, the exchange of showing body parts for beads spread to the parade routes—much to the chagrin of those touting Mardi Gras as clean family fun. It was along the parade routes where the practice became seen as exclusively women showing their breasts for "good" beads. It was this gendered dimension of the throwing game that first drew my archaeological attention. I noticed that the beads most valued by parade goers could usually only be obtained by women if they flashed their body parts.

There are several reasons for this gender-specific development. First, the vast majority of maskers, as the riders are called, are men of whom only about 10% want to see male parts. Second, there are logistical limitations faced by men wanting to show taboo body parts in a crowd. Women often show their breasts while sitting on the shoulders of their boyfriends. This protects them from unwanted groping from the crowd and makes them visible to maskers on the floats. In contrast, a man trying to pull out his penis in the crowd at ground level risks losing it, and if sitting on someone's shoulders . . . well, you get the point, so to speak.

For those choosing to show breasts, there are several ways to go. There is the classic "lift the bottom of the shirt up and over," starting the motion at the waist. This is a crowd favorite since it allows all present to share in the viewing. When one "shows" this way, however, you have to get the shirt back down before your hands are free to catch, so you are dependent on your companions to catch for you until your body parts are back in place. As a result, the surrounding crowd gets a great deal of bead wealth intended for the half-naked woman. The more common "show" technique is that planned for by the college women. You wear a loose shirt, no bra, and approach the float when stopped on a male companion's shoulders. You discretely pull the shirt forward, allowing the maskers to look down. If you wear the shirt tucked in or with a belt, you can then continue to hold the shirt out to catch any offerings dropped down the shirt.

I have not participated in showing myself. My students look at my beads and cannot believe this is the case, but I speak the truth. There are several reasons I don't participate in this part of Mardi Gras ritual. At my first Mardi Gras, a friend and I were walking through the French Quarter when we observed a woman show her breasts and then give them a good shake for the crowd. My friend, who actually looked at the woman's face, gasped, "Oh my God, that's the department secretary for the unnamed department at Big State University!" Thus, I quickly learned that even the anonymity of Mardi Gras isn't. I would like to say that my strong feminist background has prevented me from participating, but really, it is more a matter of not wanting to subject my body to that kind of unwanted scrutiny. Finally, on a purely scientific note, if I were to show at one parade, to be consistent in my sampling strategy, I would have to show at every parade. We'll talk about the problems of sampling in a later chapter.

On this occasion, however, I did make a mental note to check in on the college women to see what they were up to. The second float now approaches and we flood again out into the street. I wish I could tell you what the float was, or what even the theme of the parade was. I can't. New Orleans has the most exquisite floats you can imagine. Ethereal confections of papier-mâché and tissue paper (Figure 1.3). Nymphs and flowers bounce on nearly-invisible wires. Small lights illuminate metal foil and glitter. Shadowy faces of ancient gods emerge toward you from the flambeaux light, and yet this magic is the least appreciated aspect of Mardi Gras in the moment; all focus is on the throwing game.

This time the float is moving slower. Alex and I push forward close enough to be plainly seen by the riders of the lower deck. I make eye contact with a masker holding a nice pair of beads (bead strands are always called pairs in New Orleans), smile, and point at my cute child who is

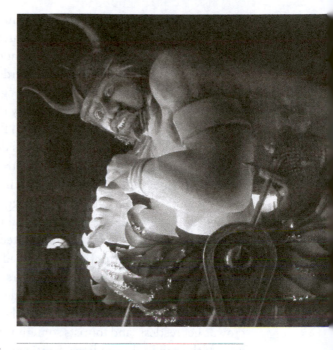

Figure 1.3. Float from a 2009 New Orleans parade.

earnestly pleading. The ploy works, the strand it tossed toward her. A large drunk man sees and brutally reaches out and grabs the strand in the air just as Alex's fingertips brush it. The masker angrily points at the man and yells at him, and others in the crowd join in. The thief is unapologetic, but soon his embarrassed companion intercedes and forces him to give the beads to Alex. We turn to thank the masker with a wave, but the float is long gone, and he has probably already forgotten us. Now that she has received a reward—a lovely thick strand of purple metallic beads featuring several coin-shaped beads emblazed with "Bacchus"—the child's confidence is boosted. She proudly puts them around her neck.

When I first attended Mardi Gras, you needed a bag to hold your plunder; the strands of beads were too short to easily put around your neck. Now, beads necklaces all easily fit around any size of head. Others have noticed this size increase, but through my excavations of Mardi Gras, I can illustrate not just how much the beads have changed in length over the years, but when and why those changes have occurred. People catch necklaces and immediately loop them around their necks. Necks quickly disappear under coils of metallic and pearl colored strands of beads. Some of the strands reach only as far as a person's clavicle, while the longest can hit even a tall person's knees when they walk. It is best to resist the temptation to coil long strands of beads into multiple loops. Instead, endure the discomfort of beads clicking against your knees; looped beads have a way of becoming chokers that in the tangled mess around your neck become impossible to remove. After a Mardi Gras parade, there is always at least one person observed with several other people trying to extricate them from their beads without suffocating them. On a cold day, the beads act as a scarf, warming you.

Now that we have caught our first strand of beads, others are easier to get. We fall into the rhythm of the parade, surging forward and backward to meet floats and retreat from bands. Our first parade bag fills, and we begin to pack our beads into a second labeled bag. After the sixth float, the parade suddenly rolls to a stop. There are many reasons parades halt. The infrastructure for most modern floats is an 18-wheeler truck frame. Floats were originally built on wagon chasses, but as demand for beads and other throws increased, it became necessary to build larger and stronger floats. Some of the floats in super krewes are composed of multiple 18-wheeler frames strung together. These monstrosities, filled with heavy throws and people, are dragged through the street by farm tractors. There is only so much weight a tractor can endure for any length of time, and sometimes the poor things just give up with an exhausted sigh and a lot of smoke in the middle of the parade. The parade in front of the disabled float will continue, only stopping if it appears the gap will be too great. Back up tractors accompany many floats, and the good folks of Blaine Kern are adept at swapping out dead tractors for new, so usually there is a small gap of no more than a block or two. If the gap between floats extends into minutes, the crowds get restless, and tourists sometimes aimlessly wander away thinking the parade is over. If the gap looks too large, frantic radio communications result in the entire parade stopping until the problem is resolved. Equipment failure is just one cause of parade stoppages. People excitedly begging for throws are sometimes run over by passing floats. Others, after a day of imbibing, suddenly fall over in a coma-like state and require medical attention—if an ambulance is required, the parade pauses to allow emergency personnel to handle the situation.

The most common stoppage is when the parade hits the viewing stands on St. Charles Street. On these stands sit dignitaries, ticket holders, orphans, and other honored groups. Each float and marching band stops to be seen. The bands perform their most complicated musical numbers at this time, and while they do so, the entire parade grinds to a halt. If you are experienced in the ways of parade-going, you have situated yourself at a point in the route where floats routinely stop, for it is during this time that the best bead-mongering can take place.

There is some bead-catching etiquette to be found among the chaos of the throwing game. Often, more than one person will catch a strand: multiple hands, raised in the air, and locked on one prize. In frenzied and aggressive crowds, the strand of beads will be torn apart rather than relinquished—particularly if the strand is determined to be "good." More often, after a few tense moments and hard staring, one person will drop the strand. Bead etiquette demands that should the opportunity arise later, that the victor should pass a reciprocal strand of beads to this person. Beads may be thrown in bunches. In their original packaging, beads can be found bagged in sets of one dozen if they are small, a half dozen, or even by threes, if they are longer and larger specimens. In particularly generous parades, riders will throw complete bags or bunches of beads together. Bunched beads are usually

Figure 1.4. Examples of the diversity of MOS bead shapes. Photograph by Alexandra Wilkie Farnsworth.

attached to one another by a stapled piece of thin paper. Generally, it is acceptable for an individual to keep a bag of beads to themselves, but there is often peer pressure from other parade goers for bunches to be split and distributed to other nearby spectators—again, particularly if the beads in question are considered to be good.

What—you may wonder—constitutes a "good" set of beads? Let us take this opportunity to look a little closer at the beads being thrown from the floats. Classification of artifacts into different groups based on how they look or where they were made is a basic and essential part of archaeological analysis. While a parade goer may simply think of beads as good or bad, an archaeologist must interrogate what physical characteristics of the objects create that cultural evaluation. Social meaning is not all we can derive from classification. We can also come to understand how certain objects changed through time and use that information to date sites.

Today, the beads are plastic and molded-on-string (MOS)—when the strand is broken, the beads stay in place. An obvious advantage of this design is that strands can be easily repaired. Repairs can, in turn be easily identified and, when recorded, can be used to understand the ways beads are recycled from one parade to another. While simple round spheres are the usual shape, molded beads can come in any range of shapes, (Figure 1.4). Bead size can range from a diameter of no more than 5 mm, to beads that are 20 mm in diameter (Figure 1.5). Length of strands also varies greatly. Today, it is rare to find a strand less than 33" (this represents the length of the strand if it were not doubled upon itself as a necklace). This size easily fits over most heads (Figure 1.6). The longest beads are 120". In a strange merger of measurement systems, all Mardi Gras beads are sold with a metric diameter, and a standard system length.

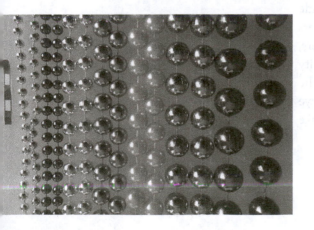

Beads come in a number of finishes—flat, pearlescent, transparent, and metallic. A small number of glow-in-the-dark beads also appear sometimes in night parades. Every color imaginable is seen, but the standard Mardi Gras trio of Purple (representing Justice), Green (representing Faith), and Gold (representing Power) remains popular. Among these beads, the ranking system is easy to

Figure 1.5. Examples of bead diameters available. Photograph by Alexandra Wilkie Farnsworth.

discern—the longest strands and the biggest beads are the most coveted. Beads that have been ornamented with a krewe's medallion are also seen as desirable (Figure 1.7).

"Fancy" beads are those that are hand-strung and feature a range of more elaborate bead shapes and stringing patterns (Figure 1.7). Necklaces can feature beads molded in the shapes of flamingoes, Mardi Gras masks, musical instruments, marijuana leaves, women's breasts, and any other shape. The strands are multi-colored, featuring metallic, pearl, and translucent beads. Sometimes, they even feature battery-operated flashing lights. These throws are more expensive for riders to obtain, as they are sold individually rather than in cases. They are delicate and strung, not molded into necklaces. They can be easily ripped apart by anxious hands. Many riders choose to hand these strands directly to individuals or to throw them encased in plastic bags to ensure they reach a recipient intact.

Figure 1.6. A young Alex models how beads are worn at Mardi Gras.

When the floats move quickly, riders throw blindly as they pass, quickly off-loading their beads to unknown recipients. Riders often attempt to throw away from the float toward the rear of the crowd to keep the mobs back. Every year there are crowd injuries. Often the injuries are stepped-on-toes, sprained ankles, or heads or faces hit by exuberantly thrown or caught beads. Sometimes, the competition for beads and other throws becomes too heated, and knives or guns are drawn. When you consider that vast amounts of alcohol have been consumed by a considerable number of parade attendees, the risks should be apparent. Despite that, violence at Mardi Gras is an exception rather than a norm. Thousands of visitors engage in stupid and potentially dangerous behavior every year and are punished no more for their follies than with a headache and sense of embarrassment.

We are now about halfway through the parade and focusing our efforts on bartering with maskers on stopped floats. A stopped float gives the riders, as well as the parade participants, the opportunity to engage one another directly and personally. The nature of the bead transaction changes; now eye contact, verbal exchanges, and bartering can take

Figure 1.7. Examples of krewe medallion beads and fancy composite hand-strung beads. Photograph by Alexandra Wilkie Farnsworth.

place. Alex is working on improving her game. She tentatively approaches the halted float. She shyly waves and smiles at a rider on the top deck. He throws his beads to someone else. She becomes discouraged too quickly and turns her gaze to another masker not realizing that the first object of her attention had selected a nice pair of beads to toss her; but finding her no longer paying him attention, he throws them to another. Several men approach the float. One bears a five-year-old child on his shoulders, and the other carries his 22-year-old girlfriend. The five-year-old's father waves to a masker on the lower deck of the float. The movement attracts the rider's attention. She notices the child and begins to hand the boy a strand of beads. The father interrupts and asks, "have you got any stuffed animals or footballs?" The masker nods, bends down again, and presents the child with a large purple, green, and gold plush football. Child and man simultaneously say thank you and fade back into the crowd.

Alex has now realized that her bead requests are likely to be fulfilled when she focuses on breaking down the will of a single rider. She makes eye contact with a rider on the top of the float. She waves, ensuring he sees her, locks eyes with him and smiles. He ignores her at first, so she waves frantically and shouts, "please, throw me something." He looks down at her and tosses her some mediocre beads. She dutifully puts them around her neck, but raises her hands to him again. "Please, medallions?" He returns to ignoring her. She yells up again, "Hey, up there, please, you got medallions?" The rider adjacent to her target looks down at her. She smiles at him and waves, and is rewarded with a dozen medallions. The first man realizes he has been shown to be cheap, calls down to her, and tosses her a stuffed animal. Now she has learned how to patiently work a rider for what she wants. She will not always be successful, but will collect a sizable collection of good throws nonetheless. Getting what you want at Mardi Gras requires strategy, as well as luck.

Meanwhile, another shoulder-sitter is attracting the attention of float riders and parade participants. A heavily made-up young woman wearing a deep scoop-necked blouse is sitting on the shoulders of her very drunk boyfriend who is wearing a local university's green sweatshirt. The girl's giggles suggest that she may have been imbibing as well. Her bright lipstick is slightly smudged, but her heavy eyeliner and mascara, foundation, and strongly highlighted hair quickly identify her as a southern sorority girl. Even at Mardi Gras, a southern lady will wear a full face. Despite her attempt to appear older and sophisticated, she is probably still in her freshman year. Pointing her out, one rider notices her approach the float and tugs at the arm of his neighbor. The two maskers bend over the rail of the float to talk to her. One pulls out a very large strand of pearl-colored beads. The woman reaches to take the beads. The masker smiles at her and pulls them away. He shakes his head and his finger, indicating that she is naughty to grab for the beads without some sort of payment. His friend indicates, through gesture, that they wish her to open her blouse and expose her breasts. She laughs, feigns shock, and then points to a bunch of fancy beads with marijuana leaf-shaped beads hanging behind the men. She makes it plain that she will only show for those beads.

By now, most of the riders on the lower deck are ignoring all other beggars in favor of watching the negotiation with the young woman. The men with whom she began bartering pull them from the nail and dangle them over her to indicate that she can have those beads. She leans over toward the men and expertly pulls her shirt neck forward, exposing her breasts for them, and them only. Her choice of shirt had signaled that she was a woman who had come to the parade prepared to participate in this kind of barter. As she exposes herself, she shimmies back and forth. Now maskers riding on the top deck have noticed her as well, and while she had only negotiated with two krewe members, she is now pelted with a large amount of beads, stuffed animals, and other throws. A number of the offerings are expertly caught in her blouse. She is unable to catch all that is offered to her. The crowd around her boyfriend has thickened as onlookers grab some of the bounty she has generated. As the float begins to move again, the riders continue to throw beads back toward the woman who had exposed her breasts. In addition to the marijuana beads that first attracted her, she also catches, fittingly enough, a large flashing strand of beads that include breast-shaped beads with nipples made of small red, flashing lights. Her boyfriend is grateful to put her down until the next float arrives. His lady-love repays him for his help by putting the breast beads around his neck. It is not unusual to see most of the booty earned by flashing women go to their boyfriends rather than themselves. There can be a whiff of prostitution's scent around the throwing game.

Riders do their best to draw out of the crowd those parade goers willing to engage in friendly barter. Sometimes, riders desire displays of nudity or affection (it is not uncommon to witness friendly kisses exchanged) or exchanges of throws for bottles of beer or other alcoholic beverages; after all, one works up a thirst when throwing all those trinkets. To attract the crowd's attention, a rider may swing the bead strand in a fast circle or dangle the strand out of reach, eliciting screams and grasping hands. Beads can be released in mid swing, so that they fly over the crowd in a perfect spinning circle, light flashing brilliantly off them as they make a graceful arc. For precision throwing, however, it is best to press the strand together into a compact lump. Beads thrown this way can go long distances and easily reach persons at the very back of the crowd. Riders can be remarkably accurate with their delivery of throws.

It is the rare southern Louisianan who does not have a friend or family member riding or marching in a Mardi Gras Parade. Knowing someone in a parade is another potential route to bead wealth. Parade goers with friends or family riding in a parade will learn not only which float the loved one will ride, but also, the side and position they occupy. Likewise, friends and family will often inform the rider of where on the parade route they will wait. In a crowd of thousands, catching the eye of a loved one is tricky. Often signs are necessary to attract attention—for shouts are often lost in the noise of the crowd. It is to the advantage of all members of the crowd to help attract the attention of a float rider. After all, just as in the case of the breast-flashing woman, the bead wealth generated from the passing of a loved one will likely benefit all in the area. Riders will let their fellow float companions know when their loved ones are in view, and most riders will "throw heavy" to their companions, friends, and families.

As the parade continues, many parade goers find their bead lust to be satiated. There is more attention paid to the passing bands and the floats. Parade goers who aggressively yanked beads from fellow attendees now hand off the throws they catch to neighbors with fewer goods. Children start to nod off in their chairs or agitate for snacks or restrooms. I am not done. I must continue to beg in earnest until the end of the parade as part of my study. My intention is to get as representative a sample of the beads available at each parade and to be able to *qualitatively* and *quantitatively* characterize the materials recovered from one parade versus another. That is part of what makes my bead study archaeological.

I have caught a decent number of beads, but nothing particularly special. While archaeologists will tell you that they are not interested in the things they find as much as they are interested in what they learn from the things, the reality is that we all like to find that unusual or exciting artifact that stands out from the rest. I walk up to a float and direct my attention to the top-most level. "Hey! Handsome! You have anything special for a California Girl?" I scream. Most of the maskers are now focused on talking to one another and drinking from plastic cups. They are taking a rest from the crowds below. One notices my frantic waving and yelling. I give him my best and, I hope most beseeching smile. I spastically wave my hands at him and jump up and down a bit more. He points at me and indicates that I should cup my hands. I do so and reach them as high as I can above my head. He leans over farther than he should have been able to if he were properly harnessed and drops something into my hands. He waits and watches as I inspect what I have caught. It is a fine strand of hand-strung glass beads. These are the sort of beads thrown fifty years ago. In post-Katrina New Orleans, glass beads are now thrown in small numbers as a way to harken back to the more traditional values of Mardi Gras. This necklace is nostalgia for Mardi Gras past-made material. I shriek and wave happily back at him as the float begins to move again, and he throws me a kiss—a gesture I have always found particularly charming among maskers. I blow one back and wave until he is out of sight. He has given me the gift of a perfect Mardi Gras moment, when the only two people who existed in the crowd were me and him. Just as when an archaeologist's trowel uncovers a complete projectile point, a sherd of decorated pottery, or a shell bead. It's a moment that can't be quantified or calculated, but is part of the wonderful lived experience of Mardi Gras.

The parade rushes on unaware of individual intrigues, and beads that are perceived as less desirable fly through the air uncaught or tossed on the ground. These discarded beads will be stomped into the muddy ground and become part of what is more typically thought of as the archaeological record awaiting recovery from the earth by future generations of archaeologists. All around in the street and on the curb and street medians, hanging in twisted tangles in tree branches and around utility lines, are intact and broken bead strands. People wave half-heartedly at the passing floats or ignore them completely as they drink and chat with friends. Finally, the last float passes, quickly followed by the flashing lights of ambulances and police cars. The parade is recognized as over when the sound of swirling brushes of the street-cleaning truck grows louder and passes. Beads left in the street await archaeological deposition of another sort—as part of a landfill deposit.

The soft clicking and clanging of beads can be heard as the gift-laden celebrants leave the parade route. Parents carry tired tots and bags of toys over their shoulders. Boxes and bead bags are salvaged to carry loot from the parade. These treasures, so frantically demanded and fought over, will remain important during the period of Mardi Gras—in this case, for 48 more hours. The best of the beads will be worn to other parades or simply around town. Elegantly dressed Louisiana matrons think nothing of wearing gaudy purple globe beads with cashmere or linen. But once Ash Wednesday arrives, the annual heyday of the bead is over. Some good strands may be strung from rearview mirrors, but most will be thrown into garages, attics, sheds, or even tossed into landfills. People who ride in parades will sort and box their beads in anticipation of the next Mardi Gras. Rethrowing of beads is common and practical. There are businesses—including bead suppliers—who will pay by the pound for used beads. Beads are repaired, repackaged, and sold as boxes of used beads the following year. It is common to catch beads that are 10, 20, even 30 years old. These are low-value beads that are often tossed in bulk to small children. Some of these vintage beads are sought by collectors and sold on eBay. Fancy krewe medallions and specialty beads can be seen being sold on ebay in the weeks following Carnival. In years past, beads thrown by Playboy in the French Quarter have sold for as much as $50.00 per strand. Only a small percentage of beads achieve this kind of exalted status. Yet, those other beads have much to tell us about Mardi Gras culture and Louisiana's place in the world. While others may soon abandon their beads in forgotten heaps, for Alex and I, bead work is just beginning. At the hotel, we will begin to analyze the beads. Our spoils will be studied closely.

As we leave the parade site, we have left a great deal of archaeological evidence behind for others to study in the future, either as debris deposited along the streets or as episodic dumping in landfills. Each parade leads to the creation of a new midden layer of crushed cans and paper cups, half-eaten hotdogs, corn cobs, crawfish and peanut shells, cotton candy cones, candied apple cores and sticks, torn masks, broken beads, unseen doubloons, snaps boxes, costume feathers, cardboard signs labeled with pleas for beads, and thousands of torn plastic bags that once contained beads. My study focuses on those who throw, and in this sense, I have followed the footsteps of archaeologists who have focused on the activities of the elite strata of society; for the parade givers are New Orleans' elite. This great pile of waste records the actions of the other 90%—the parade goers. In this stinking mass is evidence of their social activities, their Carnival diet, and the ways they passed their time. The throws left on the ground also speak to the value system of the masses—what they deemed to be offerings from the elite worthy of keeping. While I have not collected these materials, as I look at them, I am reminded that I must not render the parade goer invisible in my analyses, and that they are one of the forces that shapes what a parade giver decides to throw.

We must leave the parade now. Our materials have been collected, but now we face the task of sorting, cataloging, and analyzing the beads. Archaeologists popularly say that each week in the field represents six months in the laboratory. Even more time is spent afterward, thinking about and processing mentally what we have actually learned. So with no further ado, let us begin to discuss in earnest the ways we do archaeology.

CHAPTER 2: UNDERSTANDING ARCHAEOLOGY AND THE THROWING GAME

I lived in Louisiana from 1990 to 1995 where I completed my doctoral dissertation study that focused on African American family life from 1845 to 1950 on a cotton plantation (Wilkie 2000). I encountered Mardi Gras and the throwing game for the first time then. As an archaeologist, I was blown away by what I experienced; at the heart of the festivities is the creation of a symbolic currency system that is only meaningful for a few weeks a year! I was surprised and disappointed to learn that no one had studied this aspect of Mardi Gras. The balls, the costumes, and the floats all had received the attention of folklorists and historians, but the throwing game was itself tossed aside in academic discussions (e.g., Fox 2005, 2007; Gaudet 2001; Kinser 1990; Saxon et al. 1989; Ware 2007). When I started teaching at Berkeley in the fall of 1995, on a whim I spent my first lecture for a course on American historical archaeology talking about the many roles and uses of plastic beads in Mardi Gras celebrations. The students were fascinated and, unfortunately, had perhaps overly high expectations for the rest of the course.

One of the students had spent the previous year at Oxford and had worked with an anthropologist who was editing a volume on cross-cultural uses of beads. She told her mentor about my lecture, and I found myself invited to contribute a chapter to the edited volume (Sciama and Eicher 1998). I had at that point five years of casual participant observation invested in Mardi Gras and a large sample of material culture to write about. I wrote what I thought was a pretty good chapter (Wilkie 1998), but as I worked on it, I realized all the questions I *could* have asked of the beads, if I had collected them differently—if I had collected them in an archaeological way. You may wonder what I mean by "an archaeological way."

What Exactly is Archaeology? The Basics

Many textbooks will explain with great authority that archaeology is a Greek-derived word that means "the study of old things." That definition is fine, as far as it goes, but it is a minimalist and restrictive definition. I want you to foremost think of archaeology in two ways: first, as a mindset, a way of viewing and thinking about the world; and second, as a set of techniques and methodologies that grew out of that mindset. To think in an archaeological way is to recognize that the lives of humans take place in a physical body that occupies a material world. The material world consists of the natural world—the sky, the sea, the land, the birds, bees, flowers, trees, and so on—and human intrusions and modifications of that world—ditches, agricultural fields, walls, buildings, roads, fires, erosion, pollution, and so forth are all examples of things that humans have built into the world (Ingold 1993, 2007).

To understand this idea more fully, think of your own daily life; you wander through the world experiencing it through your senses and individual personal makeup. You may wear glasses, or have a great sense of smell. You may be tall or overweight; the physical package that is you physically shapes how you experience the world similarly or differently than other people. But "you" do not just exist as a physical being; you also exist as a social creature. You occupy different social roles: student, mother, father, child, sibling, friend, employee, and on and on. Your physical and social roles are often referred to as your *subjectivities* or subject positions.

Social roles, combined with your physical attributes, shape not just the way you see the world, but the way others in the world see you. For instance, you are treated differently when you walk into a five-star restaurant dressed in formal wear than you do when you walk in wearing shorts. While clothing is a cultural means of presenting a particular façade of yourself, your physical attributes can also shape the way that you experience both the social and physical world. A person who uses a wheelchair faces a natural and human-built world not designed for them and can find they cannot access areas that non-chair users can. They are also often treated differently in social interactions than non-wheelchair users. Gender and race are two other easily recognizable ways that people find themselves subjected to differential treatment in social interactions. Your personal, daily, lived, experience of moving through the world is called *embodiment.* While not all archaeologists may use the word embodiment, all archaeologists subscribe implicitly to the ideas I discussed above, because we all recognize that living in a material world matters when trying to understand human lives.

Humans invest a great deal of time and effort into changing the natural world into a human-controlled world. We do this on a grand scale, with modifications that cannot be moved from one place to another, such as roads or dams; and, we do this on a smaller scale by modifying natural resources to create new things that we can take along with us. Archaeologists refer to these larger modifications as *features,* such as the roads that New Orleans parades travel, and the portable human-made objects as *artifacts,* like the floats that travel those roads or the beads thrown from them.

Let's talk about the differences between artifacts and features a bit further. In Figure 2.1, A–D, you'll see photographs of several commonly found archaeological artifacts: ceramics (sometimes called pottery at prehistoric sites), glass, metal, and stone tools (lithics). While most of the objects pictured here are broken, they were originally parts of objects that people designed to be carried from place to place or kept on or near a person. If you look at Figure 2.2, A and B, you see two examples of archaeological features—both of which happen to be architectural. In the top photo, you'll see that the excavator is sitting

Figure 2.1. Commonly found artifacts: A. Obsidian flakes; B. Early twentieth-century glass medicine bottle; C. Iron artifacts from HALC, Illinois; D. European and locally produced ceramics.

Figure 2.2. Examples of archaeological features. Bottom photograph by Annelise Morris.

in the middle of a brick foundation—we uncovered that foundation through excavation. If we dismantled it by taking apart the bricks, the foundation would no longer exist. In the bottom photo, you'll see an excellent example of a feature that exhibited itself archaeologically as a set of soil stains. You'll notice that at the bottom of the excavation unit you can see what looks like a dark circular object in a light circular object. The darker circle is the stain left by a rotting wood post. The lighter circle marks the hole that was initially dug to set the post. You'll see that both are different from the surrounding soil (what the archaeologists would call *matrix*). If an excavator was not careful, these traces of what was once a hitching post would be scraped away and lost. While the stains are a very different kind of feature than the brick building foundation, neither can be transported away from the site without dismantling them.

Food remains, like the chicken wings and candied apples consumed at Mardi Gras parades, that preserve archaeologically as animal bones and plants and seeds, are sometimes referred to as *ecofacts.* Ecofacts are not made by humans, which is what distinguishes them from artifacts. They are, instead, naturally occurring and unmodified materials used by humans. Spanish moss used as bed lining would be an example of an ecofact. A tree branch picked up and used as a back scratcher would be an ecofact. The remains of the deer you shot and ate would be ecofacts. If you want to be exacting in its use, the term ecofact can get a little tricky. Consider those chicken wings, the food remains of a domesticated species that exists because of human tinkering; have we found an ecofact or an artifact? That quibbling aside; together, the traces left behind by humans, as preserved in a soil matrix, are known as the *archaeological record.* Figure 2.3 shows you some examples of ecofacts: animal bones, seashells, and plant remains.

While we use the term archaeological record to denote the totality of remains of the past preserved in the world, we do divide the archaeological record into smaller divisions. An *archaeological site* is a spatially discrete complex of associated features, artifacts, and ecofacts. In other words, it's a collection of artifacts, features, and ecofacts that you can plot on a map. That definition seems straightforward, and if you look at the regularity with which archaeologists refer to sites, you would think it's a pretty unproblematic term. As with many of the things we'll discuss in this book, it's not quite that simple. You will see references in archaeological studies to places like the ancient site of Tenochitlan, an Aztec city that was located in what is now Mexico City. Within the city, there are any number of households and public buildings that are spatially discrete clusters of chronologically associated artifacts, ecofacts, and features. Are these each individual sites, or are they just smaller places within the larger city site? After all, these associated buildings and spaces are clustered together to create the city. Because Mexico City has been continuously occupied, is Tenochitlan really a distinct site within the broader context of the site of Mexico City?

These are questions that also affect my Mardi Gras "site." Given what I described earlier, what should be my site boundaries? As I mentioned, most of the parades have routes that slightly vary from one another. I chose to collect artifacts at a location where routes for all the parades overlap. Should we consider each parade route its own site? In which case, each chronologically (or to use a more trendy archaeological term, temporally) distinct

B

Figure 2.3. Ecofacts: A. Plant remains;
B. Seashells; C. Animal bone (faunal remains).

A

C

parading episode could be seen as a site, and I have chosen to "excavate" at a point where I can study multiple overlapping sites. You can see this topic could get overwhelming to think about, but fortunately, most archaeologists are pragmatic and comfortable drawing lines around places while living with the knowledge that the reality is more blurry and complicated.

A concept that is used hand-in-hand with the term site, or sometimes to escape the bounded nature implied by it, is that of the ***archaeological landscape.*** Landscapes can be seen as larger regions over which sites are distributed. Archaeological landscapes allow us to understand spatial relationships between sites and the implications that has for social relationships among sites in the past. Landscapes can also be seen as an alternative name to the term site. Archaeologists who refer to Tenochitlan as an ancient urban landscape are not only resisting to put a boundary on that very complex archaeological place, but they are also indicating that they are thinking about relationships between natural and human elements in that space in a way that is similar to Ingold (1993, 2007) as discussed above. We could, therefore, think of the spaces where I did my Mardi Gras collections as a Carnival landscape.

Now that I have terrified you with a great deal of conceptual terminology, let us return to the notion of "things" and thinking about things. Things are very important to humans as a species. Things not only have matter, they matter. The relationship among people, their things, and the natural world is the focus of archaeology. Archaeologists are scholars who recognize that culture is not just created in the mind, but that it can also be held in one's hands and felt underneath one's feet. That is the way that archaeology is a mindset or an intellectual way of looking at the world. Within that mindset, archaeologists can be influenced by any other number of bodies of thought or disciplinary boundaries. Archaeologists can be found in history, classics, Near Eastern studies, geography, and in the American anthropology departments. The kinds of questions asked about the past may vary in each discipline, but all archaeologists share the notion that to understand the human experience through time requires you to understand the relationships between people and their stuff.

The Archaeological Toolset: Excavation

To understand relationships between people, their stuff, and the world in the past (and in the present) demands that archaeologists have a set of techniques and methods for recovering and interpreting those traces. To outsiders, the most familiar archaeological techniques are those related to excavation. *Excavation* is the controlled removal of soil to reveal spatial and temporal relationships among artifacts and features. Excavation is slow and controlled except at those times when it is fast and reasonably controlled as dictated by the presence of bulldozers.

The term excavate is now popularly used in many social sciences and humanities to denote a careful analysis that dissects sources to understand how they were created. This use of the term is true to the spirit of archaeological investigation. For archaeologists, our attention to detail is fueled by the sad irony underlying the basis of much archaeological study: when we excavate, we are essentially destroying the very thing we are studying. As we remove the soil matrix that holds in place the three-dimensional relationships between depositional events and the materials contained within them, we are dismantling those relationships. A dissection does the same thing to a biological specimen, for you can only really dissect a body once; but imagine if a historian burned a document after reading it! In an upcoming chapter, I will discuss archaeological excavation more fully with examples of how field projects are undertaken. For now, I just want to emphasize what is achieved through excavation—the recovery of spatial relationships between different traces of past human activities that can be used to understand human experiences at different times. Figure 2.4 provides a sense of what a group of university students engaged in archaeological research looks like. Excavation at its most basic is not technologically complex: trowels, dustpans, paintbrushes, levels, measuring tapes, buckets, cameras, compasses, pencils, and paper. Even with the addition of fancier electronics, such as iPads, global positioning systems (GPS), laser transits, and other technologies, excavation still requires basic tools you can get at a hardware store.

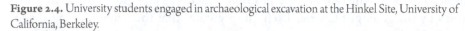

Figure 2.4. University students engaged in archaeological excavation at the Hinkel Site, University of California, Berkeley.

Our excavation records allow others to explore a site after it no longer exists in real space. What differentiates an archaeological excavation from treasure hunting is attention to recording details about where things came from. We measure and map our units of excavation, so we know where artifacts and features were located on a horizontal plane. As we remove soil, excavating down, we record the depths at which things are found. The three-dimensional location of an artifact is its *provenience*. Objects found together are said to be associated. We pay attention to changes in soil appearance and texture, and we look for evidence that will explain how things came to be where they were left—their deposition. Were the artifacts found in a pit (a feature) outside of a building (another feature), or were they simply dumped on the ground surface (a midden deposit—another kind of feature)? These are important questions to answer to understand the relationship between people and these places and things. A pit may be used only a short time and filled quickly. The garbage dumped on the surface may have accumulated over a much longer time. It is necessary to know *how* sites were created so that we can understand how and *why* the traces left behind are there.

When we see that different episodes of dumping (or deposition) have occurred on top of one another, we use the idea of *superposition* to describe the relationship between dumping episodes. The *Law of Superposition*, which was suggested back in the nineteenth century by the geologist Charles Lyell, simply states that the when looking at geological stratigraphy (different layers of rock), the topmost layer is the youngest, and the bottom level is the earliest. The principles of stratigraphy, as laid out in Lyell's Law of Super-position, are fairly straightforward: the deposits at the top are younger than the deposits in the levels below it (Rowe 1961). This is fairly intuitive; after all, most kids know that if you want to find dinosaurs in the back yard, you have to dig a really, really, really deep hole to get back to the pre-human stuff. In archaeology, we are not dealing with geological strata; Instead, we are excavating deposits created by humans that follow the same general principles in their formation as geological strata. Therefore, you will often hear archaeol-ogists talk about depositional layers instead of stratigraphic layers (see Harris 1979). Authors often like to illustrate this concept of superposition by urging the reader to think about the construction of a layer cake: in a two-layer cake, you start with the bottom layer, add icing to that, then add the second layer, and cover the whole remaining thing with icing. In terms of sequence, the oldest part of the cake is the bottom layer of cake, and the newest part of the cake would be the outermost icing layer. It's a somewhat old device for understanding this concept, but a useful one. As I'll discuss further in the next chapter, the notion of superposition has been very important in archaeological dating.

Archaeologists will often talk about *contexts*; this is shorthand for where/when a site, feature, artifact, or ecofact was situated in the world. A context is spatial *and* temporal; the context for the beads described in chapter one would be the 2009 Bacchus parade, just north of I-10 on St. Charles Street. We could also talk about the social or political contexts of the beads: four years after Hurricane Katrina, the second year of the Obama presidency, or 16 years after the legally mandated desegregation of New Orleans' Mardi Gras parading organizations. In terms of interpreting the materials archaeologists recover, these are all potentially important kinds of contexts to consider.

Some archaeologists have spent a tremendous amount of time studying how sites are formed. Michael Schiffer (1987) has developed a field called behavioral archaeology, which is dedicated to understanding what he refers to as *site formation processes*. Archae-ological sites are created through a range of different events. Foremost, human activities create archaeological sites. People make things, build things, drop things, bury, burn, and cook things. They dig holes in one spot and add dirt to build up another area. Archae-ologists study places where people did things in the past. Traces of human activities are the heart of the archaeological record. During and after archaeological sites are created, natural forces like wind, water, and critters can lead to materials being moved from where they were first deposited, or they can preserve some materials and decay others. Dry conditions, like those found in deserts, lead to better preservation of organic remains; whereas the brutal annual cycle of freezing and thawing found in the northeastern United States can lead even durable artifacts, like ceramics, to decay. Human activities shape archaeological sites long after the original inhabitants are gone

Humans impact sites in many ways, be it mining them for particular artifacts, bull-dozing them for roadways, or digging holes in them to plant gardens, and so on. Schiffer refers to site formation processes that can be linked to natural forces as N-forms (natural forms) and human interventions as C-forms (cultural forms). He argues that in order to properly interpret archaeological remains, we must understand all the transformations that have affected a site since the original deposition of materials. While not all archaeologists follow the precise strictures of Schiffer's behavioral archaeology, all practitioners recognize that paying attention to details while excavating can allow us to understand the context(s) that created the collection, or assemblage, of materials we study.

If we think about the Mardi Gras sites again, we can see how human behavior shapes the contents of the parade remains that become deposited in landfills. The beads that are swept up by the street cleaners tend to be broken or of an undesirable length or surface finish. After a parade, you will always see some people combing through the debris, looking for "good" beads that were missed in the heat of the parade. The result is that landfill deposits will not contain the most desired types of Mardi Gras beads in the same proportion as they were thrown; the bad and damaged beads will be overrepresented in the archaeological record. This is a result of human transformation processes shaping the formation of the archaeological site. A natural formation process can also be seen at play in the creation of archaeological deposits associated with night parades. Certain colors of beads, the darker colors, like deep purples, blues, and reds, are harder for humans to see in dim light. Parade goers and the people who later forage for leftover beads, are less likely to see these beads, and a wider range of dark-colored beads will be included in these archaeological deposits. In this case, the natural element involved is light.

The Archaeological Tool Set Continued: Survey

Excavation is just one tool used by archaeologists. We use *pedestrian survey,* or field walking, to walk over a property in a controlled manner to look for surface finds. In areas where there is little ground cover due to either dry conditions, burning, or plowing, archaeological sites can be found by simply walking along and looking at the ground to spot evidence of artifacts or architectural remains. Figure 2.5 shows a pedestrian survey at Fort Davis, Texas. Each flag marks a location of an artifact on the surface. When I worked in Louisiana on plantation sites, there was no better way to identify likely places to excavate than to walk through agricultural fields before the sugar cane was planted. In the bright Louisiana sun, concentrations of broken historic ceramics and glass sherds glittered fiercely and could be easily spotted some distance away. During the Mardi Gras season, one can identify where parades have passed by looking at the trees and telephone wires. While street sweepers do their best to remove surface debris from parade routes, strands of beads too high to reach remain tangled in tree limbs and around light posts and utility lines for months after Carnival.

While pedestrian survey is often one step in a field project that helps to identify sites for later study, some archaeologists focus just on using surface data to identify residential patterns or density of past occupation across a landscape. Some archaeologists will map and then collect the artifacts they encounter, which is referred to as surface collection,

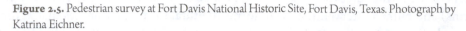

Figure 2.5. Pedestrian survey at Fort Davis National Historic Site, Fort Davis, Texas. Photograph by Katrina Eichner.

while others will engage in a "catch and release" survey, where artifacts are noted and recorded during the survey but left in place. Technologies like GPS and computer tablets have made it much easier for archaeologists to compile vast amounts of spatial, photographic, and catalog data in the field. These technologies also help make it easier to record archaeological information while preserving archaeological remains.

We use a series of other techniques, collectively known as *remote sensing,* to find and record sites without excavating them. As I mentioned before, when we excavate a site we are dismantling it; therefore, we try to treat archaeological sites as the precious non-renewable resources they are. Archaeologists actively try to conserve archaeological remains by limiting the extent of excavation. Similarly, catch and release field survey, remote sensing techniques, and other such approaches allow us to preserve archaeological resources while still studying the archaeological record. Remote sensing technologies allow us to identify and learn something about sites without disturbing them. This is particularly important when studying sites like cemeteries where we want to respect the sacred nature of a place to descendent groups.

Tools like *ground penetrating radar* (**GPR**), *magnetometers,* and resistivity meters allow archaeologists to record subsurface features without physically excavating them (Figure 2.6 illustrates the glamorous work of researchers doing a GPR survey). These machines use sound and radio waves, magnetic concentrations, or resistance to electrical currents to

Figure 2.6. GPR survey at Fort Davis National Historic Site, Fort Davis, Texas. Photograph by Erin Rodriguez.

determine where different types of features are located under the ground surface. These techniques have varying success rates from site to site, but they represent ways that archaeologists seek to minimize excavation and conserve the archaeological record where possible. It is worth noting that there are other remote sensing techniques that you may encounter in the literature. On historical sites, the use of metal detectors can be useful for identifying fence lines (barbed wire or fencing staples), collapsed wood buildings (from nail concentrations), or coffin burials (which can feature metal, particularly brass fittings). Other experiments in remote sensing have included the use of ground-sniffing dogs to attempt to identify buried human remains. One of the leading "experts" in the use of forensic dogs in archaeological settings was disgraced (and prosecuted) when she was discovered planting evidence at a crime scene (Walker, "Canine Case Closed?"). A recent tool that has been increasingly used to identify archaeological sites is Google Earth. As early as World War I, British archaeologists recognized the archaeological potential of aerial photography. A particularly enchanting discovery was the phenomenon of crop marks. In agricultural fields, the crops planted over buried architecture do not thrive as well as those that are not. When observed in the right light from airplane-height above, the stunted areas of crop growth appear as lines tracing the form of the buried architecture. Ancient field walls, ditches, Roman villas, and other such structures have been found through aerial photography. Google Earth's large database of satellite photographs have become a valuable archaeological research tool.

The Archaeological Mindset: Interpretation of Sites

I've now described many different concepts through which we describe archaeological features and sites, as well as ways that we attempt to recover spatial relationships embedded in the archaeological record. How do we actually go from those ideas to actual archaeological interpretation? I think it is best to provide an example of how these different concepts merge into archaeological thinking and interpretation.

When I teach my introductory archaeology course, to illustrate the ideas of provenience, association, and context, I have my students imagine that our lecture hall is struck by a large earthquake that buries us and our possessions. I ask them, "what could later archaeologists learn about us if they had nothing more to go on than our material culture?" Since we live near a large fault, this scenario usually provokes nervous jitters before the students start to tackle the question in earnest. Indulge me for a moment as I explain how a group of future archaeologists might approach the interpretation of a collapsed lecture hall using a basic archaeological mindset.

Archaeologists always have to wrestle with time as a variable. In studying the collapsed lecture hall, archaeologists would want to know if the site represented materials from a single chronological event or a long stretch of time. By carefully removing rubble and roof collapse from the site, the archaeologists would notice that building rubble overlaid a single living surface, the auditorium floor and all human remains and associated features and artifacts were deposited directly on this floor surface. Therefore, all of the traces were from a single depositional event—the earthquake. If they were to excavate several rooms in this classroom building, they would note that the internal arrangement of each room was similar; thus, what they learned from excavation of the largest room would provide insights into activities in the other rooms as well.

Once rubble was cleared, the archaeologists would notice that permanently fixed objects in the large room would include seats with moveable tabletops. These were aligned in rows along a sloping floor so that seats in the back were raised to a higher level than those in the front of the room. All seats faced in the same direction. Projection boards and chalkboards were mounted in the view shed of each of these seats. A single podium with an audiovisual equipment box would be discovered to be the only feature facing the people seated in the audience. Mapping these features would reveal that the room was organized so that a large number of spectators could direct their attention toward the front of the room. The writing surfaces attached to each seat would suggest that the spectators were not expected to be passive, but actively engaged with the images or person(s) at the front of the room.

Associated with many of these seats would be canvas containers that we, today, would recognize as backpacks. An examination of these bags would reveal great similarity in contents (Figure 2.7): cell phones, keys, wallets, photo identification, water bottles, textbooks, notebooks, pens, pencils, and perhaps portable snacks like granola bars. While the archaeologists would see some variation between the packs (because, of course, we are all unique and special), the repetition of certain objects over and over in the packs would suggest to the researchers that these artifacts comprised a toolkit that was necessary to occupy whatever status the room occupants held.

As for the occupants, since it was a catastrophic earthquake, a number of human skeletons would be found in the room clustered near exits and trapped in the rows of chairs (the students never like this part of the mental exercise). For the sake of our discussions, let us presume that this is an ethically astute excavation, and our hypothetical future archaeologists were asked to study all human remains of the imaginary descendant community before handing the remains over for reburial. Therefore, we can consider as well what could be learned from human remains. Bioarchaeologists—archaeologists

Figure 2.7. Typical toolkit of a Berkeley undergraduate, ca. 2013.

who specialize in studying human skeletal materials—are able to learn a great deal about an individual's life history from bones (e.g., Agarwal and Stout 2003; Baadsguard et al. 2012). Some bioarchaeological techniques have evolved out of *forensics,* which is the application of scientific methods or technologies to reconstruct evidence that can be used in legal arguments. Forensic data include determinations like skeletal age, sex, height, weight, enduring illnesses, injuries, and body modifications, such as dental work and so on. In addition, bone chemistry can reveal dietary preferences, place of birth, and exposure to pollutants. Other categories of data sometimes used in forensic anthropology, such as the determination of race, are much more controversial and of questionable use.

Some of the victims would be associated with their *toolkits*—a term archaeologists use to describe the set of items associated with the labors of a particular person or group of people. In the case of our victims, their toolkits were nicely carried together in canvas containers (backpacks). In midst of the earthquake, some victims had the presence of mind to grab their toolkits as they left their seats, while others panicked and chose to flee without their belongings. The study of toolkits in association with specific bodies would allow archaeologists to see if there were any gendered, status, or age associations for particular types or styles of artifacts in the toolkits.

Other objects associated with the bodies could be clothing. Garments can have differential preservation depending on climate, but many synthetic fabrics preserve well as would metal buttons, rivets, zippers, plastic buttons, rubber and plastic shoe soles, synthetic leathers, and shell or bone buttons or ornaments. Archaeologists would recognize that many of the humans shared a similar "uniform" or mode of dress that reflected a preference for loose-fitting clothes that could be worn in layers and shoes comfortable for walking. They would find that many of the clothing items were marked with a few particular manufacturers' names (e.g., Old Navy, Hollister, Converse). Body ornamentation in the form of rings, watches, necklaces, hair ornaments, synthetic hair extensions, glasses, and a range of body piercings would preserve. At least one student would have a strand of plastic beads with a resin "CAL" medallion—a souvenir from a recent football game—suspended from them or shoved in a pocket of their backpack.

If the archaeologists look at the age and gender distribution (the population's demographic profile), the skeletons recovered from the room would show that the majority of the population was comprised of young adults aged 18–25 years. Distinctive among the remains may be an older adult located near the front of the room, closest to the podium and projection boards, who may or may not be clothed differently from the others in the room, (certainly, during the first week of class, when I usually present this scenario, I try to be better dressed than my usual jeans, t-shirt, and sneakers). The archaeologists may find this individual to be associated with a briefcase instead of a backpack and fewer portable items than the others in the room. It is possible, but not guaranteed, that the archaeologists may recognize the faculty person as occupying a different status than the others. If the auditorium had contained a history lecture rather than an archaeology class, the professor would have immediately been identifiable. As an ethnographic point, historians are generally natty dressers and can be easily distinguished from archaeology professors.

There are many other things an archaeologist may observe without prior knowledge of university life to guide them. If they could translate the "NO FOOD OR DRINKS" signs in the room, they might laugh at the large number of discarded coffee cups and soda cans in the room. They might observe the repetition of yellow bear imagery (GO BEARS!) accompanied by the symbol "CAL" on items of clothing and artifacts found in the toolkit and suspect that the persons wearing them were somehow socially or politically affiliated to one another (for a number of historical reasons, there is little reason that any record of this university's football team would survive in the future). The archaeologists may ponder whether the victims lived during a period leading to social or economic collapse, as they observe that many of the technology-related features of the room are much older than the technology recovered from the backpacks. This observation would suggest that the victims lived in a period when infrastructure was not being invested in, which is a recognizable sign of imminent collapse of state-level society. This interpretation may be bolstered if they were to conduct *microstratigraphic analysis* (the recovery of microscopic layers of dirt) of the wall surfaces and recognize the relative thickness of layers of grime accumulated between coats of fresh paint had increased, indicating that walls had not been repainted as often as they had been in the earlier occupation of the building. They might also observe the seats were old and worn and the writing surfaces were covered with carved symbols and pictures. From this graffiti, archaeologists may get hints of mating rituals, social practices, and political attitudes of those in the room (most Berkeley lecture hall graffiti includes references to legalizing marijuana and the benefits of veganism).

Analysis of soils from victim's shoes could recover pollen or *phytoliths* (microscopic silicon structures found in some plants), and provide insights into the surrounding flora. It may be that instead of processed foods like granola bars, candy bars, and bags of chips (all artifacts), that some students were carrying bananas, oranges, apples, or other fruits or vegetables in their backpacks. These ecofacts would require paleoethnobotanists, or people who study ancient plant remains, to become involved in analysis. Chemical analysis of glass and metal objects may be used to trace objects to their manufacturing origin. Only two things would restrict what the archaeologists could learn: the questions they chose to ask and their creativity in constructing analyses that would address those questions.

I hope this scenario wasn't too tedious. I spent some time on it to emphasize that as a way of viewing the world and defining key terms, archaeological thinking is a powerful tool for illuminating social relations as enacted by people with things. I will stress again and again that archaeology is a way of thinking, and it's a productive way of thinking because materials are so important to human beings as a species. I am going to push you throughout this book to really see things, not just as noise, but as a means of communication and a means through which people create their worlds.

The Archaeological Mindset: As a Way of Asking Questions

If archaeology is a way of thinking, it is equally a way of doing. Archaeological doing starts not with a trowel but with questions. Suppose as you are hiking in a remote area, you discover a ruined structure, and scattered around it are visible trash remains. As you poked around the ruins, you might ask yourself, who lived here; what were they doing out here; when did they live here; or when and why did they leave? You might pick up objects from the ground and ask yourself, how did they use this, and what was it for? There are many other questions about the people who created, lived in, used, and abandoned this structure, but "who," "when," and "what" are essential archaeological questions—questions we ask every time we start work on a new site and every time we begin studying a new time period or part of the world. You will note that our questions do not include, is there treasure here? Nor do they include, what are these things worth, or could I sell any of this? These are not questions that archaeologists ask; for we recognize always that the value of archaeological objects is in what they can tell us about human experiences.

In any number of archaeological textbooks, authors will declare that the difference between an archaeologist and a pothunter or bottle collector (someone who mines archaeological sites for artifacts for personal ownership or to sell) is that an archaeologist goes into excavation with a research question. I would suggest that the difference is more the kinds of research questions we ask and what we intend to do with the knowledge we gain. There are many very knowledgeable pothunters who have seen more archaeological sites than trained archaeologists—you can dig a lot more when you don't worry about record keeping. They also keep their knowledge to themselves, don't pay attention to provenience, context, and associations, and only selectively collect whole artifacts of particular types.

We will discuss research questions and research design more in a later chapter, but I did want you to be thinking about what it is we expect to learn from any given archaeological site that we study. The Carnival bead assemblages we will discuss were created under very specific conditions of short duration and are best suited to understanding some very Carnival-specific questions that have larger implications for American society. There is always a question or set of questions that a researcher wants to explore when they approach an archaeological site. The archaeologist designs their research strategy around those questions. The kinds of questions asked by an archaeologist are shaped by a scholar's disciplinary and theoretical orientation. Now, some people hear the word "theory" and get anxious, for there is a strange perception in the world that theory is "hard." There are some archaeologists who like to think that there are two kinds of archaeologists: armchair archaeologists who worry about theory, and field archaeologists, who actually dig sites. The people who say this are usually people who just dig sites and expect interpretation to take care of itself.

There are, in fact, only two kinds of archaeologists: responsible archaeologists and irresponsible archaeologists. A responsible archaeologist recognizes that all of the archaeological process relies upon assumptions derived from different sets of theories. When we excavate, find different layers of soil, and interpret the lowermost deposit to be the oldest, we are drawing from theories developed in geology (superposition again!). When we analyze animal bones using comparative specimens to identify species, we are drawing upon zoology and ideas about the nature of zoological classification. When we make observations about different features of artifacts to compare them to one another to interpret past behavior, we are drawing on theories from the philosophy of science. The questions we ask and the ways we decide to answer them are also shaped by theory. A responsible archaeologist also recognizes that knowledge is produced in a social context and that this knowledge production comes with ethical responsibilities, such as the need to conserve and preserve archaeological remains as much as possible, to publish findings, to work with community and regulatory groups, and to curate materials in a way that allows others to later study the collections.

Theory shapes research questions and design. An archaeologist interested in gender roles, sexuality, inequality between the sexes, representations of the body, or parenting and childhood, is probably drawing upon a range of feminist theorizing about human sexual and gender relations. Similarly, if the relationship between humans and their environment is a focus of study, that archaeologist will be drawing upon ideas from ecology, biology, and environmental sciences. If understanding the consolidation of power, ideologies of subjugation, social inequality, or the spread of capitalistic systems is an archaeologist's cup of tea, that researcher is likely to be reading Marx and other Marx-inspired thinkers.

Different aspects of the archaeological record are going to be important to different archaeologists depending on their research questions. The artifacts are not little puzzles waiting to be solved, they are just stuff. *Data*—or the observations that we make about the world—are not waiting to be discovered in the artifacts. Data are completely created by the archaeologist. We decide that for our particular research, an artifact color is important, that its size, the material it is made out of, or the way it was made are important things to record. The artifacts merely exist. We decide, through the process of analysis, how to understand them. Similarly, different observations about the same artifacts may be important to different archaeologists. Archaeological sites are not giant jigsaw puzzles that when put together will reveal one picture. Instead, the same assemblage of artifacts can be used to answer many questions about many different aspects of human life. In the study of Mardi Gras beads, I will be subjecting the same assemblage of beads to different questions drawn from different bodies of archaeological theorizing. The beads do not change from one analysis to another, and in many cases, the characteristics, or attributes, of the beads I discuss will be the same from chapter to chapter. The pictures of human life that we create out of those beads, however, will look very different from one chapter to another.

What makes the most difference from one archaeological interpretation to another is the theoretical bent of the researcher, the questions she asks, and the data she uses to answer those questions. For instance, let us consider a collection of animal bones (also known as a faunal assemblage). A feminist archaeologist studying parenting strategies may compare the bones recovered from households with children versus childless households to see if there were particular foods or food types associated with nourishing children. Our Marxist archaeologist may focus on whether there is differential access to particular species or cuts of meat depending on a household's social status. In contrast, we may find our biologist looking at the ages of animals represented in the faunal assemblage to see if they can learn something about herding or hunting strategies. Which archaeologist is right? As long as they are rigorous and consistent in how they construct, collect, and interpret their data, each of these scholars can provide important, if very different, insights to the past.

There are infinite understandings of the human experience that can be studied from a single group of artifacts. Why is this so important to emphasize? We need to recognize that knowledge is constructed—not extracted. We live in a world that emphasizes superficial and quickly obtained "information" that is not critically consumed but swallowed effortlessly without regard to its flavor. There are thousands of collections curated in museums across the globe that are understudied. There are archaeologists who believe that artifacts excavated with less modern techniques are less "reliable" than artifacts excavated more recently; therefore, they ignore museum collections in their studies. We will be showing how incorrect that assumption is as we consider the Mardi Gras beads. After all, it's hard to imagine a less technologically sophisticated mode of archaeological recovery than catching things thrown at you!

You should think of theory as a tool that scholars use to do research or perhaps a pair of glasses that they use to see the world. During your life, you will encounter people who subscribe to only one theoretical view—a set of ideas that they will employ to understand all aspects of human life and that they will defend over all other views, sometimes to the point of absurdity. These poor folks have become ideologues and are no longer really involved in creating knowledge but are committed to preaching a particular way of thinking. Those with the quickest and most nimble minds will draw on any number of theories during the course of their scholarly life as they try to refine their own understanding of how human life is experienced. If you see theories as tools, that you control, rather than ideas that control you, you will have a rewarding intellectual life.

Now, I have spent some words discussing this for a reason. The techniques that we use in archaeology were developed during times when particular sets of theories were popular among archaeologists. We continue to use many of these techniques even after discarding the theoretical package that created them. Many of these methods and techniques are still employed by people influenced by different theories, though sometimes they need to be tweaked from one research context to another. I will be discussing in the next several chapters some of the ways of thinking about the relationships between people and things and the archaeological record that created different archaeological field and lab methods. To explain the different methods, we will be using the Mardi Gras beads that I have "excavated." Although I use the word excavation in quotes, I am quite emphatic that these objects were recovered in an archaeological way—with controls for space and time.

Contemporary Archaeology and the Study of Mardi Gras

In considering the collapsed lecture hall, you could see how a basic archaeological way of thinking—looking for patterns that reveal relationships between people, places, and things—is a powerful interpretive tool. This is the cornerstone of archaeological thinking. An archaeological lens turned upon the world can be a powerful tool for understanding a range of different issues and applications in the present, as well as the past. A specific field of archaeology that seeks to use the discipline's methods to approach modern problems is called "contemporary archaeology."

Contemporary archaeology takes many forms and has multiple goals (e.g., Buchli and Lucas 2001a; Gould 2007; Graves-Browne 2000; Harrison and Schofield 2010). One of the highest profile contemporary archaeology projects is the Tucson Garbage Project, started by Dr. William Rathje in 1973 (Rathje 1979; Rathje and Murphy 2001). Rathje recognized that landfills were one of the great public health and urban living challenges of the upcoming century. He developed a series of projects over the next thirty years that sought to document what was actually in landfills (and potentially dangerous impacts to people from those things), the nature of preservation in landfills, and what practices could improve the management of landfills. Doing what archaeologists do best, Rathje addressed these and other research questions through the excavation and analysis of materials from city landfills. Theoretically drawing on ideas from ecology and environmental sciences, Rathje was an archaeologist who was interested in the relationship between humans and their environment. Rathje's research demonstrated that even landfill engineers had little understanding of what was in landfills! Diapers and fast food packaging were popularly believed to be the largest components of landfills; instead, Rathje demonstrated that construction waste, industrial waste, and paper were the most common artifacts found in landfills. Paper not only accounted for nearly half of the volume of landfill discards, but it was found to decay much more slowly than previously thought. It would not be exaggerating to partially credit Rathje's findings for the growth of paper recycling programs across the country in the 1980s and 1990s.

Another field of contemporary archaeology brings together the field of forensics with archaeological methods and techniques to understand crime or disaster scenes. It was a sense of helplessness following the attacks of 9/11 that inspired Brown University archaeologist, Richard Gould (2007), to develop a field that he refers to as "disaster archaeology." Witnessing cleanup efforts, Gould realized that cleaning crews removing ash from building tops and streets far from the towers were inadvertently discarding human remains. The small charred fragments were unrecognizable to lay people, but large enough to potentially genetically identify individuals and give a sense of closure to a grieving family. Gould worked with police departments in New York, and later in Rhode Island, to develop this branch of contemporary archaeology in which archaeological search and recovery techniques are used to understand disaster scenes and to recover evidence and human remains. Other bioarchaeologists use skills developed in archaeology to assist in the investigation of mass gravesites for international human rights organizations (e.g., Saunders 2002; Steele 2008). Archaeological excavation techniques allow for the recovery of small evidence that can help reconstruct genocide events and identify victims while also determining those responsible for the crimes.

Working on a smaller scale, Victor Buchli and Gavin Lucas (2001b) have demonstrated the potential for contemporary archaeology to humanize persons typically seen as marginal in society. Buchli and Lucas's work at a British, two-bedroom, council house (government assisted housing) was guided by two questions: who had lived there and why had they left? Theoretically, the scholars were influenced by writings on the experiences of living in modern society and the experience of alienation from society by marginalized groups. The archaeologists spent two days making an archaeological study of the site, which had been suddenly abandoned by its renter. The survey was undertaken without knowing anything about the occupants other than what could be learned from their material remains. Review of the materials left behind showed that women and children's artifacts were found throughout the house. Some men's clothing was represented, but accounted for half as much as the women's clothing. The children's clothing suggested an older boy and a younger girl lived in the house. The archaeologists were unsure whether the men's clothing represented materials left by someone who only came to the house irregularly or if women's clothing consumption patterns were different than men's. Review of toiletries left in the house made it clear that members of the household were engaging in consenting sexual relations. The recovery of methadone prescribed to the male also indicated a heroine addiction was present in the household.

Even though the house was abandoned, many materials were left in the household. The archaeological survey revealed that the occupant had been in the process of selectively packing belongings to move but for some reason did not return to the house to recover even the packed materials. The combination of the sudden departure, the presence of a male partner with an addiction, and the archaeological evidence suggesting that the man may not have been a full-time occupant of the household, led the archaeologists to suspect the abandonment had been sudden and unexpected.

To understand the site more fully, they consulted with the housing authority and learned the house was rented to a young mother with two children. The woman received full government income support and housing benefit. The housing authority was surprised by the abandonment because the tenant had been up to date on all rent payments. Leaving the property in arrears would have made her ineligible for further services and difficult to secure other housing. By choosing to abandon the site, she became ineligible for future government support. So why did she leave? The archaeologists believed that what they had encountered was a site abandoned suddenly by a woman with her children after a breakdown in a relationship with a recovering heroine addict. The rapid departure from the house suggested that the woman had either suffered or expected to suffer domestic violence if found at the house. The archaeology revealed the dire circumstances faced by poor women attempting to leave abusive relationships and the failure of government social programs to account for these circumstances, despite statistics that demonstrate that 17% of young women who became homeless did so due to a relationship breakdown. For archaeologists, the project illuminated problems in housing authority policies. The absurdity of policies that forced this woman to choose between her family's immediate physical safety or their long-term ability to live in affordable housing is illustrated more clearly through the archaeological record than it could ever be represented in dry government statistics.

I was involved in the excavation of another contemporary archaeology site recently. In the summer of 2013, on the campus of the University of California, the field school I was directing uncovered a large stash of artifacts left in 1999 by an unknown number of homeless persons in the ruins of a campus structure. People were protecting their goods by stashing them in plastic bags and hiding them under fallen floorboards from the structure. We know the stash is no later than 1999 because we found over 100 pennies, none more recent than 1999. Newspaper accounts from late 1998 express the intent to crack down on the homeless on campus because of their involvement in drug sales. The site was covered with a deep layer of mulch to keep people from retrieving their goods, thus preserving them for us to find 14 years later. The only evidence of drug use we found was one very beat up bong that I dated to 1994. Otherwise, the materials we found included many toiletries, dress clothing, cold medicine, vitamins, frisbees, cassette tapes, tennis balls, water bottles, art supplies, and many bags (Figure 2.8). Interestingly, we found a money belt and extra pockets to sew into clothing—providing insights into the dangers of living on the streets and the need to keep one's valuables close to oneself. We excavated each stuffed bag as a feature, and are opening and recording them in the lab. Work is ongoing, but I think we're going to learn a great deal about a modern population who has been pushed to the side of our society and who has many different stereotypes associated with them. We are not trailblazers in this kind of work. Larry Zimmerman and Jessica Welch (2011) have been conducting contemporary archaeological research of homeless populations in the Midwest.

As you can see from the above examples, contemporary archaeology has an overtly political activism associated with it (Harrison and Schofield 2010). As an archaeology of ourselves, it is a discipline dedicated to understanding the social phenomenon that shape our lived experiences and that desires to contribute to the struggle for social justice. One of the strengths of contemporary archaeology is that it demonstrates that there is utility to the set of interpretive and methodological tools that archaeologists have developed for studying more remote pasts in the present.

Our Case Study: Why Beads?

So where does the Mardi Gras bead study fit into contemporary archaeology? And why do we even need a contemporary archaeology of Mardi Gras? It may not seem that the

Figure 2.8. Archaeology of homelessness. Examples of artifacts found: A. Toiletries and health related artifacts; B. Education and entertainment related artifacts.

study of plastic beads is as politically compelling as looking at the murder site of political hostages (Saunders 2002) or the site of the World Trade Center (Gould 2007). Yet, when you look at images of Carnival, you will see looped around the necks of participants, thrown in the streets and from parades, and distributed by hotels, restaurants, casinos, race tracks, and liquor companies are strands of plastic beads that are shipped by the millions from China—Mardi Gras beads. They are an ubiquitous and spreading currency in Mardi Gras celebrations of the Gulf Coast; yet, while clearly a visible and sometimes contested aspect of the Carnival season, they are always discussed as an aside or peripheral to whatever aspect of Mardi Gras is being studied.

Yet, once you notice Mardi Gras beads, you can't stop seeing them. And not just in Louisiana; they are visible at sporting events, hanging from car rearview mirrors, piled at flea markets, and tossed at Gay Pride parades. It is the simultaneous ubiquity and seemingly randomness of practices surrounding and, yet, unremarked upon nature of Mardi Gras beads that drew my attention. They are part of the politics of everyday life that connects laborers in China to parade goers in New Orleans. They are a medium through which the experiences of racism, sexism, and economic exclusivity are communicated, contested, circumvented, and caricatured. I will show you how in later chapters. In different historical contexts, people have fought for the right to both throw and catch beads as full participants in Carnival settings. The throwing game of Mardi Gras is serious play, but it is play that has not received the kind of scholarly attention it deserves.

I attended my first Mardi Gras celebration in 1991. I had heard of Mardi Gras, understood the general principles of it all as a Carnival celebration before the Lenten season began, but I did not really know what to expect of the experience. Most confusing to me was the notion of Mardi Gras beads and the throwing game. I interrogated people about Mardi Gras beads. Carnival-experienced friends and natives tried to explain.

> Friend. Well you see, the float riders, they throw beads from the parade floats for you to catch.
> Author. What kind of beads?
> Friend. You know, plastic beads. Some are short but the good ones are really long. Anyway, when the float comes by you wave and yell, 'throw me something, mister' and they throw you beads to catch.
> Author. And they just throw these at you?
> Friend. Yeah, for you to catch and wear.
> Author. Why?
> Friend. Why not? It's fun!
> Author. So you walk around after the parades wearing a bunch of plastic beads?
> Friend. Not all of the beads, just the good ones.
> Author. So, not everybody gets these beads, right?
> Author. Oh no, you go to Mardi Gras, you'll get beads. You'll get bags of beads. You won't believe how many beads you'll get.
> Author. I thought a lot of people went to Mardi Gras. How many beads are we talking about?
> Friend. Lots of beads, there are lots of beads. Everybody who wants beads gets beads.
> Author. Why do we want the beads again?
> Friend. Because they are cool, you know?
> Author. So, these are plastic beads they're throwing, because it's fun?

At this point, there is an inevitable eye roll, a dismissive wave of the hand, and the irritated headshake.

> Friend. Cher, you just have to go see the Mardi Gras. Then you'll understand.

◇◇◇◇

I went to Mardi Gras, and I did indeed get more beads than I would have imagined. While I began to understand the tempo and contours of the throwing game, I was more confused than ever. I took heart from a 1947 description of Carnival in New Orleans,

> During Mardi Gras the hotels are filled to overflowing and people sleep on cots in the corridors in fire stations and bars, in the press room at City Hall, on pool tables and park benches . . . Mardi Gras is attended by about five hundred thousand persons and hardly anybody, except the natives, has an idea of what it is all about." (Early 1947:257)

The questions I had asked before experiencing Mardi Gras remained. Why exactly did we want the beads, and how on earth did this come to be? I was surprised to learn, that despite the interest in Mardi Gras as a uniquely American festival, there was no sustained research undertaken on the throwing game. Thus began a long-term study of Mardi Gras beads.

This project is about a particular American folk tradition, but it is a much larger project through which I am grappling with larger issues of commodity exchange, globalization, racism, sexism, urban renewal, how materials and people engage, and the impacts of natural disasters on social life. Plastic beads connect each of these issues and social phenomena with the chaos of a knotted tangle . . . a mess not dissimilar to the handfuls of tangled beads thrown to parade goers at Mardi Gras.

Historical Archaeology

In this study, I have taken a documentary or *historical archaeological* approach to this contemporary phenomenon. Archaeologists working in the deep past are studying pre-literate societies—this area of study is known as *prehistoric archaeology*. Those of us who work in the more recent past—and "recent" can be as ancient as 4000 BC for the earliest cuneiform writing—have to consider the written records that a society left of itself, as well as the archaeological remains. When I'm not catching Mardi Gras beads, much of my archaeological research focuses on nineteenth- and twentieth-century sites. There is a rich documentary or archival record associated with this period of time, such as government records, such as censuses, tax rolls, judicial records, and popular culture, including fiction, magazines, newspapers, songs, and even early cinema, photographic evidence, and a range of personal papers and other ephemera that preserve thoughts. Just as archaeological materials need to be interpreted, so does archival evidence. People recorded things in writing with a sense of purpose: to document economic transactions, to remind themselves of errands to run, to stay in touch with loved ones, or even, in the case of diary writing, to present a particular wholesome image of themselves to future readers. Just as the arch-aeological record is created through the interventions of nature and humans, so is the archival record. Uncomfortable subjects may be rendered invisible with documents being intentionally destroyed or events left unrecorded, leaving archival silences. Populations denied education and literacy are likewise silenced in the archival record. Nature also takes a toll on the documentary record—which is, after all, just another kind of artifact assemblage. Papers left unprotected will rot, burn, or be sustenance for silverfish.

While the historical resources I use are curated in courthouses, libraries, and archives for more ancient documents, historians are reliant on the archaeological record. It is from archaeological sites that the earliest evidence of writing has been found, and even complete texts, like the gospels contained on papyrus and parchments of the Dead Sea scrolls, were discovered in archaeological contexts. While history and archaeology share a close disciplinary relationship, archaeology is also allied with a sister branch of anthropology—social cultural anthropology—which uses the tools of ethnographic participant observa-tion to gather its evidence in the study of contemporary society. Ethnographers learn about contemporary social phenomenon by engaging in those phenomena as self-conscious and reflective observers. By being aware of the ways one should behave as a participant in a social group, an ethnographer moves from having an *etic*, or outsider's perspective, toward a closer approximation of an *emic*, or insider's perspective of a social group's or community's world view. Just as an archaeologist understands they can never get into the mind of their archaeological subject (well, there are some, and we will discuss them soon), an ethnographer realizes that there will always be some distance between themselves and their subject, because the ethnographer necessarily views the world through their own learned, cultural values. Participant observation and self-reflexive thinking allows the anthropologist to narrow the divide between insider and outsider understandings of a social phenomenon. When I introduced you to what it is to attend a Mardi Gras parade, I was attempting to bring you closer to an insider's perspective and experience of Carnival. This makes that work essentially ethnographic.

While the basis of this study is ethnographic and archival, it is done through an archaeological lens. I think in terms of people, things, spaces, and time. Material things, whether recovered from the dirt or, in this case, the air, must be organized, analyzed, classified, contextualized, and cataloged as individual items, yet also recognized as parts of assemblages and subassemblages. This is why I present this work as a contemporary archaeology rather than an ethnography. Tim Ingold (1993:152), a scholar who has written much about people and things in anthropology, advocates for anthropologists to bring a perspective he refers to as dwelling. Dwelling is achieved through knowledge gained through lived experience. He asserts that archaeology, through the process of doing, is a form of dwelling. He writes that "it is of course part of an archaeological training to learn to attend to those clues which the rest of us might pass over (literally when they are below the surface) and which make it possible to tell a fuller or richer story" (Ingold 1993:152–53). This study brings an archaeological sense of dwelling to the experience of Mardi Gras and the throwing game, and I would suggest that an archaeological sense of dwelling separates contemporary archaeology from ethnography.

The History of the Throwing Game: Doing the Research

My research into the throwing game led me not only to parade routes and flea markets, but into archives and libraries and to sort through postcard bins. Doing archival research is a lot like excavation. You can imagine all the wonderful things you will find, but it's not until you actually dig a hole or get into an archive that you really see what you'll have to work with. Even though archives often have online catalogs that describe collections and documents, sometimes the catalog description is longer than the actual document. When I began, I presumed that I would discover in the collections of places like LSU, the Louisiana State Archives, and the Historic New Orleans and Tulane University's archives vast amounts of information about the experiences of going to Mardi Gras over the 300 years it's been celebrated in Louisiana. After all, a celebration so centrally identified with the state had to have a vast record of first-hand accounts. Within that evidence, I also expected to find discussions of the throwing game. I planned on supplementing these primary documents with newspaper stories and secondary sources.

Archives have different degrees of formality associated with them. I find Hill Memorial Library, the archive at LSU, to be one of my favorite collections to use. After passing through security and relinquishing all your pens (pencils only in the archive!), you enter a large well-appointed, high ceilinged, large oak-ornamented room with luxurious seats and tables, which is the reading room for the Louisiana and Lower Mississippi Valley Collections. You identify which collections you want to examine from online and physical catalogs, and after filling out paperwork requesting to see portions of certain collections, you sit in one of these nice seats and wait for people to bring things to you. Archives cannot stop the processes of decay that plague old documents, just try to slow the process and minimize the damage that handling them can bring. The most fragile of documents will often be microfilmed so that the originals are no longer handled. This is particularly true of nineteenth-century newspapers, which were printed on very thin, large pieces of paper (broadsheets) that do not preserve well. Newspapers are good examples of taken-for-granted documents that are tremendously valuable historical resources that users toss aside when they are done with them. Archives spend a great deal of effort trying to obtain and preserve issues of long-disbanded newspapers.

When you receive a box of documents, it is always exciting. There is so much potential. Just a few sheets away could be a casual observation written by someone a hundred years ago that provides exactly the insight you need for your research. I always get happy butterflies in my stomach when I first open a box and peer in. At LSU, I had found references to multiple diaries and paper collections that were supposed to contain descriptions of Mardi Gras celebrations. I was hoping to find information on the origins of the throwing game. When did it become common for things to be thrown from floats, and when did beads become part of the mix? Several collections had me particularly excited. Anna Farrar Richardson, who was married to a New Orleans engineer kept a diary from 1899 to 1902—a time when I believed bead throwing had begun. Emily Caroline Douglas's handwritten, 1904, autobiography was cataloged as containing a description of Mardi Gras. The Gay Papers included letters from one of the family's daughters to her grandmother about Mardi Gras in the 1870s, and as a long shot, there was a collection that contained a couple of letters to a Massachusetts man from his brother who lived on a houseboat on the Mississippi River in the late 1890s. Typically, women are better sources of social information in the nineteenth century. If they were of the middle or elite classes, they had limited opportunities in Louisiana for life outside the home, and they were dedicated correspondents to family members. Diaries were often kept with the intention of passing them along to daughters as a form of guidebook to married and family life. I was hoping to find good information.

I started with Anna Farrar Richardson's diary. The first one in the box was the 1902 volume. I excitedly read her entry for Fat Tuesday: "a cold day—growing colder—the N. wind has been blowing very hard. All the young folks went out to see 'Rex' come in. In the afternoon H. and I went down to Fellman to get some things and to my surprise we saw

'Rex' parade on Canal. I had no idea of seeing it at all. I got some overcoats for the small boys—it is so cold." (Ann Farrar Richardson Diary, Feb 10, 1902, LLMVC, LSU).

"WHAT?" I thought loudly in my head, for one has to be quiet in an archive, "I DON'T CARE ABOUT THE WEATHER! WHAT DID THE PARADE LOOK LIKE???"

With a sense of gloom I noticed her next entry. "It tires me to be in crowds and I don't care for processions." She was true to her word; in 1900, she wrote, "they all went out to the procession tonight to Lucy's again—they went there this morning too—I do not feel in the spirits for Mardi Gras" (Ann Farrar Richardson Diary, February 27, 1900, LLMVC, LSU). I was not surprised in her 1899 entry to find: "the children went to Lucy's to see the Rex procession, Morgan having gone off without his breakfast" (Ann Farrar Richardson Diary, February 14, 1899, LLMVC, LSU). Just my luck, Ann Richardson was a shut-in during Carnival and obsessed with the weather.

My luck did not improve. Emily Caroline Douglas's autobiography talked about the beauty of the parades in an abstract sense, not in any kind of personal way. Anna Gay spent a great deal of time writing to her grandmother about the costume she planned to wear to the Mardi Gras celebrations and the Mystic Krewe's Tableau, but little description of the parades except that they were magnificent. It takes time for each request for a new collection to be processed, and as the archive was getting close to "last call," I received the box containing Arthur P. Thrasher's correspondence from 1895–1898. Most of the box contained business correspondence related to Thrasher's life in Massachusetts. I found a folder, however, that contained a letter from Charles Thrasher, Arthur's brother, who was living in New Orleans for a short time as part of a business opportunity. In the letter he wrote to his brother on January 13, 1896, Charles indicated that he felt he was living in a foreign country while in Louisiana. He described a lynching and sarcastically commented on the high society members of New Orleans who would allow them as outsiders to the city to watch Mardi Gras parades but not enter "that holy of holies: the ballroom." He said little about Mardi Gras in the letter, but I found myself liking the personality that showed itself in his words. I finished the letter and then realized that there was another letter on smaller paper under it in the folder. Dated February 27, 1896, this letter described Mardi Gras! And while he only wrote a couple paragraphs about Carnival, it was his description of the floats that earned him my undying love: "the people on them [the floats] were all alive and moving, cutting up monkey shine and throwing candy into the crowds by handfuls and by the package. Bet you can imagine Alice [his wife] making a scramble for some and she got some too [sic] and brought some home" (Arthur P. Thrasher Correspondence, 1895–1898, February 27, 1896, LLMVC, LSU). One hundred years before I began my Mardi Gras study, people were already fighting one another for stuff thrown from floats.

I realized after several attempts to find period descriptions of Mardi Gras that the problem with my approach was the assumption that Louisianans, who lived each year with the festivities, would record their reactions to it. They did not. When doing research on slavery in the Bahamas, to learn about the areas where the enslaved populations had come from in Africa, I turned to early travel descriptions kept by slavers, abolitionists, and other European colonists about the African coast. While such sources have a great many potential biases to work through, there are still kernels that can be extracted. Prehistorians working in colonized areas often turn to similar documents to understand the social, political, and economic worlds of indigenous peoples at the time of contact and colonization for clues how to interpret certain archaeological remains.

In England, the *Doomsday Book,* a survey of England and Wales by William the Conquerer after his conquest of England in AD 1066, is a great example of a colonizer's document used by Anglo Saxon archaeologists to understand land tenure, settlement patterns, and farming among the Britons (Arnold 1997). We will discuss how ethnographic descriptions and documents are used in archaeological interpretation in a couple of chapters. In my case, I decided that perhaps I should take a similar tact with the Mardi Gras beads. Thrasher provided a description of the events of Mardi Gras because it was so foreign to him—Mardi Gras had been a tourist destination since at least the 1870s. Perhaps there was a body of literature aimed at visitors to explain the chaos they experienced at Mardi Gras. I soon found that my best sources on Carnival practices were travel guides to New Orleans and local newspapers who published explanatory articles about the goings-on right around the time of Fat Tuesday. In such a way, I was able to capture what was seen as ordinary Carnival practice at a particular time. This, supplemented with photos and postcards bought at flea markets, provided most of the documentary outline for my understanding of the history of the throwing game. So what did I ultimately learn? I am going to share with you a brief history of how Mardi Gras, and the current throwing game, has come to be.

The Throwing Game: What was Learned?

The throwing game did not begin with beads. It began with the throwing of flour, rocks, and mud. The tossing of trinkets is known in other Carnival settings. German *Fasnet* celebrations include *Maschkele* maskers, a woman-dominated tradition of processional. These women usually dress as clowns and perform as tricksters, satirizing local events, taunting people they encounter, and distributing small treats that relate to the theme of the costume (Tokofsky 1999). Early New Orleans Mardi Gras celebrations featured street processionals of maskers. These loosely organized processionals were likely to have been composed of groups of revelers who paraded together to entertain and play tricks on those observing them. As New Orleans' population grew in numbers and ethnic and racial diversity, Mardi Gras masks provided some with the protection and opportunity to engage in antisocial and violent behavior. Increased rowdiness verging on mob violence came to characterize these outings (Kinser 1990; Saxon et al. 1989; Young 1939).

A brief description from 1845 by a New Orleans Cotton Exchange clerk notes, "today is Mardi Gras—or Fat Tuesday. Its residents are out and in their various fantastic costumes and tonight closes the fest of the Carnival, after which comes Lent or Catholic Fasting" (Tower papers, LLMV Collections, LSU). The next day, L. F. Tower noted that the usual procession had not appeared. "A crowd of boys and rowdies annoyed them so much with mud and flour and the like that they did not make their appearance though thousands were out to look at them" (Tower papers, LLMV Collections, LSU). The following year, rain hampered the celebrations, but Tower noted that "flour was much in demand" (Tower papers, LLMV Collections, LSU).

The flour that Tower referred to was part of an initially harmless tradition of throwing flour packets or "bon-bons" at maskers. Known as *entruda* (Tofkosky 1999), the packets would explode in a poof, leaving a white coating on the costumed person. In dry circumstances, the flour could be brushed off with a laugh. In wet weather, a sticky mass could ensue. Even less pleasant is the notion of hurled mud. Also during the 1850s, bon-bons of quicklime instead of flour were thrown, causing severe injuries to eyes and faces of those unlucky enough to be hit with them (Perry 1939:20–21). Worse violence was also committed during Mardi Gras celebrations, and newspapers ran counts of how many bodies were pulled from city canals on Ash Wednesday (Perry 1939). City officials seriously discussed banning Mardi Gras celebrations in the city. It was a group of American businessmen, so goes the creation narrative, who banded together to save Mardi Gras and return orderliness to the celebrations.

The group, which called itself the Mystick Krewe of Comus, held a private ball and tableau and a public parade featuring delicate, torch-lit floats. The new phenomenon quickly developed a following, and even the elite of French Creole society ultimately accepted membership invitations, ensuring that the new form of Mardi Gras celebrations would become established (Gill 1997).

While additional krewes formed, Mardi Gras celebrations were interrupted only occasionally by events like the Civil War. The earliest credited throws were said to have originated in 1871 from a krewe member dressed as Santa Claus in the Krewe of the Twelfth Night Revellers (Hardy 1987:15). As we saw in Thrasher's description, the throwing of candy was well established in the 1890s, and maskers were throwing larger amounts. Individuals seem to have continued throwing objects on a person-by-person basis rather than on a krewe level until the 1920s.

The draw of the early parades was the beauty of the tableau scenes and parade processions. Ostentatious displays of investment of wealth in these creations clearly astonished onlookers, and the secrecy and exclusiveness of balls hosted by krewes added to the mystique of the Mistiks. In 1872, lines were blurred between self-appointed royalty of Mardi Gras and actual royalty (Gill 1997). Much ado was made of the visit of the Grand Duke Alexis of Russia to New Orleans during the Carnival season. When beads became part of the throw mix is hard to determine. Just as difficult to determine is why beads. Some have suggested that priests threw beads reminiscent of rosaries to remind revelers of the upcoming Lenten season. While this is certainly an appealing notion, it is just as likely an explanation created to explain an inexplicable material phenomenon. The earliest glass beads thrown at Mardi Gras were probably produced in Bohemia—the greatest producer of glass beads in the late nineteenth and early twentieth centuries. Incidentally, Bohemia along with Italy, was the greatest supplier of rosaries. As is often the case in folk memory, it may be that the story of the rosaries is an attempt by someone to integrate disparate bits of memory into a meaningful explanatory narrative.

The earliest description of bead throwing is recorded in the remembrances of Margaret Oneal, born in 1884. She lived in New Orleans from her childhood until 1912 when, after graduating from Tulane, she moved to the West Coast. In these reminisces that she titled "Mardi Gras (1890s)," she describes the following. "Rex's float began to move, the King waving his scepter to the crowd and throwing strings of beads and shiny jewelry, for which the crowd scrambled boisterously. Rex looked right at me and threw a diamond necklace that looked real, but a big Negro woman pushed me aside and caught it. I wanted to fight about it, but Papa pulled me away" (Oneal 1965:199).

The Rex referred to is the King of Carnival, whose parade runs on Shrove Tuesday, or Mardi Gras proper (as opposed to the Mardi Gras season, which runs from Kings' Day to Shrove Tuesday). The description of the king throwing treasure to his Mardi Gras celebrant subjects suggests that these throws were part of a royal performance. Today, the royal court rarely throws beads or anything else. In recent years, some royals have taken to having special beads noting their reign be distributed in small numbers to the crowd. Oneal mentions that she saw Rex's Boeuf Gras, which was not a part of the parade from 1900 to 1959 (Rex Organization, "Tradition"). We can use that piece of information to corroborate her memory in that she is describing an 1890s parade.

This brief description provides some possible explanation of how beads came to be part of the throws of Mardi Gras. Most of the early throws described (Hardy 1987)— whistles, rubber toys, and candies—are most likely to have appealed to tots. The beads stand out as a novelty appealing to adults. There is a parallel to them in the exclusive evening events of the Carnival season (Schindler 1997). At Mardi Gras balls, there is a tradition of giving elaborate favors to guests, particularly the ladies. It has been noted by attendees that the young ladies and older matrons receive the greatest attention at balls in terms of both call outs for dances and favors received (Tallant 1989).

A similar pattern is seen today at Mardi Gras parades in which late teenaged girls and grandmothers are the most bead-laden of adults. Sexuality has always been a part of Mardi Gras settings. It ranges from romance and flirtation on the genteel end of the spectrum to displays of nudity, simulated and real public sex acts, and the pursuit of prostitutes on the lewd end (Kinser 1990). The tossing of cheap necklaces or other faux jewelry, as well as kisses, to the ladies would fit into this tradition. The folk traditions of New Orleans Carnival include many stories of real jewelry tossed by a masker to their loved one, only to have it caught by another. If recipients perceive these items to have particular value as a token of affection from an admirer or complement of their beauty, the prestige of catching such objects increases.

Prior to the twentieth century, while throws were part of Mardi Gras celebrations, they were not apparently something that was done on a krewe-wide level. Rather, they were something done on a sporadic basis by individuals within parades. Mardi Gras historian Henri Schindler (1997:36) has suggested that bead throwing became an institutionalized part of Mardi Gras celebrations in the early 1920s and has credited Rex with originating the practice. I have not been able to confirm of disaffirm this assertion.

Evidence for pre-1920s-widespread bead throwing is sparse. Lyle Saxon (1928:61) provides a less reliable description of early twentieth-century bead throwing. Saxon reminisces about his first Mardi Gras as a child around 1901. He wrote about watching a parade and seeing maskers throwing trinkets, including beads, bags of candies, and metal ornaments, to the crowd. His description continues to include the commotion caused by a strand of beads being tossed in his direction.

> The page with the bored smile tossed a string of green beads to me. It swirled through the air over the heads of the people between us and dropped almost into my outstretched hands; but my clumsy fingers missed and it fell to the ground. Immediately there was a scramble. Robert stooped, I fell from his shoulders, and I found myself lying on the pavement as though swept under a stampede of cattle. Hands and feet were all around me but somehow in the struggle I managed to recover those beads. (Saxon 1928:38–9)

Modern readers have noted that Saxon's childhood account seems to be highly fictionalized and serves as a form of palimpsest of Mardi Gras' twentieth-century traditions (Stanonis 2001); for he also includes descriptions of King Zulu's parade. Zulu was not formed until 1909. Still, while Saxon's description does not inform us about the beginnings of the practice, we can assume that at least by 1928, beads were a coveted catch. Another late 1920s source discusses throws, but not beads explicitly: "after slowly traversing the historic route of the parades, throwing candy and confetti and kisses to the laughing friendly crowds, and tossing them occasional souvenirs qualified to confirm the proverb, 'all is not gold that glitters,' the maskers descended from their floats" (Rutland 1927:xxix).

While throws were clearly a common feature of Mardi Gras parades in the 1920s, *The Times Picayune* did not feel they warranted mention in their 1924 "Tourist's Guide to New Orleans." Perhaps the activities were not seen as genteel. Whatever the reason, the potential appeal of the throwing game to tourists may not have been recognized in 1924, but it was recognized soon after. By the 1930s, tourist-directed literature was sure to mention the practice of throwing trinkets. In 1938, the *New Orleans City Guide*, produced by the Federal Writers' Project (FWP), contained the following description of activities along a Mardi Gras route.

> Then—the first float of maskers. Hands wave and clap; people jump up and down, and everyone cries for the trinkets that the maskers carry in little bags or in their hands, shouting 'Mister—throw me something.' The trinkets are small, they are cheap, you can buy a dozen for a penny or so, but—a string of beads flies into the crowd, and the people go mad as they snatch for it. It is a belief in New Orleans that it is lucky to catch favors from passing floats. The maskers hold tight with one hand to the supporting iron pole; and with the other hand they throw gaudy necklaces and toss kisses from the mouths of their grotesque masks. (FWP 1938:66)

A 1939 copyrighted postcard book titled *Souvenir Folder of the Mardi Gras Festival and Scenic Views of New Orleans, LA,* includes several postcards that provide insights into the nature of the throwing game at that time. One scene shows the inside of a float. The maskers are bent over in the float, their hands closed as if holding something in them. On the ground, parade goers are beseeching the float with their hands in the air—a pose immediately recognizable to contemporary Mardi Gras participants. Visible on the floor of the float are several burlap-type sacks. Do these bags contain the throws? While a 1910 panorama photograph of the passage of the Rex parade shows crowds with hands down, by the end of the 1930s, this had clearly changed. Tourist literature from this period onward increasingly elaborates on the nature of the throwing game. Robert Tallant provided the following description in his 1948 book on Mardi Gras.

> As each float passed, the maskers aboard tossed their trinkets into the crowds lining the path of the pageant—a crowd who constantly yelled and begged, arms outstretched and hands waving for more and more of the bounty of King Rex, a crowd who struggled and fought with each other, sometimes sprawling to the street in an effort to seize a whistle or a string of beads, as often as not breaking and smashing and tearing apart the souvenir before any one person captured it, and behaving in general as if the junk were booty beyond price. (Tallant 1948:66)

Eleven years later, the descriptions included in the city guides seem formulaic One must mention the parades and comment on the seeming absurdity of adults fighting over beads and other trinkets.

> The best place to see a parade is from a balcony—a French Quarter balcony, preferably, if you know someone who has one, for these hang directly over the narrow streets and increase your chances of catching one of the glass-bead necklaces for which grown men and women scramble as eagerly as if they were genuine jewels from Tiffany; you have never seen anything like it. The worst thing you can say about a parade is that it ran out of trinkets (which sometimes happens) or that the maskers were stingy with them: to come home empty-handed is a misfortune to be compensated for only by the hope that next time around things will be different. People keep these souvenirs the year round, sometimes hanging them, together with their St. Christopher medals, on the mirrors of their cars. (Evans 1959:152)

Evans' point that the worst thing you can say about a krewe is that they ran out of throws is worth noting. We see that the crowd has pushed back and is no longer willing to just hope to catch a throw; they expected to catch a throw. Krewes are social, economic, and political organizations. At this time, the old line krewes were comprised of the upper echelons of society. The parade goers expected the elite to ply them with gifts.

The Times Picayune coverage depicted the throwing game slightly differently. For instance, the 1941 coverage of Mardi Gras included a parable about a crippled child who during the 1940 Carnival season could not compete to catch throws with other children because he had to hold his crutches. A kindly masker noticed his plight and assured that a giant armload of trinkets were lavished on the poor child, magically transforming his Carnival experience into one of great joy. Likewise, local coverage liked to emphasize the civic nature of the Mardi Gras celebrations by focusing on the privately funded nature of the parades and the generosity of the krewes toward orphans and the unfortunate. The orphans' section of the parade route is often mentioned in local accounts to emphasize the public good done by the secret societies.

A modern version of this narrative still exists. I have been told by a number of Mardi Gras celebrants about convents and orphanages who tape off spaces along the parade route, and how krewes throw heavily to these groups, because they recognize that the nuns can raise money for their facilities by selling the throws back to companies who will repackage them for sale the following year. A number of organizations will buy used beads and pay for them with pennies on the pound. The beads, which may or may not be cleaned, are resorted, repackaged, and resold as recycled beads for lesser cost than new beads. No one who tells these tales has ever stopped to wonder at the logic of this scenario. Recycled beads are bought at significantly less than the original purchase price. If one really wanted to support the convents and orphanages, wouldn't it be more generous to provide a check for the amount one would have spent buying the throws, rather than making the nuns and children scrape beads from the ground for resale like beggars? Ah, herein lies some of the power and class dynamics of the throwing game.

Louisianans recognize the silliness of this activity. New Orleans' resident Liz Scott (1979:12) notes that "what you catch, with luck, will be plastic beads, big aluminum coins called doubloons, and a few gumball machine type trinkets. It all harks back, some say, to the days when Royalty rode through the streets in carriages, scattering coins to the peasants. What makes the stuff valuable is the fact that you can wave it under somebody's nose and say, "look. I caught this at such and such a parade." You may note that while the descriptions include discussions of the silliness of bead lust, there have been no discussions of lewd behaviors prompted by bead lust up to the early 1980s. Although Mardi Gras became notorious for bead-related displays of nudity, it is a recent phenomenon and—as I will discuss—a phenomenon that arose as a direct result of technological changes in bead manufacturing. But I digress. Having now been more formally introduced to both archaeology and Mardi Gras' throwing game, it is time for us to embark more fully on our journey through archaeological thinking and doing.

CHAPTER 3:
A CULTURE HISTORIAN'S APPROACH TO CARNIVAL: CLASSIFYING MARDI GRAS BEADS

B ack in the dark ages, before there were cheap cell phones and widespread internet service, I went to college and majored in anthropology. For my undergraduate senior thesis, I analyzed and interpreted materials recovered from an early twentieth-century trash pit in Santa Monica, California. Graduate students from UCLA happily excavated the site when a local homeowner discovered it and called archaeologists at the university for help. They were thrilled to spend an afternoon excavating and recording the site and finding nearly intact bottles and large ceramic sherds along with thousands and thousands of broken pieces of glass, toys, bone, rubber, and metal. Once the materials were back at the Museum of Cultural History, however, they were less thrilled to take on work in addition to their dissertations and found an unsuspecting undergraduate to take on the project as a senior thesis. I was spending the summer in Los Angeles and became the unsuspecting undergrad.

One of the graduate students who excavated the site knew a bit about bottle manufacturing technology and was sure that the site dated to the early 1900s. Back in 1988, there were very few people who excavated sites as recent as the twentieth century. I had worked on a couple of sites as an excavator and had done a little analysis of historical materials, but had never analyzed an entire archaeological *assemblage.* Assemblage is the word we use to describe the totality of artifacts and ecofacts recovered from a site. All of the glass, ceramics, metal, plastic, rubber, and bone together formed the assemblage of the trash pit. If I were referring to just the glass artifacts from the site, I might refer to them as the glass assemblage, which is a subassemblage of the bigger site assemblage. Often, different materials are parceled out to specialists for analysis; but in this case, I was the only analyst working on the materials. Although the site was less than 100 years old, even when reconstructed, a number of the artifacts were completely foreign to me. As scattered pieces mixed together, they were even less intelligible. But I had all summer, and without much guidance or enough experience to know I should feel overwhelmed, I decided to start by figuring out what each of the items were and classifying them by sets of similar things.

I spent weeks fitting pieces together, first taping and then gluing them. Imagine someone took 150 boxes of puzzles, mixed all the pieces together, then randomly removed handfuls of pieces, and afterward handed the whole mess to you to sort out. That's what it was like, and it was glorious! I went home each day with my fingers glued together and little bits of tape in my hair. But before me, on the lab table, the assemblage came together. Trash pits are self-contained deposits that accumulate quickly. As a *depositional context* (meaning the circumstances through which the materials came to be deposited where they were), the deposit was a quickly filled trash pit. This means that most of the pieces of any broken object were deposited together and stayed together. At this pit, only the very top inches had been sheared off by later gardening activities, and many of the artifacts could be reconstructed. Plates, teacups, bowls, ginger jars, electrical insulators, medicine bottles, doll faces, toy saucers, mason jars, soda bottles, liquor bottles, and many other things emerged out of the broken chaos.

As I worked through the project, I began to classify the artifacts. At first, I recognized things in gross categories like "glass," "ceramic," "metal," and "rubber." Then, as I understood more of what I was seeing, I was able to classify things as "glass plate," "glass bottle," "decorated plate," "undecorated teacup," and so on. By time I was done, I was able to recognize not only specific things like "two-piece molded Barry's Tricopherus medicine bottle," but I could also understand how specific artifacts fit into subassemblages like "personal grooming," "nutritional supplements," "children's healthcare," and so on. I drew upon books published by collectors and reprints of the early twentieth-century Sears, Roebuck and Company catalogs to identify my materials and understand how they were used. I realized, later, that I had engaged in a process that was basic and essential in archaeological study. The process of artifact classification and the creation of a typology—a tool brought to our discipline by a school of archaeological thought known as culture history.

The Prehistory of Culture History

Classification in archaeology came to us first from museum studies. Before there was true archaeology as a discipline, there were antiquarians—people who roamed the world collecting ancient objects for personal collections and national museums that fed the egos of newborn European nation states at the beginning of the nineteenth century. Owning pieces of ancient Mesopotamia, Egypt, Greece, or Rome was a way for newly modern Europeans to feel like they were part of the inevitable and great march of human society. Through ownership of artifacts, they attempted to legitimate themselves as the natural and true descendants of those great civilizations (Trigger 1989). This is how temples and other architectural pieces from those ancient societies came to be housed in museums in Europe. But it wasn't just objects from these societies that were collected. The colonialist and imperialist urges that took Europeans over every part of the globe included not only the desire to conquer, but also to catalog the world. Biological specimens and cultural objects from throughout the world were collected. In the 1700s, Carl Linnaeus gave the world biological taxonomic systems, and museum curators applied the concept to human-made objects (Stocking 1987). These objects were also recovered through excavation—though not typically the kind of meticulously recorded excavations familiar to us today.

Perhaps the most famous classification was that developed by Christian Jurgensen Thomsen (Trigger 1989; Stocking 1987), who was the curator at the National Museum of Denmark in Copenhagen. Curators had previously separated objects by material and quality of craftsmanship. Thomsen became interested in knowing whether it was possible to use differences in artifact types for dating. He investigated collections that included associated artifacts from the same proveniences, especially burial assemblages. He came to recognize that stone, iron, and bronze cutting blades were not found together, and that they were associated with different forms of burial and different suites of associated artifacts. Therefore, he interpreted these assemblages as chronologically distinct, and he labeled assemblages as dating from the Stone Age, the Bronze Age, and the Iron Age. Thomsen established his chronology by 1825 and published his findings in an 1836 article. These categories have endured, and now we know the Stone Age to be divided into the Paleolithic (Old Stone Age), the Mesolithic (Middle Stone Age), and the Neolithic (New or Late Stone Age), because, really, everything sounds better when it sounds more Greek.

Joking aside, Europeans of the upper classes (the segment of society that received an education) embraced an educational system that was based in the classical writing and philosophies of the ancient Greek and Roman worlds, because they saw these civilizations as their ancestors. The gentlemen of the Enlightenment embraced Greek and Roman styles in their architecture and turned to these civilizations for inspiration in the fields of medicine and government. This strong sense of ownership of the ancient and classical world inspired the earliest archaeological work to begin in these areas. It was not unusual for young men of the elite classes of Europe and the United States to "see" the world as part of their education, leading them to traipse across the globe to see things such as the surviving architectural marvels of these civilizations—the Parthenon, the Roman Coliseum, or the Great Pyramids, for instance. These travels fueled interest in finding the locations of sites located in ancient texts, such as Heinrich Schliemann's search for the city of Troy in 1868, and inspired wealthy men of the nineteenth century to hunt for antiquities. There was no parallel encouragement for women to see the world, so perhaps it is not surprising that women only came to enter the field in large numbers in the mid-to-late twentieth century. In addition, as a field science, archaeology was seen as having a hard-drinking, rough-living side to it that was not viewed as a place for a woman. One 1960s book on archaeology complained that women shouldn't be allowed on sites because their high-heeled shoes damaged excavation (Hume 1968). Given that, it's no wonder that few women were associated with archaeology until well into the twentieth century. In fact, Heinrich Schliemann's wife, Sophia Schliemann was probably the woman most famously associated with archaeology in the nineteenth century—not as an excavator, but as the woman who modeled the golden jewelry of Troy in photographs. But I digress.

Thomsen's work set several important methodological threads for archaeology—the consideration of provenience and associations with context—and also the notion that changes in material culture can be put in order, or a series to create a chronology. This idea was central to dating archaeological sites until the widespread introduction of radiocarbon dating in the 1950s (which we will discuss shortly). But first a few words on the unintended, unfortunate legacies of age-period classification systems.

If you've ever seen an episode of the Flintstones, you know the joke behind the series is that they were the "modern Stone Age family"—the irony being, how can you be modern and Stone Aged? Yet, when we look at archaeological history, the concept of "the Stone Age" is modern—in that it is a product of modern era thinking—also known as modernity (Thomas 2004). Inherent to the notion of modernity is the idea of human progress: that through time, we improve as a species in the ways we govern ourselves, our art, our technology, and so on. Contact with the western hemisphere and explorations in Africa revealed to Europeans that there were civilizations that drew on different technologies—iron working was essential to African civilizations, and in the New World stone working was employed.

When Darwin introduced his idea of *evolution* (which biologically at the macroscale is best thought of as adaptation through differential reproduction), it was quickly taken out of context and applied to human societies with some being seen as more "advanced" or "adapted" than others (Stocking 1987). Classification systems that were developed as chronologically descriptive, like Thomsen's, were increasingly seen as a way to classify existing human societies throughout the world according to their primitiveness or sophistication. In our contemporary society, to be described as "Stone Aged" or a "cave man" is viewed as an insult meaning you are thuggish, dim, and uncivilized despite the fact that Stone Aged people gave us some of the greatest art the world has ever seen. These associations between "primitive," "stupid," and "uncivilized" have been instilled in our contemporary memory by the legacies of Victorian-era racism and imperialism.

Late nineteenth-century anthropology and archaeology developed as disciplines within the context of imperialism—and the sad history of our discipline is that we were sometimes knowingly, and sometimes unwittingly, agents of processes that helped to victimize non-European peoples and justify that victimization (Baker 1998, 2010; Harris 1968; Stocking 1987). An excellent example of this phenomenon is the case of the Elgin, or Parthenon marbles. While serving as an ambassador between England and the Ottoman Empire in the first years of the nineteenth century, Englishman Thomas Bruce, the seventh Earl of Elgin, had his agents systematically remove—through questionable means and highly contested legality—half of the classical Greek statues that adorned the Parthenon on the Acropolis in Athens. Elgin had the marbles relocated to his estate and later to the British Museum where they continue to reside but to the national ire of the Greek people. The proper ownership of these objects remains as contested today as they were in the nineteenth century. While the Parthenon marbles now receive a great deal of attention because of the Parthenon's status as an UNESCO world heritage site, atrocities that stripped people of their sacred objects and valued material culture, and even the remains of human ancestors, were common throughout the colonial period (a society's material and cultural heritage is also known as its *cultural patrimony*). This Victorian collecting was done in the name of nation building and comparative science. Any number of respected anthropologists developed models of human evolution that described the movement of human society from savagery to barbarism to civilization in three to seven steps, depending on the scheme. Ideas on social evolution were used to justify forced assimilation of indigenous peoples, or even their extermination, throughout the world.

These models of *social evolution* are often referred to as models of *unilinear evolution* because they identified only a single possible pathway for human societies to pass through. At the pinnacle of human achievement in all of these models was European society, and you can imagine that non-Europeans filled the lower rungs and were assigned statuses such as "barbarian" or "savage." Societies were not understood relative to their own histories, value systems, and achievements; but they were compared and ranked against one another based on checklists of traits, such as agriculture, trade, writing," and so on, which were used to determine rankings. It was in critical response to these models that the discipline of anthropology as we know it today developed. The scholar we credit for shepherding in this revolution in thinking was anthropologist Franz Boas (Baker 2010; Harris 1968; Stocking 1974).

Franz Boas, Historical Particularism and the Theoretical Foundations of Culture History

Boas recognized the inherent racism in evolutionary models. His response was to argue that cultures could not be compared against one another in artificially derived classifications, and they must be understood within their own historical contexts. Boas's school of thought became known as *historical particularlism*. He trained many of the great anthropologists of the first half of the twentieth century—Margaret Mead, Zora Neale Hurston, Ruth Benedict, Melville Herskovits, and Alfred Kroeber. Some have since described Boas's legacy as a-theoretical; and later critics, like Leslie White, declared him to be anti-evolution (Harris 1968). Without rehashing all of early twentieth-century anthropology, it is best to think of Boas as someone who was suspicious of deterministic models applied to understanding the human experience. He instead advocated for rigor in *ethnography* and attention to detail within individual cultural groups. Ethnography is the research tool of anthropologists who learn about other societies through participant observation—or living within a group—and informant interviews. The goal of the ethnographer is to understand the culture relative to itself not through the eyes of a judgmental outsider. Recall that Boas's predecessors were engaged in the project of classifying and categorizing societies relative to one another to determine which were the most "primitive" or "civilized." They weren't interested in understanding the societies or their histories. Boas saw ethnography as just one aspect of the anthropological enterprise. Anthropology at the beginning of the twentieth century was a holistic discipline comprised of four interrelated fields—*archaeology, ethnology* (the study of modern societies), *biological anthropology* (the study of the relationship between human body and social life), and *linguistics* (the study of language). Scholars moved across the sub-disciplines to address broad anthropological questions. Alfred Kroeber, the founder of the anthropology department at Berkeley and a student of Boas, is an excellent example of an anthropologist who worked in ethnology and archaeology while collaborating closely with biological and linguistic anthropologists to study Native California Indians.

Archaeology at this time was also dedicated to the Boasian goals of understanding the development of cultures within their own historical contexts, and recognized *culture* as the shared, *normative* set of practices and beliefs that held a community of people together. These theories of culture shaped the way that archaeology was practiced and the ways that archaeological interpretation was constructed. Anthropological archaeology became primarily dedicated to understanding *cultural history;* thus, this period of archaeology has been creatively labeled as culture history in historical studies. Studying culture history required a regional approach in which archaeologists investigated what cultures had occupied a particular area over time. *Archaeological cultures,* like contemporary ones studied by cultural anthropologists, could be identified through their material remains because every culture's distinct religious beliefs and practices, foodways, style of architecture, tools, clothing, and so on would have a distinctive assemblage of artifacts and ecofacts associated with them. By mapping the distribution of assemblages on space, an archaeologist could identify the regions inhabited by a group, or its *culture area.* By mapping artifact assemblages associated with cultural groups through time, archaeologists could understand the historical sequence of cultural groups that occupied a region.

To be an archaeologist who was involved in the work of studying cultural history, one would have to be very attentive to looking at artifact types as they clustered together in assemblages through space and time (Willey and Sabloff 1974). This archaeological focus is also excavation intensive. It requires small test excavations at many sites to recover enough evidence on the archaeological materials represented, as well as large-scale excavation at a limited number of sites to allow for recovery of chronological information. Inherent to the process of defining culture areas was the process of classifying artifacts and creating typologies that would be useful to other archaeologists working in the same region or studying the same culture group. During the period of cultural historical archaeology, many of the fundamental tools of archaeological practice were developed: artifact classification and typology, excavation, and analytical methods directed toward constructing regional chronologies. Although these tools were established as part of a particular theoretical package, they remain an essential part of archaeology today and tools that still have great utility to us. The process of classifying artifacts and creating typologies are part of the early part of any archaeological laboratory work no matter what your ultimate theoretical orientation or research questions. In other words, every archaeologist has to be a cultural historian to some degree.

Archaeological Tools: Classification

Classification is the process of sorting artifacts into types, and putting those types into an order results in a *typology.* Sounds simple enough, doesn't it? It is until you have a pile of artifacts in front of you. So let us think back to the trash pit example. The first sort

I made of the artifacts was based upon the material from which the artifact was made: glass, ceramic, bone, metal, shell, plastic, or rubber. The second sort was based on vessel form. My interest was in understanding what activities the family who created the site was engaged in. So identifying form seemed the way to go, since I was assuming that form followed function. For instance, a plate would be something you eat food from, and a tumbler is something you drink from. We can discuss the naïve simplicity that goes behind such an assumption—for instance, how many of you have a mug on your desk that you stick pens and pencils in? I could have selected other ways to sort the objects. I could have sorted based on sherd size to explore depositional processes in the pit (was there a size difference between sherds in the top of the pit versus the bottom?). Or perhaps I could have analyzed all the objects by color to see if there was a color scheme that dominated the household décor. Despite all the possibilities out there, I decided to focus on form. I did so in part because of my research interests and in part, honestly, because the materials were historical and from the same culture as myself. Thus, I recognized these vessel shapes did not require a conscious reflection on what makes a plate a plate. This is a feature of historical archaeology that can lead us to unthinkingly graft our current perceptions onto past periods of time. For instance, vessels that appear similar could have very different names and functions.

Consider the shape of the invalid feeder in Figure 3.1, which looks very much like a teapot. The spout on the invalid feeder was placed directly into a patient's mouth so that liquid foods could be poured. Without the help of the Sears catalog, I would have mislabeled any invalid feeders found at the site. But, for the most part, objects I found had similar appearances and uses to objects used in American households today.

Suppose we found a plate in an ancient site and were not familiar with its use? There are features of a vessel's construction that allow us to recognize a plate versus a bowl. For instance, a plate is typically wider than it is high, perhaps as much 10–20 times wider than it is high. A bowl, in contrast, maybe as high as it is wide. Each distinguishable characteristic of an artifact recognized by an archaeologist is called an **attribute**. **Artifact types** are clusters of attributes that are shared by all examples of a type. Within any type, there can

Figure 3.1. Similar shapes, different functions:
A. Invalid feeder; B. Teapot.

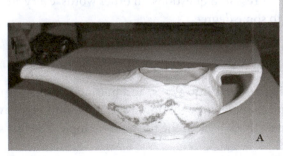

be a range of acceptable variation. How much range of variation is acceptable is, in part, a function of the analyst. Some analysts have a high tolerance for range of variation in an assemblage (and are sometimes referred to as "lumpers" because they are comfortable lumping together a number of varying forms into a single type), and some have a low tolerance (and are sometimes called "splitters" because they prefer to call each variation a separate type).

A typology is the result of whatever set of attributes an archaeologist decides to observe and focus upon. You might imagine this could lead to some strange typologies. It would be possible to construct a typology of dinnerwares that focuses only on surface decoration, hardness of the ceramic fabric, and whether the vessels had lids or not. You can see that such a typology would have merit, for lidded vessels are intrinsically different than unlidded vessels; however, in our particular cultural context, there is a great deal of variation not accounted for in that typology. And herein lies one of the great concerns of classification in archaeology: what exactly are we creating typologies of? Would the types we classify artifacts into be recognizable to the people who created and used them originally? Or are our types merely analytical constructions? This is a different variation on the problem of emic (insider) versus etic (outsider) understandings of a community's social practices and values that we discussed in the last chapter.

These very questions became the subject of a heated debate in archaeology in the 1950s between the archaeologists James Ford and Albert Spaulding. Ford argued that types were a tool or "device which is used to examine the most minute fragments of culture a student can grasp. This tool is designed for the reconstruction of culture history through time and space" (Ford 1954:56). Ford noted that if we look to ethnology as a guide, we will see that around any cultural trait in the present, there is a range of variation around a mean, and the naming of any trait is an abstraction for analytical use. Ford argued that in archaeology, ranges of variation could occur over time, as well as space. Spaulding (1953) believed that archaeologists could use statistics to discover "real" types that would have been recognizable to those who made and used the artifacts. Spaulding hoped, through the rigors of mathematics, to recover insights into the prehistoric mind. There is much validity in Spaulding's work, and statistics are a useful tool within archaeological analysis, but practitioners today generally agree that typologies are analytical tools drawn from sets of attributes that we choose to record, and that we construct to be able to answer specific questions we have about past social behavior. Would our types be recognizable to the creators and users? Probably to some degree. Do we study aspects of artifacts that they would never care about? Most certainly. Does that make our work less useful? No.

This is a debate worth understanding, because it underlines ongoing misperceptions about the practice and nature of the archaeological enterprise that endure today. Even if you had a time machine and could travel to some point in the past to ask members of a group about a particular object, you would get as many different variations on an answer as the number of people you asked. Answers could vary based upon a person's age, gender, occupation, social position, or other subject position they occupied in a society. Take, for example, a porcelain marble. To a kid, it could be a toy. To an adult who likes board games, it could be a game piece for Chinese checkers. To a baker, it could be a crust weight. To a bottle manufacturer, it could be a stopper for a cod-style bottle. To a fish enthusiast, it could be a part of an aquarium's decor. Now you hopefully also understand better why I was really naïve to think that I could automatically understand an object's single function from its form. Not all artifacts are so ambiguous as to function, but all materials possess the ability to be imbued with multiple meanings by their creators and users. Instead of being disturbing, this realization should be liberating to archaeologists. It means that our explorations into the past are only restricted by the limitations of our ability to imagine analyses that will help us address our research questions. We should be aware of the different types of types constructed by archaeologists and how they were and are used in the field.

Julian Steward (Ford and Steward 1954), another student of Boas who crossed the boundaries of ethnology and archaeology, provided the most coherent discussion of types in the archaeological record, perhaps a bit tongue-in-cheek, by discussing a typology of types. He identified four types used by archaeologists: morphological types, historical-index types, functional types, and cultural types. The first three of his types are still widely used in archaeology.

A *morphological type* is a type based on the physical or external properties of an artifact; in other words, the style of the artifact. Style is used in archaeology similarly to the way you would use it to describe a fashion trend, a musical type, or a haircut. Style basically refers to the way that something looks, and generally style is seen as an aesthetic attribute of an artifact rather than something that changes its function. For instance, you will observe a great deal of variation in the shape of bottled-water bottles. The variation doesn't actually affect what the bottle does—it contains overpriced tap water from other states.

A *historical-index type* was a type defined by form that had chronological significance, not cultural significance. For instance, from about 1890 to 1915 manganese was commonly added to glass as a decolorizing agent (Munsey 1970). When manganese-decolorized glass is exposed to ultraviolet light, the glass turns purple. Historical archaeologists, therefore, use sun-colored purple glass as a type in their classifications because it is a useful chronological index (Newman 1970). The people who consumed the contents of bottles made from this kind of glass probably cared little about this feature of the container. Steward saw morphological types and historical index types as being the two kinds of types that archaeologists commonly used to determine time and space occurrences of cultural phenomenon.

The third type Steward (1954) identified as common to the archaeological literature of the time was the *functional type*. Creating a functional type required an understanding of how an item was used—something not always possible to do in archaeological work. The functional type, which would include categories like "weapon," "food preparation," "childcare," and "personal ornamentation," was a category that focused on the relationship of an item to its cultural use. For Steward, functional types were more valuable anthropologically. There are still archaeological discussions and interpretations that revolve around function-based artifact classifications and typologies, though we have tried to broaden our understanding of functionality by recognizing that a single artifact can have multiple uses during its use-life. You will remember that in my senior thesis project, my classification system was first based upon morphological types, but as I progressed and understood the assemblage better, I was able to think in terms of functional classifications based on sets of household activities. I wish I could say that I had read Steward by that time and actually knew what I was doing! Instead, I was blundering along, reinventing the archaeological wheel.

Steward's final type, was the **cultural type**, which he defined as a type that would represent a classification of whole cultures in terms of the functionally most important features. In other words, this final type was part of the project of culture historical archaeology—a compound type that would allow us to distinguish different cultures. The notion of a culture type was abandoned when archaeology moved away from the goals of culture history.

For those of you following closely, you may be troubled that the notion of a culture type seems to be too similar to the stages of cultural development proposed in unilinear evolutionary theories that Boas worked to counter. This deserves a brief word. Steward (1951, 1956), among his accomplishments as an anthropologist, developed a theory of multi-linear evolution, which stated that human societies could change in any number of ways to adapt to changing environmental and social contexts, that the pathway of social development would not follow a predetermined route. Steward found the subject of cultural change to be something that archaeologists should explore, but he wanted to avoid returning to models that were environmentally deterministic. Steward's thinking on the dynamic relationships between human cultures and their environment would be influential on the archaeological thinking that emerged from the cultural historian's work and from broader changes in anthropological thinking.

Types of Mardi Gras Beads

When I started this project in the mid 1990s, I thought that I would have no problem learning about the history of the Mardi Gras bead traditions. After all, the beads are visible in every aspect of contemporary celebrations. Surely, I reasoned, the history of the practice is well known. I was completely wrong. Much of what is known about the throwing game is oral tradition circulated through a number of different sources without documentation. What people think they know about the throwing game is based upon hearsay, and even recent changes in forms of throws are jumbled in memory. That memories are less than reliable is not surprising. One Carnival season blurs into another. Krewes have staked out particular nights of the Carnival season to march. Some of these organizations have marched on the same night for over 100 years. Beads and throws from one season are added to those accumulated in years past—the material record is as blurred as much as the memories and jumbled together in a mass.

As in any archaeological research, when I began this project, I first had to familiarize myself with the range of artifacts I would be encountering. Throws at Mardi Gras parades are not limited to beads. Candy, stuffed animals, obnoxious plastic toys, cups, doubloons, underwear, and t-shirts are also thrown. I decided to limit my study, however, to beads, the most common and abundant artifact type.

To understand the range of types available in the present, I studied the beads I had collected at parades, visited stores that sell beads, and surfed the internet. For the contemporary beads, I could look at catalogs and talk to maskers to draw upon terminology used by those who intimately knew the materials. There is variation in names used for particular styles of beads. People who have bought and thrown beads are more likely to use catalog names; and those who have only caught beads pick up some catalog names from others or make up their own names. For instance, "globe" is a catalog name, but the same bead will often be called "disco ball" by those who catch them.

Participation in Carnival celebrations gave me an insider's perspective to what attributes were valued by bead catchers. Access to catalogs also meant that I would be able to fashion my typology around some of the attributes that were important to buyers and sellers of beads, some of which are not intuitive. For instance, bead diameters are always in metric measurements, millimeters; whereas bead lengths are always in inches. As an archaeologist, my inclination would be to use metric for all measurements. In other words, the catalogs allowed me to understand that through the *life history* of a strand of beads (a strand's existence from manufacture to deposition), different attributes were important to different bead users. Sellers and purchasers wanted to know exactly what size beads they were buying. While there is a minute size difference between 8 mm and 9 mm beads when measured in a lab, a person who catches a 9 mm-diameter bead will see it as a better bead than the 8 mm bead, and there is a price difference between them for the purchaser. Statistically speaking, most archaeologists would not find a 1 mm difference in size to be significant in many artifact classes.

Studying types of Mardi Gras beads that predated my research promised to be trickier. Until recently, there was no collectors' market for beads; so secondary sources were scant. Mardi Gras is a well-photographed event, but many of the photographs focus on the floats. YouTube features some wonderful old film footage of parades, including people throwing beads, so I was able to make interesting observations about abundance and throwing practices through time but few direct observations regarding what kinds of beads were being thrown at what time. It occurred to me that I would need to depend upon the tools of cultural historical archaeology and study as many curated examples of beads as I could find, establish a typology from those, and then hope to use archaeological tools like *seriation* (to put artifacts in a series) to sort out the chronology of these things. To build my sample, I gathered older beads that I had caught in parades. Then, I became a consumer of flea markets, thrift stores, and eBay where I sought out examples of older beads. I was immediately faced with a "type of types" problem: there are many, many, uses of beads. The plastic beads thrown at Mardi Gras could have also been children's toys or costume jewelry. Glass beads, the earliest thrown beads at Mardi Gras, could have been Mardi Gras beads or jewelry.

How was an archaeologist to sort out which vintage beads were possibly Mardi Gras beads versus some other bead? I was attempting to do a functional typology of an artifact type that had many potential uses. President McKinley and eBay (or at least an eBay reconnaissance), saved me. I observed that among the beads being sold as vintage Mardi Gras beads were strands that had paper labels sewn or glued around them. These labels indicated the country of origin and were required by law on any imports coming into the US by the *McKinley Act of 1891* and its extension in 1903 (Kovel and Kovel 1986). Why is this relevant? The tags were located on parts of the strands that would have made them highly visible if the strand of beads were worn as a necklace. As Mardi Gras beads, many of the strands were not worn, but merely thrown into a drawer, basement, or attic! This trend was true not just of older glass beads, but also more recent plastic beads with the difference that instead of being individually labeled with tags, bundles of a dozen beads were bound together with paper tags indicating the place of origin (Figure 3.2). Therefore, as I gathered examples of curated beads, I focused my efforts on examples that still had their country of origin tags. This also facilitated the creation of a typology, in which place of manufacture became an important attribute.

Through diligence I have been able to gather a collection of several hundred strands of beads that date from roughly 1920 to 1990, an assemblage of several hundred beads from 1991 to 1994, and my excavated assemblages from 1997 to 2009. For the 1920–1990 beads, I do not know when they were thrown, what other beads they may have been associated with, or how they came to be resold. Many of the oldest beads were sold from estate collections. I have two important exceptions to this trend. I was able to obtain an assemblage of beads that had been caught by a visitor to the 1947 Mardi Gras celebrations. This assemblage provides a snapshot of a moment in time of Carnival's past. As we discussed earlier, most Mardi Gras beads are saved as part of a midden assemblage, different time periods mixed together in a large mass. The 1947 assemblage is very similar to the kinds of assemblages that are found in shipwrecks or disaster sites; the materials that were being used at the moment of tragedy are still together. Shipwrecks capture what a ship assemblage contained when it went out to sea—when it was doing its most common work—shipping. We can recover the cargo as well as the belongings of the crew and the materials that supported daily life on the ship all as they were being used just up to the time of the wreck . . . well, at least in theory. The idea that you can find a site "frozen in time" is

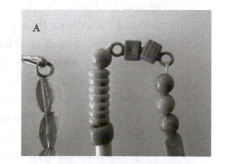

Figure 3.2. Examples of tags with country of origin found on beads: A. Made in Hong Kong impressed on clasp of hand-strung plastic beads; B. Occupied Japan, hand-strung glass beads with paper label. Photographs by Alexandra Wilkie Farnsworth.

sometimes called the *Pompeii effect*, after one of the Roman towns destroyed in AD 79 by the eruption of Mount Vesuvius. The people of Pompeii and their belongings were quickly killed by gases from the eruption blast and buried in hot ash.

The person who created the 1947 bead assemblage, by carrying the beads away and keeping them together, created a less dramatic Pompeii effect. This person was not local, and it was the only Mardi Gras they had attended. The eleven strands in this collection are unique, in that this was the first Mardi Gras celebration held following the end of World War II, and the composition of the assemblage reveals the effects of the war on the bead economy. The second assemblage is a collection of 20 beads that were caught by the same woman during her childhood in the late 1950s and early 1960s. Unlike the 1947 assemblage, this later assemblage is more typical of Mardi Gras assemblages found in Louisiana homes—the beads from six to seven years worth of parades are mixed together. Still, the assemblage is useful in that it tells us what beads were thrown during that time.

In constructing a typology of these beads, I could have used color, length, or any other number of other attributes to classify the strands. I was not interested in constructing an exhaustive typology that would account for all *stylistic variation* in the assemblage, but rather I was interested in a tool that could be used to understand the nature of the throwing game. Remember, my research questions were all focused on understanding the human-bead interactions at Mardi Gras; I was only interested in those attributes that could potentially help me answer my research questions. If I were a cultural historian, I would have constructed a much different typological system. A culture historian would have first been interested in understanding the culture that produced the beads and how these artifacts fit into their value system. As artifacts that were not made in the culture region under study (Louisiana), they would have been interpreted as artifacts that entered the culture through *diffusion* (contact with another culture). The beads thrown in Louisiana's Mardi Gras have never been made in Louisiana, but the ritual celebrations in which they are used are unique to the Gulf Coast.

Based on what I had learned from secondary sources, I decided to develop a typology founded upon the following attributes:

1. The materials from which the beads were made.
2. The country where the beads were made.
3. The method used to string the beads.
4. Whether the necklaces had a krewe medallion or not.

In creating any typology, you want your typology to be systematic in its organization, to be easily replicated by other scholars, and to be expandable when new types are encountered. If the typology can't be applied to other contexts, then it is not going to be a useful research tool. Cultural historians were trying to make their research understandable to other people working in the same region. In constructing your types, you have to decide which attributes are your primary or most important attributes—the attributes that you divide the materials by first. This is shaped by your research questions, as well as the considerations listed above.

For me, I wanted to have a typology that allowed me to look at chronological, as well as "value," dimensions of the beads. The most important attribute was a technological one that had historical and social value dimensions: whether the beads were hand-strung or machine-strung. The earliest beads were hand-strung; machine-strung beads date more recently. After the introduction of machine-stringing, hand-strung beads remained in smaller numbers as prestige items. The next sort was whether the beads were made of plastic or glass. Just as hand-stringing became marked as a prestige symbol after the introduction of machine-strung beads, glass remained a prestige item when plastic ruled the assemblages. The next sort was geographic: where the beads were manufactured. This attribute is important for understanding how the beads fit into the larger global economy. Therefore, I came up with thirteen different types (Table 3.1, Figure 3.3), but which can be expanded to include other types if different materials, manufacturing techniques, or places of origin emerge.

Within these categories, I also recorded attributes such as color, strand length, type of closure, the shape of beads, the bead finish, and if there was a country of origin tag or any evidence that the strand had been recycled or otherwise altered.

The typology accounts for all the beads: the unprovenienced and the excavated assemblages. This typology does a splendid job of illustrating spatial aspects of the assemblage—where the materials came from before arriving in Louisiana. In some ways, it turns the culture area idea upside down, for it focuses attention not on the spatial distribution of the consuming culture's practices but on the spatial aspects of where the objects originated.

Table 3.1. Types of Mardi Gras Beads, ca. 1920–2010.

Czechoslovakian hand-strung glass beads
Occupied West Germany hand-strung glass beads
Occupied Japan hand-strung glass beads
Japanese hand-strung glass beads
Indian hand-strung glass beads
Made in Taiwan hand-strung plastic beads
Made in Hong Kong hand-strung plastic beads
Made in Hong Kong hand-strung plastic beads with medallions
Made in Hong Kong plastic MOS rice beads with hand-strung center beads
Made in Hong Kong plastic MOS beads
Made in China hand-strung plastic beads
Made in China plastic MOS
Made in China plastic MOS beads with medallions

A

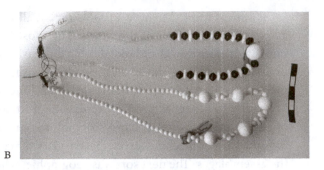

B

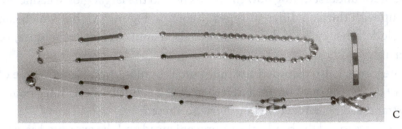

C

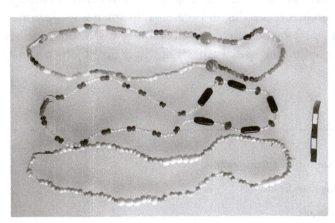

D

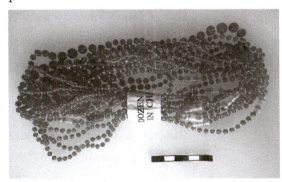

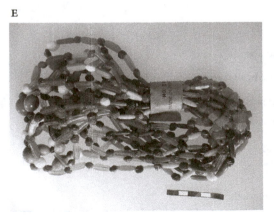

E

F

Figure 3.3. Examples of bead types: A. Czechoslovakian hand-strung glass beads; B. Occupied West Germany hand-strung glass beads; C. Japanese hand-strung glass beads; D. Indian hand-strung glass beads; E. Hong Kong hand-strung plastic beads; F. MOS Chinese plastic beads. Photographs by Alexandra Wilkie Farnsworth.

We have a somewhat unique circumstance with our beads, given that we know how they all functioned—they were thrown from floats at Carnival. The bigger question for us is what tools are available to date these beads?

Culture History and Chronology: Absolute and Relative Dating Techniques

Today, for anyone working on archaeological sites older than a few hundred years, radiocarbon dating is the standard technique used for dating sites. I will talk more about radiocarbon dating shortly. Radiocarbon dating was not developed as a technique until the 1950s. So how was dating done prior to radiocarbon dating?

Archaeologists generally lump dating techniques into two categories: *relative* and *absolute* dating techniques. Absolute dating techniques are ones that allow you to pin a calendar date on a site, whereas relative dating techniques allow you to date deposits relative to one another—older or younger. Often the two are used in concert, as I'll illustrate soon.

Dendrochronology

One of the dating techniques available to Culture Historians was *dendrochronology,* or tree-ring dating, which A. E. Douglas developed in the first half of the twentieth century at the University of Arizona. Here's a quick summary of how dendrochronology works. You've surely seen the rings in a cross-section of a tree and have heard that you can date the tree by counting the rings. Each growing season, a tree produces certain kinds of cells in the early part of the season (early growth wood), which usually appear as a light band, and another in the late season that appear as a dark band. An annual ring consists of a light and dark band. Perhaps you've also noticed that some rings are thicker than others—those patterns of thick and thin represent nature of the growing season in any given year. In a dry, cold year, a tree may add less girth to its trunk than in a wet, temperate year. Every tree of a particular species in an area has the same pattern of growth for a given year. Initial dendrochronology sequences can be built for a species can be made by using an augur to core a small cross-section of wood out of a living tree. Some species, like the bristlecone pine, can live to be 5,000 years old—this gives you a pretty good start.

Dendrochronology is based on the principle of cross-dating. This means that if you have a fragment of wood with visible rings, you can line it up with another piece of wood from a tree that lived at the same time. Using wood from archaeological sites, a long sequence of rings can be constructed, and as additional samples are found, the sequences can be extended back in time. In the American Southwest, wood preserves well in the dry, hot climate. When wood is recovered archaeologically, it can be dated using dendrochronology if the established sequences have enough time depth—otherwise, the archaeological find can be used to expand the tree-ring sequence. Although dendrochronology is another absolute dating technique, it cannot be relied on outside circumstances where there is good preservation of wood, and a chronology for local species is established (Nash 2002). It's important to remember what the date derived from dendrochronology actually tells you. That date is the year that the tree was cut down. Presumably, if the tree was felled to use, whatever was made from the wood, be it a building, fence post, canoe, a totem poll, and so on, then the creation of that artifact or feature would date to about the same time. You need to always remember that wood could also be scavenged from fallen trees some time after the tree died; or as is the case in our society today, wood planks can be salvaged from one building to be used in another, meaning that the wood can be significantly older than the structure it's used in. Still, dendrochronology is extremely useful in the areas where wood preserves, and it is generally pretty nifty as a dating technique in that it can give you an exact calendar year to work with.

Using Documents and Dated Artifacts or Events: TPQs and TAQs

For sites with written records, be they from the colonial period in the Caribbean or ancient Rome, archaeologists can use documentary records or artifacts with dates on them (think objects, such as coins, or monuments with inscriptions as popular examples), to help date deposits. Sometimes particular events can be used to date sites where the occupants had no writing themselves. For instance, certain volcanic events have global effects that include the spread of ash layers. The introduction of particular animal and plant species or even diseases to a region are potentially datable events. For instance, when "new world" crops, such as maize or tobacco, are seen in the archaeological record of sub-Saharan Africa, we know these deposits date after 1492 and similarly with the introduction of "old world" foods and technologies in the Americas. In the Bahamas, Loyalists planters relocating from the American Southeast in the late 1700s introduced raccoons to the islands. If we find raccoon bones, we can safely assume they are from deposits that date after that time. Even with datable artifacts, dating a site occupation can be tricky.

Remember my senior thesis trash pit? One graduate student thought the site dated to the early twentieth century. As I analyzed the materials, identified manufacturing methods used to mold the bottles, tracked down the dates of operation for different products represented, and pinpointed manufacturing dates for ceramic marks and patterns, I found many of the artifacts had been made in the first decade of the twentieth century. However, I also found a number of artifacts that were manufactured much later. For instance, several Hires root beer bottles found at the site had not been made until 1918. Excavation also revealed that the trash pit had just one layer of deposition; in other words, it had been dug and filled fairly quickly, so all of the artifacts had been thrown away at about the same time. Therefore, the earliest date the pit could have been filled was 1918. Anytime before that, the Hires bottles would not have existed. Does this mean that the pit was absolutely filled in 1918? No. It could have been filled even later without containing any newer artifacts. The year 1918 represents what is called a *terminus post quem* (**TPQ**), or the "time after which something happened" (Orser 2002a). A TPQ is basically a date that indicates the earliest possible start date for a deposit. As I interpreted the site, it became interesting to think about why the family who created the pit threw away a lot of older things with some newer things.

Archaeologists will also sometimes use *terminus ante quem* (TAQ), or the "time before which something happened" (Orser 2002b), when determining the possible end date for a deposit, but that is a little trickier. It is most commonly used when you know that something happened that absolutely ended the possibility of additional archaeological deposition at a site. As an example, in the backyard of my 1912 house is a trash pit. Unfortunately, a cement pad covers most of the pit, so I can't excavate it. The cement pad was laid in the 1960s, which means that the trash pit has to have been created earlier than that. The 1960s would be the TAQ for the trash pit.

In each of these instances discussed above, it is possible to tie an artifact (and therefore the deposit from which it was recovered) to a particular calendar date. As I mentioned above, archaeologists refer to this as an absolute date. Note that the absolute part of the name does not imply any greater accuracy than the date suggested. Let us consider the most commonly used absolute dating technique used in archaeology, radiocarbon dating. The introduction of this dating technique changed the archaeological landscape and eliminated the need for so much archaeological analysis to center around generating chronological typologies.

A Diversion in Which I Explain Radiocarbon Dating

To understand how radiocarbon dating works, our story all begins in the earth's upper atmosphere where cosmic rays constantly bombard the planet. These rays cause atmospheric nitrogen to break down in a radioactive isotope of carbon that has two more neutrons than the more common carbon-12 (^{12}C). As a radioactive element, carbon-14 (^{14}C) is unstable; and over time, it decays into the more stable ^{12}C. Carbon-14 joins with oxygen to become carbon dioxide (CO_2), and then it enters the earth's lower atmosphere where it is absorbed into plants through photosynthesis and into the ocean. Therefore, while living, plants absorb ^{14}C at the same ratio that it exists in the environment, and anything that eats plants absorbs ^{14}C.

In other words, all living things absorb ^{14}C in the same ratio as it exists in the environment. When any organism dies, it stops absorbing ^{14}C, and the ^{14}C in the remains begin to decay into Carbon 12. The rate at which radiocarbon decays into ^{12}C is known; it takes 5,730 years for half of the radiocarbon to decay. This is referred to as a *half-life*. Now, this is the tricky part. After something has been dead for 5,730 years, half of the radiocarbon it contained has decayed. That is one half-life. That leaves you with 50% of the original radiocarbon left in the remains, when half of that decays (leaving 25% of the original amount of radiocarbon); 5,730 years later, a second half-life has passed. You get the pattern? When 12.5% is left, three half-lives, or (5,730 times 3) 17,190 years, have passed.

Now you are probably starting to understand how potentially this could be used as a dating technique. If all creatures absorb radiocarbon at the same rate, AND the amount of radiocarbon in the atmosphere has remained constant through time, you could identify when a living organism stopped absorbing radiocarbon by measuring the amount of ^{14}C that remains in a particular organic matter compared to the amount of ^{12}C. This is achieved in a lab by burning the sample and conducting a proportional count of the decaying ^{14}C

and ^{12}C gases released. Radiocarbon is a fairly useful way to estimate the age of organic materials up to 50,000 to 60,000 years ago. After that point, there is too little ^{14}C left to reliably measure.

In a perfect world, that would be all there is to say about how radiocarbon dates work. However, the original assumption of Willard Libby, the inventor of radiocarbon dating, that the amount of radiocarbon in the atmosphere has remained constant is incorrect. The amount of radiocarbon introduced to the *biosphere* (the part of the earth that supports life) has, in reality, fluctuated slightly through time. In addition, it has been discovered that ocean waters exchange radiocarbon at a different rate, and dates on marine animal bone and shell can provide older dates (up to 400 years older) than charcoal from the same setting, which is a phenomenon known as the *marine reservoir effect*. Through independent measures, archaeologists and other scientists have sought to establish ways to adjust radiocarbon dates to take these kinds of circumstances into consideration.

The most important research has led to the creation of a *calibration curve* that corrects for variations in the earth's atmospheric radiocarbon through time. Using dendrochronology (tree ring dating), researchers have run radiocarbon dates on samples from individual tree rings of known date to construct calibration curves that chart fluctuations in atmospheric ^{14}C through time. This is some pretty creative problem solving, isn't it? At this point, there are enough tree ring sequences that have been established to allow for calibration curves that extend back 8,000 years.

Now that I've explained calibration curves, let's briefly discuss how these different elements all come together in radiocarbon dating. Most archaeologists do not run their own radiocarbon dates. There are established laboratories that do the actual processing of the samples. Most archaeologists deal with radiocarbon dates in two ways; they select the samples that will be tested, and they interpret the results that come back. When you receive a radiocarbon date from a lab, what you get is a results form for each sample that lists the laboratory number for the sample and a conventional radiocarbon date. The conventional radiocarbon date appears as a year with an error range, such as 1040±60 BP. The BP stands for before present. In radiocarbon speak, the Present is 1950, when radiocarbon dating was first developed. The ±60 represents the range of error, and the range on either side of that number that the date could fall within.

Let's look at the conventional radiocarbon date 1100–980 BP. This date range represents an adjustment to one multiple or sigma, and statistically, the object has a 68% probability of falling into that range. If we adjust the date range to two sigmas, there is a 95% chance that the object dates around 1160–1020 BP. This could be the end of the story, if we were content with just a conventional radiocarbon date. However, the lab will also provide calibration information. For instance, when I worked in the Bahamas, I excavated a prehistoric site that required radiocarbon dates. We found little carbon, so we had to use conch shells. Our date came back at 1040±60 with an adjustment to 1050±60 to correct for the marine reservoir effect, and the date was also then graphed onto a calibration curve. Once calibrated (abbreviated cal), the one-sigma correction provided a date range of cal BP 630, or cal AD 1290–1395. This means that the people living in the village I was studying were there as recently as 100 years before Columbus arrived in the Bahamas. Archaeologists generally only use BC and AD on calibrated dates, and BP without a modifier to identify a conventional date. As you can see, radiocarbon dating can be pretty complicated, but it is an extremely powerful dating tool.

So what can be radiocarbon dated? It is important to remember that radiocarbon dating is destructive—whatever sample you select to date will not be returned. So while any preserved material (including things made from plants, like textiles, basketry, furniture, etc.), or animal and human remains (skin/leather, hair, bone, etc) can be dated, it may not be in the best interests of preservation, conservation, or human rights to date these materials. Burned wood, aka charcoal, is the most popular sample to use—the material is carbon-rich and can usually be recovered in considerable amounts from human occupation sites—after all, fire hearths used for cooking and warmth are found on just about all human sites and contain large amounts of charcoal. It is important to remember that what we are dating when we date charcoal it represents the death of the tree or other burned material, not the date of when the hearth fire happened. It's generally assumed that the time between the tree dying, the wood being gathered by people, and the wood being burned is not great.

It is sometimes necessary to date an object directly by taking a sample of it. A standard radiocarbon date requires a sample of about 1 to 10 grams of charcoal (more for samples of bone or shell). In the case of highly sensitive objects, where only small samples can be taken for dating, an **Accelerator Mass Spectrometry date (AMS)** can be used. The AMS dates use an accelerator-based spectrometry unit to count all of the ^{14}C atoms rather than the decaying ones, and therefore it is more accurate with a small sample—as small as 1 to 2 milligrams. It is also more expensive.

When the Shroud of Turin, a holy object that many Christians believed was the cloth that Jesus was wrapped in for burial, was radiocarbon dated, the researchers conducted an AMS analysis given that the object is considered sacred by many Christians. Three samples were taken of 50 milligrams each that were sent to three different labs along with three control samples of known ages. Multiple labs were used to provide independent verification of the date. The resulting dates were very similar and, within a 95% probability, determined that the Shroud of Turin was made between AD 1260 and AD 1390 (Damon et al. 1989)—about the same time as the Bahamian village I studied was occupied. Is there a connection? No.

I will admit, that for someone like myself, there is a bit of mystique surrounding radiocarbon dates. I understand how they work, but it still seems magical to me that one can send a little piece of charcoal away to a laboratory and receive back a date range. For the Bahamas project, I was very excited to be running radiocarbon dates—it seemed so scientific to be carefully packaging up samples to send to the lab. One has to be careful to label all samples clearly, as well as ensure that there is no contamination of the samples. It is remarkably easy to accidentally introduce new carbon into a sample. When I received the results of the 18 dates, I was perturbed. They were close, but certainly not completely overlapping.

As I looked at them, I realized that I wasn't actually quite sure how to use them. I showed three of my prehistorian colleagues the dates and asked their opinions of how to interpret them; I received three different answers. I eventually graphed the results, picked a date range that fell within the a two-sigma range for almost all the dates, and declared the outliers to be somehow flawed. This experience only confirmed for me that there is indeed something magical and mysterious about radiocarbon dating and left me happy to return to the low-tech dating strategies of historical archaeology. While I've only discussed a couple of absolute dating techniques, there are other techniques used by paleontologists and those who study human evolution Dendrochronology and radiocarbon dating are the most commonly used by those who study past human populations.

Whew, now we'll head back to the cultural historians and how they dated sites without carbon or technology!

Dating before Radiometrics:
Relative Dating Techniques, Superposition, and Seriation

The vast majority of the human experience featured no written record, so before there was radiocarbon dating, archaeologists turned to the tools of geology and art history to sort out chronology. Relative dating techniques are so-called because the temporal sequence isn't tied to a calendar, but to the relationship of a particular object or deposit to other objects or deposits. The most straight forward type of relative dating technique employed in archaeology relies on the Law of Superposition that we've discussed before—the idea that any depositional layer is younger than the one it overlies, and older than the one above it. How do we actually apply this idea in archaeological work? To understand a sequence of deposits requires you to think through how things happened in the past. For instance, one of my archaeological projects involved the excavation of a pair of fraternity houses on campus. The first house was built in 1876 and was occupied until 1910, when it was decided to be too rundown to live in. It was then picked up off its foundation and relocated, and a second house was built on its spot. The second house was shaped like a "C" with a courtyard in the middle; we excavated in the courtyard. As we excavated, we encountered depositional layers that allowed us to reconstruct the sequence of events, each associated with a different soil deposit or feature.

A trench was dug to place the brick footings and water pipes for the first house:

1. The first house was built and the trench back filled.
2. Trash associated with the occupation of the first house accumulated around the foundation.
3. A steam roller flattened the building site.
4. A construction trench was dug for the second house, cutting through part of the first foundation.
5. The second house was built and the construction trench back filled.
6. Trash associated with the second house occupation accumulated in the courtyard.

7. Gravel fill was brought in to cover the old living surface and covered with asphalt when the university took over the building, and a raised wooden floor was installed over that.

Figure 3.4 shows the stratigraphic profile that reflects these events.

Each of these depositional events was visible as soils with different colors or textures that could be identified during excavation. The places where these different soils, fills, and construction materials intersect are called **interfaces** and are the junctures at which we interpret the temporal relationship of one depositional level to another by figuring out which happened first. If you can't determine the relationship between one episode and another, it's harder to understand your site's **depositional history**, or chronology. Once again, we see why careful excavation and record keeping is so important in archaeology. Note that I did not list dates for any of the events in the above sequence. I know from archival records about when the first house was built, when the second house was built, and when the university took over the property; and this information ties the depositional history to a calendar. This is an example of what I meant when I said that relative and absolute dating techniques are often used in concert.

There are other forms of relative dating techniques that focus on the artifacts recovered from excavation. These techniques can be used not just in sites with long depositional histories, but they can also be used to understand the chronological relationships between different sites. In Ford's (1954) discussion of types, he explained that drift, or variation in types was typical through space and time. This drift, or **stylistic variation**, is common, and can be observed in modern material culture like automobiles. Car bodies, he explained, looked different from one model year to the next, but never too different, because consumers would be unhappy with too great a change. The same kinds of subtle gradual shifts occurred in objects in societies where change was slower, and may have been less perceivable to the user than to the archaeologist. This observation about gradual stylistic change in artifacts through time is the basis of an important archaeological tool, **seriation**

Figure 3.4. Stratigraphic profile from the Zeta Psi excavation.

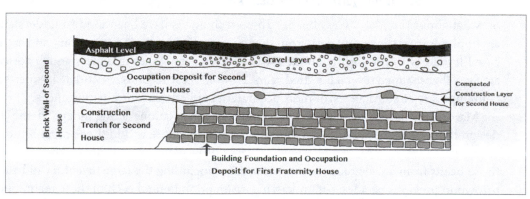

(Rowe 1961). Archaeologists use two kinds of seriation: *stylistic seriation,* which is based upon an artifact's appearance, and *frequency seriation,* which looks at how common different artifacts are relative to one another through time. Let's first consider stylistic seriation.

Stylistic seriation is to put things into a series based upon appearance (or even with something like music, sound). Marquardt (1978:258) defines stylistic seriation as "a descriptive analytic technique, the purpose of which is to arrange comparable units in a single dimension . . . such that the position of each unit reflects its similarity to other units." Stylistic seriation can be used as a dating technique if the ordering criteria are reliable chronological indicators (Marquardt 1978). For example, if I were to cut out pictures from fashion magazines over the past 30 years and ask you to put them in order, you could probably do it pretty easily. Your knowledge as a cultural insider would allow you to know which end of the fashion series was most recent. What if you did not have that knowledge, however? How would you know which object represented the oldest? This could potentially be a problem with our Mardi Gras beads, except we do know which beads are the most recently thrown. Archaeologists solved this problem in ancient assemblages by using construction sequences in conjunction with stratigraphic information from excavation (Rowe 1961).

When artifacts put into a series are also understood within a stratified depositional context, it is possible to create series that represent how artifacts and associated assemblages date relative to one another. This is, incidentally, another example of a relative dating technique. The sequences are not defined according to how they correlate to a calendrical system as are absolute dating techniques. The series could stretch over the course of 100 years or only 10. There is no way to know in a relative dating sequence just which is older and which is younger. Stylistic seriations, however, did allow archaeologists to develop chronologies by putting artifacts in stylistic order within multi-component sites and to compare styles of artifacts from one site to another. The great chronologies of Mexico, the Middle East, Peru, and the Southwest were constructed initially using just the tools of stratigraphy and stylistic seriation in the first decades of the twentieth century (Browman and Givens 1996).

The Stylistic Seriation of Mardi Gras Beads

So what about the Mardi Gras Beads? These techniques have been used to understand assemblages from the distant past, from sites occupied for multiple generations, and in the case I'll share with you shortly, about a study of cemetery stones to understand historical artifacts that spanned several hundred years. How do these techniques work in less perfect contemporary circumstances, or more accurately, perfectly chaotic circumstances?

Mardi Gras bead assemblages reflect multiple organizations acting independently to design their krewe beads, and there are thousands of people within those organizations acting autonomously to create the assemblages of beads they will throw. They choose those beads from a wide range of market sources, including the large inventory of beads thrown in previous parades. An underlying assumption behind each of these techniques is that human behavior follows particular expected patterns. In our current intellectual climate, we are prone to emphasizing the unique and distinctive subject position of every person—everyone is special! Given our wildly individualistic society, will these tools still work? There are archaeologists who study the contemporary who argue that we cannot view today's society through the same sets of ideas or methods as we do other time periods; we are too unique, too different, not just modern, but super modern (see González-Ruibal 2008, Harrison and Schofield 2010).

To explore whether contemporary archaeology can learn from old archaeology and vice versa, let us consider the assemblage of medallion beads from the Krewe of Bacchus. We spent some time together waiting for Bacchus to arrive and begging for beads, we should now examine exactly what it is we have received from this krewe over the years. When I started this project, it had occurred to me that if I stuck with it long enough, I could see if I could construct stylistic and frequency seriations from the materials. When I first experimented with doing a stylistic seriation, I decided to focus on a particular kind of bead type. One of the prized beads from any parade is an example that features the krewe's insignia. These were often called *krewe medallions beads* because the strand featured a medallion hanging from the center of the strand with the krewe's name. Since 2004, however, improvements in MOS beads has changed this somewhat. Manufacturers now cheaply produce bead molds for individual krewes that feature the krewe's names and krewe-specific images. These are cheaper than the traditional medallion beads, which were molded separately from plastic or resin and added to strands of beads by hand, and they allow for a greater number of beads featuring the organization's name to be offered to parade goers. The introduction of these beads has not led to the abandonment of medallions, but has simply created a two-tier level of medallions—the more easily obtained MOS medallions and the more difficult to acquire resin medallions.

Medallions are an intriguing artifact to consider because they are a very self-conscious self-representation of the krewe to its members and its public. In the realm of public opinion, krewes are evaluated based upon their generosity and the quality of their throws. Medallions are a means through which a krewe can establish its perceived status among other krewes, and they are a means of reaffirming a sense of continuing tradition. Remember that Ford (1954) argued that while styles can change, they shouldn't change too quickly, or they risk rejection. So I wondered, is stylistic change visible in medallions? And if so, is the change dramatic or does it follow a particular set of rules? And finally, do changes seen within one krewe have any correlation to what other krewes are doing with their medallions at the same time?

For my analysis, I recorded particular attributes for each year I had examples of the medallion bead to construct a historical typology, a la Julian Steward. I recorded the size of the medallion, the imagery on the medallion, the colors used, the material the medallion was manufactured from, the way the medallion was suspended, and the size, length, color and finish of the bead strand the medallion was suspended upon. I chose these attributes because I was hoping that one or more of them may have been a historical attribute, an attribute that had chronological significance.

Bacchus claims itself to be the first krewe to throw medallion necklaces. I cannot dispute this claim, because to date, Bacchus is the only krewe I have found that put a parade date on many of their medallions. Many krewes use a generic medallion, which, if it features a date at all, would be the founding of the krewe, not the parade year the bead was manufactured for. Because Bacchus dated their medallions, I could construct a chronological sequence for the beads that tied into a calendar date, and I could use flea market finds (unprovenienced artifacts, as opposed to the provenienced examples recovered from parades I attended) to fill in gaps in my sequence.

As best I can reconstruct from surviving material culture, Bacchus dated their medallions from 1975 to 1989, then abandoned dating until their 25th anniversary parade in 1993, and again abandoned dating medallions until 2000. Since 2000, Bacchus has thrown at least one form of medallion that featured the parade date. Table 3.2 and Figure 3.5 summarize what I have been able to reconstruct of Bacchus' medallion forms through time.

Let me quickly summarize what you see in the Table 3.2. This table describes year-by-year the appearance of the medallions. The earliest dated medallion for Bacchus is for the year 1975. For the first three years, the medallion took the identical shape of the doubloon thrown by Bacchus. In 1979, a new medallion shape was introduced—a horn of plenty. The medallion was embossed with the name of the parade. This form was used until 1981. From 1981 to 1989, Bacchus used a grape-cluster medallion embossed with the date and parade theme on the obverse side. From 1990 to 1992, the krewe seems to have used generic medallions that no longer featured the parade theme or year. The advantage of throwing a generic medallion would be that leftovers from one parade season could be thrown the following season without being dated. To celebrate their 25th anniversary in 1993, Bacchus introduced a Bacchus XXV bead and then returned to generic, transparent medallion beads until 1997. In 1997, 1998, and 1999, Bacchus used the same shape medallion, but varied the colors and finishes they used for the beads. The medallion featured the profile of a drinking Bacchus—the same image that appears on the krewe doubloons.

The millennium year of 2000 represents an important change in Bacchus medallions, for this is the year that molded and hand-painted resin medallions were introduced. The medallion features a full-frontal Bacchus face with a sticker on the back indicating "Bacchus 2000." The same medallion with a different color scheme was used the following year (2001), but a version with a voice box that said "Hail Bacchus" and a blinking-light version were also introduced. A resin medallion featuring the Bacchus profile appeared in 2002, followed by the same medallion in 2003 in an alternate color scheme with Bacchus facing the other direction. The 2003 medallion did not have the date on it.

In 2004, the medallions changed once again. This was the year that MOS krewe beads appeared. One version features the front-facing Bacchus, and another variation features representations of doubloons strung on the strand. A resin bead featuring a front-facing Bacchus, the year, and the title of the parade theme was introduced. This represents a return to one of the earliest medallion styles. Since 2004, the krewe has thrown a parade-themed bead alongside the MOS krewe beads. Beginning in 2010, front-facing Bacchus, resin medallions featuring Bacchus wearing a Mardi Gras mask also appeared. Notably,

Table 3.2. Chronology of Bacchus Medallions through Time from Curated and Excavated Collections.

YEAR	FORM OF MEDALLION	BEAD COLOR, FINISH, AND SIZE
1975	Doubloon-style medallion	Gold opaque medallion suspended on loop, purple opaque beads, 8 mm round
1976	Doubloon-style medallion	Gold opaque medallion suspended on loop, purple transparent beads, 8 mm round
1977	Doubloon-style medallion	Purple transparent medallion suspended on loop, and purple transparent beads, 8 mm round
1979	Horn of plenty, 1979, "The undersea world of BAC-CHU-STEAU"	Green opaque medallion, melted onto strand, purple transparent beads, 7 mm
1981	Horn of plenty, 1981, "The Old Testament"	Green opaque medallion, melted onto strand, purple transparent beads, 7 mm
1985	Grape Cluster medallion with profile of Bacchus, "In Vino Veritas 1985"	Purple transparent medallion attached with plastic clasp to strand, and 8 mm transparent beads
1986	Grape cluster medallion with profile of Bacchus, "New Orleans We Love You 1986"	Purple transparent medallion attached with plastic clasp to strand, and 8 mm transparent beads
1988	Grape cluster medallion with Profile of Bacchus, "20 years of Bacchus" on back	Purple transparent medallion attached with plastic clasp to strand, and 8 mm transparent beads
1990	"Bacchus" with grapes on either side	Purple transparent medallion attached by metal pins to transparent 8 mm strand
1991	"Bacchus" with grapes on either side	Purple transparent medallion attached by metal pins to transparent 8 mm strand
1992	"Bacchus" with grapes on either side	Purple transparent medallion attached by metal pins to transparent 8 mm strand
1993	Bacchus XXV on double grape cluster	Purple clear transparent medallion attached by metal pins to transparent 8 mm beads
1994	"Bacchus" with grapes on either side	Purple transparent medallion attached by metal pins to transparent 8 mm strand
1995	"Bacchus" with grapes on either side	Purple transparent medallion attached by metal pins to transparent 8 mm strand
1996	"Bacchus" with grapes on either side	Purple transparent medallion attached by metal pins to transparent 8 mm strand
1997	Side-facing drinking Bacchus	Purple, green and gold metallic on 8 mm beads
1998	Side-facing drinking Bacchus	White, lavender pearl on 8 mm beads
1999	Side-facing drinking Bacchus	Yellow, green, and purple opal transparent, 7.5 mm beads
2000	Front-facing resin Bacchus face with purple grapes, 2000	Hand-painted resin medallion suspended by metal loop on 8 mm purple metallic beads

Table 3.2 continues on page 103

Table 3.2 continued

YEAR	FORM OF MEDALLION	BEAD COLOR, FINISH, AND SIZE
2001	Front-facing resin Bacchus face with green grapes, 2001	Hand-painted resin medallion suspended by metal loop on 8 mm green metallic beads
2002	Right side-facing resin drinking Bacchus in purple	Hand-painted resin medallion suspended by metal loop on 8 mm purple metallic beads
2003	Left side-facing resin drinking Bacchus in purple and gold	Hand-painted resin medallion suspended by metal loop on 8 mm purple metallic beads
2003	Front-facing Bacchus, hand-strung, float-shaped beads	Hand-painted resin beads, hand-strung on strand, sticker with 2003 date.
2004	Front-facing Bacchus with embossed year and parade theme, "Magical Mystical Tour"	Hand-painted resin medallion on 48" 10 mm metallic teal strand
2005	Front-facing Bacchus with embossed year and parade theme, "Bacchus Super Bowl Sunday"	Hand-painted resin medallion on 48" 10 mm metallic dark blue strand
2006	MOS Bacchus front-facing medallion with crocodile, chalice, whale, and Bacchusaurus	Gold metallic, 8.5 mm MOS beads
2007	MOS Bacchus front-facing medallion with crocodile, chalice, whale, and bacchusaurus	Gold metallic, 8.5 mm MOS beads
2009	Front-facing Bacchus with purple Mardi Gras mask	Hand-painted resin on 8 mm purple metallic beads
	MOS grape medallion with mask and doubloon beads	Gold, purple, and green metallic, 8.5 mm beads
	MOS front-facing Bacchus medallion with beads spelling "Bacchus" on either side of medallion	Gold metallic, 8.5 mm beads
	MOS strands with three small Bacchus doubloon medallions	Gold, purple, hot pink, teal, green, red metallic, 12 mm beads, 42" long
2010	Front-facing Bacchus with red Mardi Gras mask	Hand-painted resin on red and gold silk cord
	MOS grape medallion with mask and doubloon beads	Gold, purple, and green metallic, 8.5 mm beads
	MOS front-facing Bacchus medallion with beads spelling "Bacchus" on either side of medallion	Purple, green, and gold metallic, 8.5 mm beads
	MOS strands with three small Bacchus doubloon medallions	Gold, purple, hot pink, teal, green, red metallic, 12 mm beads, 42" long
2011	Parade-themed bead, "Bacchus salutes our armed forces"	Hand-painted resin on red and gold silk cord
	MOS grape medallion with mask and doubloon beads	Gold, purple, and green metallic, 8.5 mm beads

Table 3.2 continues on page 104

Table 3.2 continued

YEAR	FORM OF MEDALLION	BEAD COLOR, FINISH, AND SIZE
2011	MOS front-facing Bacchus medallion with beads spelling "Bacchus" on either side of medallion	Purple, green, and gold metallic, 8.5 mm beads
	MOS strands with three small Bacchus doubloon medallions	Gold, purple, hot pink, teal, green, and red metallic, 12 mm beads, 42" long
2012	Parade-themed bead, "Bacchus Celebrates Louisiana Bicentennial"	Hand-painted resin on blue and gold silk cord
	MOS grape medallion with mask and doubloon beads	Gold, purple, and green metallic, 8.5 mm beads
	MOS front-facing Bacchus medallion with beads spelling "Bacchus" on either side of medallion	Purple, green, and gold metallic, 8.5 mm beads
	MOS	Gold, purple, hot pink, teal, green, and red metallic, 12 mm beads, 42" long

these are strung on a braided satin cord rather than a strand of beads. This had become the norm for Bacchus resin medallions through the time of this writing, in 2012.

As I looked at my evidence, I was initially disappointed. It seemed that stylistic seriation did not work for the Bacchus beads. There were constant shifts in bead color and finishes over time. A gradual drift to larger-sized medallions and bead strands could be seen, so that was interesting, I supposed. I noted that while there weren't any kind of gradual shifts in the representations of Bacchus, there was a shift from monochrome (one color) to polychrome (multiple colors) over time. Also, monochromes were reintroduced when the MOS beads were introduced. So my initial reaction to all of this was that the stylistic seriation did not really work; the medallions shift back and forth, radically varying from year to year. There is no evidence of any kind of slow change from one form to another like we see in the gravestones.

After my initial disappointment that I could not do a cool Deetz-type seriation, I did realize that there was a different kind of shift visible in my data. Clearly, the imagery used in the medallions is not the kind of historical attribute that we need to seriate an archaeological assemblage for chronological purposes. I realized that if I looked at the actual materials the beads and medallions were made out of, and the manufacture of medallions, there were clear shifts. That's how I resorted the beads into the typology shown in Table 3.3.

Now we can see some interesting trends. First, we see changes in the ways that medallions are suspended from necklaces. Plastic medallions were suspended from necklaces on metal loops, then melted into strands, then incorporated onto strands with plastic clasps, and then metal pins. Then, starting in 2004, we can see plastic medallions being molded directly onto the string. Resin medallions were introduced in 2000 when the krewe returned to using metal loops to attach them to the bead strand.

Another shift through time is in the type of bead finish used for the medallions. From 1975 until 1981, the medallions are an opaque plastic hung on 32-inch strands of transparent

Figure 3.5. Forms of Bacchus medallions through time: A. 1976; B. 1979; C. 1984; D. ca. 1990–1997; E. 1993; F. 1997; G. 2004; H. 2007; I. 2009; J. 2011; K. 2012. Illustrations by Alexandra Wilkie Farnsworth.

Table 3.3. Size of Bacchus Year-specific Parade Medallions.

YEAR	WIDTH (cm)	HEIGHT (cm)	SURFACE AREA (cm^2)
1975	4	4	16
1976	4	4	16
1977	4	4	16
1979	7	3	21
1980	7	3	21
1981	7	3	21
1983	5	7	35
1986	5	7	35
1988	5	7	35
1991	11	2	22
1992	11	2	22
1993*	10	5	50
1994	11	2	22
1995	11	2	22
1996	11	2	22
1997	8	9	72
1998	8	9	72
1999	8	9	72
2000**	6	6	36
2001	6	6	36
2002	7	7	49
2003	7	7	49
2004	7.5	7.5	56.25
2005	7.5	7.5	56.25
2006	7.5	7.5	56.25
2007	7.5	7.5	56.25
2008	7.5	7.5	56.25
2009	7.5	7.5	56.25
2010	7.5	7.5	56.25
2011	7.5	7.5	56.25
2012	7.5	7.5	56.25

*This was the 25th Anniversary medallion
**From 2000 onward, the medallions shift from plastic to resin, which is significantly heavier, so we see a trend to increasing size first in plastic, then in resin.

beads that were 8mm wide. As early as 1982, this shifted to a transparent plastic medallion hung on 33-inch long strands of transparent beads measuring 8 mm round. In 1997, 1998, and 1999, the krewe experimented with pearl, metallic, and opalescent finished plastics. Starting in 2000, medallions switched from a molded injected plastic to a resin and were hung from 42-inch metallic beads measuring 10 mm. The addition of a new type, the MOS beads in 2004, continued to use 10 mm and larger strands in metallic finishes. As early as 2003, the krewe introduced a parade-themed, hand-painted resin bead suspended on 42-inch-long, 12 mm-metallic beads.

The latest shift, starting in 2009, has been to take the parade-themed and Bacchus-head resin medallions off of bead necklaces and put them onto satin cords. Accompanying these shifts in the appearance of medallions and the materials they are made from was a gradual increase in the size of the medallions (Table 3.3). Even if we consider the iconography of the medallions, we see that several themes remain important through time, with many of the medallions from the period of 1997 onward showing imagery and forms found in the krewe's earliest medallions. This conservatism allows for continuities in a sense of krewe heritage.

Do these changes only apply to Bacchus, or can they be used to date other krewes as well? First, I compared medallions that are believed to date to the early 1980s based on oral history; each draws heavily on krewe imagery developed for doubloons and mimics the appearance of coins hung on a necklace (Figure 3.6). Each of these medallions is small in diameter and utilizes opaque plastics. During the 1980s and 1990s, Bacchus was not the only krewe to exhibit a low level of diversity in its medallion forms. Rex, Proteus, Iris, Shangri La, and the competing super krewe Endymian all adhered to continuity in their medallion form (Figure 3.6). Likewise, other krewes' medallions also underwent a shift from metal loop, to clasp, to pin-closed methods of attaching medallions to strands at

Figure 3.6. Examples of other medallions that illustrate the same stylistic sequence as seen in the Bacchus seriation by decade.

Table 3.4. Changes in Sizes of Krewe Medallions over Time.

YEAR	KREWE OF TUCKS (medallion surface area in cm²)	KREWE OF ZULU	KREWE OF ORPHEUS	KREWE OF IRIS
1985	3.75			
1990	16	16		
1995		18	48	18
1998		18	48	18
1999	16	18	48	18
2000	63	72	81	72
2003		72	100	
2004	63	72		18
2006				
2007	63	72		

roughly the same time. Resin and multi-colored plastic medallions all began to appear at the same time and correspond to celebrations of the new millennium, which sparked a growing diversity in types and numbers of medallions offered (Figure 3.6). A trend toward increasing medallion size through time is common to a number of krewes in this study, and in fact, we can clearly see that the millennium celebrations corresponded with nearly every krewe offering a larger-sized medallion. Further, these medallion sizes became the norm during the first decade of the twenty-first century (Table 3.4). Like Bacchus in 2009, the Krewe of Proteus began to offer a medallion that was hung on a cord rather than beads. We'll discuss krewes, beads, and organization identities at greater length in a later chapter, but suffice to say at this point that there are broad trends in stylistic change evidenced in Bacchus's beads that are also visible in other competing krewe's assemblages if we look at attributes of the medallions other than the iconography. My first step as an archaeologist was to identify this trend by classifying the data into a typology. Later we'll try to assess its meaning.

Frequency Seriation

There is another form of seriation, however, that is an even more precise tool for understanding the relative date of one deposit versus another between sites, and that is abundance seriation, or frequency seriation (Marquardt 1978). This form of seriation rests on the observation that most styles of things have a set trajectory of popularity—they are introduced, they become at some point as popular as they will be, and then they trail off in popularity. Archaeologically, we see this as differences in the relative abundance of one style of an artifact versus another or one type of an artifact versus another.

Popular songs illustrate this trend nicely. When a song is first played on the radio, you may hear it and think, "wow, that song is awesome, I hope they play it again." You start the hear the song more often, until it seems to be played at least once an hour, and you think, "wow, that song is so overplayed, I'm over it." And two weeks later, you hear the song and realize, "huh, they aren't playing that as much as they used to." And in a year, you never hear the song unless someone calls in to request it. If you graph that trend—the number of times played per day over time—the results will look like a battleship from above.

At anytime, there is more than one song competing for airplay; and each song will have its own popularity over time associated with it. If you were to graph the relative popularity of each song relative to one another over a six-month period, creating relational battleship curves for each of them, you would see how as one song was fading, others were peaking as still more were introduced.

So how would this have archaeological value? Suppose you excavate a site that has three depositional layers and four different pottery types that vary in proportion to one another through time. You could start to develop your battleship curves from that information. You could then see what percentages of these same types occur at other sites in the region, and use that information to build on your battleship curves until you had accounted for all the sites and created a regional chronology. Sounds almost as magical as radiocarbon dating, doesn't it? Frequency seriatiation requires that the analyst choose historical types to seriate and have a general theoretical acceptance that social time can be subdivided into analytical chunks rather than recognized as a general continuum or flow (O'Brien et al. 2000). In contemporary society, we are quite accustomed to cutting up time into organizational chunks so that we can schedule our activities—this is not a universally accepted notion of time.

It was historical archaeologists, Eric Dethelsen and James Deetz (1966) who were able to demonstrate the utility and effectiveness of frequency seriation by tying artifact styles to calendar dates in their study of gravestones in New England cemeteries. Deetz elaborated upon this work in his 1977 book, *In Small Things Forgotten,* (the book that made me an archaeologist!)

From 1680 to 1820, New England cemeteries in urban areas were dominated by three major gravestone designs: death's heads, cherubs, and the willow and urn. The death's head featured a skull with wings, the cherub was a baby's face surrounded by wings, and the willow design featured a weeping willow draping its branches over an urn. Dethelsen and Deetz (1966) realized that headstones represented a unique opportunity to test a commonly applied archaeological technique using a set of artifacts that were dated. In other words, it was an absolute dating test for a relative dating technique.

Gravestones have dates carved on them indicating the death of the grave's occupant. While gravestones were often carved soon after death, to ensure that the carving date of the gravestone was known, probate records were consulted to see when an estate paid a gravestone carver. The archaeologists counted how many gravestones of each type were in a Cambridge cemetery and plotted their distribution relative to one another through time. They found that death's heads dominated the cemetery from 1720 to 1759. It wasn't until the period from 1760 to 1769 that the first small number of cherubs were seen in the cemetery. From 1770 to 1779, a few urns appeared, but the death heads and cherubs were about equally represented. Death heads and cherubs accounted for all of the gravestones from 1780 to 1789, with cherubs dominating during that time. This represented the last hurrah of the death head. From 1790 to 1799, only cherubs and urns were found; and by 1810, cherubs had been completely replaced by urn and willow designs. When mapped, the distribution of the three types over time forms three battleship curves (Figure 3.7).

Deetz (1977) explains the shift in imagery coinciding with changes in the ways that New Englanders thought about their relationship with religion and death. The death head's popularity coincided with the period of greatest Puritan orthodoxy and acceptance of a single message about death and ressurection. The cherub represented a softening of some of the church's rigidity and influences of the Great Awakening movement in religion that emphasized personal relationships with God over predestination. The urn and willow represent the greater secularization of American life following the Enlightenment, with imagery and inscriptions focusing more on death as a period of rest or sleep-like state.

Deetz's (1977) study also considered the nature of the transition from death's head to cherub in rural New England. In Cambridge, Deetz saw the Cherub design as popular among the intellectual elite, while the death's head was favored longer by more traditionally motivated members of lower-status groups. The spread of the cherub to rural areas from Boston was slower; in fact, Deetz was able to chart it at about one mile per year. In the town of Scituate, Massachusetts, about 25 miles southeast of Boston, two men—a father and son—carved all of the community's gravestones. In their work, it is possible to trace the stylistic transformation (a stylistic seriation, for those of you taking notes!) from death's head to cherub, with some parts of the skull being deemphasized and others emphasized to create the shift. However, the artists relied upon visual punning, or more simply put, constructed their images so that they could be read in two ways. Depending upon what viewers wanted to see, they could see the cherub in the death's head or the death's head in the cherub.

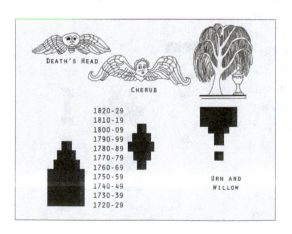

Figure 3.7: Deetz's gravestone typology and seriation (after Deetz 1996:97).

Other stone carvers around Boston made similar compromises, and there are remarkable similarities among the cemeteries of the area. Deetz (1977) interprets these hybrid death-cherubs as a way the stone carvers worked around the religious tensions that were straining communities during the Great Awakening. The elegance of the study is not only that the evidence illustrates the utility of archaeological methods and ways of thinking, but also provides a social historical context in which carvers consciously engaged with changing ideologies in their practices.

Frequency Seriation and Mardi Gras

Just as we create a stylistic seriation for the Mardi Gras beads, now let's try out frequency seriation on our assemblage. During the duration of my field project, I noticed through time that certain finishes were disappearing from assemblages and wondered if these changes would be visible in a frequency seriation. Because I was working with a relatively short period of time compared to the kinds of time periods dealt with in most archaeological settings, I wasn't sure that my sample had enough time depth for this exercise to be successful. Still, it seemed worth a shot. It was clear from standing in the crowds that certain bead finishes were growing more popular through time; was this shift clear enough to be visible in the mere twenty-year time span I had?

While we have been using curated assemblages for much of the previous discussion, here we are going to use the excavated assemblages. From 1991 to 1994, I have a **palimpsest** assemblage from the parades I went to throughout the state. The notion of a palimpsest comes from history and is used to describe a document that has been reused multiple times so that traces of overlapping fragments of writing from different times can be seen. In archaeological terms, a palimpsest exists when materials from different time periods are mixed (or more accurately, collapsed) together because there is no matrix separating them. In the Mardi Gras assemblage, there was no separation of beads from 1991 to 1994, they were all just thrown into one large bucket. That assemblage is our baseline, the actual excavated assemblages began in 1997 and continued through 2009. Figure 3.8 and Table 3.5 present the data on the relative frequency of different bead finishes through time. The table represents a composite of all beads recovered from New Orleans parades in those years so that krewe-specific trends in beads have less impact on the graph. In the graph, you will see that I have only shown the three most common types: transparent, metallic, and pearl beads. You will see from the graph that the period from 1991 to 2003 represents a clear shift in popularity from transparent to metallic beads. In the 1991–1994 assemblage, transparent beads account for 81.5% of the assemblage—in other words, the typical bead you would have caught in this parade period would have been clear. Solid-colored opaque beads were the second most common, at 9.8%. By 1997, we can see that the popularity of different bead finishes had already shifted a

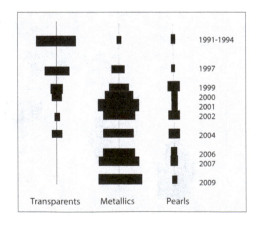

Figure 3.8: Frequency seriation of Mardi Gras bead finishes.

Table 3.5. Relative Abundance of Beads by Finish (%).

YEAR	TRANSPARENT	METALLIC	PEARL	OPALESCENT	OPAQUE	MARBELIZED
1991–1994	81.5	3.9	2	2.8	9.8	
1997	50.8	29.5	6.6	6.6	6.6	
1999	26.1	46.6	21.9	.4		
2000	18.5	64.3	12.4	1.2	4.9	
2001	.5	87.5	10.4	1	3.2	
2002	11.6	67.8	19.7	.3	.5	
2004	19.6	65.3	20.7	1.2	.6	
2006		73	12.6	.6		.6
2007		78.6	16.9	2.5	13.1	2.5
2009	.3	90.9	6.4	2		.3
2010	2.9	82.3	8.8	2.9	2.9	

great deal. Transparent beads were still the most common, having accounted for 50.8% of the assemblage. Opaque beads were replaced in popularity by metallic-finished beads, which account for 29.5% of the assemblage. By time we get to the year 2000, metallic bead finishes become established as the most common bead thrown at Mardi Gras, a position it retained to the end of my study. After 2006, transparent beads barely occur at Mardi Gras.

Pearl beads, which at different times have been the most highly valued beads thrown at Mardi Gras, demonstrate their growth and decline in popularity through time in which they comprised only 2% of the bead assemblage from 1991 to 1994. Later, they peak in 1999 when pearl-finished beads accounted for 21.9% of the bead assemblage. Until 2006, pearls comprised from 10 to 20% of the bead assemblages each year. In 2009, we saw pearl-finished beads drop to only 6.4% of the assemblage. In 2010, the pearls demonstrated no meaningful change in abundance and represented 8.8% of the assemblage. As I will discuss in chapter nine, this change in frequency (and therefore popularity) of pearl beads may be related to changes in the throwing game and to displays of nudity.

If we think about the trends we saw in the stylistic seriation, it seems that Bacchus's shift from opaque to transparent beads coincides with the replacement of opaque beads with transparent ones in popularity. Certainly, Bacchus's use of transparent medallions through the first part of the 1990s puts them in alignment with broader popular finish choices. In 1997, 1998, and 1999, the krewe experimented with alternate finishes to transparent—metallic, opalescent, and pearl finishes—before settling exclusively on metallic beads as the strands from which to hang their medallions in 2000 and to mold their MOS medallion beads from 2004 onward. By then, it would have been clear that metallic beads were the most popular with parade-goers. The medallion itself, switched from plastic to hand-painted resin. While not as elegant or tidy as Deetz's gravestone study, the tools of stylistic and frequency seriation have a role to play in the interpretation of Mardi Gras materials. Even the chaos of Carnival bends to the established habits of human beings.

The tools of stylistic and frequency seriation have further utility for us as we consider the contemporary artifacts of Mardi Gras. While the discipline of archaeology no longer attempts to identify culture areas and culture types as the main focus of our disciplinary work, the tools developed by archaeologists remain vital interpretive tools. You now have some familiarity with some archaeological ways of thinking and the bead assemblage, but before we go further, I must discuss with you the broader questions and research methodology that shaped this project. To do this requires that we consider the ideas of processual archaeology.

CHAPTER 4:
PUTTING THE SCIENCE IN ARCHAEOLOGY'S SOCIAL SCIENCE

I n some ways, I put the float before the mule in the last chapter, for I started to introduce my evidence before I explained my methodology. My early exposure to theory in archaeology was the writings of archaeologists like Lewis Binford (1967, 1972, 1981), Patty Jo Watson, Steven LeBlanc, and Charles Redman (1984); so to this day, it is engrained in me that archaeology must start with a question and follow with a plan for answering that question. These archaeologists, part of what was once called "*new archaeology*" or now as *processual archaeology*, emphasized the importance of developing a research question and a design for research before ever putting trowel to earth. To introduce you to the ideas and methods of cultural historical archaeology, I have betrayed my indoctrination by talking about the beads before discussing "why" the beads and "how" the beads.

Methodology was important to cultural historians; controlled, stratified excavation was perfected by that generation of archaeologists (e.g., Rowe 1961). The theoretical underpinning of culture history—that culture was shared and bounded and generally resistant to change—created an archaeology whose questions, methods, and goals were focused on recovering data related to addressing "who," "where," "for how long," and "in contact with whom?" Cultural change was not a focus of culture historians, in part because theories about change were like the evolutionary and environmental determinism that Boas's historical particularism had struggled against. Besides, answering those other questions that cultural historians were interested in was a labor-intensive enterprise. Diffusion, or the spread of a cultural practice, trait, artifact type, or style from one culture to another through contact, was the most popular explanation for cultural change. Diffusion and stylistic drift, a concept we saw employed by Ford (1954) in stylistic seriation, were satisfying explanations of culture change for many culture historians.

During the 1940s and 1950s, there were debates about what other questions can be asked through archaeology. Julian Steward suggested that cultural change could be a bigger part of archaeological investigation. In a 1938 article, Julian Steward and Frank Setzler suggested that archaeology was no longer making the kinds of contributions to anthropology of which it was capable. They worried that the obsession with minute descriptions of ceramic paste and temper distracted archaeologists from thinking about questions of cultural process—how cultures came to be what they were—and that archaeologists offered description but no explanation. It would be 20 years before Steward and Setzler's (1938) call for an archaeology that considered human ecology and cultural process would be answered.

Walter Taylor (1948) later published his dissertation, in which he offered a different type of archaeology—a conjunctive-approach archaeology—that would push beyond the descriptive enterprise that archaeology had become. Taylor suggested that archaeology should be more holistic and consider a wider range of material evidence from archaeological sites—including dietary and other evidence than just pots and points. Taylor's work was a bit premature and a bit too aggressive in denigrating the work of practicing, well-established archaeologists. Yet, we have seen some of his specific ideas coming to fruition in what is called processual and *post-processual* archaeologies. Taylor's 1948 work, *A Study of Archaeology,* is now widely read in graduate seminars even though it had little influence on most of his contemporaries.

A number of factors converged by the late 1950s to prepare archaeology for a paradigm shift. Many historians of archaeology will point to the development of radiocarbon dating as the deathblow for culture history; all those complicated regional chronologies based upon deeply debated typological systems were rendered unnecessary. This is a bit of a false claim, in that while revolutionary, radiocarbon dating was not always as precise in detailing relative chronological relationships because of its range of error. However, it did become possible to tie all of those regional chronologies based on artifact sequences to a calendrical scale. It wasn't technology that was necessary for the archaeological revolution—it was a shift in thinking.

Changes in anthropology and the broader academy contributed to archaeology being open to making broad-scale changes to its methods and theories. Expanded funding from the National Science Foundation (NSF) of disciplines like archaeology started in 1957 (NSF website, "Timeline of NSF History") and meant that there was an external stimulus for archaeology to develop scientific rigor in the ways advocated for by people like Binford. Not only was there funding, but there was also a radical change in the demographics of the academy. The GI bill opened up a college education to returning war veterans, and ultimately, their children after them. The men who finished bachelor degrees right after the war were the graduate students and freshly minted PhDs who developed processual archaeology. Importantly for them, the expansion of universities meant that there were actually an abundance of faculty positions, which favored the hire of younger scholars. Archaeology was not the only discipline to benefit from an influx of new thinking resulting from the GI bill. Computer technology was developing, which allowed for the processing of large amounts of data—larger evidentiary sets than could be easily manipulated by hand.

The most important changes that led to what became the new archaeology were changes in thinking. Anthropology had moved on from historical particularism. Anthropologists, like Julian Steward (Steward and Murphy 1977) and Leslie White (1959), reintroduced ideas based on evolution back into anthropological discourse, but this time with careful use of vocabulary that made it clear they were proposing different conceptualizations of social evolution. For Julian Steward, it was the idea of cultural ecology—that humans and their environment shaped and were shaped by one another in a mutualistic and ever-dynamic relationship. Leslie White (1959) envisioned cultures as systems that needed to harness more and more energy to sustain themselves; thus, cultural complexity could be measured as the ever-increasing ability of societies to harvest more and more energy out of their environment. In 1960, Marshall Sahlins and Ellman Service wrote a paper that outlined an evolutionary model that recognized "bands," "tribes," "chiefdoms," and "states" as the stages of social evolution, which proved to be particularly influential in archaeology. Although this classification sounds much like the old savage, barbarian, and civilization scheme of the nineteenth century's unilinear evolutionary models we discussed in the last chapter, the Sahlins and Service model was different. They did not define each group by a set of trait lists (like writing and mono-theism), but based their model on the kinds of *subsistence* (food) economies, forms of social organizations and government, and residential patterns.

Archaeology was uniquely situated to contribute to the growing anthropological interests in the mechanisms of social change, cultural ecology, and the development of *social complexity*. These were arenas that required the insights of time depth, something that archaeology had—thanks in no small part to the work of the culture historians. It was not surprising, therefore, that it was a student of Leslie White, who led the charge for a new archaeology.

Lewis Binford was a charismatic young scholar who was influenced by the neo-evolutionary movement in anthropology. In his famous 1962 essay, "Archaeology as Anthropology," Binford clearly situated himself as someone interested in cultural change and human/environment interactions by citing the works of Sahlins, White, and Steward. In his essay, he lamented the apparent disconnect at the time between the goals of anthropology and the contributions of archaeology. He further noted that while anthropology sought to explain and analyze the range of human social forms throughout history, archaeologists only contributed to the explication side of things. He argued that to enter into the realm of explanation, archaeologists had to think about the nature of culture more broadly and particularly the ways that societies lived with their environment.

Following Steward's (1954) lead, Binford called for functional analyses of artifacts (although he didn't cite Steward) and suggested that archaeologists hurt themselves by assuming all artifacts were equal in a given cultural system. Additionally, Binford iden-tified three artifact classes that archaeology could use to explore change through time. He called the first functional artifact type *technomic* and described these as artifacts whose form and nature arose most directly from the environment. Technomic artifacts were likely to be related to activities like subsistence. For instance, a group living on a coast was likely to have artifacts related to fishing and acquisition of marine sources—a cir-cumstance not expected for desert cultures, whose technomic artifacts would be very different. The next functional group were artifacts that played a *socio-technic* role—artifacts that served to connect people together in a culture—such as artifacts related to kinship. The final functional group of artifacts were *ideo-technic*, or artifacts that signified the ideological rational of the social system; figurines of gods were examples of ideo-technic artifacts for Binford. He went on to suggest that while archaeologists had easiest access to understanding technomic artifacts, that given the right circumstances, archaeologists could reconstruct past social and ideological systems that artifacts had functioned in.

While his categories were tedious, the most compelling part of the article was Binford's example of how the Old Copper culture of the Midwest could be understood using these new frameworks. Copper was used to make tools in the Archaic period (about 3,000–6,000 years ago), and then in the Middle and Late Woodland, the material was used to make only nonutilitarian objects. Archaeologists of the time generally saw this as a sign of technological devolution. Using the ideas of Sahlins, White, and Steward, Binford proposed a different interpretation. He first discussed how copper was not a particularly smart choice for tools because of the tremendous energy input required to manufacture them, and he suggested that perhaps their value in the cultural system was related to symbolic power. He showed how copper objects, through time, were found in highest concentrations far away from mines, and he interpreted them as objects of prestige value that became increasingly concentrated in the hands of the elite as cultures in the area became more socially complex. He demonstrated that a set of artifacts that had been misinterpreted as having a technomic role were better understood as having a social function—reinforcing social status and hierarchies.

The article was compelling, and Binford gathered around him a following of bright young graduate students and influenced a generation of scholars to take up the new archaeology. Now, thinking differently is hard when you are used to thinking a particular way. Binford's calls for a new archaeology were met with resistance in the form of, "Well, how do we do this? We clearly need new methodologies!" Binford did not need a new methodology to reinterpret the Old Copper culture. He simply needed to turn his thinking around. Still, there was a perception that the new archaeology needed new ways of doing, and certainly, new areas of archaeological methods and methodological concerns grew out of processual archaeology.

So what did the new archaeology, really demand? First, it is important to understand that Binford was not asking archaeologists to think about culture in different ways. For processual archaeology, culture was still normative—a set of bounded practices shared by all members of a society. Binford called on archaeologists to change their focus from cultures in times of stasis to cultures in times of change and to explore all the issues about social development being put forward by the neo-evolutionary thinkers who were writing in anthropology. Binford and those who followed him embraced the idea that the primary question archaeology should ask is "why" and that archaeology should be explanatory not descriptive.

In response to those archaeologists wanting a new way of doing archaeology to make the new thinking easier, Binford argued that the discipline needed to rethink its ways of thinking about the doing of archaeology. He turned to the philosophy of science, particularly thinkers like Hempel (1942, 1966) and Popper (1959) and proposed that arch-aeology needed to draw upon the hypothetico-deductive method in order to generate *general covering laws* to explain *cultural change*. This is a loaded sentence that requires further explanation.

The Hypothetico-Deductive Method

What would be an example of a *hypothetico-deductive method*? This term refers to a means of conducting scientific research in which a researcher starts with a research question and then considers all the reasonable and testable possible answers to that question; these possible, reasonable, and testable answers are *hypotheses*. By saying a hypothesis is testable, we mean that it is possible to identify what evidence would be necessary to support that hypothesis. The research is designed to collect that evidence and to determine which hypotheses are refuted (proven wrong by the evidence) and which ones are not refuted. In this kind of scientific method, you cannot prove your hypotheses; you can only disprove them. A hypothesis that cannot be disproved after much effort is considered to be a theory. To call something a theory is to use some pretty strong scientific language; thus, evolution is a theory that is accepted in the archaeological community as fact just as Einstein's theory of relativity is accepted in physics. The only stronger language is to call something a law, such as Lyell's Law of Superposition, or the Laws of Thermodynamics. When Binford called for archaeology to come up with laws that governed cultural change, it was a mighty ambitious goal.

Zooarchaeology and an Example of the Hypothetico-Deductive Method

So let's consider an example of the hypothetico-deductive method in practice. I codirected an archaeological project in the Bahamas at a site called Clifton Plantation (Wilkie and Farnsworth 2005). The site dated from the late eighteenth to the early nineteenth centuries, and we excavated trash deposits (*middens*) from house yards associated with the enslaved African population of the plantation. The plantation was situated on the ocean, and we recovered large amounts of fish bone from the site. The study of animal remains from archaeological sites is a specialized field of analysis called *zooarchaeology*, or archeozoology in places like Europe. Zooarchaeology is one of the specialized fields of analysis that developed out of processual archaeology, so this is a particularly useful case study to discuss. Zooarchaeology looks at the relationship between human beings and animals as evidenced through archaeological remains, such as animal bone and shell most commonly, but also by looking at field arrangements, barns, animal-husbandry related artifacts, or even images of animals on artifacts or in paintings. Often, zooarchaeological remains are associated with subsistence activities—humans eating animals—but work animals, companion animals, and even sacred animals (in art and burials) can be recovered archaeologically. The fragments of animal bones recovered from archaeological sites can be used to possibly identify information as diverse as which parts of which animals are represented at a site, the relative abundance of one animal species to another, the age of an animal at slaughter, the season in which an animal was killed, which cuts of meat were favored over others, and butchering and cooking techniques among many other things. Zooarchaeological analysis is possible because while all species have unique features about their individual bones and skeletons shared with others of their kind, all birds have the same bones in their skeletons, as do all fish and all mammals. With the aid of a skeletal comparative collection, a decent-sized piece of bone can be identified as to its *skeletal element* (what bone it is) and what species it is from.

At Clifton, I was interested in answering two basic research questions. First, what fish were consumed by the enslaved people, and second, how did the enslaved people acquire the fish? The first question required determining which species were represented at the site through the identification of faunal specimens. The second question required me to think further about the social and technological processes through which people could obtain fish. I considered several possibilities.

1. The fish could have been caught by independent families within the village.
2. There may have been one person who fished within the village who then distributed the fish.
3. The planter, or an agent of the planter caught the fish, and they were distributed as rations.

Each of these is a hypothesis. What evidence could I look for to answer this question? In thinking about the first possibility, since the enslaved Africans living at Clifton had competing demands on their time, I would therefore expect to see them using methods that would allow them to catch fish with little time investment. This could be done by spear fishing or by using set lines (a fishing pole with a series of hooks that is left with bait on it either during the day or over night and then checked at intervals for fish), fishing pots (a cage that is dropped with bait in it that has an entrance that fish can enter but not exit), or a fishing net. If different families were all involved in fishing, I would expect to see a diversity of fishing-related equipment, such as net weights, fishing hooks, or tools for fishing net repair at houses that had fish remains. If one person in the village did most of the fishing, we would expect to find no evidence of fishing from all of the houses except one. If no one in the quarters were fishing, and the families were being provisioned with fish by a fisherman in hire of the planter, we would see no evidence of fishing-related artifacts in any of the quarters.

There were implications for the *faunal assemblage* (bone assemblage) depending on what method of capture was used. With nets, one gets a wide range of species of different sizes that are caught at one time. An enslaved person using a net would be doing so from shore. If a professional fisherman, with a boat, was using the net, however, they would be heading to deeper waters and catching different, larger species than someone setting out pots or nets close to shore. Close to Clifton's shores is a rich reef environment inhabited by snappers, grunts, squirrel fish, jacks, porgies, parrot fish, and an occasional grouper. In deeper waters, there are tuna and mackerel to be caught. I would also expect that if a fisherman were engaged to do the fishing, we would see species that live farther from the shore. If enslaved people were doing the fishing, I would expect to see species that inhabit the reef just offshore.

A fisherman using pots will also gather a variety of species, but whatever the species, they will be of a relatively consistent size, because they are all getting trapped through the same-sized pot opening. Line fishing would look much like net fishing in terms of the size and diversity of species; though species that can bite through line, such as parrotfish, would not be present. Spear fishing seeks to capture larger fish, such as groupers and big parrotfish, and leaves a distinctive hole in the fish's bone where the spear pierces them.

So what did we learn from the analysis? First, the vast majority of the fish recovered from the quarters were no more than a pound in size—what are called pan fish because they fit in a pan. Grunts, snappers, and jacks were most common. Because of the consistency in fish size and the diversity of close-to-shore reef fish represented, this suggests at least some fish were being caught in pots. None of the small, less-desirable-to-eat-species (like sergeant majors, trunk fish, or trumpet fish) were represented in the assemblages, which suggests that if nets were used, unwanted species were culled out. None of the bones included any signs of harpoon or spear damage, nor had hooks damaged any of the mouth or gill-related elements of the skeleton. In contrast, when I looked at the fish bones from the planter's house, I realized that the planter's family was consuming large, deeper water fish like mackerel. These species were not represented to any large degree in the enslaved African people's village.

Within the enslaved African peoples' village, only one house had any number of fishing-related objects recovered: some nails that seemed to have been intentionally bent into hooks and a piece of coral carved into a net weight. I did learn, talking to some Bahamian fisherman, that pots are the easiest of fishing equipment to maintain, and their use would not necessarily leave a noticeable archaeological trace. So my conclusions were limited. I feel that the evidence disproves the hypothesis that there was a professional fisherman provisioning the village. Instead, based on the evidence of the consistent fish size, I think the villagers were collecting the fish themselves using pots. I do not feel like I have the evidence necessary to disprove either hypothesis one or two given that fish pots would not necessarily leave an archaeological trace. To further explore my question, I would need to engage in additional archaeological work after devising an archaeological test that could recover evidence that could disprove one or both of the other hypotheses. For now, I have been comfortable with the conclusion that the enslaved people at Clifton were supplementing their diets with reef fish caught in fishing pots just offshore from the plantation.

Making Archaeology Scientific: Other New Methodologies of the New Archaeology

This is how the hypothetico-deductive method works in archaeology, and it is a clear example of the vision Binford had for archaeology to become more scientifically rigorous. To Binford and his followers, it was clear that what archaeology needed was to develop methodologies that were scientifically rigorous—meaning an emphasis on *empirical data* collection (statistically verifiable results) that sought to look at a wider range of archaeological materials than was typical during the cultural historical period. So what are some examples of the new kinds of analyses archaeologists conducted?

Paleoethnobotany

New emphasis was placed on reconstructing subsistence strategies, which according to Binford are the clearest manifestation of the human-environment interaction and the easiest to reconstruct from archaeological data. Zooarchaeology and *Paleoethnobotany*, the study of plant remains, developed rapidly under processual archaeology. Just as zoo-archaeology looks at the human-animal relationship, paleoethnobotany looks at human-plant relationships (Hastorf and Popper 1989). Plants are not as sturdy as bone and preserve archaeologically only in particular circumstances and in particular ways. Paleo-ethnobotanists study *macrobotanical remains* (seeds, corncobs, wood, and roots) that can be see by the naked eye and *microbotanical remains*, which require the use of a microscope to be seen. Preservation of macrobotanicals requires particular sets of environmental conditions. For instance, cooking hearths (fireplaces) are great places to search for plants remains that have been burned and carbonized (made into charcoal), these remains are recoverable, and often identifiable. A lovely feature of charred plant materials is that they float, so in a process called, unsurprisingly, *flotation,* a soil sample from a feature expected to preserve plant remains is processed in a water tub (flotation tank). The materials that float to the surface are removed from the surface of the tank (this is called the *light fraction*), and anything that sinks is recovered from a fine wire mesh screen at the bottom of the tank (Figure 4.1). In addition to charred seeds and wood fragments, small mammal bones, fish bones, scales, shell fragments, and even small artifacts like beads can be recovered in this mix of small things called *heavy fraction.* Plant

Figure 4.1. Soil flotation set-up. Photographs by Annelise Morris and Gloria Keng.

material can also survive in very dry climates (such as desert caves) and in water-logged or frozen circumstances.

Microbotanical remains need more sophisticated recovery techniques. The most commonly studied microbotanical remains are **pollen** (plant reproductive products), **spores** (the reproductive products of fungi), **starches** (the energy storage units of plants), and **phytoliths** (small silica structures that are in the cells of many plant species). Pollen, spores, and phytliths can be recovered from ground sediments in a lab setting through a series of procedures involving acid washes and centrifuging. The recovered samples are mounted on microscopic slides and viewed at magnifications as high as 1,000 × for identification. Starch grains are also often recovered from the surface of stone cutting and scraping tools, cooking pots, griddles, or grinding stones. Pollen is airborne matter, which can travel far from where it was released by a plant; however, a study of the relative abundance of different pollen types at a site is invaluable for understanding prehistoric environments. Phytoliths are more likely to be preserved in the same area where the plant that created them died. It has been possible for paleoethnobotanists to identify phytoliths from wild versus domesticated varieties at archaeological sites, making this kind of analysis very important for the study of ancient domestication and farming practices (e.g., Hastorf and Popper 1989, Piperno 2009).

A unique opportunity for the study of macro and microbotanical remains presented itself in the frozen and mummified body of Ötzi the Iceman. Ötzi, as the remains are affectionately called, was discovered in a thawing glacier in the mountains along the Swiss-Austrian border. Ötzi has been radiocarbon dated to having died sometime between 5350–5100 BP, which corresponds to the late Neolithic period in Europe. This means Ötzi lived during the earliest farming days of human beings (Rollo et al. 2002). Archaeologists were thrilled with the preservation of organic material culture associated with this Neolithic man. In addition to animal hides, artifacts made from plant materials, such as a woven grass mat or cape, a yew tree bow, sapwood arrows, a birch bark box containing maple leaves, and two birch fungi that were believed to have medicinal uses were recovered (South Tyrol Museum of Archaoelogy, "Ötzi;" Rollo et al. 2002). These are examples of the most amazing kind of macrobotanicals. Finds like the body of Ötzi and his material assemblage remind us how many uses for plants ancient peoples had, as well as how much of that material is lost to us through decay. Ötzi's body has also been an unusual source of microbotanical data. The contents of the Iceman's intestine and colon have been studied for insights into his diet and where he may have lived. Ötzi would have absorbed pollen by breathing, drinking water, and eating. Pollen species that were related to foods he ate, as well as plants that existed in his place of residence, would have been represented. Pine trees, cereal, and fern spores and flowering plant pollens representing 30 different types were among the most prominent floral remains in Ötzi's system. Using fecal matter from Ötzi's bowels, a team of researchers led by Franco Rollo (Rollo et al. 2002), were able to extract genetic matter from different plant and animal species that had been components of the man's last meals. Archaeologists are still exploring the different ways the study of ancient genetics can contribute to our understandings of the relationships between humans, plants, animals, and their environments.

All of the kinds of specialized analyses mentioned above have their roots in the period of processual archaeology. The recovery of these traces from the archaeological record required new methods in the field, and their analyses demanded new laboratory techniques. The development of new techniques and methodologies was not limited to subsistence studies. New dating methods were explored and developed as were new ways of storing and processing data. We'll talk more about some of these innovations later.

One of the most important hallmarks of the new archaeology was a strong commitment to the appearance of scientific rigor in research design and field and laboratory techniques (e.g., Binford 1981; Harris 1979; Schiffer 1987; Watson et al. 1984). For me, the works of Charles Redman (1973, 1987) have always been sources that I turn back to when thinking through a research project. Redman emphasized integrating field and lab research when designing a project; while also recognizing that during the process of doing a project, it can become necessary to alter your design to accommodate new information. There is a certain amount of absurdity involved in the process of designing archaeological research: we have to anticipate what evidence we will find before we ever excavate it. I will be talking more about the intellectual goals of processual archaeology as we consider how we can use the bead assemblage to understand regional distribution systems and the relationship between Mardi Gras celebrations and environmental circumstances. For now, I want to demonstrate how the attention to methodological issues and research design brought to archaeology by the processualists shaped my Mardi Gras research.

Designing Mardi Gras

Whether artifacts are collected from the surface, the ground, or in my case, the air, you need to have a plan of research that links the questions you want to address with clear goals of what evidence needs to be collected in what ways to make that happen (Redman 1973, 1987). This makes a great deal of sense as a way to conserve resources like time, labor, and money spent on fieldwork; for example, there is no need to excavate an agricultural site in a rural area if you want to study urban ceramic production. Yet, you would be surprised, in absence of a research design, how many researchers would love to excavate their entire site and try every possible technical artifact analysis to "just see" what they can learn. This is not how knowledge is produced. That's not to say that questions like, "I wonder if we had tried such and such" does not lead to valid experimentation and discovery—it does. But "eureka" moments in science ultimately arise out of disciplined practice not desperate flailing of arms and minds. Since Mardi Gras, by its nature, can involve a great deal of desperate flailing of arms, it seemed to me that it was especially important to go into Carnival with a plan. I understand this is a bit antithetical to the spirit of Mardi Gras, but sometimes it is necessary to make sacrifices to maintain scientific rigor.

When I first envisioned this project, I planned on conducting very short-term, focused data collection of no more than a field season or perhaps two. I was interested in a mainly comparative study of the throwing practices of different krewes. My original questions were straightforward.

1. How do throws vary from one parade to another?
2. Are there differences in bead quantity or quality from one parade to another?
3. How does location affect bead assemblages?
4. Are krewes using bead selection to create a material identity for themselves?
5. Is there evidence of recycling in the bead assemblages, and if so, is it datable?

The only way to answer these questions was through an archaeological intervention. Assemblages had to be collected in a methodical manner, kept separated by parade, and be analyzed with a consistent set of standards. Now, at this point, some of you may be thinking that this project seems like a bit of a boondoggle, an academic excuse just to visit Mardi Gras, a trick worthy of the infamous trickster governor of Louisiana, Huey Long, himself. (This populist governor of Louisiana once wanted to build a new stadium for Louisiana State University's football team, but the legislature would only fund new dorms. Long's answer? He built dorm rooms into a new stadium.) Why on earth would I need to do this study as a contemporary archaeology project when surely there must be documents and other sources? So for the doubters, let me discuss a bit about the site formation processes of Mardi Gras assemblages.

Problems of Site Formation Processes

Binford and other processualists understood the archaeological record to be something that existed in the present, but if we understood how it was formed, we could use it to understand behaviors in the past. The study of site formation processes, or **taphonomic** processes, at archaeological sites, grew out of the concerns of processual archaeology to understand how the archaeological record was created. As we've discussed previously, Michael Schiffer (1987) has conducted the most rigorous sustained consideration of the ways that natural (earth, wind, fire, water, growing plants, burrowing animals, etc.) and human (dredging, excavating, filling, backfilling, flooding, mining, etc.) processes modify the archaeological record through time. Most of the processes that go into forming what we will refer to as the Mardi Gras bead record are related to human activities.

Let us just take a moment to consider the life course of a bead after it is taken out of its plastic shipping bag and thrown at a parade (Figure 4.2). During Carnival season, individuals acquire new beads from parades, purchase, or other bartering transactions. Come the end of the Mardi Gras season, some strands will be evaluated as "good" and sent to friends in other states or used to decorate homes, offices, and cars; while the lesser beads will be tossed together with those of previous years. This creates something we discussed a bit earlier—a palimpsest, which is an assemblage where chronological relationships are collapsed upon one another with no matrix between to keep materials from different periods of time separate. These piles of beads may be permanently removed from the Mardi Gras cycle and left to accumulate year after year. There is a market for used Mardi Gras beads, however, and beads can be bundled by color, shape, and length,

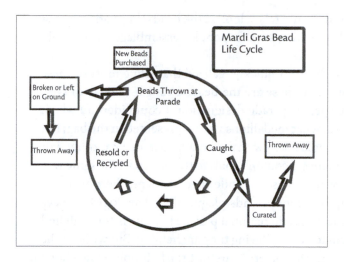

Figure 4.2. Life history of beads.

and sold either back into the formal bead market, to a company that will repackage and resell the used beads at a lower case price, or the informal bead market through garage sales, newspaper ads, or craigslist. Others, desperate to make space in attics or basements, will give their lesser beads to friends or family members who ride in one of the many parades that occur in southwestern Louisiana leading up to Mardi Gras. And every year, more beads come in from China, renewing the cycle each year.

So consider this, how is one to study what beads are being thrown at Mardi Gras in any given year? If you study bead catalogs and store contents, you will only gain partial insights; new beads brought into the state are a small portion of the entire bead population available for throwing. The krewes negotiate their own packages, and with Chinese factories willing to do smaller and smaller personalized bead orders, it is not possible to document all the varieties of beads that may be available. Further, because each rider is responsible for purchasing his or her own beads, there is no centralization of bead purchasing even at the krewe level, although some krewes offer packages of beads for sale to members. To understand the geography and history—the temporal and spatial dimensions—of the seemingly constant annual ritual, a an archaeological intervention is required. The atemporal bead assemblages found in many a Louisiana home are not unlike the village middens and trash heaps studied by archaeologists; just as the temporally discrete acquisitions of one-time visitors are similar to archaeological features found in a soil matrix. Even though the throwing game is a modern phenomenon, which takes place in a well-documented society, the social dimensions of the throwing game and the insights about our society they communicate can only be understood through an archaeological approach that emphasizes the detailed examination of the beads themselves. To obtain samples of beads from any given parade requires someone to be there to take a sample with controls for space, time, and sampling strategy—the hallmarks of archaeological investigation. So, perhaps now you understand why an archaeological approach is the only way to understand this American festival tradition, but you are still not convinced that Mardi Gras' throwing game is worth the attention. Well, Cher, give me the rest of the book for that.

Data Collection and Sampling

In 1997, when I was first playing with the idea of undertaking this study (I mean, doing a preliminary field survey), I asked graduate students and faculty in the Department of

Geography and Anthropology at LSU if I could take a look at the beads they had caught at Mardi Gras that year. I was hoping that looking at other people's assemblages would help me to develop a research design.

Several people brought me bags of beads. I quickly realized that while most of these assemblages had a temporal provenience ("these are the beads I caught Sunday in New Orleans"), they did not have a more specific parade designation. I could identify which parades they had attended by looking at what medallions were represented in the bag, but not which of the unmarked beads were associated with a particular parade or another. For me, this was simply a matter of provenience. I couldn't analyze the materials the same way I could for the materials I had recovered myself. While inconvenient, there were no further consequences. However, unprovenienced finds plague all archaeologists. I have worked on a number of sites located in state and national parks. Helpful visitors will find artifacts on the surface and bring them to you, believing they are helping. But without the context, this information is useless to us; the materials are just trash. It doesn't take long for a number of well-meaning visitors to completely dismantle an archaeological site. One of my graduate students was recently working at a Fort in Texas, trying to sort through materials that had been picked up by park staff and visitors over the years. The Fort had two distinct occupations: one before the civil war and one after. Conveniently, the two phases of the forts were represented by two sets of buildings on different alignments: one on true north and one on magnetic north. When surveying, it was possible to determine which materials were associated with each occupation despite the short period of time separating them. The post-war occupation included cavalry units of African American soldiers—the famous Buffalo soldiers. While we were interested in learning more about the Buffalo soldier's occupation, the materials that had been picked up were a mixture of things from the two forts, and without knowing where they were found, it was impossible to separate out which materials were from which time period.

I realized certain questions could only be addressed if data collection took place in a controlled manner. I had to excavate the Mardi Gras parades, pulling artifacts, as it were, out of the sky. Any one who collected beads for me, would have to conform to the same standards of data collection, or I would not be able to use the samples they collected.

I was able to identify what types of evidence I would need to gather in terms of the kinds of assemblages I would need to create and the observations (data) I would have to collect from each artifact (Table 4.1). There were some other issues to sort out, however. I needed to choose a place to "dig." I had already narrowed my study to New Orleans, but where along any parade's route should I collect my artifact samples? The new archaeologists brought debates about sampling procedures and sample sizes to the discipline. To sample is simply to select a portion of something. Anything that we take out of the archaeological record is already a sample of what was once there—not everything preserves in the archaeological record. It is both impossible and irresponsible to attempt to excavate an entire site, so any archaeological sample is a sample of a sample (Redman 1987; Watson et al. 1984). Remember that archaeology is a destructive science, and we dismantle the thing we are studying. If we were to excavate an entire site every time we ran an excavation,

Table 4.1. Questions and Evidentiary Requirements.

RESEARCH QUESTION	DATA NECESSARY TO ANSWER QUESTION
How do throws vary from one parade to another?	Discrete samples from each parade to be studied, gathered during the same Mardi Gras season.
Are there differences in bead quantity or quality from one parade to another?	Since bead finish, length, width, and shape all have differing values associated with them, it would be necessary to quantify not only the abundance of beads but the overall quality of the assemblage based on average bead size and length.
How does location on the parade route affect bead assemblages?	This would require multiple samples to be taken along the parade route.
Are krewes using bead selection to create a material identity for themselves?	This would require comparison across assemblages to see if particular colors, shapes, or finishes of beads were associated most strongly with one krewe or another.
Is there evidence of recycling in the bead assemblages, and if so, is it datable?	Attributes, such as flaking surface finish, bead discoloration, medallions predating the year of the parade, or evidence of bead repair on a strand would be observed and recorded.

we would not be leaving materials for future generations of researchers to study. In addition, many sites have areas that are sacred or otherwise important to communities in the present; there are simply parts of certain sites that should not be excavated unless they are somehow threatened with destruction.

Archaeologists make many sampling decisions as we design research, some more consciously than others (Neff 1993; Plog 1978; Shott 1987; Watson et al. 1984). We decide how much of a site we are going to excavate and where in a site we will excavate; those are sampling decisions. When we decide to sift the soil matrix through a mesh screen, we are making a sampling decision to retrieve artifactual and ecofactual data that may not be visible to excavators. Once it has been decided to sift the dirt, then one has to decide what size screen mesh to use. Choosing to use a quarter-inch screen means you are deciding to sample those artifacts that are bigger than that size only. Some people decide they want to recover a "complete sample" of all materials and will do flotation of the dirt to remove the light fraction and then collect all the heavy fraction) to be sorted through. Usually, when an archaeologist decides to collect a larger sample of materials from each excavation unit, they are also committing to excavating a smaller volume of matrix from the overall site. The kind of sample is also shaped by what you are studying. As you'll recall from our discussion of zooarchaeology and paleoethnobotany, these are fields that require the recovery of specific kinds of archaeological evidence.

Dating techniques like radiocarbon dating, dendrochronology, and obsidian hydration require the collection of particular kinds of samples. We've discussed radiocarbon dating and dendrochronology already, but let us say a few words about **obsidian hydration**. It is a dating technique developed in processual archaeology. Obsidian is a volcanic glass that has excellent mechanical traits for the creation of stone tools. It has few inclusions and allows for the creation of narrow, sharp blades. Obsidian contains about 1% water. At the time when it is flaked, the exposed face of the stone will appear clear and glassy, but over time, the water in the obsidian will move to the surface and create an opaque looking layer. In cross section, the thickness of this layer can be measured under a microscope. The older a flaked face, the thicker the obsidian hydration layer. A researcher who has a number of obsidian tools from a single site, can remove small portions of the tools to examine the thickness of the hydration layers to determine relative to one another which tools are the oldest. If the properties of a particular obsidian source are known, and the rate that the layer forms has been dated through independent means, such as radiocarbon dating, then, the thickness of the layer can be used to calculate an absolute date.

Sampling concerns can shape what kinds of sites and features archaeologists target in their research designs. If an archaeologist wants to conduct an intensive study of environmental conditions and human environmental interactions, then it makes sense to focus excavation on certain limited contexts that are expected to be rich in those kinds of evidence, such as fire pits. If an archaeologist is interested in understanding the use of architecture at a site, that researcher will need to excavate a larger horizontal exposure of a site to locate and identify architecture (or select a survey interval with a remote sensing device that will allow for the identification of subsurface architectural remains). Further sampling decisions are made in the laboratory. Sometimes it is not possible to analyze every artifact recovered, so a sample is taken of the sample recovered from excavation. This is particularly true when artifacts are being subjected to a labor-heavy or technology-expensive analysis. What is important is that the sampling decisions made are appropriate for the work to be undertaken.

The new archaeologists spent a great deal of time talking about sampling strategies and what kind of sampling in the field was most appropriate for what forms of statistical analysis (e.g., Longacre and Graves 1976; Nance 1981; Redman 1987; Watson et al. 1984). You will see references to "probabilistic sampling strategies" and "nonprobabilistic sampling strategies." A **probabilistic sampling strategy**, also sometimes called a **random sampling strategy**, avoids using prior knowledge to rank the selection of one sample over another. In other words, every sample, be it a spot to excavate or a recovered artifact or ecofact, has equal chance of being selected. Archaeologists, to ensure randomness, would use random number tables to select samples—a fancy version of drawing lots out of a hat. How might this actually work in an excavation setting? Suppose we were going to excavate the debris that accumulates along the parade route during Mardi Gras celebrations. We would superimpose a grid of units over the extent of the site and assign numbers to each excavation unit. If we had 1,000 units and intended to excavate 1% of the site (that would be 10 units for those of you who are math whizzes), we could then use one of the many random number generator computational programs available on the web to generate 10 random numbers that fall within our sample unit universe. Those 10 would be the units that we excavate.

Now, if you've ever looked at lotto drawings, you've seen that random drawings can result in clustering of numbers. For instance, a recent powerball drawing resulted in the numbers 1, 17, 20, 25, 37, and 44 being drawn. On an archaeological grid, clustering can result in one part of a site being tested more than another part. To ensure coverage across the site, some archaeologists would use something called a *random stratified sampling strategy*. They would divide their study areas into large blocks that were subdivided into smaller grids and randomly select units to excavate within each of these bigger blocks to excavate. Why might someone use a stratified random sample? Suppose you are studying a landscape where there are different kinds of environmental zones? For instance, a river cuts through a portion of the site. You may be interested in knowing if different kinds of activities are taking place close to the river than are taking place farther from the river. Or suppose you are excavating in a large city, and you want to ensure that you are excavating samples from different neighborhoods. Then a random stratified sampling strategy may be for you. Ultimately, the biggest shortcoming of random sampling is that we usually know something about our site before we dig that affects how we want to approach the excavation of the site. When we use our judgment and prior knowledge to make sampling decisions, we are entering the world of nonprobablistic sampling.

A *nonprobabilistic sample* uses some sort of ranking or prior knowledge to select a sample. "Hey, look, there's a privy, I think we should excavate that to get our sample of household trash" would be an excellent example of an archaeologist making a non-probabilistic sampling decision. Suppose you want to make sure that you test each part of a site equally. You may decide to excavate every 10th unit in a grid. This would give you consistent coverage across the site and the resulting map would look like a checkerboard. This would be a *systematic sample,* a particular kind of nonprobablistic sample. These are also sometimes called judgmental samples, because the researcher is using other information available to make a decision about including a sample or not in the analysis.

Cultural resource management (CRM), a field of archaeology that deals with impacts of modern construction on archaeological remains, makes widespread use of nonprobablistic sampling in archaeology. In CRM, the research area is dictated by the boundaries of the construction project not the boundaries of the site or the research needs of the archaeologist. For example, on the Berkeley campus, I conducted a CRM excavation that had to test the boundaries around a parking lot to see if any portion of a nineteenth century plant conservatory was still preserved. We knew from Sanborn maps that the majority of the building was probably under the parking lot, but only had the edges around the parking lot to test—not ideal sampling. I will admit, as well, that the thought of excavating a big glass house full of flowerpots was not exciting to me, but it was what the project required. I diligently went through the process of constructing research questions and doing the testing. We found, even in the small area we had to test, great preservation of foundations and other features, and two years later were contracted to excavate under the parking lot as part of the environmental compliance process. Importantly, even though I was not excited to excavate this structure, I became intellectually engaged with the project, and it ends up that the site I would have never chosen to excavate has become one of the most important for understanding campus life in the nineteenth century. Development destroys a great many archaeological sites each year; many are never tested. Archaeologists in CRM are on the frontlines of recovering information that would otherwise be lost forever, while also being on the cutting edge of using new technologies and analyses. There are some archaeologists who would argue that probabilistic sampling strategies represent a commitment to the purest science (and, of course, probabilistic sampling relies on randomness of the studied population, which is never the case in human behavior), but the vast majority of archaeologists rely on some sort of prior knowledge when selecting parts of sites or assemblages to sample. There are many examples from CRM archaeology that demonstrate clearly that important archaeological research is conducted even when archaeologists have little control over the selection of where to excavate or survey.

Before I discuss my sampling strategies for the Mardi Gras project, it may be useful to tell you a bit about an archaeological project that involved traditional archaeological excavation to illustrate how research design and sampling can work on a real site. I mentioned before that I worked on a fraternity site on the University of California campus. My foremost question in developing the excavation strategy was "has any archaeological trace of the fraternity house built in 1876 survived?" If the answer to that question was yes, then I had a series of other questions to ask; but determining if there was any archaeological trace was foremost. The only area that could contain any portion of the original foundation was the area that was the courtyard for the second fraternity house. During the university's occupation of the second building, there had been a series of antigravity tanks in that courtyard that had been supported by large concrete piers. My sampling strategy for excavation was completely nonprobablistic; the placement of excavation units was decided by where the undisturbed areas of the courtyard were. Because the courtyard was going to be completely destroyed by an upcoming seismic retrofit, our goal was to excavate as much of the undisturbed area as possible; after four weeks, whatever we did not excavate would be destroyed and the information lost forever. Because of previous uses of the courtyard, we knew that the amount of the site left intact would be small, thus our targeted excavation strategy.

But there were other sampling decisions to make. I had the students use jackhammers to break through the asphalt that overlaid the site and shovels to remove most of the layer of gravel that was under the asphalt but above the original ground surface of the courtyard. Before reaching the bottom of the gravel layer, I had the students switch to digging with dustpans and trowels. I didn't want to risk digging through any features that may have been visible on the surface underlaying the gravel. With shovels, it would have been easier to accidentally dig through features. This is also a set of sampling decisions. I wasn't concerned about any evidence that may be recoverable from the gravel fill layer. I wanted to make sure we had a complete sample of what features may have been preserved below it. We sifted all soil through eighth-inch screen so that we could recover small artifacts and ecofacts. We took soil samples from barbeque pits discovered during excavation. Because we recovered so much brick and mortar rubble, we decided not to collect any brick or mortar fragments that were smaller than a quarter in size.

Each of these decisions were sampling decisions made based on the research questions and on the realities of effective time management and operational concerns. For instance, *wet-screening,* or using water to wash sediments through a small screen mesh, which leaves behind very small ecofacts and artifacts, is one method used to increase the amount of materials recovered from an archaeological site. Wet-screening is messy (think lots of mud) and requires an area where water can run off, and even, preferably, be recycled to minimize waste. In our asphalt-covered part of campus, there was no place suitable for wet-screening our matrix (soil) through screen smaller than one-eighth inch so we decided instead to take soil samples for later flotation.

Time was of the essence in this project, thus the decision to limit the size of brick fragments collected; we could learn more about the site by spending more time excavating and less time picking out miniscule pieces of brick. Sampling strategies and research design may be part of a scientific archaeology, but that doesn't mean it's not pragmatic as well. Archaeological excavation is expensive, and it is a foolish archaeologist who doesn't consider the budget when planning fieldwork.

Although the Mardi Gras project did not involve the removal of dirt, the collection of beads in an archaeological manner still demanded the development of a research design and sampling strategy. Just as the area of the frat house we excavated was constrained by time, the Mardi Gras sample size would be limited to whatever I, and my assistants, could catch at any given parade. Any parade has a limited duration, and in many ways, excavating a parade is not unlike being in a salvage archaeology situation, with archaeologists frantically working in front of bulldozers waiting to demolish their sites. Using a consistent team would ensure that variations in factors like height, attractiveness, aggressiveness (including willingness to show body parts), would not lead to wild variation between samples.

In terms of artifact recovery, there were also sampling decisions that had to be made about catching practices. I instituted a "you-have-to-keep-everything-you-catch" policy. Sometimes during parades, people will stop catching because they are bored, or toss undesirable beads on the ground, or pass them to some kid (because in the heat of a parade, a kid will accept any beads, no matter what). Therefore, my team members had to consistently keep anything they caught, no matter how crappy the beads or how much pressure they received from others to share. Because I was accompanied at all times by a munchkin (aka my daughter Alex), I also had to institute a policy about being handed beads for the kid. Therefore, a parallel policy, "we-have-to-accept-all-beads-offered-to-the-kid" was implemented to also be consistent from one parade to another. That way, any impact on assemblage quality that the presence of a child created would be shared equally from one parade to another. To protect the overly enthusiastic child, there was also the

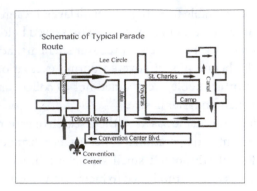

Figure 4.3. Schematic map of representative parade routes.

policy "I-don't-care-how-nice-it-is-don't-pick-it-up-out-of-the-street-sludge." Again, each of these policies was implemented to maintain the scientific rigor of the collecting strategies while also protecting the health of project participants.

Where to actually sample along the parade route also had to be determined. Most of the large parades that walk through New Orleans travel similar routes, with major differences resulting from where the specific parade begins and ends its procession. I had initially intended to institute a larger team who would be spread out at different parts of the parade route but ultimately decided that this introduced too many potential variables and was too hard to organize labor for. This part of the project was abandoned. The Riverwalk Convention Center (made infamous during Hurricane Katrina) and the Superdome (made infamous during many poor seasons of play by the New Orleans' Saints) are the end points for many of the parades. For our samples, I selected an area that was travelled by each of the parades, a section of St. Charles street, just southwest of Lee Circle. Figure 4.3 gives you a general sense of the routes that parades follow.

This area was advantageous for a number of reasons. First of all, it is not an area that attracts hoards of tourists. Tourists are found most thickly distributed along Canal Street, which is the closest part of the parade route to the French Quarter. Visitors, and no small number of locals, move like the tides between the Quarter and the parades, and they flow onto Canal Street for the spectacle of the parades and ebb back into the Quarter for the more-adult entertainments to be found there. Beads caught at the parades are used to fund Bourbon Street debaucheries! To the southwest of my selected spot, are residential areas that are thickly lined with ladder seats for children. It is impossible to navigate around these contraptions. Closer to Lee Circle, the police line the street on both sides with crowd control gates that limit one's ability to approach the floats and barter. Therefore, in terms of access to beads and ability to engage with and observe floats, I selected a place that would allow us to maximize the sample we collected. Furthermore, parking was available reasonably close to this area, as were reasonably clean restrooms. Do not let any archaeologist claim that they never factor in logistics when setting up a field project—they are lying. Everyone needs to know where the nearest running water to their site is.

The Field Seasons

I did my first serious collections of beads in 1998 and 1999 when I attended parades in Baton Rouge and New Orleans. Based upon the results of this work, I wrote a small research grant proposal that would allow me to pay for membership in a super krewe, so I could participate in Mardi Gras from the supply side, and stay in New Orleans for the final week of the 2000 Carnival season. The questions posed above were the driving force behind my research. I attended 10 parades in New Orleans, including super krewes, the older "mainline krewes," an all women's krewe, and Zulu, the historically black krewe that parades on Mardi Gras morning before the krewe of Rex (Table 4.2). The breadth of parades attended would allow me to compare parades of different statuses, gender, and racial composition. My experiences as a rider in a parade would hopefully provide me with insights on the throwing game not available to me from the ground (see the next chapter for more on this). The intent was to conduct one in-depth year of research and publish a paper or two on the nature of the throwing game.

It is the nature of archaeological research that you find things you did not anticipate in your excavations. During a field school in the summer of 2013, I was directing excavations at the University of California's student astronomical observatory, which was built in the 1870s and abandoned and partially demolished in the 1970s. We were expecting to find artifacts associated with the use of the building but were surprised to find more information about how local homeless populations used the site in the 1990s, long after it was abandoned. The logical rigor of a research design drafted before any evidence has been collected can quickly fold under the realities presented by fieldwork. In the case of the homeless people's deposits, we had to quickly develop a methodology for recording each of the plastic bags we found stashed, and the items contained within them.

Similar kinds of surprises awaited me in the Mardi Gras research. It had not occurred to me that 2000 was a momentous year to be participating in Mardi Gras—the millennium! Krewes announced that this would be a Mardi Gras to celebrate with particularly extravagant throws. I had a wonderful sample of how each krewe was potentially trying to outdo both its own history of giving, as well as outdo the other krewes. It was a great year to collect bead samples, but it raised other questions. Was there really an escalation in qual-ity or quantity of beads, or was this just krewe propaganda? What would happen next year? Would the krewes have to keep their heightened levels of gifting the following year? And if they were less generous, how would crowds respond?

Having ridden in a parade, I now understand the power of the crowd to shape bead selection; nothing was more disappointing than seeing one of your strands of beads dropped to the ground, discarded as unworthy of keeping. The memory of what was popular and what was not shaped maskers' purchasing decisions for following Carnival seasons. Through successive years, the consumer could exert pressure on the throwing game, demanding better and better beads. I realized that I needed more evidence and planned to gather data for just one more year.

In 2001, I was able to attend three New Orleans parades, and two in Baton Rouge (Table 4.2). I had bead assemblages from the 1997, 1998, 1999, and 2000 parades. Now, my research was self-funded. I was in Louisiana on sabbatical during the 2001–2002 academic year, which allowed me to easily attend Carnival celebrations and gather another year of materials. I truly intended to end the project that year. I now had thousands of Mardi Gras beads from over a dozen parades over a four-year period. Surely that was a large enough

Table 4.2. Excavated New Orleans parades.

YEAR	NEW ORLEANS PARADES											BATON ROUGE PARADES				POINTE COUPEE PARISH PARADES		
	Bacchus	Endymion	Iris	Krewe of Midcity	Orpheus	Proteus	Thoth	Tuck	Truck	Rex	Zulu	Spanish Town	South downs	Orion	Mystick	Kings	Lions	Livonia
1997	X											X						
1998							X					X	X					
1999					X		X					X	X		X			
2000	X	X	X	X	X			X	X	X	X							
2001	X				X	X						X	X					
2002					X	X						X	X					
2003	X									X		X	X	X				
2004					X							X	X			X	X	X
2005																		
2006					X	X							X			X	X	
2007					X	X						X	X			X	X	
2008																		
2009	X			X	X	X						X				X	X	

sample for my contemporary archaeology project. Except in the fall of 2001, a terrible thing happened, the destruction of the World Trade Center Towers on September 11. I watched as Louisianans draped themselves in patriotic garb and hung flags—leaving them hanging until they were in shreds—from every building and car. Would Mardi Gras go on? And how would the tragedy shape the celebrations?

I was able to attend Mardi Gras celebrations in 2003, and 2004, and I declared 2004 to be my last Carnival celebration before writing a book on the project. By then, I was trying to consistently sample from parades in New Orleans, Baton Rouge, and the rural parish of Point Coupee (Table 4.2). Trends in my data suggested that it would be interesting to look at the flow of beads from urban areas to rural peripheries and to see what differences could be seen in assemblages. The project had continued to develop additional sidelines of research—something that happens in any long-term archaeological project. For instance, when I started excavating sites on the University of California campus, I was originally interested in student daily life. As I had the opportunity to excavate a growing number of sites, I recognized the potential to look at how students and faculty were involved in broader social debates about gender, science, and education.

I did not attend Mardi Gras celebrations in 2005, a misstep given what happened in August of 2005. Even as Katrina's survivors were being pulled from rooftops, residents of Louisiana and the world alike began to ask whether the city could or should celebrate Mardi Gras again. There were practical matters—bead orders were made in October, hotel reservations were similarly booked early, and floats had to be designed and built—would the city be ready to handle the logistics of even just preparing for Carnival? There was also the emotional aspect, with so many lost lives and fortunes, could the state really stomach the idea of celebrating? There was a Mardi Gras celebrated in 2006, and I was there. I stood in my usual place on the parade ground, surrounded by families who used to live in the 9th ward and were now forced to call Houston, Texas, home. A woman cried to me and said, "You know, I just had to be here, I had to be home for this. This is normal." And we nodded and patted one another and agreed; if the city's heart was still beating, the best time to search for a pulse was at Carnival.

The Carnival seasons of 2006 and 2007 were inversions of everything I knew to be Mardi Gras. The city of Baton Rouge's celebrations grew to double their previous size to accommodate families who had relocated from New Orleans and still wanted to participate in Mardi Gras. The beads told the story of the disaster and the rebalancing of population in Louisiana in a way no other source could. I was unable to attend Mardi Gras in 2008, but returned, at last, for a final season in 2009, when for the first time my evidence suggested the renewal of New Orleans as Carnival's center.

In the table listing the years and parades for which I collected samples, you will note that there are gaps (Table 4.2). For instance, you will see in 2000, when I was focusing my attention on attending as many New Orleans parades as possible, there are no Baton Rouge parades represented. In 2005 and 2008, financial considerations and obligations at home prevented me from attending Carnival. Life interferes in research, no matter one's best intentions. To fill in gaps in my samples, when and where possible, I asked friends and colleagues who were attending parades to keep their beads from different parades separate and to allow me to catalog them. This allowed me to acquire data from a broader range of parades than I could have done on my own, but it resulted in some years with a small sample size. One of the advantages of having a clear research design and set of methodological protocols for an excavation is that it ensures consistency in data recovery, even when different excavators and analysts are involved. For instance, excavations have been taking place at the ancient city of Çatalhöyük, under the primary direction of Professor Ian Hodder of Stanford, since 1993 (Çatalhöyük: Excavations of a Neolithic Anatolian Hoyuk, "History of the Excavations" http://www.catalhoyuk.com/). During that time, the project has included collaborators from many different universities: Berkeley, Stanford, Cambridge, Poznan (Poland), Istanbul and Selcuk (Turkey). A commitment to a shared set of protocols and research design allows consistency in such large collaborative projects involving multiple research teams.

In analyzing the Mardi Gras beads, I had a set of protocols that I followed as part of the research design for my project. For every bead strand in each assemblage, I recorded the following: strand length (in inches); bead shape (using commonly agreed upon names if available, naming them if not, and illustrating or photographing each shape type); spherical bead diameter (in mm); color(s); finish; method of manufacture (hand-strung or MOS); whether there was any evidence of alteration, repair, recycling, and descriptions (and illustrations or photographs) of medallions. While beads were kept separated by parade, it is possible to collapse assemblages into bigger groupings. For some analyses, I consider New Orleans parades in a given year as one assemblage (as I did in the previous chapter's frequency seriation) for comparison with Baton Rouge or rural parish parades. In other comparisons, I compare single parades to one another. Because I collected beads in the way that I did, I can always create larger data sets from the individual parades or years.

While there are gaps in the assemblage, this characteristic makes the bead assemblage more akin to assemblages excavated from traditional archaeological sites, it shares the messiness that is characteristic of real life. Some years I have bigger samples than others. Some parades I have been able to consistently attend over the last decade, and others I have only been able to attend sporadically or once.

This is no different from the challenges we face in other archaeological settings. For instance, remember that fraternity site excavation? My team and I were excavating to learn about the fraternity of Zeta Psi's occupation of two houses in the same location: one that was built in 1876 and occupied until 1910; and the second house built to replace the first house and occupied from 1911 until 1956, when the university took it over. Our strategy to locate the foundations of the first house worked; we did find a ten-foot-long portion of intact foundation from the 1876 house.

As I mentioned in our discussion of superposition, our excavations revealed a series of different depositional layers (better described as depositional events) that told us about the building sequence of the second house relative to the first. One of those depositional events was the accumulation of household trash (a midden) around the foundation of the first house during its occupation. The artifacts and ecofacts from this midden are small and very broken, but they provided a great opportunity to study everyday life in the fraternity from 1876 to 1910. There was not the same kind of thick, clear trash midden associated with the 1910 to 1956 occupation of the house as there was for the first house. However, associated with the occupation of the second house, is a 1923 trashpit that was used by the fraternity. From that context we had hundreds of artifacts that included lots of ceramics, many intact alcohol and medicine bottles, toothbrushes, large animal bones, parts of furnishings and lampshades (clearly quite a party was had), and many other objects that were easily identified, which provided a much larger glimpse into the lives of the fraternity brothers in the 1920s. I recovered good archaeological data from both occupations at the site. I just don't have the same abundance of artifactual materials for the earlier 1876–1910 occupation as I did from the 1923 trash pit. The 1923 trash pit was great, but represented only one moment of time in the 40 plus-year-occupation of the second house. The materials offer different kinds of possibilities for interpretation. Figuring out how to work with what you find and to make the most out of it is one of the fun challenges of archaeology

So, now you have been introduced to the beads that we will use to address socio-technic and ideo-technic questions about, among other things, economic relationships, regional distributions, gender and sexuality, the construction of communal identities, struggles for symbolic power, and the uneasy relationship between human social life and the environment . . . but not quite yet. There is the little issue of how one actually goes about interpreting archaeological data.

Archaeological Knowing

The cultural historians focused most of their interpretive efforts on understanding chronological relationships. In England, archaeologists of this time period were not tied to anthropology departments, but instead saw their discipline as either independent or part of history. They were as much constrained by the need to work through chronologies as their American counterparts, but did not have the same disciplinary lashback against evolutionary theories. In his important work, *Man Makes Himself*, V. Gordon Childe (1936), looked at how the technology behind artifacts could be used to understand how groups adapted to local environments. As someone influenced by Marxist theory, his interests in production, technology, and the environment is an excellent example of someone who was interpreting artifacts within a different theoretical orientation than culture history. Still, as someone who also saw himself as a historian, Childe asserted in his work that the form adaptations took were shaped by a group's history. Although separated by an ocean, archaeologists were still in dialogue, and Childe's work no doubt influenced ideas in the US that became processual archaeology.

Some writers during this period of research did ponder the interpretive constraints of the archaeological record. C. F. Hawkes (1954) wrote that archaeologists should think of different aspects of society as being like rungs of a ladder with technology at the bottom, economics above that, social arrangements above that, and ideological aspects of society at the top rung. Archaeology, he suggested, could hope to most completely reconstruct the technological and economic activities of a past society, but only rarely get at social practices, and almost never be able to reconstruct past ideological beliefs. Hawkes' ladder clearly had to influence Binford's notions of "technomic," "socio-technic," and "ideo-technic," with the important difference that Binford thought proper attention to the practices of science within archaeology would make the socio-technic and ideo-technic aspects of society easier to reconstruct.

But how does one go from the empirical to the interpretive? Processual archaeology was shaped by a number of theoretical influences, although they are rarely acknowledged explicitly in the writings. The work of his advisor, Leslie White, is clear in Binford's notion of culture as an adaptive organism that harnesses energy from the environment. Likewise, his understandings of societies shifting from one level of complexity to another is drawn from neo-evolutionary thinkers like Sahlins and Service (1960), Julian Steward (1944) and Steward and Setzler (1938), who were interested in understanding how societies developed from simple political and economic forms to complex ones. Binford's later attention to cultures as an adaptive system was influenced by cybernetics theories developed by early computer designers (Raab and Goodyear 1984) and the functionalism of anthropologist Radcliffe-Browne (1952), who saw culture as comprising a set of co-adaptive structures that served to keep a society functioning. None of these thinkers, with the exception of Steward, were archaeologists. Nor were they confronted with the problem of going from empirical data (841 pot sherds of type A, 361 baskets of nonlocal fibers, 900 pieces of obsidian debitage from quarry x) to anthropological interpretations (the people of Broken Pot site were engaged in trade of pots with the people of Torn Basket that allowed the two groups to peacefully share access to an obsidian quarry that existed on their territorial boundary). Going from stuff to the actions that created the patterned distribution of the stuff has always been the greatest challenge and fun of archaeology. And yes, archaeology is fun!

The krewes of Mardi Gras celebrate Greek and Roman gods, and to many archaeologists, the charismatic Binford seemed like an inhabitant of Mount Olympus whose every proclamation seemed filled with wisdom and keen insight. In reading (and writing) intellectual histories, it is hard to explain the role that charisma and force of personality can have in shaping a discipline. Binford often seemed infallible to those who adopted new archaeology; but while the great Roman god, Jupiter, may have been able to incubate his half-human son, Bacchus, in his leg; Binford's ideas about how to cope with the question of "how do we get from data to interpretation" did not spring fully formed from his thigh like a Roman god. Instead, processualism developed over time as part of a disciplinary dialogue involving many archaeologists. Binford was often a strong voice in these discussions, but he was not the only one. Much of the theorizing of processualism focused upon the idea that archaeologists needed to focus efforts on understanding how the archaeological record we excavate in the present came to take the form we find it in.

First, it was necessary to understand what "noise" had affected the record between the time it was created and the time it was studied. As we discussed above, this noise is seen as site formation processes, which can either be natural or human in source (Harris 1979; Schiffer 1987). Binford (1991:23) advocated that archaeologists embrace Charles Lyell's idea of uniformitarianism from geology to understand how processes affected archaeological sites. Uniformitarianism has two key points: first, natural laws are constant in space and time; and second, processes now operating to mold the earth's surface should be invoked to explain the past. Just as culture historians used the principles of geology to excavate and recover chronological relationships between artifacts and sites, Binford drew upon nineteenth-century geological principles to understand how sites changed through time.

Once the processes of archaeological deposition were understood, it was necessary to understand what behaviors were represented by the patterns of material culture uncovered. Binford (1981:91) referred to this as *middle-range research,* which others in archaeology ultimately began to call *middle-range theory.* Sociology also has a set of theories called middle-range theory, but their ideas and practices bear little resemblance to those in archaeology (Raab and Goodyear 1984).

Binford defined middle-range research as consisting of "actualistic studies designed to control for the relationship between dynamic properties of the past and the present" (1981:23). It was necessary, he poetically wrote, to keep "our 'empirical' feet on the ground and our heads in the 'theoretical sky'"(Binford 1981:21). A number of tools were seen as a means of going from archaeological pattern to interpretation of behaviors that it represented. The most important were *ethnographic analogy, ethnoarchaeology, and experimental archaeology.* Each of these middle-range tools came into play in the Mardi Gras study.

Ethnographic Analogy

Ethnographic analogy is using ethnographic information to interpret archaeological patterns. Ethnographic analogy was not a new tool in archaeology. The culture historians working in the southwest had used the *direct historical approach* since the first decades of the twentieth century (Steward 1942). The direct historical approach involved starting with a known ethnographic group, locating historic period sites associated with that group, and then proceeding backward through the archaeological record from the ethnographically known to the unknown. Such an approach allowed for different contemporary practices and materials of the group to be traced into the past. Analogies between the contemporary group and the archaeological remains were used to interpret materials.

Discussions arose in processual archaeology about what is an appropriate analog to use (e.g., Ascher 1961; Binford 1967). Archaeologists were sometimes using analogies that seemed highly problematic. In particular, the !Kung people of the Kalahari desert of Africa were a well-studied contemporary hunter-gatherer group. Studies of how the !Kung related to their environment were prevalent (e.g., Bentley 1985; Hassan 1978; Lee 1972). The range of species they utilized over the course of the year was known, and how far they would travel to obtain resources was also known. These became standards that were sometimes used by archaeologists to understand prehistoric hunter-gatherer information (e.g., Winterhaulder and Smith 1981). Yet, how appropriate was it to use modern hunter-gatherer cultures like the !Kung of the Kalahari to understand ancient hunter-gatherers in Europe or North America? If archaeology saw the human experience as so universal that you could use modern peoples to understand ancient ones, did we really need archaeology at all?

Binford (1967) provided what was probably the most elegant case for how a systematic approach to the ethnographic record could be used to interpret the archaeological record. He took the example of a set of archaeological features that he had excavated at a site in south-central Illinois. The features were a cache of carbonized corncobs that were found nested in the remains of burned twigs in an oval-shaped hole that was about 30 × 26 × 32 cm. The features had straight sides and flat bottoms, and all were filled at the top with a grey loam soil that suggested they had been intentionally capped. Some had occasional minor oxidation of the soil at the mouth of the pit. Because these features were so similar, Binford inferred they shared the same function within the site. He then noted that features like these had been found elsewhere in the middle and lower Mississippi area with extremities in distribution from Georgia Creek to the East and the Texas Caddo to the West. He also showed that in each case, these features were associated with domestic structures, not public buildings. Again, because of their clear similarity to one another, he inferred that these features found at different sites had the same use. Because the fires they contained had only charred the plant material, not completely consumed it, he believed that these pits created a great deal of smoke and, for convenience sake, referred to them as smudge pits.

Binford then turned to the available ethnographic record to draw upon the works of early anthropologists and accounts by early European visitors, which gave him a body of evidence that dated from the colonial period and 1900–1950. He systematically reviewed the ethnographic record for the area of the distribution of the features but also the surrounding areas where the features were not found. He found that Native American groups in all regions regularly used pits like these for smoking hides to make them into usable leather; however, he found only three groups who were explicitly described as putting corncobs in their smudge pits. Early references for the Creek and the Natchez described the use of corncobs, and a recent reference for the Arapaho also made reference to using corncobs in hide-smoking pits. The Creek and the Natchez are both groups who lived in the area where the archaeological features are distributed. The Arapaho do not, but Binford suggested the recent observation may indicate a post-reservation practice. Therefore, based on his rigorous survey of the ethnographic literature, Binford argued that corncob smudge pits should be interpreted as having been used for hide smoking.

Ethnoarchaeology

A distinct field of inquiry called *ethnoarchaeology* developed as part of middle-range research. Ethnoarchaeology involves archaeologists doing particular kinds of ethnographic research with the explicit goal of understanding the archaeological record. Ethnographers did not always record the kinds of information that would be useful to archaeologists; therefore, archaeologists decided to do the work themselves. I experienced this to some degree myself. A friend, who was a social anthropologist, collected beads for me from different small neighborhood parades she attended in New Orleans over the years. While what she brought me was always interesting, the assemblages also were shaped by her own particular observational interests and curation practices. Her assemblages included sexually themed throws like condoms and dental dams, silly toys, and only beads that she thought were pretty. Overall, her assemblages give a very different set of insights into Mardi Gras material culture than the controlled collections I made.

Ethnoarchaeology studies may involve working with contemporary craftspersons to understand practices related to the production of pottery, basketry, metalwork, food preparation, farming, and so on. Or they may involve studies of time allocation, how much time a person in a group spends on particular tasks each day, to understand the relative importance of particular tasks represented archaeologically. Douglas Bird and Rebecca Bird (2000) conducted ethnoarchaeological research to investigate how much children contribute to food foraging and what might be the archaeological implications? Until recently, children have not received much attention from archaeologists; though clearly, there were proportionally as many children in the past as there are now, if not more. As life expectancy increases, adults come to comprise a larger proportion of the overall population than they do when life expectancy is shorter. Bird and Bird suspected that child labor was underrepresented in archaeological models.

Bird and Bird (2000) utilized a range of theories that were developed in biology called **optimal foraging models** to explain foraging behavior in animal species. These models became popular first in the 1980s as a way to understand relationships between hunter-gatherers and their environment (e.g., Boyd and Richerson 1985; Winterhalder and Smith 1981), and they remain popularized in the anthropologically controversial works of Jared Diamond (e.g., 2005). The models are based on an assumption that living creatures want to acquire as many calories as they can for the least amount of work. This leaves them more time for reproduction, because ultimately, an individual life form is only successful in the grand evolutionary scheme if it passes its genetic material down to the next generation. Optimal foraging is part of a broader package of theories in biology known as **sociobiology**, which is ultimately interested in how evolutionary forces work on animal communities. In anthropology, sociobiology is often seen as at odds with anthropology's disciplinary focus on the role of nurture (culture/society) over nature (biology/genetics) in human society.

Bird and Bird's (2000) version of sociobiology is of the type embraced by archaeologists who consider themselves, human behavioral ecologists; they were interested most how humans create efficient relationships with their environments. They suggest that perhaps children haven't been accounted for in foraging studies of this sort because children are not sexually reproductive. Still, children have a vested interest in reaching adulthood (and therefore becoming reproductive eventually), and, the Birds argue, are likely to contribute to their own subsistence. They studied shell-fishing strategies among Meriam

Islander children of Melanesia on the northern edge of the Great Barrier Reef. On average, 600 calories per day of the Meriam diet is derived from coastal foraging: collecting marine turtles, fishing with hand lines onshore and offshore, and collecting shellfish. The Birds focused their study of children's versus adult's foraging by studying their shell-fishing strategies. Other scholars have suggested that children's activities in foraging are most likely related to children learning how to forage from adults (and therefore, children's foraging would archaeologically, look like adult foraging).

The Birds thought that models should consider the different physiologies of children versus adults and question the assumption that children's foraging would look like that of grownups. In their ethnoarchaeological study, they followed 47 adults (age 16 and up) and 35 children (ages 5–15), recorded the species they gathered, their foraging strategies, and their processing behaviors to see what each group brought back to the home site (the modern equivalent of the archaeological site). The results of their study are intriguing. First, they found that children gather in groups of children—the same groups that they play in—and learn from one another, not adults. There were three species that accounted for 90% of what children foraged, and none of them are species that adults forage for. While adults selected for larger prey, choosing to select the largest examples, and passing over smaller specimens, children collected every specimen they encountered (which sounded an awful lot like the way my daughter collected Mardi Gras beads). Further, children did not process any of the shellfish they gathered at the site of collection but carried them all back home to process. Children were found to be slower at collecting food but quicker at processing it, meaning that while their caloric expenditure for foraging was higher, their processing costs were lower. This means that adults should be selecting for larger (more calorie specimens) to make up for more energy spent processing, while children might as well pick up every example even if it takes longer, because they spend less energy making the food consumable.

So what are the archaeological implications of this? First, if children are picking up every example of a species they encounter, they will be introducing smaller specimens into the archaeological record. The inclusion of smaller individuals of a key species, if only adult optimizing strategies are being considered, tends toward interpretations that identify the foraging of smaller examples as evidence of resource depletion (an adult will only choose the biggest examples available). Based on Bird and Bird's study, if children's foraging behaviors are factored in, however, all sizes of a food species should be represented., Secondly, the inclusion of lesser-utilized species is also seen in optimal foraging as people needing to expand the breadth of species they are consuming because the highly ranked species are not as abundant as needed. So again, children's contributions to subsistence could be misinterpreted archaeologically as evidence of environmental stress. Bird and Bird's study is an interesting example of ethnoarchaeology, but it also illustrates how methodology is explicitly related to theoretical orientation. For instance, the Birds' theoretical interests made it important that they collect data related to caloric intake, processing time, and collection time. Another researcher, whose questions were focused on understanding children's foraging behaviors may have focused more on the social interactions that take place within children's groups. While each set of researchers may have been studying children collecting shellfish, the kinds of evidence they collected would be very different. This study reinforced to me as well, the usefulness of having a child help me collect Mardi Gras beads, her presence ensured that we had a greater representation of what the total bead universe in any given year was. It also occurred to me, that a whole other study that compared the Mardi Gras beads collected by a child versus an adult from the same parade would be interesting to undertake and would be a way to test the Birds' results in another social setting.

Experimental Archaeology

The third type of middle-range research that developed as part of processual archaeology was *experimental archaeology*. Experimental archaeologies are attempts to understand some cultural or taphonomic processes through replicative experiments in the present. Attempts to recreate ancient technologies are a well-known example of experimental archaeology. Archaeologists have engaged in learning flint knapping (making stone tools), butchering animals with stone tools, or testing different pottery-firing techniques (e.g., Coles 1979; Hill 1978; Jones 1980; Schiffer et al. 1994). Experimental archaeology gives archaeologists the opportunity to test ideas out in nonarchaeological settings. In the previous chapter, I described Dethlefsen and Deetz's (1966) death's head, cherub, and willow and urn study of gravestones. The original paper for that study was subtitled, "Experimental Archaeology in Colonial Cemeteries."

Haskel Greenfield (1999) has provided an interesting example of how experimental archaeology can be used to understand the more remote past. Archaeologists recognize that metal working from the Neolithic period to the Bronze Age became an important technology in European societies. Metal was a rare enough commodity that broken metal tools seem to have often been recycled, thus leading to them being less represented archaeologically. Further, the metal is susceptible to decay, which means that only a proportion of metal tools survive in the archaeological record. Archaeologists recognize that metal tools came to replace stone tools, but given the spotty archaeological record, the speed and extent of that replacement through time is difficult to know. Greenfield decided to determine whether it was possible to identify differences in cuts on bone made by metal versus stone tools, and therefore, study the rate of replacement of stone tools by metal ones.

For the experiment, Haskell limited his attention to cut marks, defined as a slice, rather than a chopping or sawing motion. He made his experimental cuts into a soft pine board to ensure consistency in hardness of the material being cut and the angle at which the cutting took place. Bone has too many variations in hardness and angle depending upon the part of the bone being cut, and he wanted to control for as many variables as possible in his experiment. He used a controlled number of steel cutting blades (which has a similar cutting strength to bronze) of different blade shapes and thicknesses to make the metal cut marks, and stone tools from one of the sites he was studying to make the stone cuts. He made silicon molds of the cut marks and observed them under a Scanning

Table 4.3. Results from Haskell's Experimental Archaeology.

TIME PERIOD	DATE RANGE (CALIBRATED)	% OF CUTS MADE BY STONE TOOLS	% OF CUTS MADE BY METAL TOOLS
Middle Neolithic	4500–4200 BC	94.12	5.88
Late Neolithic	4200–3800 BC	90.91	9.09
Late Neolithic	3800–3300 BC	83.72	16.28
Eneolithic	3300–2500 BC	86.36	13.64
Early-Middle Bronze	2500–1500 BC	15.38	84.62

Electron Microscope (SEM) to note differences in the cuts. Clear identifiable differences between cuts made between the two materials were visible! Metal cuts were clearer and straight-edged, stone-tool cuts were more v-shaped and angled in one direction versus the other. His experiment demonstrated that differences between metal cut marks and stone cut marks on bone were identifiable.

The next part of the experiment was to determine if the differences were visible on archaeological materials. Haskell chose materials from the sites of Petnica and Ljuljaci in the eastern-central Balkans. This was a part of Europe where metallurgy developed autonomously (as opposed to being introduced from another area); therefore, any changes in ratios of stone tool cuts to metal tool cuts would represent growing acceptance and use of the new technology. His study provided remarkable results (Table 4.3). Haskell discovered that during the period from 2500–1500 BC (the Early to Middle Bronze Age), that replacement of stone tools with metal ones happened very quickly. He was surprised, however, to see that his results also suggested that pre-Bronze Age copper tools were used in small but consistent amounts for cutting during the Neolithic. Conventional archaeological wisdom had held that copper tools were not sharp enough or strong enough to be used for cutting. Haskell's work is an excellent example of a replicable archaeological experiment that developed a new technique for analyzing archaeological materials.

Middle-Range Research and Mardi Gras

So where is the middle-range research in the Mardi Gras project? Some might argue, that like the Dethlefsen and Deetz (1966) project, all of the Mardi Gras bead project is a form of experimental archaeology. After all, aren't I just "testing" different archaeological methods and theories with the Mardi Gras assemblage? While using the Mardi Gras bead assemblages to "test" whether stylistic and frequency seriation works on modern materials could be seen as experimental archaeology, that represents just one facet of this research. Ultimately, the Mardi Gras bead project is an archaeological study of a contemporary social phenomenon, which draws upon insights from ethnoarchaeology, ethnographic analogy, and experimental archaeology.

Graduate student Katrina Eichner and I did engage in some experimental archaeology as we attempted to restring some broken strands of glass beads. We learned a great deal about the embodied practice of beading and realized it is much more difficult to get a strand tightly strung and to look symmetrical than we thought. We learned that for the tightest stringing, you cannot tie the strand off at the finding (or closure), but have to make your knot about one inch or two from the closure and double string the strand. The experiment in restringing has informed some of my understandings of the production of the glass bead strands. I have also used documentary accounts of Mardi Gras' past in different parts of my interpretation as a form of ethnographic analogy. I might also point to my experiences riding in a super krewe as an example of me conducting an ethnoarchaeology of Mardi Gras to better understand the material patterning I saw in the bead assemblage. That was certainly part of my intent in participating as a masker in Mardi Gras celebrations, but as I'll discuss in the next chapter, between the time when Binford was writing about his conceptualization of middle-range theory and when I donned a mask to ride in a super krewe, some new ideas had emerged in archaeology about the nature of our archaeological subjects and the role of the archaeologist in the interpretive process. I was as greatly influenced by those shifts in thinking as I was by the practices and methodologies of processual archaeology.

CHAPTER 5:
MARDI GRAS AS LIVED, SOCIAL, AND EXPERIENTIAL

An Archaeological Creation Story

O n the first day, the lands of archaeology were created, and they were peopled by a folk called the cultural historians. They worked hard and toiled much in the earth while they learned to put pots into categories. Although the work was plentiful, the culture historians longed for more. On the seventh day, the archaeology gods created Lewis Binford. Binford came with commandments from the Great God Science, and together, Binford and the people created processual archaeology. And the archaeologists saw that it was good and true, and they worked to understand the vast systems of the world. But into the processualist garden came the foreigner, Ian Hodder, who said, "I have been touched by another god, and that god wants you to think about what actually is goodness and truth? What is the context and history for this truth and goodness? Shouldn't archaeology think about people, not systems?" Some archaeologists agreed, and they left the farmstead of processualism to till other lands where the harvest was a multi-vocal, contextual archaeology that embraced ambiguity and subjectivity. And now today, the children of Binford and the children of Hodder wage a great war for the lands of archaeology.

A variation of this story is told in many archaeological textbooks, though perhaps with less snark. We like to simplify intellectual histories by setting up shifts in thinking as battles between particular "big men." Instead, practitioners of a discipline circulate and discuss ideas, sometimes for a long time, before one or two thinkers crystallize those thoughts into a coherent vision. Binford packaged ideas into what became processualism, and Ian Hodder, who we will now discuss, became the person who pulled together a comprehensive critique of processualism's shortcomings. Processualism and post-processualism have come to be characterized as archaeologies that emphasize subjectivity (post-processualism) and objectivity (processualism), a characterization that perhaps is used most by processualists who see themselves as doing work that is "real" (see Flannery 2006). The reality is that post-processualism draws upon the rigorous methodologies of processualism while attempting to grapple with the politics of doing archaeology, which include, but aren't limited to, understanding the diverse subject positions that existed in the past. Post-processual archaeologists consider the role of the researcher in the production of knowledge, how archaeological knowledge is used, consumed, and appropriated, and the notions of ownership that surround heritage. Because the questions that post-processualists ask of the archaeological record have changed, the intellectual and methodological tools they draw upon have also shifted.

This is not to say that processual archaeology hasn't changed. Social identity, the politics of doing archaeology, and the role of symbolic systems and meaning in the manipulation of power and maintenance of social inequality are issues now explored by some archaeologists who would define themselves as processually leaning or "processual plus" (Hegmon 2003, 2005). If you were to ask an archaeologist what "kind" of archaeologist they are, you will find that most archaeologists do not define themselves today as "processual" or "post-processual." Instead, they self-identify based on the kinds of issues they study, the materials they study, or their regional or temporal focus. These range of subjectivities indicate that the legacies of culture history, processualism, and the post-processual critique all contribute to how any archaeologist thinks. New kinds of archaeology continue to emerge. Archaeology is a much more theoretically diverse discipline than the one encountered by Binford or Hodder. Feminist, phenomenonological, post-structuralist, Marxist and neo-Marxist, practice and performance theories, Darwinian evolution, network, and science and technology studies theories, are among the bodies of thought that now shape archaeological thinking and provide labels that archaeologists use to self-identify. Don't worry if you don't know what all of these bodies of thought are about. We'll be discussing them more fully in upcoming chapters; I list them now so that you can see the philosophical diversity that characterizes this period of archaeology. I now introduce you to the origins of the post-processual critique and the ideas that formed the critique. I also introduce you to the archaeologies of phenomenology, or post-processual archaeologies that have embraced the notion of being-in-the-world and embodiment as part of an archaeological methodology, and the ways that these ideas shaped some aspects of the Mardi Gras research.

The Post-Processual Critique

Just as some archaeologists felt constrained by archaeologies that focused on developing the idea of culture areas; some archaeologists got frustrated with some of the ways processual archaeology developed through time. When I explained sociobiological reasoning behind the Meriam Islanders shell-fishing study, did any of you wonder, "doesn't anyone eat food just because it tastes good?" Or maybe, you wondered if changing the fuel in the smudge pit changed the smell of the smoke, and pondered which fuel smells best?

Processual archaeologists tend to favor research questions that are BIG and focused on understanding change across large areas of land through vast amounts of time (e.g., Flannery and Marcus 2012, Kirch 2007; Pauketat 2007, 2009). Why do societies shift from a hunter-gatherer subsistence system to agriculture? How do long-distance trade net-works develop? What factors lead to the development of social stratification and the creation of state-level societies? How do hunter-gatherers develop strategies for resource intensification? These are essential and fascinating questions, but, when you are looking at society-level changes, it is easy to gloss over the textures and variations between sites, material culture, and households within those cultures that existed; you are looking for the shared patterns, not the noisy differences. Some people believed it was exactly those noisy differences that were interesting to consider.

The post-processual critique is best described as yet another shift in the kinds of questions archaeologists wanted to ask. Ian Hodder (e.g., 1985, 1986, 1991, 1997) is often credited with starting the post-processual movement in archaeology. He certainly put a name to it (1985), though he claimed at that point to only want to reform processual archaeology. Other archaeologists also hoped to reform archaeology. Archaeologists expressed frustration with the failure of the new archaeology to construct general laws of cultural change that were not "Mickey Mouse" (Flannery 1982), and Raab and Goodyear's (1984) review of middle-range theorizing hoped to spur improvements in archaeology's approach to theory building.

Other archaeologists, however, were already asking and addressing different research questions about social identity, which considered the agency of people in the past, and actively thought about the politics of doing archaeology. In the United States, I would point to Robert Ascher's and Charles Fairbanks' (1971) study of an African American slave cabin that used black voices drawn from the Worker's Project Administration's oral histories; James Deetz's (1977) study of the Georgian mindset; Robert Schuyler's edited volume on ethnicity (1980); Kathleen Deagan's study of race and ethnicity at St. Augustine (1983); and Mark Leone's (1977, 1982) work on the experience of space in Mormon temples, his thoughts on potential for neo-Marxist theorizing, and the recovery of mind as examples of important works that foreshadowed the post-processual critique. It is not surprising that these are works written by archaeologists who worked on historical period sites. Access to the documentary record meant that archaeologists not only had information about their sites, which may have included names, ages, family relationships, economic data, among other kinds of evidence, but they also had to deal with understanding the specific contexts in which their subjects lived. Another important foreshadowing of the post-processual critique came in the development of feminist archaeology. A 1984 paper by prehistorians Margaret Conkey and Janet Spector was the first serious engagement with explicitly feminist theorizing in archaeology. Each of these authors were dealing with issues that became part of the post-processual critique. It is not surprising, therefore, that Ian Hodder referred to the works of Leone, Deetz, and a 1982 unpublished gender paper by Margaret Conkey, in his 1985 article, "Post-Processual Archaeology."

Forces outside of archaeology also shaped the need for the post-processual critique. Native Americans did not see the relevance to their communities of processual archaeology's interpretations focused on systems and behavior, and they resented destructive analyses—such as radiocarbon dating and isotopic analysis to understand diet—that were being conducted on their ancestors' remains without their permission. *The Native American Graves Protection and Repatriation Act* (NAGPRA) was passed into federal law in 1990 after years of bitter debate among archaeologists and between Native peoples and archaeologists (Watkins 2006). The mishandled discovery and excavations of the African Burial Ground in New York City, which provoked outrage from African American communities throughout the United States, also in 1990, demonstrated to skeptics that an archaeology that consulted with different aspects of the public and concerned communities was absolutely needed (LaRoche and Blakey 1997).

So what was the nature of Hodder's critique? The following points came to form the core of the critique of processualism (Hodder 1985). First, people are active and self-aware; this is a feature of the human experience that is lost in processualism which represents people as helpless cogs of the behavioral system. Second, processualist archaeology lost culture from its vocabulary. They used the word behavior instead even though the concept of culture and social life were central to anthropology. Third, processualism lost history along with culture. Social change, argued Hodder, is always historically situated and subject to contextual and cultural particularities. And fourth, human behavior is not always rational and predictable (as is theorized in disciplines like optimal foraging models) despite processualists' wish that it were so.

So what was his answer? Hodder (1985) suggested that we needed a theory of social action that allowed archaeologists to understand human decision making and negotiations within a contextual history. He argued that we should think of style as evidence of cultural attitudes, but look toward materials' meanings, which humans achieved through processes he called "evocation," "ambiguity," and "context." Evocation was the process through which one references another—the way the US Congressional building is supposed to evoke a sense of classical Greek temples to reinforce ties between the US and the birthplace of democracy is a good example—but we've also discussed how the early Bacchus bead medallions were intentionally evoking the Bacchus doubloon. Ambiguity is when an object can be read in multiple ways. Hodder used the example of how a safety pin could be used to hold cloth together or worn through the nose of a Punk rocker. Without a context, the artifact has the potential to be read in multiple ways. Likewise, the meaning of bead color is ambiguous. In a Mardi Gras parade, the color green is associated with the idea of justice; in St. Patrick's day parades, the same green beads are associated with Irish pride. Context is the cultural setting in which the object is situated and given meaning. As we will see, whether a particular strand of beads would be considered "good" or not is dependent upon its temporal context. Beads that were valuable in the 1990s are now average today.

To illustrate his argument, Hodder presented a discussion of current interpretations of Neolithic houses and burial monuments in Western Europe. The current understanding of Neolithic burial monuments at the time was that they were territorial markers built in times of stress—their role and meaning in society were ignored. Hodder then described the formal similarities between long burial mounds in Western Europe and earlier and contemporary long houses in Central Europe. The two structural types included similarities in construction, shape, placement, orientation, and elaboration of doorways. In addition, each of these structural types were divided into three chambers and were flanked on their two long sides with ditches. So what did these similarities mean to those who lived in them? Hodder observed that for Neolithic peoples, who were—based on archaeological research—organized around lineages, the ability of one lineage to become stronger than another was not based on access to arable land—which would have been plentiful—but on the ability to reproduce labor. In such a setting, the role of women and their reproductive work in the household would have been highly valued. Based on Hodder's ethnoarchaeological work on similarly organized societies, the domestic sphere would have been elaborated in social life. Men gained power and prestige as lineage headsmen from the successes of women's domestic roles; therefore, the burial monuments, which were markers of male power, came to reference domestic structures.

Although Hodder (1985) was clearly trying to evoke Binford's 1962 article, "Archaeology as Anthropology," with the structure of his paper, his case study lacked the definitive "ta da!" of Binford's Old Copper culture study. There are very important ideas in this early work that are elaborated upon and developed by Hodder and other archaeologists. At first glance, it may seem that Hodder's focus on history and context called for a return to culture history. This is not the case. He called for an archaeology that doesn't consider "process without culture, social systems without individuals, adaptive change without history, science without the subjective" (1985:7). Also, his interpretation is not ecological. It considers a social process that is instead historical and would not be considered in a processual framework. By using the word social rather than culture, Hodder is not using a normative view of culture; social life is negotiated between consciously engaged people, not passively mimicked from generation to generation. He calls for an ethnoarchaeology in which the archaeologist participates as more than an outsider. For an archaeologist who does not attempt to understand the cultures in which he/she works cannot claim to have examined all relevant variables. There are two other things achieved in this article, which I think are particularly important. Hodder talks about men and women (bringing gender into archaeological research in a meaningful way), and he talks about the politics of doing archaeology. He notes that all research is political, and with its dehumanized representations of persons being helpless cogs in an all powerful system they can't change, it would seem to naturalize totalitarian rule in human societies. Hodder notes that it is all a little too Orwellian for his tastes.

Just as Binford's call for a new archaeology was met with demands for new methodologies, so was Hodder's work. In 1991, he called for the replacement of processualism's hypothetico-deductive reasoning with **hermeneutic reasoning**. The hypothetico-deductive method limited archaeologists' ability to understand the internal logic of past societies, because the process of generating and testing hypotheses was limited by the understandings of the scholar creating the hypotheses and never encouraged interpretive engagement between researcher and data. In other words, data and theory were always kept separate and distinct from one another.

Hermeneutic thinking was a spiral, or dialogic, between parts and the whole. A scholar would be fitting pieces into an interpretive whole at the same time as constructing the whole out of the pieces. "We measure our success in this enmeshing of theory and data (our context and their context) in terms of how much of the data is accounted for by our hypotheses compared to other hypotheses. This working back and forth between theory and data, this absorption in context and texture tends to be more concerned with understanding the data in their own terms and in using internal, as well as external, criteria for judgment" (Hodder 1985:8). Note that Hodder was not calling for the abolition of scientific process, but a revision of the interpretive process. At different times, he referred to his flavor of archaeology as "contextual" or "interpretive." It was the term post-processual, however, that continued to be used to label the archaeologies that arose after Hodder's critique.

In 1997, Hodder discussed how field methodology also needed to shift in an interpretive archaeology; and he noted, quite elegantly, that "interpretation takes place at the trowel's edge," and excavation data already include interpretation. Not only does the process of thinking about what the traces we uncover mean begin as we excavate, excavation itself is an interpretive process that includes decisions about what to record, what not to record, and the decisions about how to make those records. Even the subjectivities of an excavator can shape initial interpretations of field evidence (Gero 1996).

In his work, Hodder (1997) urged excavators to be critical of assumptions, to be reflexive about affects of archaeological assumptions on different communities, to maintain relational and contextual thinking, and to bring multi-vocality into the interpretive field process by listening to fieldworkers and visitors understandings of the evidence. Hodder urged archaeologists to surrender the authority as experts that they claimed for themselves under the umbrella of doing "big science." Critiques of Hodder's vision included complaints that he wasn't aware of the proper intellectual heritage of hermeneutic thinking (Harald and Olsen 1992), that his approach was too relative and subjective, and that he invalidated all archaeological research by claiming that we could not make claims to accurately reconstructing the past (Flannery 2006). Others adopted some of his critiques by including community partners and descendants in research designs or modifying research questions to look at gender and other social identities. Others, still, took advantage of the new freedom to develop alternate archaeologies and created new areas of study and theorizing.

One of the important new bodies of archaeological theorizing and distinct practice to arise following the post-processualist critique during the early 1990s was **phenomenological archaeology**. Christopher Tilley (1997), Barbara Bender (Bender et al. 2007), and Julian Thomas (1996) are most commonly associated with this form of landscape archaeology, which became particularly important in Britain and was influenced by thinkers like Martin Heidegger and Maurice Merleau-Ponty (Thomas 1993; Tilley 1994). Phenomenology considers firsthand experience of phenomena in the world. Since all human understanding and experience of the world is three-dimensional and filtered through the senses of the body, it is the act of doing and experiencing that creates reality. Archeologists advocating for phenomenological approaches argue that understanding how places were experienced in an embodied way is essential for archaeological interpretation. Part of the aim of this work was to break away from the Cartesian mind/body duality that shapes much of Western thinking about the human self.

Tilley (1997) suggested that travelling across landscapes where prehistoric features were located allowed archaeologists to access their embodied experience of a place in a way that two-dimensional maps would not allow. Thomas (1996) argued that because humans experience the world in time, understanding for any person was developed over the course of a lifetime. As occupants of the modern world, archaeologists could never experience things as prehistoric peoples could but only understand the past through the lenses of our own socially structured experiences. Phenomenologists embraced hermeneutic ways of thinking and used their self-reflective experiences of the landscape to create understandings of prehistoric monuments.

Clearly, phenomenological approaches can be seen as a post-processual reimagining of ethnoarchaeology and experimental archaeology. Hodder had advocated that ethnoarchaeology be more participatory though never to the degree advocated by Tilly or Thomas. As you may imagine, phenomenological approaches were subjected to a chorus of critiques (see Bruck 2005 for a particular coherent review and critique). For some, the phenomenologists replicated the work of early British antiquarians (read this as "a-scientific"). For others, their failure to recognize that bodies are themselves social products meant that they were only creating a white male view of the past. Others raised the more basic question of how on earth can a late twentieth-century person, walking over a late twentieth-century landscape with prehistoric monuments, hope to recreate the experience of Neolithic peoples? Still, phenomenology has made important contributions to archaeology and has encouraged archaeologists to think about spaces of control, embodiment, and the sensuality of the human experience in ways previously unknown in the discipline.

For myself, I see embodied experiences as one of the aspects of the past to consider, but it is not the whole of my research aims. For the Mardi Gras project, I was necessarily involved in the embodied experience of attending parades by participating in several parades as a masker. How to classify this work though, is a bigger question. Attending parades was a critical part of fieldwork to obtain a number of my samples in a systematic, consistent, and controlled way. This demonstrates clear influences of processual experimental and ethnoarchaeologies. Yet, if I was not worried about having a controlled sample, I could have simply allowed others to collect the bead data—and indeed, some years I did out of necessity. It was that embodied experience of attending parades that allowed me to understand the contexts in which beads were recovered and the social practices they were situated in. It was those embodied experiences that allowed me to understand the assemblages others had collected. In that sense, I conducted an ethnoarchaeology of the type advocated by Hodder (1985).

Those experiences were necessarily channeled explicitly through my short, white, female body. Sights I saw were different than those experienced by someone shorter or taller. Perhaps my experience of the smells and sounds were different as well. Maybe others aren't hit so strongly with the chemical smell that wafts up from a newly opened bag of beads; maybe others do not find their hearing overwhelmed by the background buzz of tractors, marching bands, and shouts that makes it impossible for me to hear others speaking to me in the midst of a parade. Yet, those experiences ultimately informed my understandings of the material assemblages, as I put the pieces of information I had acquired together into an interpretive whole.

Riding in the Super Krewe: An Embodied Experience

I had intended to study only the objects of Mardi Gras. As I became more involved in the study, I realized that I could not artificially separate the things from the ways they were used, the ways they communicated, and they ways they were communicated with—what some have referred to as the social lives of the things. This is why the study is anthropological and archaeological, rather than an art historical. I will admit, I do "like" Mardi Gras beads as objects. They of things are of varying levels of attractiveness. I still find myself unable to resist picking up a large strand of hot pink metallic beads when I see them. The shine across the surface of a marble-sized bead in the light attracts my eye. The feeling of the smooth surface against my fingers, the weight of the strand against my palm, and the sound of the beads clanking together are undeniable sensual aspects of the beads. These are attributes accessible to any viewer engaging directly with the object, but their own embodied experience of the objects may differ.

The beads have other properties and attributes, which only become apparent in the course of using them. The larger beads, with their greater weight, can be thrown farther than smaller beads and should be used to reach the back of the crowd. The elongated bead shape of the style called "twist" is less prone to tangling than the round and faceted beads, which makes them easier to separate and throw quickly as single strands. The smaller the bead, the easier they are to repair by twisting the ends against one another or melting them together. These are attributes of the beads that only become meaningful in particular contexts. To better understand the beads, I needed to participate in Mardi Gras, not just on the catching end of the throwing game, but also on the throwing end. My Louisiana friends and colleagues drew upon available networks and managed to get me nominated into membership of one of the super krewes. Recognizing this as a rare opportunity, I gathered the mental and financial resources necessary to ride in a New Orleans parade.

Since Hurricane Katrina, it has become more common for outsiders to have the opportunity to join krewes just to ride. The parades are large and expensive to maintain, and as part of the City's tourism savvy, they have recognized that this is a way to generate a different branch of Mardi Gras tourism. I imagine that the experience of riding with a bunch of out-of-towners with no previous Carnival experience would be very different. I was fortunate enough to ride with a group of experienced Louisiana riders in an organization that advocated for a particular kind of politics.

The Krewe of Orpheus was formed following the 1991 ordinance mandating the racial integration of krewes that parade as a mixed-sex and race organization celebrating New Orleans' diverse arts heritage, particularly music. My goal was to understand the embodied experience of New Orleans Mardi Gras from the perspective of a rider at the top of the float, rather than a spectator at the street level. And to this end, it was an extraordinary experience, one that I was able to participate in during the 2000 and 2001

Carnival seasons. I also rode in a small community-based parade in sugar country in 2005, which was an experience that taught me much about how racial politics affect the social geography of Carnival and the playing of the throwing game; but that is a story for later.

What one catches at a Mardi Gras parade is a combination of luck, skill, and product availability. If no one is throwing a particular type of object, you will not get it. It is that simple. Not so simple, as I quickly learned, was deciding what to throw. The krewe sent some guidelines for amounts of beads to throw that would allow them to last throughout the parade, a pricelist for the krewe-specific throws (cups, medallion beads, and doubloons), and several pre-fixe bead packages. It is important to recognize that krewes build a reputation not just on the quality and beauty of their floats, but on the generosity of their throws. In the case of super krewes, in addition to attendance by the riders and their guests, tickets to the balls are also available to the public at expensive prices. The parades march into the Riverwalk Convention Center (made infamous during coverage following Hurricane Katrina) or the Superdome, and riders throw beads to the ball guests. Therefore, there had to be enough beads to throw not only to the parade goers, but also to throw heavily to the paying "guests" and family and friends. Krewes will always exaggerate the number of beads one needs to purchase.

The advantage of pre-fixe packages is that it could be picked up a few days prior to the parade, and they are a mixed assemblage of large and small beads, medallions, and special objects. For the person who had a sense of how much they wanted to spend, these were very useful. I ordered one of these packages as my base, and my local contact picked up the beads for me when they were available. I was travelling from California just a few days prior to the parade. A friend provided a list of his 1999 bead purchases (Table 5.1), which I used to shape my purchasing decisions. At first, I was content that I had purchased an adequate amount of beads. After all, I had spent $840.00 on, essentially, a bunch of plastic beads and cups I was going to throw away (Table 5.1). As parade day approached, however, I began to fret as to whether I was being generous enough. I have learned this is a common malady that affects riders. The day before the parade, I went to Mardi Gras Annex, then one of the largest suppliers of Mardi Gras throws in the city, and supplemented my assemblage. I purchased a range of hand-strung beads, stuffed animals, Carnival masked-dolls, several Frisbees, and several footballs and basketballs in Mardi Gras colors totaling another $85.00. I based my decision not on knowledge of how these throws would be received by others, but based upon the kinds of throws I had caught and liked. I was hoping that others would like the same things as me. My three-year-old daughter was already a fan of Mardi Gras stuffed animals, and I had arranged a special packet of things to hand off to her from the float (which was not included in the parade tally gathered from Orpheus that year). In this, I was also like many other riders.

The resulting assemblage of throws was absurd to behold: cases of beads, a case of cups, a sack of doubloons, and two trash bags of "special" beads and stuffed animals. This being my first riding experience, I had no sense of how to prepare my beads prior to the parade. My informants told me to just wait until parade day; it was easier to unpack at the float. The parade was to start rolling at 6PM on Lundi Gras. I was to arrive to start

Table 5.1. Examples of Beads and Throws Bought for Orpheus in 1999 and 2000.

Orpheus 1999 Bead Purchase (not the author's assemblage).

AMOUNT	TYPE OF THROW (FINISH, LENGTH, DIAMETER)	COST PER UNIT ($)	TOTAL COST ($)
2 cases	Krewe cups	65.00 per case	130.00
1 case	Metallic medallion beads, 4 gross per case	125.00 per case	125.00
1 case	Metallic purple-green-gold, 60" 14 mm, 13 dozen strands	125.00 per case	125.00
40 dozen	Pearl, 48" 8 mm	570.00	570.00
10 dozen	Metallic, 48" 8 mm	Bought as part of above	
40 dozen	Transparent, 48" 8 mm	Bought as part of above	
40 dozen	Metallic Faceted, 33" 8 mm	Bought as part of above	

Total: $950

Orpheus 2000 Bead Purchase by the Author

AMOUNT	TYPE OF THROW (FINISH, LENGTH, DIAMETER)	COST PER UNIT (USD)	TOTAL COST (USD)
1 case	White pearls, 72" 14 mm, 10 dozen case	90.00 per case	90.00
Package A from krewe			750.00 for entire A package
1 case	Orpheus medallion beads, 4 gross per case	135.00 per case	
1 case	Orpheus throw cups, 250 cups per case	65.00 per case	
1	Insulated travel mug	6.00 per mug	
100	Gold Orpheus theme doubloons	18.00 per 100	
100	Red music legend doubloons	17.00 per 100	
1	Orpheus cloisonné doubloon	35.00 per doubloon	
2	Orpheus logo baseball cap	12.00 per hat	
4 cases	metallic beads, 33" 7.5 mm, 60 dozen case	65.00 per case	

Table 5.1. Continued on page 157

Table 5.1. Continued

AMOUNT	TYPE OF THROW (FINISH, LENGTH, DIAMETER)	COST PER UNIT (USD)	TOTAL COST (USD)
1 case	Metallic beads, 48" 8 mm, 48 dozen case	100.00 per case	
1 case	Metallic beads, 48" 12 mm, 24 dozen case	100.00 per case	
2 dozen	Mardi Gras-themed stuffed animals	2.00 an animal	48.00
1 dozen	Small jester dolls	12.00 for a pack of dozen	12.00
5	Jester MOS beads	5.00	5.00
10	Hand-strung fancy strands	2.00 a piece	20.00

Total: 925.00

to load up at 8 AM. The New Orleans Convention Center, which in 2000 was free of the horrible images of huddled Katrina refugees that would forever stain the nation's sense of the place, is an incredibly long building, stretching for over a mile on the bank of the Mississippi River.

Cars lined up on the street parallel to the parked floats outside the convention center. People were unloading piles of boxes and trash bags similar to mine. I had the sense of being at an airport on the Wednesday prior to Thanksgiving. Cars that snaked in a long line occasionally made a sudden movement to snatch an unexpectedly vacated parking spot. After much sitting on the horn and armed with aggressive driving skills developed in California, my family pulled up to the curb by my assigned float, and we off-loaded my precious haul. I was abandoned with my beads so that the car could be parked in less chaotic circumstances. The noise and jostling of so many people with identical piles of stuff was unnerving. I was shocked to see that the pile of boxes and goods was nearly as tall as me, and for the first time, it struck me that the float seemed awfully small to accommodate all the goods that we had. My musings on this subject were interrupted by the arrival of my krewe sponsor and friend and the float captains.

Each float has at least one captain to oversee the rest of the maskers during the parade. This is a title of some prestige, and it recognizes effectiveness in organization and long-time dedication to the organization. Our captains were a married couple who had been parading with the krewe since its inception. Our float was one of the largest in the parade, an electric-lighted monstrosity that was three 18-wheelers linked together. The captains had hosted an orientation event a month before the parade so riders could get to know one another prior to the parade. They had come up with the seating chart, so to speak, for the float that assigned spaces according to who was friends with whom, as well as issues of gender and experience.

Experienced riders, particularly men, were positioned on the lower floors of the float. Parade goers often approach the floats during stops, and people in spots like the densely crowded areas of Canal Street can be aggressive at times. There was concern that women may not have the physical strength (or perhaps courage) to push off people who might try to cling to or climb up the floats. The lower float position also allows for greater negotiation with crowd members. Kisses, beer, and displays of nudity are all best negotiated from the bottom tier of the float; thus this is also a reason, perhaps, to place men at the float's lowest level. In addition, off-duty New Orleans police officers were reserved spots on the lowest level of the float. The officers were provided throws and costumes by the krewe, with the recognition that their unmarked presence would provide security support if parts of the parade became hairy.

I had collected my costume for the day, and had the eyeholes in my mask cut larger to my specifications. New Orleans ordinances require that riders stay masked for the duration of the parade, and that they wear a harness that attaches them to the float. The costume featured a hood that covered my hair and much of my head and a gold foil mask that covered most of my face apart from my mouth. I chose not to wear lipstick that would clearly identify me as a woman. The blocky smock-like shirt and unisex pants that comprised the rest of the costume disguised all hints of a feminine shape. The costume provided me with perfect anonymity. Joseph Roach (1993) has noted the built-in legal inequities in New Orleans' ordinances about Mardi Gras activities. One such inequity involves the ability of maskers to protect their identity during the extent of Mardi Gras parades, and with the protection of one's identity came the license to behave outside of one's normal practice.

My costume and boxed lunch collected and my mask prepared, I faced the most daunting task of my parade preparations, figuring out how to get my throws up the rickety stairs of the float to my riding position without hurting myself or dropping my cargo on top of those below me. Once the goods were up to the second floor of the float, I would have to face the task of making my haul and myself fit into an area about the size of a telephone booth. I had been placed in an enclosed cab at the front of the train-shaped float, essentially, the engineer's spot. I would share this space with one another person, who happened to be an acquaintance. One of us would throw to one side of the street, the second, to the other side of the street. We also got to toot the train's horn.

We were fortunate to have a contained space that would house most of our throws. What we lacked, however, was much wall or ceiling space. Maskers will bring hammers, nails, and hooks to modify the float on the morning of the parade to create hanging space for beads and bags of throws. The purpose of this is multi-fold. Many maskers like to display their finest throws for crowds to see. Large stuffed animals, strands of ornate, hand-strung beads, large and long strands of beads, umbrellas, and other novelties can be seen displayed near a masker (Figure 5.1). This serves to incite the crowd and can attract attention to particular riders. The people most effective at attracting Mardi Gras loot are focused on finding maskers who have the particular object they desire. Seeing who has what allows for targeted solicitation. Our position, while providing us with a decent amount of space, would limit some of our ability to initiate negotiations.

Hanging throws from nails provided another useful function. To grab hanging objects required repeated bending over. It also becomes important to understand how to pace oneself. The parade rolls for about three hours, depending on delays. It is a serious problem to run out of throws before the end of the parade. And with ball guests expecting our arrival as well, we needed to have beads in reserve. Some maskers will isolate those throws intended for the ball by divide their throws and then hanging all the throws intended for distribution for the first half of the parade. At the half-way-point, one quickly unpacks and hangs the remainder of the beads (or what is perceived as needed). If one has thrown too heavy, exhausting bead supply before the first half, they simply duck down and sit on the floor of the float to take a break or focus on inciting the crowd. On any float, there is likely to be a number of people who have "bought heavy" who are willing to give beads to other maskers to throw if they run short. Riders are generally not interested in having large amounts of beads left over after a parade. Who wants to repackage those things and lug them back down the stairs? Some people do, but at the end of the day, laziness does factor in, and the best solution for many is to just throw the rest of it off the float to the crowds just outside of and in the convention center. The float captains

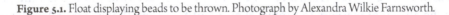

Figure 5.1. Float displaying beads to be thrown. Photograph by Alexandra Wilkie Farnsworth.

facilitate these decisions and strategies during the parade by letting the maskers know when they have hit the parade's halfway point.

These were all things I would learn during the actual parade. I still faced the daunting task of loading my gear onto the float. Moving on a Carnival float is like moving around on an airplane during a flight when the beverage cart is blocking the aisle between you and the lavatory. Everyone is engaged in the same activity, best described as trying to make size-eight feet fit into size-five shoes. Early in the day, everyone was filled with good spirits and looked forward to having a good parade run. They flattened themselves as best as possible against the float while I lugged boxes of goods by them. On my first several trips up the stairs, I was amazed at how much the float bounced in response to movement on it. I was worried that we were in for a very bumpy and uncomfortable ride. As more of us loaded our throws, however, the float felt more and more stable.

I noted this observation to one of my float mates, who laughed and explained that the floats required special suspension so that they could accommodate all the added weight of the throws. He assured me that the float ride would get bumpier as we neared the end of our ride and most of our throws were gone. Once the boxes and bags of throws were safely in the cabin of the train, it was time to decide how to unpack and organize them.

In 2000, most beads were packaged in plastic bags within cardboard boxes. Ordinarily, each bag would contain one dozen beads attached together with a strip of brown stapled paper that identified the beads as having been made in China. For long strands with large beads, however, bags may only contain six strands or even just three. For average to medium length beads (up to 48" in length and 10 mm in bead diameter), it is typical for a case to contain one gross or 144 strands of beads (Figure 5.2). Then common among the post-parade debris in the streets of New Orleans were mashed cardboard boxes and torn plastic baggies, tossed or lost from floats during the frantic unpacking of beads during the parade, now beads are some of the most commonly seen garbage (Figure 5.3). A delightful development of the past several years has been the replacement of cardboard boxes with vinyl, handled bags that contain the plastic bags of beads. Krewes who sell beads to members will often have their emblem emblazoned on these bags (Figure 5.4). Krewe members will keep these bags as souvenirs, use them to cart away excess beads, or throw them to the crowds. Catching a vinyl bag is an excellent way to take one's Mardi Gras haul home. It also creates a strange, and definitely false, sense that Mardi Gras has somehow become "green."

My cab companion and I sorted through our respective beads. We were able to hammer nails received from other riders into the back wall of the cabin. From those, we hung our fancy

Figure 5.2. Packaging of beads. Photograph by Alexandra Wilkie Farnsworth.

Figure 5.3. Post-parade debris after Spanish Town parade rolled by. Photograph by Alexandra Wilkie Farnsworth.

beads. There were a few hanging nails under the window opening that we would throw through. I opened and hung a number of "throwing beads," which back then meant basic 33" strands with 8 mm diameters in purple, gold, and green. I was amazed how quickly the space filled and how many beads were still in their packages. I tried several different ways to arrange the lot and finally decided to build myself a seat out of the boxes. Crowds on the streets endure long waits for parades to appear, but their wait is nothing like the wait endured by those in the floats. Piles of bags surrounded my feet, and my bags of stuffed animals and other novelties were wedged behind me. Somewhere in the mess, I lost my boxed lunch, and when I found it hours later, it was unworthy of human consumption.

As maskers unloaded their throws, they carefully watched what others unloaded. This was both out

Figure 5.4. Plastic krewe bag used to package beads. Photograph by Alexandra Wilkie Farnsworth.

of a sense of professionalism—"oh, how do you find that bead is to throw? I found they tangled easily last year, but mine were smaller"—as well as interest in what unusual things others might have. Bead lust is not limited to the parade goers. Fellow maskers would wander by, inspecting beads and asking for examples they liked, offering to trade for ones they had. As a junior member of the float, I was more often than not, at the short end of the exchange but was not perturbed by the situation.

A newspaper article from 1973 described the organizing of throws on Thoth's floats. The article describes riders bragging about how many gross of beads they had purchased, and it describes them stealing from one another during the course of loading as part of a joking relationship between krewe members, who mocked one another for having so few beads.

In 2000, the internet was just starting to be a major alternate bead source. Several of the krewe members had alternate sources of beads—guys who mysteriously sold beads out of the backs of their trucks, others who knew a guy who knew a guy who sold beads cheaper. Those who thought they had a particularly good source, were careful to keep details to themselves; for their suppliers only had a limited number of cases that they sold in any given year. Today, in addition to well-known terrestrial sources of beads, there are multiple sources that compete against one another on the internet, and most are significantly cheaper than the prices offered by the krewes to their members.

Beads loaded, we went for a last stretch of our legs and use of the bathroom. Port-o-lets travel on the floats, but using them is not something that one wants to contemplate, particularly if a woman. This was also a discouragement to drinking too much beer. The floats had to move to the start position for the parade well before the parade was to begin rolling. We were parked on Napoleon Ave., but the parade did not start until the intersection of Napoleon Avenue and Tchoupitoulas Street. As the floats made the right-hand turn onto Tchoupitoulous, the jugglers, marching bands, stilt-walkers, horseback riders, and other auxiliary members of the parade would be integrated in between the floats. Until the float passes that intersection, we were not to start throwing beads. This was not followed. The families who lived along Napoleon Avenue clearly expected us to throw them beads.

Katrina introduced the nation to poverty Louisiana-style, but for outsiders, it can be difficult to recognize the difference between the truly destitute, the working-class poor, and the emergent-middle-class based on architecture. Louisiana's climate is not kind to the faces of her houses. Beautiful painted façades are brutalized by the heat, humidity, and onslaught of tropical rains in the summer, and icy rains in the winter. And there is the extra insult added by the pollution of the petrochemical companies that line the Mississippi. A paint job that may look presentable for 20 years in a reasonable climate is appalling in 5 years' time in Louisiana. The house façades along Napoleon suggested their residents had other financial priorities than repainting the house every five years.

There was no frantic begging and no insistent demands that we must hand over goods. People wandered by wanting to chat, and if we had something they found particular interesting, they would ask. A few floats in front of us, someone distributed some footballs to a group of older children. The footballs were tossed through the air—back to the floats, where they were tossed back, or over the floats, to children on the other side. As I looked up and down the length of the parade, I could see clusters of people walking along, inspecting the floats, receiving occasional throws, and waving their appreciation. People on the floats were chatting to one another. Some climbed down to walk around or seek out a restroom or a place to purchase beer or soda, I saw beverages and chips traded for beads and other throws.

Some residents stayed on their porches where they gently rocked and watched. Maskers would experiment with their throwing arms and try to toss beads into their laps or across their porches. Tree limbs and power lines caught many of the beads, hanging like a new-fangled plastic Spanish moss from oak trees. In the distance, it was possible to hear the brassy mumble of practicing marching bands. Occasionally, a fast-driving black vehicle bearing a "Blaine Kern Studios" placard would pass us. The parade featured many electric lights and moving parts; last minute adjustments to the electronics, the mechanics, or the decorations are always necessary.

I enjoyed the peacefulness and tranquility of our wait time. No great distance away, masses of humanity assembled to watch the two evening parades. We were to be the second. The parade in front of us had not marched for several years, and there was speculation that there may be great delays as a result. As the sun faded, however, a greater sense of urgency overtook us. There is only so long you can sit perched on beads without feeling some fatigue of the nether regions. Finally, the lieutenants called to us, "hold on, we're about to move!" The float moved with a great lurch as the tractor finally exerted the power necessary to move us. We were not moving quickly, but after hours of inertia, movement was a frightening novelty. Masks were quickly re-donned, harnesses reattached, and throws surveyed. We stopped and started multiple times, pausing as marching bands slipped between the floats. As we grew closer to the intersection of Napoleon and Tchoupitoulous, the songs played by the bands became audible. What had been the distant roar of the crowd became louder. Nothing can prepare one for the onslaught of sights and sounds that strike you as your float turns onto Tchoupitoulous Street.

Watching a parade, you expect that maskers can see you, that they are aware you are there and clearly should want to throw something to you personally. I have been in the crowd when masking friends fail to hear me shout their name and didn't see me jumping up and down to get their attention. I could not understand how such obliviousness was possible until I rode in a parade. The experience overloads one's senses. The sounds of shouting, the drone of the tractors, the din of multiple marching bands, and sound systems of businesses and individuals competing for the soundscape is overwhelming. It took me several minutes to sort out what I was hearing. Visually, the movement of the float is fast enough between stops that it is hard to pull out individual faces from the crowd. A blur of hands—hands of all sizes and colors—wave in a flurry. The faces below them are hard to discern, all one gets is an impression of movement—waving hands and shouting mouths.

Louisiana is an olfactory challenge in the best of times. The humid and hot climate, combined with the petrochemical companies, means that there is always a putrid smell underlying everything in the state. Perhaps this constant reminder of mortality is why Louisianans embrace Carnival as they do. Mardi Gras assaults the olfactory sense as well. The pleasant smells of hot dogs, cotton candy, roasted nuts, boiled crawfish, and fried chicken are all but overpowered by the smell of sweaty, drunk, agitated humans and the diesel of the tractors. As a masker, instead of stopping and gawking at this scene, or as you are paralyzed by it, you are supposed to grab plastic beads to throw to the masses. It was a verbal nudge from spectators that drew me to action.

"Hey, up in the cab, you gonna throw anything?" I snapped to life. I had these piles of beads I was sitting atop and more hanging from nails. They were there to throw! I quickly tossed a strand of beads, then another and another. I loaded my right forearm with several dozen beads, pulling one at a time from my arm to toss into the crowd. The float was moving quickly, it seemed. I could not see to whom I was throwing; all was a blur of waving arms and shouting upturned faces. I realized two things quite quickly. First, one must throw in a way that assured the average person had a chance of getting beads; we could not throw a single strand of beads at a time, because the crowd was too dense, and the float was moving too fast. Second, there was no way I would ever get through my pile of beads if I threw one strand at a time. I removed a dozen strands from my arm and hurled them into the crowd. I was able to see them separate in the air, twirl apart, glitter briefly in the lamplight, and at least four dozen people lunge themselves into the air to receive them. I quickly added a second dozen to the air. "All right," I thought, "this is what I am supposed to do."

From the vantage point of the float, what one sees is very much dependent upon where along the parade route one is. In neighborhoods, crowds are not so deep, and often, the most visible parade goers will be the small children sitting on ladder seats. In commercial areas, crowds are denser and deeper. There are still those who will cordon off sections of road medians or other open public spaces for their groups, and there are those who lug stepladder chairs into these areas. But for the most part, crowds are more fluid in the commercial areas, often moving in a wave with the floats.

A note on children: small-sized children are often the hardest to please with throws. Because little children tend to be cuter than many of the drunken, shouting, and pushing adults along the parade route, it is particularly appealing to throw to them, thus making a rejection of a throw by a cute child all the more difficult to bear. For these littlest ones, beads lose their charm after a while, and it is not uncommon to throw beads to a child only to see them pass them to a parent. Likewise, there is limited diversity in stuffed animals available if one sticks with the Mardi Gras-themed ones. There are really only so many bears in jester outfits, and purple-, green-, and gold-colored crawfish, alligators, or fish that any child needs. How hard to be so jaded by throws at a young age! To put the amount of throw wealth a well-placed, decent-looking child can accumulate into perspective, my daughter remembers fondly the year that she acquired 26 stuffed animals in a four-day visit to Carnival. Her eyes will mist up when she tells the tale, and I cannot help but think of seasoned fishermen reminiscing over great hauls of the past. Often, by the end of a night parade, the little ones propped atop the ladders are slumped over, sleeping, or in a very dream-like awake state. Older children are fully consumed by bead lust and will grab and keep anything thrown to them. They just aren't as cute.

I tried to match my volume of throwing to the demands of the crowd and registered these changes in social geography as the difference between periods of high-demand throwing and lesser-demand throwing. When the crowds were 10 people deep, it was easiest to throw bunches of beads and let the crowd distribute them among themselves. We had driven for an unknown amount of time, when suddenly the parade lurched to a stop. The front of the parade had reached the viewing stands. Now, each marching band would pause and perform. Each float would stop to be evaluated by city dignitaries and those who had bought or received grandstand tickets. I was exhausted when we stopped and sank to the floor to evaluate the mess of dropped beads and torn bags. My companion in the cab had a similar reaction. We looked at one another. Do you believe this? We asked one another. This is crazy! How will we keep up? This was supposed to be fun, but it felt a lot like work. I drank deeply of a bottle of water and looked out over the crowd.

People had flooded off the curb to be close to the float. They were calling and negotiating with maskers on the bottom level of the float. A lost looking man was at the perimeter with a little girl, not much older than mine, on his shoulders. As she smiled and waved, it was clear she was having a better time than her dad. Some large beads were around her neck. She noticed me and waved. I waved back, which caused a greater amount of waving. Very cute. Her dad must have felt her weight shifting back and forth and looked up and saw me waving. Our eyes met, and I held up a finger indicating he should wait a moment. I bent into the cab and opened my bag of stuffed animals. I selected a cute stuffed purple bear dressed in a jester's costume. I leaned way out of the cab, held it in my hand, and indicated he should move in close to catch it. Others saw what was happening and let him through. He caught the bear one-handed, evoking a happy shriek from his daughter, who grabbed it from his hand and hugged it fiercely. Stuffed animals were a common throw at smaller town parades but were not always common in New Orleans. I had made, at least for that moment, the little girl's parade. I was hooked. Now I understood how this could be fun. I began to work the crowd. Until we passed the grandstand, the rest of the parade was characterized by a flow of stops and starts and a blurred crowd contrasted with periods of personal interaction.

What makes you want to throw to a particular person? There are a lot of motivations. Someone catches your eye because they are attractive, seem to be having a good time, reminds you of someone, has a great costume, makes eye contact and talks to you or waves, or sometimes they just make you laugh. These are positive experiences that you want to reinforce. There are also negative behaviors visible from the floats. Throwing objects at people has long been a way of expressing a negative opinion at Mardi Gras, and this is true for maskers as well. Sometimes, you see someone acting like a jerk—stealing beads intended for a child or being too aggressive. Then you will see a masker hurl a bunch of beads at that person—or more accurately, their head. I am not condoning such behavior, merely describing it. The person rarely gets the throw that hits her/him, and those who were subjected to the bad behavior receive the throws and reap the joy of seeing them punished.

I have decided to throw to a particular person just to practice my aim or throwing technique. It is good to get a sense of how far you can throw particular sizes and shapes of beads. I learned quickly that it is dangerous to try to throw beads in a spinning arc. They are too hard to control and you can randomly hit people. It is better to wad the beads up in your hand to throw underhand tosses within 20 feet and overhand for greater distances. There is a certain fun in trying to throw the beads to the people at the edge of the crowd to test one's aim and strength. Some enterprising people will hold signs with bullseyes or other targets for you to throw at.

I quickly learned how to pace my throwing. Shorter beads have to be thrown quickly. People are looking for bulk with those, and as the parade goes on, and they have caught as many of the normal sized beads as they care to have, you might as well throw them still packaged in the bag. In contrast, long beads, or fancy hand-strung beads, can be made to last. During a stop, you can pull a long strand of beads out and alluringly dangle them in front of the crowd. You can twirl them, run them back and forth in your hands seductively, or, if you are wearing some of the long beads you intend to throw, you can take them slowly off your neck in a bead striptease. This incites the crowd and burns time. This would be the point, if one were to solicit some sort of exchange for the beads, to start negotiations. Most maskers do not expect anything more than human contact and a smile and wave in exchange for throws. While displays of nudity are most commonly discussed as examples of things bartered for beads, they are not the only, and certainly not the most common. The most common bead exchange I witnessed was the trade of good beads for beer, water, soda, or food. One gets very thirsty with the shouting and throwing. A lot of folks along the parade route have coolers. A two-dollar strand of beads can get you a can of American beer.

If a masker is worried about running out of beads, s/ he may trade a good pair of beads to get a bunch of little beads. I have also seen beads traded for beads, and beads traded for baseball hats ("Hey, I love the Dodgers, will you give me that hat for these beads?"). It is not always clear that the person trading really wants the object or is merely seeing how far they can push people. There are also the romantics who will ask a pretty girl not to show their body parts, but to come and plant a kiss on the masker's face. Clearly, this only works for maskers on the bottom level of the float, and in circumstances when said pretty girl is on someone's shoulders. To steal a kiss from a woman in front of her male companion is definitely in line with the spirit of Mardi Gras's bawdiness.

The parade moved quicker once we were past St. Charles Circle. When we made the turn onto Canal Street, our senses were overwhelmed—light as bright as daylight, the choking smells of smoke bombs, tobacco, weed, urine, sweat, street food, and beer and a roaring crowd that seemed, impossibly, four times louder than anything we had experienced. People stood 20 or more deep wedged between street barriers at the front and buildings at the back. People covered multiple stories of balconies, sometimes screaming at us from above to throw beads upward. There were no faces. Occasionally there were breasts; but mainly there were hands, urgently waving and begging hands in an endless sea of need. The floats were lighter now, and the tractors pulling us sped up. The crowds here were unpredictable; there would be no pausing unless a serious malfunction or injury occurred. Now we were driving to get through the parade route and enter the Riverwalk Convention Center where the guests of our ball, Orpheuscapade, awaited us. The crowds followed us to the convention center.

Many of the riders stopped throwing at the end of the route, reserving stocks of beads for ball guests, as we had been ordered. Entering the convention center was like entering another dimension. Beautifully gowned and tuxedoed guests waved and begged for throws as the parade slowly wound past them—the entire parade of floats— driving into the convention center. We parked, and my float mates and I jumped off the float and ran to join the spectators … collecting some beads of our own, until all of the floats were there and parked. I had thrown all of my beads. But others had not and were planning on unloading the float the next morning. It was past midnight. Every muscle in my body ached with exhaustion, and my ears rung with the sounds of the crowd. In a daze, I ate the meal that others had paid over $100 per person to enjoy. I couldn't stay for the dancing and stumbled out of the convention center. I don't remember the ride back to my hotel or even undressing and getting into bed. There was too much to process and no mind left to process it with. It had been glorious.

CHAPTER 6
TECHNOLOGY AND SOCIAL CHANGE

A quick explanatory note: now that I've introduced you to the general ways that archaeological thinking has come to be, in each of the chapters to follow, we will focus on a single interpretive theme that characterizes a body of archaeological investigation and scholarship. Mardi Gras beads are easily tangled; human lives are no different, with different aspects of lived experience entangling. Archaeologists often try to narrow their focus on one particular topic—but in the process of trying to free one aspect of human life from the archaeological record, they often find that they cannot separate one thing from the others. How can we think about subsistence without technology? Or discuss food without recognizing how it relates to ritual, gender, or social identity? As a rider on a float, the temptation is to just pick up the tangled mass of beads and hurl it to the crowd. We will do no such thing here. We will attempt to cleanly and distinctly discuss the different threads that have characterized groups of archaeological research programs. When necessary, we will drop one to follow another, with the hope being at the end, we see the ways they are all interwoven, thus allowing us to see the big messy tangle that is the human experience.

The first strand we'll begin to talk about in this chapter is technology, but in doing so, we will also discuss the intimately entangled issues of labor and the evolution of social complexity. Many of these issues are explored archaeologically over grand expanses of time, something that we do not have in our twenty-something years of Mardi Gras evidence. Still, even though we are not dealing with deep history in our Carnival study, insights drawn from archaeological studies of technology will help us in our analyses of the bead assemblages.

Archaeologies of Technology

Living in the twenty-first century, we tend to think of *technology* as related to engineering or industry. For anthropologists, however, a society's technology is the sum of their shared knowledge regarding how to make things and extract resources. Technological knowledge includes not only how to make a stone tool but also where to get the materials to make the stone tool and how to use the finished stone tool most effectively. Technology under such a definition doesn't have to be a thing. It can be knowledge about things, such as plants or other resources, that are encountered and extracted from the environment. Technology separates humans from other animals; other creatures may be able to use tools, or be taught to fashion them, but humans and their ancestors alone have picked up a stone and seen the potential to create something new. Early hominid studies pay particular attention to quality and craftsmanship of the earliest evidence of technology, which dates to around 2.6 million years ago (e.g., Semaw 2000).

Technology has also been seen as one of the most accessible areas for archaeological analysis. It is something that can be studied from any artifact by simply asking the questions, "how was it made?" and "how was it used?" For archaeologists interested in social evolution, increased technological complexity is seen as linked to social processes like *craft specialization* (when a society focuses on intensively producing one type of good over others, for instance, pottery or shell beads) and increased social complexity (e.g., Arnold 1995; Brumfiel and Earle 1987; Kuijt and Goring-Morris 2002; Shackel 1996). Archaeologists are interested in answering the "how was it made" question but have been most interested in understanding the relationship between technology and the ways it shapes the broader social system. Archaeologists recognize that changes in one part of a society inevitably impact other parts of the social world. Binford identified technology as the base on which other parts of the social world were built . . . remember his technomic category?

How was an Item Made?

Archaeologists interested in how things are made approach their subject in different ways. Some focus on the embodied experience of making something. This can be done by looking at the stages of production that go into making an artifact, or by looking at the impacts of the labor on people's actual bodies. Other archaeologists consider the thought processes that go along with the process of making things—what is called the cognitive steps of production—part of *cognitive archaeology.* For archaeologists, studying the earliest of humans and their technologies, this is particularly important. What changes in thought allowed early humans to make complex artifacts that would have been impossible for their ancestors to make? Were these technology-using behaviors hard-wired into the early humans (like the way a bird makes a nest), or were they learned. And if learned, can we see evidence of the learning process in the archaeological record?

For this discussion we'll first look at how bioarchaeologists approach understanding relationships between technology and the body and then consider a methodological tool of cognitive archaeologists: the chaînes opertoire.

Bioarchaeology of Labor

Bioarchaeologists look literally at the impacts of different forms of technology on the bodies that use them. While we think of bones as solid and unchanging, during an animal's lifetime, bone is a living tissue just as any other body part. It responds to stresses and pressures placed on the body, is affected by long-term nutritional deficiencies and long-term health problems. Human bone provides a record of a person's lifetime experiences at the individual level, and when a collection of skeletons from the same community is studied, at the population or demographic level.

The repeated strenuous activities that a person engages in are recorded in the skeleton in the form of evidence of well-developed ridges for muscle attachments, stress fractures from overwork, and conditions like osteoarthritis from chronic joint stress, which appear as extra growth of bone tissue at joints. Some of the most harrowing and illustrative examples of labor's impact on the body have been seen in bioarchaeological studies of the skeletons of enslaved African Americans (Blakey 2001). Consistently, male and female skeletons studied from enslaved populations demonstrate evidence of heavy labor loads indicated by exaggerated development of lifting muscles on the upper arm bones and early degeneration of the back bones and shoulder joints. Plowing, shoveling, and moving heavy exertion could all be contributors to this kind of body stress. Overwork has been demonstrated in some populations to lead to bone breaks from over stress. These heavy-labor demands on the body are typically coupled with evidence of poor diet and violence-incurred fractures and head injuries. While the experiences of enslaved African American peoples represent an extreme of how technology can reshape the skeleton, at different points in human history it is possible to see how certain shifts from one technology to another have resulted in decreased health. Worldwide, the shift from primarily hunting and gathering economies to primarily agricultural ones has been found to be a physically difficult one for human beings, with dietary deficiencies, susceptibility to long-term disease and increased osteoarthritis and vertebral degeneration being common (see Buikstra 1984; McClung De Tapia 1992).

Bioarchaeologists have noted that differences in men's and women's labors can be seen in the skeleton. In their study of prehistoric coastal Native California populations, Phillip L. Walker and Sandra Holliman (1989) studied skeletal populations to examine the effects, if any, that the shift from a generalized hunter-gatherer subsistence strategy to one more focused on marine foodstuffs had on the population's skeletal health. They studied close to 1,000 skeletons that dated from 3500 BC until the time of contact and found that osteo-arthritis increased in all persons through time, with men being more affected than women. The scientists hypothesized that the greater incidence of osteoarthritis in men may have been related to men spending more time engaged in strenuous repetitive work like fishing.

Having now considered the ways that technology can physically shape humans, let us turn our attention toward the ways that people shape their technologies.

Chaînes Opertoire

One of the more well-known tools in archaeological technology studies has been the concept of the *chaînes opertoire,* or "operation chain," which was developed in French Paleolithic archaeology to understand stone tool production. The original intent behind the technique, which French archaeologist A. Leroi-Gourhan first advanced, was to move beyond tool types based on shape to grasp that assemblages of lithics were artifacts that are methodologically interlinked—the tools are a by-product of complex production technologies. A chaînes opertoire approach emphasizes the need to study the tools that people used to produce lithics along with all of the waste materials resulting from stone working. The intent was to comprehend stone tools through the ways they were made (Bleed 2001, 2011; Bar-Yosef and Van Peer 2009:104; Sclanger 1996). A stone knife or arrowhead can be produced in a variety of ways, getting to a similar shape. By focusing on technology, archaeologists could realize the practical and technical skill involved in tool manufacture, the choice and selection of raw materials, the shape modification necessary to create a particular set of items, and the spatial organization of a lithic economy (Bar-Yosef and Van Peer 2009).

What would be an example of a chaînes opertoire? You probably follow multiple chains of operation every day as you stumble through your routine. Are you a coffee drinker? Then you may start your morning by filling your coffee maker with water, measuring out and grinding your beans, pouring the ground coffee into a filter-lined brew basket, replacing the basket, aligning the pot and pushing the "on" button. This would be an example of an operational chain—if you fail to follow a step correctly, you will end up not only with a bad cup of coffee, but going to that chain coffee shop with the odd mermaid logo. Wait, you probably did that anyway, didn't you?

In Paleolithic studies, the chaînes opertoire also became associated with particular analytical methodologies. Flint knapping is a **reductive technology**—you start with something big and end with something small (Bleed 2001, 2011). Therefore, in some contexts, it is possible to take all the pieces of stone that went into making a tool and refit them. Yes, that sounds appallingly difficult—and it is—but this technique was developed for a period of time, the Paleolithic, when the main focus of lithic technology was preparing a platform core from which relatively uniform, long, slender flakes, could be removed. In that archaeological context, where you have instances that a person sat in one place and made a core, removing flakes as necessary and discarding those flakes in the same area, then refitting becomes possible. All the various pieces that were struck off the core stayed in the same area. Reconstructing a core allows an archaeologist to reproduce the steps that a knapper went through to make the tool and the step-by-step process an ancient human went through to create that tool.

For some archaeologists, the chaînes opertoire provides an opportunity to get into the human mind, which is a field of archaeology known as cognitive archaeology (Bleed 2011). Creating something complex like a stone tool requires particular kinds of skill mastery. Bleed has noted that in a reductive technology, the ability to avoid mistakes is particularly important—one wrong flake removed, and a tool is destroyed. He has suggested that ancient flint knappers did not learn through rote memorization—a kind of learning that leads to greater mistakes—how to make tools. Bleed suggested they used something called **"mental models"** which is an understanding of the sequences that had to be followed in order for the process to have the right end result. Such mental models might involve mnemonic devices to help the maker remember the steps of the process. Through elaborate rehearsal, a level of practice that engrains actions, practices can become second nature and mastery can be achieved. Bleed notes that he has found archaeological evidence of knappers who left a tool part-way made and then returned to the core to finish the project. This would only be possible if the maker understood the process as a series of steps that could be halted and later resumed. Such interruptions would be impossible if a producer was merely following steps by memory and without understanding.

Some of the implications of Bleed's emphasis on mental models are that we should archaeologically see evidence of the learning period. It should be possible to see improvement through time in the work of particular persons, as well as see evidence of learners in the form of tool failures and poorly executed final products. In her study of Sylvester Manor Plantation, Katherine Howlett-Hayes (2013) focused on understanding how the technologies of enslaved Africans and enslaved Indians at the New York plantation affected one another. She found that African plaster making and iron technologies came to be adopted in local Indian pottery-firing techniques. She also found evidence that Indians were teaching Africans, who had long abandoned knapping technologies, how to fashion stone tools—as demonstrated by the recovery of tools clearly made by novices in enslaved African American contexts.

Reconstructing operational chains allow us to look at the stages of the production process for any artifact, and can also help us to identify the social and spatial arrangements of labor. What use is the notion of the chaînes opertoire for our study of Mardi Gras beads? By using documents as a kind of ethnographic source, it is possible to interrogate the bead assemblages for evidence of their steps of production. And by excavating the sequences that went into creating a particular strand, it is possible to better surmise the limitations of, and changes in, the technology. Understanding the evidence of the manufacturing process also makes it easier to cognize the alterations beads underwent following their manufacture. So let us quickly consider each of our bead types and the processes and steps that went into producing them.

How the Mardi Gras Beads Were Made and How They Changed

For a number of the beads in our study, we have to consider two separate sets of production processes: the production of the beads and the production of the bead strands. Until we reach the discussion of MOS beads, these two separate processes have been collapsed into one, with the strand and the bead being formed simultaneously.

Much of the discussion in this section will focus on the development of Mardi Gras beads from 1918 to 1990, before the beginning of my archaeological excavations. Our considerations are based on what we can glean from items that exist as curated objects but that have no more information than general provenience. It is best to think of this as similar to the kind of museum study that an archaeologist may conduct before going into the field. You may wonder why I even need to review the early Mardi Gras beads; I discuss the early technology of Mardi Gras beads because it becomes important to understanding changes in the throwing game that take place during our study period. In other words, to understand why the changes took place, we need to understand what the changes were. Remember the nature of the bead assemblages thrown each year at Mardi Gras—they are accumulative—with beads from previous years re-thrown for years before they disappear from parades. If we want to understand recycling in parade contexts, we also need to know roughly when these things were manufactured. The archaeologist Gavin Lucas (2005) quite rightly observes that what makes something perceived as part of the past is that it is recognizably different to people in the present.

Archaeologists often use manufacturing techniques to create chronologies for artifacts, such as the Stone Age, Bronze Age, and the Iron Age systems we discussed earlier. Figuring out the relative ages of Mardi Gras beads has proven complicated. Folk memory is of little help. *Oral history,* or the process of interviewing people about their memories of the past, can be a fruitful source of evidence for archaeologists. Archaeologist Larry Zimmerman and his colleagues (Zimmerman et al. 1991) used oral histories gathered from Native Americans whose tribes had preserved stories about the events that happened at the Battle of Little Bighorn. Zimmerman compared these oral histories with US military accounts of the battle and archaeological evidence related to the fighting. Zimmerman and his associates found that the Native American oral traditions about the battle were more in alignment with the archaeological data than the "official" military reports that sought to minimize the scale of the military's failures. Oral histories have been used by archaeologists to locate sites, identify artifacts, and learn about site histories (Wilkie 2000). It's best to think of oral history as a cousin to ethnography—whereas ethnography requires the immersion of an observer in a living culture, oral history depends on the memories of those who lived in a society at a particular place and time. Needless to say, some informants are better than others, and some kinds of memories more reliable than others. Like any other evidentiary source, oral histories need to be evaluated.

Unfortunately, oral histories have not been very useful for understanding when particular bead manufacturing technologies were introduced to Mardi Gras. This is in part because people didn't necessarily pay as close attention to the form of the beads as an archaeologist would (here is a great example of an archaeologist fixating on attributes that were not important from an emic perspective). But it is also because the practice of rethrowing beads year after year leads to blurred memories of what kind of bead actually appeared first. Among those with memories of Mardi Gras long past, there is a general understanding that glass beads predated plastic beads, and that is about it. Many people only remember the Czechoslovakian glass beads, and some may remember the Japanese beads and even blame them as the reason that glass beads were outlawed at Mardi Gras. The thin, fine glass was dangerous to catch—shattering and embedding shards in hands and feet. These beads were labeled with their country of origin on each individual strand, an attribute that made it easy for people to know where the beads were manufactured. The Indian beads were bundled by the dozen, so they had no tags that survived on individual strands. As a result, no one remembers the Indian beads—dealers conveniently classify vintage Indian beads as Czech to sell them at higher prices.

The few sources that recognize Indian beads usually put the chronology as follows: first there were Czech beads, but then the Czechs became communists. So people switched to Japanese beads, but they were unpopular. So people switched to Indian beads, until all glass was outlawed. When the outlawing took place varies in folk memory from as early as the 1950s to the 1960s. I caught a strand of glass Indian beads—clearly recycled from another parade due to the chipping on a number of the beads—at my first Mardi Gras in 1991. Clearly, then, glass beads were thrown in small numbers much later than the 1960s.

The Czech-Japan-India sequence from oral history is appealing to a modernist way of thinking, which emphasizes progress with newer things replacing older things, and it made sense to my archaeological desire for things to be chronological and orderly. In looking through newspapers for references to beads, however, I found that Czech beads were mentioned quite late in the literature. Looking at Czech history as related to manufacturing and glass production, this actually now makes sense. The Czech glass beads became unavailable not because of anti-communism sentiment among Mardi Gras goers, but because the communist government of Czechoslovakia decided to focus on heavy industry after World War II; so no beads were manufactured after the changeover. In the 1960s, the Czech government realized this was a mistake and started to support the bead industry again, and sure enough, Czech beads bearing a tag marking them as products of the state-sanctioned industry appear again at Mardi Gras.

Having been exposed to the thinking of processual archaeology (see chapter four), I hope you are asking yourself about my sample size—just how many beads am I including in this part of the study to discuss bead technology over the course of 60 plus years? The answer to that question is in Table 6.1. While the sample is admittedly small, through close consideration of these objects, it is possible to begin to understand the technological and social processes that shaped the throwing game in the period leading up to my archaeological study. Archaeologists always have to contend with the specter of the unknown in their analyses (what other materials are out there that I didn't find?). Archaeological knowledge always grows in an additive, as well as synthetic way. We discover new objects, literally, as we excavate more sites and, in doing so, add

Table 6.1. Numbers of Beads by Broad Type in the Curated Collection.

PLACE OF MANUFACTURE	GENERAL TYPE	NUMBER IN COLLECTION
CZECHOSLOVAKIA	Hand-strung glass beads	80
OCCUPIED WEST GERMANY	Hand-strung glass beads	4
OCCUPIED JAPAN	Hand-strung glass beads	10
INDIA	Hand-strung glass beads	34
HONG KONG	Hand-strung plastic beads	45
TAIWAN	Hand-strung plastic beads	1
HONG KONG	MOS plastic beads	60
CHINA	MOS plastic beads	151

more evidence to our interpretive narratives. This is part of why publication is such an important part of the archaeological enterprise—by reading the results of other people's findings, we have access to a greater pool of archaeological evidence than any single researcher could accumulate themselves.

Chaînes Opertoires for Mardi Gras Beads

How does using a chaînes opertoire approach tell us something about changing technology and labor relations in the production of Mardi Gras beads? What this analysis will reveal is the attempt by manufacturers to balance labor costs and product quality as demand for Mardi Gras beads increased through time.

For all of the hand-strung bead examples, there are going to be two very different sets of manufacture processes. First, the beads have to be manufactured, and secondly, the strands have to be strung from those beads. In describing the operational chains for each of the beads, I have greatly simplified the representation of the steps. I am looking at the production of each bead type as a step with one step for each different bead type represented in a strand. The creation of the clasp is another step; the manufacture of the string the beads are strung on is a step; and the stringing is a step. I assume that you recognize this is for ease of discussion, and the within each of the processes, a number of individual steps of manufacturing would have taken place.

Techniques for Making Glass Beads

Glass beads produced in Czechoslovakia, Japan, Occupied Germany, and India, were thrown at different times from Mardi Gras floats. While each region has its own sets of labor organizations and practices, the technologies they use to create glass beads are generally shared. Most glass beads were produced in the following ways; they were wound, drawn, molded, or blown (Kidd 1978). While there were variations on these methods, or additional modifications that beads may underwent following initial production, these four techniques account for all glass beads.

Wound glass beads are produced by heating glass to a workable state and then wrapping thin strands of hot glass around a flux-covered wire. The flux allows the bead to be removed from the wire, which forms the hole. Drawn glass beads start with a piece of hot glass (or gather) on the end of a blow tube. A small bubble of air is blown into the glass. A second pontil is attached to the gather, and it is stretched to create a long hollow tube, beads are made from the cut or broken tube. The resulting beads may be tumbled to smooth their edges. Molding can be accomplished by pressing hot glass into molds, with needles used to pierce holes through the hot glass. Blown glass beads are made individually over a hot lamp that brings the glass to a malleable state for shaping.

The Czech Operational Chain

The Czech glass bead strands involved the most steps (Figure 6.1). In looking at our chains, I have greatly simplified the steps. A single strand may include molded, wound, drawn, and

Figure 6.1. Operational chains for production of hand-strung glass beads, hand-strung plastic beads, and MOS beads.

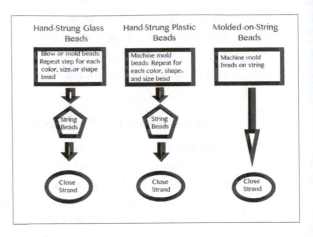

blown beads. Each of these has a different manufacturing step associated with it. Glass beads of different colors are made in different manufacturing episodes. Most strands contained at least four different colors of beads and no fewer than four bead shapes, with some containing as many as 10 different bead shapes. This means that a strand of beads could represent a minimum of four different production processes (one for each bead shape and or color) Therefore, multiple production steps had occurred before the beads ever came to be strung. To illustrate this, look at the bead strand illustrated in Figure 6.2. When you account for all the bead types and colors represented in this strand, there are nine different beads representing nine different episodes of glass preparation and blowing to make all the beads in the necklace.

With the exception of the beads recovered from immediately after the end of World War II, all of the Czech bead strands have metal clasps. The production of these represents another step in the operational chain that must be completed before stringing. The creation of the string is another process. Czechoslovakian glass beads dominated Mardi Gras from about 1918 until 1938 when the ethnic Germans who dominated the glass-blowing industry in the country were forced out as part of an ethnic cleansing by the Czech government (Kirschbaum 2006. Beads were produced at the household level with machines and molds owned by individual families (Stepanek 1922). The glass strands during this time period exhibit a lot of diversity and creativity with many playful bead shapes, such as elephants, peanuts, shoes, and children appearing in addition to

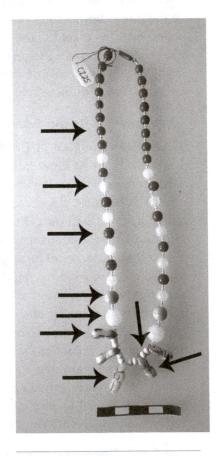

Figure 6.2. Example of Czechoslovakian glass strand. Photograph by Alexandra Wilkie Farnsworth.

traditional round and cone-, oval-, and tube-shaped beads. Most strands were strung to have from three to seven large beads adorn the bottom of the strand (Figure 6.3). I originally thought this was primarily an aesthetic attribute of the strand.

The beads were strung by making a double hitch around the finding (the clasp). After stringing the beads, the string was doubled back through the beads, and the strand was tied off about an inch from the finding. This allowed the strand to be tightly tied, which also ensured that strand was stronger than if a single strand was used. This technique, while resulting in a stronger strand, required the attentive counting of the beads and attention to bead size during stringing to ensure symmetry.

Home-based industries provided beads to suppliers who negotiated global contracts. Samplers from Czechoslovakia traveled to potential markets to develop products tailored to the needs of each market (Jargstorf 1997). After the World War II, the Czech glass industry was in chaos, and Occupied Japan became a source of beads. It was not until 1958 that the Communist government of Czechoslovakia decided to revitalize the glass industry. Production was still essentially done at the household level, but now all beads had to be channeled through a single global supplier—the Czech state-created Jablonex company. All Czech beads distributed during this time had to have a Jablonex tag on them. Thereafter, in contrast to the earlier Czech beads, there is little diversity in the shapes of beads found in the strands, and only one stringing pattern is found. There are never more than three different bead types represented in the post-war Jablonex bead

Figure 6.3. Stringing patterns with heavier beads strung at bottom of the strand. Photograph by Alexandra Wilkie Farnsworth.

strands, representing a reduction in the number of steps necessary to make the bead strands. As we will see, this brings the Czech bead industry in line with the other glass bead manufacturers now competing for the global market. Therefore, we can see in the material culture record the impacts of the Czech government's control over the industry, as well as the impacts of economic competition.

German Glass Bead Chain of Operations

The only examples of German glass Mardi Gras beads were recovered from the 1947 assemblage. Those made in "Occupied Germany US zone" are all molded beads. The beads are no more than two different sizes, and no more than two different colors are found in any strand unlike the more ornate Czech strands made at the household level that could include nine different operational steps to make the beads for the strand. The German strands exhibit no more than three steps for individual bead production. Like the Czech beads, the strands have clasps and were tied off an inch from the clasp. The ethnically German, Czech refugee bead makers settled in an area they named Neu Gablontz after the former glass bead capital of what had been known as Bohemia. The technologies were, therefore, identical in both places. The German beads are examples of minimalist Mardi Gras strands with basic round and oval shapes and white and green glass as the only colors represented. As was the case with the Czech beads, the German beads were strung to have several large beads suspended at the bottom of the strand.

Japanese Glass Bead Operational Chain

While the Czech and German glass industries were historically linked, Japan had its own history of glass working. Beads made in Occupied Japan are monochromatic, round, and mold-blown glass beads that represent just one operational step for production. After the end of occupation, the Japanese beads continued to be mold blown, but started to include long drawn, or cane, beads. Colors were limited to amber, green, blue, or clear with some of the clear beads metalized to appear gold or silver. With the post-occupation Japanese beads, it is more common for each strand to include three, and sometimes four, different bead types representing more of operational steps. The appearance of gold could be achieved by blowing silver nitrate into amber colored beads (Francis 1999). The Japanese strands are the longest of the beads and have no clasp. Beads were tied off at the bottom to form a tassel that dangled at the end of the strand (Figure 6.3). The lack of clasp increased strand length but would have reduced the time and skill necessary to string the beads and made it easier to achieve symmetrical designs.

Indian Beads Chain of Operation

Indian Mardi Gras glass beads were molded or wound. With the exception of being manufactured out of Indian glass (which has a very high gloss), they are identical to the Czech and German beads—with good reason. Following World War II, a number of German glass-bead makers relocated factories, including molds, to India due to the presence of cheap labor in that newly independent nation (Francis 1999). The Indian strands have clasps, but the strands are tied off on the clasp. This reduces strand strength but would, as in the case of the Japanese beads, require less skilled labor. The Indian beads rarely achieve symmetry in stringing. The Indian strands normally had no more than two or three different beads in a strand, but also followed the style of often having larger beads at the bottom of the strand seen in all the other manufacturers. Indian beads seem to have been popularly thrown in the late 1960s and early 1970s as glass beads were being

Figure 6.4. Example of modern Indian glass Mardi Gras strand. Photograph by Alexandra Wilkie Farnsworth.

pushed out of Mardi Gras. More recently, glass Indian beads have been reintroduced in small numbers (Figure 6.4). These beads are lamp wound and drawn, and typically only two shapes are represented. The small seed beads that make up most of the strands are multi-colored. These newer beads have no clasp and are long enough to easily fit over a person's head. Despite being longer, the strands are delicate and light compared to the older Indian Mardi Gras beads.

In the Mardi Gras glass bead assemblages, we see two of the markets attempting to imitate the technology and aesthetic of the original Czech Mardi Gras beads. Imitation is said to be the sincerest form of flattery, and if that is so, we see a lot of flattery in the archaeological record. British colonial period sites throughout the world dating to the late eighteenth and early nineteenth centuries are covered with English attempts to flatter the Chinese. The English potteries created a blue-green glaze to decorate their earthenwares to make them the color of the highly desirable Chinese porcelains. They also used blue hand-painting and transfer-printed patterns to imitate the decorative styles and motifs found on Chinese ceramics (Noel Hume 1969). Some English companies even put "Chinese" maker marks on the back of their plates to make them seem like authentic imports. Archaeologists have found examples of similar processes taking place in the ancient Classical world. For instance, in the ancient Aegean, many societies imitated the pottery decorative styles of Crete (Knappett and Nikolako poulou in press). We see in the Mardi Gras beads another kind of emulation happening—as plastic beads come to be more commonly produced, the manufacturers of these items attempted to make them look like glass beads.

A Different Chain of Operation: Manufacturing Plastic Beads

The introduction of plastic beads represents a shift in technology resulting in a very different set of operational chains. Plastics are broadly defined as materials that are softened by heat and set into lasting form when shaped into a mold (Katz 1984). They may be made of natural materials, such as amber, horn, or shellac. They can also be made from semi-synthetic material, such as celluloid, which is formulated out of cellulose from plants, or fully synthetic substances, such as those that are created out of coal or oil. All plastics can be separated into two main categories: thermosets and thermoplastics (Beck 1980:2). Thermosets undergo permanent transformations during heating, or vulcanization. Once they are heated, they are permanently shaped. Thermoplastics are heat sensitive but solid at room temperature. A thermoplastic can be reheated and reformed; recyclable plastics are all thermoplastics. Mardi Gras beads are thermoplastics.

There are literally hundreds of different plastics, and it can be very difficult to distinguish between different types. The hand-strung beads and the early MOS beads appear to be examples of polystyrene, which is a rigid, hard thermoplastic with a high surface gloss that is naturally clear, but can be colored to be opaque or different translucent colors. Polystyrene is one of the cheapest available and can be pigmented with an endless number of colors. It can be either injection molded or mold blown (Beck 1980). The MOS beads that have metallic finishes, on the other hand, seem to be polyethylene—another inexpensive plastic. The most common means of forming plastic beads are injection molding and mold blowing. Injection molding involves the forming or molding of plastics from powdered or granular thermoplastic materials. The plastic materials are heated and then forced by a ramrod or vacuum into a mold where the plastics undergo pressure, are cooled, and when sufficiently set, removed from the mold (Beck 1980:41). Injection-mold machines were experimented with as early as the late nineteenth-century, but the first fully automatic injection-mold machines were patented in 1937. The MOS beads are injection-molded, as are many of the beads that are hand-strung. A method for molding and mechanically cutting multiple plastic beads simultaneously was developed in 1942 and patented in 1946 by J. Casalino (US Patent 2,392,459).

Mold-blown plastics are hollow in shape, and this is the technique used to create vessels like bottles and jars. The earliest patent for this process was granted to William Kopitke, May 16, 1944 (US Patent 2,349,177). His invention led to the ability to make seamless large beads used on some hand-strung strands. Importantly for Mardi Gras beads, the process that allows for large numbers of beads to be colored, metalized, or pearlized at one time was developed in 1962 and patented July 20, 1965 (US Patent 3,196,064) by Phillip Tell of Orange, NJ. A review of US patents shows that the technology necessary to make individual plastic beads was in existence before World War II. In the United States, with the coming of the war, all non-military uses of plastic were suspended. It would not be until the 1950s that plastic throw beads would first become possible for use in Mardi Gras. Review of documents related to Mardi Gras, however, suggest that plastic beads were not prevalent at Mardi Gras until the late 1960s and early 1970s.

The plastic beads, manufactured and strung primarily in Hong Kong, were designed to look like the shapes, colors, and finishes of glass beads. The ease with which large numbers of beads could be produced at a time, with minimal labor supervision, meant that strands could have a larger diversity of bead types in a strand. Stringing was still done by hand. Originally, clasps were made of white metal, but in time, a variety of different

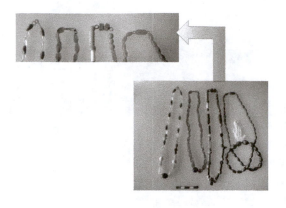

Figure 6.5. Examples of clasps used on plastic hand-strung Mardi Gras beads. Photograph by Alexandra Wilkie Farnsworth.

plastic clasps were used (Figure 6.5). The plastic bead stringers followed the technique used by the Czechs and Germans and tied the strand off about an inch from the clasp. The strands I have encountered are all perfectly symmetrical. The plastic hand-strung beads also feature larger beads at the end of the strand.

Chinese Hand-Strung Plastic Beads

Since at least 1990, Chinese hand-strung plastic beads have become some of the most coveted bead throws; they can cost $5.00 per strand. The Chinese hand-strung beads are symmetrical and tied off using a metal tab that closes over the knot. The strands are generally 33" and longer and feature both large plastic and hand-painted resin beads. These are usually handed, rather than thrown, to parade goers due to their fragility and tendency to break easily, hurling beads in every direction. The beads often have humorous, regional, or Carnival themes, and it is common to see strands fea-

Figure 6.6. Example of modern, hand-strung, Chinese "fancy" Mardi Gras beads. Photograph by Alexandra Wilkie Farnsworth.

turing rubber duckies, oysters, crawfish, shrimp, pirates, princesses, Mardi Gras masks, king cakes, or bare breasts (see examples of these bead types in Figure 6.6).

MOS Operational Chains:
Collapsing Bead Manufacturing and Stringing in One Step

In contrast to the complicated steps required in the processes described above, the MOS beads require no craft skills to string. Instead, unskilled laborers feeds string through the machines, cuts them to the appropriate lengths, and seal them using a plastic tube closure, melting bead ends together (Figure 6.7) or connecting the ends of the strand together with an embedded hot wire. The basic technology for MOS bead manufacture was developed in the early 1970s and patented in 1981. Levine Irving of Calabassas, CA, submitted a patent for "Apparatus for molding strand-mounded plastic members" October 1, 1973. The proposed machine would mount thermoplastic materials directly upon a string medium using a bifurcated mold. Irving explicitly stated that he saw his apparatus's main application to be molding decorative beads.

Figure 6.7. MOS closures and multi-component strands. Photograph by Alexandra Wilkie Farnsworth.

By 1975 MOS beads were part of Mardi Gras celebrations. Our dated Bacchus medallion from our stylistic seriation in chapter three is the earliest, definitively dated MOS bead in the assemblage. It also demonstrates that MOS beads were appearing in Mardi Gras soon after Irving's patent was applied for but long before the patent was approved in 1981 (US Patent 4,295,813).

Based on observation, the early MOS beads were molded in a single mold plate. They had two finished ends that were slightly smaller beads on long necks. These were designed to fit into a polyethylene (same plastic as Tupperware) tube so that it could be opened and closed to fit around a neck. These bead strands were quite short in length—from 14 to 18″ when opened. Strands with finished ends do not appear to be longer than 24″. After that length, the length of the strand is wider than the mold plate that produces them. Therefore, the strand is left uncut and moved to mold the next section. I have recovered 24″ strands that are clearly from a 12″ mold but left uncut and with a duplicate set of clasp beads appearing in the middle of the strand.

Most manufacturers, however, when manufacturing longer strands, used molds that had no clasp beads. The resulting strands would look uniform and could be cut to any desired length. The problem was how to close them. The claspless Hong Kong MOS beads were fused shut by melting the ends of the strand together. This was not a particularly satisfying solution, for beads closed this way break easily. The 1975–1981 Bacchus medallions all feature strands that were melted closed, and in 1979, 1980, and 1981, medallions were fused onto strands through melting. If there was any finish added to the bead, such as a pearl or metallic coat, the melted ends would disrupt the appearance of the strand by adding a black melted section. The more secure solution was to heat a wire and insert it into the two beads that ended the strand (Figure 6.7). These are much easier to repair and are stronger.

Starting in 2004, we see the introduction of a new variation on MOS beads. Krewes like Bacchus and Thoth, have begun to have krewe-specific MOS molds designed. Thoth used a repeating pattern that could be molded to any length Bacchus strands, however, attempted to reproduce the look of medallion throw beads; except the Bacchus medallions were molded directly on the strings. The portion of the strand featuring the medallions was molded on one plate, and the strands were made longer by adding a length of plain round beads. The MOS krewe beads allow the organization to throw a greater number of theme beads. By using the same mold each year, the krewe can ultimately reduce costs.

Krewes have not abandoned year-specific beads; however, they are still throwing resin-based medallions that are cheaper to produce in small batches and that feature the year's parade theme.

Molded-on-string beads have a very different appearance and characteristics than the beads that preceded them. All previous beads, with the exception of the examples from Occupied Japan, were multi-colored. Molded-on-string beads are monochromatic. Multiple colors can only be achieved on MOS beads by either twisting multiple strands of MOS beads together or by fusing sections of different colored strands together. In addition, while multiple different shapes are possible on MOS beads, the majority of strands only feature one or two unique shapes on a strand. Glass beads used on Mardi Gras strands tended to be of a relatively small size and typically no wider than 0.5 or 0.6 mm. To create a larger glass bead required greater materials and labor expenditure. To mold a larger plastic bead required more materials, not labor.

What Changes Due to Technology

The switch to MOS beads was not just a technological shift, but also had a profound effect on the appearance of the throwing game. Consider this quote in which New Orleans' native, Sandra Paluzzi, describes her memories of Mardi Gras beads:

My hometown is New Orleans. In fact it is because of Mardi Gras that I gained a love of beads and started collecting over 45 years ago. One of the things most people assume is that the 'throws,' i.e. beads, doubloons, and trinkets, have always been cheap plastic. All the way back to the early part of the century and in the 1950s when I began going to the parades the beads were made from glass and came mostly from Czech sources and then from Japan. Any type of bead you can imagine were thrown, from fragile mercury bugles and hollow rounds to flower, animal, and geometric shapes. Some necklaces were more ornate and balanced while some looked like floor sweeps strung randomly of mostly pressed beads ... The first plastic beads were strung and some were just as intriguing as their glass counterparts. (Paluzzi, "Mardi Gras Beads")

Ms. Paluzzi's quote emphasizes the visual diversity of the beads, be they hand-strung glass or plastic. Note that she doesn't describe beads as being of different lengths. Just as forging larger beads required a different labor investment for glassworkers, changing the length of a hand-strung strand of beads has labor implications as well. When we look at the average length of beads by geographic origin (Table 6.2.), we can observe an interesting trend: size remains consistent across space and averages about 16 or 17" in length for necklaces with clasps and about 22" for necklaces without clasps. Given that Czech beads were thrown as early as the 1920s, and the latest beads in the curated study sample date to the 1980s, that is a remarkable degree of consistency. For the assemblage of 889 beads, almost all of which were MOS beads manufactured in China and acquired at parades from 1991 to 1994, the average length of a strand of beads was calculated at 21.7", with the range

Table 6.2. Average Strand Length by Type.

PLACE OF ORIGIN	TYPE OF BEAD STRAND	AVERAGE STRAND LENGTH (in)
Czechoslovakian	Hand-strung with clasp	16.6
Czechoslovakian	Hand-strung no clasp	26 *
Occupied Japan	Hand-strung no clasp	21
Japanese	Hand-strung no clasp	22.1
Occupied West Germany	Hand-strung with clasp	16
India	Hand-strung with clasp	17.1
Hong Kong	Hand-strung with metal clasp	17
Hong Kong	Hand-strung with plastic loop clasp	18
Hong Kong	Hand-strung with square pop bead	16
Hong Kong	Hand-strung with oval pop bead	17.1
Hong Kong	MOS with plastic tube clasp	16
Hong Kong	MOS rice bead with added bead no clasp	22
Hong Kong	MOS rice bead with no clasp	22
1991–1994 Mardi Gras Assemblage	Plastic MOS beads	21.7 average

*(longer length to fit over head)

being from 15 to 48″. The median length was 18″. Again, remarkable consistency is evident in bead length. This quickly changes in the 1990s and after. The average strand length thrown in New Orleans in 2010 had grown to 43.66″, double the length of those thrown only 15 years earlier. This is an example of what Ford would have called drift within a type; yet, in this case, there is clearly drift toward longer and wider beads.

So there are two questions here. First, why was there continuity in bead length for so long. And second, why did it suddenly change? We'll be coming back to these questions shortly.

Our Chaînes Opertoire in Summation

When I first started working with the curated beads, I expected that my chaînes opertoire would demonstrate that more finely strung beads were older and that the asymmetrical strands were more recently manufactured. In part, this notion was based on archaeological work in California on the shell-bead manufacturing industry among Native Californians during the Mission Period (1790–1821). Archaeologists have demonstrated that the Spanish introduction of glass beads into Native trade networks led to inflation in the indigenous bead market, which then led to a rapid decline in bead quality. What were once beautifully shaped and ground olivella shell beads evolved into quickly split-in-half shells with crass holes punched through them (Heizer 1978). I wondered if a similar process was taking place with glass bead stringing as more competitors entered the Mardi Gras market. I hypothesized that as more necklace makers competed to fill the demand for Mardi Gras beads, there would be fewer skilled workers entering the labor pool, and management would have less interest in quality control. Instead, the operational chain analysis shows a slightly different process.

First, in our earliest bead manufacture, we see all of the work of bead making—the making of the beads and the stringing them—based in individual households who were tied to the global market. These early bead strands contained a variety of bead shapes, colors, and creativity in their stringing. Through time, we see smaller numbers of bead colors and shapes in the individual strands, which would reduce labor time invested in the manufacture of the beads, and would simplify the stringing process (less complicated designs). Some manufacturers further simplified the stringing process by eliminating clasps or changing the way the string was attached to the clasp.

With the introduction of machine-made plastic beads, we see a shift from house-based manufacture to factory-based manufacture. The skilled labor necessary to design and build the machinery used in the factory setting is located in a geographically different location. This reduced the number of skilled laborers involved in bead production while increasing the number of beads made at a time. Skilled labor was involved in the stringing of these beads, which rivaled the oldest Czech glass beads in symmetry and complexity of stringing pattern.

All skilled labor was removed from the manufacturing process with the introduction of MOS beads. Unlike the original house-based industries of the Czech glass makers, where all skilled labor was necessary for the entire process of bead production and stringing, no skilled labor is required on-site for the factory, fully mechanized production of the MOS beads. The introduction of this technology is accompanied by a reorganization of labor spatially and in their skill levels. Hopefully, you can see how there would be archaeological implications if we were to attempt to physically excavate sites concerned with bead manufacturing. For the Czech sites, we could excavate sites where the beads were made and strung. To study the later period, we would be looking at how technologies developed in the United States (as indicated by the patent histories) were used in factory production in Hong Kong and China. This is no different than the dilemma of lithics specialists who need to study the quarry sites where obsidian is mined and shaped into blanks, and the sites where the blanks are fashioned into finished tools (e.g., Shackley 2005).

Impacts of Technology Change

We have now spent some time discussing the "whats" of how archaeologists think about technology, but you may be wondering about the "whys." Why do archaeologists care so much about how something is made, and why does it matter if the way something is made changes? New ways of making things may require labor be divided up between different tasks. In nineteenth-century British pottery businesses, the creation of high-fired ceramics on an industrial level required a number of different specialized craftsman working together in the factory. The people who spun the pots, the people who ran the kilns, the people who decorated the ceramics, and the people who packed the goods for the global market, are just a few examples of the *task differentiation* that took place within the manufacturing of pottery. This is different from ceramic production seen in many small-scale societies in which a single person may find the clay, form the pots, build a fire, and fire the pots in their household area.

Remember that Lewis Binford urged archaeologists to search for universal laws of cultural change? Processual archaeology was influenced by evolution-minded anthropologists who were interested in understanding the development of social complexity. In evolutionary thinking, any change in an organism is an adaptation reacting to forces of natural selection. In archaeology today, there are two fields of the discipline that have developed from processual archaeology's generalized neo-evolutionary roots, *evolutionary archaeology* or *selectionist archaeology,* and human behavioral ecology. Each of these subdisciplines are concerned with understanding human technologies for the roles they play in cultural change.

Evolutionary Archaeology

Evolutionary archaeologists think of each human society as a form of organism. In biology, each living thing has a genotype—its actual DNA code—and a phenotype, the physical manifestation of that code. Evolutionary archaeologists see the material culture of a society as its phenotype. Therefore, all archaeological traces of a society are traces of its phenotype. Evolutionary archaeologists focus on artifacts as the phenotypic expression of human populations, which are or are not affected by forces of selection. Changes in the appearance/traits, frequency, or types of artifacts that make up a phenotype are typically seen as evidence of forces of selection acting on the population; whereas continuity in artifact traits is seen as most likely the absence of selective pressures (O'Brien and Lyman 2000). A shift in material culture, under this model of thinking, represents an underlying shift in the cultural genotype and, therefore, is an evolutionary change. Since changes in genotype happen as a result of either mutation or natural selection, evolutionary archaeologists see change in material culture as evidence of evolutionary adaptation. Therefore, in their minds, if technology shifted, then there was an evolutionary reason.

Evolutionary archaeologists see their enterprise as having two parts. The first is to construct a lineage of the artifacts to demonstrate which are related through a line of heritability from one to another (in other words, which artifacts arose from which artifacts). The second is to identify the mechanisms that led to change. The typological tool that the selectionists use is *cladistics,* which is drawn from biology. Cladistics is a system of classification based on the proportion of measurable characteristics that traits have in common.

Evolutionary archaeology is popular in North America and highly controversial. Some outsiders to the subdiscipline see it as taking all of the anthropology out of archaeology, because people are no longer the main focus of study, and because all of human life is seen in biological evolutionary terms. For those who practice evolutionary archaeology, they see themselves as being the only archaeologists who still hold the mantle of science in the field. Its development as a field was certainly, in part, a reaction to the perceived marshmallowy-soft nature of the more post-modern of post-processual archaeologies. Evolutionary archaeology is self-defined as a science of the archaeological record. The selectionists have argued that they focus on understanding macroscalar processes of evolutionary selection, but that the work of behavioral ecologists is compatible with their work, as they focus on microscalar interpretations (O'Brien and Lyman 2000; Winterhalder and Smith 1981) and are therefore compatible. We'll talk more about human behavioral ecology (which you were introduced to in our ethnographic analogy in chapter four) shortly.

The Evolutionary Archaeology of Mardi Gras

On the surface, it would seem that Mardi Gras beads have no place in the world of evolutionary archaeology, but selectionists would argue that forces of evolution continue to operate on us in the present. Therefore, it is completely valid to apply this theorizing to contemporary assemblages. As artifacts, the beads have to be part of the phenotype of Louisianans. In creating our review of bead technology, we have created the sort of artifact lineage that is the basis of evolutionary archaeological interpretation. We have failed, however, by talking in terms of types. Let us consider what would happen if we thought of the changes in the beads through time in terms of cladistics (Figure 6.8).

In terms of attributes, in chapter three, we used place of origin as one of the major organizing principles of the typology. I used this attribute because it is part of the historical context in which the beads were created. This is not an attribute inherent in the phenotype of the artifact, however. If we focus only on physical attributes, it leaves us with a slightly different-looking classification—one that is clearly based on technological attributes. The most noticeable differences between the beads are what they are made of (glass or plastic) and how they were strung together (by hand or by machine). By focusing on the physical attributes, we are left with a classification that has only three categories: hand-strung glass beads, which gave rise to hand-strung plastic beads, which gave rise to MOS plastic beads (Figure 6.8). In this classification, we clearly see the technological

Cladogram Describing Evolution of Mardi Gras Beads

Plastic Beads

MOS

Hand-Strung Glass Beads

Hand-Strung Plastic Beads

Figure 6.8. Cladogram for evolution of Mardi Gras beads.

innovations and changes in bead manufacturing taking center stage. An evolutionary archaeology doesn't have to focus on technological traits; they just happen to be the physical features that emerged in our study, and incidentally, why I'm discussing them in this chapter!

The next step, according to O'Brien and Lyman (2000), is to identify and describe the factors that led to these traits being selected for. In the parlance of evolutionary archaeology, any traits that disappear were not selected for, and therefore not adaptive. Whereas, any traits that continue and are elaborated upon were selected for and adaptive. So, if we look at this cladogram as a function of time, we can see that all three of these types still exist. However, while glass hand-strung beads were once the most abundant, they were replaced in significance by hand-strung plastic beads, which in turn, were not as adaptive as the MOS beads. The hand-strung plastic and hand-strung glass beads, by still existing in the population of Mardi Gras beads, must have some sort of enduring selective advantage. If we had archaeological information for a broader expanse of time, we would be able to construct frequency seriations for comparing the relative abundance of glass hand-strung beads versus plastic hand-strung beads versus plastic MOS beads through time to demonstrate their changing popularity. And in fact, selectionist archaeology makes use of frequency seriation in exactly this way (e.g., O'Brien et al. 2000).

From ethnoarchaeological research, we know that hand-strung and glass beads have higher prestige in Mardi Gras interactions, thus explaining their continuing evolutionary advantage and endurance. Within the MOS population, we can see drift within the type toward larger beads. It would seem from this analysis that the change to a technology that allowed for the beads to be manufactured directly on the string was adaptively advantageous. We can see how in this kind of analysis, technology, which our culture defines as "adaptive" becomes an important prime mover in Darwinian evolutionary archaeological interpretations. So to this point, I think we've managed to create an understanding of the beads that is true to the intentions of evolutionary archaeology. We described the cladogram in evolutionary terms, but we haven't yet identified the mechanisms that triggered these changes.

Have we learned anything new about the beads by taking an evolutionary archaeology approach? Perhaps not, but the framework does provide archaeologists with a structure for organizing their data. The framework does not, however, contribute much to the explanatory enterprise of our archaeological project. The larger explanation provided by evolutionary archaeology—that natural selection drives change—doesn't actually help with understanding the specific cultural-historical contextual mechanisms that triggered those changes.

I am, personally, not an evolutionary archaeologist because I have always been more interested in *microscalar* (small groups of people over short periods of time) levels of archaeological investigation rather than the *macroscalar* (large populations over large periods of time). The Mardi Gras study encompasses a very short period of time archaeologically speaking—20 years of excavated evidence and 100 years of curated collections—not a period of time best suited to the evolutionary scale of analysis favored by selectionist archaeology. A different field of evolutionary-influenced archaeological thought focuses more on the microscale.

Human Behavioral Ecology

I started my graduate career as a human behavioral ecologist, though that is a title for the field that came later. At the time, I was interested in applying the ideas from *optimal foraging theory* to understanding the relationships between complex hunter-gatherer societies and their environment in Southern California from 2000 BP until contact in the 1500s. California is a particularly exciting place to study hunter-gatherer lifeways, and optimal foraging theories were seen at the time as an important tool for understanding them.

Hunter-gatherer populations make a living by harvesting naturally occurring resources from the environment and taking advantage of different foodstuffs available throughout the year. To be a hunter-gatherer requires a broad understanding of many, many different plant and animal species, where and when they can be found, and how to most effectively harvest them. Hunter-gatherers usually have to be mobile, moving from one location to another on a seasonal cycle, perhaps settling down in larger groups during some parts of the year when a particularly rich resource is available.

In California, oak trees provide a calorically rich and seasonally abundant resource that became a staple for many Native California groups: the acorn. In particularly abundant years, Native Californians could gather enough acorns to feed their families for several years (Heizer 1978). This meant that prehistoric Californians were hunter-gatherers who could become *sedentary*, living in permanent villages year round, and send out smaller groups of people to specialized harvest sites to procure other animal and plant resources seasonally. But oak trees weren't the only rich resource available to Native Californian peoples. The Pacific provided a wealth of foodstuffs along the coasts and in the waters. Abalone, clams, and mussels could be recovered from the shore and shallow waters, and tuna, sharks, rays, halibut, and rock fish swam in the oceans along with sea mammals like harbor seals, sea lions, sea otters, dolphins, and whales. Plenty of calories were available as long as a community had the right knowledge and means.

One narrative (and as we continue through this book, I'm going to reiterate again and again that there can be multiple, complementary narratives to explain what happened at any archaeological site) to understand California's prehistory is that of a number of tribes who successfully learned to take more and more energy from their natural environment over time, which allowed them to support ever-growing populations. The process of getting more and more energy from the available environment is referred to as *intensification*. Intensification is always accompanied by changes in technology. When people live in one spot, it also gives them the opportunity to invest more time in the places where they live and work. When a community can procure enough food to feed itself for some period into the future, it also gives them time to develop other pastimes: art, leisure, or perhaps other kinds of economic labors—such as specializing in a particular industry.

Jeanne Arnold (1987), working in the Channel Islands off the coast of California, has archaeologically documented the development of a shell-bead industry on the islands. The beads were traded to the mainland for other goods, such as deer meat, obsidian, and other goods. Groups on the mainland also harvested obsidian, chert, and other stones for trade. Tool blanks were quickly flaked at quarry sites and traded to other people who would finish the tools. When a village or society focuses on developing a particular industry above all others, it is known as craft specialization. Together, craft specialization, sedentism, subsistence resource intensification, and the development of social organizations to regulate the administrative challenges of coordinating labor, trade, and community living are all recognized as part and parcel of humans developing *social complexity*.

The settlement of the Channel Islands and the exploitation of their rich resource base was only possible through an important technological development: the ocean-going plank canoe (Arnold 2007) The ocean-going canoe was a technology that could be developed, in part, exactly because coastal California hunter-gatherers had time left after they had fed themselves to experiment with new ways to do things. The site I was studying was an inland village that was engaged in trade with coastal and island groups. The village residents provided deer meat and probably plant foods, in exchange for marine fish, shellfish, and shell beads.

As you can see from my brief discussion of prehistoric California, understanding subsistence systems is essential to understanding how societies develop from small, simply organized communities, to large, complexly organized ones. Understanding the technomic realm of technology and subsistence was one of the immediate goals set by Binford for processual archaeology. *Human behavioral ecology* (HBE), the other archaeological school of thought that influenced by ideas of evolutionary processes of adaptation and developed to address questions surrounding the relationships between people and the environment. Human behavioral ecology typically focuses on understanding strategies of resource acquisition, like the Bird and Bird (2000) case study discussed earlier and the social impacts that arise from those strategies. Technology plays heavily into these kinds of interpretations; technology is a means through which productivity can be increased. Human behavioral ecology draws its theorizing from ideas developed by animal population biologists in the field of *sociobiology*. E. O. Wilson developed by this line of thinking in the 1970s (Wilson 1975).

Sociobiologists focus on understanding how we can see evolutionary forces at play in present-day populations. Evolution is ultimately about natural selection, the processes through which particular genes become more represented in a population than others. This change in gene representation is ultimately achieved through differential reproduction—some creatures have more surviving offspring than others. So, while the end effect of natural selection is seen at the population level, it is dependent upon the all the organisms within that population trying to have as many babies as possible—or at least having as much sex as possible. And to have a lot of sex requires time to pursue sex, which means you, I mean an organism, has to take care of all those other tasks that are required to support itself, like eating, drinking, and sleeping. If an organism is able to do those things efficiently, then they have more time to pursue reproduction; those that are most efficient have the most time to pursue reproduction. Therefore, within sociobiology, a body of research developed that studies how animals work to most effectively get their food from the environment. The goal is to achieve the most calories in the least amount of time. The resulting bodies of theory that models food-getting strategies are called optimal foraging theory, and it is used a great deal in HBE archaeology to look at how human societies organize their time, labor, and technology in food acquisition.

Now, it may be that some of you are considering this self-reflexively and thinking, wait a minute, getting more time to pursue more sex is not the same thing as getting more sex! And you would be absolutely right; there are other things that need to happen. You need to find a potentially willing partner, convince that partner that you would be a good contributor to the genetic pool, and make sure that you win out over others who are offering their genetic material to the partner before you actually get to reproduce. You know, a typical night at the bar scene? These are part of the social aspects of sociobiology.

Sociobiology recognizes that animal societies have practices or behaviors that serve to sort out the best genetic contributor from the lesser genetic contributors. They have social systems that ensure the biggest, strongest, and most ferocious get to reproduce if that ensures the healthiest offspring; or, the gentlest, smartest, most nurturing get to reproduce if that is what is best for the population. There is no "consciousness" on the population level but just a bunch of competing strategies toward reproduction that coexist at any moment of time in a population. Only time will tell which strategy is most successful evolutionarily speaking. And at any time, circumstances in the environment may shift to favor one strategy over another.

Suppose you have an organism that lives in a resource rich environment that allows females to raise and support offspring without help from a mate. In such circumstances, the best interest of the male is to impregnate as many females as possible without investing any additional time or energy to raising those offspring and to ensure his maximum reproductive success. Therefore, in such a system, females would select among potential mates for the biggest, strongest, healthiest male to impregnate her to ensure her offspring are likely to be healthy and not require additional help to raise. In such a social system, you get the emergence of alpha males who have more access to mates than other males. Suppose the environment shifts, however, and all of a sudden, resources are scarce and to successfully raise offspring requires the work of both mother and father? All of a sudden, the males whose reproductive strategies focus on monogamy and contributing to the rearing of a smaller number of offspring becomes more reproductively successful than the alpha male whose male offspring are dying before adulthood because they are off spending their time chasing sex partners.

Incidentally, are you recognizing any of these ideas from pop culture? There has been a lot of discussion on dating sites about alpha males and beta males and which are better to date, as well as lots of sites telling men how they can be an alpha. All of these are examples of appropriations of sociobiological thought in popular culture. See? You can learn many things from archaeology. The alpha male/beta male talk relevant to human dating arises from the fact that many primate societies have social systems with troops where an alpha male lives with multiple females that bear his offspring. Research has shown that in some baboon species, for instance, beta males—the less aggressive males—can be sexually successful by secretly wooing and helping the neglected female members of a troop until some of them decide to leave their alpha to set up house with the beta (who becomes an alpha). Typically, the Internet sites intended for men tout the importance of being an alpha male, while the women's sites are advocating that women seek beta males for long-term relationships. For members of the Lesbian-Gay-Bisexual-Transgender (LGBT) community among my readers, you'll know that different shades of sociobiology have infiltrated your dating scene as well.

My intent is not to provide a complete discussion and overview of sociobiology. However, a lot of archaeologists talk about and use ideas from sociobiological theory—like optimal foraging models—without acknowledging the underlying ideas about maximizing reproductive success that underlie the models or discussing whether that is part of the theoretical package that they are embracing when they use the models. The assumption underlying all of the foraging models is the notion that all animals seek to maximize the efficiency of their food gathering, and that people have the drive to be efficient in their labors. That innate drive to be efficient has to have a motivation, and the motivation supplied by sociobiologists is a sexual one.

You need to understand that for sociobiologists anything can be explained by the drive to have access to more sex. Altruism? Another strategy for getting access to more sexual partners! Pursuit of artistic endeavors? A means of consolidating social respect that can translate into more sexual partners. The shortcoming of applying sociobiological thought to human beings is that we often demonstrate a decided lack of commitment to efficiency, and despite sociobiology's protests to the contrary, we do, as a species, have interests that are not always easily translatable back to reproductive fitness. Still, it becomes an interesting archaeological question to see when humans choose to be efficient and rational, and when they do not. Foraging models have given us a means of evaluating the efficiency of human labors and technologies. We noted that for anthropologists, the notion of technology includes not just the material culture that is used to make things or extract resources, but also the knowledge about those subjects. This means that changes in labor organization to make certain tasks more efficient, a redesign of a tool, or a new way of engaging with resources in the environment can all be measures of technological change. You can imagine in each of these circumstances that changes in technology can have impacts on other parts of daily life in any given society.

So archaeologically speaking, what might technological efficiency look like? Archaeologists usually assume that people make rational decisions about where to live. Hunter-gatherers should make their camps in areas that are close to potable resources and adjacent to or very close to the resources that they are exploiting in a particular season. Agricultural societies are expected to live in locations that are situated amongst arable (farmable) lands with good access to water for human consumption and irrigation. Access to other resources, such as raw materials for pottery making, or sites for quarrying stones for tool production, may shape decision making about settlement location.

In chapter five, we talked about phenomenological approaches to understanding landscape. These developed as part of post-processualism. Processual archaeologists developed a different range of methods and analyses for studying how humans occupied and used a landscape through time. Collectively, these methods are known as *settlement pattern analysis,* and were influenced by methods for understanding space developed in the field of geography. These tools allow archaeologists not only to look at the relationships of individual sites to their immediate landscape, but to one another.

At the most basic level, archaeologists plot the locations of sites on a map and look at how sites are distributed relative to different kinds of soil types, vegetation types, topography, and access to water to look for patterning in site placement. Sites are usually classified by their use. Domestic sites are expected to be residential and have a wide range of day-to-day activities and technologies/artifact types associated with them. Specialized activity sites, such as a workshop (like a kiln or quarry site) or a seasonal short-term resource exploitation site (like a butchering or seed-grinding site), are expected to have a narrower range of specialized artifact types associated with them. For instance, a butchering site may include discarded scrapers (for hide preparation) or knife blades (for cutting the meatiest parts off of the bone). Also included in the range of site types may be ceremonially or ritually important sites, that have feasting or other functions.

To understand why a particular location may have been desirable for settlement, an archaeologist may do a *site catchment analysis.* A catchment area is the distance from a site that people may be reasonably expected to wander to utilize local resources. Based on vague ethnographic analysis, the original site catchments for hunter-gatherers were proposed to be 10 km, and 5 km for agriculturalists (Vita-Finzi and Higgs 1970). It takes about an hour to walk 5 km, and two hours to walk 10 km. The notion was that if people had to walk farther than that from a site, the community would be better off to just move their settlement. Some people do site catchment analyses by simply drawing a 5- or 10-km-circle around a site. Others take into account topography or other natural features of the landscape that may have increased travel times, and adjust their perimeters accordingly. Then they evaluate the landscape contained within using any available information that may shed light on the ancient environment. In the United States, the Department of Agriculture has created soil maps of the United States. Since certain plants need certain soil characteristics to thrive, it is possible to reconstruct the environment or the agricultural potential of the catchment area. Clays suitable for pottery production will also show up on soil maps. In terms of technology, site catchment analysis can be a useful

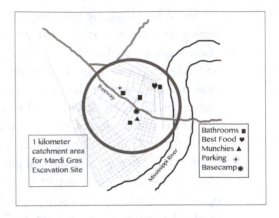

Figure 6.9. Site catchment for the Mardi Gras parade site selected for bead procurement.

tool for understanding what resources (raw materials, access to transportation, power, or suitable soils) may have influenced where a site was located.

I pondered site catchment analysis relative to the site that I selected for my Mardi Gras bead research. If I drew a catchment around my parade spot, what resources would we find that I had selected for? We discussed the pragmatic logistics of archaeological fieldwork a bit previously, but site catchment also provides a means of thinking about why individuals stake out particular routes of a Mardi Gras parade for spectating. The spot where I watched parades was one that I had committed to before I was engaged in this research—so clearly there were features of that landscape that drew me. I found that I was generally unwilling to walk beyond 1 km in any direction from the collection site (Figure 6.9). The car parking and bathroom was a half kilometer from my parade spot, and my favorite restaurant to get Shrimp Po-boys was within 1 km in the other direction. When one considers the crowds that fill New Orleans during Mardi Gras, the walking time between those spots is probably equivalent to the time it takes to walk 10 km anywhere else in the world. Perhaps you are amused that someone who engages in the irrational behavior of collecting and counting Mardi Gras beads behaves in a rational and predictable manner when it comes to choosing a settlement location.

It is also important to understand how different sites are related to one another on a landscape. Remember the sedentary California hunter-gatherers? By the time the Spanish missionaries rolled their way through what they called Alta California, the Native peoples of California settled along the coastal regions were living in permanent villages of over 1000 people. Connected to these villages were numerous satellite sites where plant gathering and processing, quarrying, and hunting took place. In the next chapter, I'll discuss central place theory, which is used to understand the economic relationships between these kinds of large and small sites, and other types of spatial analysis in archaeology that help us understand relationships between communities in regional settings. At this point, let's try to look at technological relationships between people and their environments and return our attention to what these archaeological notions might be able to tell us about Mardi Gras.

Foraging for Beads Part I:
Human Behavioral Ecology and Choosing Which Beads to Throw

So what insights can the ideas from HBE bring to our study of Mardi Gras? If we think of beads as a resource to be gathered, then we need to recognize that beads are acquired at least twice. First, those who throw them acquire them, and then they are actively foraged at parades by attendees. I'm going to first focus on those who throw the beads, since their initial set of decision-making processes affects the composition of the Mardi Gras assemblages. This is a bit of a flipping of the classical HBE study, in that, I'm interested in how maskers can most efficiently disperse a resource rather than gather it. However, I think a number of the same concerns are still in play. The thrower achieves prestige through the throwing of beads. Under an HBE model, they would want to do this in such a way that they get the most return for the least amount of investment of personal resources.

For modern societies, resources invested in bead acquisition would usually be thought of in terms of currency units. Human behavioral ecology usually thinks in terms of calorie investment. It is not unreasonable to think of currency as translatable to calories—each currency unit could be translated into the number of calories a laborer must burn in order to earn the currency necessary to acquire any good. For a lower-paid worker, each currency unit would require a higher caloric investment than that of a higher-paid worker. If we think about caloric investments, we should recognize that the calories expended to purchase beads are not the only calories at play. There are also the calories expended distributing the beads. Carrying, loading, and throwing the beads all take a calorie investment. Throwing greater numbers of heavier beads requires a greater calorie investment on the part of maskers.

Clearly there is a new set of attributes that may shape bead selection that should be considered in our analysis. There are the symbolic dimensions of value, aesthetics, and perception of worth, which may make one strand more desirable than another. The quote above from Ms. Paluzzi suggests that aesthetic principles shaped perceived value. In my experience, I didn't want to see my beads rejected, and I attempted in the second year to select beads I thought would be desirable. This part of the equation is difficult to measure calorically. However, more basic attributes also come to mind. Beads that are easier to carry and to throw will require a lower caloric investment. We need to consider, then, attributes related to design and weight that could affect distribution, otherwise known as throwing.

Mardi Gras beads are unusual necklaces in that they are not intended for wearing but for throwing. A Mardi Gras guide from 1987 (Hardy 1987), when MOS beads were still a relative newcomer, provides some interesting insights into form and function of beads. One rider indicated that he preferred the strands that had graduated beads (smaller toward the clasps and larger toward the middle) because they were easier to throw with the weight distributed that way. Another complained that the "rice" beads being introduced were too light to throw. I have seen packs of rice beads that have a heavy bead added to one end, presumably to improve throwing weight.

These observations intrigued me. Were certain beads actually designed as throw beads? Was the shape an adaptation to their use? I decided to experiment with tossing examples of the different bead types—yes, this is an example of experimental archaeology! I quickly established that the graduated beads were easier to throw—but only if you were throwing the beads as if they were a frisbee—with a sideways flick of the wrist (you can use this movement in an upward or outwards direction). The beads thrown today are much bigger than those of yesteryear, and to use a frisbee throw would be to risk hurting crowd members or even fellow riders. Today, as I described, strands of beads are gathered in a bundle in one's hand, and tossing is typically done overhand or underhand. But how was it done in the past?

Two testable questions occurred to me. First, is there any way to determine whether people threw beads differently in the past? And secondly, if they did, are there attributes of the earlier glass beads that facilitated throwing? To answer the first question, I went to that great archive that visually depicts the entirety of the human experience: YouTube. There are a number of short films featuring Mardi Gras parade footage from the 1930–1970s. Sure enough, analysis of footage revealed that the frisbee throw was the throw of choice for beads. The Frisbee throw does create a wonderful visual in the air—the strand spins as a perfect circle. During daylight, faceted glass beads or even some of the translucent hand-strung plastic beads could catch the light and create a glittering spectacle sure to incite the crowd's bead lust. One of the changes ultimately brought about by the introduction of MOS beads was a shift in the bodily performance of throwing the beads!

As for our second question, the continuity in bead strand length now makes more sense. An 18-to-21″ strand of beads would be easier to throw like a frisbee than a longer strand. The design of the stringing layout on many of the Czech beads, with the heavier beads strung on one end of the strand, also makes sense; it is a similar design to the graduated MOS beads that were favored for throwing. Similarly, the addition of the tassel on the Japanese beads is also explained. These beads are particularly light and would have been hard to throw efficiently. It does seem that some beads were strung in ways that would facilitate throwing by increasing the weight of the strand at one end.

But while a slightly heavier bead would be easier to throw, maskers also have to accommodate the weight of beads in loading the floats and throwing the beads. The floats also bear increased weight load when heavier beads are selected. So let us look at weight of the different types of beads (Table 6.3). For this exercise, I have provided the length

Table 6.3. Average Weight in Grams per Inch for Each Mardi Gras Bead Type.

BEAD DIAMETER	WEIGHT IN GRAMS PER INCH	WEIGHT IN KILOGRAMS PER GROSS FOR A 48″ STRAND
7	.45	3.11
8	.53	3.66
10	1.42	9.81
12	1.64	11.34
16	3.33	23.02
20	3.83	26.47

of the strand weighed, and calculated a weight-per-inch ratio to make the beads more comparable. I have also calculated, based on these strands, what a gross of this type of bead would weigh. You will see that the beads got lighter through time. This means that as parade goers demanded more and more beads, the maskers were able to accommodate without destroying their budget or their floats by switching to lighter glass beads and then lighter plastic beads.

While the example is only intended to be illustrative, it convincingly demonstrates that weight could have been an important consideration when selecting beads. The Czech beads, which were universally lauded as the most beautiful of the beads thrown, were, per inch, the heaviest beads thrown at Mardi Gras until the 1990s. The appeal of the Japanese beads is particularly evident given how light they were, but they broke easily and were dangerous to handle. The switch to plastic hand-strung beads provided significant advantages to maskers. They were significantly lighter, cheaper, and from a distance often indistinguishable from the glass beads. Both the cheaper price and the lighter weight allowed maskers to purchase and load more beads onto the floats without structurally taxing them. Since crowds measured the krewe's generosity by abundance of throws, krewes could theoretically increase their prestige without increasing caloric expenditure, to use the HBE way of thinking, by simply switching from glass to hand-strung plastic beads.

Remember how I mentioned that the selectionist archaeologists see HBE as complementary to their work? In this case, by looking at the beads through an HBE lens, we have identified the mechanism for the selection forces seen in the development of the beads (to use evolutionary archaeology speak). Our study does illustrate a problem encountered with the switch to the MOS beads. The MOS beads also provided a way to increase the number of throws while decreasing caloric investment, with one snag; the beads look completely different from the glass and plastic hand-strung beads, and the difference is visible from a distance. Remember that it is only once maskers switch to throwing MOS beads that we see the introduction of clear size drift within the beads. So why do the MOS beads suddenly begin to increase in size? This seems contradictory to the trends we have demonstrated in the rest of the history. The shift to heavier and heavier beads seems to be, to use the words of the evolutionary archaeologists, maladaptive. Something else happened—something related to the technology shift resulted in a fundamental change in the dynamics of the throwing game.

Human behavioral ecology models have provided an interesting way of demonstrating that there is some rational decision making that goes into the selection of beads to throw. Unfortunately, HBE models focus on tangible outcomes that can be measured in clear ways—technological output, return on calories, and labor efficiency. It has no way to measure intangibles like prestige. Say a masker burnt 25,000 calories working to earn the money to purchase her/his throw beads, and another 400 calories throwing them over the course of the parade. How can we measure whether the prestige and other benefits the masker got in return were worth his or her investment? We cannot. So while HBE models have helped us to identify design factors that may have shaped the throwing game, it cannot be used to answer all of our questions. Our analysis has also indicated that clearly economics come into play in the bead manufacturing process. The technological changes emphasize a shift from labor-intensive to less labor-intensive technologies. There will be definite economic dimensions to these shifts that we now need to consider as well. We will continue to develop this thread in the next chapter; however, for now, I want to look at the other half of the bead foraging equation—the acquisition of beads from parades by parade goers.

Bead Foraging Part II: Human Behavioral Ecology and Catching Beads

Thus far, I discussed how HBE models are entrenched in sociobiological thought, which in turn, is somewhat obsessed with sex. Well, Mardi Gras is the only instance of foraging that I can think of where a person can take the resource they've acquired and then trade it directly for some sort of sexual access. If you watch a parade on Canal Street, just a block away is the French Quarter where one can use beads to barter for kisses, gropes, and displays of body parts usually not on display; and really, who knows what else (I've seen things in the French Quarter that I don't really possess the language to describe). You can literally take the beads you catch on Canal Street and "spend" them on Bourbon Street. Therefore, perhaps HBE models are best suited for looking at strategies of bead acquisition.

Optimal foraging theory is a set of predictive models describing how an efficient forager will act in given resource environments (just as site catchment analysis is based on the idea that people will limit their travel times between regularly exploited resources). One of these models deals with circumstances when resources are not uniformly spread across the landscape, but occur, instead, in patches where some are richer than others. If you have ever been berry picking, you have probably encountered this phenomenon—some parts of a bush just seem to have more than another. The models predict that a forager will gather from the densest resource patches until the patch is depleted relative to the resource density of the patches surrounding it. The forager will continue through the environment gathering until the resource density is evened out across patches. How might this look archaeologically? Suppose you have a hunter-gatherer population foraging for shellfish. They will select for the largest specimens of any given species until all the creatures of that size have been harvested and only then harvest the smaller specimens. In the Meriam Islander case study, you'll recall that children failed to follow these models, but the adults did.

A strict application of the patch model is not possible for a parade, which is a moving resource. In that sense, the parade goers are more like fisherman during the salmon spawning season; we can sit at the river's edge with a net and hope to catch as many as possible as the fish pass by. I'm sure if we were to discuss fishing with people from the Klamath Falls area, they would have definite ideas about which where the best areas to catch salmon, and Louisianans are equally likely to have ideas about the best bead-catching locations. While not all adults approach Mardi Gras hoping to catch as many beads as possible, a surprising number of Louisianans do; and just about every Mardi Gras-seasoned New Orleans native has very strong ideas about where the best part of a parade route to catch beads is. This means that the parade route is perceived to be "patchy;" bead resources are thought to be distributed more abundantly in some areas than others. Whether or not parades are indeed patchy is something that we can test, and during the Carnival season of 2000, I designed a sampling strategy to do just that. A friend and her husband attended two of the same parades that I did, but in different locations. For the Orpheus parade, I attended with my group in my usual spot on St. Charles Street, while she settled in at the end of the parade route. Common wisdom suggests that the end of the parade route is the best place to be because the maskers who were pacing themselves to conserve beads during the rest of the route are now off-loading the last of their beads, so they don't need to pack them up again after the parade. It was generally thought that people at the end of the parade would get more and better beads than someone standing earlier in the parade route.

In comparing the end of the parade assemblage with the mid-route assemblage, it appears that some of the folk wisdom may be correct. Even though we were both situated in spectator crowds of similar density (we were both in the front line of the parade, with about four additional lines of people behind us, and with enough room on either side to move several feet back and forth), the end-of-route group received an average of 22.5 strands of beads per person compared to the 13.5 strand average caught by my mid-parade-route group. In terms of bead quality, the average length of strand at the end of the route was 36.8" (with a range of 32 to 46"), not statistically different from the of 37.4" average strand (with a range of 20 to 70") caught mid-parade. The average bead diameter for the end of the parade route was 8.5 mm, which was noticeably smaller than the 9.1-mm average caught mid-parade. Medallion beads accounted for approximately the same proportion of each assemblage (26.7% for end of the parade and 33.3% for the mid-parade). Where the end-of-parade-route group clearly won over the mid-parade-route group was in the highest prestige categories. The end-of-parade group caught two hand-strung "fancy" strands, whereas the mid-parade group caught none. While pearl finished beads comprised 14.8% of the mid-parade group assemblage; over twice as many pearls (29.5%) were caught at the end of the parade. Overall, it does appear if one is trying to acquire the kinds of high-status beads that will facilitate sexual bartering in the French Quarter and that the end of the parade route is a rich patch to exploit.

As we have seen in our archaeological discussions, travel time between resources and home bases needs to be considered when evaluating foraging strategies. Highly contested in Mardi Gras folk wisdom is whether it is better to catch beads on Canal Street (near the French Quarter) or in one of the neighborhood sections. Some people are adamant that despite the deep crowds on Canal, maskers throw heaviest to the tourists. In addition, these people argue that the tourists are generally befuddled and drunk and fail to catch as many beads as the drunk but seasoned parade goers who watch in the neighborhoods. Canal Street is better, they conclude, because you are close to the French Quarter and can quickly take your bead wealth to Bourbon Street to expend on sinful behaviors (after all, you need something to repent for during Lent). On the opposing side are people who argue just as strongly that the parades throw heaviest to the locals and reward natives with greater bead wealth than the tourists. Therefore, while competition may be steeper, everyone will catch better beads in the neighborhoods. So despite the greater distance one needs to travel after the parade to the French Quarter, the difference in wealth makes that travel worthwhile.

To test this perception of patchiness/resource density, my friend and I again took different parade vantage points. I took a rare departure from my usual parade spot and stood in the crowds on Canal Street, while she settled on Napoleon Avenue in a quieter neighborhood to watch the procession of Rex. While there were many measures in which the end-of-parade sample and mid-parade-route sample were equivalent, there was no doubt following this test that there was a clear winner in all categories. The Canal Street group, despite having very experienced bead catchers, averaged three strands per person. The Napoleon Avenue group averaged 18 strands per person. The average length of strand caught on Canal was 29.4″, whereas Napoleon was 43.7″! The average diameter on Canal Street was 8.0 mm, and 8.9 mm on Napoleon. While not many pearls were caught on Napoleon (5.0%), none were caught on Canal. In short, the Canal group did not catch any beads that were valuable enough to use for bartering in the French Quarter. The time we saved by being close to the Quarter was meaningless because we were not able to gather the resources necessary to fund anticipated debaucheries. That said, one could merely go to the French Quarter stores and buy beads, but that's not really the point of the study.

We see in both of these Mardi Gras HBE examples how knowledge about resource acquisition, an aspect of technological know-how, shapes the effectiveness of resource exploitation. Sometimes information is a forager's best tool. In the next chapter, we'll discuss how the ability to trade for what you want and need is pretty helpful, and we will explore archaeologies of trade and exchange.

CHAPTER 7: MARDI GRAS GIFTS AND BEAD EXCHANGE

In 1991, I attended my first Fat Tuesday. I had driven from Baton Rouge with a group of LSU folks to attend a full day of festivities. We started with Zulu, then Rex, and then the Elks Truck parade, which never, ever, seemed to end. We wandered through the French Quarter, saw things I would have never imagined could take place on public streets, and then found ourselves a table at a restaurant where we could eat, rest, and use a clean bathroom. We decided we wanted to stay for the last parade of Carnival: the Mystick Krewe of Comus. We had heard that Comus still paraded with wagons, their procession lit by flambeaux. They were the first krewe to have ever marched and the last krewe to parade each Mardi Gras season.

The floats were beautiful—ethereal, delicate, flowers and fairies gently moving in time with the movement of the wagons. Throws were not abundant, but we were pretty tired of catching things by this point. I had a cup and a doubloon both bearing Comus' emblem and was satisfied. As the last float arrived, I waved happily at the maskers and one saw and pointed at me. With a great flourish, he tossed me a bundle of beads. They glittered and sparkled in the torchlight, and I caught them easily. They were 33-inch, faceted metallic beads in red, white, and blue, a decent catch in 1991. I squealed excitedly, in part because they were the only beads I had caught that day intended for me, and I waved to the masker who was now growing smaller in the distance. He saw and dramatically threw me a kiss. It was a lovely gift with which to close my first Mardi Gras.

Gift Giving

What kind of a gift was it, though? "Gift" is a loaded term within anthropological thought thanks to the works of Marcel Mauss and others he inspired. Anthropologists recognize gift giving, or *reciprocity,* as one of the most basic forms of exchange that humans engage in. While most of us now live in a currency-exchange economy where we purchase goods with monetary units that have been attributed with standardized value, there have been many other ways to regulate exchange relationships in the past. And the kinds of economic system that a society has is intimately tied with some of the factors we discussed in the previous chapter: level of social complexity, the type of subsistence system, and nature of settlement patterning. For Mauss, gifts are never free. A giver imparts a part of oneself in the object s/he gives, and in doing so, it is a transaction that transcends ordinary commodity exchange. A gift creates a social bond and obligation between giver and receiver. A gift represents a convergence of spirit and object called inalienability; meaning you can never separate the thing from the person who gave it (Mauss 2011 [1954]). If this is the case, what is the social obligation I have to the masked member of the Krewe of Comus?

Some critiques of Mauss have argued over whether there are indeed "free gifts" (Strathern 1988; Laidlaw 2000). An example of a free gift would be a panhandler receiving money from a stranger on the street whom they may never encounter again. Are Mardi Gras beads examples of "free gifts" from masked parade goers to parade attendees? Are beads given with no expectation of repayment or reciprocity? Perhaps the intangible value of a smile is repayment enough? These are answers we will explore further in this and later chapters. For now, we should recognize that gifts are part of a series of social and economic relationships that archaeologists recognize under the title of "exchange." Let's consider this further.

Types of Exchange Relationships

I have introduced reciprocity as when you receive a gift that you are expected to return in some way—perhaps by giving a similar valued material gift at some point in the future or by providing labor of a similar value. Many of us engage in reciprocity systems, which tend to be informal and bound by trust (for example, you may say to a friend, "hey, I'm a bit short of cash, if you buy me my coffee today, I'll buy yours next time"). In small-scale societies, where people know one another (or their lineages/families) well, this kind of informal reciprocity occurs. You can probably think of any number of reciprocity relationships that you are engaged in that have different time scales associated with them: the exchange of birthday presents, wedding gifts, baby shower presents, graduation gifts, and so on. While birthdays are predictable, not everyone has a birthday the same time of the year; nor will all of your friends get married or have children at the same times (though there will be times when it feels like they are). Gifting is serious business, and in contemporary American society people do judge the gifts received, and givers are judged by the gifts they give. We are all probably familiar with the phenomenon of "regifting" when someone gives a gift someone else has given to them. In our contemporary society, this practice is perceived as not properly "paying back" one's social obligation to a previous gift giver.

Bartering is a form of exchange where goods or labor perceived to be of similar value are traded at the same time. There is debate in the anthropological literature over where the line between reciprocity and bartering lies, if there is indeed a line at all. Again, trust is often believed to be a component of these exchange systems, and exchange partners may be members of particular family groups (lineage) or particular villages. Trade partners may be people one would also consider as appropriate groups to marry with—people can be gifts as well.

With greater social complexity, it becomes more difficult to limit trade relationships to groups that are well known and trusted. Once this happens, it is more important to standardize units of exchange. In the last chapter, we discussed shell-bead currency that was used by California Indians leading up to the time of contact. Beads were traded in strands that were reportedly measured in units determined by wrapping them around a person's fist (one wrap around the fist would = one unit, two wraps around the fist would equal two units, etc.) (Heizer 1978). The earliest archaeological evidence of human writing systems are records of trade accounts, as evidenced in cuneiform tablets written by the Sumerian peoples dating from the fourth century BCE (Daniels and Bright 1996).

Trade as Seen on the Landscape

With complexity also comes the development of market places—spaces dedicated to trade. If you have the chance to visit New Orleans, be sure to visit the French Market. It is a sprawling line of open buildings filled with the stalls of fruits, vegetables, prepared foods and terribly tacky souvenirs, and it dates back to the earliest days of the city. Here people came to buy things that had been brought down the Mississippi or were destined to travel up it. In earlier days, the market would have been a place to buy animals, fruits, vegetables, cloth, baskets, ceramics, and any number of home-manufactured goods. As I walk through the endless stalls of stale pralines and embarrassing shirts, I like to imagine the building in the time when Louisiana was still a parcel of land tossed back and forth among the French, Spanish, and English. Then, the market was filled with the sounds of chickens, pigs, a dozen different European and African languages, the smell of flowers and freshly caught fish, and a blaze of moving color. Such places would have been familiar not only to colonists across the Americas but to anyone who had lived in a large settlement since the earliest days of human urbanization at Çatalhöyük (discussed in chapter four).

Archaeologists interested in understanding the flow of commodities between places and different kinds of market settings have often drawn upon a theory developed in geography to study modern cities: *central place theory* (CPT). Walter Christaller, a German urban geographer, developed CPT to understand the economic relationships between cities and their surrounding rural areas. Christaller (1972) hypothesized that population clusters like villages or cities developed as distribution centers that served local populations. People would travel the least amount of distance necessary to get goods. He saw consumable products as dividable into high-level and low-level goods. Low-level goods would be those consumables that you need to replenish regularly and don't want to travel far to get. These goods would be available in small settlements.

In contrast, high-level goods are luxury items, which are things that are acquired less often. To keep providers of those goods in business requires a larger population to support them, thus it is in the largest settlements where the broadest range of goods are available. These large settlements are central places (cities in Christaller's model), while smaller residential areas (Christaller used terms like towns, villages, and hamlets) have smaller populations and a more limited range of goods available. Medium-sized sites serve as intermediary trade spaces between central places and small settlements. There will always be more, smaller settlements than large settlements; the larger central places serve a larger territory than smaller settlements. Each central place will serve multiple smaller settlements of medium and small scales.

Because people want to minimize travel time, says the CPT model, settlements of each scale will be evenly distributed across landscapes to serve the populations dependent upon them. Why do we care archaeologically? If we can identify central places, then we can understand the relationships between different types of settlements within a region and gain insight into the economic landscapes in which they operated. Now, Christaller developed his model in a flat part of Germany where market access had been a prime motivation for settlement placement. Waterways and topography can be problematic natural barriers to settlement and trade between settlements. Social attitudes about territorial boundaries or sacred or symbolic features of the landscape can also influence settlement choices. However, archaeologists have found CPT to be useful for understanding archaeological landscapes. Ian Hodder (yes, that Ian Hodder) used a number of geographic theories to understand the prehistoric landscape of Britain (Hodder 1972). Hodder decided to explore whether CPT could explain the relationship between walled cities in Roman Britain. He mapped the known major walled cities, and then constructed Theissen polygons around the sites. *Theissen polygons* are generated from a set of sample points (in Hodder's case, each city represented his sample point). Each polygon defines an area of influence around its sample point in such a way that any location in the polygon is closer to the center point than any other sample point. Say what??? It's actually quite simple, what you do is draw a line between each adjacent point that is half way between them, and when you look at the areas created by the intersecting lines you'll see you have formed a number of polygons (see Figure 7.1). Central Place Theory dictates that this should reveal that smaller sites cluster equidistant from one another and from the centers. What Hodder's analysis revealed is that the distribution of the walled cities and the smaller settlements did indeed conform to the expectations of CPT, particularly when the impacts of waterways, which would have affected trade accessibility, were accounted for. Hodder suggested that the factors shaping settlement were administrative, as well as market driven, since the Romans preferred to rule their colonies with a highly structured governmental system.

As I looked at Hodder's data, I wondered if it were possible to attempt a similar map for the distribution of Mardi

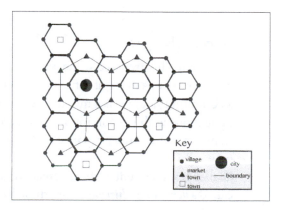

Key

● village   ⬤ city
▲ market   — boundary
  town
□ town

Figure 7.1. Schematic showing idealized arrangement of different site types around central places; after http://watd.wuthering-heights.co.uk/mainpages/sustainability.html.

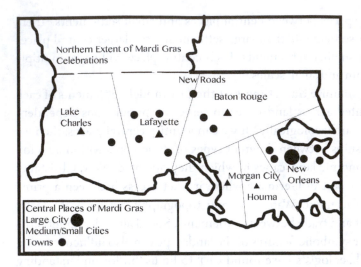

Figure 7.2. Geographic distribution of Mardi Gras celebrations in Louisiana showing distribution of smaller parades clustering around cities hosting larger Mardi Gras celebrations. In the case of Baton Rouge, we can see that New Roads falls within the territory of Baton Rouge. And archaeologically, we saw the redistribution of beads from Baton Rouge to New Roads.

Gras parades in southern Louisiana. Three major cities host Mardi Gras celebrations, New Orleans, Baton Rouge, and Lafayette; but a host of suburban areas and smaller towns also host Mardi Gras celebrations. Since Mardi Gras is only celebrated in the southern part of the state, we can only draw lines midway between each of these cities. However, if we plot the smaller parades, we see that with one exception, they do cluster very neatly within the territories of each of the larger cities (Figure 7.2). The one exception is the town of Morgan City, which seems to fall equidistant between the two centers. Morgan City is located deep in the wetlands of southern Louisiana, and I wondered whether this circumstance increased the travel time between either Baton Rouge and Morgan City or New Orleans and Morgan City. If the gods of MapQuest are to be believed, the difference in travel time is only two minutes; therefore, Morgan City really doesn't clearly fall into the territory of one city or the other. Given this, it would be interesting to visit Morgan City's Mardi Gras parades and see if there is material evidence of closer relationships with one city or the other. Unfortunately, I have only been to Morgan City's Shrimp and Petroleum Festival. But what do these spatial divisions represent in terms of the other Mardi Gras celebrations? We will explore that question further later in this chapter.

Why Exchange?

We've already discussed some of the "whys" for exchange; it cements social relationships between groups living at different sites; it allows for access to goods that are remote from a community; and it is a medium for establishing and maintaining social hierarchies and obligations within a community and across a region. Exchange is also an important economic survival strategy, particularly for people in marginal or highly seasonal environments. In the Andes of South America, the mountain environment creates particular challenges. Different altitudes create different ecological niches leading to what has been called a *vertical archipelago*—with each ecological zone existing like an island surrounded on either side by different environments, with different natural resources, and different potentials for resource exploitation. Andean archaeologists have long argued that reciprocity and exchange systems linking these different mountain islands enabled the survival of all Andean peoples. Traditionally, archaeologists have argued that kinship networks (family connections) linked different environmental zones in the Andes and were a major driving force in the development of exchange systems. This trend toward the development of trade across environmental zones is known as *ecological complementarity* (Lazarri 2010). The domestication of llamas some 5,000 years ago facilitated exchange among mountain peoples. While llamas cannot carry the weight of humans, they are very effective pack animals, and llama caravans moved goods across the Andes. When the Spanish encountered the Inca Empire, they found a well-developed road system that enabled the movement of goods and peoples across the Inca Empire. Lower elevation agriculturalists would trade foodstuffs and other resources up the mountains in exchange for llama meat, wool, and other resources. The llama caravans still operate in the Andes and often use roads built by the Inca and even earlier societies in the Andes (Tripcevich 2008). One way that Tripcevich is studying llama caravans using ethnoarchaeology (he's travelled with modern caravans) and *Geographic Information Systems* (GIS) to record and analyze spatial and visual data recovered during that study.

New tools, such as GIS, in archaeology provide archaeologists with an understanding of the relationship between sites on ancient landscapes. And, GIS allows researchers to layer multiple sets of spatial information (maps) on top of one another. Tripcevich (2008) considers landscape features like topography, road systems, canals, and other waterways. The affects they have on travel time can be accounted for, as well as features on the landscape that have sacred or other social meaning. Through GIS, archaeologists like Tripcevich can study the spatial relationships between and among sites and resources, and incorporate phenomenological evidence into their data. For instance, what is it like to travel a trade route through mountain passes? What are the experiences brought on by climate change and dropping oxygen levels as one ascends into the mountains? What are the views of the landscape one experiences along different parts of the journey? Are there human settlements in view always, or does the landscape block one's view and give a sense of isolation? These are questions that could have had as much impact on the ways that ancient peoples designed travel as did the location of resources, and through creative applications of GIS, archaeologists can address a broad range of questions about past people and landscapes.

Recognizing Trade Items

We talked about recognizing that trade existed on a landscape level, but within an artifact assemblage, how do archaeologists recognize trade or exchange goods? For cultural historians, the tools of typology were important. Remember that cultural historians used the concept of the "culture area" to understand the chronological and geographic boundaries of past cultures, and that the culture area was defined by a set of shared artifact types that were reflections of the shared cultural values of the group that used them. Any objects that were not part of the recognized artifact types associated with a particular culture area were seen as trade goods. Cultural historians understood cultures to be stable and resistant to change. One mechanism for cultural change was through the diffusion of new ideas from other cultures via mechanisms like intermarriage or trade. Therefore, it was important to understand trade and exchange as a source of new materials and ideas.

Remember our site catchment analysis? This archaeological tool is also related to identifying evidence of exchange; trade goods can be identified as those resources or materials recovered from a site that are not found near the site. The idea is that when objects that were made (or made of materials) whose source was far away, people obtained those goods by trading for them. Processual archaeologists added new means of recognizing trade goods through the identification of non-local goods or raw materials based on techniques like chemical sourcing of the clays or lithics used to make artifacts. They recognized that non-local raw materials could be traded as well. Objects like obsidian points could be made at a site out of imported materials. They may look stylistically like other points made in that region, but tracing the material back to its geological source would allow the archaeologist to reconstruct trade relationships between sites and source areas. In chemical sourcing—using the analytical technique *x-ray fluorescence* (**XRF**)—a machine uses x-rays to excite a material so it releases photons (fluorescing). Each element within the material responds in a way consistent with its atomic structure. By measuring the photon response, the XRF machine allows one to see the relative abundance of different elements within the material and to compare the archaeological materials with samples from known sources. Or, if the source isn't known, it allows one to look at how relatively abundant within a site different sources are, and in that way, identify the exotic versus common materials.

The XRF analysis can be performed on stone, metal, ceramic, and glass. It has been very widely used in North, Central, and South American archaeological settings to source obsidian. There are, compared to, say, clay sources, a finite number of available obsidian sources; so the chemical signatures of the various sources are well known. For many years, you would hear of archaeologists who would claim to identify obsidian sources by visually examining them. The use of XRF has demonstrated the fallacy of this assertion, and XRF provides an invaluable tool for archaeologists studying exchange (Shackley 2005).

Archaeologists have spent some time thinking about the relationship between things and the distance they have travelled. **Down-the-line trade models** demonstrate that in ancient societies, the further away something gets from its place of manufacture, the more rare it becomes. The mechanism for this is that at every stop along a trade route, a recipient of goods will keep some of what they acquire for themselves, to sell locally, or to give as gifts. This means that each time trade goods are exchanged from one village to the next, the volume of the goods decreases. Down the trade line, there will be evidence of decreasing numbers of a particular item as it gets farther from its place of origin until there is no more of it left to trade. Archaeologically, we see this as a decrease in the abundance of par-ticular artifact types it gets farther from their manufacturing site (this observation is also called a *distance decay model*).

It's important to remember, however, that the number of stops involved is very important. Say we were looking at goods coming into the United States today from China. Those goods have to cross the ocean before they land in Los Angeles or Oakland. There are few opportunities for selling the goods before reaching port in California; therefore, we would expect to see the "decay" in the abundance of the goods to begin at what is actually a great distance from China. It would be at the port where certain amounts of the goods would be off-loaded for local sales, while others are loaded onto trains for cross-country shipping, that we would see decay begin. By looking at rates for decay across space for different artifacts in a region, archaeologists can begin to look at trade routes.

Mary Helms (1993) has suggested that in looking at trade goods, we need to consider how elites manipulate access to trade goods to build their own prestige and naturalize their authority and power. Objects of high artistic value or that have been obtained from great distances, become physical manifestations of the power the elite have to control the acquisition of these goods. There is a general acceptance that the farther something has traveled, the more prestige that it holds for those who possess it. As an example of this phenomenon, in Mesoamerican societies the elite classes seem to have controlled access to green obsidian, And points made from this material often appear as part of ritual *caches* (intentional clusters) but not as part of tool kits used by commoners.

Recognizing Types of Trade Archaeologically: An Example from Oakley Plantation

Even in contexts where an archaeologist can draw insights from the archival and oral historical record, the range of different kinds of exchange relationships that occupants of a site were engaged in can be difficult to sort out. By way of an example, I'm going to take a brief detour through another Louisiana site—one whose only Mardi Gras connection is that one of the members of the planter family was invited to multiple carnival balls each year in the late nineteenth century. The site is Oakley Plantation where I excavated two houses associated with African American families who were employed by the Matthews family to work in the planter's residence and in the plantation yard—the area immediately surrounding the planter's house (Wilkie 2000).

The first house was built in the 1840s for an enslaved family, abandoned during the Civil War, and rebuilt in the 1870s to house the Matthews' cook, the widowed Silvia Freeman and her family of five children. After Silvia's death, sometime in the early 1900s, two of her daughters, Delphine and Eliza, continued to live in the house with their daughters, who moved out upon reaching adulthood. Delphine and Eliza continued to live in the house until each of their deaths. Delphine outlived Eliza, passing sometime in the 1930s. There are three distinct depositional layers around the house, each of which corresponds to an occupation (enslaved people's occupation, first Freeman occupation, and second Freeman occupation). The layers allow us to distinguish the practices of the different households.

The second house, located about a five-minute walk away was a house built in the early 1920s by Samuel Scott and his wife, Nettie. Sam Scott worked in the yard area of Oakley Plantation where he maintained farm equipment, cared for animals, and conducted general house maintenance. Nettie would eventually replace Delphine Freeman as the Matthews' cook. The Scotts were the Freeman's closest neighbors; the majority of the African American farming families who lived on Oakley lived over one mile away. The oral historical, documentary, and archaeological records combine to demonstrate the variety of exchange and labor relationships that tied together the Freeman, Scott, and Matthews families. And these sources illustrate the challenges archaeologists face in trying to illuminate the nature of exchange relationships in contexts with fewer lines of evidence to draw upon.

The economic life of Silvia Freeman, who worked as the plantation cook, is the only one clearly marked in the documentary record. Isabelle Matthews, owner of Oakley until her death in 1899, was a better record keeper than her daughters, Lucy and Ida, who inherited the plantation. Isabelle kept an inventory of goods that were lent from the kitchen to Silvia, maintained records of purchases made by tenants at the small commissary in the planter's house, and kept copies of the accounts she had with merchants in the nearby town of Bayou Sara, where tenants and employees of Oakley could make purchases on credit. From these records, it is possible to look at how Silvia Freeman spent the $4.00 per month she earned.

To put Silvia's $4.00 per month in perspective, at the same time, white wage laborers could expect to make about a dollar a day. On her $4.00 per month, Silvia supported her five children. House servants were notoriously underpaid in the South, and employers often gave employees hand-me-down clothing and household goods as "gifts." White employers saw these "gifts" as a demonstration that they and their employees had a relationship more akin to familial than professional. Employees were often referred to by diminutives of their first names, a practice that only further served to juvenilize them. Silvia Freeman is referred to in a number of the documents by Isabelle Matthews as "Silvie." In both Freeman assemblages, this kind of power differential in gift giving is seen when the Matthew's archaeological house assemblage is compared with the Freeman's assemblage.

There are multiple examples of matching ceramic patterns in each house of very expensive porcelains and transfer-printed decorated ceramics. I also recovered parts of toy tea sets from the Freeman house that match examples left by the Matthews family that are now displayed in the Oakley House Museum. Related to the practice of gift giving was the practice of toting. Toting was when cooks would take home leftovers from the planter's kitchen to their families. In looking at Silvia Freeman's commissary and store purchases, she bought salt pork, molasses, corn meal, and sometimes, milk. The archaeological materials demonstrated that her family also consumed beef, chicken, and eggs, and glass artifacts included multiple examples of Mason and jelly jars—food containers that presumably contained fruits and vegetables. Clearly, Silvia Freeman was obtaining food through other avenues, and toting very well could have been one of those avenues.

To understand Silvia's economic life more fully, I decided to tally Silvia's purchases against her known income. I found that she often operated on a dollar or two of debt by buying goods on account at Bayou Sara, as well as the commissary, and she took small amounts of her salary as cash (typically no more than 25 cents at a time). At the house site, we found a number of pennies and nickels that had been lost through the floorboards, which attests to Freeman's access to currency. Among the stores she frequented were pharmacies in Bayou Sara, and medicine bottles were among the artifacts found at the house. When I calculated how much she spent on different categories of goods, I found some strange things going on. For the three years that there were commissary records for Freeman, she was spending sometimes as much as 25% of her annual income on the purchase of tobacco! My first reaction was, "whoa, this woman had a mean habit." But I reconsidered the pipes from the site (cigarettes were not common, tobacco was most commonly consumed with pipes or as snuff). The pipes from the site were the stoneware elbow pipes that were commonly included free in a pouch of tobacco. Interestingly, however, there was only a small number, and none of them had any indication of having been used to smoke! There was no burning of the clay and no sticky residue. They were most likely used not for smoking, but for blowing soap bubbles—a popular children's pastime even then. I thought back to the commissary records. I had noticed that in a few instances Silvia Freeman had been recorded making purchases for other tenants on the plantation—small sacks of cornmeal, clothes, and so on. I then realized that I was possibly seeing evidence of bartering. Silvia was one of only a few African Americans living on Oakley who received a wage. The other community members were sharecroppers.

Sharecropping was an exploitive labor system that replaced enslavement after the Civil War. A planter would provide a tenant family with a parcel of land for a year under the condition that they would split 50-50 the resulting crop at the harvest. Tenants had to rent equipment from the planter and buy their seed and anything else they needed (say food, clothing, school supplies, shoes, and medicines) for the year on credit from the planter. At harvest time, at a meeting called "the settle," the sharecropper would turn over half of their crop, and from what remained, all of the year's debts would be paid. You can probably guess that this usually didn't end well for the sharecroppers. Typically, a sharecropper would end the year in debt and have to stay on the plantation another year to pay off the debt.

Yes, this was slavery under a new name, but without the cash resources to buy land, African Americans in rural areas had few opportunities. Sharecroppers did what they could to minimize debt to the planter; they hunted wild food stuffs, and often the women and children of the family would raise food crops in gardens near their houses and help in the cash crop fields. Families would barter with one another for goods. Education was one way to escape, but many families necessarily were dependent on their children's labor. Schools were under funded, and African American communities raised money to ensure a longer school year. Churches often did double duty as schools. At Oakley, Mt. Pilgrim Baptist Church, located adjacent to the plantation, served as the local African American school.

So how does Silvia Freeman fit into this? As someone with access to cash, she could purchase items for other people and trade them for fresh foodstuffs grown by the share-cropping families. Tobacco could only be obtained with cash or on credit; it didn't grow well in the area. Silvia could help members of the Oakley community access goods they needed and minimize their debts; the preserves and mason jars, fresh eggs, and possibly some of the meat recovered from the site may have been obtained through bartering. This was not merely a magnanimous act of charity on Silvia's part. She was spatially isolated from the rest of the African American community, and she would have been potentially considered with suspicion by other tenants given her close association with the planter family. Participating in barter with sharecropping families would have linked her closer socially with the rest of the community. Her children attended the school at Mt. Pilgrim, and the house assemblage contains a number of writing-related artifacts like inkwells, a school slate, and a pen nib, which would have also served to tighten her network to the community while potentially giving her children tools to escape plantation life.

So you can see that we have a rather complicated set of exchange relationships at Oakley; Silvia Freeman participated in a currency exchange system, bought goods with her wages with currency and on credit. She was the recipient of gifts intended to keep her in a socially subordinate position to her employer who used the gifting practice as an excuse to keep Freeman's salary low. At the same time, Freeman was engaged in a bartering system with fellow community members, which was a relationship that also had an expectation of mutual support. These are three types of exchange happening simultan-eously within the household.

But I'm not quite done; we have evidence of yet more gift giving at Oakley. Remember the Scott family? Excavations at the Scott house revealed that they owned a matching set of ceramics manufactured by the Homer Laughlin Company of Ohio, which were decorated with a distinctive orange flower pattern. These were much newer and different than the ceramics used in Delphine and Eliza Freeman's house; yet, from the second Freeman occupation, I recovered a plate that matched the Scott's pattern. And from the Scott's house? I recovered a ceramic pattern that matched one of the patterns used by the Freemans that was not found at the planter's house; therefore, it was unique to Eliza and Delphine's household. So what does this mean? Were the Scotts and Freeman's trading plates? In a sense, yes. I think the two households were engaged in reciprocity in the form of food sharing—being neighborly and bringing one another plates of food from time to time. On several of those occasions, a plate was broken and discarded at the borrower's home. The plates were not the items of exchange. They were the vehicle for transporting what was being exchanged—food! Here we see evidence of reciprocity with a very different intent than the gift giving of the planter to the Freemans. Here, there doesn't seem to be an intention to produce a relationship of inequality because the gift giving was mutual, not a means of masking social and racial inequality.

I hope I have illustrated how we can form very nuanced understandings of exchange relationships in historical archaeology. In prehistoric settings, it can be difficult to sort out the nature of the exchange relationship represented by goods. Some archaeologists have suggested that instead of attempting to name a specific type of exchange system, we should think in terms of how goods circulate within a society (Lazarri 2010). Trade suggests a primarily economic motivation, while circulation emphasizes the variety of social relationships that can lead materials to move throughout a social landscape.

Marisa Lazzari (2010), who studies archaeology in the Andes has suggested that archaeologists have often thought foremost about the economic value of objects in their archaeological interpretations and in doing so may be missing some of the social value of goods. She refers to small numbers of obsidian artifacts that are regularly found in eastern lowland Argentinian sites where access to this resource is limited. She noted that although the obsidian is of a better quality for napping than local stones, the people who were using the obsidian did not invest any greater effort in knapping it, nor did they save it for fancier tool production. Overall, the pattern of use neither suggested that the communities were particularly seeking out this obsidian resource, nor that they valued it more than local resources.

This contradicts the idea that something more distant is more valuable. So why is the obsidian even in this area? Lazzari notes that barter transactions today are started with the exchange of small gifts. The obsidian could have been given out as small gifts by traveling vendors to potential trade partners to open negotiations. Or it reached the area through a number of short-to-medium distance exchange systems that introduced the materials into the region along with more desired trade goods. In each case, it was the symbolic act of giving that was more important than the present; thus, the obsidian was not used any differently than any other lithic material.

Buying, Bribing, and Bartering with Beads

So Let us now consider further how we can look at gift giving, exchange, or generally, circulation, in the Mardi Gras beads assemblages. The economics of the throwing game are complicated to disentangle, because there is a complex gift economy (the throwing of beads from floats to parade goers without return favors) and an interrelated bartering economy (exchanges of beads for tangible items like displays of nudity, gifts of beer, or other beads) that are intermeshed within the commodity exchange system in which the beads were initially produced. These different exchange relationships affect one another in strange, and sometimes unpredictable, ways. Fortunately, archaeologists have been dealing with these kinds of issues at a variety of different sites. I'll now address different aspects of the economies at play in the throwing game. I discuss the throwing game as a kind of feasting ritual that operates at different scales at different places. I look at how beads are redistributed throughout the state over the course of time. I work through how we can get at the monetary economies behind the throwing game, and then I introduce two different theoretical frameworks—systems theory and actor network theory—that archaeologists have used to create synthetic and integrated interpretations of complex, interconnected sets of social and economic relationships in archaeological settings.

The Throwing Game as a Feast

An archaeological parallel to the kind of gifting dynamic we see at Mardi Gras is the staging of feasts in prehistoric settings. Feasting is understood as forms of ritual acting that involve the communal consumption of food and drink (Joyce and Henderson 2007: 650). When archaeologists refer to ritual, we do not necessarily mean practices related to religious beliefs—a way the term is often interpreted in popular usage. Instead, a ritual means a practice performed within a particular context that is done repeatedly according to particularly prescribed steps. Something that is part of ordinary practice but takes on different significance in particular settings are ritualized. It can be said that all of Carnival is a ritual event, given that it is an annual event that takes place at the same part of the calendar each year. The parts of each parade, the expectations of how floats will be organized, and the appearance of particular floats within particular parades are practices that have become ritualized and taken on special significance in the minds of those who participate.

Archaeologists interpret feasts as having different social purposes; many suggest that large-scale feasting at a communal level was/is a means of political maneuvering between factions competing for political power (Dietler 1990, 2006; Pauketat et al. 2002). Whereas smaller scale feasts may have been used to reinforce ties between households and lineages (Pluckhahn et al. 2006). Large-scale feasts often take place in particular ritualized spaces, such as shared public spaces like plazas, or in association with ceremonial centers. Large-scale feasting is represented archaeologically by the rapid deposition of archaeological materials that include large amounts of meat that sometimes includes rare or particularly prestigious cuts of meat or species, and prestige items, such as objects of scarcity, particularly high workmanship, or items of specialized function.

Large-Scale Feasts in Honduras

In a study of feasting at the site of Puerto Escondido, in Northern Honduras, archaeologists Rosemary Joyce and John Henderson (2007) looked at changes in cacao consumption related to feasting practices from the period of 1600 to 200 BCE. In the earliest deposits, they found cacao (the plant from which chocolate is created) was served in the form of an alcoholic beer made from cacao beans. From 1400 to 200 BCE, however, the consumption of cacao shifted from fermented to non-fermented beverages, whose preparation had a highly visible component. The architecture during this time shifted from private domestic compounds to publically visible, large-stepped platforms. At the same time, there was a shift to elaborately decorated vessel forms that were used to frothing chocolate beverages, as well as increased diversity in the flavorings (represented by plant remains) added to the chocolate.

Joyce and Henderson (2007) suggest that the feasts using the cacao beverages were used to build solidarity and create hierarchy. By making the brewing more visible, *actors* were foregrounding the labor and creativity that went into the manufacture of the beverage and demonstrating particular skills in creating versions of the beverage that would be distinctive in flavor, which brought more prestige to the feast giver. They conclude that what distinguishes a feast from other food consumption "is not simply the amount of food, the diversity of the foodstuffs, or the provision of things normally not consumed. It is also the experience of being a consumer of dishes created through extra labor, with special skill, and served with some level of distinction" (Joyce and Henderson 2007:652).

Small-Scale Feasts in the American Prehistoric South

Working at the Kolomoki site (cal AD 350–750) in Georgia, archaeologists Thomas Pluckhahn, J. Matthew Compton, and Mary Theresa Bonuage-Foreund (2006) found evidence in a house site trash pit that they believe was associated with small-scale feasting. Large-scale feasting has been found at the site associated with the tops of ceremonial earthen mounds, but this house site is located well away from the mounds. The pit they studied was deposited rapidly and includes a rich array of ecofactual and artifactual evidence. Animal bones from the site demonstrate that 99% of the animal remains recovered were from the front and back legs of deer. These are the meatiest portions of these animals, but at other deposits at the site, all elements of the deer are represented, distinguishing this pit as unique. Other deposits at the site also contain a much broader range of species represented than the white-tailed deer, fish, turtle, and bird found in the feasting deposit.

Another unusual feature of the deposit was the great range of plant materials that are associated with medical uses in the ethnohistoric literature that were found in the pit. One of the species, a member of the St. John's Wort family, was represented by 43 seeds in the sample—one of the more abundant plant species. St. Andrew's cross, a species of the St. John's Wort family, is recorded in the ethnographic literature of the area as having many medical uses, including treating diarrhea, venereal disease, snakebites, and unwanted pregnancies (Pluckhorn et al. 2006). The archaeologists see this as a feast that was related to curing rituals. The archaeologists found no indication that special ceremonial vessels were used during the event that created the deposit, which providing to them further evidence that this was a small-scale feasting event used to create solidarity among a set of households or lineages rather than a community-directed event.

Feasting Mardi Gras Style

At first glance, it may seem that these studies have little bearing on Mardi Gras, but Carnival parades are not unlike an ancient feast. Each parade is hosted by a set of sponsors (the krewe) who provide the floats, the maskers, and the throws that are distributed to the crowds. Just as the gift of a feast creates a potential social obligation (be it political allegiance, a sense of community solidarity, or an assortment of family connections), the gifts given at Mardi Gras, and the public performance of that gift-giving, also creates a sense of connection to a particular parade. Make no mistake, while feasting is the giving of the gift of food and entertainment by the wealthy members of a society to their peers and underlings, it is a form of economic exchange, with wealth being redistributed from the top of the social hierarchy to those below. These are gifts that come with clear obligations—expectations of loyalty in times of warfare, expectations of fulfillment of tribute obligations, and a whole range of other social obligations.

The feasting literature in archaeology got me thinking not only about the throwing game as a public performance in which different Mardi Gras organizations competed against one another for perceived dominance but also about how different scales of Mardi Gras parades serve different functions to different communities in Louisiana (Figure 7.2). For this, I will compare three different scales of parades that have different audiences and goals: the parades of New Orleans, the parades of Baton Rouge, and the parades of the rural town of New Roads (located just across the Mississippi River from Oakley Plantation where Silvia Freeman and her family lived).

The audience for parades in New Orleans is international. It attracts visitors from across the state, the country, and the globe who participate in the feast that is Mardi Gras. Feasting at Mardi Gras takes two main forms: the private, elite balls thrown by the krewes, and the public parades experienced by members of all social classes and backgrounds. Parades within Baton Rouge have a much narrower audience; the Krewe of Southdowns primarily serves the community of South Baton Rouge, and the Krewe of Spanish Town draws all of Baton Rouge and its neighboring communities. The parades at Pointe Coupee, some 30 miles west of Baton Rouge, in a mainly agricultural parish, are directed toward the small number of towns that surround the oxbow lake of False River. The throws recovered from these three settings should reflect differences in both the audiences the parade organizers are hosting, as well as the intent behind the feast. So let us now consider whether we can see material traces of large and small feasts. Now we are going to begin to consider more closely the individual archaeological assemblages excavated from different Mardi Gras to tell us more about their social meaning.

Scales of Parades

If we think of Mardi Gras organizations as different political factions maneuvering against one another for power or prestige as they might in an ancient society, then the practice of marking of materials with krewes' or organizations' names becomes quite interesting. Joyce and Henderson (2007) argued that the performance of distinctiveness was important in feasting settings. If we look for evidence of distinctiveness within Mardi Gras assemblages, then any throw marked with an organization's name is significant. We will discuss the specifics of krewe medallions more in the next chapter; however, for now, we will focus on which krewes have materials that identify their organization and those that do not.

We quickly see that there are clearly differences between parades that fall along geographic lines. The most diverse assemblages of krewe-emblazoned throws are associated with the New Orleans parades; most of the organizations at a minimum throw three different types of krewe-marked artifacts. In addition, Proteus (red/white), Rex (purple/ green/gold), Zulu (black), and Endymian (sky blue) have used krewe-specific bead colors that further serve to mark the identity of their organization. This pattern would be in keeping with archaeological patterns associated with large-scale feasting and distinctive material culture for feasting performances.

Only two of the four Baton Rouge parades sampled throw medallion beads. The South-downs parade is a small local affair that marches through a south Baton Rouge neighborhood and sometimes throws parade-themed doubloons. Mystique Krewe d'Capital is likewise a small, local parade. The two parades with medallion beads, Spanish Town and Orion, are two of the three organizations that parade in the city center of Baton Rouge. The third parade, the all-women Krewe of Artemis, also throws medallion beads with their krewe name. Artemis parades at the very beginning of the Carnival season and wasn't sampled for this study. These three parades, though, seem to be engaged in local competitions with one another but are not operating on the same scale as the New Orleans parades.

In contrast, the parades of Point Coupee parish do not mark themselves with any distinctive throws, although there are reports that the Community Center and Lions' parades have each thrown doubloons. Individual groups or organizations within the towns or parishes contribute floats. The Lions' club sponsors the Livonia parade the Saturday before Mardi Gras. The Community Center and Lions parades in New Roads march on Fat Tuesday. The town of New Roads has a population of about 5,000 people, and the area around False River, the oxbow lake on which New Roads is situated, has about 15,000 people. During Mardi Gras celebrations, it is typical for the area to draw upward of 80,000 visitors from neighboring parishes.

The Community Center parade has been parading since 1922, and it is the oldest parade outside of New Orleans. Although few news media or other Mardi Gras literature refers to it as such, it is also an African American organized event, and the parade features African American royalty. Louisiana has a long history of separate and unequal facilities, and segregated Mardi Gras parades are one social artifact of that history. As we will see in later chapters, understanding the history of race relations, racialization, and racism in Louisiana is necessary to answer some research questions we will pose of the Mardi Gras assemblages. Carnival in New Roads is no different, and the Lions parade is the predominantly white parade (with a white court) of the day. The parade began as a small children's procession organized by local mothers, but the Lions began sponsoring and organizing the parade in 1941 as a fundraising event. On Fat Tuesday, the members of the Lions block New Roads' only street and solicit a minimum recommended donation for entry. The Lions organization is reported to have contributed over 1.5 million dollars to local charities since its inception.

For both parades, kings are selected by secret committees. The kings are typically local businessmen; whereas the queens are local college students. Dukes and duchesses are selected from the local high schools. It is not only the Carnival celebrations that are segregated in New Roads. The spaces of the town are also racialized with the white population's housing concentrated between the railroad and the waterfront of False River and the black's between the railroad and the Mississippi River. Parade goers also are segregated through practice with the majority of black viewers concentrated in their neighborhoods.

Unlike the processions of New Orleans or Baton Rouge, where a number of the organizations are using parades to negotiate for dominance over one another through their demonstrated generosity, there was a different agenda to the New Roads Parades and the dual racialized organization of Carnival celebrations. The community there gathered to reinforce racial solidarity and to reenact the politics of segregation through an illusion of separate but equal Carnival participation. Part of this enactment entails rendering invisible that one parade is predominantly black and the other predominantly white. The limited throwing of krewe specific beads that might identify one parade versus the other is one way this can be achieved.

Feasts Increasing: Bead Inflation, 1921–2004

A feature of any kind of feast, whether it is a meal or a Mardi Gras parade, is its inevitable comparison with the celebrations that preceded it. This puts pressure on those who sponsor the feast to escalate the scale of the festivities—either through elaboration of materials or performances (as seen in Joyce and Henderson [2007]), increased abundance, or increased quality of the feasting experience. Can we see evidence of this process in the Carnival celebrations of Louisiana? And is there a difference between the different regions where parades were excavated?

Importantly, the period under study included time before and after Hurricane Katrina. Therefore, any trends noticed in the bead assemblages also have to consider how this 2005 tragedy impacted and reshaped the contours of Mardi Gras celebrations throughout the state. At this point, our focus will be on the period from the beginning of the throwing game until 2004. Prior to excavations beginning in 1997, I have only a few windows that allow us to reconstruct the nature of the throwing game. These include: 1) the composite collection of beads that date from 1991 to 1994, which were caught during Mardi Gras celebrations throughout Louisiana and provide a baseline for comparison with the later assemblages; 2) the curated examples of earlier glass and hand-strung plastic Mardi Gras beads that we have discussed previously; and 3) the textual and visual documents from earlier carnival celebrations that provide some insights into the dynamics of the throwing game.

Measuring Wealth—Abundance Versus Quality: Historical Perspectives

Using documentary and ethnographic sources, it is possible to construct an important shift in the throwing game—a shift from a focus on quantity to one on quality. In the early days, to catch a throw was a rare event, and one to be celebrated. Over time, krewes threw more and more items, which have led to greater expectations of abundance at parades. Once we get to the 1980s, however, we clearly see a shift to expectations of quality throws, not just abundant throws. We can see in our archaeological sample, increased demands for quality and quantity, which has also led to greater diversity and innovation in Mardi Gras throws.

Quantity Matters

In 1984, *The Times Picayune* (February 22, 1984) interviewed masker Buddy Charouleau, on the occasion of the 60th anniversary of the founding of the Krewe of Carrollton. Charouleau joined the krewe in 1936. He recalled that the dues were $12.00 to ride, and that a gross (a dozen dozen, or 144) of beads cost $6.00. Given the time period, those beads would have originated in Czechoslovakia. This would put a strand of Czech beads at about $0.04 per strand. To provide a contemporary comparison and convert for the rate of inflation, those would cost about $0.64 a piece in 2011. Charouleau did not discuss how many beads he would buy. Parade goers could not expect to catch a throw at every parade. Underscoring this point, the local newspaper provided parents with tips about how to avert disappointment by bringing small favors that they could then pretend to catch for their children! Footage of the 1941 Rex parade shows maskers clearly throwing objects, including beads, drawn from bunches of a dozen. Boxes are visible on some of the floats. Footage from what appears to be the Elks of Orleans parade that followed Rex clearly shows lots of small trinkets being thrown (Mindsmedia, "New Orleans Mardi Gras 1941 in Color"). A 1949 *The Times Picayune* article (February 27, 1949) discussed the Elks Truck Parade that ran after Rex (we'll be discussing this parade further in a few chapters). The article relayed, "the bags of Trinkets to throw from the truck set them back about a cent a piece. Each person throws about 300 articles." Again, not everyone attending a par-ade could reasonably expect to walk away with a throw given the number of objects being distributed.

By 1954, Mardi Gras footage shows maskers wearing shoulder bags that they are throwing objects from. The footage posted October 13, 2007, on YouTube by wolfieredi ("Mardi Gras Exposed: 1954") shows footage of Zulu and Rex. The maskers on several of the Rex floats are clearly throwing glass beads to the crowd. At this point, there is no evidence that floats were modified to load greater quantities of beads. In some shots, it is possible to see cardboard boxes on the floats in front of the maskers. Maskers take handfuls of the boxes' contents and hurl them upward toward the crowd, which suggests they are small favors and candy.

In addition to showing the parade's distinctive tinfoil-decorated, animated floats, 1956 footage of the Krewe of Midcity's parade (tv.boingboing.net) also clearly shows the addition of racks designed to hold bunches of beads. Footage from 1957 street scenes of maskers shows, among others, four little girls in costume walking together; two are clearly wearing Czech-type Mardi Gras beads (Trilussa, "Mardi Gras 1957, High Quality"). Clearly by this time, the abundance of throws had substantially increased.

Rex was reported in 1960 to have thrown 80,000 doubloons—the minted coins that were popular in the 1960s–1970s as throws (Hardy 1987). *The Dixie* reported in 1972, that Rex was throwing 500,000 doubloons. This represents an increase of 525% in a period of just ten years! Footage from a mid-1960s parade (Whoopwaah, "Mardi Gras in the 1960s") shows racks on parade floats that contain what appear mainly to be hand-strung plastic beads. Maskers can be seen tearing apart the binding holding the beads together, and in some cases, throwing them as multiple strand bundles. Again, this seems like definitive evidence that the feasts became more and more generous with throws through time.

In 1973, an advertisement for Carnival Mart in *The Dixie* stated that the main manufacturers of the beads were located in Hong Kong and Taiwan, and that beads 24″ in size would sell for $2.00 and up for a gross (Carnival Mart Ad, Dixie, February 13, 1973). Averaging just over a penny per strand, these beads were significantly cheaper than the glass beads thrown in 1936 with a starting price of $.05 a strand when converted to 2011 prices. To put this into perspective, the short MOS transparent beads, measuring about 16–18″ today sell for about that price. A photograph accompanying the article shows the maskers' arms covered with hand-strung plastic beads. While the article cites prices for 24-inch bead strands, I have found no hand-strung beads of that length, all of the hand-strung beads I have found are 18″. Only MOS beads are found in that length in the curated collections.

The 1973 prices help to contextualize a 1972 article in *The Dixie* on the Krewe of Thoth, where maskers are described as unloading a few million strands of beads. "Plastic bags, packing boxes and laundry bags crammed full of beads are loaded onto two-wheeled carts and trundled into the den. Outside the door, krewe members crush out their cigarette and go inside to load the beads onto the floats" ("Thoth Prepares to Ride", February 13, 1972). The article describes "cheap riders" with 100 gross, and others with 150 and 185 gross of beads. They suggested that the average person brought on about $200.00 in beads (about $1,060.00 converted to 2011 prices), but given the cost of beads at about $2.00 or more a gross, it seems that some members were spending significantly more.

Also writing in 1973, Sarah Searight had this to say about Mardi Gras throws.

The carnival throws are a fairly recent extravagance, giving rise to such concerns as the Cutprice Novelty Company, and Pressner's Carnival Mart advertising "beautiful and distinctive throws from Japan and Hong Kong." *It is difficult to see distinctiveness in the mountain of beads accumulated for Carnival* [emphasis added] (though people will debate the relative merits of a string from Hong Kong versus a string from Czechoslovakia) but grabbing for throws is reckoned by many to be half the fun of Mardi Gras. Usually it is taken so seriously as to threaten the carnival spirit. Maskers on board the floats sometimes spend two hundred dollars or more on their sacks of throws. (Searight 1973:267–268)

What we see in the historical record is an indication that the trend in the throwing game was toward throwing greater and greater numbers of beads. We looked previously at the comparative weights of beads thrown in relationship to the problem of supporting greater and greater bead weight on small floats. Ultimately, the plastic beads were lighter than the glass, as well as cheaper, making them the perfect throw bead. As we saw in the previous chapter, during the previous 60 years of Mardi Gras celebrations that included glass and plastic beads, bead strands did not shift significantly in length; they hovered from about 16–18" for strands with clasps and 16–22" for strands that had no clasps. The pressure exerted on maskers during these times was for greater and greater number of beads, not longer beads.

Quality Matters

By 1987, there is evidence that differentiation of Mardi Gras beads based on length and finish appeared. A 1987 article in *The Times-Picayune* noted that (March 2, 1987, "Carnival Throwaways") an estimated $8.6 million dollars were spent on throws in New Orleans, and that the average krewe member spent $350.00 (about $694.00 converted to 2011 prices). The long pearls and gold beads were said to sell for $5.00 a dozen ($.42 a strand, $0.90 when adjusted for inflation), while 3.50 to $5.00 a gross was more common. Many people bought typically 100 gross, and a local retail source allowed people to layaway. By this time, the common beads thrown were transparent MOS beads, and a small number of recycled hand-strung Hong Kong beads still thrown as late as 2009.

For the more recent past, it is easier to reconstruct the price structure for beads of different types through time. In the 1990s, Arthur Hardy's *Mardi Gras Guide* regularly featured advertisements by a company called Big Wheel Novelties. During the 1990s, it is remarkable how consistent the pricing in beads remained, and if anything, became slightly cheaper (Table 7.1). There may be several factors contributing to this phenomenon. An informal review of Chinese bead manufacturing sites indicates that many of the companies that now provide Mardi Gras beads were founded 1990–2000. Greater numbers of suppliers could potentially lead to decreases in cost. Similarly, the US dollar 1994–2005 remained remarkably strong with exchange rates of over eight Chinese Yuan for every dollar (Oanda.com, "Historical Exchange Rates") making it possible for US merchants to buy better beads from Chinese suppliers for fewer dollars (Table 7.2).

On the New Orleans end, it appears that Louisiana suppliers also started pushing the sale of longer strands of beads, perhaps taking a larger profit on the larger-sized beads. When one compares beads recovered at parades from 1991 to 1994 and parades in the late 1990s (Table 7.3), there is clear evidence that the trend toward longer beads had begun, with the beads caught in 1999 being on average 55.2% longer than beads caught between 1991 and 1994. Bead prices had stabilized or even decreased slightly, which facilitated this shift from the perspective of those buying the beads, in that they could purchase larger beads without radically increasing the amount they spent. Based on the prices cited for Big Wheel Novelties' beads, one could purchase large numbers of shorter beads supplemented by a certain number of the longer beads.

Table 7.1. Prices of Beads Sold by Big Wheel Novelties and Accent Annex 1990–2009.*

BEAD TYPE	1991	1995	1999	2004	2007
18″ grad trans		.02	.02		
21″ 7 mm trans			.04	.04	
24″ 6 mm trans	.02		.02	.03	
33″ 7 mm metallic		.08	.05	.06	.05
33″ 10 mm metallic					.11
42″ 10 mm metallic		.17	.40		.15
42″ 12 mm metallic			.40		.20
48″ 8 mm pearl	.25	.21	.29	.25	.10
48″ 12 mm pearl			.37	.49	
60″ metallic twist			.99	.24	.12
60″ 12 mm pearl			.69		.27
72″ 12 mm pearl			.77		.71
72″ 12 mm metallic			.77		
72″ 18 mm metallic or pearl					1.60
96″ 18 mm pearl			2.63		1.72
96″ 18 mm metallic			2.63		1.05

*Prices have been converted into dollars per strand (not adjusted for inflation).

When we look at the composite 1991–1994 assemblage, we can see that the average length of a strand was 21.7″. By the early 1990s, we get a sense that something may be shifting in the throwing game (Table 7.3). Only 9% of the assemblage caught between 1991 and 1994 is comprised of bead strands that measure over 32″, and only 2.9% of the assemblage are beads that measure 46″ or greater. The vast majority of the beads are transparent or flat opaque colored (see Figure 3.3). Among the 889 beads are 18 strands of faux pearls (2.1% of assemblage). The shortest strand of pearls recovered was 28″, and the longest was 48″. The average length of a pearl strand was 37.8″, which was significantly longer than the average. Metallic beads were also rare in the assemblage, accounting for 4.1%. Like the pearls, these beads were found in longer lengths, with the shortest at 24″, and the longest at 48″. The average metallic strands thrown were 32.6″. In this assemblage, we can see the beginning of bead inflation, or a trend toward longer and wider beads, as well as a ranking system that selects for particular finishes of beads. Do these trends continue in the excavated samples from 1997 onward?

Table 7.2. Exchange Rate, Dollars to Chinese Yuen and to Hong Kong Currency.*

YEAR	DOLLARS TO YUEN	US TO HONG KONG
1978	1.68	4.68
1979	1.55	5.00
1980	1.55	4.97
1981	1.70	5.58
1982	1.89	6.06
1983	1.98	7.2
1984	2.33	7.9
1985	2.94	8.27
1986	3.46	8.26
1987	3.73	8.23
1988	3.73	8.23
1989	3.77	8.12
1990	4.79	7.8
1991	5.335	7.7
1992	5.528	7.7
1993	5.7934	7.7
1994	8.5651	7.7
1995	8.3505	7.6
1996	8.3142	7.62
1997	8.2898	7.717
1998	8.2789	7.75
1999	8.2761	7.75
2000	8.2784	7.79
2001	8.2743	7.79
2002	8.2669	7.99
2003	8.2672	7.787
2004	8.2664	
2005	8.1838	
2006	7.9646	
2007	7.5972	
2008	6.9404	
2009	6.8212	

*Only 1.75% of the 1991–1994 assemblage could be attributed to manufacture in Hong Kong, looking at this table, the cheaper costs of labor in China, combined with the increasingly favorable exchange rate probably caused shift from Hong Kong manufactured beads to Chinese manufactured beads. Many Hong Kong firms shifted manufacturing to China to also take advantage of cheaper labor, so it is entirely possible that the firms that New Orleans consumers worked with continued to be in Hong Kong. This is also the reason why Taiwanese beads could be invisible archaeologically—the bead tags only show us where they were manufactured, not the nationality of the corporation that owned the factories.

Table 7.3. Average Bead Length by Year and Region.

NEW ORLEANS

YEAR	1991–1994	1999	2000	2001	2002	2003	2004	2006	2007	2009
BEAD LENGTH	21.7	33.7	33.7	36.1	38.2	38.5	33.5	40.8	43.7	43.7
% CHANGE FROM PREVIOUS YEAR		55.2		7.1	5.7	.8	-13.0	21.8	7.1	
BEAD DIAMETER		8.6	8.5	8.7	8.4	8.8	9.1	9.8	9.5	10.3
% CHANGE FROM PREVIOUS YEAR			-1.2	2.4	-3.4	4.7	3.4	7.7	-3.1	8.8
AVERAGE NUMBER OF BEADS CAUGHT PER PERSON PER PARADE (BPP)		32.6	22.1	22.6	32.1	23.3	25.3	26.6	14.3	31.6

BATON ROUGE

YEAR	1991–1994	1998	1999	2001	2002	2003	2004	2006	2007	2009
BEAD LENGTH	21.7	29.7	32.9	35.1	31.9	36.8	37.2	38.3	40.6	37.0
% CHANGE FROM PREVIOUS YEAR		36.8	10.8	6.7	-10.0	15.3	1.1	3.0	6.0	-8.8
BEAD DIAMETER MM		7.3	7.1	8.2	7.9	8.4	9.0	8.7	10.	9.2
% CHANGE FROM PREVIOUS YEAR			-2.7	15.4	-4.8	6.3	7.1	-3.3	20.6	-12.3
AVERAGE NUMBER OF BPP CAUGHT IN EACH PARADE		2640.6.5	38.1	37.6	46.5	35	44.9	60.5	80.3	66.2

POINT COUPEE

YEAR	1991–1994	2004	2006	2007	2009
BEAD LENGTH	21.7	30.3	38.6	39.2	37.0
BEAD DIAMETER		7.6	8.2	8.1	10.4
BPP		21.6	22	10	12.7

The Excavated Assemblage

Understanding inflation is important for the symbolic exchange system of Mardi Gras (how much prestige one receives for the perceived value of one's throws), as well as the monetary economic system (how much one has to spend on beads to acquire that symbolic capital). This raised some analytical issues. Each parade has its own context and history, and if I were to focus on understanding inflation just within individual parades, I would also have to do a contextual analysis of other factors that may affect each organization. For instance, was the krewe celebrating an anniversary? Did they have a drop or increase in membership? Did they change the pre-made packages of throws available for krewes to throws? In short, I wanted to understand inflation at a regional level, not a smaller scale. Therefore, the research question I asked was, "is inflation visible across time and does the rate of inflation differ between cities?"

We can assume to a certain degree that each city has its own supply centers and local bead market that is tied to the larger regional and global markets. I wanted a macroscalar view of bead assemblages on a city level so that I could compare inflation rates between large-scale parades (New Orleans), medium-sized parades (Baton Rouge), and smaller community-based parades (Pointe Coupee).

Although I'm speaking of these parades as if they were autonomous units, these are not disarticulated systems. Remember our CPT map of Mardi Gras parades (Figure 7.2)? The large cities of Lafayette, Baton Rouge, and New Orleans have a host of smaller parades that cluster around them. What our CPT does not do, however, is attempt to look at the relationship between those three cities. Baton Rouge and Lafayette have little interaction with one another, but they both have strong connections to New Orleans. New Orleans has historically been the central place for Mardi Gras in Louisiana. The large parades of New Orleans are a source of beads for mid-sized and small-sized parades. People attending parades in New Orleans will take the beads they catch there and rethrow them in other parades. This is, incidentally, a perfect example of the down-the-line trade models we discussed earlier. Beads sold into the recycled bead economies also serve to move beads from New Orleans to other areas. The easiest way to demonstrate this phenomenon archaeologically is through a consideration of the distribution of rethrown krewe medallions (Table 7.4). We can see that beads recirculate in New Orleans, with some krewes throwing recycled medallions from other krewes. Overall, it would seem that such an activity would be frowned upon by krewes trying to assert their prestige over another by marking their gifts with their krewe logos. Rethrowing in that context could lead to bead confusion by recipients—are they enjoying the generosity of Rex or Bacchus? Perhaps for this reason we see rethrowing of krewe medallions happening with greater frequency in Baton Rouge, where New Orleans krewe beads are rethrown nearly every year. Rethrowing of New Orleans beads is also seen in the small town of Livonia, in Pointe Coupee.

While New Orleans krewes rethrow New Orleans' beads, and Baton Rouge and Livonia rethrow New Orleans beads, we have no unambiguous proof of Baton Rouge beads being rethrown in New Orleans. The movement of these goods is away from the center, not

Table 7.4: Rethrowing of Krewe Medallion Beads.

YEAR	NEW ORLEANS	BATON ROUGE	POINT COUPEE
1999	Krewe of Orpheus rethrows Endymian medallion	Spanish Town rethrows 1998 Bacchus, Endymian medallion Southdowns rethrows Rex medallion	No data
2000	Krewe of Iris rethrows Krewe d'Etat medallion	No data	No data
2001		Spanish Town rethrows Rex medallion Southdowns rethrows Orion medallion*, Endymian medallion	No data
2002	Krewe of Proteus rethrows 2 Krewe of Tucks medallions		No data
2003	Krewe of Rex rethrows 1 Thoth, 1 Endymion, 1 Bacchus, 1 pink flamingo*	Spanish Town rethrows 1985 Krewe of Bacchus	No data
2004		Spanish Town rethrows one Krewe of Midcity, 1 2001 Krewe of Bacchus	Livonia parade rethrows 1 Rex and 1 2000 Bacchus medallion

*Pink flamingo could be a Spanish Town rethrow, but it's unclear.

toward it. People go to New Orleans to get beads; New Orleans does not go elsewhere for its beads. In the 2003 Rex assemblage, there is one example of a plastic flamingo medallion that matches medallions thrown by that time in the parade of Spanish Town in Baton Rouge. The medallion is not krewe-specific, however, but is one sold through the catalog and online merchandiser "Oriental Trader." Therefore, we cannot demonstrate that it is clear evidence of a Baton Rouge bead that was rethrown in New Orleans. As we'll discuss, flamingos have a loaded iconography all their own and strong associations with gay culture. Spanish Town parade is, among other things, a gay pride parade. A 2003 flamingo bead in New Orleans is more likely associated with marking gay identities than a Spanish Town parade identity. Based on the evidence, New Orleans is the center of bead redistribution in the state, with the other places being satellites. Archaeologically, anyone who works on colonial sites has seen this phenomenon with Chinese porcelains. The world clamored for Chinese porcelains due to their beauty and high quality; the Chinese had no use for the world's ceramics, therefore, the flow in the ceramic industry was one way.

Rethrowing of unmarked beads is harder to trace in the assemblages unless the beads are of a chronologically distinctive type, like the hand-strung Hong Kong beads, or if they have obvious signs of repair or age. From an archaeological perspective, looking at the rethrowing of generic beads only gives us a sense of chronology, not geography, like the medallions. An advantage of MOS beads is that when a strand breaks, it can be repaired. The beads are repaired by melting the ends together, which gives a very distinctive look (Figure 7.3). As beads age, some of the metallic or pearl finishes also begin to peel, which is another sign of reuse that was observable in the assemblages. Table 7.5 details evidence of reuse in the assemblages. Bonnie Clark (2011), studied a remote, late nineteenth-century Hispanic settlement in Colorado and found that isolated from major commercial centers and generally cash poor, the occupants of the households she studied were creatively reusing materials in the household. Food cans were saved and reused for storage. Children played with bailing wire to create their own toys; even rifle cartridges were collected and reused after being shot, probably to scare coyotes away from the hen house.

Reuse has implications for economic analysis of any of the Mardi Gras assemblages. We can see that in 2003, a 1985 Bacchus medallion bead was still in circulation. The Hong Kong hand-strung beads were no longer available for sale in the primary market by the mid-1980s, but were still being rethrown as recently as 2009 in Baton Rouge. We have to acknowledge that a certain percentage of the beads thrown in any given year are possibly 10 to 20 years old, or perhaps even older! The same selection pressures that shape purchasing decisions for new beads, however, are likely to shape the purchasing of reused beads; in other words, we would expect there to be selection for the longer, bigger recycled beads. In 2007, it was possible to see vendors openly selling boxes of beads marked as "recycled," where beads were sorted by length, but not bead shape, finish, or diameter. As a result, these boxes were actually more expensive than purchasing beads of the same length with small diameters—the logic being that the mixed case was likely to contain a number of better quality beads.

When we look at average bead lengths and diameters recovered from each region during the course of the study, we see some striking trends (Table 7.3). In each area there is a general increase over time in the length and diameter of beads thrown at parades, but variations occur with some downward dips experienced in places at different times. These differences reflect different strategies employed to demonstrate generosity. The highest

quality beads were consistently thrown in New Orleans. Throughout the period of the study, New Orleans shows steady increase in bead strand length from 1999 through 2003, increasing from an average of 33.7" to 38.5" before dropping to below 1999 lengths in 2004. Bead diameters in New Orleans were more volatile during this time with periods of increase followed by years of decrease; but an upward trend is still visible overall. Bead diameter hit a city high in 2004 (Table 7.6). This suggests that in 2004 what we are actually seeing

Figure 7.3. Examples of MOS beads exhibiting wear and evidence of repair. Arrows indicate where strands have been reclosed by melting beads together.

Table 7.5. Evidence of Rethrowing of Beads 1997–2004.

YEAR	PARADE	LOCATION	EVIDENCE OF RETHROWING
1997	Bacchus	New Orleans	4 repaired strands
			1 Hong Kong hand-strung
1998	Spanish Town	Baton Rouge	1 multi-colored strand made by melting other strands together
1999	Orpheus parade	New Orleans	6 repaired strands
	Spanish Town	Baton Rouge	4 hand-strung Hong Kong strands
2000	Bacchus	New Orleans	2 repaired
	Iris	New Orleans	3 repaired
	Orpheus parade	New Orleans	3 repaired
	Orpheus ball	New Orleans	3 repaired
	Rex	New Orleans	8 repaired (including medallions)
	Thoth	New Orleans	1 repaired
	Tucks	New Orleans	3 repaired
	Zulu	New Orleans	16 repaired
2001	Spanish Town	Baton Rouge	10 repaired
	Southdowns	Baton Rouge	3 repaired
			1 strand Hong Kong hand-strung
2002	Orpheus	New Orleans	2 repaired
	Spanish Town	Baton Rouge	12 repaired
2004	Orpheus	New Orleans	5 repaired
	Spanish town	Baton Rouge	15 repaired
			1 Hong Kong hand-strung
	Livonia	Pointe Coupee	3 repaired
			1 Hong Kong hand-strung

is throwers adjusting their throws to include wider beads and a corresponding slight sacrifice in length. Part of any bead throwing strategy is how much to throw. If we look at the average number of beads caught per person (BPP) per parade, we see the largest numbers of beads caught in 1999 with an average of 53 BPP. This drops to 22.6 in 2001 and 22.1 BPP in 2000. It increased in 2002 to 32.1 BPP then went back down to 23.3 BPP in 2003 and slightly up to 25.3 in 2004. Therefore, we can see a trend toward decreasing the number of beads thrown as the quality of beads increases.

In Baton Rouge, we see steady growth in length and width until a dip in both in 2002 followed by another upward trend (Table 7.6). The overall trend is an increase through time in bead size and strand length. Beads do not reach the lengths or diameters that we see in New Orleans, but the rate of increase is roughly equivalent to the increases we see

Table 7.6: Comparison of Bead Inflation by Region over Entire Length of Study.

REGION	% INCREASE IN STRAND LENGTH	% INCREASE IN BEAD DIAMETER
NEW ORLEANS (1999–2009)	29.6	20.2
BATON ROUGE (1998–2009)	24.6	26
POINTE COUPEE (2004–2009)	22	36.8

in New Orleans. Where Baton Rouge differs from New Orleans is that we see an increase in the average number of throws per parade in Baton Rouge. This is not a function of individual maskers being more generous—it is a function of parade length.

In New Orleans, parades are kept at a constant number of floats from year to year, with most parades having from 20 to 24. The parades in Baton Rouge are additive; they could be as long as necessary to accommodate participants and only recently have come to limit their sizes as the parades swelled to contain as many as 100 floats. What we see in both Southdowns and Spanish Town during this period is increased participation in the parades. The longer the parade, the greater the number of throws caught. In particularly long parades, it is possible to get catcher's fatigue, which leaves greater numbers of beads to be caught by those still trying. If you consider New Orleans' numbers again, this means that even in the lower-catch years, a person attending a New Orleans parade was probably catching on average one strand of beads per parade float.

We have only a few years of samples from Point Coupee, and only one that predates Hurricane Katrina. That 2004 assemblage (Table 7.6) is what we would expect for a parade hosted by a smaller community. The average strand length is shorter than either New Orleans or Baton Rouge, and the number of beads caught per person is reasonably high at 21 strands BPP.

Comparing Bead Values through Time

One question this analysis raises is, do the changes we see represent a real change in the financial investment made by the masker who threw these beads, or are these trends the result of bead prices through time? What do these shifts in quality and quantity mean? This requires us to be able to compare the beads to an absolute rather than relative scale (the same problem faced by archaeologists in chronology).

Historical archaeologist George Miller was interested in solving a similar problem for English earthenware ceramics commonly found on sites worldwide from the 1780s onward. He researched pottery archives, reconstructing price charts for different types of wares and vessel forms year by year. He noticed that there was a ranking system, in which plain wares were always the cheapest available vessels, followed by minimally decorated wares, like factory turned slip wares and edged wares. The second-most expensive category of earthenwares were hand-painted decorations, which required more labor costs to create; whereas transfer-printed vessels were always the most expensive wares produced. This relationship was consistent through time, although the degree of price difference between the categories varied from year to year. A transfer-printed bowl would sometimes cost four times as much as a plain bowl, and in other years only two and one half times as much.

Miller (1980, 1991) used this archival information to create a ceramic index system, with a plain decorated bowl always being given a value of one, and all other vessels of different wares being assigned a number that represented how many times more expensive that ceramic was than a plain bowl. That way, archaeologists could compare the value of assemblages from different sites and times to one another to determine how households were making expenditures on ceramics. Since ceramics were a way of communicating wealth and gentility of a household, this was a pretty handy tool. Archaeologists were able to show that some middle-class families of the mid-nineteenth century were choosing to purchase more expensive tea wares, which were used in entertaining, and cheaper table wares that were used privately by family members (see Spencer-Wood 1987). There are definitely shortcomings to Miller's index. It became difficult to figure out which index year to use for any particular artifact—should one use the production year or the deposition year? The purchase price, if bought new, would have been based on its date of production, but what if the ceramic was broken long after it was purchased? Did it really have the same value in the household then? And what about the circumstance that most households accumulate different vessels at different times? Should one use multiple years of the index for one assemblage?

To avoid these issues, Miller suggested that archaeologists use a mean ceramic date (MCD), or an average of the average production dates, to determine what year of his chart to use. An MCD was a tool developed by Stanley South (1977), which is based on the notion of frequency seriation. Every historical ceramic type is known to have a beginning and end date of production. South reasoned that each artifact type is most likely found at its production mid-point, when it was most popular. Therefore, if you averaged all the averages from the ceramic production dates together, you would get a date of deposition for your archaeological deposit. It is tricky math that works well for sealed deposits that were created quickly, but not so well for middens, which tend to be deposited over a long period of time. The MCD also does not really account for the impacts of human behaviors, like curation. My senior thesis site was a great case in point.

The Cordes family used a lot of much older plates and bowls and teacups—perhaps things that were inherited from family members—which gave the site an MCD of 20 years older than the occupation of the site. Calculating a mean production date on the glass artifacts came up with a date much closer to the documented occupation in the early 1920s. Interestingly, the MCD became a useful way to talk about the curation of heirlooms rather than its intended use as a means of dating a site's occupation. Archaeological tools are handy that way, you can always figure out ways to apply old techniques to new ways of thinking or new problems.

So despite the problems, is there a way to make a Miller type system apply to the Mardi Gras beads? We have a few challenges that Miller did not face. First, there is no equivalent of a "plain bowl" for Mardi Gras beads. Beads are priced according to finish, length, and diameter size. The combination of these elements is not consistently offered from one distributor to another from year to year. As we have seen, Mardi Gras beads have undergone symbolic inflation, with beads that were once acceptable now rarely ever thrown. So we don't have a base artifact type to relate everything to like Miller did. I attempted to create a price system a la Miller that would have covered the period from 1990 to 2009. To be blunt, it proved more frustrating than really necessary to illustrate how the method works. So instead, I have three years, 1999, 2004, and 2009 in which I have been able to construct relatively comprehensive sets of price data to demonstrate how this could work with the Mardi Gras beads while also giving us a sense of change through time.

Different bead companies sell beads in different lot sizes. Some sell them by the dozen, some by packs of a dozen, and some by the gross. The lot size is also determined by the size and length of the bead. Transparent throw beads are often sold in packs of five gross per pack, while 96" strands of 18mm are sold in packs of three strands. So the first thing I did was convert things into strand prices. Because there is not one constant standard size and diameter of bead type, I decided that I had to convert things into real dollars, which means, of course, factoring in for the rate of inflation afterward (which I did using conversion rates widely available on the internet). When it was not possible to find an exact bead's price, I used the closest length-diameter-finish combination available to me, rounding down as a matter of practice as to not artificially inflate the value of the assemblage.

To illustrate this technique, I have selected the 1999, 2004, and 2009 assemblages from the parade of Orpheus (Table 7.7). The average strand length from this parade in 1999 was 42.4", 43.6" in 2004, and 48.2" in 2009. There were 100 strands recovered from the 1999 par-ade, which would have cost $20.13. The 2004 assemblage, contained 116 strands and would have been valued at $25.28 in 2004. The value of the 87 beads recovered in 2009 had a value of $28.51. If we convert the value of the earlier assemblages to 2009 prices, then the 1999 assemblage has a value of $25.68 and the 2004 assemblage, $28.48. The greatest abundance was thrown in 1999, less in 2004, and the least in 2009, so even though we see relative consistency in the value of the three assemblages, we see a shift to fewer beads. If we convert the assemblage values into average strand prices, then we see that the average strand thrown in the 1999 assemblage was $0.25; the 2004 sample was $0.25; and the 2009 set was $0.33. For 1999, the assemblage is comprised of more high- and low-quality beads, and fewer mid-quality beads, ranging in length from 24 " to 100". In 2004, the beads were more concentrated in the middle-quality range with lengths of 32–60". In 2009, only one strand of beads measured 32", but the rest fell in the range of 48–60". In 2009, the strands recovered measured from 42" to 70".

So what have we learned from this exercise? If our parade samples are representations of the entire sample thrown, it suggests that maskers attempt to budget a consistent amount toward the purchase of beads each year, but within that budget have shifted from

Table 7.7. Economic Comparison of Orpheus Assemblages from 1999, 2004, and 2009.

	1999	2004	2009
AVERAGE STRAND LENGTH (in)	42.4	43.8	48.2
TOTAL NUMBER OF STRANDS CAUGHT	100	116	87
NUMBER OF BEAD STRANDS CAUGHT PER PERSON	50	39	29
VALUE OF ASSEMBLAGE IN YEAR CAUGHT ($)	20.13	25.28	28.51
VALUE OF ASSEMBLAGE ADJUSTED FOR INFLATION TO 2009 ($)	25.68	28.48	28.51
INFLATION-ADJUSTED AVERAGE STRAND VALUE ($)	.25	.25	.33

a strategy of throwing greater numbers of beads to throwing increased quality of beads. In other words, the throwing game is shifting from one of abundance to one of quality, and it is a shift clearly documented in the archaeological assemblage.

Explanations of Change

What these analyses allow us to see through time is an elaboration of the throwing game with new attributes of the beads coming to have meaning and value. How can we explain this new development in the throwing game when it was preceded by at least 70 years of a different trend? Processual archaeologists used systems theory to explain the relationships between different components of social life. The original intent of archaeologists using systems theory was to use formalized mathematical systems theory to model culture change. It became clear that such an enterprise was impossible to employ in archaeological settings (Salmon 1978); therefore, archaeologists turned to general systems theory, which was more descriptive than predictive. *General systems theory* as developed in archaeology was concerned with understanding how parts of a society articulated and interacted with one another and how changes in one part of a system would lead to changes in the overall system. Archaeologists called changes that occurred from outside of the system "kicks" (Flannery 1968). Archaeologists broke cultures down into its components to understand how culture change came about.

Flannery (1968) put forward one of the most successful uses of system theory to explain the shift from foraging to sedentary agriculture in Mesoamerica. Flannery examined five different systems of resource procurement that were taking place in Mesoamerica: maguey procurement, cactus fruit procurement, tree legume procurement, white-tailed deer procurement, and cottontail rabbit procurement. He used the seasonality of these resources, in combination with archaeological remains, to understand the annual scheduling cycles that Mesoamerican foragers lived by.

Flannery argued that seasonal scheduling—decision making—was part of a "deviation-counteracting" feedback system that prevented the intensification of any one resource over another and was designed to counteract short-term shortages in any particular resource. Without any changes to the system, he argued, the system would stay in equilibrium and not change. However, he argued, a "kick" had happened to a sixth, otherwise minor procurement system—wild grass procurement. Genetic changes to several of these plants led to the "kick" that became domesticated species. Zea mays, the wild form of corn, in particular, experienced genetic changes that made it an increasingly profitable crop to develop and harvest, which led to an amplification of that system over all others. Other procurement systems, like deer hunting, were rescheduled around maize planting and harvesting. With increases in farming, the exploitation of seasonally available waterfowl in areas becomes evident in regions where winter farming was not possible. Flannery demonstrated how using the terminology of systems theory allowed archaeologists to recognize links between different parts of the subsistence economy.

What then of Mardi Gras? Can we see a kick occurring in the bead economy that made it advantageous to change the way that beads were acquired and redistributed? I looked for possible economic changes that may have shaped bead acquisition from 1990 to 1994 that might explain bead inflation. Flannery's systems theory drew heavily upon the same economic theorizing as HBE, expecting that humans behave in a rational economic manner. I investigated whether there may have been an economic reason for changes in the throwing game that would lead to selection for larger beads. I have heard it expressed by Louisianans that a strong US dollar compared to the yen led to bead inflation. This cannot be true for the early period of MOS manufacturing, when the dollar was not particularly strong against the yen, and during the period of the early 1990s when the exchange rate held steady. Our cost analysis above demonstrated that assemblages thrown in different years represent similar expenditures once adjusted for inflation, but alteration in the composition of the assemblage reflects new values. Economics do not provide enough of an explanation for the shift in the throwing game to explain the incredible inflation we see in bead width and length during the study period.

The kick seems to be the introduction of MOS bead technology. We do not see changes until after the introduction of MOS beads. As we discussed in the last chapter, as the demand for beads grew, krewes were faced with a growing weight problem. The switch from one bead source and type to another was driven not only by cost but also by bead weight. The graduated MOS strands provided a cheaper, lighter bead that would allow krewes to continue to throw heavy. There is no reason that the game should have shifted at this point to include rankings of quality rather than quantity—the system could have continued in equilibrium with the throwing game involving greater and greater tribute of shorter, smaller beads. The switch to a quality and quantity ranking has lead to significantly greater bead weights, greater than anything before experienced in the throwing game! The switch doesn't make sense.

In Flannery's example, the switch seems rational— because Zea Mays exhibits genetic traits that make it more profitable to cultivate, the system shifts to intensify Zea Mays harvesting. Wait a minute. Let's review what I just said. It is the plant that does something that causes the shift. The plant makes people do something. It has agency. Not as a person has agency, mind you, but in the way a plant has agency. Sociologist Bruno Latour (2005) (and his collaborators) has developed the idea of object agency in *actor network theory* (**ANT**), as has anthropologist Timothy Ingold (2007) in his meshwork theory.

Generally speaking, ANT and meshwork theory both look at how people and things create interrelationships of meaning to one another in a complex network. In ANT, objects, just as people, have the ability to act (agency), in a way that makes them even (symmetrical) within a network. Now, Latour is not suggesting that people and objects act in the same ways as they act upon one another. People act in the way of people, and objects act in the manner of what they are. A building forces people to walk around it if they want to be on the other side or to move through it using its existing doorways, stairways, and elevators. It is the building's physical form that shapes it ability to act. Ingold's meshwork theory expands on ANT by recognizing that climate and geography—weather, mountains, oceans, temperatures, wind, sky, in short, the world—are also part of the meshwork in which people and objects generate meaning and life. These approaches differ from systems theory in that they focus on meaning rather than economy, and that they recognize more explicitly humans in relationships with the material world.

Like systems theory, ANT and meshwork theories have the great potential to become descriptive rather than explanatory. Both of these takes on humans-in-the-world theories are much more complex than I have described here, but for our discussion, these are the important ideas to take away. Some advocates for ANT in archaeology have proposed a new field—*symmetrical archaeology*—as a way to reorient the discipline away from processual archaeologies and the archaeologies that followed. They argue that the symmetry principle does away with the objective/subjective divide that has characterized recent archaeological practice and theory, (Olsen et al. 2012; Shanks 2007; Witmore 2007). The notion of symmetry is drawn from ANT and argues that all components of a network should be recognized as having equal ability to act, be they human, material, or technological. As means of an archaeological example, Witmore (2007) argues that a symmetrical approach forces archaeologists to recognize that the very process of excavation reveals the relationships between human action, materials, and technology and their shaping of one another. The archaeologist using tools interfaces with the archaeological record (material traces left by the actions of past people engaging with one another, materials and technologies) in a way that erases those traces. Through the mediation of technologies, archaeologists transform them into different kinds of representations that are also material and exist to be "read" or used and transformed by other archaeologists into interpretations. One cannot disentangle these engagements between the material, technological and human.

Drawing an example from my own archaeological experiences working at Clifton Plantation in the Bahamas (see chapter four), we found that the use of the land through time was intimately connected to how the original people who settled the property lived on it. The first residents of what became Clifton Plantation, the Lucayan Indians, settled a pair of villages in the 1300 and 1400s near established freshwater sources and to take advantage of a natural bay with sandy beaches that facilitated boat landing. They created a central plaza that was clear of vegetation and structures. Following them, the earliest

European colonists in the mid-1700s built their first stone houses in this same cleared area with access to drinking water and established a well. For these earliest residents, the primary transportation mode was the sea. The stone houses and the well were reused by Wylly. By Wylly's time, in the early 1800s, the island of New Providence had a developing network of roads that allowed transportation across the island. Boats remained important, so Wylly expanded the plantation. He reoccupied the structures at the beach, used the natural harbor, and added a new planter residence and enslaved people's village along the new road. By putting these residences on display along the road, Wylly was also displaying his wealth and power to those who traveled the roadway. After the end of the plantation system, the stone structures and walls built in previous times continued to shape the way the landscape was used. Plantation roads are still used for beach access, and people camp and cook by the stone houses on the beach where the Lucayans once lived. Periodically, people pour bleach into the wells to use the water. The stone walls that outlined the agricultural fields serve as visible pathways across the overgrown property, connecting the interior road to the sea. Although the walls are crooked and bend— meaning that it is a longer distance between the road and the beach—people still use them to mark the pathway rather than cutting new paths. Instead of building new houses, the enslaved people's village has been reoccupied multiple times, and the fields marked behind them replanted rather than cultivating new spots. We see that the previously built environment has shaped the way that people have interfaced with that landscape long after the original builders have been forgotten. This idea that things have agency is both the brilliant dimension of ANT, as well as the aspect that many find controversial. You'll note that in talking about ANT and systems theory, we have drifted back into the realm of technology as well. As I mentioned in our previous chapter, it is hard to separate technology from economy in many settings. In the case of the Mardi Gras beads, the symbolic economy was shaped in a real way by changes in the beads affected by the change in technology.

You'll note that I was careful to emphasize that Latour and others do not argue that things have the same kind of agency as humans, but agency that emerges out of the material or object's nature. I am not interested in trying to construct a network for the beads; that does not serve my interpretive needs at this point. What I do want to explore is the notion of the beads doing something to the throwing game. So how can considering the agency of the beads affect our understanding of the social world in which they are used and have meaning? As cited above, the 1973 quote about Mardi Gras beads proclaimed, "It is difficult to see distinctiveness in the mountain of beads accumulated for Carnival." Let us consider that quote further as it applies to the beads that would have been commonly found in 1973. The remaining glass hand-strung beads and the plastic hand-strung beads would have looked quite similar. They were all the same lengths, used the same general shapes and colors, and while they were made of different materials, all followed the same principles of stringing patterns.

The MOS beads offered potentially different attributes. They were also short, but because they were monochromatic and had one style of bead per strand, their differences could be easily distinguished. The first MOS beads were either transparent or opaque. Then, metallic, opalescent and pearl finishes were available by the early 1980s, though, at greater expense. The other variable that could be manipulated was the length of the strand or the size of the bead. Each of these attributes clearly stood out and made strands easy to compare against one another. Parade goers and celebrants in the French Quarter created rankings of the beads based on these attributes. Their preference for metallic and pearl finishes over transparent, and for wider and longer strands, shaped the purchasing decisions of the maskers.

Maskers selected MOS beads for two primary attributes: price and weight. But the beads had other attributes that acted upon the throwing game to change it. The beads themselves caused the changes in the throwing game. MOS beads have any number of attributes that allow them to act in different ways for different participants in the throwing game. It is the creativity of expression possible through Mardi Gras beads that we will explore for the rest of this book.

CHAPTER 8
SOCIAL IDENTITY

When I first began attending Mardi Gras parades, I found myself perplexed by the variety of materials I would catch. Everyone seemed to throw purple, green, and gold beads—the colors of Mardi Gras first decreed by Rex in the late nineteenth century; but beyond that, some krewes seemed to throw other colors of beads in abundance. Some threw necklaces bearing their krewe's initials, while others just threw a logo that as parade goers we were supposed to recognize. Some krewes threw things broadly signifying aspects of Louisiana culture or Mardi Gras celebrations; and some krewes threw things that were esoterically and specifically related just to their own organization. There were things that seemed to be inside jokes, and I wasn't able to catch the punch line. As I became more acquainted with the practices of Carnival, I began to understand more of the self-referencing systems and the signals that I was supposed to read in the throws. And in so doing, I became more of an insider to Louisiana culture. Material culture is like that; it can have many different meanings and different levels of significance to different users.

This is how material culture becomes a powerful means for people to express a sense of shared group identity. We experience this use of meaning-loaded material culture in our society all the time. At sporting events, fans of opposing teams wear different colors. Certain fashion labels are more important to some groups than others. We see people wearing red to indicate support for AIDS research and pink for breast cancer. Black armbands can indicate mourning and yellow ribbons support for political hostages. The mermaid has gone from being a nautical sign to one indicating the availability of overpriced coffee. Jeans denote casualness, a business suit professionalism, and jeans with a blazer is the uniform of archaeology conferences everywhere. When we talk about people using materials to situate themselves within a particular social group, we refer to this as the process of identification and the study of group identity.

How does one group of people distinguish themselves from another? This question has always been of central concern to archaeologists. For unilinear evolutionary thinkers, the answer led them to sort cultures in a rank order. For cultural historians, differences between groups of people, as evidenced by differences in composition of assemblages, allowed for the delineation of distinct cultural groups. Processual archaeology recognized that differences between people, as evidenced by toolkits or burial assemblages, could be

Strung Out on Archaeology: An Introduction to Archaeological Research by Laurie A. Wilkie, 239–268.
©2014 Left Coast Press, Inc. All rights reserved.

a way to distinguish between different kinds of subsistence strategies or social organization. For each of these sets of archaeology, culture was normative and shared. Difference meant differences in level of social development, differences in cultural affiliation, or differences in status within the society.

It is important to note from the onset, that archaeologists no longer think about social identity as a static, essentialized trait list as the cultural historians did. We now recognize that the beauty of using materials in this way is the ability to shift and change how identification takes place. For instance, in American society the color blue is often associated with baby boys and pink with baby girls. This however is only a recent phenomenon—in the 1920s, pink, seen as a stronger color, was for boys, and the delicate color blue was for girls. It was reversed in the 1940s. People are creative, innovative, and hard to pin down—making the process of identification more fun to study archaeologically.

Possible differences other than insider/outsider, or commoner/elite within a society were first considered in the field of historical archaeology where archaeologists understood they were studying sites in which ethnicity and race existed as identities within society (e.g., Ascher and Fairbanks 1971; Deetz 1977; MCGuire 1982; Schuyler 1980). Historical archaeologists looking at ethnicity were limited by the prevalent anthropological theories regarding ethnicity of the time, which focused on understanding ethnicity as an identity that created boundaries (Barth 1969) and did not yet address ethnicity as a politicized and situational identity but as a group that existed as a subset of larger society.

A number of historical archaeologists looked at ethnicity as standing in opposition to assimilation and searched for materials that served as "ethnic indicators" in assemblages. This is very much a normative, cultural historical approach to ethnicity. Roberta Greenwood's study (1980) of materials from Chinese American sites in California is an excellent example of how this kind of approach worked. Greenwood correlated the percentage of Chinese artifacts found in the archaeological assemblages to the degree of Chinese ethnicity/culture the occupants of the sites retained. A site with more Chinese artifacts was more Chinese than sites with fewer Chinese artifacts. Imagine if an archaeologist applied that thinking to any American household assemblage today? The entire United States would be characterized as culturally Chinese! While the logic seems absurd to us today, at the time, any attempt to understand differences in cultural practices within a dominant society was new and innovative in archaeology.

James Deetz (1977) also struggled with how to account for social difference within colonial society. He took a different route, drawing upon *structuralist thought* as used by the folklorist Henry Glassie (1975) to study folk housing. Deetz worked with the structuralist idea that any culture has a set of mental templates—ways of thinking—that shape the way people in that society make and do things. In his book, *In Small Things Forgotten*, Deetz looked at the transition among Anglo American colonists from a Medieval way of thinking to a Georgian mindset, which was shaped by the principles of the Enlightenment. He demonstrated how table wares, trash pits, house design, and gravestones all shifted in form as mindsets shifted. For instance, Medieval architecture was characterized by asymmetry, and an open floor plan may have included not just people living in one room but also their animals. Georgian architecture, which became popular during the Enlightenment featured great attention to symmetrical layout and space that was separated into multiple, functionally specific rooms. For Deetz, this shift in design mirrored a shift in the way Anglo Americans thought about domestic spaces. Deetz also introduced the African American families of the eighteen-century settlement of Parting Ways, Massachusetts as an example of a contrasting mindset. Deetz demonstrated that the people of Parting Ways lived by a different set of cultural ways of thinking; therefore, they structured their daily lives differently, built different styles of housing, used different pottery, and had different burial practices. The houses of Parting Ways did not resemble Medieval Anglo houses or Enlightenment Anglo American households. They looked like houses found in compounds in western-central Africa and were interpreted as evidence of continuity in an African worldview. While structuralist ways of thinking have been highly critiqued for their emphasis on western mind-body dualities and static approaches, Deetz's use of structuralism was extremely forward thinking. It allowed him to focus not on the recovery of specific artifact types to identify differences, but on the daily practices of everyday life that created different material worlds for different people.

In his critique of processualism, post-processualist Ian Hodder (discussed in chapter five) called upon archaeologists to rethink materials and consider the ways they are actively used in the construction of social life rather than as just a reflection of social values (which is a structuralist way of thinking) (Hodder 1979, 1982, 1986). He noted that archaeologists should consider the agency of individuals within society and explore the relationship between the structures of society and individual people (often called actors or **agents** in social theorizing), which is an idea that follows Anthony Giddens' **structuration theory** (1983), and Bourdieu's (1977, 1990) notions of the **habitus** and **doxa**.

In structuration theory, actors live within the structures of society—its rules, norms, and sets of acceptable practices—but they are conscious of these rules and work to manipulate them to their own advantage. Giddens recognizes that the cumulative effect of individual's actions lead to unintended social change; therefore, agency and structure are in a recursive relationship, where each makes the other. This recursive relationship is what he calls structuration. A good example of structuration would be the recent elevation of thrift store shopping to the status of "cool." A combination of a weak economy and a growing green movement promoting the reduction of one's carbon footprint has led more and more people to seek out secondhand clothing. For business owners, secondhand and consignment stores offer a business model that involves less investment in pricey inventory; and in a weak economy, these are the safest kinds of business risks to take. Individuals decide to look for decent secondhand clothing due to political and/or economic motivations. The unintended consequence of these decisions has been an increased number of thrift and secondhand clothing stores, a growing interest in vintage fashion, and the completely unexpected popularity of the song "Popping Tags." No one got together and decided, "let's make thrift store shopping a popular trend;" it was the combined effect of individuals all making similar decisions.

Bourdieu's social theorizing was, like Giddens', a critique of structuralism. For Bourdieu, habitus is the sense of cultural propriety and normative order that a person develops from childhood and through their everyday practices and experiences. Habitus serves as a structuring structure, but it does so at the individual level and shapes how they will approach new experiences and domains. Culture, therefore, is lived and experienced in the every day. Doxa—another concept proposed by Bourdieu—is the set of taken-for-granted realities embraced within a society. They are learned as part of the habitus, and as such, habitus can serve to reinforce social hierarchies and structural inequalities within society by making those structures seem inevitable and natural. In Zeta Psi, the Berkeley fraternity house I excavated, while all members of the household were brothers, the upper classmen were the "elders of the house." Their position as house leaders was enforced through a series of practices (these would be the habitus). For instance, at mealtime, the senior classmen sat at the head of the table, and were served food first. This mimicked the structure of mealtimes in patriarchal families, where the head of household was served first, and it was a way of naturalizing the power of the upper classmen (doxa). In contrast, not only did freshmen eat last, but they were also responsible for the bulk of household chores—putting them in the structural position of the "women" of the house. All members participated in these practices, no matter their status, for it was understood that one's position in the house would increase in prestige the longer one was there, and all would eventually sit in the seats of privilege.

Agents within Bourdieu's theorizing are limited in their ability to affect change on society, but despite this serious shortcoming, the notion of habitus has proven popular with archaeologists in part because it allows for artifacts to carry different meanings to different users. Men, women, children, the elderly, the infirm, all living together can then be understood to potentially experience the material world in very different ways. Archaeologists have found structuration theory and practice theory a productive means for thinking about concepts such as tradition and ethnicity (e.g., DeCunzo 1995; Jones 1997; Lightfoot et al. 1998; Pauketat 2000).

Lu Ann DeCunzo (1995) excavated the site of the Magdalene Society in Philadelphia (in existence from 1800 to 1850). Magdalene societies (named after Mary Magdalene) were reform houses focused on rehabilitating "fallen" women—women who had been sexually promiscuous, worked as prostitutes, or otherwise engaged in behaviors that were seen as outside the realm of acceptable womanhood of the time. DeCunzo found Bourdieu's notion of habitus to be a useful tool for understanding the way reformers approached the institutionalization and rehabilitation of women that entered the asylum. The reformers believed that salvation relied on women relearning proper discipline and womanly behavior. Based on the materials recovered archaeologically, women in the asylums lived simple existences with plain and simple material culture, a bland diet, and an emphasis on hard work and regimented schedules. In other words, through exposure to a new habitus, reformers hoped to instill the doxa of proper womanhood in these fallen women.

Theories of practice, including, but not limited to, the ideas of Anthony Giddens and Pierre Bourdieu have been used by archaeologists to examine different subject positions that may have been occupied in past societies: gender and sexuality (DeCunzo 1995; Gilchrist 1994), ethnicity (Jones 1997; Lightfoot et al. 1998), social class (Beaudry et al. 1991), and race (Wilkie 2000). Theories of practice have been popular because they focus on the importance of day-to-day routines—the kind of activities that are best represented in archaeological remains. Most practice theories recognize some degree of agency for actors, but they also recognize the constraining aspects of social norms on human action.

Also inherent in practice theories are different degrees of consciousness of the actors engaged in day-to-day actions. Bourdieu's actors are often engaged in routinized behavior that they take for granted without much self-reflection. Giddens' actors may recognize their own motives for acting in particular ways, but they do not necessarily understand the larger-scale implications of their actions. Judith Butler's performance theory offers yet another form of practice theory, in which Butler's actors are engaged in self-conscious, embodied performances of public identity that they shift according to time and context (Joyce and Meskell 2003). I will explain Butler's ideas in more detail in the next chapter; but for now, just recognize that unlike Giddens and Bourdieu, whose actors do not necessarily think about the consequences of their actions, Butler's people are actively thinking about what they are doing and how what they are doing will be perceived by others.

Social identity has proven itself a slippery concept. A number of different subjectivities are lumped under the category "social identity:" race, sex, gender, class/social status, ethnicity, occupation, age, and so on. How does one actually manage to study all of those things embodied in one person? Some archaeologists choose to see, instead, multiple social identities embodied in one person and focus interpretively on one aspect of identity foremost. A number of archaeologists have again raised the concern that too many archaeological conceptualizations of their subjects impose a Western mentality on the past. This extends not only to the mind-body duality we discussed before, but also to the idea that bodies are bounded. In much of Western thought tradition, the boundaries of the person end with the boundaries of the body. One body equals one person. This is not a human universal. Following the work of anthropologist Marilyn Strathern (1988) and her idea of the"dividual", or social person, some archaeologists interrogate the notion of what constituted a person in the past, because they recognize that not all individuals were given full person rights depending on their age, gender, or other statuses. In many societies, children are not considered full persons until they reach puberty. In the US, there are a series of age-related markers that serve to highlight the road to full personhood: a driver's license at 16, voting at 18, drinking at 21, and then, full personhood at 25 when you can rent a car. In addition, in many societies an individual's personhood may have extended to their belongings (Clark and Wilkie 2007; Fowler 2004; Joyce 2009; Meskell 1999) and beyond one's life. During debates about NAGPRA and repatriation, a number of Native American groups argued that interfering with their ancestors' mortal remains disturbed their ability to live in the afterlife. This is an important example of personhood extending beyond life that has a recognizable material manifestation.

Others are concerned that "identity" is too static and essentializing a term. Remember that much of post-modern theorizing that has influenced thinking among archaeologists who embraced the post-processual critique emphasizes fluidity and prefers to defy categorizations and focus on recursive relationships between people and society. For this reason, some archaeologists discuss processes of identification—again, bringing us theoretically back to the notion of performance, or the ways that people choose to intentionally (or unintentionally) present themselves.

Performance of Social Identity in Mardi Gras Parades

Performance theories represent an interesting avenue for exploring social identification within the Mardi Gras krewes. Mardi Gras celebrations are carefully and self-consciously planned by participants. For Krewes, their parade is the most public face of their institution, and everything from the parade theme, float designs, the costumes, to the music, and yes, the throws, are planned during the entire year leading up to the celebration. As noted, Krewes are judged by parade goers according to their generosity with throws. Krewes also compete with one another in other ways. Exclusivity, lavishness of balls, civic engagements, philanthropy, beautiful and innovative parade floats, or the ability to attract high-visibility celebrity participants are ways that krewes compete against one another. Krewes are engaged in highly self-conscious representations of their organizations as they prepare for and celebrate the Carnival season. Bacchus, for example, is known for its celebrity kings and lavish parade with grand floats that make all things Bacchus, such as the Bacchasaurus float featuring a purple dinosaur wearing laurels around its head. Orpheus prides itself as the krewe that celebrates New Orleans' rich musical history and honors famous local musicians in its parade. The historically black Zulu reminds parade goers of histories of racial discrimination while also expressing a strong sense of pride in links to an African homeland.

Throws are a means of constructing krewe identities for the public through the performance of throwing. Zulu provides one of the most coveted throws of the Carnival season, their hand-painted and decorated coconuts. Muse, an all female krewe, works to develop throws that are innovative and feature tongue-in-cheek feminist themes and has begun to throw hand-decorated shoes in a sort of homage to Zulu's creativity. Rex, Bacchus, and other krewes develop new throws that they hope will become popular new Mardi Gras traditions. Krewes will often publicize new throws they are introducing prior to a parade to build excitement and encourage crowds to beg for the new item.

In the excavated bead assemblages, by analyzing one parade versus another, it should be possible to see ways that material culture is used to create a shared, krewe identity that is communicated to the crowds. The MOS beads offer a distinct advantage over the hand-strung beads. It becomes possible to use color in an inexpensive way to communicate a krewe identity—in the same way that sports teams use colors to self-identify. We will look at how krewes use the materiality of beads to communicate about their organization to the public and ways that materials may be used within the krewes to suggest differences in social status. We will also see evidence of ways of self-identification that crosscut Krewes and creates shared identities that are broader reaching than individual organizations.

Representation of Self in 2000

I first envisioned this project as a short-term survey exploring how krewes differentiated themselves while trying to establish their relative prestige against one another. I was intrigued to see how krewes balanced issues of quality versus quantity in the throwing game (see chapter seven). One way to do that was through generosity in krewe-specific articles. These items tend to be valued by parade goers because they are a memento of a particular parade. The sense I get from parade goers is that a parade that is generous with generic throws but fails to provide any krewe-specific gifts is viewed less favorably than a krewe that provides fewer overall throws but more krewe-specific items. In addition to medallions, krewes will throw plastic cups, frisbees, doubloons, koozies, hats, t-shirts, underwear, bracelets, and stuffed animals depending on the parade (for an example of the diversity, see Figure 8.1). All of these items are highly prized, but in the last ten years the beads have been the most common and the most enduring.

The earliest krewe-themed throws were the aluminum doubloons that Rex introduced in the early 1960s. These featured the krewe's logo on one side and the theme of the parade and date on the obverse side (Figure 8.2). These were highly popular and widely collected; the popularity of the doubloons is what probably prompted Bacchus to use a representation of their doubloon on the first medallions. There are several drawbacks to doubloons as throws. They are harder to catch in the air, and if they hit the ground, you have to stomp your foot on top of it to claim them; otherwise, you will find your hand quickly and thoroughly stomped by someone else. Having to pick anything up off the ground at a Mardi Gras parade is a risky proposition; there are nasty, nasty, things on the ground. After a parade, it is not uncommon to see doubloons left lying in the primordial sludge that accumulates at the curbside during the Carnival season. The doubloons are not worth the risk of exposure to whatever lurks in that goo. At night parades, doubloons are even harder to see. They have become less popular and are most likely to be tossed gently directly to a particular person or handed out individually by riders on foot or horseback.

Seemingly functional throws—cups—printed with the krewe's name and parade theme were widely popular in the 1980s and

Figure 8.1. Throws caught at the 2009 Spanish Town parade; note the wide range of flamingo-themed artifacts. Photograph by Alexandra Wilkie Farnsworth.

Figure 8.2. Examples of Mardi Gras doubloons.

1990s but have also faded in popularity. For parade goers, they are useful at the parade and used to consume beer from kegs and are then discarded among the growing pile of trash, which makes them not a particularly popular throw with landfill managers. They crunch under foot, and there are only so many you can carry in a tall stack. It is typical to see freshly thrown cups that hit the ground never be picked up along parade routes, and that circumstance alone is enough to discourage maskers from throwing too many of them.

So beads remain the most popular of the commonly available krewe throws. The beads are not particularly useful; but you will see krewe beads strung around rear view mirrors in cars, hanging in offices, decorating Christmas trees (a very popular reuse of Mardi Gras beads), and they are popularly rethrown in smaller parades that have no medallion beads of their own. A krewe's prestige is built as well through the practice of rethrowing. A krewe is seen as particularly generous if they throw so much that people who went to the parade have enough to throw as well. Even someone who has never attended the parade firsthand learns of the krewe by catching beads that have been redistributed.

Relevant to this discussion is the subject of how krewes are categorized in the popular literature. Categories of krewes include old-line krewes, super krewes, all-women's krewes, Zulu, and everyone else. Zulu, as the only New Orleans all-black krewe (NOMTOC is another all black krewe that parades across the river in Algiers), has not been historically lumped in with other categories of krewes but recognized as unique. Racial unease that still marks social life in Louisiana has probably prevented Zulu from being classified as an old-line krewe, which it most certainly is by original definitions.

Classifying Krewes

When I began attending Mardi Gras in 1991, the term "old-line krewes" was used to designate parading organizations of long duration that had maintained their traditions of membership and parading since the nineteenth-century, and it included the krewes of Comus, Proteus, Momus, and Rex. In 1991, the city council of New Orleans passed an ordinance that revoked the right of any organization to obtain a permit to parade if they could not prove that they were integrated. The ordinance forbade discrimination against potential members based upon race, color, sex, sexual orientation, national origin, ancestry, age, physical condition, or disability. Of the nineteenth-century krewes that were still parading, Momus, Proteus, and Comus decided to stop parading rather than reveal their membership or change their selection processes. The members of these societies were highly secretive, and parading represented only one dimension the organization's activities. Rex quickly agreed to comply, but remained the only recognized old-line krewe parading until Proteus returned in 2000.

Super krewes were those organizations that were founded recently, and they had lesser emphasis on strict selectivity of members. The ability to pay the dues and nomination for membership by a current krewe member was all that was required. These krewes emphasized giant floats, abundant throws, and excess in all things. As mentioned before, Endymion was the first super krewe. It was founded in 1967 and followed by Bacchus in 1968 and Orpheus in 1993. The public perceives super krewes to be the most generous of the krewes, because they throw more and better beads than other parades. The general sense of the old-line krewes is that they tend to be "cheap" and throw fewer beads. Other krewes fall somewhere in between.

In 2009, Arthur Hardy, a well-known popular historian of Mardi Gras, reclassified krewes and determined that old-line krewes should be a term that referred to the style of parading rather than the age of the parade. Hardy also decided that Rex and Zulu (which informally paraded as early as 1901, but became more formally organized in 1909), should be classified as super krewes along with Endymion, Orpheus, and Bacchus, while krewes that still paraded with floats designed on a wagon base should be referred to as old-line krewes. To be a successful historian of secret societies requires Hardy to be as much a spokesperson for, as scholar of, the krewes. Hardy has always been a particular fan of Rex; therefore, I read his redefinition of krewe classification as a concern on Rex's part that their parade was not perceived as as important as the super krewes in the popular imagination. In putting Zulu in the category of super krewe rather than old-line krewe, Hardy avoided the discomfort of tweaking the noses of the old-line krewes who revolted against the 1991 desegregation ordinance, but it allowed him to recognize Zulu, historically, as well as today, as one of the main attractions of New Orleans' Carnival season. The all-women Krewe of Iris was founded in 1917 and has also maintained strict traditions in membership and parading, but it was not included as an old-line krewe. Iris was among the krewes that reacted strongly against the ordinance of 1991; they did not want to incorporate men into their membership. Hardy also identified the Knights of Babylon, the Krewe of Hermes, and the Krewe of Proteus as old-line krewes. As an archaeologist, I read Hardy's reclassification with great interest. It reminded me of the debates that one sees during the intellectual period of culture history in archaeology, in which archaeologists debated the chronological and geographic boundaries of a particular culture area. Just as Ford and Spaulding (see chapter 3) debated whether archaeologists created real types with their classification systems or just useful analytical constructs, I found myself wondering whether Hardy's classification system had any use in the real world of Mardi Gras.

Hardy has published annually for several decades a popular guide on Mardi Gras for tourists and is consulted regularly on all things Mardi Gras; so I expect that his definition will endure. However, if we look at the data recovered from the 10 New Orleans parades excavated in 2000, we can see other ways that krewes can be classified using archaeological data based on their throwing strategies.

In retrospect, 2000 represents a bit of an anomaly because it coincided with millennium celebrations when many of the krewes were increasing the abundance and quality of their throws to mark the event. It was that year when Bacchus introduced a hand-painted resin medallion; Orpheus introduced a heavier and larger, metallic medallion; and Zulu, Tucks, and Thoth moved to multi-colored, larger medallions. The Krewe of Rex has for years thrown a distinctive opaque purple, yellow, and green plastic hand-strung necklace featuring a yellow crown medallion that says "Rex." In 2000, for the first time, I collected MOS strands that had gold Rex crowns hanging from them. I haven't been able to confirm if this was the year they were introduced, but it seems likely. Parade goers, however, did not see the generosity of 2000 as a one-time event; as seen in the previous chapter, bead inflation picks up from 2000 onward.

The parades attended during 2000 (Table 8.1) included the super krewes Bacchus, Endymion, Orpheus, the old-line Krewe of Proteus (who was returning to parading for the first time since 1991), the historically long-established krewes of Rex, Zulu, and Iris,

Table 8.1. Medallions Thrown by New Orleans Krewes in 2000.

KREWE	AVERAGE LENGTH OF BEAD STRANDS CAUGHT (33.7" = NEW ORLEANS AVERAGE)	NUMBER OF MEDALLIONS	MEDALLIONS AS A PERCENTAGE OF TOTAL BEADS CAUGHT AT PARADE	OVERALL NUMBER OF BEADS CAUGHT PER PERSON AT PARADE
BACCHUS	46.1	6	7.7	26
ENDYMIAN	27.3	7	3.1	74.7
IRIS	33.2	6	6.3	31.6
OKEONOS	32.6	1	8.3	3.6
ORPHEUS	47.7	8	9.8	41
PROTEUS	36.4			4.5
REX	42.1	16	34	11.8
THOTH	33.9	1	2.3	14.3
TUCKS	35.6	7	14.9	15.7
ZULU	33.5	13	29.5	14.7

and the more recently founded (since the 1950s) krewes of Thoth, Tucks, and Okeonos. This cross-section of parades allows us to look at differing strategies used by organizations in the throwing game as well as allows us to determine if there is any truth to classification system of the krewes. Table 8.1 lists each of the parades excavated in 2000 and the average length of the bead strands thrown, the number of medallions recovered from each parade, the percentage of the parade beads that were medallions, and the average number of beads caught per person at each parade. I used these measures so that we can compare the relative representation of krewe-specific beads for each organization and the overall abundance and quality of each assemblage.

Household Archaeology and Mardi Gras

I will, in this discussion, speak of each krewe as if it is a separate entity or almost, a person, and for the sake of Mardi Gras, each krewe is. Outside of burial contexts and certain kinds of historical period sites, individual actors can be difficult to identify archaeologically. Most of the deposits archaeologists study were created by multiple people who were somehow connected to one another in their routines of daily life. Archaeologists try to recognize subgroups that existed within past communities by looking at the organization of features across space. Field boundaries or walls, architectural remains, plazas, and roads, are examples of archaeological features that could have served to delineate segments of society in the past. Through ethnographic analogy, oral history, or archival work, spatial features can be recognized as having distinctive social meaning. For instance, it was through the ethnographic observation of kivas as the ritual spaces of Puebloan peoples in the American Southwest that the distinctive circular rooms found in Ancestral Pueblo sites were identified as such spaces.

One of the most important social spaces that archaeologists study is that of the household. While anthropologists agree that households are the smallest meaningful social group that humans form, what a household looks like through time and space—both in terms of what people and what physical materials comprise that place—is often tricky to determine (Wilk 1988). Households are economic, social, and sometimes political units, and they may be autonomous or linked to other households. A single household may occupy multiple buildings (think of a farm complex where a household may include a residence, barn, silo, outhouse, toolshed, etc.), or multiple households may occupy a single building (think of a dorm or an apartment building). Who the members of the household are can take a variety of forms, even within a single society.

There is often a strong desire among archaeologists to equate cohabitation with kinship—the idea that family members live together. But cross-culturally, we know this isn't the case now or in the past. In just the recent past, the archaeological sites I have worked on include a variety of household forms. Delphine and Eliza Freeman, of Oakley Plantation, set up a household where the unmarried sisters resided together and jointly raised their children. They lived together in one structure, but all of their food preparation was done in the separate kitchen building that was part of the planter's residence. The fraternity site of Zeta Psi was a single household comprised of unrelated young men (who may or may not have been related to previous generations of men who had lived in the house), who nonetheless, called one another by the kinship term "brother." The fraternity also housed another pair of unrelated young men—the Chinese or Japanese house servants and cooks who were hired by the fraternity. These men lived in quarters spatially isolated from the rest of the house and did not socialize with the fraternity men, nor were they granted the status of fictive kin.

At Clifton Plantation, the planter wanted to encourage European forms of marriage among the enslaved Africans and provided a stone house to each of the married couples on the plantation to raise their children. In many West African societies of the time, however, men and women lived in the same household compound, but not the same structure. Women were seen as potentially dangerous (*polluting,* to use an anthropological term), to men's spiritual and physical health when they were menstruating or breastfeeding; thus, even married couples did not always live together. At Clifton, the beach houses far from the village were used as barracks for single men and women. The archaeological evidence suggests that married women would temporarily live in the women's barrack at different times, perhaps to accommodate cultural ideas about pollution.

The Cordes, who created the deposit that became my senior thesis site, were the only household I've worked on that fit the modern sterotype of a married couple with their descendents coresiding in a single structure. And by no means have I discussed all the household variations I have encountered! If we have this many different house types represented in the recent past, just imagine the wonderful diversity that had to exist in the past!

So how is an archaeologist to sort this out? Since anthropologists agree that communities are composed of households, and households are the smallest meaningful social unit of society, it stands to reason that those things that make up a household should be replicated over and over again in a community. So archaeologists look for features that are repeated. At a site where there is little preservation of architecture, like in many prehistoric California hunter-gatherer sites, archaeologists look for features like cooking hearths as evidence of distinct households. In Mesoamerica, at prehistoric Maya sites, households usually consist of multiple structures built around a central plaza or compound with some sort of ritual space for the veneration of shared ancestors and perhaps some of those ancestors buried within the compound area (Gillespie 2000).

It's worth asking that if a Mardi Gras krewe can be seen as a kind of household, what are the material manifestations of that household? Most of the New Orleans parades are multiple float parades sponsored by a single krewe/household; while other parades are sponsored by multiple groups/krewes who each contribute a component. You can see this is not unlike the farmhouse-apartment building duality. Some parades with 20 floats may represent one household, whereas some parades of 20 floats may represent 20 households. At the bare minimum, a krewe household is represented materially by a number of people who self-identify as part of the same group and have a name for their group, which they have somehow labeled themselves with. Often, the group's name will be emblazoned on clothing or on a banner or painted on the float. Communication of group identity may also be achieved by riding a float decorated with their name, throwing items emblazoned with their name, and wearing matching costumes.

For multi-float krewe households, the different components of the household demonstrate their affiliation through a shared parade theme, throws marked with their shared name, shared costumes, shared design elements on the floats, and to make affiliation absolutely clear, floats that are part of the parade are visibly numbered. Within the single household parades, other groups, such as marching bands or dance troops, may participate in the parade, and they will mark themselves in all the same kind of ways that households in multi-household parades distinguish themselves. Some of the invited groups often include military recruitment floats or veterans organizations. While these groups have their own floats within the larger household's procession, these floats conspicuously lack numbers.

Susan Gillespie (2000) has suggested for archaeologists interested in understanding family, social dynamics, and incipient stratification within past non-state-level societies that the idea of the "house" is a much more productive intellectual concept for us to use than alternative terms like "lineages." She points out that ethnography demonstrates that households are arenas where wealth and prestige are communicated, as well as places where power can be consolidated. Although she is writing specifically for the purpose of understanding ancient Mesoamerica, her arguments, and the ideas of household archaeology in general, are useful for understanding types of Mardi Gras parades.

While we saw earlier that the material evidence of the krewes can be understood through the model of households, this isn't just a conceit on my part. The documentary record of Mardi Gras also demonstrates the corporate identity of these organizations. Krewe members act as part of a single household. Newspapers, tourist guides, and Louisiana natives refer to krewes as singular beings, with statements such as, "Rex makes his appearance at . . .," or "Iris will follow her usual route." Members of the krewe are judged as part of a collective. I will follow this convention in my analysis, but I recognize that the bead assemblages caught are the result of a structuration process—individuals buying beads, knowing what the krewe recommended as guidelines, knowing what was popular with crowds, and then using their agency to create the assemblage of beads they would throw. The assemblage is the unanticipated outcome of all of those separate decision-making processes by individual actors. No matter what the generosity or stinginess of individuals within the parade organization, all are judged collectively as part of the larger corporate group.

If we look first at abundance (Table 8.1), or which krewe throws the most, we see the krewes fall into three natural clusters based on their generosity. The top cluster is Endymion, Orpheus, Iris, and Bacchus. It is worth noting that Endymion, Orpheus, and Bacchus fall in the first tier and are all considered to be super krewes under Arthur Hardy's old and new classification system. Tucks, Zulu, Thoth, and Rex form the second cluster.

Hardy classifies Zulu and Rex as super krewes in his new Mardi Gras typology, but super krewes are judged in folk wisdom to be the most generous of krewes. The least generous krewes, based on this measure, are Okeonos and Proteus. A quick word on Proteus, we'll consider this krewe more closely in a later chapter. They returned to Mardi Gras in 2000 to find themselves dislodged from their parading slot by a new super krewe, Orpheus. They clearly underestimated ways that bead economy had changed since 1991, and their maskers were under provisioned. They struggled for years afterward to catch up.

How do our krewes compare if we use the criteria of bead quality to compare them? As we discussed previously, bead length is a measure of quality used by parade goers to evaluate generosity. The average length of a strand of Mardi Gras beads thrown during the 2000 Carnival season was 33.7″. This average provides us with something to compare the parades against. Again, we see the beads falling into three natural clusters (Table 8.1). Orpheus threw the longest average beads, followed by Bacchus, and surprisingly to me, Rex. Each of these krewes threw beads that were well above the average for the parade season. The next cluster of krewes all threw at or just around the average for New Orleans: Proteus, Tucks, Thoth, Zulu, Okeonos, and Iris. Falling below the city average was Endymion.

When we now compare the bead length to number of strands caught per person, we see strategy emerging. The super krewes of Bacchus and Orpheus threw both "heavy" and "good," which fits into the popular notion of a super krewe. Endymion, the super krewe who threw much "heavier" than the other two super krewes, did so by sacrificing quality for quantity. Similarly, Iris, who threw heavier than Bacchus, threw only average length beads. Rex, who was the third lightest thrower, made up for stinginess by throwing some of the longest beads. Okeonos threw lightly of average length beads. Zulu, Thoth, and Tucks consistently threw an average amount of average beads.

When I looked at these results, I didn't see a convincing case for designating Rex or Zulu as super krewes based on their participation in the throwing game, and I wondered if looking at patterns of medallion distribution would provide additional insights? While I have provided the number of medallions included in each parade assemblage, this raw number is not as important as understanding what proportion of the overall assemblage was marked with krewe names or iconography. When we sort our krewes by this measure, we see yet a third set of clustering. Rex has the highest percentage of krewe marked beads (34.0%) followed by Zulu (29.5%) and Tucks (14.9%). The second cluster includes super krewe Orpheus (9.8%), Okeonos (8.3%), Bacchus (7.7%) and Iris (6.3%), with the lowest cluster being Endymion (3.1%), Thoth (2.3%) and Proteus (0). Rex, Zulu, and Tucks appear to have selected to expend more resources on krewe-themed beads than non-krewe beads of higher quality or greater abundance. The result is an assemblage that strongly communicates the identity of the organization, and suggests these krewes have a strong sense of shared identity. By looking at medallion design through time, we can also get a sense of how Krewes see themselves within the history of Mardi Gras. To do this, we will now expand our consideration of krewes and their beads to before and beyond 2000.

Communicating Tradition

Among the New Orleans krewes I studied are four groups that have been parading for over or close to a century: Rex (1872), Proteus (1882), Zulu (1909), and Iris (1917). These krewes use imagery and form of their medallions to communicate a sense of organizational heritage and tradition. Rex may no longer be considered an old-line krewe by Arthur Hardy; but, Rex and Proteus, the only two nineteenth-century organizations still parading, share similar strategies in the design of their krewe beads. Iris is the oldest surviving all women's krewe. For them, tradition is also a way to communicate a commitment to family values and womanly propriety. Zulu, as the only historically African American parading organization, uses continuity in medallion imagery to maintain a historical connection with the political sensibilities and commitments of the society.

Demonstrating Endurance

Rex was founded in 1872 by a group of New Orleans businessmen to celebrate the visit of Grand Duke Alexis of Russia to the city for Carnival (Gill 1997). Rex, drawing from the Latin language, was to be the king of Carnival, a royal worthy of welcoming royalty to the city. The krewe's other aim was to develop an attraction that would draw tourism to post-Civil War New Orleans, an aim perhaps reflected in the krewe's motto, "*Pro Bono Publico*" (for the public good). Rex has had an undeniable long-term impact on Mardi Gras celebrations. They chose gold (power), purple (justice), and green (faith), to be the colors of Carnival, and this palette is still used to signal Mardi Gras—whether in the choice of bead colors thrown, the colors of icing on king cakes served during the Carnival season, or the colors of crepe paper and other decorations. Rex is closely tied to the Boston Club, a private New Orleans organization whose membership continues to contain New Orleans' most elite. The membership of Rex selects their king each spring, but their decision is kept secret until Lundi Gras when Rex's identity is revealed and profiled in local papers. Rex is a prominent citizen of the city who is also usually known for his philanthropic activities. His queen is also selected in the spring but not revealed until Lundi Gras. She is typically a debutante and daughter of a well-placed krewe member.

The Krewe of Rex has resisted the urge to branch out heavily into new forms of throws and new representations of itself. While other krewes regularly change their medallion designs or offer multiple versions of beads each year, Rex continues to throw its distinctive hand-strung, tri-color Rex crown medallion and metallic strands featuring the same crown. In doing so, Rex maintains a visible connection with their legacy of distinctive contributions to Mardi Gras history. Rex's historical contributions to Mardi Gras are seen in another way throughout just about every Mardi Gras parade in Louisiana. The purple, green, and gold Mardi Gras colors decreed by Rex in 1872 are abundant in nearly every Mardi Gras parade I excavated in Louisiana during my study (Table 8.2). The introduction of MOS beads and their monochromatic coloration has allowed for Mardi Gras colors to be highlighted inexpensively in throw beads in a way that was not possible

Table 8.2. Color Distribution of Beads Thrown by Krewes in 2000.

% BEAD COLOR (ALL FINISHES COMBINED)	1997	1999	2000	2001	2002	2003	2004	2006	2007	2009
PURPLE	26.1	17.6	17.3	18.6	15.5	15.9	15.7	20.6	13.0	10.5
GREEN	13.1	23.7	25.3	14.4	14.3	29.8	10.2	11.7	16	18.8
GOLD	15.2	15.2	14.1	16.9	21.7	19.4	24.4	8.8	11	19.1
RED	13.1	3.7	4.3	16.9	7.7		10.7	32.2	31	19.1
BLUE	2.5	2.5	2.6	5	3.3	4.9	6.6	3.7	5	3.3
SILVER	4.5	4.5	2	3.4	3	8.3	3	5.6	6	8.2
BLACK	2.5	2.5	2.5	.8						.3
WHITE	8.7	22.2	20.5	15.2	20.5	11.8	25.4	10.3	3	6.9
CLEAR					.3		2	.5		
PINK	8.7	2	3.1	3.4	1.5	7.6		5.1	11	12.8
GREY		2								
ORANGE		.4	.5		.6				1	
YELLOW			4.1		2.4					.7
COPPER		1.6								
MULTI-COLORED STRANDS	2.1	2	3.5	5	9.2	2	2	1.4	3	.3

with hand-strung beads. Symbolically, it could be said that any krewe that flies his royal colors is recognizing Rex as the king of Mardi Gras.

Proteus, named for the God of the Sea, is only eight years younger than Rex, but its departure and return to parading left it in a strange position. Proteus had a signature bead, which like that of Rex, was a short, hand-strung strand with a simple medallion. While Rex features the purple-green-gold combination, Proteus threw a monochrome red strand with a white seahorse medallion, signifying the sea god. Also like Rex, to demonstrate that the old krewe was not out of touch, in 2001 they threw a more fashionable update of their medallion—a silver seahorse on a red metallic strand. More so than any other krewe, Proteus brands most of its throws by either color or with its krewe logo. In 2000, 2001, and 2002, the colors red and white dominated the throw bead assemblage (Table 8.3). In 2006, 67 of the 70 beads caught were red (95.7%), and in 2009, in conjunction with the apparent complete replacement of the hand-strung medallions with the new metallic ones, we see red (72%), followed by silver (18%), dominating the color assemblage. Perhaps it is not unintentional that Proteus also has the lowest incidence of the purple-green-gold color scheme of Mardi Gras that all other parading organizations draw upon, throwing well

Table 8.3. Color Distribution of Beads Thrown by Krewe of Proteus through Time.

	2000 (%)	2001 (%)	2002 (%)	2004 (%)	2006 (%)	2007 (%)	2009 (%)
PURPLE	12.5		4.2	3.6	5		
GREEN	12.5	5	2.8	3.6			
GOLD	12.5	5	4.2	3.6			
RED	37.5	55	23.9	32.7	93.5	100	72
BLUE			1.4	1.8	2.5		
SILVER							18
BLACK							
WHITE	25 0	35	40.8	50.9			
CLEAR							
PINK							
GREY							
ORANGE							
YELLOW							
COPPER							
MULTI-COLORED STRANDS			22.5	1.8			

under the New Orleans average in every year (Table 8.2). Unlike other krewes, Proteus does not hail Rex.

On the University of California campus, I have encountered two archaeological examples of households that used particular designs or colors to assert their group's identity. You'll probably not be surprised to hear that one of them was the Zeta Psi fraternity. Among the ceramics recovered from excavations of the house were multiple examples of hotel porcelains by the Onondaga Pottery Company of New York, which bore the crest of the fraternity. The crest-decorated ceramics were used at rush dinners, during the recruitment of new pledges, and would have reinforced to guests whose hospitality they were receiving. The crest contains symbolic representations of the values of the fraternity, and viewing the crest while eating would remind the members of those values as they shared a meal with their fictive kin. The second site where I found ceramics of a particular color and design being used to communicate a sense of shared identity was in the women's house club of Casa Hispana. Formed in the late 1920s as a communal living group for women students, Casa Hispana was a themed house, whose members were to share a passion for Spanish language and culture. With a field school, I excavated the house where the group lived from 1932 to 1935. The women chose a set of blue California art pottery, often called by the name Fiesta ware, for their house ceramics. These ceramics were available in many different colors, but the choice of blue is likely to be linked to the University of California colors of Blue and Gold. While these ceramics have no connection to Spanish culture, they were perceived as having ties to Hispanic California, and for reasons I do not really understand, a number of Mexican restaurants surrounding the Berkeley campus to this day use Fiesta wares (which are still made by Homer Laughlin Pottery Company of Ohio) as their restaurant wares. In each case, a household of unrelated people who were trying to create a sense of shared identity intentionally used ceramic design and color to do so.

Gendered Identities

In the next chapter we will explore sexualized and gendered dynamics of Mardi Gras, but I consider the Krewe of Iris here briefly. Iris is another krewe that has retained its original medallion design—a yellow or purple transparent medallion featuring an Iris. In the past, some of these medallions featured the parade year (I have seen examples from 1985), but as best I can tell, this part of the mold has been left blank, creating a generic and timeless bead. The decision to maintain one style of medallion through time is also a statement about tradition and continuity. At least in 1999, in addition to throwing the classic medallion, Iris threw a silver metallic parade-themed bead: "Iris Dreams of Hollywood." In its parade history, Iris has emphasized the importance of tradition, including their commitment to wearing full-length fitted gowns, full-face Carnival masks, and white gloves while parading. The krewe exudes a particular kind of lady-like elegance in their parade. I understand that a coveted throw to catch at an Iris parade is a pair of ceramic beads. I have failed to ever see these, and I do not know when they were introduced. However, the use of ceramic would get around ordinances prohibiting throwing glass beads. I suspect these are most likely to be porcelain beads, which would also add to the image of refined and elegant womanhood performed by the krewe. Porcelain has long been associated with well-to-do women (Wall 1994). In the nineteenth century, middle class women in New York used expensive porcelain tea sets to entertain the wives of their husbands' business associates. Archaeological study of houses from New York's Greenwich Village area revealed that women chose to spend more money on porcelain tea wares for entertaining non-family members than on the ceramics they used for their own families (Wall 1994), which shows how conscious women were of how their material wealth would be evaluated by their guests.

Racialized Identities

Early efforts to study race and racism archaeologically were hindered by normative notions of culture. Just as we saw in the example where Roberta Greenwood (1980) and others looked for artifactual markers of ethnicity, archaeologists were hoping to find material signatures that indicated race, which was conflated with ethnicity. In studying African American sites, archaeologists looked for artifacts that were either made in the same way as African materials or looked like African materials, and they generally assumed that assimilation had occurred when they could find no evidence of race. Their problem was a theoretical one; they were looking for race as if it were real instead of a socially constructed and imposed identity.

It is important to understand that both race and ethnicity are socially constructed identities that are historically situated and ever-shifting. It is often tempting for people to think that race is real and that it has a biological basis; after all, we can "see" race, right? For several years, while living in Baton Rouge, I would walk the dog of an elderly neighbor. She knew I was not a Baton Rouge native, and I suppose felt that she was being helpful when she pulled me aside one day. "That neighbor of yours," she said to me in a confidential whisper, "the one who lives across the street, you cannot tell by looking at him, but he is a black man!" I looked at her with an expression she read as confused rather than appalled, and she elaborated; "he looks white, all right, but his family is black." The legacy of one-drop laws in the United States, which designated anyone with any African ancestry as black, makes identifying people who may have been racialized as black based on appearance a ridiculous task. Race is socially constructed, not a biological reality. If you "cannot tell by looking at someone," it is not a real physical phenomenon. At a genetic level, with all modern humans descending from a common African heritage, we are ultimately all African. Other groups that have been constructed as "not white" in nineteenth-century America are now constructed as white by American society—eastern Europeans, Irish, and Italian immigrants (see Orser 2001, 2007).

Archaeological studies have shifted from trying to identify race and ethnicity to understanding processes of *racialization* (how categories of racial designation come to be), *ethno-genesis* (the formation of ethnic groups), and the material traces of living in a racialized society. Looking at how racism shaped consumer habits among African American communities has proven a fruitful avenue of research. Paul Mullins (1999) explored consumer practices among Annapolis African American families in the late nineteenth and early twentieth centuries. He found that the black families he studied favored national brands when purchasing goods. While national brand-name goods were slightly more expensive than buying local goods from bulk at general merchandisers, the quality of the goods was more consistent and better than might have been obtained from a local seller. Black customers found themselves being short-changed or sold lesser quality goods, such as spoiled or moldy food or flour, by white storeowners. Brand name, nationally marketed products were packaged elsewhere without regard to the color or socioeconomic status of the person who would ultimately purchase the goods. Mullins did not look simply look for a material signature that would allow him to identify black families, but was concerned with understanding how racism and social inequality shaped everyday life.

In the history and material culture of the Zulu Social Aid and Pleasure Club, we can see how one Mardi Gras organization uses Carnival as a platform for asserting for African American equality, civil rights, and ancestral pride. The Zulu parade is one of the highlights of the Mardi Gras season. The predominantly black organization parades as Zulu warriors wearing black face paint and grass skirts. You might think that this costume has a comedic effect, but that is not the case. The face makeup worn today features a large white circle surrounding one eye and an ever-so-slightly downward facing white mouth. When a masker smiles in Zulu face makeup, it only increases the downwardness of the character's mouth. The effect is entirely different from the big rolling eyes and large gaping smile that typified the early twentieth-century white, black-faced minstrel traditions that Zulu is critiquing. The Zulu warriors are mysterious, serious looking, and otherworldly.

Zulu has a king and queen. While the king now dresses in regal garments rather than the rags the first King Zulus wore, he wears the black face garb of the rest of the maskers; Queen Zulu wears a gown and crown to rival any of the queens of the white courts and wears no face paint. She is a woman of accomplishment in the black community. For instance, the 2012 Zulu queen was Dr. Tanyanika Phillips, an oncologist well-respected for her medical practice as well as her fund-raising efforts in support of cancer research and care (WWL TV, February 12, 2012).

Zulu stands in distinct contrast to other Mardi Gras parading groups in New Orleans, in that it refers to itself as a social aid and pleasure club, not a krewe. This self-designation serves to emphasize its distinctiveness from the white krewes it lampoons, as well as signifies the group's historical connection with African American community's self-help and uplift movements. Just as many of the old-line krewes have a philanthropic mission to their organization, Zulu is committed to a range of community projects, including mentoring young people, sponsoring scholarships, and fund raising for health and community initiatives (www.kreweofzulu.com). Putting forward a royal court of successful black business people and leaders is part of the politics of Zulu. As far back as the 1940s (Early 1947:276), Zulu's queen was treated regally and accompanied by a court of equally beautifully dressed women. With black women being stereotyped in US media as overly sexualized and unequal to white women in beauty and gentility (see Collins 2000), there are politics to the way Queen Zulu is presented to her public.

The Zulu Social Aid and Pleasure Club was not founded per se; it emerged from a neighborhood group that paraded through the French Quarter as early as 1901. The group was called the Tramps, and was probably part of a ward-based African American benevolent society. Benevolent or mutual aid societies were common in African American communities and served to provide members with health care and burial insurance. The Tramps first marched as Zulus in 1909 with William Story as their king; he was decked out in ragged clothing and a lard-can crown with a banana stalk scepter (www.kreweofzulu.com/history, accessed October 12, 2012). While popular folklore places the origin of the Zulu name as inspired by a local musical featuring the song, "there will never be a king like me," I suspect the choice of the Zulu warrior was a more socially conscious one. The Zulu kingdom in southern Africa embarrassed Victorian England with an impressive early victory in the Anglo-Zulu war despite Britain's overwhelming technological advantages. The Zulu were feared. Evoking of a Zulu warrior reminded white populations that African peoples would react to unjust treatment. It was a message that would have resonated for New Orleans' African American population, who lived with the daily outrages of the Jim Crow south. Zulu was formed at the same time that black thinker Marcus Garvey's pan-African movement was gaining attention in the United States (Baker 1998). The first Zulu parade featuring wagon-based floats took place in 1915, and the Zulu Social Aid and Pleasure club was incorporated September 20, 1916 (www.kreweofzulu.com/history). While the press represented Zulu in the racialized terms of the time, the parade was loaded with social commentary with the appropriation of black faces critiquing minstrel shows that featured white performers mocking African Americans and the raggedy king satirizing the overblown ceremony of the white Mardi Gras krewes and their royal courts.

First published in 1928, folklorist and Louisiana writer, Lyle Saxon, provided a description of seeing Zulu when he was a child. Critics have pointed out that Saxon, born in 1891, was unlikely to have encountered Zulu as a child. But from our perspective, we can take his description as typical of the procession as of 1928. He describes Zulu and his court approaching on a barge.

> In a tattered Morris chair, the King sat. He represented a savage chieftain, but whether from modesty or from fear of cold, the Zulu King wore, instead of his own black skin, a suit of black knitted underwear. There were bunches of dried grass at throat, ankles, and wrists, and a sort of grass skirt such as hula-hula dancers wear, and he wore a fuzzy black wig surmounted by a tin crown. In his hand he carried a scepter—a broomstick—upon which was mounted a stuffed white rooster. There were some tattered artificial palm-trees at the four corners of the royal barge, and a strip of red cloth was draped from palm to palm. Four henchmen, dressed almost exactly like the king—save that they wore no crowns—were capering beside him . . . . I saw that the king and his followers had improved upon Nature's handiwork by blackening their faces and by putting stripes of red and green paint liberally upon their cheeks and upon their black union suits (Saxon 1941:26–27).

> Saxon recognized the social satire involved in Zulu, noting that "this custom has continued for many years—a sort of burlesque of the grander Mardi Gras of the white people, and it provides the note of humor which is lacking in the great parades" (1941:26).

While Zulu's own historians have found references to undecorated coconuts being handed out by Zulus as early as 1910, Saxon describes how the parade included a wagon where fish were fried, and the Zulu king gave bites of fried catfish to his followers, particularly women who stopped the procession to give him a kiss. A 1947 travel guide for New Orleans stated about the Zulu king that "on his head he wears a crown made from a gasoline tin gilded to catch the shining sun. Sometimes he carries a broomstick for a scepter, topped with cock feathers, sometimes a banana stalk, or a loaf of Italian bread. He wears black tights, a patchwork vest, and a grass skirt. But over his motley attire he trails an ermine robe . . . . Following the royal float, warriors and medicine men ride in the palmetto jungles where papier-mâché beasts roam, serpents slither through the bush, and grass-green snakes sway from moss-hung trees." (Early 1947:275).

Early (1947) describes Zulu parading all of Fat Tuesday and throwing coconuts and favors to followers. She also understands that the procession's intent was not only to celebrate but to also satirize: "Zulu's extravaganza is a witty travesty of the white folks' Mardi Gras. On his rattrap float, trailing clouds of tarnished glory, he mocks the white parades and in his mangy robe, he mocks their Kings. His hilarious floats burlesque all the gaudy show of the white Krewes. His horned medicine men imitate their Dukes, and the Big Shot of Africa caricatures their Captains" Early (1947:276). The coconuts thrown by Zulu were, and remain, the most highly prized throw of their parade. A 1949 *The Times Picayune* article (Feb 27, 1949) discussed Zulu's throws for the year.

> It is estimated there will be 10,000 coconut favors to be distributed to the throngs along the way. But in view of the cranial hazard, they are to be handed down gently and not tossed out promiscuously, as in the past. The parade chairman, a shoemaker in private life, is presently employing his shoe finishing machinery to smooth off his some coconuts so that Zulu greetings can be pasted on them. The chairman declared the coconut favors will go to visitors, whenever possible, as the visitors value them as souvenirs. 'The local folks break 'em open and eat 'em' he remarked sadly.

Today, the coconuts are usually painted in gold or black and decorated with the year of the parade in glitter or paint; sometimes they are adorned with feathers or fake rhinestones. More ornately carved coconuts will be labeled with the organization's name and distributed (Figure 8.3). In 2009, to celebrate the 100th anniversary of the Zulu parade, the organization introduced a half coconut hanging from a thick strand of beads. The coconut, turned sideways so that the three "eyes" of the coconut are visible and looking like a face, is a important reoccurring image in Zulu's medallions.

Zulu took advantage of the monochrome MOS beads by adopting black beads as a signature color for their organization. As early as 1989, Zulu has thrown black beads and medallions. Zulu has so successfully become associated with black beads that no other krewe regularly used them as of 2009. In 1999, Orpheus used a black medallion as one of their throws, perhaps to emphasize their commitment to a racially integrated organization? I have seen no evidence that they have used it since. It is uncommon to even see Zulu beads rethrown—so strong are the associations with the organization and by extension, blackness. The social landscape of Louisiana remains highly racialized with segregation of black and white populations in daily life being the norm and interactions highly regulated by particular sets of economic and social practices.

The earliest dated Zulu medallion I have found is a 1989 coconut medallion. In 1990, the two-sided medallion featured a profile of King Zulu on one side and the coconut

Figure 8.3: Examples of Zulu coconut throws from 2009, 2010, and 2011. Photograph by Alexandra Wilkie Farnsworth.

face on the other. In 1991 and 1992, the coconut face was on one side, and the other side featured an African animal, which served as the parade theme. The medallions (Figure 8.4) were mounted on MOS beads that featured a pattern that evoked strings of seeds. To celebrate the millennium in 2000, a black medallion painted with green, gold, and white, was introduced. Since that time, Zulu has offered different medallions each year, some

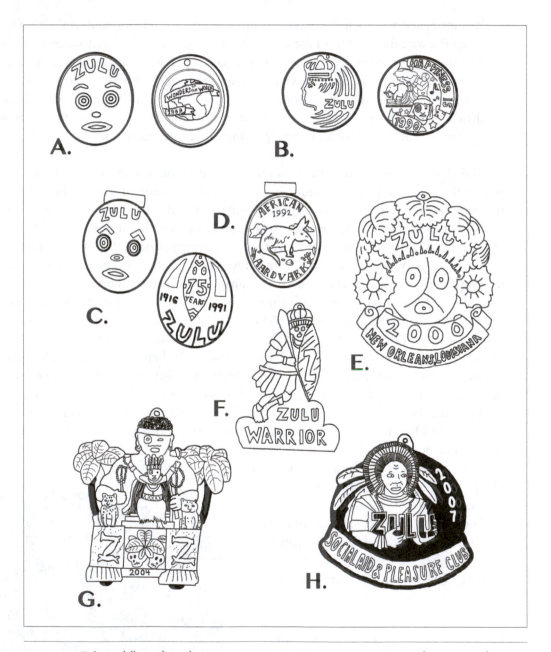

Figure 8.4. Zulu medallions through time: A. 1989; B. 1990; C. 1991; D. 1992; E. 2000; F. late 1990s; early 2000s; G. 2004; H. 2007. Illustrations by Alexandra Wilkie Farnsworth.

Figure 8.5. Examples of resin Zulu court medallions: Left: generic duke medallion; Right: queen medallion with Desiree Glapion Rogers. Photograph by Alexandra Wilkie Farnsworth.

featuring green highlights, and others red. Recall that red and green were the colors of the original face paint worn by the first Zulu warriors. In this way, the organization highlights connections with its historical past. The Zulu warriors and the coconut are the two most common images employed in the medallions. In recent years, the imagery of the warrior has shifted to de-emphasize the black face makeup and accent the warrior's masculinity with a pointedly muscular physique.

Special medallions honoring each year's king and queen have been thrown since at least 2000. These are molded in resin and depict the royals and their accomplishments (Figure 8.5). The 2000 medallion honoring Queen Desiree Glaspian Rogers references her college degree at Harvard. This kind of representation of the royalty is unique among parading organizations, and, speaks to the organization's political sensibilities. Other Zulu-themed throws include stuffed fabric dolls representing members of the Zulu court (the witch doctor, Mr. Big Shot of Africa, the mayor) and Zulu warriors, cups, toy spears, and frisbees.

Zulu's membership is focused on the local New Orleans community, with members coming from all socioeconomic and occupational backgrounds. The famed coconuts are decorated by krewe members, keeping costs down, and meaning that these favors represent a unique piece of Mardi Gras art. The 2000 bead assemblage demonstrates clearly how members attempt to negotiate between minimizing costs, yet providing throws that clearly demonstrate that Zulu is as generous as any krewe in New Orleans. Zulu throws a high percentage of organization-themed beads compared to other parades. Of the 44 strands of beads recovered in 2000, 14 (31.8%) were black in color. The other two colors found in the medallion, green (18.2%) and white (15.9%), comprised a significant

Figure 8.6. Zulu bead animal caught in 1991. Photograph by Alexandra Wilkie Farnsworth.

proportion of the assemblage as well. The Zulu assemblage also demonstrated a greater percentage of beads that were being recycled from previous parades. If we look at incidences of repair, 17 of the 44 strands of beads had been previously broken and repaired by melting (38.6%). Two 33-inch strands of silver metallic beads had been spliced from six different pieces to create each strand. Three of the strands demonstrated great originality—multiple strands of different colors had been melted together to create multi-colored strands, of the type that are expensive to acquire new. Four more of the strands were early MOS beads. Three were translucent, dating their production to as recent as the mid-1990s, but a fourth was a white opaque style that has not been commonly thrown since the late 1980s.

I observed other parade goers catching strands of beads that had been made through creative twisting of segments of bead strands around longer strands to create complex looking strands of great beauty. My favorite of the Zulu throws, however, are also a product of bead recycling; these are little animals that have been created by twisting a short segment of MOS beads around one another to create a little animal (Figure 8.6). These bead animals were tossed by the handful, with parade goers not always realizing what they were. The first time I caught one, I was standing near an African American woman who was thrilled to catch several; she showed and explained to me what they were. Like the coconuts, the animals show an investment in Mardi Gras of personal time and ingenuity that cannot be purchased.

In Zulu, we see an organization with a long, rich history of politicized action against the racialized environment of Louisiana. For Zulu members, to be charged with being cheap or throwing poor beads would be an accusation laden with hundreds of years of racial discrimination—a history of enforced economic inequality. Through scholarship programs and uplift activities, Zulu maintains a commitment to improving the lives of African American families in New Orleans as part of a 100-year-old tradition. The parade is just one public face of the organization, but it is a performance in which Zulu is able to mock the krewes of elite white New Orleans. Remember that performance theory emphasizes that actors are conscious of how their performances will be read by viewers. For Zulu, parading offers the opportunity to perform in ways that serve to simultaneously mock and subvert the racial power structure of this country, if only for a few hours, by giving a public face to successful members of the African American community and by creating a circumstance where white parade goers find themselves begging for gifts from black maskers.

Forging an Identity

A study of medallion design through time can provide insights into the developing identity of a krewe and how it presents itself to the public. In two different Mardi Gras parades, it is possible to see how a sense of organizational identity emerges and develops over time. I will discuss the Krewe of Tucks and how its medallion styles have changed as the krewe has developed a stronger sense of self-definition. I also discuss Baton Rouge's Spanish Town parade, a local parade that is composed of many small krewes rather than a single one. Despite the diversity of groups that march in Spanish Town, over the last ten years it is possible to trace the parade's development of a shared, corporate identity. I see these as examples of how material culture can be used to understand the process of ethnogenesis— or how a shared social identity emerges through shared histories and practices.

Drawing upon shared lithic technologies and understandings of landscape, archaeologist Steve Silliman (2004) used the concept of ethnogenesis to understand how Native Californian laborers after the Mission period formed new shared identities in California's nineteenth-century ranching society. This shared, California Indian, ethnicity existed in distinction with Mexican, *Californios,* and American ethnicities that established themselves in the territory and provided Native Californians not only with a sense of shared heritage and historical experience but with an alternate trade and social network that facilitated access to economic and social resources in a highly racialized society.

Tucks

The Krewe of Tucks was founded in 1969. The story is that a pair of failed flambeaux hopefuls from Loyola University in New Orleans decided to found their own krewe, which they named after a now-defunct pub, Friar Tucks. The krewe was non-exclusive and did not even require a nomination for membership from an existing member. The ability to pay was the only requirement (with the growth of the krewe's popularity, this has changed, and now recommendation from a member is required). The parade was a local, nighttime truck parade until 1983 when it first marched during the daytime. Its route extended to downtown New Orleans for the first time in 1989, a circumstance that indicated it had become a large-scale parade. The krewe embraced irreverence for Mardi Gras tradition as their hallmark. The earliest medallions thrown by the krewe demonstrated not so much the creation of their own identity but the definition of what they were not. Two early Tucks medallions have been found. One is an exact copy of Rex's iconic purple-yellow-green, hand-strung, plastic medallion, except the Rex crown has been replaced with a small, yellow, Friar Tuck (Figure 8.7). The other is a strand of beads featuring a black Friar Tuck. With these medallions, Tuck was poking fun at the kings of Carnival and rulers of Fat Tuesday, Rex and Zulu.

By 2000, Tucks (Figure 8.7) had developed a multi-colored medallion that was defined by their own ideals rather than merely satirizing those of another. The medallion featured a well-lubricated Friar Tuck sitting on a beer barrel and toasting revelers. His green robe and yellow barrel with purple accents clearly situate Tucks within Mardi Gras as it own

Figure 8.7. Tucks medallions through time: A. late 1980s; early 1990s; B. 1999; C. 2000; D. 2007. Illustration by Alexandra Wilkie Farnsworth.

entity. In 2004, the krewe pushed the boundaries of humor further and redesigned the medallion to show the good Friar sitting on the toilet, plunger and beer in hand, and toilet paper handy (2004). What we see in these transitions is a solidification of the Krewe's sense of self-identity. This is exactly how archaeologists expect ethnogenesis to look in the material record. Tucks original medallion design, playfully referencing Rex's medallions, defines the Krewe of Tucks as what it is not—it is not Rex. The changes in the medallion design, however, illustrate the development of the krewe into something more than "not Rex," and as an organization with its own iconography and continuously developing comedic identity.

Spanish Town

The Spanish Town parade is the biggest parade celebrating Mardi Gras in the city of Baton Rouge. The parade was established in 1982 by a krewe calling itself "The Mystick Krewe for the Preservation of Louisiana Lagniappe" (MKPLL). Lagniappe is a Cajun term generally used to mean, something a little extra. For instance, if a baker gives you an extra cookie when you buy a dozen, it would be an example of lagniappe. The MKPLL still organizes the parade, collects fees, runs the ball, and so on, and was responsible for selecting the krewe's mascot: a pink flamingo wearing a top hat, sunglasses, and bow tie.

Histories of the parade refer to Spanish Town, the section of Baton Rouge, surrounding the state capital, as a "questionable" neighborhood when the parade began. What these histories gloss over is that the questionable-ness of the neighborhood was related to its large gay population who was involved in gentrifying the beautiful nineteenth-century homes in the neighborhood. As of 2005, the parade was prominently listed on sites highlighting gay Mardi Gras celebrations. This history of the parade is glossed over, and while gay pride is still part of the celebrations (rainbow pride beads are seen on a number of the floats), conservative Baton Rougeans take their families to the parade, enjoying the generosity and political satire, completely ignorant (willfully or otherwise) of the parade's sexual politics. Each float that participates in the parade is sponsored by a unique krewe; therefore, the parade is best described as a confederation of krewes, or to return to our discussion of household archaeology, it is the apartment building of parades. What we see in Spanish Town through time is the material diversity that arises from the participation of multiple autonomous krewes, as well as a growing tendency of these krewes to express through their throws an affiliation with the aesthetic sensibility of the founding krewe. An attendee at the parade is likely to walk away with bunches of hot pink pearl and metallic beads and probably some sort of representation of a flamingo—either in the form of a medallion, a stuffed animal, sunglasses, or a pink feather boa. In 2009 (Table 8.4), nearly 34% of the beads caught at Spanish town were hot pink in color. The parade has not always had a sense of thematic unity in terms of throws.

When I first started attending Spanish Town parades in 1991, there was little sense that there was a mascot or color scheme for the parade. When I began excavating Spanish Town in 1998, this largely remained the case, as evident in the color distribution of the beads caught (Table 8.4). In 1998, no throws were caught that gave any sense of a corporate identity among the floats. In 1999, however, I caught my first flamingo throw, a brass medallion of a stylized flamingo in a top hat, in pink and black enamel, and mounted on a hot pink strand of beads. I thought it quite strange. In 2001, one of the krewes, the Krewe of Boo Hoo, had their own resin medallion manufactured that featured a pink flamingo.

Table 8.4. Distribution of Beads by Color from Spanish Town Parade.

COLOR	1998	1999	2001	2002	2003	2004	2006	2007	2009
	N=178	N=171	N=213	N=364	N=77	N=426	N=898	N=647	N=1090
PURPLE	24.6	19.1	21.9	23.4	16.8	18.1	16.8	18	14.5
GREEN	24.0	29.7	26.2	31.5	24.7	23.5	19.8	22.9	17.2
GOLD	11.7	25.8	20.9	19.3	14.3	22.3	18.4	20.6	17
RED	4.1	2.2	3.2	5.5	2.6	2.3	4.6	2.2	1.6
BLUE	4.7	1.7	3.7	1.1	11.7	4.2	5.6	5.6	2.9
SILVER	2.9	.6	2.2	5.8	1.3	4.5	6	5.6	4.5
BLACK			.5			.7	2.7	.2	.2
WHITE	7	12.9	14.9		7.8	9.9	6.9	4	5.8
CLEAR						.5	.1		
HOT PINK	7.6	3.4	5.3	5.5	16.9	11.5	17.7	19.7	33.8
ORANGE	.6		.5			.9		.2	1.2
MULTI-COLORED	2.9		.5			.7	1.4	1.1	1.2
YELLOW	9.4	.6			3.9	.7			.2
GLOW IN DARK						.2			
COPPER		1.2							
GRAY	.6								

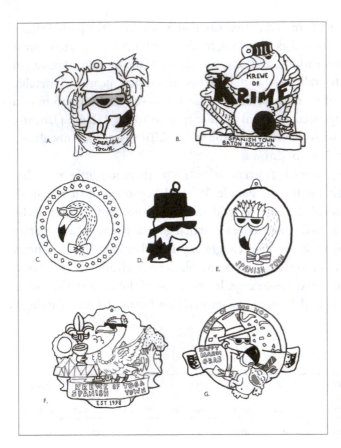

Figure 8.8. A variety of parade-wide medallions could potentially be caught from any float in the parade, while the krewe medallions would only be thrown from the float sponsored by that specific krewe. The variety of parade-wide and krewe-specific medallion beads thrown at Spanish Town is seen here: A. Parade-wide resin medallion; B. Krewe of Krime resin medallion; C. Parade-wide resin medallion; D. Parade-wide enameled brass medallion; E. Parade-wide resin medallion; F. Krewe of Toga resin medallion; G. Krewe of Boo Hoo resin medallion. Illustrations by Alexandra Wilkie Farnsworth.

Another float threw a generic plastic medallion featuring a pink flamingo. Party catalogs, like Oriental Trader, which is a popular source of throws for smaller parades, features a number of Hawaii and Tiki themed beads, including flamingo beads, both as medallions and MOS beads (Figure 8.8). Flamingos again disappeared from the assemblages in 2002 and 2003, but roared back in 2004. That year I caught another flamingo in a top hat, two multi-colored flamingo medallions, one Krewe of Boo Hoo medallion, and three resin flamingo strands. Flamingos appeared again in 2006 in the form of MOS beads and in 2009 with MOS beads and three other flamingo medallions. Throws caught also included flamingo stuffed animals, neck wraps, and sunglasses (see Figure 8.1).

More interesting than the increased number of flamingo artifacts, however, is the trend visible in the bead color scheme of the parade. We see hot pink comprising 7.6% of the assemblage in 1998, 3.4% in 1999, and 5.3% and 5.5% respectively in 2001 and 2002. In 2003, however, the percentage triples, to 16.5, dips slightly in 2004, and then builds steadily in 2006, 2007, and 2009. Note that the assemblage sizes for 2002, 2004, 2006, 2007, and 2009 are particularly large and provide the clearest evidence of the trend (the 2003 sample was not collected by me, and I am suspicious that the excavator was selecting for particular kinds of beads over others).

So what may be the explanation for the rapid increase? Clearly, by 2004, the parade was on its way to creating a clear, shared identity. This process accelerated, however, in 2006 and beyond. I suspect that impacts from Hurricane Katrina are the explanation. Baton Rouge experienced a large population increase overnight as a result of Katrina. The Spanish Town parade, with its policy of accepting groups to contribute floats, was a natural place for displaced New Orleanians to join in local Mardi Gras festivities. The parade swelled to double its previous length. I believe that previous participants responded to the swell of newcomers by embracing more firmly the iconography of the parade, while newcomers, wanting to behave in a way that conformed with their new surroundings, likewise, adopted the colors and mascot of the parading organization. If they had previously been involved in New Orleans krewes, this would have been part of their routinized expectation—or their habitus—if you will. The result is evident through time—the crystallization of Spanish Town as a hot pink, flamingo-loving parade group. If we continue to think of each krewe within Spanish Town as a separate household, we could argue that we are seeing through time the creation of a stronger sense of ties and affiliation between the households of Spanish Town's parade.

Conclusions

In this chapter we have seen how groups use material culture to communicate a range of subject positions and performances of identity. While the discussion has focused on Mardi Gras beads as the medium of communication, any artifact has the potential to reveal dimensions of social discourses about age, gender, social status, kinship, or group affiliation, be it pottery, lithics, figurines, or rock art. In the next chapter, we'll delve more deeply into how archaeologists have used feminist and queer theory to examine gender and sexuality.

CHAPTER 9
GENDER AND SEXUALITY
IN THE THROWING GAME

I fell in love as soon as I saw them; they were so deliciously contradictory. A large resin, hand-painted, erect penis medallion was suspended on a shiny metallic strand of gay pride, rainbow beads held by a man unsuccessfully soliciting a woman to show her breasts. I had to have them. It was the end of the parade, so I thought my chances of talking the masker out of them was pretty good. I ran up to the float and began to barter, jogging alongside the float as it moved the last few blocks of the parade route.

"Can I have those please?"

"Show me your tits and you can have them!"

"Oh come, you don't want to see these, they're mommy tits, you just want to give me the pretty beads!"

He looked at me unimpressed.

"Come on, show me anyway."

Clearly a different tactic was necessary. I've not shown my breasts as part of a commodity exchange, and I wasn't about to start. I would have to be crass in the name of science.

"Listen," I say, still jogging to keep pace, but now holding on to the float so I can get a little closer to him.

"Here's the real deal. You can't handle seeing these boobs."

Now he was intrigued.

"Why not?"

"Well," I said, maybe throwing my shoulders back slightly as I jogged,

"These tits are so awesome, that if I showed them to you, you'd never be happy looking at another breast as long as you lived."

I paused to take a breath—both for effect and because I wasn't used to jogging this far—and closed the deal, "Really, it's for your own protection."

At this he laughed, and said,

"Well, I really want to see them now, but here you go!"

He tossed me the beads. I held them up triumphantly laughing as I returned to where my friends were standing and noticed my twelve-year old daughter staring at me. Oh, oh, I thought, she's going to need therapy after her terrible mother exposed her to pornographic Mardi Gras beads. She got a little smirk on her face and shook her head. "MOM!" she said, rolling her eyes in an exaggerated fashion. "Put those away!" Oh, oh, I thought, I'm going to need therapy to deal with her teenage years; she was not nearly as appalled as I would have liked, and that smirk would haunt me!

Engendered Archaeologies

Engendered archaeologies emerged as an important arena of archaeological theorizing following the post-processual critique. In the last chapter, we began to discuss gender as one recognizable axis of social identity, which can be interpretively approached through practice and performance theories. Gender, like race, has been a difficult subject to broach archaeologically, not because it is difficult to study gender from archaeological traces, but because we live in a society where gendered roles and inequalities are so ingrained in everyday practice as to seem naturalized. The study of gender in archaeology came out of a body of political theory—feminism.

That's right, I said the "F" word—feminism. Why is feminism so derided? Gender inequality is so naturalized in Western society that any attempt to draw attention to it often provokes powerful (and negative) responses, which target those who question inequality as "unnatural" or "unfeminine" women, the common stereotypes of feminists. The only body of thought that competes with feminism for the most derided in the public imagination, thanks to the Cold War, is Marxist-influenced theories (see next chapter). Feminism has been so besmirched in the last two decades, that many people do not really understand what the points of feminism are, so let us just have a little review.

In the interest of full self-disclosure, I foremost self-identify as a feminist archaeologist who looks at how gender, race, and class inequalities intersect in everyday life, and how communities respond to social inequality. Feminist practice demands that we understand how our own lived experiences (our subjectivities) enter into our research. Why am I choosing to tell you this now? So that I can underscore that feminist theory is embodied and lived. And because if I had told you sooner, some of you would have been appalled and put down the book before you ever got to this chapter.

Feminism has a distinct political agenda; its goal is to achieve social, economic, and political equality among the sexes. Some of you may be worried about the notion of politics shaping theory. Pish posh. All theory is political and subject to politicization; it is merely a matter of being aware of the political discourses in which intellectual movements are situated. Unilinear evolution was situated within politics of imperialism and eugenics, with its emphasis on some societies being better adapted for survival than others, and the extinction of entire races of people as part of the "natural order." Part of the post-processual critique was that the systems theory approaches of processual archaeology naturalized political systems where strong elite controlled all aspects of society. Commoners were powerless cogs in the system unable to exert influence on the societal structures that shaped their lives. While Hodder proposed using agency and practice theories to understand the relationship between individual actors and social change, the Marxists scoffed at archaeologies of practice for looking at the individual human scale as part of a neo-liberal plot that served to create the illusion of free will and prevent the development of class consciousness that was necessary for true social revolution to occur. Feminists accused the Marxists of ignoring gender inequality that crosscuts class divisions, and so we go around and around. My point? To reiterate, all theory is political, so just embrace it, and be sure you know what ideas you are aligning yourself with when you take a particular theoretical position. Hopefully, after getting through this book, you'll have some exposure to the different bodies of thinking that underlie a lot of political and social debate!

First-Wave Feminism

Feminist theory is often discussed as having come in three distinct "waves" (Freedman 2003; Walters 2005); the first wave corresponds to the late nineteenth- and early twentieth-centuries suffrage movements when women demanded civil rights equal to those of men. The first wave of feminism was successful in getting women the vote, improving educational and employment opportunities for women, establishing women's right to control family size through contraception, and changing notions about women's sexuality and ability to socialize in public. The return of GIs from World War II led to a re-entrenchment of Victorian domesticity in American homes, as women were forced to vacate jobs for returning GIs had left and were pushed back into the domestic arena to raise the baby boomers.

Kim Christensen (2012) has conducted a very neat archaeological study of one of the important first-wave feminist thinkers, Matilda Gage, who lived with her husband and family in upstate New York and was part of the feminist and abolitionist movements in that area. Christensen excavated the Gage house and found evidence of the ways that Gage's political actions made their way into hers and her family's everyday life. Social movements of the mid to late nineteenth century were often conducted within the spaces of the household. Abolitionists had meetings over tea and invited speakers to address groups in someone's parlor. Both women's suffrage and abolitionism were seen as movements that were potentially threatening to the fabric of American society. Anyone who visited the Gage house could have been concerned that they were consorting with dangerous, unpatriotic radicals (an accusation sometimes hurled at those fighting for reform). Visitors would have been reassured upon entering the Gage home, however. Christensen found that the Gages stocked their house with the kinds of materials expected to be found in any respectable middle-class home of the time—white ironstone ceramics in the Gothic pattern—which would have been recognized by observers as a promotion of family values and extolment of the sanctity of hearth and home. Christensen also found an unusual number of tobacco pipes with patriotic themes molded on them, such as bald eagles and stars-and-stripes banners. Pipes are artifacts used near the face— the same area people look when engaged in conversation. Anyone speaking to Mr. Gage while he smoked would have seen the patriotic themes on the pipes. The activist Gages,

Christensen realized, used material culture in their home to make the statement that they were ordinary, patriotic citizens. It would appear that feminists have always felt like they have to counteract the accusation by others that they are unpatriotic.

Second-Wave Feminism

The second wave emerged in the 1960s, when predominantly white, middle-class, educated, female baby boomers came of age and questioned gender ideologies that dictated women should only be mothers and housewives (Walters 2005). They demanded equality in the workplace, equal pay, control over their reproductive lives, and the ability to choose to pursue career over family. Second-wave feminist theorizing emphasized that gender roles, or the ways that members of a particular sex are expected to behave in society, are socially constructed and historically contextualized. Gender roles are the product of gender ideologies that exist within a society at a particular time and place. They are not natural or biological; they are social constructions. Just as race is not biologically real, gender is not biologically real. For second-wave feminist theorizing, there are men, and there are women; but the roles men and women play in society are not biologically determined.

The ongoing legacies of the second wave are less clear: the glass ceiling remains; the Equal Rights Amendment failed; women still make less than men for the same labor; and a range of economic and social structures continue to prevent women from joining the workforce. A particularly salient critique of second-wave feminism was that it was a middle-class political movement that failed to consider issues of concern to working-class women, who were disproportionately women of color who faced additional historical inequalities in American society. For women who occupied the lowest socioeconomic rungs of society, it was not a question of whether or not to work. Employment was necessary for their survival; but, issues such as maternity leave, leave to care for sick family members, affordable childcare, and freedom from sexual harassment, abuse, and violence in the workplace were not addressed in feminism. In terms of scholarly legacies, second-wave feminism provided important critiques of the practice of science and demonstrated how androcentric (male-centered) biases shaped supposedly neutral scientific practices.

Third-Wave Feminism

Third-wave feminism developed in the 1990s and 2000s in response to multiple critiques of second-wave theorizing. There is no unified feminist third wave, but a lot of swirling, frothy, third-wavey water. Women of color wrote about how their experiences of American life differed from those of white middle-class women. Theorists like Giddings (1984) and Spelman (1988) looked at how women of color's experiences of being female, of color, and poor left them at the intersection of multiple inequalities. Writers like bell hooks (1994) and Angela Davis (1983) explored the role of the beauty industry and how racialized notions of beauty led to internalized self-hatred by women of color. Writers, such as Roberts (1997), focused on social justice issues. Patricia Hill Collins (2000) looked at how historical representations of women of color continued to fuel contemporary stereotypes and inequities.

The work of Judith Butler (1990) became important to the lesbian-gay-bisexual-transgender (LGBT) movement. Butler, in works such as *Gender Trouble* (1990) and *Bodies that Matter* (1993), problematized the notion of sex as a fixed category and demonstrated that sex and gender are signified through societies and time via repetitive acts of performance. She argues what sexual and gender performances are possible in a given society are shaped by what is seen as possible in that society. For Butler, feminists have created a problem for themselves by reinforcing a male-female binary that fits into normative understandings of heterosexuality. She envisions a feminism that doesn't try to define womanhood or manhood, but interrogates how sexuality and gender are constructed in a particular time and place. The idea that gender and sex are fluid and performed rather than essentialized identities is the basis of queer theory—one of the third waves of feminism.

Did you get that? You only think you have male parts or female parts because that is what society has led you to believe are the performative options. In the early 1990s, Saturday Night Live had an ongoing skit featuring a character called "Pat." Pat was completely sexually and gender ambiguous by US standards of manhood and womanhood. Each skit featured a build up where the other characters thought that a clue about Pat's identity would be revealed only to have some additional layer of ambiguity added to the mix. The Pat character provokes uncomfortable laughter precisely because we want to fit people into particular categories. Importantly, it is not Pat's biology that the other characters look to in order to understand the character's sexual identity; they interrogate what Pat does for clues. It is Pat's failure to perform a recognizable sexual or gender identity that frustrates them! Butler would say that the problem isn't Pat; the problem is our society's pathological need to categorize all human performance of desire into one of two categories. You can understand why this work has been so important to the LGBT community.

Another realm of third-wave feminism has been a rebellion against stereotypes of feminists as anti-men, anti-beauty products, anti-sex, and anti-sexy. Instead of condemning pornography, these feminists embrace it as a meaningful way of exploring their own sexuality and enriching sexual relations with their partners. High-heels are not tools of torture; they are means of empowerment and the construction of female self-esteem. Make-up provides another means of self-expression. It is okay to want to be feminine and girly without sacrificing your right to be viewed as professional and equal to men. Some argue that if beauty and sex appeal are tools through which women can manipulate the patriarchal system, they should use these tools to their advantage (Scott 2004). These are the lipstick feminists, and they are controversial within feminism.

The debates the lipstick feminists provoke are intriguing. Some point out that women who participate in the fashion industry—even as consumers—are enabling the abuse of female workers who make up 90% of sweatshop laborers. Kat Banyard, founder of the social activist group UK Feminist, in her recent book, *The Equality Illusion* (2011) discusses how the sex and beauty industry co-opted the language of feminism to sell their products as tools of empowerment, but likens pornography to videotaped prostitution with consent as an impossibility. She argues that the exploitation of women in the beauty and sex industries harms not only women, but also men, who are exposed to hard-core pornography at such a young age that it cannot fail to shape life-long intimate relationships. A theme of recent feminist theorizing more broadly has been to explain how patriarchy and its ideologies oppress men, as well as women—men need to be enlisted in the feminist cause, not just for the sake of their female family members and loved ones but for their own sake as well. While Banyard refuses to condemn women who feel that manipulating society's beauty standards is a means of empowerment, she makes it clear that she believes participating in that culture creates the problem. Lipstick feminists counter that feminism is once again attempting to create a one-size fits all movement that is exclusive rather than inclusive. You may be wondering what any of this has to do with archaeology, but we will be encountering a krewe of lipstick feminists shortly.

Political protest and action is part of feminist practice—whether it is stereotypical types of protests like pitching one's corset (first-wave), burning bras (second-wave), or rejecting anything that smells of gender normativity (third-wave). While third-wave feminism doesn't have the same kind of unified political movement or goals associated with it that its predecessors had, continued struggles for reproductive rights, work-place equality, equal pay, and gay marriage rights all continue to be foci of feminist action. Mardi Gras is a realm where gender protest is possible through participation in krewes or as a participant in street celebrations. We'll return to this idea shortly.

And how does this swirling mess of politics and lived practice fit with archaeology? Archaeologists have attempted to deal with these debates, using feminist theorizing both to interpret archaeological remains, but also to interrogate the way knowledge is produced within the discipline. Joan Gero (1996) demonstrated that men and women excavate in ways that over or under represent the importance of the evidence they have uncovered along gender lines. Other archaeologists have looked at citational practices and demonstrated how male archaeologists are more likely to be cited than a female archaeologist even when they are writing on the same subject.

Second-Wave Feminist Archaeologies

The greatest challenge to archaeologies of sex and gender has been one of imagination. When archaeologists first proposed that gender should be a part of archaeological study (Conkey and Spector 1984; Gero and Conkey 1991; Seifert 1991), they were met with skepticism by archaeologists who said it wasn't possible to see gender in the archaeological record. The response to such critiques is: can you really see social stratification or resource intensification in the archaeological record? No; we see material evidence and patterns of behavior that reflect those things. The search for behaviors associated with culturally prescribed gender roles or ideologies is no different. The earliest engendered archaeology was still very much working within a processualist framework and trying to reconstruct the past while embracing a structuralist understanding of the relationship between materials and cultural beliefs. It is believed that we should be able to find artifacts that reflected gender systems (Conkey and Spector 1984).

Women's Labor in the Aztec Empire

Elizabeth Brumfiel (1991)—using divisions in labor as her entrée into discussing fabric and food preparation in the Aztec world—provided an outstanding case study demonstrating how changes in economic demands of the Aztec tax system forced changes in subsistence. All members of Aztec society were required to work for the government, either in physical labor or through production of goods for the empire. Iconography from the period shows that women were involved in fabric and food production, thus allowing Brumfiel to speak of those activities as gendered. Through time, increased production of tribute cloth was evidenced by changes in distributions of spindle whorls recovered archaeologically.

Food production in Aztec homes was represented by two important artifact types: griddles for preparing tortillas and cooking pots for preparing stews. Brumfiel expected that as production in cloth intensified, there would be a corresponding decrease in griddles. This was because tortilla production is very labor intensive, and women would have had less time to invest in food production and would favor quicker ways to prepare stews. She was surprised to see the opposite was the case—tortilla production increased. She realized that there was a good explanation for this—demands on all of the household labor increased. Men would be called away from the home as labor for public works like roads and would require portable foods to consume while away. Stews may be easier to prepare, but you cannot easily carry them with you. Brumfiel's study demonstrated how understanding labor in a gendered way provided new insights into how home life was shaped by demands of the empire. Brumfiel's case study also shows one of the mental blocks of anyone doing engendered archaeology—artifact attribution. The notion that gender has to be a binary system is very difficult to work around. There is a desperate desire to separate artifacts into "boy things" and "girl things."

In historical archaeology, where it is commonplace to identify a site's occupants through documentary evidence, archaeologists tried to circumvent the "boys things" and "girls things" by excavating sites that were known to have been occupied only by women. Thus, we have archaeologies of women's boarding houses, brothels, and reformation homes (e.g., Costello 2001; DeCunzo 1995; Seifert 2005). Others focused on artifacts of domesticity that women used in socializing and caring for family (Wall 1994).

A body of evidence that became a focus of interest was skeletal remains and their associated burial goods. The idea is that biological sex is real and morphologically identifiable, and that gender is culturally grafted onto the physical body. Things found with sexable bodies can be interrogated for evidence of patterning to determine whether there are recognizable "girl things" and "boy things" and things that fell "in between." As long as you don't embrace Judith Butler's notion that sex isn't real, and you ignore the forensic reality that a significant proportion human skeletal materials are sexually indeterminate, this is a productive strategy. Many Native American descendent communities are not interested in having their ancestors excavated; therefore, much of the gender work in Europe has focused on mortuary remains.

Third Genders in a Dakota Cemetery

Mary Whelan (1991) provided an excellent case study of how mortuary remains, in association with biologically sexed skeletal remains can reveal insights into past gender ideologies. Whelan examined materials from the Black Dog Burial site, which was a nineteenth-century Santee Sioux cemetery from Minnesota. The human remains in the cemetery were excavated in 1968 and reburied in 1988. No destructive analysis was conducted on the materials, and no materials deemed sacred by the tribe were studied in order to adhere to the best ethical standards of the time. The Santee Sioux were an egalitarian group with a mixed subsistence economy of foraging and horticulture. They lived in large villages of over 200 people in the summers and smaller groups during the winter. Cemeteries were arranged linearly along river terraces. The Santee Sioux first exposed bodies for primary decomposition on raised scaffolds and then buried the remains. Of the excavated burials, nearly all (95%) dated between 1835 and 1855 and contained 39–41 individuals. One burial had no intact remains; 11 were single burials; and the remaining 12 burials contained more than one individual. In the case of multiple burials, one individual was primary, with others placed on the left side of that burial. Biological sexing was used to determine whether particular artifacts were associated with one sex or another. Twelve of the individuals were sexed (six men and six women), but sex was indeterminate for 27–29 of the remains. Sixteen of the individuals were identifiable as adults and 16 as juveniles.

Small and medium-sized beads recovered from the burials showed distinct patterning. Medium-sized beads were found associated with men, while smaller beads were found with women. Whelan suspected these differences resulted from different modes of dress. Blue, white, green, yellow, and light blue beads were exclusively found with women, while red beads with white cores were found only with men. Thirty-seven different categories of artifacts were recovered from the burials; 26 of those categories were only associated with adults. These included fishhooks, lead net sinkers, lead shot, musket balls, gunflints, pipes, and strike-a-lights (flints that were used to create a spark for starting fires). Whelan used the number of artifacts associated with each burial to look for status differences between individuals. She found the average number of artifact types per adult was 13.6. Three males and three females had more than 13; one male was recovered with 34 different types, and one female had 30 different types, which suggested to Whelan that men and women had equal access to status.

Whelan found that there were no artifacts that were exclusively found with either men or women. But she did find that only seven individuals were associated with pipestone pipes, mirrors, and pouches. Every identified male was associated with these artifacts, and one woman. The Santee Sioux are ethnographically known to have recognized three genders: men, women, and individuals who may have had the body of a man or woman, but the spirit of the opposite sex from their body. These individuals were seen as having two-spirits, and upon adulthood chose to live as the opposite sex from which they were raised. Their decision was typically the result of a shamanistic intervention or spiritual vision. Whelan suggested that the association of otherwise male artifacts with this person may indicate that she was a two-spirit. Whelan's work is important in that it demonstrates the ways that human remains can be ethically and responsibly used to explore gender in a way that recognizes more than just male-female binaries.

All-Female Krewes: Second-Wave Feminist Approaches to Mardi Gras

Woman protested the formal structures of Mardi Gras by forming their own krewes as early as 1917. The women's krewes of Venus and Iris held their own balls and tableaus but had no public celebrations. In 1941, the Krewe of Venus declared that men had controlled the public face of Mardi Gras for too long and decided to hold their first public parade. The women had their own floats and dressed in beautiful gowns. The presence of women publicly parading was offensive to many, and taunts of "prostitute" and "whore" were among the catcalls thrown at the women. The crowd also apparently revived the old Carnival practice of hurling objects at maskers—women were pelted with eggs and tomatoes. World War II interfered with Venus's plans to continue parading. The Krewe of Iris did not begin parading until 1959 (Winkler-Schmit 2007). As discussed previously, Iris adheres to traditions that emphasize formality and genteel womanly behavior.

Within the Mardi Gras bead assemblage, I have artifactual materials from one all-women krewe, Iris (2000), and a krewe that was formerly all women but began to accept male members in 2001—the Krewe of Shangri-La (2002). This krewe was originally based out of Chalmette across the river from New Orleans, but it began to parade in the city starting in 2000. In the 1980s, Shangri-La was a large parade featuring over 1,000 members. Membership declined, and the krewe has not resumed parading since Hurricane Katrina. At the time this assemblage was excavated, although Shangri-La had integrated, they were still a predominantly women's parade. Therefore, I will talk about the assemblage as an example of a women's parading organization.

More women-only krewes are not featured in the study due to timing conflicts. The high season of Carnival is the last two weeks before Mardi Gras. The most prestigious time slots for parading are the last days before Mardi Gras. Iris occupies a space on Saturday and is the female krewe that marches closest to Fat Tuesday; but their parade is scheduled at the same time as Spanish Town's in Baton Rouge. As I mentioned before when discussing methodology, my typical travel was to fly on Friday, after class, to attend the Southdowns Mardi Gras Parade, then Spanish Town on Saturday, then—when energies permitted—Sunday and Monday in New Orleans to attend Bacchus, Proteus, and Orpheus, and to New Roads for Tuesday's King's and Lion's parades. One consequence of this sampling strategy, I realized later, was that I was systematically missing the women's parades. Apart from Iris, women's krewes do not parade on the last days of Carnival. The wildly popular Muses, who we will discuss shortly, parade on the Thursday before Mardi Gras, and Artemis, the all-women's krewe of Baton Rouge, parades two

Fridays before Mardi Gras. There is a kind of chronological segregation within the Carnival season that limits the national exposure women's krewes can obtain. The greatest media coverage of Carnival corresponds to the period from Friday to Tuesday. With the two female krewe assemblages, I am able to conduct the kind of comparative study of single-gender sites that was typical of early, engendered historical archaeology. Are there patterns within the bead assemblages that mark a krewe as male or female? I will discuss each of the assemblages relative to other parades excavated in the same year. For this analysis I was not as interested in the relative wealth of the materials the krewes offered but whether there were any other trends in bead selection visible suggesting a gendered pattern. I considered bead finishes and diversity of bead shapes found in the assemblages. The results are contained in Tables 9.1 and 9.2. I started by looking at whether there were any bead shapes that may be perceived as more "girly" (hearts or roses for example) or "manly" (footballs or other sports themes) and found each of the assemblages included one or two examples that could be seen as one or the other but none in any patterned way. I then decided to see if there were any broader differences in the aesthetics of the assemblages; did any krewes throw assemblages that included more different shapes than the others? Again, no clear pattern emerged.

If we look at Tables 9.1, which shows the comparisons for 2000, and 9.2, which shows the 2002 comparisons, we see that the women's Krewe of Iris threw a wider range of bead shapes than any of the men's krewes, but the same general percentage of her assemblage was comprised of round beads. The diversity in bead shapes was likely the result of artifact recycling; the assemblage contained many transparent strands, which by 2000 included up to 20 or more years of recycled beads with a wide range of variety in shapes. In 2002 (Table 9.2), Shangri-La did throw fewer round beads than either Bacchus or Proteus, but

Table 9.1. Comparison of All-Male Versus All-Female Krewes from 2000.

BEAD FINISH BY PERCENTAGE	IRIS	REX	BACCHUS	THOTH
TRANSPARENT	37.9		3.1	34.1
METALLIC	47.3	75.6	60	46.3
OPALESCENT	2.1	7.3		
OPAQUE	2.1	19.5		
PEARL	10.5	4.9	37.2	19.5
DIFFERENT-SHAPED BEAD STRANDS	9	6	6	5
PERCENTAGE OF ASSEMBLAGE THAT WAS ROUND BEADS	79.2	69	76.9	86
AVERAGE STRAND LENGTH (in)	33.2	42.1	46.1	33.9
AVERAGE STRAND WIDTH (mm)	7.5	8.7	8.4	7.6

Table 9.2. Comparison of All-Female and All-Male Kewes in 2002.

BEAD FINISH BY PERCENTAGE	SHANGRI-LA	PROTEUS	BACCHUS
TRANSPARENT	17.7	15.1	2.6
METALLIC	74.5	42.2	80.2
OPALESCENT	.7		1.3
OPAQUE	3.5		
PEARL	3.5	40.8	15.7
DIFFERENT SHAPED BEAD STRANDS	6	2	6
PERCENTAGE OF ASSEMBLAGE THAT WAS ROUND BEADS	61	98.5	81.8
AVERAGE STRAND LENGTH (in)	34.9	32.4	41.4
AVERAGE STRAND WIDTH (mm)	8.1	7.75	9.1

she threw the same number of different patterns of bead shapes as Bacchus (six different shapes each). Proteus threw a limited number of different patterns (two). So it is unclear whether there is any gendered meaning behind the differences in practices. Remember that I noted that one of the problems in archaeological studies of gender is the strong desire to separate things into two neat piles of girls' things versus boys' things. This analysis shows the weakness of such assumptions.

Does this mean we cannot get at gender in the archaeological record, as some would claim? Not at all, it just means that being gendered male or female does not seem to have any impact on the look of the beads these groups throw. We gain different insights if we look at the gendered representations of the krewe's identities through the medallions. This is not a matter of looking at boy things versus girl things but looking at the practice of how gendered characters are used or not used as a mode of self-presentation by the group. So for this analysis we will focus on the iconography of medallions from the krewes (Figure 9.1). Now we see that Iris shows a female figure on her medallion; Bacchus and Thoth throw medallions with male figures; and Rex and Proteus throw medallions with symbols that signal a male character (the crown-embossed "REX," which is the masculine form of the Latin word for ruler, and the seahorse is a symbol of the male sea god, Proteus.). Only Shangri-La throws a gender-neutral medallion, for the krewe is named after a mythical place (Shangri-La) and renowned not for a ruler but a state of mind— eternal peace, youth, and happiness. It is interesting that the organization that became one of the largest women's parading organizations chose to deflect attention away from her gender. This may also indicate why it was possible for Shangri-La to re-emerge as a mixed gender krewe as its female membership dropped.

Now, keeping in mind that we are looking for patterns of different practice that may have gendered implications, let's look back at our 2000 and 2002 comparisons. If we compare the bead finishes found in the all-male and all-female krewes, some interesting patterns do emerge that are broader than "boys" versus "girls" (Tables 9.1 and 9.2). In both years, the female krewe's beads are similar to the smaller male krewe than the larger all-male super krewe. In 2000, Iris and Thoth each threw larger numbers of transparent beads than Rex and tended to have slightly smaller-sized beads (an effect of throwing the greater number of transparents, which tend to be shorter and smaller). The same trend is seen in 2002, with Shangri-La sharing more commonalities with Proteus than Bacchus. Again, each of these parades threw greater numbers of transparent beads. Is this merely a reflection of krewe size, or is there something else going on?

If we were to take an economic interpretation of this pattern, we would simply account for the greater percentage of transparent beads as evidence that these krewes threw less expensive beads because they are smaller krewes and cannot afford more expensive beads. This interpretation does not hold up, however, when you consider that Thoth and Proteus are throwing large numbers of pearl beads (and we now know why those pearls are so important, don't we?). If we bother to ask the question—whether there is a gendered dimension to this pattern—then another possible interpretation emerges. When transparent beads are included in bead catalogs from 2000

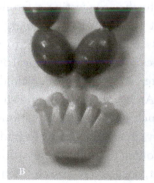

Figure 9.1. Krewe medallions:
A. Proteus, B. Rex, C. Bacchus,
D. Iris, E. Shangri-La, F. Thoth.

onward, distributors often advertise them as "children's throw beads." The short transparent beads are not popular with the adults because they have fiddly clasps, and in the bartering economy of the throwing game, little symbolic value. Children love the seemingly child-sized, small colorful beads. Because the adults don't want them, they are perfect to throw to a child to ensure the *child* catches it without an adult menacing them. There is historical precedent for child-sized beads. I have examples of Czechoslovakian beads that were described by vendors as "children's beads" because they are slightly shorter in length and used smaller-sized beads (Figure 9.2). Some archaeologists have tied miniaturization of artifacts in archaeological sites to the practices of children or associations with children. Being child-sized may have implications other than practical ones. Bill Sillar (1994), in his study of offerings made on alters in the Andes, has noted that small clay representations of household goods are often found on altars. He thinks that the small size of these objects is explicitly related to the ways that the Andean peoples viewed the relationship between children and the spiritual world. Children were often seen as less human than adults, and had closer ties to the spiritual world as a result. Using child-like objects as offerings may have been a way of evoking this closeness in ritual practices.

Thoth is known as the "parade of shut-ins" because its route passes 14 different health facilities. As a daytime parade, it attracts large numbers of families. Proteus, likewise, promotes their parade as having a family atmosphere—something that the women's krewes promote about themselves. What we may be seeing through a comparison of these assemblages is not a gendered difference between men's and women's parades, but a difference between family and non-family oriented parades. Thoth was among the male krewes who were not throwing significantly bigger pearls, further suggesting a family tone rather than an adult one. Thus we see, emerging from the Mardi Gras assemblages, the ability to study generational dynamics and the archaeological presence of children. It is interesting to consider children as little social actors. Archaeologists tend not to consider children very much in their interpretations, perhaps because so many archaeologists were traditionally male and were looking to replicate the world they knew in the past. Yet, once you realize children existed in the past, they pop up in most archaeological sites. They played in abandoned house sites—even in Mayan times (Hutson 2000)—and made toys out of abandoned artifacts (Clark 2011). At Clifton Plantation, parents swept up household debris in their yards to protect

Figure 9.2. Example of child-sized and adult-sized glass Czechoslovakian beads. Photograph by Alexandra Wilkie Farnsworth.

their children's bare feet from broken glass, ceramics, and sharp fish bones (Clark and Wilkie 2007). Even the Zeta Psi fraternity included a number of toys in both house assemblages—including parts of a toy tea set. Many of the men would have had younger siblings themselves, and as college students, they occupied a liminal space between childhood and adulthood. They lived in a neighborhood that included small children, and apparently the house attracted children to the house to play.

Archaeology has branched out to explore a broader range of women's issues, such as archaeologies of childhood, mothering (Baxter 2005; Sofaer-Derevenski 2001; Wilkie 2003), and how childbirth and nursing impact long-term material bone health (Agarwal 2010). Some of the most exciting research has drawn upon the work of third-wave minority theorists (see Battle-Baptiste 2012; Franklin 2001) to interrogate intersectionalities of race, gender, and class.

Archaeologies of Sexuality: Third-Wave Feminism and Mardi Gras

Also developing out of engendered archaeologies is an interest in sex, sexuality, and desire (Voss and Schmidt 2000). With a world population of over six billion, I think we can all safely agree that sexual activity leading to reproduction is alive and well in the modern world; and reproductive sex represents only a small proportion of the human sexual experience. Archaeologies of sexuality look at how sexuality is perceived and marked on ancient landscapes, such as Fietosa's (2013) study of love and eroticism in ancient Pompey, where she used inscriptions and graffiti on walls to understand sexual attitudes and practices. Other studies recognize that sex is a power relationship, and that sexual politics has shaped relationships between indigenous peoples and colonizers (Voss and Cassella 2012). Still others look at sex as an economic transaction (e.g., Casella 2000, Seifert 2005). I can almost imagine you looking at me with a quizzical expression. How on earth, you are thinking, is any of this possible to study with Mardi Gras beads? I was a little worried about pulling this off myself, but I will be discussing the sexual power dynamics of Mardi Gras: how desire is created through the selection of particular throws, and the queering of Mardi Gras since Hurricane Katrina.

The Sexual Politics of Mardi Gras—Historical Context

American Mardi Gras developed in the historical context of the period of slavery. The southern plantation system depended not only on the control of black enslaved bodies, but it also required strict control over the behavior and sexuality of white women (Fox-Genovese 1988). Just as Mardi Gras has provided a means for African Americans to critique and push against racism and its racialized societal structures, for women Carnival has been an arena in which to voice dissatisfaction with society's constraints. Ways that women pushed against the system included using the open spirit of Mardi Gras to engage in forbidden activities and to enter spaces otherwise off-limits. Throughout the history of

Carnival, women who pushed against social boundaries found themselves punished by the patriarchal power structure.

Mardi Gras ritual, as constructed by the white male krewes, is structured to reinforce and normalize the white, male, power that rules New Orleans residents' experiences of the everyday. These are the kinds of gender inequalities that feminist archaeologists like to interrogate. The secret societies of Comus and its imitators, first organized as a means of imposing control on the chaos of Mardi Gras; it was a chaos that included enslaved people celebrating unchecked in masks and costumes, and women, both respectable and unrespectable (i.e., prostitutes) intermingling in those same street festivities.

Transgressive Behaviors

Roach (1993) has noted that the krewes have always shown themselves to be outside of the rules set for the rest of society. They paraded in complete masks in opposition to New Orleans city ordinances forbidding masking. They assembled in organized processions when similar activities were banned for others. From the beginning, the krewes marked themselves as bigger than the laws that governed the rest of the populace's movements. As members of the city's most elite families, the New Orleans krewes flaunted their social, economic, and political power. Part of that expression of power took the form of dictating how others could participate in the celebrations. Women and people of color have structured positions within the Mardi Gras constructed by the krewes. Young women could aspire to being part of a Mardi Gras court as a debutante, but otherwise, their aspirations beyond that would be to someday be married to a man who serves as king of a krewe organization. Mardi Gras balls were a space in which young women from elite families were evaluated for their marriage potential—their ultimate position in society manipulated by the male-run krewes.

Provocative Dress

One forbidden practice women engaged in was cross-dressing, which has historically been a favorite of maskers at Mardi Gras. Accounts of women dressed as men, wearing pants, riding in coaches, and smoking cigars can be found in the historical record of Mardi Gras from the nineteenth century onward. There are also reports of men cross-dressing at Carnival from the mid nineteenth century onward. On the floats and tableau's presented by the Mystick Krewe of Comus, female roles were played by men in drag. Yet, as early as 1857, women were arrested at Mardi Gras for cross-dressing as men (Wilkie 1998). Women who participated in Mardi Gras were often labeled as degraded women—a euphemism for prostitutes.

Storyville, the legally sanctioned red-light district of New Orleans from 1898 to 1917, butted against Canal Street between Basin and Claiborne Aves., was easily accessible to the French Quarter whose boundaries began south of Rampart (Rose 1974:72). Brothels were busy during Carnival, as they took advantage of the surge of visitors that came to the city to celebrate. The "Ball of Two Well-Known Gentlemen," first held in the district in 1882, is a particularly famous example of the sex industry co-opting Mardi Gras traditions.

The ball featured fancy dress and all the trappings of krewe balls with the important exception being that ladies honored in the ball were prostitutes, or the favored New Orleans term, *demi-monde* (Rose 1974:20). Prostitutes were commonly seen masking and celebrating in the streets during Mardi Gras, and in addition to several sporting newspapers published in the city, fliers were distributed to visitors promoting particular bawdy houses.

While the prostitutes were used to being visible in public contexts, women who would otherwise have been reticent to draw attention took advantage of Mardi Gras to engage in risqué behavior. In the early twentieth century, women who costumed as pirates and ballerinas were popularly seen in street celebrations (Mitchell 1995). Both of these costumes allowed for women to show off their legs and the shape of their figures in ways otherwise denied to them. After World War I, women continued to cross-dress, now also donning military uniforms brought home by veterans. The military costumes provoked less rebuke than they may have 50 years earlier. Men mocked women's assertiveness with cross-dressing of their own by wearing clothing that would have been more immodest than even the more-daring women wore. Some of the cross-dressers were clearly mocking women, others, emulating them. Several Mardi Gras accounts refer to police approaching immodestly dressed women to arrest them only to find that the beautiful woman is a man. For men, exploration of homosexuality and homoerotic desire is part of their taboo Carnival experience. Women also took advantage of Carnival's freedoms by dancing in the streets, publicly drinking, and publicly smoking. Mardi Gras tradition holds that Fat Tuesday was the only day women were allowed into the famous Sazerac Bar, and they flocked there to enjoy the bar's signature cocktail that day. We can see that this is an excellent example of how women work to subvert societal restrictions placed on their movements, dress, and behavior.

Nudity

While provocative clothing that allowed for the expression of sexuality has long been a part of women's Carnival experiences, it was not until recently that the throwing game became entangled in the sexual politics surrounding the struggle between self-expression and imposed societal control over women's sexuality. No element of the throwing game is more infamous than the display of female breasts in exchange for gifts of beads. Native New Orleanians despair of the reputation these activities have given to Mardi Gras celebrations and are quick to blame tourists for the behavior. While there is no doubt that visitors add to the nudity mix, the illusion of anonymity combined with alcohol abuse prompts women who would never consider displaying body parts for beads to do just that. Sociologist John Kilborn (1992:11), who conducted a sociological study of breast displays at Mardi Gras, claims that the practice can be traced back to the 1975 Carnival season when a group of women on a balcony showed their breasts and then held a sign stating something along the lines of "we'll show you our tits if you show us your dick." Note there is no mention of beads entering these transactions. What is interesting to me is not that people flash body parts at one another, but the ritualization of the practice as a commodity exchange—beads for breasts. In this case, the "I'll show you mine if you show me yours," is clearly an act of reciprocity with no materials entering into the exchange. However, at some point beads become a currency for bartering sexual access. The question to answer then is when and why does that happen?

The earliest mention I have found that explicitly discusses exchanges of nudity for beads is from *The Times-Picayune,* 1986. Because the quote is so important, I'm going to include a long excerpt from the article.

> The clientele of Lafitte's in Exile Bar on Bourbon Street did not let the cold put a stop to a more recent tradition probably peculiar to the French Quarter.
>
> In fact, the people who were willing to drop their drawers or lift their shirts—depending on their gender—for long strands of expensive cut glass and fake pearl beads, did not seem to notice the cold at all. The beads were offered by a group of young men who collect on the balcony of the bar to dangle the coveted beads over the head of potential exhibitionists. (*The Times-Picayune*, February 12,1986)

Lafitte's in Exile promotes itself as the oldest, continually operating gay bar in the country, because it has occupied its current location since 1954; therefore, it is safe to assume that there was a homoerotic element to the requests to see penises. Bourbon Street features a number of gay bars, and the gay community of New Orleans is long established.

Although described as a "relatively new" practice in 1986, the practice quickly spread in the French Quarter and along parade routes. The budding archaeologist in you should be asking why this happened at this place and time? After years of relatively little innovation in the throwing game, why did this new element enter into practice? I pondered this for some time before coming to a conclusion.

The answer is simple; the date of the nudity displays corresponds to the widespread introduction of MOS beads at Mardi Gras. In other words, people get naked for beads at Mardi Gras because bead technology changed. Technology change led directly to cultural change. How's that for an unexpected answer? But wait a minute, why didn't I talk about the nudity and technology in the technology chapter? Why did I save it for so late in the book? Let's face it, the technology chapter would have been more interesting with a little skin being shown! The answer to that is also simple—it was only when I started asking questions about gendered dynamics in the throwing game that I asked the question that led me back to the technology. This is also the nature of archaeological research—you have to keep asking a lot of questions that force you to think about your evidence in a variety of different ways before you start really understanding your assemblages. This is both Binford's hypothetico-deductive method and Hodder's hermeneutic thinking brought to their best possible outcomes. It's not about asking one right question, it's about continuing to ask more and more questions. Both Binford's way and Hodder's way will get you there—the key is to keep with it long enough to have your "Eureka" moment.

But I digress. I need to explain why the technology change led to the cultural change. In this case, it is not the economics of the beads that deserve our consideration, but the communicative potential of these beads. To this point, we've talked about the economic implications of the switch to MOS beads—the economics were the motivation for the shift, combined with weight factors—but this is another unintended consequence of the shift. Just as the MOS beads made inflation happen, the MOS beads made people flash their body parts.

MOS beads are as diverse as the hand-strung beads are in appearance, but the ways that they differ from one another is standardized. While hand-strung beads can feature any number of combinations of bead shape, color, and finish within a single strand, MOS beads are limited by the constraints of the manufacturing process. Within a strand, color must be relatively uniform, finish is uniform, and bead shape and size is uniform. Length, bead size, color, shape, and finish can vary from strand to strand. When two strands are held against one another, it is very easy to quickly evaluate which strand is "better." The same physical attributes of the Mardi Gras beads that led to bead inflation created the nudity dimension of the throwing game.

The second question we should consider is why did the pearl strands become popular as "tit beads?" I think a convergence of factors led to this historical development: the introduction of MOS beads into the throwing game beginning in the mid-1970s and becoming the predominant bead thrown by the 1980s; the growing safe sex movement; and the widespread popularity of a rock song that made a particular sex term part of mainstream slang. Just as Deetz identified evidence of visual punning in the death's heads carved by New England stoneworkers, I believe that the use of pearls for displays of nudity is a visual pun on the term, "pearl necklace." For those unfamiliar with the term, sometimes more politely referred to as "mammary sex," it means to ejaculate on a partner's neck or chest. The development of nudity for beads corresponds to growing awareness about HIV transmission and the safe sex movement. Ejaculating outside of one's partner was part of the rhetoric of the early safe sex movement, with mammary sex being promoted as safe sex practice that required no penetration. Before the AIDs epidemic, mammary sex was seen as a way to prevent pregnancy and STDs.

In the beads for nudity exchange, a man who showed his penis, or increasingly, a woman who showed her breasts, was rewarded with a pearl necklace. The ZZ Top song, "Pearl Necklace," was released in 1981, and the lyrics clearly refer to the pearl necklace the woman in the song wants being a sexual act, demonstrating that the slang was already well-known by that time. Not only did the MOS beads provide physical attributes that allowed some to be more highly valued than others, they also provided a physicality that could be used in material word plays.

Kilborn's (1992) sociology thesis from LSU represents the only systematic study of displays of nudity at Mardi Gras that I have encountered. Kilborn and his research team conducted the study between February 9–12, 1991, which focused on French Quarter displays of nudity. His records indicate that his team witnessed 409 breast exposures and 63 penis displays. He does not specify in his thesis whether or not he is recording male or female breasts, but given the time and effort taken to quantify what percentage of nipple had to be shown to count as a display, we might assume that he defined breasts as only occurring on the female body. It is actually quite a shame that he did not include differentiation between male and female shows (men do commonly lift their shirts to attempt to get beads from women)or his counts of bra and non-nipple shows. Those particular kinds of displays demonstrate women attempting to find a liminal space between nude and dressed, and are, to forgive the pun, also revealing.

The 1986 newspaper article references displays of nudity for beads as "probably peculiar" to the French Quarter, and suggests the practice did not yet have high visibility along the parade routes. By 1990, however, showing breasts for beads was an established practice at parades, with the greatest likelihood of encountering an exposed breast being along Canal Street where the parades come closest to the French Quarter. The truly drunk and self-confident flasher will display her/his breasts by lifting the shirt up and over the chest. The more modest will approach a float and pull their shirt forward at the neckline, providing only those above with a view. This second approach also ensures that the flasher will recover most of the rewards from her efforts; when one is pulling down their shirt, it is hard to simultaneously catch beads. The more modest approach is also less likely to draw the attention of the New Orleans Police (NOPD).

Enforcement of laws preventing public nudity is inconsistent. The city benefits from the national reputation Mardi Gras has for drunken frivolity and does not want to discourage those tourism dollars. Yet, the city does not want to deter families from visiting the city, nor do they want to alienate the local population. In 1999, NOPD was engaged in a particularly heavy-handed crackdown on public nudity and arrested 350 people during the Carnival season. In the month prior to the 2000 Carnival season, bars were provided with placards to post informing clients that plain-clothes officers, who would be stationed throughout the French Quarter, were poised to make arrests, and warning that restaurant balconies identified as nuisances would be shut down (*Bangor Daily News,* February 28, 2000).

Crackdowns in the French Quarter are uncommon. Displays of nudity above the waistline are usually ignored there and tolerated along parade routes, especially at night as long as it is on Canal Street where few families attend the parades. The fear of exposing children to lewdness fuels many of the arrests outside of the French Quarter, not only in New Orleans but also in other parts of the state. Women who show their breasts are the target of arrest along parade routes, not the maskers who solicit and reward the flashers.

New Orleans has been recently trying to clean up the national reputation of Mardi Gras. According to a recently strengthened city curfew policy, children under the age of 16 must be accompanied by an adult, if entering the French Quarter after 8pm, to protect them from the booze, nudity, and violence that characterizes the quarter, according to NOPD Commander Jeffrey Walls. The curfew is year-round, not just during Carnival. The curfew was in effect for the 2012 Carnival season and resulted in 170 arrests (out of 816 Carnival arrests[news.blogs.cnn.com/2012/02/20/strict-new-french-quarter-curfew-nets-almost-200-mardi-gras-arrests/]).

Archaeologies of the Mardi Gras Sex Trade

So how do we get at any of this archaeologically? Is it possible to see evidence of sexual bartering in the archaeological record of Mardi Gras? Archaeologies of sexuality have been challenged by this very question. Most studies of sexuality have focused either on representations in art, statuary, and monumental architecture (e.g., Joyce 2009; Joyce and Meskell 2003; Meskell 1999) or explicit explorations of sites where sex was known to have taken place (e.g., Seifert 2005), such as brothels or women's penitentiaries (Cassella 2000). Archaeologists have tried to follow the directive of Judith Butler that we should attempt to understand how desire was constructed in different social settings. Therefore, when studying brothels, we should not just look for evidence of how prostitutes dealt with the mechanics of the sex trade—treatments for VD or contraceptive needs—but how they designed their space to evoke desire. This then leads us to look at furnishings, the aphrodisiac properties of the foods served, and the inversion of Victorian domesticity that served to create a space where men felt comfortable acting outside of the norms and restrictions of polite society. At home, a Victorian man was expected to use the correct fork (or spoon or knife or cup, etc.) for each dish. He was to chew with his mouth shut, never let his lips touch his fork, and make no disagreeable sounds with his body. In contrast, at a brothel, a man could eat Oysters out of the shell with his fingers, drink straight out of the champagne bottle, gamble, laugh, yell loudly with his friends, and use vulgar and shocking language—all in a space that was designed to look like his parlor at home. The prostitutes were the ultimate in naughty Victorian housewives (Wilkie 2010).

How then do we understand desire within the bead assemblages. If we were to look only at iconography suggestive of sexuality, we would be left with a limited sample: the penis bead I discussed at the beginning of the chapter, a strand of pride beads, and a hand-made medallion made out of a coconut, which was painted hot pink and decorated with glitter letters "WTF," (to my eye, it looks like a giant misshapen scrotum; Figure 9.3). I caught no beads depicting naked women, no condoms, no pornographic pictures (though a friend of mine caught gay porn trading cards and condoms at Krewe de Vieux).

Within each of the assemblages are pearl beads—the beads that were marked within Mardi Gras practice as associated with sexualized displays of nudity. You may remember that I presented a frequency seriation of bead finish in chapter three (Figure 3.8). Pearl finished beads in that analysis were a small but pervasive part of Mardi Gras from 1991 through 2010. Our frequency seriation showed that the beads peaked in popularity between 1999 and 2004, with a slight depression in 2000 and 2001. The slight decrease corresponds to the advertised police crackdowns in 2000 and 2001. Pearls never regained the same levels of popularity after Hurricane Katrina.

Based on ethnographic evidence, we know that these beads were used to barter for displays of nudity. We should consider them as artifacts that were used to communicate desire—desire on the part of the giver to gain a form of sexual access to the recipient. I wondered if the beads, as a potential currency, could be indicative of a masker's

Figure 9.3. Examples of sex-themed beads and throws recovered from Mardi Gras parades.

intentionality to participate in sexual bartering. After all, I have observed maskers opening solicitations by prominently displaying a long, thick strand of pearl beads. I decided to draw on the thinking tools of processual archaeology to see if I could imagine tests of the materials that would allow me to "see" sexual barter in the assemblages. I found the exercise useful.

Hypothesis 1. In parades where maskers intended to solicit nudity, since bigger beads are more likely to attract sexual favors, we should see the greatest amounts of resources expended on the acquisition of pearl beads. This would result in high numbers of pearl beads that were of greater quality than other beads in the assemblage.

Archaeological Expectation: Since the bigger beads are more likely to attract sexual favors, we should expect to see pearls from a given assemblage with longer average lengths and/or diameters than the overall assemblage average. Krewes that do not have pearls that are longer or wider than the average beads they throw were not planning on engaging in sexual solicitation.

Hypothesis 2. Soliciting nudity in the Mardi Gras setting is a way for male maskers to reinforce patriarchy by enforcing that the female body (and by extension, their sexuality) is something that can be bought and be controlled by men.

Archaeological Expectation: The greatest differences between average pearl length and/or diameter will be in the assemblages of all-male krewes.

Hypothesis 3. Patriarchy in Louisiana is racialized, and to enforce white supremacy, African American men were racialized as predators of white women. White supremacist groups accused black men of assaulting white women so they could justify racial violence against black men.

Archaeological Expectation: In a parade focused on expressing African American success and philanthropy, as well as promoting positive images of black womanhood, we should expect to see little to no evidence of members of Zulu participating in this aspect of the throwing game.

While these hypotheses are couched more in the theories of feminism than the human behavioral ecology of processualism, you should see that any question can be framed in a hypothetico-deductive framework. The tools of processual archaeology can be used for any research question. To evaluate each of these hypotheses, I calculated the average length and diameter width of white pearls recovered from parades in New Orleans and Baton Rouge (the two cities where displays of nudity were regularly reported along parade routes). Table 9.3 shows the result of these analyses, and includes reference to whether the krewe was male-only, female-only, or mixed. I was not necessarily expecting to see any particular trends from this analysis, but was surprised at the results. The all-male Krewes of de Capital (1999), Bacchus (2000), and Rex (2000), exhibit particularly significant differences in the strand length, diameter of the pearls they threw, and the average lengths and widths for the parade. In the case of Bacchus, the average bead thrown in 2000 was 46", whereas the average length of the pearls they threw was 72". Rex threw strands of pearls that were almost twice as long as the average bead they threw (80" for pearls, 42.1" for average overall). Both Rex and Bacchus threw pearls with an average diameter of 11 mm.

The only coed parade that showed a significant difference in pearl and overall bead length was Spanish Town, which threw slightly wider pearls than the overall average. Since Spanish Town is a parade made of multiple krewes, some of which are male only, and the parade relishes its bawdy reputation, this is not a surprising circumstance. Through time, the difference in size between pearls and other beads decreases, with some fluctuations on a krewe-by-krewe basis. As expected, though, for different reasons, neither Zulu nor the all-women's krewes exhibited significant evidence of participation in the breasts-for-beads bartering game. While pearls were generally slightly larger and longer in most parades, this is probably a function of them being highly valued beads among all crowd goers, and therefore a choice of maskers for their "good" beads.

Table 9.3. Length and Diameter of Average Pearl Strands Versus Overall Parade Average for Men's Versus Women's Krewes.

YEAR	KREWE NAME AND LOCATION	MALE, FEMALE OR COED?	LENGTH OF AVERAGE STRAND (in)	LENGTH OF AVERAGE PEARL STRAND (in)	DIAMETER OF AVERAGE BEAD (mm)	DIAMETER OF AVERAGE PEARL (mm)
1999	Spanish Town, Baton Rouge	Coed	33.3	45.7	7.3	9.5
1999	Southdowns, Baton Rouge	Coed	26.6	37.9	5.9	7.6
1999	Mystick Krewe de Capitale	Male	30	50	7.4	12
1999	Thoth, New Orleans	Male	32.25	42.5	8.2	9.53
1999	Orpheus, New Orleans	Coed	42.4	52.45	8.6	9.1
2000	Orpheus, New Orleans	Coed	41.5	35.4	9.6	9.5
2000	Bacchus, New Orleans	Male	46.1	72.4	8.4	11
2000	Rex, New Orleans	Male	42.1	80	8.8	11
2000	Okeanos, New Orleans	male	32.6	48	7.6	8
2000	Zulu, New Orleans	Male	33.5	39	7.2	7.5
2000	Endymian, New Orleans	Male	27.3	38.3	7.6	8.3
2000	Thoth, New Orleans	Male	32.1	42	7.6	8.18
2000	Tucks. New Orleans	Male*	36	40.6	8	8
2000	Iris, New Orleans	Female	33.2	38.5	7.6	8.6
2001	Bacchus	male	35.5	37.8	8.4	8.4
2001	Orpheus	Coed	38.4	72	8.4	12
2002	Spanish Town, Baton Rouge	Coed	31.6	39.8	7.8	9.2

Table continued on page 292

Table 9.3. Continued from page 291

YEAR	KREWE NAME AND LOCATION	MALE, FEMALE OR COED?	LENGTH OF AVERAGE STRAND (in)	LENGTH OF AVERAGE PEARL STRAND (in)	DIAMETER OF AVERAGE BEAD (mm)	DIAMETER OF AVERAGE PEARL (mm)
2002	Orpheus	Coed	40.19	46.8	8.5	9.2
2003	Spanish Town, Baton Rouge	Coed	38.7	41.7	8.4	8.3
2004	Bacchus	Male	48.6		11.8	
2004	Orpheus, New Orleans	Coed	43.6	47.7	9.3	11.96
2004	Spanish Town, Baton Rouge	Coed	36.4	47.6	8.9	12
2006	Spanish Town, Baton Rouge	Coed	34.9	47.3	9	10
2006	Orpheus	Coed	44	50.2	11.3	12.9
2007	Spanish Town, Baton Rouge	Coed		45.57		10.4
2007	Southdowns, Baton Rouge	Coed		56.54		9.18
2007	Orpheus, New Orleans	Coed	47.2	52.6	10.2	12.55
2009	Spanish Town, Baton Rouge	Coed	34.7	51.62	9.2	10.8
2009	Bacchus, New Orleans	Male	43.3	53.3	10.8	11.71
2009	Orpheus, New Orleans	Coed	48.2	44.8	10.76	10.8
2009	Proteus, New Orleans	Male			8.8	

So what can we conclude about displays of nudity at Mardi Gras? First, the material evidence demonstrates that some maskers clearly came to Carnival with the intention to solicit displays of nudity by purchasing high "quality" pearl beads. What was their motivation? A human behavioral ecologist would say they did so because of the biological imperative to increase one's access to sexual relations and by extension increase reproductive rates. A feminist would say that the ability for men to demonstrate that they could "buy" sexual access to women through bead wealth in a public setting like Mardi Gras reinforces and naturalizes the social power that patriarchal systems grant to men based on their sex.

What about the women who show their breasts? A human behavioral ecologist may argue that by showing their desirability through the collection of large numbers of quality beads, a woman is positioning herself to attract the best possible mate to father her children. Her participation in the bartering game provides her with material evidence, in the form of beads, of her sexual desirability to others at the parade. A feminist might argue alternatively that these women are dupes to the patriarchal system in which they are enmeshed, or that these women are attempting to demonstrate their ownership of their own bodies by flouting conventions that frown on public nudity. Participants in the bartering game meet with differing motivations for and understandings of their actions. Feminist theorizing emphasizes multi-vocality and recognizes multiple subjectivities that exist in any social negotiation. For some women, the decision to flash one's breasts is empowering, and it allows them to exert control over their own sexuality in a society that attempts to control it in hundreds of different ways. The act, in many ways, desexualizes the breast, removing it from an erotic context, which could be seen as a woman's way of reclaiming the breast for herself. A feminist reading of the transaction could just as easily condemn the woman who flashes as contributing to her own sexual subjugation. Feminism encourages us to consider multiple possibilities simultaneously.

Throwing around Feminist Politics: Muses

A krewe founded more recently, the Krewe of Muses, represents a different approach to women's parading, and in pushing the boundaries of women's public behavior has recently found itself mired in a not-as-friendly-as-portrayed rivalry with an all-male krewe. Muses was founded in 2001 by Staci Rosenberg, a New Orleans real estate attorney, who was jealous of the friendships and revelry her male coworkers enjoyed as part of memberships in krewes. She founded Muses for professional women as a krewe with a smart aleck sensibility. The krewe was named after the nine Muses, and each year an honorary Muse who has contributed to some aspect of New Orleans life embodied by one of the nine sisters is selected to ride with the krewe.

The krewe has spent a great deal of time developing their girly-themed throws. The medallions feature high-heel shoes, lipstick cases, stuffed animals, teddy bears, lip gloss, manicure sets, and change purses. My daughter and I finally attended Muses as I was finishing this book (see chapter 13 for more details), and most of our catches were not beads but magnets, stuffed vegetables, re-useable high-heeled shoe ice cubes, a laser pointer, blinky rings, and bead-catcher nets (Figure 9.4). The clear embracing of the iconography of lipstick feminism—high heels and lipstick—in the krewe's medallions is fascinating. In a nod to Zulu, the krewe decorates high-heel shoes with glitter that they toss from their floats. The Muses are lipstick feminists—professional women and artists who have fought their way up in New Orleans society, but have embraced the material

Figure 9.4. Examples of Muses' lipstick feminist throws. Photograph by Alexandra Wilkie Farnsworth.

trappings of the performance of southern beauty. Their floats often have a woman-centric bawdiness to them, which shows an embracing of female sexuality. Based upon New Orleans' on-line polls, the krewe has quickly become one of the most popular parades of the Mardi Gras season with locals.

The krewe tries to have a feminist sensibility on a global scale, and here we can see how politics can affect economics. The 2005 documentary, *Made in China,* which explores conditions within a Chinese bead factory, worried Staci Rosenberg and Krewe of Muses creative director, Virginia Saussy. As a result, they visited China to see the factory that made their throws. In an interview, Saussy stated,

> We had seen a horrifying documentary on bead factories, and it kind of freaked us out. The bead factory was really nice, actually. It had a purple, green, and gold entrance and everyone wore purple, green, and gold uniforms. A lot of young women, they live in a dorm next door to the factory. We said, 'We should have brought a video,' and the owner said, 'No! Don't tell them you throw them off of floats. They think they're making very popular jewelry.' And they are. It is extremely popular and in demand for a very brief period. (Rawls, 2012 "Krewe of Muses Mardi Gras Throws")

We might question whether the visit was really enough to oversee working conditions, but it does demonstrate some awareness of the criticism that lipstick feminists ignore the plight of women who work in sweatshop labor.

The popularity of Muse has drawn the attention of the Krewe d'Etat, who marches the Friday night after Muse. Krewe d'Etat was founded in 1996 and has a highly secretive membership, which is reportedly drawn from former members of Comus and Momus, two old-line krewes who withdrew from parading after the passage of the city's 1991 desegregation ordinance. Krewe d'Etat is known for its political and social satire in their floats and has been one of the most popular parades with locals. In 2011, Krewe d'Etat featured a float called "the Triple Sow Cow," which featured an ice-skating cow decorated with a Muses logo. The program for the parade distributed by the krewe included the following description of the float.

Our version of this now classic move features a certain 'krewe' of whirling dervishes whose spins on things have slung mud (and ice) on many others in the past. But this time, the high-heeled mudslingers are in for the Tonya Harding treatment themselves. Watch for the old footwear that might be flung from this float. Who knows, perhaps this year these full-figured skaters might even be able to witness this spectacle, rather than once again riding in our wake.

I want to take a moment to deconstruct this text, because it is a classical piece of anti-feminist writing. Note the insults to the physical appearance of the women, comparing them to cows and sows. There is a racialized reference to whirling dervishes, a Sufi group. Louisiana has a conservative population who can harbor distrust of non-Christians. To compare the women to an Islamic sect, in that Louisiana mindset, is communicating that they are a threat to American society. There is also the implied threat of violence with the reference to the "Tonya Harding" treatment; recall that Tonya Harding was thrown out of ice-skating after her boyfriend knee-capped competing national skater, Nancy Kerrigan. We see the patriarchy of Mardi Gras attempting to punish women who have pushed too far on acceptable boundaries.

Muses was tipped off about the float, and protestors along the Krewe d'Etat parade route booed the float and yelled "moo." In 2012, Muses threw a special cow medallion that said, "moo," and bore the inscription, "how a-mooosing." Another action by the krewe drew media attention and sparked debate. During the 2012 Krewe d'Etat procession, spectators in the crowd put coaster-sized stickers on the floats, and even on some of Krewe d'Etat's maskers (who must have been quite drunk not to realize they had been stickered). The stickers featured the Krewe d'Etat logo, a skull wearing a jester's hat, with a red high heel shoe stabbing it in the eye socket, with blood coming out. The image was also found spray-painted outside of Krewe d'Etat's headquarters, or den.

Krewe d'Etat was not a-mooosed and threatened legal action against the culprits, but did not directly accuse Muses' organization. Tommy Mitchell, spokesman for Krewe d'Etat stated "there may have been people who may have taken a float we had in our parade last year a little bit to heart, not as if it was in the fun of Mardi Gras," he said. "But it's all in good fun and satire. It's not personal."

For their part, Muses did not deny knowledge or participation. The following is the statement offered by the krewe's publicist, Denise Estopina, to *The Times-Picayune*.

> With all the serious issues facing our city, this is much ado about nothing, " Estopinal wrote. "Trying to elevate this to something other than a prank is absurd. Last year, a lot of people were upset about d'Etat's depiction of Muses on one of their floats, which was considered mean-spirited. Perhaps this resulted from that. (New Orleans *The Times-Picayune*, February 27, 2012)

Comments on local newspaper websites and blogs tended to condemn Muses for being unladylike and unclassy for pulling this prank. This particular comment is worth noting: "it's all fun and games until some yuppie, mother-of-two gets popped with misdemeanor charges for vandalism. Also, a shoe in the eye with blood squirting out?? Is that a threat of violence? What would happen if a male group did this to a female group?" (Coviello 2012). The writer fails to acknowledge the threat of violence implied by the original Krewe d'Etat float. Little has changed during the last 100 years, women are still being punished by the patriarchy of the New Orleans when they attempt to bring change to Carnival or dare to respond to inequality.

So what are the archaeological implications of this? Let us look again at the material culture of women's Mardi Gras groups. The Krewe of Iris was breaking new ground in 1941 when they first paraded, and they emphasized through the materiality of their parade their identity as women with ornate dresses and long feminine ball gloves; and they were promptly attacked as unlady-like and had rotten fruit thrown at them during their parade. Muses has pushed a material iconography of girl-power with pink girly-girly wigs and throws that emphasize high-heel shoes, make-up, teddy bears, and flowers. Muses has also been critiqued by male rivals as presenting an "unlady-like" presence. Let us contrast this with Shangri-La, the former all-female krewe who did not push their identity materially as a female krewe but who peacefully converted to a male-female krewe with no fuss or controversy.

Remember first-wave feminist Matilda Gage? She arranged her material household life so that visitors would not be offended by her radical feminist views. Shangri-La seems to have taken a similar approach to not rocking the material boat. Iris and Muses seem to be taking a different tact, one similar to in-your-face first-wave feminists like Alice Paul, who constantly and publicly badgered Woodrow Wilson about the issue of women's suffrage and went to prison as a result. You may have heard of Alice Paul in history class, but have probably not heard of Matilda Gage, even though she was the more prolific author. Alice Paul, Iris, and Muses have all chosen to spread their message not only through words, but with things—and the thingness of their message made them more threatening to their rivals. Perhaps this is an excellent illustration of why archaeology matters—things endure longer than words.

Queering Mardi Gras

Our trip through feminist theory would not be complete without some archaeological attention to queer theory, and queer Mardi Gras. Queer archaeology has also found a niche. Advocates of queer archaeology argue that too much of archaeological interpretations in sex and gender presume a heteronormative (straight) subject position and, in doing so graft contemporary sexual identities and norms onto past societies (Voss 2008). So far, much of queer archaeology has succumbed to the same blinders as the early gender work, in that archaeologists are attempting to find sites and artifacts that can be pinpointed as queer instead of straight (see Casella 2000). But this arena is developing and represents one of the cutting edges of feminist archaeology (see Joyce 2009).

So what do we mean when we talk about a "queer archaeology"? The use of the term "queer" came into gay activism and sexuality studies in the 1990s as a way to take back a term of hate speech in an empowering way and to problematize the presumed binary be-tween heterosexuality and homosexuality. Writers, such as Sedgwick (1990), have argued that the heterosexual-homosexual binary has always been an asymmetrical one, with the "unnaturalness" and "deviant" presumed nature of homosexuality used to naturalize the supremacy and normalness of heterosexuality. Yet, queer theorists rightly argue, there is no clear line between heterosexuality and homosexuality—how about Katie Perry, who sang about kissing a girl and liking it while married to self-reported sex addict Russell Brand? How about the football player who grabs his teammate's rear after a great play? Just as there is a problem trying to put archaeological materials into clear "boys" versus "girls" categories, sexual acts are open to social interpretation and definition that are time and place specific. In the nineteenth century, for instance, it was expected that college women would have romantic attachments to one another that might include passionate physical intimacies (D'Emilio and Freeman 1997).

The category of "queer" includes a wider range of sexualities and gender expressions, compounded by other "outcast" positions, such as race, gender, or class, to complicate the homosexual-heterosexual binary and to challenge assumptions of *heteronormativity*, which should be understood as the uncritically accepted idea that normal sex is heterosexual sex, and all other sex is somehow deviant (Hennessy 1994–1995:34). As I discussed previously, the ideas of sexuality and performance developed by Judith Butler are essential foundations of queer theory, and queer archaeology.

Queer archaeology has been described by Voss (2000, 2010) and others (e.g., Dowson 2000; Geller 2005; Ransley 2005) as a commitment to "an opposition to the normative" or explicitly as countering heteronormativity. The idea of queering archaeology is a politically powerful one, which continues to have little impact on archaeology in general. There may be a continued perception that a queer archaeology is only concerned with studying gay populations, a perception Thomas Dowson sought to dismiss in his introduction to *Queer Archaeologies*. Dowson (2000:163) asserted that "queer theory is thus definitely not restricted to homosexual men and women but to anyone who feels their position (sexual, intellectual, cultural) to be marginalized." That said, queer theory provides an intellectual toolbox for understanding the experiences of gay populations and, importantly, for forcing archaeologists to consider other possible models for sexual expression in the past other than those we encounter today.

To finish our discussion of engendered and feminist archaeology, I want to briefly consider Spanish Town again, not just as a gay parade, but as a parade that employs a particular kind of performance mode that is seen as historically associated with gay performers—"camp." As I will now discuss, camp serves as a mode of performance used by groups excluded by heteronormativity. Camp has been alternately described as an aesthetic, style, or sensibility often associated with gay men (Isherwood 1954) and a mode of performance (Rodger 2004; Meyer 2010). Camp involves the use of irony, theatricality, and an over-the-top stylized aesthetic. Cleto (1999) refers to camp as a "mode of performance that exposes the artifice of what passes as normal." Camp is most often discussed relative to performances, be they performances in music videos, film, television, theater or language.

I would argue that there is an element of camp to any Mardi Gras parade. Inherent to the notion of camp is materiality. It is through the reading of excess and irony, be it clothing, makeup, hair, accouterments, set design, movement through space, or speech acts that camp is recognizable to the parade goer. When one watches the Mardi Gras royalty wearing costumes covered in feathers and rhinestones on floats decorated with papier-mâché flowers and the heads of Greek Gods, one cannot help but recognize that the makers are drawing heavily from camp norms. This excess is a hallmark of camp performances, and the bead inflation that we've talked about in earlier chapters demonstrates the need for krewes to increase the "quality" of beads they throw to maintain the appearance of excess. Because of their abundance, beads are actively used as part of all krewes' camp performances of self-identification.

While some authors who write about camp doubt that straight people can authentically perform camp (e.g., Meyer 2010), Spanish Town is the parade whose performances should be universally accepted as camp. It is a gay-organized parade whose material performances valorize John Water's campy 1979 movie, *Pink Flamingos,* and who use ironic commentary in parade themes to mobilize like-thinking groups in Baton Rouge. John Water's white trash homage, *Pink Flamingos* became a cult hit in the gay community following its release, and propelled drag star, Divine, to camp stardom. The idea behind the movie, that bad taste is better than no taste at all, has inspired a number of Spanish Town's parade themes (Table 9.4). A review of the themes illustrates that the gay sensibility of the parade is becoming more overt, particularly as demonstrated by the 2013 theme, "A Spanish Town Twinkie Ate My Ding-Dong," which was ostensibly to commemorate the demise of the iconic bakery, Hostess.

The neighborhood of Spanish Town in downtown Baton Rouge is the oldest residential area of the city. By the early 1980s, efforts to revitalize the old neighborhood's houses were associated with a growing gay population. Historian John Sykes has attributed the start of the parade to "a bunch of gay guys and other Bohemians too broke to go to New Orleans" who decided to parade down Spanish Town Road (McMains 2010).

Table 9.4. Year-by-Year Spanish Town Themes Showing Evidence of Camp Influences.

Year	Theme
2013	A Spanish Town Twinkie Ate My Dingdong!
2012	It's Conival Time!
2011	BP Blows and Wiki Leaks
2010	XXXpress It
2009	Buy Yeaux Bailout
2008	Flamingeaux Phil Predicts
2007	Quit Flocking Around and Pink Your Own Theme
2006	FEMAture Evacuation
2005	25 Flockin' Years
2004	Flamingos Gone Wild
2003	La. Purchase – Name Your Price
2002	Pink, White and Blue – Show Me Your Colors
2001	2001 – A Spaced Out Oddity
2000	XXcessive MMadness
1999	Leathers and Feathers
1998	Politically Incorrect
1997	See No Evil, Hear No Evil, Speak No Evil
1996	Top Ten Reasons to Mardi Gras in Spanish Town
1995	Manias
1994	Neatness Counts
1993	Krewesing Spanish Town
1992	Louisiana's Dirty Laundry
1991	What If?
1990	What A Long Strange Trip It's Been
1989	Hollywood Comes to Spanish Town
1988	Louisiana – A Fantasy State
1987	Louisiana, A Royal Miss
1986	Poor Taste is Better Than No Taste at All
1985	Urban Olympics
1984	*$@# Big Brother
1983	CATS
1982	Every Man a Mardi Gras King

Today, a Spanish Town parade attendee is likely to catch bunches of hot pink pearl and metallic beads, and some sort of representation of a flamingo—in the form of a medallion, a stuffed animal, sunglasses, pink feather boa, frisbee, or cup. By 2013 (see chapter 13), nearly one-third of the beads caught at Spanish Town were hot pink in color. As I mentioned in chapter eight, Spanish Town's material expression of its identity as a queer krewe has grown through time. In 1998, no throws were caught that gave any sense of a corporate identity among the floats; however, the release of the film "Pink Flamingos" onto VHS may have inspired one masker to throw plastic dog poop (the infamous final scene of the movie features star, Divine, eating dog excrement). In 1999, I caught my first flamingo throw, a brass medallion of a flamingo in a top hat. A growing range of flamingo beads and throws were caught in 2001. Since that time, flamingo throws have been a consistent part of the Spanish Town parade. As the parade has become larger and included larger numbers of non-gay participants, the camp aesthetic of the parade has increasingly become the enduring material legacy of the parade.

In 2009, I caught a throw that suggests that members of Spanish Town see themselves as part of the same material and political parading tradition as the parade of Zulu, which has long been an outsider to white Mardi Gras. A hot-pink coconut, decorated with "WTF" in glitter letters was thrown from one of the floats (Figure 9.2). The object takes the familiar camp object of the Zulu Social Aid and Pleasure Club and merges it with the queer camp of Spanish Town. Emblazoning the familiar expression "WTF" on an object that is vaguely obscene yet indeterminate and appropriately embraces the attitude of Spanish Town's performativity.

Camp provides one arena of queer theory to understand gay Mardi Gras performances, but simply using queer theory's call to question heteronormativity provides other opportunities to make gay participants visible at Mardi Gras, as well as recognizes how Carnival is unto itself, a celebration about queering social norms. New Orleans has long been the site of an active gay culture. The Clover Grill began to sponsor the Gay Mardi Gras beauty pageant in the late 1950s, with sponsorship later passing to Café Lafitte's in Exile—the site of our earliest confirmed bartering exchange of beads for nudity. In 1968, a gay writer observed, "while Straight America comes to be something that they are not … Gay America comes to be something they are but cannot often be the rest of the year" (quoted in Mitchell 1995:142). By the late 1950s, at least one gay krewe was sponsoring a ball, and by the 1960s, the gay krewes of Yuga, Amon Ra, Apollo, Armenius, Celestial Knights, Dionysius, Memphis, Olympus, and Petronius were openly holding balls.

In New Orleans, gay street celebrations are common on Bourbon Street, where bears, bikers, transvestites, and transsexuals gather to drink, dance, and revel. There is a political sensibility that can also be found during Carnival. It is not uncommon to be handed condoms in the quarter or pamphlets about safe sex. In 1991, the NO/AIDS Task Force distributed Mardi Gras beads with medallions shaped like a safety pin, declaring "Play Safe/no AIDS taskforce" (Figure 9.5). This organization, founded in 1983, claims to be the oldest HIV/AIDS service organization in the Gulf South (NoAIDS Task Force,

"History"). Since 2000, gay pride beads have been thrown not only in the French Quarter but also from floats including the super krewes of Bacchus and Orpheus.

While gay Mardi Gras exists as a separate part of Carnival celebrations, it is also becoming part of mainstream Mardi Gras celebrations. The Spanish Town parade is an important case in point. After Hurricane Katrina, relocations of people to Baton Rouge increased the visibility of this parade and led to larger and larger numbers of floats participating each year. While I will discuss this more in chapter 11, the post-Katrina influence of Spanish Town on the aesthetic of Mardi Gras is clearly visible in New Orleans assemblages. The hot pink beads of Spanish Town become popular in New Orleans krewes, and have also become some of the most expensive beads being thrown (Table 9.5). While pearls were once the largest and widest of the monochrome MOS beads thrown, a consideration of beads recovered from Orpheus and Bacchus parades clearly shows that hot pink beads are now all the rage. Bacchus has even begun to make MOS medallion beads in hot pink, as had the parade of Hermes in 2013. For each of these krewes, the hot pink medallions were the largest of the MOS medallions thrown.

Spanish Town was founded as a local neighborhood parade in the predominantly gay neighborhood of Spanish Town. As we discussed earlier, the hot pink beads and flamingos selected by the krewe as their themes were part of a gay Carnival aesthetic. That aesthetic is now shaping how straight and LGBT communities experience and celebrate Mardi Gras in New Orleans, as well as Baton Rouge! I think it is fair to say that the spread of the pink beads should be seen not simply as the result of *diffusionism* of a style from one part of the state to another, but should also be actively interpreted as evidence of the queering of Mardi Gras. Diffusionism was used by cultural historians to explain the spread of objects from one place to another through trade or other contacts. It was a passive kind of culture change, with groups merely adopting new items. Whether the adoption of a new item represents the adoption of a new set of accompanying ideas or not was a less interesting question to cultural historians who tended to see cultures as enduring entities resistant to change. I would argue the spread of beads in this instance is emerging from a spread of ideas; I am not implying some sort of neo-conservative nightmare of a contagious homosexuality spread through Mardi Gras beads. I am saying just the opposite. At a time when social attitudes about homosexuality are shifting toward tolerance and acceptance, we see the wider embracement of a gay aesthetic within Mardi Gras. It is hopeful commentary on our times that the beads have spread from a gay pride parade that is the most popular family parade in the city of Baton Rouge.

Figure 9.5. "Play safe-No AIDS Taskforce" medallion caught in 1990 in the French Quarter. Photograph by Alexandra Wilkie Farnsworth.

Table 9.5. Changes in Hot Pink Beads Post-Katrina.

Hot Pink Beads as a Percentage of Beads Thrown in New Orleans over Time (excludes transparent pale pink beads)

YEAR	1999	2000	2001	2002	2003	2004	2006	2007	2009
PERCENTAGE OF BEADS THAT WERE METALLIC HOT PINK	1	1.4	1.5	1.5	3.2		5.1	11	12.8

YEAR	PARADE	LOCATION	% OF HOT PINK BEADS THROWN	AVERAGE BEAD DIAMETER (mm)	AVERAGE HOT PINK BEAD DIAMETER (mm)	AVERAGE BEAD LENGTH (in)	AVERAGE HOT PINK BEAD LENGTH (in)
2002	Spanish Town	Baton Rouge	5.5	7.8	7.8	31.6	35.4
2003	Spanish Town	Baton Rouge	16.9	8.4	8.5	38.7	41.4
2004	Spanish Town	Baton Rouge	11.5	8.9	9.8	36.4	40.7
2006	Spanish Town	Baton Rouge	17.7	9	9.5	34.9	38.7
2009	Spanish Town	Baton Rouge	33.8	9.2	10.9	34.7	43.9
2004	Orpheus	New Orleans	1.6	9.3		43.6	
2006	Orpheus	New Orleans	8.8	11.3	11.1	44	44.7
2007	Orpheus	New Orleans	15	10.76	11.71	43.6	44.6
2009	Orpheus	New Orleans	11.4	10.76	13.25	48.2	51.75
2003	Bacchus	New Orleans		9.1	8.7	41.4	35.5
2009	Bacchus	New Orleans	21.9	10.8	11.71	43.3	69.3

Another way I think a gay aesthetic is entering Mardi Gras is in the color composition of throw bead packs. Remember that at the beginning of my study, packages of beads were often combined in purple-green-gold Mardi Gras-theme colored packs. In recent years, a new color assortment has become popular: a six-color set featuring purple, green, gold, pink, blue, and silver; these are the colors of the rainbow, which when thrown as a package have the same visual affect as throwing rainbow pride beads. I haven't yet quantified this trend, but am working on it for another project. Archaeology often works that way; the process of working through ideas causes new ideas to emerge for consideration. Speaking of new ideas, in the next chapter, we'll discuss the ways a set of nineteenth-century ideas continue to provide critical thinking space for archaeologists as we ponder Marxism and ideas of power and archaeological interpretation.

CHAPTER 10
ESTABLISHING POWER
AND PRESTIGE THROUGH BEADS

The switch from riding in a New Orleans super krewe to a float decorated the night before by volunteers from the local animal shelter was a bit shocking for me. While my spaces in the cabins of Orpheus' floats were never roomy, I did have roofs over my head and a solid wall behind me. Now Alex and I found ourselves precariously perched on a crepe-paper-decorated trailer with a number of children dressed as adoptable pets who were being closely supervised by their parents as the trailer-float lurched along as part of the Lion's parade in New Roads. Alex was having a great time, as would be expected for any reasonably good-humored seven-year-old who finds herself dressed as a kitten and riding a Mardi Gras float.

I, on the other hand, was feeling some unjustified annoyance toward the other float riders. The well-meaning organizers of our float had told participants there would be beads for the children to throw, and apparently, I was the only person who didn't believe them and had bought additional beads for my own child. There is nothing sadder than a thrown-out float at a small local parade. In New Orleans, no one knows who you are; but, in a local parade, you rarely wear a mask and your trailer-based floats leave you pretty much face-to-face with your disappointed crowd. To parade with no more throws is a particularly terrible ride of shame, and I wasn't going to allow Alex to experience that for her first-ever Mardi Gras ride! I had bought several cases of beads, some footballs, stuffed animals, and frisbees for the kid to throw. It was much less than I would have purchased for New Orleans; the parade was shorter, and Alex's ability to throw was significantly less than mine. I was going to be unwrapping beads and keeping the child provisioned rather than throwing myself. We should have had plenty.

Now that we were only half way through the parade, everyone else was thrown out and expecting Alex to hand over her beads, but for that to happen, they had to get through me. Now you need to know that I was raised in a household that strongly emphasized self-reliance and hard work. (for minimal pay, if my parents were the employers) And I feel it acutely when I arrive prepared for something and those who didn't prepare expect me to cover for them (this is the group project syndrome in classes, right?). And it cost me money to be prepared, money that I spent, and they hadn't.

Strung Out on Archaeology: An Introduction to Archaeological Research by Laurie A. Wilkie, 303–331.

It irritated me, but still, I wasn't going to let the other kids have a spoilt Mardi Gras, nor was I going to risk an uprising of the masses on the float who would attempt to strip us of our wealth for the good of the commoners. I gave packets of beads to the other kids on the float, (and cut them off when I saw their parents throwing the beads instead of the kids—I wasn't throwing beads, why should they?) I spent the parade rationing the beads so that they would last throughout the parade and that so Alex wasn't denied her rightful proportion. Really, I was a bit of a jerk. Most of the adults on the float had probably never been in a parade before either. I should have just let everyone throw like mad and we could have experienced the ride of shame together. But at the time, I couldn't bring myself to think that way. Bead madness had possessed me. Now, I absolutely realize how absurd it was to feel possessive of something I had bought to throw away—really, did it matter if it was given away to the masses or to the others on my float? Yes, I realized. Yes, it did matter—at least in the logic of Mardi Gras. Those other people were getting credit for the beads we had acquired to throw and for throwing. Even if fleeting and momentary, the ability to throw beads to a begging parade goer gives you a sense of power and prestige. So while the experience was frustrating, and I'm a bit ashamed of how I felt about it all, the experience gave me further insights into the strange draw that is the throwing game, as well as some potentially unflattering personal insights that required further reflection later on.

An archaeologist working from a human behavioral ecology or evolutionary perspective speaks of social difference in society in terms like "social stratification" and "social complexity." Because researchers using these theoretical perspectives are interested in long-term, macroscalar changes, their concerns are not so much about the events and strategies that allow particular people or segments of a society to consolidate and control resources but about the economic and technological developments that make it possible for certain groups to become elites. It was Marxist-influenced thinkers who called upon archaeologists to think about issues such as how is power consolidated in a society, and how do elites manipulate materials, architecture, and landscapes to give the impression that their ruling position is both natural and inevitable?

Surely you've heard of Karl Marx and understand the basics of his theory of social evolution? Marx believed that the history of humankind was marked by class struggle between the haves (the bourgeois) and the have-nots (the proletariat). In capitalism, the bourgeois controlled the means of production—basically production sites, production technologies, and raw materials. The proletariat only controlled their labor, which they had to put out for competitive sale on the free market—a circumstance that kept labor costs low. The proletariat labored to make goods that they then could not always afford to purchase themselves (this is referred to as *alienation*). Marx believed that such structural inequalities could not endure, and revolution would occur. The proletariat would rise up and take back the means of production for themselves and create a classless society where access to the means of production and wealth was equally shared. This is a very simplistic introduction to Marx, but hopefully you get the point.

Few archaeologists draw directly upon the writings of Marx in their works, but instead draw upon Marxist thinkers (neo-Marxists), like Michel Foucault, Martin Heidegger, and

Jürgen Habermas. These writers were concerned with understanding why class revolutions were not a more common feature of the human experience—how was it that the lower classes continued to labor under unfair conditions, alienated from the fruits of their labor, without uprising? A great deal of thought in neo-Marxist writing focuses on mechanisms of control that serve to structure inequality in society, the ways elites use *masking ideologies* to prevent labor from creating a class consciousness, and the ways that labor is disciplined through experiences of the everyday (Barrow 1993; Gorman 1982). A masking *ideology* is basically a set of ideas that serve to keep a worker from seeing the realities of the inequalities they live with on a daily basis. What would be a good example of a masking ideology? This is a tricky thing to come up with an example for simply because masking ideologies are so entrenched that people often take offense when something they believe to be true is suggested to not only be false, but that they are a "dupe" to the system for believing it.

So here's an example. It is generally believed in the United States that we are a democracy where every person has an equal say in the government (one person one vote). But in presidential elections, this is not the case. For the president and vice president are actually elected by electors in the electoral college. Each state gets the same number of electors as they get congress persons—meaning that smaller states are disproportionately represented in the electoral college. As a consequence, each person in a small state has more representation in the electoral college than people from larger states—and in no case does the popular vote actually serve to elect the president or vice president. It is only every four years, during the election season that US citizens have to confront that the idea of one person one vote is an ideology that masks the multitude of inequalities inherent between voters in the electoral college.

What would be an example of archaeological evidence of a masking ideology? An excellent example comes from historical archaeology and involves the idea of *fashion* and *emulation*. Before I talk about the archaeology, I should quickly explain the ideas behind these terms. While we usually think of fashion as related to dress, fashion is a term that refers to a prevailing style or mannerism at a given time and place. The archaeological tool of frequency seriation, you'll remember, basically charts the popularity of different styles—or fashions—relative to one another through time. Fashion is often a means of creating distinction between different social categories of people. For instance, we saw it was the prevailing trend—or fashion—of the elite in Mesoamerica to keep green obsidian for their own exclusive use (see chapter seven). Emulation occurs when the fashions of one group are copied by another.

In consumer capitalist societies, where fashion becomes a means of establishing a class identity and involves the purchase of luxury goods—the elite use materials to distance themselves from everyone else. Think high-end, brand-named goods like Burberry with its distinctive tan and black plaid as an example. Yet, have you ever seen copies of Burberry for sale? Of course you have, it's easy enough to copy the look of Burberry so less-wealthy people can have Burberry style. This is an example of emulation. Why would you want knock-off Burberry? Because when you are seen wearing or carrying it, it looks as if you are more well-to-do than you are. A Marxist would say that when members of the lower classes engage in emulation, they are dupes to consumer capitalism and the notion that they can purchase class or social equality by possessing goods like the elite. Or alternately, a Marxist could also see it as an attempt by the lower classes to subvert the naturalized position of the elite by using material culture that they try to control for themselves. Of course, emulation can be seen as one reason fashion shifts—those trying to maintain their distinction have to shift the fashion after it becomes common. Again, it's useful to think about those battleship curves created during frequency seriation. Generally, as one style becomes common, others are introduced that gradually come to replace the style that is going out of fashion. We can now see how an archaeological method designed by cultural historians to understand site chronologies can be used by evolutionary archaeologists to understand phenotypic frequencies, and by Marxists to look at processes of emulation. The tools of archaeological thinking are infinitely malleable.

In historical archaeological sites dating to the late eighteenth and early nineteenth centuries, we see wonderful examples of the process of emulation. You might recall that I talked about the worldwide popularity of Chinese porcelains during that time as the pinnacle of fine ceramics available. People desired the elegant translucent and hard ceramics with their beautiful blue hand-painted designs. Josiah Wedgwood devised an earthenware ceramic that had a white body, and when covered with a bluish-tinged glazed and decorated with blue hand-painting or Chinese-influenced decorations, it looked remarkably like Chinese porcelains. In other words, Wedgwood's ceramics emulated Chinese porcelains. Wedgwood's English ceramics were of lower quality, but much cheaper and more abundant than Chinese porcelains; therefore, they were accessible to the members of the industrial revolution's growing middle class in England. Wedgwood's ceramics of this style, which we call pearl wares, were copied by other potters and were popular globally as a strong, cheaper alternative to Chinese porcelains until the 1830s (Hume 1970).

Because Marx wrote his original manifesto as a critique of modern industrial capitalism, there have been debates about the appropriateness of using Marxist theory to interpret past societies prior to the industrial revolution. Capitalism is a particular mode of production in which individuals sell their labor on the market rather than the results of their labor. Labor does not own the means of production. Instead, the machinery and tools needed to create industrial products are owned by an elite class whose interests are represented by a management class that serve as "middle men" between labor and capital. While Marx's writings have an evolutionary bent to them, in that he formulates the stages of labor development that must occur before a socialist society can emerge, this model is specific to the nineteenth century. Issues of economic and social inequality, however, did occur in the past; so Marxist-influenced thought is appropriate for shaping archaeological interpretations and has been used to understand prehistoric societies (McGuire 2008; Saitta 1997, 2007; Thomas 1996).

An important branch of Marxist thought in archaeology draws on critical theory. Critical archaeology, developed by Mark Leone and his collaborators in the Archaeology at Annapolis project (Leone 2010), calls for a politically self-reflexive archaeology that seeks to reveal how the elites consolidate power while duping labor into believing that power is inevitable. For critical archaeologists, the goal of archaeology is not to reconstruct the past from evidentiary traces so much as to use the past as a mirror that allows us to better understand the how structures of inequality in our own society are created and maintained through masking ideologies. The hope is that understanding how one has been duped by the system will be liberating (or *emancipatory*) for the lower classes. Armed with the emancipatory knowledge that a critical archaeological perspective can provide, contemporary American society will have the tools necessary to dismantle the controlling structures of corporate capitalism, or at least that is the hope. Just as feminism has a distinct political agenda, so does critical archaeology. Feminists want sexual/gender equity and to dismantle patriarchy; critical archaeologies want to dismantle capitalism. Archaeology, bringing you social revolution one site at a time! Don't laugh (okay, you can chuckle a bit), but, archaeology and passions ignited over archaeological sites have had some profound social and political impacts at particular places and times, as discussed in the case of the Greek Elgin Marbles housed at the British Museum or the African Burial Ground in New York City. Although the historical circumstances that led to the development of industrial capitalism are unique to a particular time and place, critical archaeological perspectives have the potential to be a powerful tool in prehistory. There is power in language. For instance, the transition from a hunter-gatherer economy to agriculture was accompanied by a decrease in human health as evidenced in skeletal remains that demonstrate portions of populations experienced regular periods of hunger and malnutrition (e.g., Sutton 2010). These conditions are often described as evidence of chronic resource or food shortages. We know that the societies in which these agricultural shifts took place were also undergoing social changes that involved the creation of elite classes. Imagine we used a word like "poverty" to describe what these ancient peoples were enduring? By a simple change in word choice, we see the past as a place where humans worked through the same problems that we struggle with today.

There are ethical questions raised when applying modernist perspectives on past peoples—doesn't it do a kind of symbolic violence against a people to use their history as a tool for writing about contemporary society? You will remember that a similar critique of phenomenological approaches to the deep past has been put forward, and goes back to a central issue raised by post-modernism and post-processualism—can we ever get beyond the lenses of our own experiences to ever get a "real" understanding of the past? Some archaeologists believe that you can never get past our own subjectivities, so any account of the past we write is merely an account of ourselves, while others believe that we have the philosophical and methodological tools necessary to confront our own belief systems in our interpretations.

Marxist approaches in archaeology have enjoyed the greatest success in historical archaeology, where Mark Leone (2010), Matthew Johnson (1995), Randall McGuire (2008), Paul Mullins (1999), Charles Orser (2007), and others have forcefully argued that historical archaeology, as the study of the modern world, must deal with the spread and entrenchment of capitalism as a main focus of its research. Mark Leone has conducted thought-provoking work regarding how landscapes and perspective were used by colonial architects and gardeners to create landscapes that naturalized power held by the elites and the subordinate position of others in the colonial city of Annapolis. The city was designed during a period when architecture known as Georgian was in vogue. Recall that Jim Deetz discussed "Georgian" as a cultural state of mind that came to distinguish the cultural practices of Anglo Americans from their Medieval predecessors and other cultural groups that lived in Massachusetts.

For Leone, Georgian is not a cultural phenomenon but an ideological one. He argues that the Georgian ideology took advantage of new scientific tools like surveying instruments to impose human control over nature in the form of highly designed city plans, such as the one of Annapolis, which was set on a pair of circles, one featuring the state house, the other the central church. Both structures were built on the highest part of the city, naturalizing their interlinked roles—church and state—as the foundation of Annapolis society. After the formation of the US government, with its ideological separation of church and state, the courthouse had a tower added that increased its height and demonstrated its visual dominance on the landscape and over all other parts of society (Leone 2005).

On a smaller scale, Leone has studied the garden of colonial capitalist William Paca. The garden is highly symmetrical and partitioned in a way that emphasized the human rule over the natural world. The so-called natural world of the day included Native Americans, who were being displaced from ancestral lands, and enslaved Africans, who had been forcibly removed from homelands and transported to North America. Leone argues that tight control over perspective and even time in the garden serves as a way of enforcing and naturalizing social inequalities in Annapolis's society by underscoring the white capital's ability to organize and control the natural world. Though he does not discuss sexual and gender inequality, women were also perceived as part of the natural world, so Leone's interpretations could include the naturalizing of white patriarchy (Leone 1982, 2005).

Leone's work is controversial. Hodder, in particular, critiqued it because Leone presumed that only the elite knew what they were doing in their control of the landscape. Other peoples were merely dupes who had the ability to read the landscape, as was intended, but were not clever enough to understand they had been manipulated into that particular reading. From my perspective, perhaps it isn't necessary to presume that the gardens or even the city layout were designed to dupe the general populace. Perhaps, it is enough to demonstrate that this is how the elites told themselves their actions were justified. Certainly, as we observe US society, particularly at election time, we can see ways that different political groups spin narratives about the political "other" that they use to justify their economic and social policies. Much of that rhetoric is not directed toward the entire voting population, but the core constituency of a particular party. Maybe Paca's main audience was other elites, who were duping themselves into believing they were naturally fit to lead.

While Marxists primarily use class as their means of interpreting social relations, an important term in analyses of prestige is the notion of symbolic capital, developed in Bourdieu's (1984) work, *Distinction*. Symbolic capital is non-material wealth that one accumulates in social interactions. It is wealth that has social currency, and can be used to consolidate power. Remember Silvia Freeman, the African American cook at Oakley who used her access to cash to help sharecroppers in her community gain access to luxury goods like tobacco? Archaeologically, we could see that Freeman received farm produce, such as eggs or canned foods, in exchange for the items she bought; but we should also presume that she acquired symbolic capital as well in the form of gratitude from the people she traded with. Likewise, it could be said that generosity in the throwing game is about maskers attempting to accrue symbolic favor with parade goers, and the Louisiana public more broadly. In 1991, the krewes' threat that the passage of the anti-discrimination ordinance would kill Mardi Gras was a blatant attempt to cash in symbolic capital with the people of the city and state; they hoped that the public would come to the defense of the krewes.

Masking Ideologies in the History of Mardi Gras

Let us take another look at the structure of Mardi Gras parades so that we can see how materiality can be used in the service of elite ideologies. The krewes' celebrations have a public and a private face. In the private realm of balls, the elite classes communicate and re-enact their social relationships with one another. The parades, however, are a public performance, intended to enact the krewe's relationship to the masses of New Orleans' society.

The processional begins with the krewe's royalty, seated high above the street-level crowds and equal to those persons who are watching the parade from balconies; these are people who either own property along the parade route or have connections that allow them to access these locations. The position of the royalty relative to the crowd re-inscribes society's inequalities in a way that serves to naturalize them. The structure of the royal court also serves to naturalize gender roles within society, with the women isolated on a separate float. The queen is honored for her youth, and her wifely and motherly potential. Flambeau-carrying black men accompany the night parades. Their position at the street level, combined with their role as the only visible laborers in the parade setting serves to naturalize the position of African Americans as a laboring class within southern society. In a real material way (and if it's material, we can understand it archaeologically), the floats serve to construct a narrative about the relative role of white men, white women, and people of color for parade-goers to read and internalize.

The throwing game also serves as an enactment of the elite's benevolence toward the parade crowds. The original form of the Carnival throwing game, with observers throwing flour pellets at maskers, could never do within the structure of krewe-organized Carnival. To have items thrown at the floats would shatter the illusion of the naturalized hierarchy the krewe presents. City ordinances, passed when Comus initiated parading, outlawed the throwing of objects at maskers and served to protect krewe members from behaviors that would undermine their positionality.

Ultimately, by co-opting and inverting the throwing game from one where maskers were thrown *at*, to one where they threw *to* the crowds, Carnival krewes found another way to reinforce their status as the naturalized leaders of New Orleans' society. The generosity of a particular krewe becomes a metaphor for the generosity of the organization to the city during the rest of the year. Rex's motto, For the Public Good, in this light takes on additional meanings. Rex's reign—both during Carnival and after—is in the best interest of the city, and for the organizations' rulers to no longer control New Orleans would not be in the best interest of the city's populace. The krewes' parades then become an annual ritual in which the position of New Orleans' elite is reinforced to, and applauded by, the spectators of the parade. As the tourist trade grew, the crowds themselves became a validation of the krewes' might—here were crowds, and the money they brought with them to the city—and came to honor the elite of New Orleans.

The elite are themselves ranked, with different krewes commanding different levels of prestige behind the closed doors of Carnival. Comus, as the oldest, holds the highest place in New Orleans society. Rex may be the king of Carnival, but he is the offspring of two members of Comus. Momus appeared a year after Rex, and soon after, Proteus. Proteus was founded in 1882 primarily by businessmen associated with the cotton exchange, and it was unusual among the krewes in that it featured a significant number of Creoles among its membership. The krewe sang the praises of French history in its second parade, attempting to counter the Anglo-centric American krewes. As such, Proteus was probably the only one of the old-line krewes associated with Mardi Gras that included significant numbers of Catholics, which was, ironically, originally primarily celebrated as a Catholic holiday. In 1890, Comus and Proteus fought over who could parade on Mardi Gras day—traditionally Comus's parade day. The two parades ended up colliding while travelling opposite directions on Canal Street. As the king of Comus and the king of Proteus were about to come to blows, a spectator is said to have interceded by taking hold of Proteus's horse and leading him away, which demonstrated that while both were kings, Comus reigned supreme (Tallant 1948).

The popularity of the parades provided krewes with a unique opportunity to communicate their ideological positions to their viewers. James Gill (1997) has written an outstanding political history of the krewes in New Orleans. He relays in detail the overlap between membership in krewes, elite city clubs, and the white supremacy movement during and beyond the period of Reconstruction. During Reconstruction, Mardi Gras pageants became forums for critiques of the federal government.

Most infamous was the Mardi Gras of 1873, when in the midst of statewide violence over the contested elections for the Louisiana governorship, Comus staged a tableau featuring Darwin's *Origin of Species*. Character designs included caricatures of federal and state republican officials as different animals, supposed "missing links." The tableau featured a barely disguised representation of an African American as a gorilla who ruled over all society—a clear commentary on the enfranchisement of African American voters during Reconstruction.

Shortly after Comus's ball, white supremacists in Colfax, LA, dragged 59 African American men from a prison and lynched them. Racial violence was the norm rather than the exception. The membership of the Boston and Pickwick clubs formed a group called the White League that plotted to take over the Louisiana government from the republicans by any means necessary. They raised an army, and all out war involving several thousand men battling against the 550-strong police force of the city erupted September 14, 1874. White Leaguers captured the city and inaugurated their own governor. Papers lauded the takeover as a victory for the white race, now saved from "Africanization." The battle became known as the Battle of Liberty Place, and it is a powerful demonstration of the vested interests the krewes had in maintaining the system of racial privilege they enjoyed since the antebellum period. The interference of the krewe men in state politics did not end with Reconstruction. It continued through the twentieth century, as krewe men colluded against populist politician Huey Long and later interfered in attempts to desegregate schools (Gill 1997).

It was in the late 1960s, as national politics shifted in favor of desegregation and civil rights, that the old-line krewes found themselves to be anachronisms. In 1967, the super krewe Endymion was founded, and one of its explicit goals was to be populist. They had a king selected by lots and a generosity with throws that surpassed all other krewes. Bacchus, who was founded the following year, decided to use a celebrity king, and selected Danny Kaye, a practicing Jew, as their first king (Gill 1997:212). Mardi Gras was shifting and getting away from the old-line krewes. But that does not mean that krewes did not continue to compete for the public's attention.

Now we can see the added poignancy of King Zulu's message to the crowd as he paraded the same day as Rex, interrupting the procession of the king of Carnival, with his band of grass-skirt wearing, coconut-throwing, warriors. How better to undermine the masking ideologies of Mardi Gras' white elite than with Zulu's in-your-face use of black-face? It is particularly fitting that Zulu surpasses Rex in popularity and is for many the most anticipated parade of Fat Tuesday.

It was the city ordinance, put forward by Dorothy Mae Taylor, that forced the desegregation of any krewes that wanted to parade on public streets, however, which demonstrated at last that city hall was not completely controlled by New Orleans' white elite. In a 2012 *Times Picayune* article, the impacts of the ordinance were considered. James Henderson, a long-time member of the Algiers-based African American krewe NOMTOC (whose name is an acronym for New Orleans' Most Talked of Club), and member of the Mayor's Mardi Gras advisory committee, had this to say about Taylor's motivations. "Her ordinance had more to do with economic opportunity, not actual participation in Mardi Gras parades.... I think the elite Mardi Gras organizations were viewed as a network to a better job, better opportunities, a link to the 'better' people in the city, and if you couldn't crack that, then you could never be upwardly mobile" (Nola, February 12, 2012).

The networking importance of being involved in the high-profile krewes should not be underestimated. As an example of how krewe royalty move in high circles, corresponding with the first black US president residing in the White House was the entrance of a Queen Zulu into the inner circle of the executive branch. Barack Obama's social secretary is Desiree Glapion Rogers, a Harvard graduate, and Queen Zulu, 2000, who tossed me a lovely medallion that year (Figure 8.5).

Power and Prestige at Mardi Gras

When we consider the role of Mardi Gras in reinforcing social inequality and the existing class of elites in New Orleans, the throwing game takes on a new edge. It is play, but it is serious play. Popularity as a parading institution provides a particular set of platforms for communicating with the masses. Satire is a powerful medium of political commentary, and visual comedy is the medium of Mardi Gras floats. But, to get audiences to attend your parades to hear your message requires, in today's Carnival, for you to be generous. That there is a perceived value to using Mardi Gras parades as a forum by the old-line krewes is evidenced by the creation of Krewe d'Etat—reportedly created by members of Comus and Momus who wanted to return to parading, but did not want their old-line krewe organizations to appear to kowtow to the 1991 ordinance. Better to start afresh with a new group. Krewe d'Etat, has a political edge to its floats, and they regularly skewer local politicians and comments on political issues in the state. They generated attention when they were formed for their commitment to a "traditional" Mardi Gras and for throwing glass beads in small numbers.

Apart from political platforms, what else does a rider get in return for the money they spend on throws? Quite a bit of real capital is expended to join a krewe and purchase enough throws to distribute over the course of 3–4 hours. Speaking of my own experiences riding in three parades, there is the thrill of the experience of seeing the crowds and their absolute hunger for your throws. It is gratifying to watch the smile of gratitude or triumph that lights up someone's face when they successfully catch a desired throw. But there is also something extremely satisfying, after Mardi Gras has ended, in being able to drop into conversation that you were part of a particular parade. As someone living outside of Louisiana, the symbolic capital that I accrue from having been part of Mardi Gras is small compared to what a Louisianan can earn. For the more exclusive krewes, membership is restricted to the elite echelons of Louisiana society, and the people one interacts with in business and political realms of life are the people who one parades with. The most elite krewes do not reveal their membership, but anyone familiar with Louisiana's social calendar would be able to determine if any of their friends or colleagues were members of the organizations. The most elite do not need to identify themselves as such. The symbolic capital accrued by locals can be immense, and the creation of a new krewe is a means of creating new alliances. It is serious play, indeed.

Power and Prestige in Prehistory: An Example from the Hawaiian Islands

The wealthy and powerful of a society intermingle, and materials are a means of doing this—thus the importance to archaeologists of understanding how exchange relationships and the circulation of prestige goods were created and maintained in the past (see chapter eight). But let us look again at the idea of social stratification, but this time, through the lens not of social complexity, but as a process through which some people come to hold power over others and the ways that they manage that power. Let's take a quick trip to Hawaii for this discussion, because, well, who wouldn't like to visit Hawaii?

At the time of European contact in the late eighteenth century, Hawaii was home to a complex society of competing, ranked chiefs and their followers. Hawaiians lived in a type of social-political organizations that are called **chiefdoms** by archaeologists, drawing on the works of Marshall Sahlins and Elman Service (1960). In chapter four, we talked about the work of these scholars having an influence on processual archaeologists in chapter four. These anthropologists came up with a model for explaining the evolution of one form of human social-political organization. The simplest and smallest form of human social integration is considered to be a **band**—a small cohabitating group of families who live and work together cooperatively and with no one having structural power over another— this is said to be **egalitarian.** Hunter-gatherer groups living in marginal environments are examples of bands. The groups may gather in larger numbers in times of greater resource abundance (say, for instance, in the rainy season or when a particular clustered resource is available for harvest). Any differences in their rank arises from their particular skills or personality—what is known as **achieved status** in anthropological circles. A chiefdom develops when a number of things happen; first, population increases, and subsistence strategies improve to feed that population and perhaps create a surplus. Certain lineages (family lines) within a group come to control greater resources than others. This is where settling in areas can allow for the control of raw resources, technological innovation, craft specialization and exchange—all the things we've talked about in previous chapters—can all come into play. These actors or groups of actors consolidate power by redistributing those resources strategically (reciprocity) to others. Through time, certain lineages come to have **ascribed status**—status achieved through birthright rather than achievement— and leaders come to be drawn from those families. A group that is primarily organized around kinship groups, has hereditary leaders, craft specialization, exchange, and social inequality consisting of at least two social classes (elite and commoners) is typically called a chiefdom by anthropologists. In **paramount chiefdoms,** there may be a hierarchy of chiefs within the society, with paramount chiefs at the top of the hierarchy. When forms of government become highly centralized, entrenched, and maintained by a bureaucracy with a small number of elites at the top of society, the bureaucrats in the middle, and the masses at the bottom, there is said to be a **state-level society.** Examples of ancient state-level societies include ancient Egypt and the empires of the Romans, Olmec, Aztecs, and Inca to name just a few.

Archaeologist Patrick Kirch (e.g., 1990, 2012) has dedicated his career to understanding the long-term development of the chiefdom-level societies in Polynesia. He has paid particular attention to the Hawaiian Islands where the volcanic environment and natural history of the islands created different sets of challenges for cultivation. The uneven distribution of raw resources (such as stone used for making adzes, pearl shell for fishhooks, and large koa trees to build canoes necessary for movement within and between islands) and farm land across the islands allowed for small groups of people to come to control access to particular resources in the islands. Control of economic resources and goods brings power.

Early settlements in Hawaii demonstrate that people lived in household clusters where architecture did not vary much from cluster to cluster, which suggests less social distinction between households. Household clusters included ritual spaces where offerings were made to the spiritual world. Kirch has noted, however, that from AD 1550 to 1800, clear differences are seen emerging in house clusters. Commoners lived much as they had before, but the elite lived in complex architectural buildings that were accompanied by stone platforms and walled temples. Excavation at some sites revealed that temples began as modest structures and were elaborated through time. Kirch believed that this trend of improvement may represent the rededication of temples by successive chiefs through time as a physical way to demonstrate their greater power over the previous chief.

Perhaps one of the most memorable displays of power used by Hawaiian chiefs is a practice that began in the late prehistoric period but increased after contact with Europeans—the use of human bone to make artifacts such as fishhooks. The source of the bone is believed to be warriors from enemy chiefdoms who were killed in warfare. By using the enemy's body, not only does the victorious side demonstrate their absolute defeat of their opponents, they also take the person's spiritual power (*mana*) as their own. Thus, we see the Hawaiian chiefs using the authority of ascribed status, wealth, spiritual authority, and fear as some of their tools to enforce their power positions in their societies.

Power and Prestige in Mardi Gras: Perspectives from the Beads

The Mardi Gras excavations provide a number of ways to look at how power and prestige is negotiated through Mardi Gras. We will look first at the struggle of the Krewe of Proteus to earn back respect of parade-goers as it goes head to head with the super krewe Orpheus on Lundi Gras. Orpheus has its own internal struggles for prestige, as evidenced by changes in medallions that have created divides within the parading organization and threaten to undermine its communal identity. We will also explore whether or not ball goers have access to greater bead wealth than the people who stand on the street during parades.

Monday Night Fights

We have already been introduced to the krewes of Proteus and Orpheus. What we have not discussed is the two parades' relationships to one another as they struggle to win the hearts of Monday night parade goers. It is only a recent phenomenon that Proteus finds itself sharing Monday night. Since its founding in 1882, the Krewe of Proteus marched on prestigious Lundi Gras, the night before Shrove Tuesday. As other parades shifted from floats built on wagon chasses to larger and larger floats pulled by motorized vehicles, Proteus and Comus maintained their ethereal small floats. Lit by flambeau carriers, the delicate paper flowers, fish, waves, and other real and mythical sea creatures that inhabit the floats have a life to them that isn't possible on the larger sturdier modern floats. Today, in watching Proteus, one gains a sense of the mystical and other worldly atmosphere experienced by parade goers in the time before electric lights.

After the passage of the 1991 city ordinance, Comus never returned to parading; they preferred to protect the ways of its secret society. When Proteus returned in 2000, they were the only major prime-time parade that still built its floats on a wagon base. During the nine-year gap, profound changes had come both to Monday night and to the throwing game. From 1991 to 1994, as discussed before, the average length of a strand of beads thrown in New Orleans was 21.7" long, and because most strands featured beads of graduated sizes with the largest bead measuring about 5 mm, diameter was mainly meaningless. In 2000, the average length was 33.7" long and a diameter of 8.7 mm. This shift in size means that Proteus was returning to a Mardi Gras world that contained much, much, heavier beads. For all of Proteus's beauty, Proteus had a major throw problem. Unlike the double- and triple-deckered floats of the modern era, the wagon chassis of yesteryear was not designed to carry tons of plastic chotchkies. Alas, poor Proteus has preserved the wonder of Mardi Gras like no other krewe, yet it suffers continuously from the reputation of being cheap.

Proteus used to own Monday night alone, and its cheapness while commented on, could not be compared to any other parade. Comus, like Proteus, also was not seen as one of the more generous krewes. The older krewes were more concerned with the prestige earned from age and membership exclusivity. Membership of old-line krewes like Comus, Momus, Proteus, and Rex is drawn from generations of legacies, and an invitation to join is a sign of being someone important in New Orleans society.

When Proteus stopped parading, Lundi Gras was too important a night to leave open. The last weekend leading up to Shrove Tuesday is the peak of tourism to the area. Parades fill Saturday and Sunday; super krewes Endymion marches on Saturday and Bacchus on Sunday. To leave Monday empty would risk the loss of tourists to the city. Parades are the family oriented part of Mardi Gras, the element of Carnival celebrations that are most participated in by the local population. There has long been a tension between residents who believe the city sells out tradition by developing the tourism profile of the city, and, as we have seen, they are often vocal in protesting lascivious behavior they believe to have been introduced to the celebrations by the influx of tourists.

Harry Connick Jr. is known to those outside New Orleans as a crooner and sometimes actor; but, to New Orleanians, he is also the son of a popular former DA, Harry Connick Sr. Connick organized a new super krewe to fill in the Monday gap. This new krewe, to be called Orpheus and celebrate the musical heritage of New Orleans, would not only be racially integrated but would be the first large krewe to have mixed sex membership. The parade marched for the first time in 1993 and quickly established itself as a spectacle.

Ultra long floats, like the Smokey Mary train and the sea monster Leviathan, as well as the towering Trojan horse float, quickly became icons. Orpheus not only took over Proteus's parade night and route; it also took over its krewe colors and threw lyre-shaped medallions evoking the Trojan horse in transparent red plastic (Figure 10.1).

Proteus stayed away from Carnival from 1993 to 1999, but returned in 2000 with a small number of Jewish and African American members and a reported $50,000 worth of beads. To put this into perspective, this would purchase about 950 gross of average beads for the entire parade. Orpheus in 2000 suggested that riders each purchase 10 gross per person. Proteus in 2012 had 260 riders on 20 floats; Orpheus had 1,200 riders on a similar number of floats. Even if the little wagons of Proteus overflowed with trinkets, they could not compete with the Leviathan of a parade that followed them. Orpheus's floats are built on 18-wheeler truck beds, and many feature three levels of maskers. Orpheus has space to accommodate a lot of throws on its floats, and the burden of appearing generous is spread among more participating maskers.

So there was Proteus in 2000, one of the most exclusive and ancient of Mardi Gras organizations. They returned to a Lundi Gras they had to share and were given the position of parading before Orpheus. What was once a proud old-line krewe had been delegated to a warm up act. The humiliation was completed when, after the parade, crowds declared Proteus to be cheap. A comparison of assemblages caught from each parade illustrates the depths of Proteus's bead problem. First, let's compare generosity, measured in New Orleans as who throws the most beads and the best beads. In terms of raw numbers,

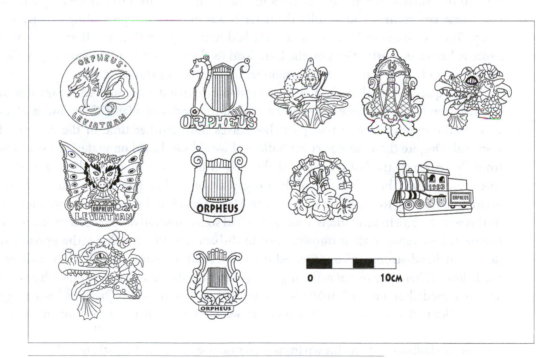

Figure 10.1. Orpheus medallions. Illustrations by Alexandra Wilkie Farnsworth.

Table 10.1. Abundance of Bead Wealth Caught at Proteus Versus Orpheus through Time.

YEAR	PROTEUS: TOTAL BEADS	PROTEUS: BEADS CAUGHT PER PERSON	ORPHEUS: TOTAL BEADS	ORPHEUS: BEADS CAUGHT PER PERSON
1999	n/a	n/a	92	46
2000	9	4.5	107	53.5
2001	20	10	35[*]	17.5
2002	71	23.7	162	54
2004	61	20.3	123	41
2006	70	23.3	117	39
2007	29	9.7	69	23
2009	68	22.6	116	38.7

* heavy rains

you can see that one regularly receives twice as many beads from Orpheus as from Proteus (Table 10.1).

So what about the quality of those beads (Table 10.2)? Once again, Orpheus clearly outranks Proteus by throwing on average, beads that are 8 to 12 inches longer than those thrown by Proteus. This trend continues in bead diameter, with Proteus keeping a fairly consistent commitment to smaller diameter beads and 2009 representing a fairly big jump. The measures of bead value are stacked against poor Proteus. Remember that Proteus has severe restrictions on the bead load its floats can carry. By throwing smaller shorter strands, they can increase the number of strands they throw.

So the question we should ask is, does Proteus care that it is considered cheap? It is an organization that offers one of the most beautiful parades of Mardi Gras, and it gives viewers the opportunity to transport themselves into another time in the history of Carnival. Despite these unique contributions, I would say, based on materials excavated from Proteus over the last decade, that the answer is a resounding yes, they care. They care a great deal. The public face of their organization is their parade. Proteus is clearly aware that the way to consolidate prestige in Mardi Gras is to improve its image through its throws. Despite its limitations, Proteus has had some innovative strategies to maximize the perceived value of their throws. Prior to disbanding, Proteus threw the previously described, hand-strung, 17″, opaque, red strands of beads featuring a small white seahorse medallion. When they began marching again, they introduced a new version with a silver seahorse medallion on a 33″, MOS metallic red strand (Figure 10.2). Orpheus has a range of medallions it throws. There is a basic krewe medallion that can be thrown by any member who purchases it, which features the krewe's name and a lyre. There are also float specific medallions that are thrown from premium floats like the Leviathan or the Smokey Mary. These are thrown only from those particular floats (Figure 10.1). As discussed,

Table 10.2. Quality of Bead Wealth Caught at Proteus Versus Orpheus through Time.

AVERAGE BEAD LENGTH (in)

YEAR	PROTEUS	ORPHEUS
1999	n/a	42.4
2000	33.5	47.7
2001	37.1*	38.4
2002	32.4	40.2
2004	30.5	43.6
2006	30.6	44
2007	33	43.6
2009	36	48.2

*One 100″ strand recovered had significant impact on average length.

AVERAGE BEAD DIAMETER (mm)

YEAR	PROTEUS	ORPHEUS
1999	n/a	8.6
2000	8.4	9.6
2001	7.85	8.46
2002	7.75	8.8
2004	8.02	9.3
2006	8.2	11.27
2007	8	10.04
2009	8.8	10.76

earlier, Proteus throws a higher percentage of the medallion beads than Orpheus throws, even when converted to number of beads per person (Table 10.3). Proteus's medallions, however, are significantly smaller and simpler. In 2008, Proteus did introduce a high-end fancy medallion featuring blinking lights. This, however, was a rare throw. The choice to throw medallion beads has weight implications as well.

Let us compare the weight differences between different medallions, as shown in Figures 10.1 and 10.2. You can see that the decision to throw medallions adds significant weight loads when you start to multiply the weight of a single strand by the many 1,000s of beads thrown from each float. Let's just quickly calculate out the weight implications for Proteus versus Orpheus if you have 10 riders on a float each throwing 10 gross of basic medallion beads from each respective organization. You can see that the weight differences, even in the same relative category of bead, are quite striking (Table 10.4).

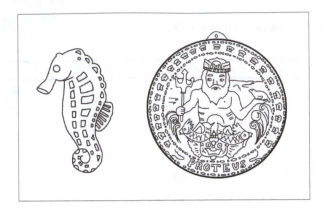

Figure 10.2. Proteus medallions: On left, typical seahorse medallion used on hand-strung and metallic plastic beads; on right, plastic blinkie medallion. Illustrations by Alexandra Wilkie Farnsworth.

Proteus has introduced other kinds of krewe emblem wares to throw from it floats that attempt to deal with the weight issue. One year, the krewe introduced a "water bottle," which weighed 11 grams. While half the weight of the medallion bead, the throw had the disadvantage of looking like empty trash, and never really (excuse the Mardi Gras pun) caught on. More popular are the Proteus "cozies," or can holders. These objects are foam covers to put your beer or soda can in. In the hot temperatures of the deep South, cold drinks sweat (or glow, if they are a lady's beverage) and the cozie keeps one's hands dry while holding the can. The cozie weighs just under 12 grams (Figure 10.3).

In 2009, however, Proteus introduced an innovation that represented a variation on the bead theme: a gel seahorse containing a three-colored blinking light suspended on a red string (Figure 10.3). Despite the three watch-type batteries contained in the seahorse, this object only weighs 18 grams, slightly less than the traditional medallion bead. In 2009,

Table 10.3. Abundance of Medallions for Proteus Versus Orpheus.

YEAR	PROTEUS: NUMBER	ORPHEUS: NUMBER	PROTEUS: NUMBER OF MEDALLIONS PER PERSON	ORPHEUS: NUMBER OF MEDALLIONS PER PERSON	PROTEUS: % OF OVERALL BEADS	ORPHEUS: % OF OVERALL BEADS
1999	n/a	9		4.5		8
2000		18		9		16.8
2001		3		1.5		8.5
2002	2	21	.7	7	3.2	12.9
2004		2		.6		1.6
2006	54	1	18	.3	77.2	.7
2007	29	1	9.6	.3	100	.8
2009	34	1	11.3	.3	58.6	.9

Table 10.4. Weight Differentials between Medallion Beads Thrown by Proteus and Orpheus.

PROTEUS		ORPHEUS	
MEDALLION BEAD TYPE	WEIGHT IN GRAMS	MEDALLION BEAD TYPE	WEIGHT IN GRAMS
Hand-strung medallion (2000–2004)	19.85	Trojan horse (1993–1998)	27.88
Silver seahorse on 33" beads (2004 to present)	22.31	Lyre medallion (1998–1999)	29.77
Battery-operated blinkie medallion (2007 to present)	110.18	Metallic lyre (2000+)	52.27
Jelly blinky seahorse (2009 to present)	18	2000 Plastic leviathan	83.92
		2003 Resin leviathan	116.62

three of the medallions caught were these seahorses. One was the fancy Proteus blinking light, and the remaining 33 were the traditional medallion beads. As I'll discuss further in chapter 13, our 2013 Mardi Gras trip revealed a new innovation in beads among those krewes that see themselves as old-line or traditional Mardi Gras krewes. With Proteus participating, there was the reintroduction of hand-strung plastic bead medallions. Instead of the shorter hand-strung medallions of yesteryear, the new Proteus medallion beads are 38" long and feature red and pearl beads with silver seahorse medallions (Figure 10.4). These fancy medallions are of a much higher quality than comparable MOS medallion beads, weigh less than many of the high-end krewe beads—coming in at 72.5 grams—and crowds seem satisfied, for now, to catch smaller numbers of excellent beads.

So despite limitations of weight on the kinds and volumes of throws Proteus can distribute, the organization has made a seemingly conscious effort since 2006 to position itself as a more generous krewe. In terms of head-to-head comparison with Orpheus, Proteus has also more effectively branded itself. If we look at the color distribution of beads recovered from each parade, we see some interesting trends (Table 10.5).

When Proteus first began marching again, red and white were the most common colors thrown.

Figure 10.3. Experimentation with lighter throws by Proteus: cozies, jelly seahorse, and water bottle. Photograph by Alexandra Wilkie Farnsworth.

The following year, 2001, white, or in this case, faux pearl beads, were the most common bead thrown. When Proteus exited Mardi Gras, pearls were highly coveted throw beads. While not throwing in abundance, the krewe did attempt to throw quality beads. In the years that followed, however, metallic beads became more popular, and pearls have steadily decreased in popularity. Keeping to the krewe's theme colors, red was always the other dominant color thrown by the krewe, eventually coming to dominate. In 2009, silver replaced pearl as the other important color, which caused the bead assemblage to match the colors contained on the krewe's medallion beads. Now, remember, each member of the krewe purchases their own beads. They have made selections that demonstrate a decision to express participation in a corporate identity through their throws. A bag of beads from Proteus is easily identified as such, not only from the number of medallions included, but the color scheme of the remaining beads.

Orpheus, in contrast, does not have assemblages marked by the same kind of consistency. Prior to 2006, the most commonly represented color was gold, but not by any great margin. In fact, purple and green, the "official" Mardi Gras colors, are more often than not, the other most represented colors. Many cases of beads are sold in what are called PGG (purple-green-gold) mixes. In 2006 and beyond, there is no pattern to the color distribution. There appears to be no official krewe color theme for Orpheus. When the parade first started, their earliest medallions were black and red. I did wonder whether this was intentionally a play on Proteus and the race politics that reshaped parading on Monday night. It seems to be a kind of playful commentary that Proteus, with their red and white theme color and white membership, was replaced by the multi-racial krewe of Orpheus, with red and black beads. Again, we see visual punning potentially at play in the throwing game. Whatever commentary may have initially shaped Orpheus, however, was not enduring. The krewe has not established a corporate identity through their throws

Figure 10.4: Hand-strung Proteus medallion caught in 2013.

Table 10.5. Color Distribution in Proteus Versus Orpheus Throws.*

KREWE	1999	2000	2001	2002	2004	2006	2007	2009
PROTEUS	n/a	Red (37.5)	Red (55)	White (40.8)	White (50.9)	Red (95.7)	Red (100)	Red (72)
		White (25)	White (35)	Red (21.5)	Red (32.7)	Blue (2.5)		Silver (18)
		Gold (12.5)						
ORPHEUS	Gold (23.9)	Gold (23.3)	Gold (31.0)	Gold (41.2)	Gold (35.4)	Green (20.2)	Green (22.5)	Gold (22.5)
	Purple (14.6)	Green (16.6)	Purple (17.2)	White (24.6)	Purple (20.5)	Purple (17.7)	Purple (18.3)	Green (20.2)
	Green (10.4)	Purple (13.3)	Green (10.3)	Purple (8.8)	Silver (14.2)	White (17.7)	Gold (15.5)	Purple (14.9)
	Red (6.3)	White (13.3)	Red (10.3)	Green (8.8)	White (14.2)	Gold 15.3)	Pink (15.5)	Pink (11.4)
	Black (6.3)		White (10.3)					

* Colors are listed from most to least abundant. Numbers in parentheses represent percentages.

the way Proteus has, and it has invested less and less in beads that are labeled with their organization name.

A final thought on these comparisons. We need to also contextualize these assemblages relative to what happened in August of 2005—Hurricane Katrina. You'll note changes in the patterning of both assemblages beginning in 2006—the first Carnival after Katrina. The timing of the hurricane left many wondering whether Mardi Gras could or even should be held in 2006. Beads are ordered by krewes in the fall, and many did not order the amounts they would have ordinarily or were unable to order special throws. More importantly, however, the post-Katrina assemblages hint at the economic differences between the members of Proteus and Orpheus. While Proteus seems to have made a conscious effort to reposition itself as a generous krewe post-Katrina, Orpheus shows signs of disunity, with fewer medallions being thrown and little evidence of a community identity expressed through throws. Orpheus's membership is not exclusively drawn from the elite of New Orleans and includes a number of working class people. Orpheus is a super krewe, and membership is as much a matter of ability to pay as through any kind of social connection. It may be that the krewe membership of Orpheus was more disrupted by Katrina than that of Proteus and what we are seeing is the effects of the hurricane on the organization's community, with the loss of original founding members. In 2013, Orpheus's members adopted new MOS medallion beads, which makes the krewes branding more clear, and perhaps suggests a revitalization in the krewe's membership.

Proteus's attention to its throws seems to be paying off for them in the world of public opinion. The following quote is from a blog article about Muse's unique throws. Proteus is specifically mentioned by Muses creative director, Virginia Saussy.

> The generosity of super krewes has raised expectations for how much should come off a float, and if the skies aren't darkened with beads and cups, some find a parade wanting. Saussy, who watches parades when she's not riding, says appearances are deceiving. 'Proteus is as generous as Bacchus,' she says, 'but 10 riders to a side create a very different impression from 30 to 40 on two tiers.' Decisions regarding what to throw are likely simpler for Proteus. The old line parade seems to throw more and longer beads than it once did, but most feature its iconic image, a seahorse. (Rawls 2012)

A travel site promoting 2013's Mardi Gras is more blunt, "Proteus was once known as the most miserly in the area of throws. However, the trinkets now include 60" red and white pearl necklaces, plastic tridents, and polystone medallions" (http//www.mardigras neworleans.com/schedule/parade-info/parades-proteus.html).

Proteus's experiments with throws since rejoining Mardi Gras in 2000 have paid off; the krewe is gaining the favor of the Mardi Gras crowds. What is not clear is why the krewe cares. Is it attempting to rebuild damage done to its reputation by being seen as anachronistic and racist when it pulled out of parading in 1992, or does it have some other agenda? The only insight we have is a statement from Proteus's official, Gary Webster, in 2000 when the krewe returned to parading. "The world's changing, and we're changing with the world. It's an evolution. What I'm trying to stress here is that it is going to happen" (Nolan 2012).

Webster's choice of the word evolution is ironic given its context in the history of Mardi Gras, but, perhaps the old-line krewes have evolved since Comus featured *The Origin of Species* to protest the Africanization of Louisiana. In 2008, Rex introduced African American debutantes at his ball for the first time, something that would have been nearly impossible to imagine in 1993. The comparison of materials from Proteus versus Orpheus provides a unique archaeological opportunity to see how two sets of elites compete to create memorable feasts in an attempt to jockey for the most prestige. In the case of Proteus, we can see the material strategies they employed to impress their audiences and rehabilitate their former image as miserly and cheap. Proteus's elaboration of their material culture to achieve more prestige among parade goers and secure their power base is not unlike the chiefs of Hawaii who created more elaborate temples to state their supremacy.

What are other ways that krewes attempt to woo their audiences? Do they treat some audiences differently than others? We have the opportunity to address these questions by comparing assemblages caught at Mardi Gras parades versus balls.

Street People and Ball Guests

Float captains in Orpheus explained to riders that it was important to put aside "good beads" to throw to the ball guests once we rode into the convention center. While others crowded along the streets, braving rain in 2002, guests who had purchased tickets for Orpheuscapade, the krewe ball, awaited the arrival of the parade indoors, enjoying music, dancing, and drinks. The first time I experienced this, I was flabbergasted as the entire parade drove into the cavernous convention center. The roar of another crowd greeted us; this crowd, however, wore tuxedos and gowns.

"Remember, throw heavy!" We were reminded, "these are our guests!"

Some of the guests were friends and family of the krewe members, but others were guests who had paid hundreds of dollars for the privilege of our hospitality. In a day of strange experiences and sensory overload, I think perhaps nothing of my Mardi Gras experience struck me as more odd than people in evening wear begging for beads. Finally, I was experiencing the inversion of societal norms that Mardi Gras was so famous for! I found myself wondering, as I watched our guests drape strands of beads around their necks, whether my fellow riders had indeed thrown heavy. I had dutifully put aside some beads, and threw all that I had left. I was returning to California and had no desire to cart more beads than necessary back with me. Others I rode with were involved in other parades or planned on participating in Orpheus the following year. By the end of the ride, I had also noted other riders, who had "thrown out" their entire stash before the end of Canal street, were frantically asking fellow riders for beads or scraping their hands on the floor of the float, searching through the debris of plastic bags, wrappers, and cardboard boxes for strands of beads that had dropped during our throwing frenzy.

So do ball guests get better beads? I had the opportunity to compare one ball assemblage from 2000 and two from 2001 with the assemblages excavated from the Orpheus parade (Table 10.6). While the results are mixed, overall, the assemblages caught by the ball goers were of a higher quality in that they were consistently larger and longer than the beads caught at the parade—but not necessarily by a large margin. The 2000 parade's average length was 42.7″ versus an impressive average of 52.8″ caught at the ball. In 2001, the parade's average length was 38.4″ with one ball average being 42.8″ and the other 47.0″—less than the quality of the beads caught in 2000. The average diameter of beads from the 2000 parade was 9.6 mm versus 10.9 mm caught at the ball. The following year, the parade average was 8.46 mm, whereas the ball-caught beads averaged 9.8 mm for one ball attendee and 10.0 mm for another.

In both years, more medallions were caught when attending the parade than the ball. It is interesting to ponder whether this was part of a conscious choice by maskers to throw more krewe-branded items to people on the street rather than save them for ball guests. One of the 2001 ball assemblages included a significant number of short transparent beads (20.7% of the beads caught). These "cheaper" beads are often thrown either to children or when a masker is trying to extend the life of his/her better throws. Tossing them at the

Table 10.6. Beads Caught at Parades Versus Balls: An Example from Orpheus.

	2000		2001		
	PARADE	BALL	PARADE	BALL	BALL
AVERAGE STRAND LENGTH (in)	47.7	52.8	38.4	42.8	47
AVERAGE BEAD DIAMETER (mm)	9.6	10.9	8.46	9.8	10
% MEDALLIONS	9.5	4.4	7.8	3.5	7
% OF ASSEMBLAGE WITH TRANSPARENT FINISH	2.6			20.7	
% OF ASSEMBLAGE WITH METALLIC FINISH	63.6	77.7	91.4	58.6	95.3
% OF ASSEMBLAGE WITH PEARL FINISH	28.9	17.8	2.9	12.1	4.7
% OF ASSEMBLAGE WITH OPALESCENT FINISH		4.4	2.9	6.9	
% OF ASSEMBLAGE WITH OPAQUE FINISH			2.9	1.7	

ball suggests to me that a rider was nearly thrown out and tossing the last of their backup beads to ball guests.

There was a greater proportion of quality beads thrown at the 2001 ball than at the parade, which was a change from 2000, where many more pearls were caught on the street. I might cynically suggest that given the 2001 police crackdown on nudity, Orpheus's male riders may have been left with more pearls at the end of their ride than they had hoped. Overall, it would appear that attending a ball where beads are thrown does provide one with a better sample of beads than standing on the street. Whether the difference is enough to justify spending several hundred dollars to attend a ball is open for discussion. From the perspective of those who do the bookkeeping for a krewe, there should be great motivation for guests to feel they were treated generously; the ball tickets, along with krewe member dues are the major income generators for the krewe. Happy guests are more likely to return the following year. That happiness is in part dependent upon the maskers, who have all paid for their own throws, to cooperate and save good beads for the ball guests. The analysis of materials here suggests that overall, krewe members attempt to comply.

Social Status within the Krewes

Within krewes there are differing levels of status—at the high end, there are the krewe presidents, and of course, the royal courts. Each float also has one or two captains. The float captains are the den mothers of the float; they ensure maskers comply with ordinances requiring harnesses and masks, and they prevent the throwing of boxes off the float. They also serve as the point person if something goes wrong on the float.

Many parades feature maskers on horseback. As these men ride in full costume with hoods rather than the masks that typically cover float rider's faces, I always find myself transported back to the period of Reconstruction, wondering if this is what it looked like when the Knights of the White Camellia (Louisiana's nineteenth-century version of the Klan) rode through plantation quarters. I find these men terribly ominous and frightening looking—their features are not discernible; they are inscrutable. While float maskers give the appearance of enjoying what they do, this is hard to tell about the horseback riders. Horses have little room for throws, so the riding lieutenants, as they are often called, have their own special doubloon that they toss along the parade route. In some parades, these doubloons are slightly thicker and have a following of collectors.

In addition to these roles, there are also divisions that arise within the parade. For the super krewes, particular floats become iconic of the large parades. At least in Orpheus, this has manifested in the creation of a hierarchy of floats. For Orpheus, the Smokey Mary and the Leviathan became what the krewe calls premier floats. They have float-specific beads and throws that the riders can purchase to throw. Riders also pay an extra fee to ride on a premier float and have the right to purchase the float-specific beads for the Leviathan or Smokey Mary. In 2002 and 2003 (I have no evidence that this practice extended beyond 2003), Orpheus had individual resin medallions for each of the parade floats made. They sold them at an additional premium; the idea was that parade goers could attempt to get a float-specific medallion from each float. It was not clear to me, as an attendee in 2002 and 2003, if someone from every float had bothered to purchase the float-specific beads. What we see through time from Orpheus is after 2002, there is a complete decline in the number of medallions thrown, (Table 10.7) and less of a shared krewe identity is visible in the

Table 10.7. Orpheus Krewe-specific Beads through Time by Type.

YEAR	NUMBER OF GENERIC KREWE MEDALLIONS RECOVERED	NUMBER OF FLOAT SPECIFIC MEDALLIONS RECOVERED
1999	8 generic	1 Leviathan
2000	12 generic	6 Leviathan
2001	3 generic	
2002	13 generic	7 Leviathan, 1 Smokey Mary
2003		
2004	1 generic	1 Leviathan
2005		
2006	1 generic	
2007		
2008		
2009		1 Smokey Mary

throws. In 2009, the only Orpheus medallion caught was a resin Smokey Mary. As I reported above, however, this downward slide seems to have been corrected sometime between the end of my excavations in 2009 and 2013 when I popped back for a quick Mardi Gras visit to find Orpheus throwing many MOS krewe beads; although the 2013 assemblage contained float-specific, blinky jelly medallions for the Trojan horse and Smokey Mary.

In Zulu, there seems to be some differentiation of throw medallion based on status. There are the previously discussed resin medallions thrown by the royal court, but I have also seen on the secondary market "Zulu warrior" medallions that do not seem to be specific to a parade year. While there are different quality levels of krewe beads, Bacchus's different medallions do not appear to be float specific. Based on trends visible in Orpheus during their experimentations with float-specific medallions, creating visible social stratification in the material culture of the parades seems to hinder the overall sense of corporate identity within the krewe.

Parade of the People: The Elks Truck Parade

One last group needs to be discussed here, the Elks Orleans Truck parade that passes along Rex's route following his last float on Mardi Gras. The truck parade began in 1935. The truck parade was born out of one motivation—why should the rich boys have all the fun? The parade is not a krewe, it is a starting point and a route. The parade is coordinated and judged by the Elks, but it appears that the main criterion for membership is a truck and a whole lot of Mardi Gras spirit.

The term vulgarization is another word used in Marxist circles to describe the ways that the practices or materiality of the upper classes become copied in the lower classes. Vulgarization is when something that was high brow is made low brow to appeal to the masses. For instance, one could certainly consider the Bugs Bunny cartoon short where Bugs and Elmer Fudd do their own retelling of a Wagner opera ("Kill da Wabbit, Kill da Wabbit . . .") as an excellent example of vulgarization. Using trucks for floats instead of the beautiful highly designed floats found in the Krewe's parades would also be a form of vulgarization—it allows the lower classes to participate in an activity that had been restricted to the upper classes.

An archaeological example of vulgarization would be the popularity of bric-a-brac in Victorian parlors in the nineteenth century (Mullins 2001). Bric-a-brac was a range of decorative items that included things like vases, figurines, statuary, and cheap prints that were popular and are found in every nineteenth-century household site excavated in the US. Many of these items were copies of classical scenes, figures, or fine art objects that were made in cheap, readily available commodity form. Want to demonstrate that your taste isn't just in your mouth? Buy yourself a classical-theme-inspired porcelain figurine for your hallway. There is question about whether this process involves emulation or irony—are the lower classes sincerely imitating the upper class as part of buying into ideologies of equality, or is the use of these objects an appropriation that is charged with conscious intentionality to assert equality with the upper classes. See the important difference? Are the people dupes or usurpers?

The material culture of the truck parades raise the issue of vulgarization in a Carnival setting. The truck parades are no Rex. The trucks aren't typically much to look at, but some people do decorate their trucks and compete for prizes for best decorated. Krewe of Elks, Orleans, is described on Mardi Gras websites as having been founded in 1935 and as "a group of over 50 individually designed truck floats that parade following Rex down St. Charles Ave. The organization is formed by 4,600 male and female riders." (www.mardir-grasneworleans.com/schedule/parade-ifno/parades-elk-orleans.html). This description presents a much more coherent vision of what really happens when the 80 or so trucks drive by. Writing in 1947, journalist Robert Tallant described the trucks as follows.

> It was the Elks who organized the Krewe of Orleanians in 1935, one of two loosely knitted groups of maskers who follow Rex on Mardi Gras aboard the decorated trucks. Until then truck rides had been popular for years, but they had been unconnected and individual affairs that rolled haphazardly through the streets, appearing along the parade routes at unpredictable hours or confining their activities to outlying sections of the city. Now they are an integrated part of Mardi Gras, contributed much beauty and humor and merriment to the day, and, in a way, replaced the custom of decades before when most of the city's maskers had followed Rex during his procession through the city. (1994:166)

What you experience at the truck parade is a lot of really happy, screaming, waving, and drinking people, who aren't ready for Mardi Gras to end, throwing you every leftover bead they're done with. The procession has no shared or corporate identity; there is nothing to thematically unite the massive array of trucks. Some are ornately decorated with satirical themes and crepe paper; others are basically trucks with beads in them. The Elks offers prizes for the best floats, but apparently that's not enough of an enticement for everyone to participate in decorating. Their good spirits are infectious, and it is one of the few parading experiences in New Orleans where one feels they stand on equal footing with those in the parades—who generally wear no masks.

The trucks move fast and throw heavy. The assemblage for 2000 (Table 10.8) had an average strand length of 36.9". Only five of the 166 strands caught measured over 48" in length. The average bead diameter was 8.05 mm, with 88.3% of the assemblage measuring between 7.0 to 8.5 mm in diameter. In other words, this was an assemblage comprised mainly of cheap throw beads—but a lot of them. Metallic finishes accounted for the majority of the assemblage, followed by opalescent beads, then pearls and transparent beads.

The high incidence of opalescent finished beads is interesting in terms of the idea of vulgarization. Opalescent beads look a great deal like the higher-priced pearl beads from a distance. Once they are in your hands, however, it is clear they are not the same

Table 10.8. Beads from the New Orleans Elks' Truck Parade.

Number of beads caught per person	88
Average length of strand	36.9"
Average bead diameter	8.1 mm
Beads by finish (%)	
Transparent	1.8
Metallic	77.5
Opaque	.6
Opalescent	11.3
Pearl	8.8
% Strands that showed repair or heavy reuse	31.9
Number of different beads shapes represented	14
Number of throws identifying the parade	
Medallions of other organizations represented	Tucks, Zulu, Bards of Bohemia

thing. My friends and I used to joke that the opalescent beads were poor people's fake, fake pearls; whereas the richer folks bought the better quality fake, fake pearls (and yes, as parade goers, we did regularly rate throw quality). The analysis of the beads from the truck parades suggests just that—that the truck riders want to throw the best beads they can without spending too much. Therefore, the opalescent are attractive. Further, given the high degree of rethrowing of beads happening at the parade, we could also interpret the higher incidence of opalescent at the parade another way; the people riding the trucks have selected the higher quality pearl beads to keep for themselves and are throwing away the less prestigious ones. An analysis of color distribution of the beads thrown by the Elks demonstrates that most of the beads thrown are purple (18.1%), green (19.8%), gold (15.6%), and white (10.6%). The purple, green, and gold colors of Mardi Gras are almost equally represented, as they are in the mixed packs of one dozen beads sold in PGG packs. The slight underrepresentation of gold may represent that this color was withheld from rethrowing at a slightly greater rate than the other two colors.

So are the Elks ideological dupes or social critics? To answer this question, I believe, requires understanding the historical context in which the formalized truck krewe developed.

Louisiana has a strong populist political history, which never flourished more than it did under the governorship and senator-ship of Huey Long in the late 1920s and first half of the 1930s. As a US senator for Louisiana in 1934, Long created the "share our wealth" program with the motto "Every Man a King." The slogan became a motto for Mardi Gras as well, where for a day, even the poorest man could imagine himself royalty.

Perhaps it is not accidental that the Elks decided to organize the trucks into a more organized presence in 1935. In January of that year, a paramilitary group called the Square Dealers, with reputed ties to New Orleans' old-line krewes (Gill 1997), engaged in armed skirmishes with Louisiana's National Guard in Baton Rouge in an attempt to take over the state government. The uprising failed, but Long was assassinated in the Louisiana State Capital building September 8, 1935. The man who killed Long, Dr. Carl Weiss, was the son-in-law of a judge and long-time opponent of Long, Benjamin Henry Pavy. Long's bodyguards shot Weiss dead—63 times. Long later died in surgery from a gunshot wound to the abdomen. Long hated the elitism of Mardi Gras, and to disparage his memory, it is popular in Mardi Gras histories to report that he intended to abolish Mardi Gras. Long's attitude, that Mardi Gras, like wealth, should be shared by all, lives on today in the Elks parade. In bringing populist tradition into Mardi Gras, the Elks and other truck organizations took on the Carnival traditions of the elite in their own festive way, claiming Carnival for the people. The Elks may throw fewer faux beads, but apparently they were not dupes to the attempts of the old-line krewes to naturalize their power.

I mentioned before that we see English ceramic manufacturers used to make wares that imitated the look of Chinese porcelains but were cheaper, which allowed the growing number of middle-class consumers created by the industrial revolution to have things that looked like the things owned by the noble classes. More recently, in the late nineteenth century, we see pressed glassware in archaeological sites doing the same kind of work. Victorian and Edwardian table etiquette was complicated by arcane sets of practices that dictated that specialized cutlery and service vessels be used for every imaginable thing that may be consumed at a table. To have these objects in ceramic would have been very expensive indeed, and it was out of the reach of those with upwardly class ambitions. However, the US glass industry stepped in to fill the gap with vessels that were made out of inexpensive glass (not crystals). These vessels were blown in molds that made objects appear to be hand-cut crystal in every shape you could desire. This is another classical example of the process of vulgarization.

I worked on a site in Alabama (Wilkie and Shorter 2001) that was home to an African American family during the 1870s and 1880s. This family, the Perrymans, was pragmatic and invested their limited income primarily in the purchases of land. This did not preclude them, however, from wanting to have material items in their household that marked them as part of the emergent black middle class. At the site containing the Perryman family's cast-offs, we found pressed glass celery vases (you know you need a special vase to serve your celery in, right?), spooners (for rinsing your spoon after stirring your ice tea), covered butter dishes, candy dishes, and an assortment of other pressed glass artifacts that would have been substitutes on the Perryman table for crystal or porcelain vessels of the same shape.

Does this mean that the Perrymans were emulating the upper classes (who almost exclusively were white)? Or were they involved in creating the materiality of a new black middle class? The glass objects don't give us an answer one way or the other, but ultimately, when I considered all the materials from the site along with other decisions made by the household, I decided the evidence supported the latter interpretation. The Perrymans were involved, as the first generation of freed slaves raising families and buying homes, in creating something new with materials that would have strongly communicated to white families that they were all symbolically sitting at the same table. I've included this example because there are often times in archaeology where more than one interpretation is possible. Sometimes, it is possible to find a different line of evidence to use to try to choose between interpretations—and sometimes it's not.

We see that Marxist approaches to archaeology allow us to consider the symbolic and ideological dimensions of power struggles in ways different than the economic models of status that we discussed as part of HBE. Is one approach more valuable than another? Hopefully, by now you know that the answer depends upon your research questions.

CHAPTER 11
REBUILDING, REINVENTING, REVITALIZATION, AND BEAD BLEED

We stood on the neutral ground. I don't think it was raining, but in my memory there is a soft drizzle falling on all those gathered. We had all come for one reason, not because we felt like celebrating, but because we were there to show solidarity and love for an ailing loved one. If the patient was to make a recovery, we wanted to be there to provide comfort and encouragement; if it was instead a deathbed we were attending, we wanted to there as well. It was February 27, 2006; the first Mardi Gras after Hurricane Katrina, and incompetent levy-building by the federal government had ravaged the city of New Orleans. We awaited the arrivals of Proteus and Orpheus. The pre-parade festivities were muted; we huddled around and talked in quiet groups. The pre-parade drive through the city had been sobering. It wasn't my first time in the city since the hurricane, but the changes in the city were still shocking, and the slowness of the rebuilding made the city seem abandoned.

As a result of Katrina, the permanent population of the city of New Orleans was reduced overnight from 500,000 to 150,000 people. The scale of the devastation is difficult to explain. I drove through the city in October of 2005 as part of an LSU group. The only people we saw outside of the French Quarter were armed military personnel in tanks and jeeps. We drove through sections of the city where you could find no occupied houses, no open businesses. Grass was growing up in cracks on the highway on ramps and exits. In the ninth ward, there were houses that had boats on their roofs . . . desperate families had climbed out of holes punched through their roofs into waiting boats. When rescue units in helicopters and larger boats arrived, family boats were left tied to chimneys. As the water receded, the boats were left stranded on roofs.

Four months later, during Carnival, there was little noticeable change. The boats were still on roofs, the streets still filled with weeds. Occupied houses could be identified by the blue tarps that covered roofs. Most of the houses had spray-painted symbols by their front door—not graffiti, but a marking system used by rescuers to identify how many living and how many dead had been recovered from the structure. So many houses had broken windows and holes punched in their roofs, and few had blue tarps. In some neighborhoods, the only sound was the hum of generators that kept FEMA trailers powered.

There had, understandably, been intense discussions about whether or not Mardi Gras should be observed in 2006. There were logistical issues—areas storing floats had been impacted by the hurricane. Beads and other supplies were typically ordered and readied by October. More importantly, there were emotional issues. Over 1,200 people lost their lives in New Orleans in the aftermath of the hurricane. How could anyone celebrate? What was there to celebrate?

Media coverage of the hurricane and its aftermath rendered visible deeply entrenched racial biases that shaped relief efforts at the state and national levels. Louisiana Governor Kathleen Blanco pushed for National Guard troops to treat New Orleans as hostile territory, authorizing guardsmen to draw weapons on desperately terrified citizens who had been trapped without food or water for days. Survivor Cynthia Delores Banks, in a 2006 interview, summed it up as follows.

> There has been a great awakening for those who didn't know that these kind of inhumane mindsets exist. The way people were hovered over with guns like they were criminals, rather than victims. Something good has got to come out of this because it has been exposed to the nation. So they're poor. They don't need to be treated with dignity? I could not be rich if it were not for the poor. I had the opportunity to watch people hide food in America: during the storm, after the storm, right now. They don't know if they're going to have it tomorrow. (quoted in Penner and Ferdinand 2009: 69)

At the federal level, relief efforts were no better organized, and the nation was appalled as New Orleans men, women, and children huddled on roofs. Citizen-organized efforts to take boats into the city to assist rescues were prohibited by state- and federal-sponsored agencies, even as people were dying. There were many reasons to not have Mardi Gras that year. When the city of New Orleans announced it would host 2006 Mardi Gras celebrations, reactions were mixed. Walter Frances, a 57-year-old New Orleans man who lost family and property, expressed a common opinion to CNN at the time of celebrations; "I really don't think the city is prepared. There's so much that still needs to be done. There's so many homes that are still vacant, there's so many people that have not had the opportunity to come back because they have no place to live" (quoted in Patterson 2006). Arthur Hardy, the recognized leading historian of Mardi Gras, expressed most succinctly the opinion of the other side of the debate, which was "to not have Mardi Gras would be like skipping Christmas" (quoted in Patterson 2006). It wasn't that those in support of having Mardi Gras were callous; the heart of their argument was that if the city lost something so central to its self-identity as Mardi Gras, then there was little hope of successful rebuilding.

One survivor posting on the NOLA blog (NOLA is an affectionate abbreviation for New Orleans, LA) blog wrote,

> Ask anyone picking through the mold and wreckage of their home: Why are you doing this? Why not just turn your back and walk away? 'I'm trying to save what I can,' they answer as they search for their most precious treasures: the photo albums and

mementoes that remind them of who they are and people they love. Mardi Gras is a treasure worth saving. It is part of what makes us who we are. It is a celebration of community, a time when all races and classes take to the streets and enjoy what we have in common. Anyone who thinks that Mardi Gras is just for rich people has never seen a truck parade, the Mardi Gras Indians or a neighborhood marching group. (Watts 2006, NOLA Blog)

The satirical newspaper, *The Onion* even got into the debate, with a fake survey of people on the street who were asked what they thought of the idea. One answer was, "that sucks. You know how hard it is to get a chick to take off her dive mask, remove her rebreather, roll up her scuba suit, and show her tits?" (*The Onion*, "Mardi Gras 2006?")

There were economic issues at play, as well (Table 11.1). Before Katrina, Mardi Gras attracted large number of tourists to New Orleans, but it only represented a small portion of income brought to the city by tourism. The New Orleans Jazz and Heritage Festival is another large draw to the city. New Orleans is a convention and trade show capital that drew 3,261 conventions in the pre-Katrina days of 1999 (Gotham 2005). Conventions are booked years in advance; it was urgent for the city to demonstrate they were quickly rebuilding, or they risked delaying the city's economic recovery. In addition to the service industry, which depended upon tourism, float, and costume designers along with musicians and performing artists were a particular niche of the New Orleans economy, and they needed the annual celebrations for their livelihoods.

The 2006 parade season was compressed into eight days instead of 11 with all parades following a route along St. Charles Street, which avoided the worst devastation. National

Table 11.1. Estimates of Mardi Gras' Economic Impact on Louisiana, Compiled from the Work of James McClain of UNO (Hardy 1998:33).

YEAR	AMOUNT IN MILLIONS OF DOLLARS
1986	239.2
1987	275.3
1988	309.6
1989	330.6
1990	487.9
1991	499.1
1992	579.9
1993	567.7
1994	660
1995	929.1
1996	810.6

Guard units helped supplement security usually provided by the NOPD. Floats in New Orleans and Baton Rouge were particularly scathing in their political commentary that year. Maskers walked wearing blue tarps. The synchronized lawn-mower team of Baton Rouge's Spanish Town parade danced as hurricanes and tarp-covered buildings with their lawn mowers to the sounds of the Scorpion's "Rock Me Like a Hurricane." Critiques of FEMA, Governor Blanco, and "You've done a heck of a job, Brownie" Bush were plentiful, as were floats depicting the indignities of living in a flooded shell of a city. As I talked to other bystanders at parades in New Orleans, I found many of my fellow parade watchers were dislocated New Orleanians who had returned from Houston, Dallas, and other Texas cities to get a taste of the food—a whiff of memory of their old life. Many avoided visiting their homes because they heard from friends and relatives that their property and homes were destroyed. But they came to see the parades—the familiar krewes and floats that were part of the shared experience of Mardi Gras. One woman, down from Houston with her children said to me, "I don't know what's going to happen now (to her family), but I know one thing, someone owes me some good beads."

Archaeologies of Depopulation and Collapse

Archaeology has long been interested in societal collapse and social disintegration. In the field of contemporary archaeology, many practitioners focus on the experience of alienation in a late-modern global economy (e.g., González-Ruibal 2008). In part, the obsession with disappearance is part of the modern obsession with "ruins." As a mindset, modernity embraces the notion of progress. To see evidence of progress, one must have evidence that the past was different, and ruins associated with long-gone societies are material manifestations of just that. Some of the supposed great mysteries of archaeology—the disappearance of the Mound Builders of central North America or the disappearance of the Maya of Central America—are two pertinent examples.

Myth of the Mound Builders

In the nineteenth century, American natural historians were perplexed by the great earthen works found concentrated in the Ohio, Illinois, and Mississippi river valleys. These fantastic ruins were evidence of complex societies with the ability to organize enough labor to construct monumental architecture. Where had these great ancients gone? In the minds of white colonizers intent on fulfilling self-prophesized manifest destiny, the local Native American peoples were incapable of such feats, and alternative groups were suggested as possibilities. The Celts, the lost tribes of Israel, Vikings, or extensions of the great civilizations of Central America were all put forward as candidates. The question of who were the Mound Builders was not settled definitively by anthropologists until the closure of the frontier when indigenous peoples were no longer seen as an ongoing military threat or political obstacle (Feder 2006).

Just as reports of the death of American Indians and their cultures have been greatly exaggerated, the Maya are also alive and well, having not disappeared but just relocated out of the urban decay that seems to have plagued their city centers. Movements of people from city centers to peripheries gave the impression of collapse when archaeologists were intent on only excavating city centers. In many American cities, we would also see an archaeological pattern that suggests collapse if one didn't look at all the residential zones built immediately surrounding urban centers.

There are archaeological studies of collapse that are not merely dupes to mythologies of modernity. Archaeologists are paying greater attention to long-term human/environment/ climate relationships and seeking to understand anthropomorphic changes to environments that occurred over long stretches of time. Such work has the possibility of illuminating further our contemporary society's impact on global ecology and climate. To return to the Maya and the depopulation of the central Mayan lowlands during the Classic period (AD 250–900), B. L. Turner and Jeremy Sabloff (2012) have proposed a systems theory model that attributes a collapse of governing organizations to human-caused deforestation and periods of increased aridity that over taxed the social-political structure of the Mayan states. Note that saying that a government system has dissolved is very different from claiming a people have disappeared. The Turner and Sabloff (2012) work is part of a new and growing interest in understanding sustainability successes and failures in ancient societies.

Archaeological Studies of Epidemics

Depopulation, rather than merely relocation, was a tragedy that affected Native American populations at the time of contact. Old World diseases, to which American indigenous peoples had not been exposed, took a terrible toll on native peoples. One of the debates in archaeology has concerned how quickly disease spread after first European contact. Did depopulation begin in a significant way in the fifteenth century? And if so, does this mean that native peoples contacted earlier already had been decimated by diseases? Or did depopulation correspond to first physical contact with European colonists? Gary Warrick (2005) has looked at bioarchaeological, archaeological, and documentary resources to ask this question of the Wendat-Tonontate (or Huron-Petun) group of Ontario, Canada. Europeans recorded an epidemic hitting the Wendat-Tonontate territory in 1634.

Warrick wanted to know if this was the first European-caused epidemic to hit the area. He used information about frequency of hearths at domestic sites predating 1634 to estimate pre-contact occupation densities to compare with the earliest recorded population information recorded by French Jesuits in the area. To study the population from archaeological remains, he used two measures: the number of households (as represented by archaeological hearths) and mortality evidence recovered from human remains excavated from an ossuary. An ossuary is a specific kind of burial context that includes the bones from multiple individuals. Cultures who create ossuaries generally do so as part of the practice of secondary burial. Upon death, bodies are left to skeletonize (either passively, through burial, exposure or excarnation, the removal of the flesh with knives or scrapers). Based on a ritual or other calendar cycle, the bones of the recent dead would be gathered at buried together. Ossuaries are important contexts for understanding demographic

· · · 337 · · ·

trends in past populations through bioarchaeology. For the Wendat-Tonontate study, archaeological estimates of paleopopulation calculated that a hearth would have served a family group of 10–11 people. Warrick found that there were no changes in hearth density at domestic sites until after 1634, when sites are abandoned and hearth density decreased to six people per hearth. Similarly, bioarchaeological data from repatriated ossuaries demonstrated low juvenile and adolescent mortality rates in pre-1634 mortuary remains, whereas a 1636 ossuary demonstrated that only 40% of adolescents were surviving, which is a profile typical of populations hit by diseases like smallpox that differentially impact adolescent populations (Warrick 2005).

Warrick's analysis, using multiple lines of evidence, suggests that disease impacts from Europeans were not serious among the Wendat-Tonotate until large numbers of European children were brought to the colony. It provides new understandings of depopulation and disease transmission in the colonial period while suggesting that European diseases did not necessarily predate physical European contact.

Katrina caused depopulation of New Orleans, but in this situation, movement of populations accounts for most of the demographic shift. In looking at post-Katrina Louisiana, we see populations that have undergone massive relocations and must learn how to socially integrate with one another. While Baton Rouge, one of the main areas in Louisiana that gained population, is only 80-something miles north of New Orleans, its Mardi Gras traditions are very different in scale and audience than those of New Orleans. How are these population shifts manifested in the throwing game?

Changes in Population, Changes in Mardi Gras

Katrina rearranged the people of Louisiana. The evacuation, intended to be temporary, was the initial movement of people. When the extent of destruction to the city became apparent, people rushed to find longer-term accommodations. Settlement decisions were made based upon location of extended kin networks, friends, and access to work. Even krewe connections came into play. Leonard Smith, who was rescued from his roof during the flood and evacuated with three busloads of survivors to Houma, noted he knew someone from Zulu who lived there and described being visited in the shelter there by Houma residents (Penner and Ferdinand 2009:30).

A comparison of the 2000 and 2010 census demonstrates the extent of the relocations. While some people did return to New Orleans, the parish of New Orleans experienced a 29.1% decline in its population from the 2000 to 2010 census (http://www.census .gov/2010census/). There is a racialized aspect to the population change in New Orleans. Post-Katrina New Orleans has been described as noticeably whiter and wealthier. Pre-Katrina, the black population of New Orleans represented 67% of the city, and only 60% after the hurricane. Despite an overall federal investment of 45 billion dollars in the city, only 25% of the city's 4,200 public housing units had been rebuilt as of 2011, which has also led to a decrease in the numbers of working poor. African American refugees have found new opportunities elsewhere. Lena Johnson, a sixty-year old African American, New

Orleans native now living and working in Dallas, was able to finish her college degree and begin graduate work in Texas. Although she has no intention to return to New Orleans, still she noted in an interview, "I miss Mardi Gras . . . that was part of the fabric of being a citizen" (Mildenberg 2011).

As New Orleans parish population decreased, Ascension and Livingston parishes, the two suburban parishes that border Baton Rouge, had considerable population gains, each grew by just under 40%. St. Tammany Parish, located to the north of New Orleans parish, grew in population by 22.2%. Changes to Pointe Coupee, the rural parish across the river and about 30 miles west from Baton Rouge, are not clearly visible in the census because of other demographic forces. The rural parish had been generally losing population. However, the town of New Roads is located on False River, a large oxbow lake of the Mississippi, which is popular for recreation. The area has long been a popular site for fishing camps. After the tremendous growth around Baton Rouge due to Katrina refugees, however, traffic congestion from Livingston and Ascension parishes made False River an attractive alternative for full-time residence. While 30 miles from Baton Rouge, the commute is largely traffic-free and cuts through sugar cane fields. Commuters from Pointe Coupee enter the city via the "new" Mississippi River Bridge on I-10, directly into downtown, and close to LSU. The area around False River, particularly the eastern shore, enjoyed a building boom. Camps were demolished and replaced with large luxury homes. I know a number of LSU and state employees who were among the people who relocated to Pointe Coupee; so many in fact, that I was surprised that the changes were muted in the ten years between censuses. The changes are visible in the Mardi Gras beads, however.

While archaeologists have been interested in understanding long-term relationships between human societies and their environments, recent attention to the issue of global warming in the contemporary period has led archeologists to realize that our work has the potential to contribute to policy discussions regarding proactive ways humans can prepare for climate change based on the ways people have responded in the past. Areas that have received long-term archaeological attention and that have richly detailed environmental and social histories constructed from the archaeological record are particularly valuable for looking at how humans respond to changing climate. The Four Corners region of the American Southwest provides particularly poignant examples of how vulnerable human achievements are to shifts in climate and the ways that societies respond to environmental crisis (e.g., Blinman 2008; Cordell and McBrinn 2012; Kohler and Varien 2012; Kohler et al. 2010).

The archaeological history of the Four Corners region can best be characterized as a temperature- and rainfall-led dance that moved prehistoric populations across the landscape. By 200 BCE (corresponding to the archaeological culture known as Basketmaker II, which lasted from about 1500 BC to 50 AD), the people of this region were becoming dependent on maize agriculture. The topography of the area features elevations ranging from 600 to 4,200 meters above sea level. The landscape is a mosaic of areas that have enough water and warm enough temperatures to support maize agriculture and those that do not. Over the past 2,000 years, where windows of agricultural opportunity have shifted according to short- and long-term environmental changes, the prehistoric peoples of the area have modified their settlements in response. What may appear as abandonment at any given archaeological site may merely be evidence of people moving to a higher or lower level elevation as temperatures and rainfall levels increase or decrease.

During the Basketmaker II period populations were dispersed throughout the area. Household clusters were organized around a new, shared-ritual system that manifested itself architecturally in the building of distinctive circular-shaped rooms—kivas—which occurred in multi-family homes and were used in ritual practice. Abundant rainfalls and appropriate temperature ranges allowed for the development of mid-altitude areas.

The following period, Pueblo I (AD 750–900), corresponds to increasing population growth and density as demonstrated by the appearance of villages that could contain up to 100 household clusters. Dry-land agriculture was intensified to meet growing food demands of the larger population, and the elaboration of some ritual spaces suggests that there social hierarchies developed in some areas. Temperatures rose during this period, which forced populations into higher elevations and caused the abandonment of mid-level elevations by AD 800. Then, in the late AD 880s, severe and persistent droughts led to the abandonment of the upper elevations, and some sites were "killed" through ritual burning.

Following the abandonment of the higher elevations, in the Pueblo II period, people returned to the areas they had farmed in the earlier Basketmaker III period (AD 500–750), and likewise returned to a settlement pattern of clustered households that were more dispersed over the landscape. At the household level, families were able to store enough surplus to serve as buffers for less productive crop years. Once again, evidence of ceremonial elaboration becomes apparently by AD 1040 with the construction of distinctive stone architecture ceremonial centers (referred to as Chacoan ceremonial complex) like those found in Chaco Canyon. While these stone-built areas were rooted in space, the communities that surrounded them shifted between farming areas as necessary to use the best-suited agricultural locations. Again, population starts to grow, and there is evidence that much of the region is coming to participate in shared ceremonial practices and exchange.

By the early twelfth century, however, the climate dealt the peoples of the Four Corners region a double blow—cooling temperatures and increased drought frequency severely reduced the area available for maize agriculture. During this period, known as Pueblo III, Chacoan type buildings cease to be built, population growth stops, the dry areas are abandoned, long distance trade stops, and evidence of increased violence is suggested by the study of skeletal remains. The climatic changes were so enduring that by 1300, Pueblo peoples abandoned much of the Four Corners region and relocated to the Northern Rio Grande region where better rainfall allowed he continuation of farming practices. The Rio Grande experienced massive population growth during this time.

This example has at least two different important archaeological lessons to teach. First, the culture sequence presented here, the Pecos classification, is a product of the culture history period. For the culture historians, the archaeological evidence spoke of a series of different cultures with different social organizations, pottery types, house types, and settlement types that replaced one another through time. Second, a shift in perspective to one that emphasized explanation of change brings out a different set of interpretive understandings: one that sees not collapse, but an ongoing set of dynamic relationships between groups of people and their environment against a backdrop of climate change.

Effects of Population Redistributions on the Throwing Game

One of the immediate impacts of population growth on Mardi Gras was the ballooning in size of local parades. After Katrina, new residents to the area sought to participate in local parades, and Spanish Town grew greatly. By 2011, the parade had grown from 40–50 floats to 120. The parade became so long that it lapped itself, causing traffic and policing problems. In 2012, the city imposed maximum float numbers on Baton Rouge parades; the city capped parades at 85 with an additional 5 discretionary floats for dignitaries (Martin 2012).

We previously discussed some of the changes in Spanish Town's parade presentation of itself post-Katrina and the growing influence of that parade's queer aesthetic among New Orleans parades since 2004. We see a similar situation occurring in Pointe Coupee (Table 11.2). The increase could be due to a combination of two factors: Pointe Coupee parade participants rethrowing beads caught in Baton Rouge, and Baton Rouge transplants participating in Pointe Coupee parades. In 2009, at least one float that appeared in Spanish Town parade also drove in the Lions' Pointe Coupee parade.

When we look at the rethrowing of beads at Mardi Gras after Katrina, there is an interesting trend visible in the beads. While New Orleans beads are still being rethrown in Baton Rouge parades, the beads thrown in 2006 and 2007 were all pre-Katrina medallions (Table 11.3). Despite the larger and larger numbers of beads thrown at Baton Rouge parades, there was no evidence of fresh bead stocks coming from New Orleans. The same circumstance applied to Pointe Coupee, where Baton Rouge beads were thrown alongside old New Orleans beads. It was not until 2009 that we have our only evidence that post-Katrina beads made their way to Baton Rouge—the Spanish Town assemblage includes a 2007 Zulu medallion. While circumstances may change, as of 2009, Baton Rouge had taken on a new position as a major center of Mardi Gras for Pointe Coupee and replaced New Orleans in that role. But New Orleans was re-emerging as the center for Baton Rouge.

Table 11.2. Increase in Hot Pink Beads in Pointe Coupee Parades.

YEAR	PERCENTAGE OF BEADS THAT ARE COLORED HOT PINK
2004	1.4
2006	.6
2007	4
2009	14.3

Table 11.3. Rethrowing of Krewe Medallions, Post-Katrina.

YEAR	NEW ORLEANS	BATON ROUGE	POINTE COUPEE
2006		Spanish Town: 2 pre-Katrina Thoth	
2007		Spanish Town: pre-Katrina Thoth and indeterminate-aged Rex	Kings parade rethrowing pre-Katrina Bacchus, Ralph and kacoo's (Baton Rouge) LSU football beads
2009	Proteus rethrowing post-Katrina Krewe d'Etat	Spanish Town: pre-Katrina Krewe of Midcity, Bacchus, Tucks, Rex, and 2007 Zulu	

Bead Inflation

The trend toward increasingly large and long beads did not end with Katrina. If anything, we see an acceleration of the phenomenon following the hurricane. In New Orleans, the average strand length in 2006 increased from 33.5″ to 40.3″, while in Baton Rouge, a modest increase in 2006 was followed by a jump in 2007, bringing the city average up to over 40″ (Table 7.2). Pointe Coupee also experienced a large jump in average bead length, with strands increasing from a 33″ average to 40″.

As early as 2008, others started to publically comment on what I had already been documenting archaeologically—that beads had undergone incredible changes. An associate feature editor for *The Times Picayune* made the following observations after watching large numbers of Mardi Gras beads being sucked up by street cleaners following a parade.

> I've been here long enough to recall the cheapie, post-glass-era but pre-long-bead strands that barely fit over your head. I dove for them like they were gold. Now, 33-inchers are about the shortest sold, and even they've become like the parsley on your dinner plate: A nice touch of color to fill an empty spot, but totally dispensable. Ground fodder. Keepers have to be at least 48 inches (that's to the bikini line). And even then, the size of the individual bead can make or break the desirability rating. And, like the juiciest of e-mails, they've got to have attachments: rubber duckies; blinky things; big, colorful krewe medallions. My teenage son came home with a miniature bottle of Jaegermeister (fake) swinging from his neck. Yes, even the 48-inchers have to have added sex appeal. Length has to hit 60 inches (crotch-length) to be a sure thing for saving. (Gist 2008)

Writing about the quest of Muse to develop ever more creative throws in 2012, writer Alex Rawls noted that,

Once, glass beads were the cherry throw of Mardi Gras. Today, they've made a slight comeback for those nostalgic for their heyday, but no amount of retro fondness has sparked resurgent interest in the choker-length strings of plastic beads that closed with a clasp, the beads that became the red-headed stepchildren of Carnival. Today, 33-inch strings of metallic beads are the bottom of the line and often land unloved, only to be raked up by inmates before they'reshipped to the Island of Misfit Throws. (Rawls 2012)

Recall our frequency seriation battleship curves back in chapter three? In that graph, we see transparent beads drop off quickly after 2004. Right after the hurricane, there were concerns that warehouses containing stocks of recycled beads had been destroyed by flooding. Did Katrina rush the demise of the unappreciated transparent beads?

Rapid bead inflation following Katrina is probably in part related to a desire on the part of maskers to overcompensate for the shortage of krewe-themed items available that year, as well as a conscious effort to express through the beads that nothing had changed. There were signs, however, that things had changed. The throwing game may have a length limit. There are beginning signs of bead fatigue. There is a slight drop in average strand length and diameter from 2007 to 2009. This corresponds with the implosion of the US economy in 2008 and may reflect a direct response to the changed economic circumstances of maskers. Still, newspaper accounts for the 2011 Mardi Gras season reported bead sales were better than expected for that year despite concerns about the economy. That said, as I'll discuss below, there is a convergence of other factors occurring that may indicate that the throwing game is about to undergo another significant shift in the next few years.

Archaeologies of Tradition and Revitalization

We have discussed how archaeologists have looked at cultural change. Sometimes in a society, change means an intentional return to an older set of practices through the evoking of *tradition*. We call this *revitalization*. To explain how revitalization works, we need to have a brief chat first about what we mean by tradition. Tradition can be defined as when a group of people evoke their understanding of their history to explain why things are done the way they are and to justify why things should be done the way they are. A number of archaeologists have recognized that the ideas of practice theory, particularly as developed by Giddens and Bourdieu (see chapter five), offer powerful theoretical tools for understanding the ways that communities maintain traditions—through the everyday routines of daily life.

Susan Alt (2001) provides an excellent example of how we see a sense of tradition at play in the archaeology of Cahokia and its outlying areas. Cahokia was a prehistoric city that thrived along the Mississippi in the area now known as St. Louis. At its peak, Cahokia included over 100 flat-top and temple mounds, and the elite of Cahokia had influence over much of the Mississippi Valley. Cahokia developed as a massive population and cultural center quickly around cal AD 1050–1100, in a period known as the "Big Bang." In Cahokia, the period of the Big Bang coincides with the relocation and reorganization of residential areas in the site, the development of a large central plaza, the building of monumental architecture, changes in pottery technologies and styles, introductions of new building techniques and types, increases in social inequality, and massive movements of people as labor was needed for the construction of monuments. The need for labor and the output of new materials during this period had to impact not only the people of Cahokia, but the surrounding settlements as well, which Alt refers to as the greater Cahokia community. In addition to the continued occupation of previously established sites, new villages were established surrounding Cahokia, with evidence of the new architectural techniques and intensified craft specialization of typical of Cahokia.

Yet, as Alt studied the archaeological remains of two sites just outside of Cahokia in the uplands, she recognized that not every community was adopting the complete Cahokia package. At the sites of Knoebel and Halliday, each village maintained its traditional layout with houses surrounding a central compound or small plaza—a layout that had been found in Cahokia prior to the Big Bang but was eliminated as part of the construction of large monument-filled plazas and the movement of residential groups to new areas. At each of these sites, Alt did see some incorporation of Cahokia technologies or aesthetics into the villages. For instance, houses became bigger, and shell-tempered ceramics—a technological innovation of Cahokia—were adopted, even though shell was not the best temper for the local clays. Some stylistic elements of the new Cahokia architecture were incorporated into buildings, but building techniques remained the same. So what was the reason for new villages in the Cahokia "suburbs" looking like Cahokia and older villages not? Alt drew upon the ideas of practice theory. She argues that the power of tradition (Giddens' routine or Bourdieu's doxa) led inhabitants of the older villages to adopt only those parts of the Cahokia lifeways that did not contradict their established ways of doing things. Those practices that were seen as core to who the community was were not changed or were modified only in superficial ways.

What were some of the long-term effects of this adherence to tradition? An analysis of pot and food storage vessel sizes from Cahokia versus the sites of Knoebel and Halliday showed that the vessels from Cahokia were much smaller. The village arrangement of Knoebel and Halliday, with their central spaces, encouraged people to engage with one another and to share food storage and meals. At Cahokia, the shift to new residential forms served to disrupt community formation and provide insight that perhaps tells us something as well about how the leaders of Cahokia managed to so completely control their populace. By breaking down older established social relationships within the existing communities, the leaders could reduce resistance to their authority.

So we can understand tradition as something that archaeologists can study the influences of in the archaeological record. Revitalization is when a culture actively revives what they perceive to be an older set of traditions in order to respond to social, political, economic, or climatic upheavals. The Ghost Dance, a religious movement that gained many Native Americans incarcerated on reservations under federal rule in the last quarter of the nineteenth century is an excellent example of a revitalistic movement. The religion was founded under the teachings of a Paiute prophet known as Wovoka to his followers and Jack Wilson to his detractors and the US government. Members of the religion believed that by returning to the spiritual values and traditions of their pre-contact worlds, that the Great Spirit would overthrow the Europeans and return their lands to the way they were (Brown 2001).

Archaeologically, William Turnbaugh (1979) noted that ethnohistoric accounts from the northeastern United States and eastern Canada, in conjunction with archaeological evidence, demonstrates that Native American populations revitalized ritualism surrounding tobacco ceremonies during the early colonial period as a response to European colonialism. He notes that for many sites throughout the region, tobacco pipes are the only indigenous manufactured artifact that increases in abundance and variety of styles during the early colonial period, demonstrating the importance of this particular artifact type to its users. Revitalization provides a means of calling on tradition in times of stress. Certainly, Hurricane Katrina created the kinds of stress among New Orleanians that could manifest themselves in revitalization movements.

Reclaiming and Revitalizing the Throwing Game

Prior to Katrina, New Orleans' growing numbers of residents were expressing frustration with the trend of Mardi Gras toward lewdness and commercialism over "traditional" and family oriented practices like masking and a focus on enjoying parades. In an article on urban festivals, Keith Gotham (2005) shares some of these views as expressed on the eve of the Hurricane. While some of the views he cites are more extreme (such as a person who sees Mardi Gras as turning the city into Sodom and Gomorrah), the following quote seems to reflect the views of New Orleans residents with families; "you have to practically keep your children in or take them out of town for Mardi Gras. They cannot grow up with the tradition of Mardi Gras because of the nudity that takes place all over the city during this time of year. It is not a traditional part of the Mardi Gras scene and other things that hurt people and property such as Silly String, voiding on people's property, that's a total lack of respect for your fellow human being and their property" (cited in Gotham 2005:238).

Katrina provided a unique opportunity to rethink and reorient Mardi Gras' public face and reputation. Advertising campaigns outside the state have emphasized Mardi Gras as a family celebration and pointed out that adult-only activities are restricted to the French Quarter. There are traits in the material assemblages of Mardi Gras that reflect the repositioning of Mardi Gras as a revitalized celebration.

Louisiana State Pride

The 2000 Mardi Gras season saw the introduction of beads that tipped their hat to the distinctive features of Louisiana's culture and natural resources (Figure 11.1). Some MOS strands featuring crawfish and alligators were thrown by Endymion and Thoth in 2001, and Shangri-La in 2002. None of these beads appeared again in New Orleans after 2002.

The only post-Katrina example of a Louisiana-specific bead thrown in New Orleans were two wetlands organization beads caught at Bacchus in 2009 (Figure 11.2). These

Figure 11.1. Louisiana State pride beads.

Figure 11.2. Louisiana storm warning beads caught in 2009 at Bacchus.

particular beads were associated with the Wetland Campaign, STORM WARNING, which uses the opening day of the hurricane season to educate the public about the role of wetlands in protecting coastlines from storm damage. In 2005, the organization used blue tarps to dramatize how high flood levels would rise in the French Quarter if a hurricane hit the city—three months later, Katrina hit. The beads caught at Bacchus were advertising the upcoming STORM WARNING IV gathering, held in southern Louisiana May 30–June 1, 2009 (http://www.stormwarning4.com/).

Louisiana theme beads first appeared in Baton Rouge in 2001; a crocodile was thrown at Spanish Town in 2001 and a chili pepper from the same parade in 2003. In 2004, Spanish Town threw more crawfish beads. Post-Katrina, we see more elaborate and varied Louisiana-specific beads thrown at Spanish Town. The 2006 parade throws included MOS shrimp beads, a fleur de lis medallion, and one crawfish. In 2009, two long, hand-strung strands featuring Louisiana seafood were caught as was a strand with an oyster medallion and an MOS strand featuring crab, redfish, and crawfish (three of Louisiana's most prized seafoods). This celebration of Louisiana's seafood bounty is somewhat sad and ironic given the massive British Petroleum (BP) oil spill that would occur just over a year later.

While increasing numbers of Louisiana-themed beads were caught in Baton Rouge for the years 2006, 2007, and 2009, it is surprising similar beads are missing from New Orleans parades. There are multiple interpretations possible for this. Post-Katrina, all Mardi Gras krewes had a harder time recruiting members, and more resorted to accepting out-of-staters as riders through their websites. A decrease in local riders would lead to lower diversity in beads thrown, and less of a desire to express state pride. There is also the possibility that New Orleans riders continued to feel disconnected from the rest of the state

Figure 11.3. Bacchus 2012 medallion.

following Katrina. The Louisiana pride beads are showing up post-Katrina exclusively in Spanish Town—the parade that received the most refugees from New Orleans of the parades. Is it possible that for survivors, beads become a means of expressing pride in their home state? Or is it that occupants of the state capital, where the parade takes place feel a greater need to promote the state in their celebrations? Or perhaps there is another reason? We do not have evidence that allows us to pick one interpretation over the other, but one of the attributes that makes the beads such powerful materials for communication is that ambiguity and the ability to imbue them with multiple meanings.

Although outside my excavation window, in 2012, the State of Louisiana celebrated its bicentennial anniversary. Bacchus celebrated the event with a special medallion that had a bicentennial theme (Figure 11.3), so perhaps a shift to more pro-Louisiana beads will be more apparent in New Orleans in upcoming years.

Revitalization: Glass Beads Return

For me, one of the more interesting turn of events has been the reintroduction of glass beads in the throwing game. I had heard that Krewe d'Etat threw some glass beads from their floats in a nod to Mardi Gras traditions, but I had not met anyone who caught said beads. The Krewe of Muses (Figure 11.4) had glass beads made for their organization in 2004. Their beads feature clear, blue, and green beads, a clasp, and decals placed on the clear beads with the Krewe's logo. I was given a strand of these beads by a Muses rider who told me they were going to be given to friends and family rather than thrown from the floats. The strands have a tassel and are reminiscent of the Japanese glass beads (and the few Indian strands that copied them). The addition of the Krewe's logo adds a modern twist.

I did not encounter glass beads firsthand at a Mardi Gras until 2009, when I was thrilled to catch a strand at Bacchus (Figure 11.5). Those beads had no clasp and were strung with several large beads (12 mm by 5 mm ovals) set at intervals with smaller (2 mm) beads strung between them. That same year, the man selected to be king of the Lions' parade in

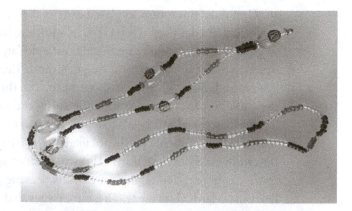

Figure 11.4. Glass beads from the Krewe of Muses, 2004. Photograph by Alexandra Wilkie Farnsworth.

Figure 11.5. Glass beads caught at parades in 2009, 2010, and 2013. Photograph by Alexandra Wilkie Farnsworth.

New Roads was a local historian, who decided to throw glass beads from his royal float. I wasn't able to catch any of those strands, but found a broken strand that had been left on a tree. That strand looked very different from the Bacchus ones; it had no set stringing pattern but did have larger glass beads (averaging 5mm) that looked more like the Czech strands.

Even though I officially closed my study in 2009, one of my undergraduate students went to Mardi Gras in 2010 and brought me her beads to analyze. Her group was generally in a festive haze the Friday night they attended parades, so they couldn't remember the name of the parades they watched, but among their beads were three glass strands. Since Krewe d' Etat is the primary parade the Friday before Mardi Gras, these beads may be examples of that group's famous yet elusive beads. These strands were consistent with one another and were of the same length, mixed, predominantly red beads averaging about 3–5 mm with no clasp. Beads like this are currently being sold as Mardi Gras beads on eBay, as are a range of other glass Mardi Gras beads, in a growing variety of styles and designs (Figure 11.6).

Other krewes have followed suit. Not surprisingly, Proteus has apparently joined the glass bead wagon. In a 2012 travel site description, Proteus was touted for throwing "rare glass beads," like those thrown in the 1950s and 1960s, as part of their parade emphasizing tradition (http://goneneworleans.about.com/od/mardigras/p/Proteus.htlm).

Certainly, the return to glass beads makes a very clear statement about nostalgia for the "good old days" of Mardi Gras. In addition, based on a review of websites, each strand of glass beads costs no more than about a dollar, less than a strand of hand-strung plastic beads, which can run up to $4.00 per strand. They are also cheaper than the average resin krewe medallion, which cost about $1.50. The throws are seen as rare, which makes them desirable to the crowds. And importantly, and ironically, the glass beads are on average, lighter than the plastic beads that originally were selected to replace earlier glass beads due to their lighter weight! While not likely to be part of the calculus that is driving maskers to purchase glass beads to throw, these particular artifacts also have the advantage of being more easily recycled than plastic beads, leaving a smaller carbon footprint and creating less post-Mardi Gras waste. These are issues that at least some Louisianans are beginning to worry about post-Katrina and post-BP oil spill.

Verdi Gras: Bringing the Other Green into Carnival

Prior to Katrina, Louisianans were not concerned with the environmental movement; really how could they be with an economy that has long depended upon the petrochemical industry? The Mississippi River corridor from Baton Rouge to New Orleans, which is home to the state's highest concentration of petrochemical plants, has long been known as "cancer alley" (Perlin et al. 1999). Even recycling programs were hardly participated in. New Orleans had been ready to scrap its recycling program prior to Katrina. "It's a cultural thing," said a spokesman for the mayor's office, "We have a hard enough time convincing people to put their trash in the can" (Fausset 2012).

For Louisianans, garbage has been one way of judging the success of the Carnival season—the more tons of trash removed from public streets by sweep cleaners at the end of Fat Tuesday, the bigger the success. This is not to say that there were not critiques of Carnival excesses prior to Katrina. Arthur Hardy, historian of Mardi Gras, lamented in 2001 that "more and more people not only expect to catch a lot of stuff, but they demand it. They've come to view the parades as an exercise in shopping, that they're going to get

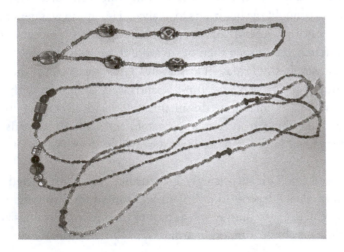

Figure 11.6. Glass beads being sold for Mardi Gras. Example on far left is purple, green, and yellow colored beads using the traditional colors of Mardi Gras. Photograph by Alexandra Wilkie Farnsworth.

something free . . . [Mardi Gras] is incredibly rich, culturally, historically . . . . Everything is buried in this crush of plastic and beads and screams and demands for more" (quoted in Gotham 2005:237).

The 2005 documentary, *Mardi Gras: Made in China* (Redmon 2005), critiqued parade goers as hedonistic, selfish, and icons of all that was wrong with Western society. The film contrasted parade scenes with an account of labor conditions in Chinese factories where plastic Mardi Gras beads are produced by underpaid, mainly female, staff, who are likely exposed to serious health hazards as a result of their work. Although a bleeding heart liberal myself, I found the documentary to be simplistic in its juxtapositions. The documentary did lead the Krewe of Muses, as described earlier, to visit China to inspect the factory where their beads are produced.

In a post-Katrina world, sustainability has become an issue with greater resonance to some Louisianans (others still find using the trash can challenging). Post-hurricane studies demonstrate that the loss of the coastal barrier islands and wetland coastal areas due to subsidence caused by the petrochemical industry was a contributor to the intensity of the storm surge that struck mainland Louisiana (Rego and Li 2009). The barrier islands would have cut the storm surge. The tossing of pro-wetland preservation beads in the 2009 Bacchus parade demonstrates one example of this new awareness.

In the 2008 article "Gist, In the throes of bead-flation," (*The Times Picayune*, Feb. 2, 2008), a New Orleans writer pondered issues of sustainability while watching clean up after a Mardi Gras parade. "So there I stood, watching the great bead roundup after Alla and pondering all this waste in a world where green universally has come to symbolize not faith, nor money, but sustainability. How many of these throws end up in our landfills? Does the plastic ever break down? When some future ancestors mount archaeological digs, what will they make of the things? Will they think us tasteless and tacky?" Hmm, well, perhaps this archaeologist affectionately finds them a little tacky. The greening of Mardi Gras has slowly begun. In 2009, it was apparent that many krewes had switched from buying beads packed in cardboard boxes to vinyl, zippered bags bearing the krewe's insignia, or a general Mardi Gras theme. In contrast to the cardboard boxes, which were torn and tossed into the street during parades, the bags are highly desirable to parade goers as a souvenir of the parade and a useful way to cart throws home. A number of krewes have switched from bead-mounted medallions to lighter-weight flashing medallions like those of Proteus. These have the advantage of being desirable catches because they weigh less. They are battery-powered, however, which creates another kind of environmental hazard. In 2010, Bacchus introduced string-mounted resin medallion. The silky nylon cord is lighter, cheaper, and also has a smaller footprint without sacrificing the krewe emblem (Figure 11.3 illustrates this form of medallion).

In 2012, an organization started by Holly and Kirk Groh, called Verdi Gras, began working toward increasing awareness of Carnival's carbon footprint. The pair claim that 25 million pounds of Mardi Gras beads arrive in New Orleans each year, with only 2% ever recycled (Cutler 2012). The couple is hoping to make recycling bins part of Carnival parades and get people to rethink throws, not eliminate them. They cite Zulu coconuts and decorated shoes thrown by Muse as examples of cherished throws that are made with recycled products. The organization was said to have 130 members as of the 2012 Carnival season (Fausset 2012).

Archaeologists are familiar with recycling in the archaeological record. The earliest evidence of human writing—clay cuneiform tablets—found new lives as foundation footings and construction fill after they had served their use as documents (Schmandt-Besserat 1992). On late nineteenth- and early twentieth-century sites in the US, we see evidence of wear on the bases of glass soda bottles that had been returned and refilled many times. It is not uncommon on prehistoric sites to find examples of older lithics that have been retouched (resharpened by removing more flakes) and reused in new contexts, or in historic settings for broken glass sherds to be used to make scraping and cutting tools (Wilkie 1996). Native peoples in the California missions would make game pieces out of broken ceramics (Farnsworth 1992). People have always creatively reused and repurposed artifacts.

My archaeological research suggests that there has long been recycling in Mardi Gras—but that it takes the form of rethrowing rather than recycling of the bead materials themselves. Recycling can include the repair and rethrowing of broken beads, purchasing previously thrown beads, or using Mardi Gras beads to create new pieces of art. Arc Enterprises has been selling recycled beads for years, but recently brought recycling to parades themselves. The group, Arc, which is a non-profit dedicated to developmentally disabled children, has introduced a "catch and release" float in New Orleans parades that collects unwanted beads directly from parade goers at the end of parades (McCash, February 10, 2012 "Catch and Release Trailer Brings Instant Mardi Gras Bead Recycling"). Recycling and reusing the beads, Arc r uses the proceeds for its programs for adults and children. The organization also has recycling locations throughout the city and regularly has bead drives (www.arcgno.org). At the Arc float's debut in 2012 at the Little Rascal's parade in the New Orleans suburb of Metarie, it was pelted with 1,000 pounds of throws. The float was following three parades in 2012.

Another recent initiative is the group LifeCity's proposal that a system be put in place that would encourage the exchange of the beads for tokens from businesses that could be used to access clean toilets during Carnival. This program is still hoping to take root. Of concern are the large numbers of tourists who catch large numbers of heavy beads that they have no reasonable way to transport home and elect instead to toss them in the garbage.

How prevalent has recycling been since Katrina? This is not an easy question to address. Taking a conservative approach, there are four circumstances that can be used to identify beads that have been thrown in a previous Mardi Gras parade: 1) the presence of beads with krewe logos other than the parade being attended; 2) the recovery of bundles of beads that do not have a country of origin label binding them and that are a mixture of different lengths, finishes, diameters, and shapes; 3) beads that have clasps identifying them as made in Hong Kong; and 4) beads that display evidence of repairs or other damage like the flaking of finish or missing or cracked beads.

These are the conservative criteria I used for this analysis. There are other beads that are likely to be rethrows, particularly the transparent beads. I have not found evidence that new transparent beads in lengths less than 33 inches are still being manufactured, making it likely any transparent beads of this type recovered from parades in 2003 and later stayed in circulation through rethrowing. However, I'm not comfortable making a blanket attribution that all of these types of beads are definitely recycled from earlier parades because there were still bundles of transparent beads with country of origin tags being caught in 2009. Despite Alex Rawl's assertion (above) that there will never be nostalgia for the short transparent beads, I'm unwilling to discount that possibility. Therefore, the numbers represented in Table 11.4 represent the minimum number of rethrown beads represented in an assemblage. I used composites for each city to tabulate this data.

Recycling has been ongoing in Mardi Gras, but I suspect with the green movement, the meaning of recycling has changed. In the past, recycling beads was a way to purchase more beads at a cheaper price to give the appearance of being more generous. A sign of conspicuous consumption is to be thrown an unwrapped bundle or bag of beads with its original tags. When I first attended Mardi Gras, any size bead thrown as part of a bundle was an extremely good catch. Now, bags of 48-inch-long beads or longer are necessary to cause a draw of breath. In that context, to throw a recycled bundle of beads would deflate the symbolic value of the throw because clearly the wealth investment on the part of the masker was not the same as if the beads were new.

Recycled beads did not occur thrown as bundles until the 2006 assemblage from Baton Rouge. In 2013, I caught my first recycled bundle of beads from New Orleans—it was wrapped with a green Arc label that encouraged recycling. In Baton Rouge, recycled beads were prominently displayed in local bead outlets as of 2009 and were priced higher

Table 11.4. Percentages of Assemblages Recycled.

YEAR	NEW ORLEANS	BATON ROUGE	POINTE COUPEE
1998	n/a	2.5	
1999	5.7	.6	
2000	5		
2001	.9	7.9	
2002	2.7	2.2	
2003		1.4	
2004	.5	.9	1.6
2005			
2006		3.7	
2007		25.8	3.8
2008			
2009	4.5	7.4	7.8

than new beads of equivalent length—a circumstance that suggests there was symbolic capital associated with being "green." Home to LSU, the capital city of Louisiana prides itself as being hip and socially conscious, so perhaps there is a conscious display of political correctness going on there with the recycled beads. That said, the number of recycled beads caught at Spanish Town in 2009 is a smaller percentage of the overall assemblage than they were in 2007. There is no clear trend that recycling is becoming a larger part of Mardi Gras than it had been previously.

That recycled beads occur at a much lower level in New Orleans, however, suggests that there are different value systems regarding recycled beads in that city where much of the Carnival performance is directed toward non-locals. This would also fit with our discussion of different scales of Mardi Gras parades being different kinds of feasts. At a feast where an elite group is trying to convince the populace of their wealth and generosity, regifting could be seen as diminishing the prestige of the gift. Even as the Baton Rouge parades grow in size and attendance, the vast majority of people watching the parades are from the immediate area. As sustainability movements grow in New Orleans, it will be interesting to see if this shifts. Just as some Louisianans are beginning to think about sustainability in Carnival, the excesses of Mardi Gras and the throwing game are spreading to other parades and arenas of popular culture. It is a phenomenon I have witnessed with fascination over the last decade, and which I refer to as "bead bleed."

Bead Bleed: Mardi Gras Beads *Everywhere*

Bead bleed is in some ways, deeply connected to bead recycling, but to understand the connection between the two requires us to think more broadly about the life cycle of beads. I have not found figures estimating how many beads go into landfills each year other than those put forward by the Verdi Gras organization. I would suggest that while Mardi Gras beads are likely to be a landfill nightmare, that far more of the beads stay above ground than 2% suggested by the Grohs' Verdi Gras organization. To develop effective recycling and reuse programs demands a better understanding of the life cycle of a Mardi Gras bead. The Grohs' organization has focused their attention on the production part of the artifact's life, its manufacture in China from raw products produced in the Middle East, and its distribution in the form of sales to maskers and then ultimately, distribution to parade goers. The Grohs then assume that beads are either given to organizations for recycling (the most likely source of their 2% estimate) or dumped. The archaeological research I've conducted shows that beads have a much more complicated biography, or life history, than that.

Artifact Biographies

Following the lead of the material culture scholar Kopytoff (1986), archaeologists have come to understand that artifacts have their own social histories or biographies. *Artifact biographies* explore how an object's significance changes whether or not the object is physically modified (Mytum 2003-2004:112). Harold Mytum conducted research in Dublin, Fermanagh, Galway, Louth, Monaghan, and Ireland to look at how an artifact biography approach could illuminate our understandings of social relations created and maintained through cemeteries. While many of the stones have simple biographies, and most of their meaning is associated with their erection and their short-term use by survivors as a place of commemoration, their later life is more associated with their role in creating a larger landscape of commemoration. Processes of erosion, vandalism, or removal can all contribute to the end of a gravestone's life course. Instead of being removed, some stones may become tipped over and buried, leaving the possibility of rediscovery and re-erection.

The most interesting practice that Mytum observed is that the stones had active lifetimes that extended across multiple generations. One such stone that Mytum recorded was erected to honor a man's mother and father (who died in 1805 and 1808) and four of their children. Later added to the stone was the name and date of death (1866) for the man who erected the stone. Following that inscription was another line of text, which was later removed, and then the addition of another family member, who died in 1880. At this point, the stone's surface was very covered with inscriptions, and smaller and smaller letters were being used to fit it in. The family was not discouraged, and managed to squeeze in between other lines of text four more names and death dates, with the last being 1891. This particular stone had a long life course, during which it remained an important point of commemoration and family identity for over 80 years.

While Mytum demonstrates how a single object can have a long and active social life, Cornelius Holtorf (2005) goes several steps further and challenges us to consider the long, varied life of one the world's best known archaeological sites: Stonehenge. Today, the Stonehenge is a heritage site that is "protected" from vandalism and modification. Yet, Holtorf points out the maintenance of the site and repairs to some of its components as acts of preservation and restoration are themselves forms of modification. It is a Neolithic site, a Bronze Age Site, an Iron Age Site, a Roman Site, and a Saxon site. During Stonehenge's long life, it has come to mean many things to many different peoples at different times, including today. How can such a site be "authentically" restored to any given period? And how should one recognize that what previous users may have seen as vandalism, was seen by those who took over the site as simply using it in ways that made sense to them. While Holtorf ultimately wants us to question notions of authenticity, vandalism, and preservation, he makes a convincing illustration of how humans constantly reuse and remake the things they find that others have left behind.

How can the idea of an artifact life history enrich our understanding of Mardi Gras beads and the phenomenon of bead bleed (see Figure 4.2)? In the case of the beads, their potential for use and reuse is part of an annual ritual cycle. Let us review the potential life paths our beads could follow. A certain number of beads do die at the parade site. They become broken, dropped in the primordial slime, and left untouched, wrapped around overhead wires, or wound around street signs, lamps and fence lines. At night parades, it is particularly easy to miss beads, and perfectly good strands lie in the street. Following parades, you can see families packing up beads and carting them away. There are always people visible who are pulling large strands of beads out of trees, off of street signs, or picking up strands from the ground that have been abandoned by the over-burdened, or were simply missed. Beads that fall in the street are usually left there. If the beads were caught early in the Mardi Gras season by locals, the "best beads" will be culled out and worn to subsequent parades or given to friends who missed parades. Packets of beads are sent to family and friends in other places. Some of the beads get hung places, like rear view mirrors or on nails, or draped over doorknobs or stuffed animals. Some beads get hauled out to decorate the Christmas tree. And a whole mess of them accumulate in a massive, tangled mass, somewhere in the house. At some point, those beads are cleaned out in estate sales, yard sales, donated to charities, or gifted to friends or family members who participate in parades.

As best I can tell, from five years of living in the state and an intimate association of nearly 20 years, most Louisianans who live in parts of the state that celebrate Mardi Gras are either in a parade themselves or know someone in a parade. When I began my project, I had imagined creating a museum-worthy collection with complete assemblages of beads thrown by different parades through time. While I have representative examples of parade assemblages from different years, and a complete assemblage for 2000, I found my research collection to have exceeded curation capacity when I completed field research in 2009. I carefully culled examples of all types and medallions, representative lengths and dimensions, and kept examples of beads from every Carnival year so that technical physical analyses can take place on the beads. I then engaged in my own catch and release program. I sold five banker's boxes of beads—earning myself $100.00—and gave ten groceries bags worth to friends who parade in Southdowns. Oh, by the way, I realize that I am in murky ethical waters by engaging in the sale of artifacts. We'll touch on archaeological ethics in our next chapter.

What about tourists and their beads? In 2013, I asked several hotel workers about whether beads were dumped in rooms, they said usually not. I have never seen a tourist dump a strand of Mardi Gras beads at the airport. Never. I check the cans. They buy extra suitcases and haul the stuff home. They give their friends beads, hang others around rear view mirrors, like they've seen done in New Orleans. They give the beads to school groups to have Mardi Gras parades or use them in their own Mardi Gras parties; and when they get tired of them, they give them to thrift stores or sell them in flea markets and garage sales. I've been able to fill in gaps in medallion series with Bay Area flea market discoveries. There is also a growing collectables market associated with Mardi Gras items, particularly post-Katrina. Look around you; you'll be surprised how many places you see Mardi Gras beads.

It is these after-lives of beads that have facilitated the spread of Mardi Gras beads throughout the country. The trend is a function of their life biographies that extend beyond their time in parades. As we saw in the archaeological assemblages, some of the beads I caught were manufactured as many as 30 years earlier. Even when they break, beads are still repurposed. Small bits can be used to make the Zulu animals. Broken strands can be sewn on costumes, glued on paper to make mosaics, or wrapped around other strands of beads to make home-made fancy beads, which can be re-thrown yet again.

Beads don't really die, but they do bleed, and as they bleed, they spread. They are infectious. For archaeologists working in the period of culture history, this spread of beads would be seen as evidence of diffusion—evidence that cultures had been in contact and shared ideas and materials with one another. For processual archaeologists, the distribution of beads out from Louisiana and other Mardi Gras-celebrating states would indicate the presence of long-distance trade networks, with the beads in remote locations serving as prestige items to be redistributed. For post-processualists, any number of interpretations could be made depending on one's theoretical bent; but most would agree that there was some communicative potential that the beads offered to those who decided to employ them in new social interactions. So who would be right? Let's look at some of the places beads have popped up.

St. Patrick's Day Parades

The first casualties of bead bleed were other Louisiana parades. St. Patrick's Day parades in New Orleans and Baton Rouge have come to develop their own bead culture. Let's look at one last set of assemblages: beads caught in the 2003 and 2004 St. Patrick's Day parade in Baton Rouge (Table 11.5). This parade first rolled in 1985, and beads were part of the parade from the beginning. The New Orleans' Irish Channel parade is older, dating to 1962. I don't know when beads were first thrown in that parade, but the St. Patrick's Day parades in Louisiana feature food throws in addition to beads. Potatoes, carrots, and cabbages—ingredients for Irish stew—are thrown. I have also seen cans of corned beef handed out along the route. If we compare the 2003 and 2007 assemblages, you should immediately be struck by the color distribution. Green is dominant in both assemblages, with pearls, silver, and gold, the colors of treasures that might be found in the pot at the end of the rainbow, also featured prominently. Green and white pearl combination strands appear in these parades as well. The other colors represented, particularly the purple and hot pink, are evidence of rethrowing from Mardi Gras parades.

Rethrowing is visible in both assemblages, and New Orleans Mardi Gras beads from the same year are often included. Mardi Gras predates St. Patrick's day on the calendar. Note, therefore, that these parades provide a much-needed release from the good behavior of the Lenten season, as well as an opportunity to quickly off-load one's Mardi Gras beads on the public. These are parades that throw heavy, and each year has BPP rates of over 75 strands. In 2003, the major material signal that this assemblage was associated with St. Patty's day rather than Mardi Gras was the color composition of the assemblage. By 2007, however, there was a radical shift in the number of St. Patrick's Day-specific beads being thrown. Resin leprechauns (the family friendly harp-holding version and the obviously drunk version) were popularly thrown, as were shamrock medallions and shamrock MOS beads (Figure 11.7).

Table 11.5. St. Patrick's Day Parade Beads.

	2003	2007
AVERAGE STRAND LENGTH (in)	38.5	37.4
AVERAGE DIAMETER SIZE (mm)	8.1	9.2
DISTRIBUTION OF BEADS BY COLOR %		
WHITE	25.2	7.3
GREEN	52.7	51.9
GOLD	7.7	12.4
SILVER	2.2	8.6
PURPLE	4.4	9.2
BLUE	2.2	1
RED	1.1	1.6
PINK		4.1
GREEN AND WHITE	3.3	2.5
RETHROW	1 2003 Bacchus medallion	3 Rex 1 Orpheus 1 Orion 1 Proteus 1 Krewe of Midcity
ST. PATRICK'S DAY SPECIFIC BEADS		2 shamrock MOS beads 1 shamrock medallion 3 leprechauns with harps resin medallions 1 drunk leprechaun resin medallion 1 plastic medallion "St. Patrick's Day Parade" 1 hand strung green metallic and white pearl necklace with smiling frog beads

Why did Mardi Gras beads bleed into St. Patrick's Day celebrations? First, both St. Patrick's day and Mardi Gras are events tied to the Catholic religious calendar, despite their appropriation by a wider range of celebrants. It was in the St. Patrick's Day parades of New Orleans where the bead throwing began—a circumstance that cultural historians would find unsurprising. Bead throwing could be seen as part of the practices of the culture region where the artifacts were found. Both processualists and post-processualists would agree that the elaboration of the beads into distinctive types for particular types of parades, however, suggests that there is more to it; after all, it if were merely a matter

Figure 11.7: St. Patrick's Day parade beads recovered from Baton Rouge. Photograph by Alexandra Wilkie Farnsworth.

of throwing beads at parades, you wouldn't need beads that look differently. Specialization could be seen as evidence of increased social complexity or social elaboration. It also suggests that some fundamental attribute or attributes of the beads are useful for doing some sort of social work within that society. We will explore this idea further shortly.

It was expected that 122 St. Patrick's Day parades would roll in 2013 in the United States. Parades throughout Louisiana throw beads. In addition, I have confirmed it has become popular to throw Irish-themed beads in Chicago, Savannah, and New York City. Starting in 2009, the clothing chain Old Navy began to sell St. Patrick's Day shamrock beads for the holiday. In fact, President Obama has been photographed at the Chicago parade wearing a neck-full of green metallic beads. I suspect that the bead throwing may have received a corporate nudge. Pictured prominently in the Chicago parades are floats sponsored by Anheuser-Bush, which leads us to another transmission vector of bead bleed—alcohol companies.

Vice Beads

Alcohol companies and casino franchises have been quick to enter the bead business. Gambling came into Louisiana in the early 1990s, in the form of Indian tribal casinos and riverboat gambling. More recently, Harrah's opened the only land-based casino permitted in the state in New Orleans by the convention center. Harrah's gives beads to visitors, as do the riverboats. Beads shaped as dice feature either snake eyes or rolling a combination of "seven" are regularly caught at parades as are card-shaped beads featuring the ace of spades. Beads are now regularly thrown at casinos outside of Louisiana and are particularly visible in Las Vegas casinos, where they are thrown on casino floors by scantily clad casino employees and sold in casino souvenir shops.

Since at least 2001, Budweiser has had a float in the Spanish Town parade. They regularly throw purple, gold, and green bracelets with the Budweiser logo, bottle openers, mug-shaped beads, and medallion beads. In 2001, they threw a beautiful cozie made out of metallic beads and designed to be worn around the neck. I was fortunate enough to receive one, and was immediately offered $50.00 for it. I turned down the offer and have never regretted it (Figure 11.8). Alcohol-themed beads are less commonly thrown at parades, perhaps because cards and dice could be related to non-gambling games and are therefore more ambiguous in their meaning than alcohol-related beads.

Alcohol-related beads are more often distributed by alcohol companies in the French Quarter during Mardi Gras; they then enter the parades as rethrows. Mardi Gras beads are now regularly provided to bars to give to patrons during particular holidays. A student provided me with a Mardi Gras strand of Bud Light beads he received at a Berkeley, California bar in 2008. In fact, students alerted me that Corona has begun distributing beads during Cinco de Mayo, as has Michelob. Perhaps my favorite strand of beads brought to me by a student is the strand that combines sex and booze—a Miller Light medallion mounted on a rainbow strand of beads that was thrown during San Francisco pride (Figure 11.9).

Archaeologically, what would we say about the appearance of these beads in Mardi Gras and other contexts? Here I think the tools of neo-Marxian thinkers could be useful. What if we think of the alcohol beverage sellers and the casinos attempting to create a masking ideology regarding their products? In other words, what does the use of beads

Figure 11.8. The image on the left provides a representative sample of the alcohol manufacturers who promote their products at Mardi Gras with specialized throws. The cozie on the right is a particularly spectacular example of a Mardi Gras-specific beer promotion. Photograph by Alexandra Wilkie Farnsworth.

Figure 11.9. Gay pride beads. Photograph by Alexandra Wilkie Farnsworth.

attempt to communicate or conceal? The city of New Orleans embraces the motto, "Let the Good Times Roll," and alcohol has clear associations with Carnival settings. For purveyors of alcoholic beverages, the distribution of beads at Mardi Gras is an obvious ploy to advertise products they are selling. Outside of the Mardi Gras context, the alcohol beads hope to evoke the festive spirit of Mardi Gras and its associations with intoxicating good times. The casinos are also advertising their product; but they are attempting to create an association between Carnival and gambling that is not part of or inherent in the celebrations. They are instead trying to naturalize an association between good times and gambling. The mother in me is troubled that these objects appear with as regularly as they do in the stashes of beads caught by small children. That said, the cigarette companies do not throw beads, but that doesn't stop one from seeing elementary school-aged children smoking at Mardi Gras parades in Lafayette.

More Sexually Transmitted Beads

Archaeologically, it is not unknown to find examples of elites in one culture appropriating the material goods and rituals of elites in other cultures. Narragansett Indian chiefs in New England adopted some British garments as part of their dress to demonstrate their status and relationship to European elites (Rubertone 2001). And of course, the elite of Europe, after contact with the indigenous peoples of the Americas, adopted the consumption of tobacco and chocolate as practices that demonstrated their access to rare and exotic foodstuffs. While the consumption of tobacco by Europeans failed to include the spiritual and ritual associations with tobacco consumption found in Native America (Turnbaugh 1979), as we saw in the discussion of feasting in Central America (chapter seven), the elaborate preparation of chocolate as part of feasting was part of a ritual to impress feast-goers. Chocolate preparation within elite Spanish colonial contexts maintained a certain degree of ritual practice associated with it, and consumption of chocolate in Spain and her colonies was associated with the elite classes.

In 1997, when I started talking about beads in California, several people told me that bead throwing had started to appear in gay pride celebrations in San Francisco. We've already discussed the importance of gay participation in shaping contemporary Mardi Gras rituals and its contemporary aesthetic. It's not surprising that the gay community was at the leading edge of taking the throwing game to new locations. Rainbow beads were being thrown in San Francisco in the late 1990s, but did not appear in Louisiana bead outlets until 2000. I bought a bunch of pride beads to throw my first time as a rider, in part to see if people had any understanding of their meaning. In 2000, they did not. By 2004, there was a broader understanding of the symbolism behind the rainbow, and reactions were mixed. In several cases in New Orleans, I saw rainbow beads allowed to drop untouched, despite being of good quality. At this point, I can confirm that Mardi Gras beads are thrown in San Francisco and Austin gay pride celebrations. Online vendors now offer a wide range of pride beads, and I have caught opaques, metalics, and opalescent pride beads in Louisiana from the parades of Orpheus in New Orleans and Spanish Town in Baton Rouge (Figure 11.9). With the exception of the complex negotiations I entered into to get the penis pride beads, catching pride beads has not required any particular bargaining technique (see chapter nine).

How should we consider pride beads archaeologically? Here is an instance where we need to reinforce the importance of context. A strand of pride beads recovered from a pride parade, Spanish Town, or the recognized gay section of Bourbon Street, are less ambiguous than such beads found in other parade settings. As was the case with the penis beads, the person throwing the beads did not seem to be challenging any notions of heteronormativity through his Mardi Gras performance; in fact, to be demanding I show my breasts in order to get the beads, he was most definitely enacting a performance of patriarchy! This, despite the fact he was part of Spanish Town's parade!

While I believe that the rainbow flag and rainbow decorations in general are increasingly recognized as having associations with LGBT pride, rainbow beads can be ambiguous because it is more difficult to access whether such beads in other settings represent a statement of gay pride or acceptance on the part of a masker or the person rethrowing pride beads, or the appropriation of pride beads for other reasons (for instance, aesthetic). For subaltern (ostracized) groups, the ambiguity of the bead message is part of its communicative strength, allowing group insiders to recognize one another in covert ways. As evidenced by the Miller Lite rainbow beads thrown in San Francisco, however, marketers recognize the power of using rainbow beads in advertising; and as acceptance grows, we may see more explicit forms of signaling in the form of rainbow beads.

Figure 11.10. Sports-related bead shapes and medallions. Photograph by Alexandra Wilkie Farnsworth.

Sports Events

Sports beads appear regularly in Mardi Gras parades in small but pervasive numbers. Louisiana State University's colors are purple and gold, while Tulane's are green and gold. Therefore, purple and green football-shaped beads are the most commonly found, with purple increasing in years that LSU has a good season. With New Orleans regularly hosting the Sugar Bowl, Superbowl, and Final Four, it was only a matter of time before Mardi Gras beads became part of sports boosterism. Popular memory points to the 2002 Superbowl held in New Orleans as the start of the sports team beads.

I was able to get Cal football beads starting in 2005. Football-shaped beads in team colors are now commonly seen in high school and college football games across the county. Sports themed beads include footballs, soccer balls, hockey pucks, and basketball-shaped beads (Figure 11.10). Baseball and Nascar have somehow escaped any large-scale bead following as best I can tell to date.

Archaeologically speaking, the bleed of Mardi Gras beads into sports is directly a result of the beads communicative powers. The beads are able to quickly visually communicate the team affiliations of audience members at a sporting event. At any distance, the fact that the beads are shaped like baseballs or footballs is probably less visible to observers, but the colors will be clear. The bead shape is probably most important to the wearer who is trying to communicate an allegiance to a specific type of sports team to those in his/her immediate vicinity. While sports team beads started in New Orleans, the practice of wearing the beads of one's team colors could diffuse very quickly given the nature of the social interaction involved. Because fans of sporting events seem to feel that they are competing with the fans of other teams in their boosterism, if one team's fans begins to wear their team's colors, others will quickly follow suit. Not only do teams move across landscapes to play other teams, fans of a team will follow their team. In such a way, the beads can also travel quickly. The spread of sports-themed beads among fans seems to be a classic example of culture history-style diffusionism.

Other Manifestations of Bead Bleed

Katrina contributed to bead bleed in unexpected ways. In Los Angeles, a local café sponsored a fund-raiser for hurricane relief, selling Mardi Gras beads. When relief organizations went to Louisiana, thankful Louisianans did what they do for guests; they treated them with warmth, hospitality, and gave them beads to take away as souvenirs. It is probably no coincidence that post-2005 we see beads as visible components of fund-raising events. A 2007 mailing for a breast cancer walk-a-thon features smiling women, walking and wearing bright pink beads. Just as sports teams are associated with particular team colors, different social causes have also come to be branded with particular colors. We have seen breast cancer pink; AIDs red; the military's black armbands, and yellow associated with hostages, to name just a few. Again, the wearing of a color allows for a quick communication of affiliation with a cause or political agenda. Following 9/11, red, white, and blue beads communicated a particular subject position very clearly.

Spread of Mardi Gras and Mardi Gras Beads

And of course, Mardi Gras beads as part of Mardi Gras celebrations have spread. Mardi Gras parties throughout the US include Mardi Gras beads. And Mardi Gras bead throwing has not been contained to the US. I was fortunate enough to visit Honduras in 2007. While there I saw the end of a local parade in San Pedro Sula celebrating a harvest festival. Imagine my astonishment when a float decorated as a yellow, green, and purple crown drove by, with its riders happily throwing stands of plastic beads to the crowd! Honduras was one of the Latin American countries that provided labor during the initial construction boom in the city following Katrina. Honduran labor has a long history in Louisiana, with seasonal workers travelling to work in the sugar fields. The laborers returned home with a case of bead bleed. Again we can see a case of diffusion that would make a cultural historian proud—the materials and ideas have travelled from one place to another through a group of translated people. Still, it is interesting to ponder what set of associations led a group of Honduran farmers to celebrate their harvest with a Mardi Gras float.

We've nearly come to the end of our travels together. In the next chapter I want to address some lingering issues, not the least of which is, why on earth have these plastic beads taken on such widespread popularity, not just in the US, but beyond?

CHAPTER 12
DID YOU CATCH THE
METHOD AND THEORY?

S o we have come to the end of our journey together—nearly. We're still sitting on that porch, and it appears I have talked your ear off all night. The last beer bottle is nearly empty, the sky is beginning to turn pink, and really, we should both get some sleep. We have just a few matters to wrap up first. While we have covered a lot of intellectual territory, there is a great deal more archaeology out there that we haven't discussed. I won't attempt to discuss it all in these last pages, but just generally let you know what else is out there to consider. No field project is perfect, and a large part of the archaeological learning process is realizing what you really should have done instead of what you did. So I'll share some of that with you. There are several ethical issues that we need to cover as well: issues that have been raised by this project and about the nature of contemporary archaeology practice. And finally, I want to wind up with a brief concluding statement about what you should be taking away from all this.

Picking up some Dropped Strands

Archaeology is a large and diverse field that is always growing and developing in new directions as new technologies and ideas open up different avenues of research. Methodologically, I have not really covered the fields of archaeological science at all, but have focused on physical, macroscalar levels of analysis, rather than chemical and microscalar levels of analysis. We have only superficially talked about radiometric dating techniques. While we discussed radiocarbon dating, we haven't discussed **Potassium Argon dating**, which uses the relative decay rates of radioactive potassium into argon gas, a process that has a half-life of 1.3 million years (making it the dating technique used to date ancient human ancestors), or **thermoluminescence dating** (**TL dating**), which measures the naturally occurring background radiation at any place and time that becomes trapped within soil and nearby objects. The technique is mainly used for dating pottery, which of course, is made out of soils. When the pottery is fired (as long as firing reaches a temperature of over 450 degrees centigrade), the TL levels are set back to zero and start to accumulate again. Therefore, if the background radiations levels are known, then TL can be used to calculate the age of a ceramic artifact directly by measuring how much radiation it has stored since it was fired. TL is most commonly used for dating pottery, fired lithics, or heated sediments. A related technique is optically stimulated luminescence (OSL), which measures the emission of light from a material that has been stimulated in some way. All objects store light energy so the technique could be revolutionary in archaeology if the kinks get worked out; but after nearly 40 years, they haven't. Because of the difficulties of sorting out the background radiation levels, it is not as precise as radiocarbon dating (Feathers 1997). The technique of TL seems to be used most frequently these days by art historians and collectors trying to authenticate the age of ceramic objects for museums or private collections.

I could have used TL dating or OSL to date the plastic or glass Mardi Gras beads, but the range of error would have been bigger than useful. Likewise, the strings of the beads could have been dated using AMS radiocarbon dating. But the difference between beads made in 1930 and 1950 would likely be obscured in the range of error—making the application of these dating techniques to any of my objects an expensive exercise in learning less than I already knew. Some archaeologists have tried to use the principles of obsidian hydration to date historic glass artifacts, but this has not been particularly successful because there are simply too many glass manufacturers using different recipes to be able to identify sources (Lanford 1977).

In terms of other realms of archaeological science, I originally intended to include some x-ray fluorescence (XRF) studies of the beads as part of this work. This analytical technique allows us to look at the chemical components of artifacts, and it can be used for sourcing materials and understanding technological processes. You'll recall that we talked about the role of XRF in obsidian sourcing studies in a previous chapter.

I did some initial XRF on the beads to look at lead content. You'll recall that there was a massive recall of toys manufactured in China due to dangerous levels of lead content. In my collections, I have beads that can be dated to particular years of manufacture—I wondered if there were any lead issues for the plastic beads, especially given you see so many children handling them. When one handles too many beads, there is a black smudge that accumulates on one's hands that really is worrisome. Initial XRF readings, however, demonstrated that lead wasn't a problem, but that we were seeing very high levels of chemicals associated with fire retardants. A survey of consumer sites demonstrates that this is a concern for all plastic jewelry. I am planning on expanding this work as soon as possible, but it just wasn't possible to do it properly for this particular book. Perhaps I'll need to write a sequel: *The Archaeological Science of Mardi Gras*.

While particularly useful, XRF is only one of a large number of technologies employed in archaeological science. The study of stable isotopes (such as carbon, nitrogen, and strontium) and other elements (like lead) accumulated during a person's lifetime and contained in their bone has been used to study ancient diet, the introduction of domesticates, gender relations, and place of origin (for instance, see Price et al. 2012). The ability to recover ancient DNA has opened entirely new fields of research—not only into human populations, but also into the populations of plants and animals that they used and the diseases they suffered from (e.g., Shapiro and Hofreiter 2012, Barnes and Thomas 2006,

Xie et al. 2006). Likewise, while I tried to include some case studies that involved evidence drawn from animal and plant remains and introduce you to the basic recovery techniques used archaeologically, we did not cover all of the complex methodologies that go into reconstructing ancient environments and human/plant and human/animal relationships. That would have also required a different book.

What I have tried to do is introduce ways that archaeologists seek to understand different aspects of human life through material culture. In terms of realms of human experience, we have not really covered kinship systems, or explicitly addressed theories of culture change and post-colonial theory. Post-colonial theorizing has been particularly important in the development of indigenous archaeologies, which I will discuss momentarily as we consider the ethics of archaeological practice. Perhaps the most glaring omission, however, is an in-depth discussion of archaeologies of religion. Has it occurred to you that this study is an archaeological study of religion? All of the excavated assemblages have been from celebrations tied to the Christian calendar: the period from King's Day until the beginning of Lent, and celebrations of St. Patrick. In Louisiana, these celebrations are part of devout religious practice. The state universities in southern Louisiana do not have classes on Ash Wednesday to allow students to attend religious services. Many students appear in the afternoon with ash prominently smeared across their foreheads. The St. Patrick's parades are tied to masses and feature prayers at their start. Yet, there is no religious iconography that appears in any of these celebrations.

I looked through the entire assemblage looking for evidence of beads that may have some sort of religious something. Among the curated glass Mardi Gras beads from Czechoslovakia are three Muslim prayer beads that were incorporated into two different strands. The first has a medallion that praises Allah in Arabic, the other strand features beads with the star and crescent. Intriguingly, the people who I bought these strands from did not recognize the beads as having Islamic significance. The owner of the first strand assumed the writing was Czechoslovakian; the second thought the latter beads were referencing New Orleans, known as the Crescent city (Figure 12.1). Old manhole covers in the city actually feature a crescent moon surrounded by three stars, so the interpretive connection made by the gentleman is sound, and a wonderful example of how artifacts are reinterpreted to fit into particular contexts. There are three strands of generic fish-shaped MOS beads that were caught at Spanish Town. If I wanted to really push interpretive boundaries, I could argue that these beads closely resemble the fish icon used as short hand to represent Christianity and may represent an attempt to inject religious decorum into the festivities. Ethnographically speaking, Mardi Gras celebrations do feature a certain number of participants who hold signs near Bourbon Street warning of the impending apocalypse and describing what happens to sinners. They don't throw beads, and their presence is part of an archaeological silence.

What does this say of archaeology that we cannot identify a religious celebration from its material culture? This goes back to the challenge of archaeology, the need to interpret human life from material traces. Religion is a set of ideological beliefs put into ritualized practice. We can find ritualized practices associated with particular symbols,

Figure 12.1. Comparison of Muslim prayer beads contained on post-WWII Czechoslova-kian Mardi Gras bead strand and the well-loved New Orleans water company manhole cover, which is shown here both as it exists in the wild and as represented on a 2013 throw.

but we do not find religion, per se. However, if we were to look at the distribution of Mardi Gras celebrations throughout the state, we would quickly see a pattern that emerges. There are no celebrations of Mardi Gras in the parishes of Louisiana that were settled by protestants. Although just across the river from Pointe Coupee, the parishes of West and East Feliciana do not celebrate Mardi Gras. They were settled by Anglo and Scottish Protestant immigrants, while Pointe Coupee was settled by the French. New Orleans and Baton Rouge were French, and then Spanish cities, which gave them a strong Catholic heritage. At the landscape level, then, an archaeologist could recognize that Mardi Gras was a ritualized celebration that occurred in areas with greater numbers of Catholic churches than Protestant ones. Those archaeological tools of association and context come to our aid. Therefore, if we take a settlement pattern approach and take another look at my central place map of

Mardi Gras celebrations (Figure 7.2), you'll see that this map doesn't just tell you about the relationship between different Mardi Gras parades. It also tells you where Mardi Gras doesn't happen, and in doing so, tells you about where high concentrations of Catholic versus Protestant populations are in the state of Louisiana. In other words, the material evidence of where Mardi Gras parades occur allows us to map which religions are practiced where.

Archaeological Ethics

We discussed NAGPRA, and some of the resulting discussions regarding archaeologists' obligations to descendent communities, but the world of archaeological ethics is infinitely larger than the issues related to the excavation of human remains and repatriation. Though development of new technologies dependent upon the destructive analysis of bone, such as DNA studies, means that the ethical debates revolving the study of human remains will take new directions. Interpreting materials is an overtly political act, and the things we say about people and their things can have real impacts on real people. Three years ago, I received an email from a woman who was a descendent of the family I studied for my senior thesis project. Apparently, my thesis is scanned and available on the web, and she found it. Remember that the thesis was written in 1988. I am not sure that I still have a copy of the thesis! At the time of the study, I had located one of the other descendants and interviewed her about her family, and talked to her about the project but had not located this second descendent. This second woman was very polite in her email, but had found my discussion of medical products from the site upsetting. From her understanding of her grandmother's values, those materials should not be there at all. Her grandmother had been a Christian Scientist and did not use medicines.

Historical archaeology has many "gotcha" moments when we recover evidence of people doing things they claimed they hadn't, it is one of the realities of human nature. I could have dismissed the woman's concerns as someone unhappy with the story revealed by archaeological materials. However, I was disturbed at the idea that this woman felt that I had dishonored her grandmother in some way, and I was very aware that archaeological interpretations are not fail-proof. So I went back into the senior thesis, twenty years after I had written it, to look at what I had said. There were quite a few medicine bottles recovered from the site, but as I looked at them, I realized that there were two categories of materials that I hadn't distinguished as an undergraduate. There were drugs that were associated with treating some sort of tuberculosis or other chronic lung condition, but the rest of the pharmaceuticals were *preventative* products—things you would use to maintain health—like cod liver oil, malt extracts, fig syrup, castoria, and an enema kit. There were no specific women's cures or children's cures.

I wrote back to the woman and asked if it was possible that her grandfather used medicines to treat his pulmonary tuberculosis (the disease that killed him), while her grandmother worked to keep the children healthy rather than to treat them when sick, and explained what I was seeing in the products that made me think that way. She wrote back, saying that fit perfectly with her memories, her grandfather wasn't really religious, so he didn't follow the same beliefs as her grandmother. I assured her that in any further publications that resulted from the site I would make that distinction clear. The experience reminded me that no matter when we conduct a piece of research, we are always accountable to it.

Some people would argue that I was modifying my interpretation to merely make a descendant happy. I see it differently; the woman provided me with information I had not had access to previously—her grandmother's belief system—and once I understood that, it changed the way that I looked at the archaeological materials. The kinds of healthcare related items had to be understood in a set of very different meanings. Collaboration did not weaken the validity of my interpretations; they strengthened them, providing me with greater nuance and insight that my 19-year old self had when originally classifying those artifacts.

Imagine how many insights archaeologists lose when they fail to engage with the communities they study. In North America, indigenous people were often excluded from the process of designing archaeological research, a phenomenon that became heightened when archaeology emphasized the "science" part of its social science identity during the ascendancy of processual archaeology. The growing field of *indigenous archaeology* (Watkins 2001; Nicholas 2010; Atalay 2012) imagines how the field could be if the perspectives of indigenous peoples not only shaped the design and interpretive process, but the methodologies and presentation of archaeology.

The Mardi Gras research described here did not have a formal community partnering element to it—to identify myself in the crowds risked the methodology of the project. My fellow maskers knew I was riding to learn more about the experiences of the throwing game. I have protected the identities of maskers I rode with, so that their Carnival masks stay firmly in place by not naming or quoting any of them. My interest was not in examining the social dynamics of krewes, but the interaction between rider and parade goer. I am happy to talk to any maskers or krewe representatives who take issue with any of my interpretations. Archaeological interpretation is a dialogic process that involves many voices (Joyce et al. 2002), and discord is part of that process.

Another important ethical issue facing archaeologists that I encountered during the Mardi Gras project was the problem of curation. Archaeology is a destructive science, we dismantle the archaeological record to understand and study it. Record keeping and the curation of the archaeological materials in a facility where others can access them is an essential part of responsible excavation. If nothing else, I want you to take away from this book the idea that any archaeological assemblage has the potential to address multiple research questions from multiple theoretical perspectives. Museum collections and state and federal repositories are an important component of archaeological information management. Curation is forever, however, and collections are expensive to maintain and keep.

Space is at a premium, and in addition to charging for curatorial space, facilities often have standards regarding what kind of archaeological materials they will and will not curate. For prehistoric pottery, some facilities will only accept decorated body sherds or rim sherds—artifacts that are seen as diagnostic. Historical archaeological sites have some of the strictest limitations on them, with some facilities refusing to take anything younger than 50 years, and others refusing to curate unconserved metal, undecorated glass, undecorated ceramics, and any architectural remains. Increasingly, "catch and release" is being undertaken at sites excavated under cultural resource management laws, with historical materials being reburied rather than curated. This archaeological editing presumes that we can predict what will be important to the research of future archaeologists.

I was frustrated to find myself facing the same pressures. At this point, the bead assemblages I still physically have are curated in my lab. I had the vast bulk of the materials curated at a house in Louisiana. When I lost access to that space, I had to move quickly to choose which materials were important to save, while letting other materials go. Hopefully, there is enough of the collection still preserved, along with the accompanying catalogs of the full assemblage, that it can be used for further research if anyone so desires in the future.

I mentioned that when forced to off-load my assemblage, I sold a portion of it. If I were working on a traditionally excavated site, this would be one of the gravest ethical violations I could commit. When we do things to create a market for archaeological objects, we are contributing to the destruction of archaeological sites. The demand for artifacts from the classical worlds remains high, and the American Institute of Archaeology reports that 85 to 90% of classical artifacts on the market are unprovenienced and likely to have been recently looted from ancient sites (Archaeological Institute of America, http://www.archaeological.org/events/10009). In the US, states regulate archaeological resources on a state-by-state level, unless the sites are contained on federal lands, in which case, the federal government is responsible for oversight. In Georgia, the Society for Georgia Archaeology presented staggering statistics for the level of destruction of archaeological sites in that state. Recent reliable studies in that state estimate that urban-ization and development in Georgia have destroyed 50,000 archaeological sites. Since only 100 sites in the state have received rigorous scientific archaeological study, the people of Georgia, they note, have destroyed 500 times more sites than they have studied (http://thesga.org/2005/04/loss-of-georgias-archaeological-heritage-detailed/). It's not my intent to scold Georgia. Estimates for other states are just as depressing. The State Historical Society for Wisconsin estimates that 80% of archaeological sites that have ever existed in the state have been destroyed (Wisconsin Historical Society, "Preservation of Wisconsin Archaeological Sites"). The destruction of the monumental Bamiyan Buddhas (built in 507 AD) by the Taliban in 2001 drew international criticism and heightened awareness of the vulnerability of world heritage sites to willful destruction and terrorism, but every day, thousands of smaller, just as potentially insightful sites are destroyed willfully and through neglect.

In Peru, a series of important Moche tombs were discovered by pothunters and looted. Archaeologists became aware of the site when never before seen gold figurines, pottery, jewelry, and other mortuary objects came onto the international art market. There are international laws forbidding the sale and trade of illegally excavated goods under the terms of the UNESCO convention. Archaeologists were able to track down the location of the looted tombs, and ultimately found the site, which incredibly had another tomb shaft that had been missed by looters. One of the archaeologists involved with the project, Christopher Donnan of UCLA, studied and wrote about objects that came from the looted tombs in an effort to reconstruct what had been in them and how they fit with the materials from the excavated tomb (Alva and Donnan 1993). Donnan was accused of helping to authenticate and increase the value of the collections of looted artifacts by giving them scholarly attention. Donnan has maintained that his work has allowed for the identification and preservation of other sites that would have undoubtedly been otherwise destroyed.

The secondary market for antiquities is a serious problem that affects the preservation of archaeological sites worldwide (Atwood 2006). Often, the looting is done by impoverished descendants of the people who created the sites, who participate in selling antiquities for small sums to supplement meager incomes. This has led Cornelius Holtorf (Holtorf and Ortman 2008, Holtorf 2007) to argue that the notions of both the archaeological record and looting are specifically Western concepts that are part of a colonialist attitude. Who are outsiders to say how a society should use the remains of their past? Needless to say, there has been heated response to Holtorf's ideas, which are interpreted in some sectors as an attempt to deconstruct the discipline of archaeology into oblivion (Kristiansen 2008).

There is a growing secondary market in Mardi Gras collectibles, including beads. By doing this book, and tracking down what was thrown where and when, I am providing information that can be used in that secondary market. In my case, while the archaeological sites I studied are ephemeral, they are not part of the archaeological record in the traditional sense until they are thrown out. Given the lack of long-term curation space for the Mardi Gras beads and the demand for recycled older beads, in an ironic turn, my decision to both sell and give away the artifacts has kept them from entering the archaeological record (landfills), at least for now. Perhaps more ironically, the objects I sold were never archaeological in a traditional sense. I created an archaeological assemblage from a non-archaeological context (no beads were taken from the ground) by collecting the materials in an archaeological way. It was my intervention—me working in an archaeological way—that gave the beads archaeological value. That archaeological value was lost when I dismantled portions of the bead assemblage. In that sense, I'm no better than a looter. I stripped the beads of their archaeological meaning and sent them back off into the world, beads without histories. But lots of archaeological materials are stripped of their archaeological meaning—by not curating undecorated sherds, by not excavating particular kinds of features, by dumping unconserved metal, or reburying construction materials. Archaeological ethics and the politics of preservation is a large and complicated area in the field. As for my own part in the destruction of the archaeological record, I have mixed feelings. I would have preferred to curate the entire assemblage. Whoever wishes to study my excavations will be dependent solely on my field notes and analyses, which

Figure 12.2. Bags of beads recycled from 2013 carnival season by the author. The type of bag on the right is more traditionally used as a 50-pound sack for crawfish. Photograph by Alexandra Wilkie Farnsworth.

accompany the remaining assemblages. On the opposite side of the argument, I have curated examples from every parade year, so that a representative sample of the range of types are available to be studied. By "de-accessioning" (removing an object from a museum or archival collection), I have created space that allows research to take place on more recently excavated collections from other sites. This has allowed my graduate and undergraduate students space to work on their research. Figure 12.2 shows the bags of beads that we donated to a Verde Gras station after the 2013 Carnival season. This does not include the four bags of beads and krewe throws we kept for curation. Museums face a similar dilemma: how do we balance limited available space in a way that allows older collections to still have research value, and new research to take place. In terms of selling the beads (I also gave many away), I'm not actually creating further demand for Mardi Gras beads. The people who bought the beads from me are going to throw them away free to other people.

Directions not Taken

The Mardi Gras sites are the most ephemeral I have ever encountered, they exist only in the space of a few hours. If they are not excavated within that window, there is little opportunity to collect evidence from them. The archaeological intervention necessary to collect beads on a parade-by-parade basis, merely bagging the assemblages separately, is so simple, but so completely beyond the embodied practices of Carnival goers, that few people save their beads this way.

I conducted this project during a period of time when I co-directed an archaeological project in the Bahamas that became entangled in international protest and intrigue, conducted four years of excavations on the University of California campus, and wrote four other books. I've talked about some of those projects throughout this book: the excavations at Oakley Plantation in Louisiana, Clifton Plantation in the Bahamas, the Perryman house site in Alabama, and the fraternity house at Berkeley. Each of these sites were more traditional archaeological sites, and three of them (Oakley, Clifton, and the Perryman house) have been interpreted for the public in historical museums. The continued engagement with the Mardi Gras project—some would argue the least archaeological of all of them—continuously led me to think more deeply about issues I was confronting in the archaeological study of more distant pasts. This project was something I was doing as a side project out of a sense that there could be something fascinating here, but it was never the focus of my full attention until I had a chance to write this book as part of a sabbatical leave.

I will admit, that even I have been shocked at how much can be interpretively drawn from these assemblages. Contemporary archaeology is still a very new discipline in the United States, and it wasn't until 2003 that I realized how large a community in England was becoming interested in developing the field into a serious discipline. Much of the contemporary archaeology was landscape based, and none of it involved sustained, multi-year fieldwork. I was developing this project as I went along, and the path I was creating was little travelled.

I cannot change what I have already done, but, if I were to start a second phase of the project, I would continue to follow developments in New Orleans and Baton Rouge Mardi Gras. While I chose to collect beads from only one location for each parade, I would be interested in knowing how location along a parade route affects or doesn't affect resulting bead assemblages. This would require a larger research team. Any volunteers out there? I would focus more attention on the spread of the throwing game to other parts of the country. What new forms would the throwing game take? Will it tend toward the antics of pre-Katrina, or are other parts of the country too conservative? What are growing Mardi Gras celebrations, such as the sponsor-driven parade in St. Louis, MO, like? All archaeological projects are like this. You address one set of questions, and a series of related or completely new questions arise. Every year, these sites are being created. Just over the short period of time I studied the throwing game, there have been significant changes.

Thinking In and On Archaeology

For me, the initial research hook for this project was to create a project similar to the grave-stone project conducted by Dethelsen and Deetz (1966). I thought that this contemporary archaeology project could be a useful way to illustrate how different archaeological techniques work with pretty, glittery, objects. As I continued, the project solidified for me how the most important tools in our archaeological tool kit are not our methodological techniques, but the frameworks that we use to think with. I came out of a graduate program that was heavily influenced by human behavioral ecology. While conducting my dissertation research in Louisiana, I was fortunate enough to get to know a number of the human geography faculty at LSU. I was first exposed to the social theorizing that was part of the post-processual critique through discussions with them at departmental parties and at beer night. It was as a young faculty person at Berkeley where I really began to engage in depth with writings that developed out of the post-processual critique in archaeology: feminism, critical theory, agency and practice theories, critical race theory, and more recently, actor network theory.

As I mentioned, I see myself falling back on feminist theory more than any other school of thought, but by no means do I limit myself to feminist writers. I have come to think of theory as a pair of glasses. When you need to see things close up, you grab some bifocals, when the sun is too bright and you need to filter it out, you put on sunglasses, when you're trying to see faraway, you need your distance glasses or binoculars. You get my point? A pair of sunglasses is useful in the daytime, but are they really the best thing to use at night? Theories and schools of thought are frameworks designed to support particular idea structures. Different theories fit best in trying to answer different research questions. Despite the processualists' attempts to discover one large overriding theory of culture, it is not out there (Figure 12.3). Humans are creative, innovative, stubborn, conservative, rational, and irrational all at once. There is no one set of theory that can contain us. Those scholars who think there is just one school of thought that explains all of human experience are wearing another kind of glasses: blinders. They become ideologues whose work becomes stale and repetitive. I don't advocate that all theories are equal, or that different schools of thought should be combined willy nilly. We have seen that the application of evolutionary ideas to race theory leads to terrible outcomes like eugenics movements. What I do advocate is that understanding the relative strengths and weaknesses of a particular set of ideas is absolutely necessary.

Methodology walks hand-in-hand with theory. You cannot ask a research question without operating within a particular theoretical framework. Nor can you design a research methodology without understanding the kinds of evidence necessary to address your research questions. Archaeologists often divorce method from theory in the classroom, teaching the history of theory and method in different semesters, or teaching lab or field classes that have no discussion of the theoretical framework or research questions that drive the analysis or excavations. Even more surprising, are the archaeologists who claim they do not need theory, that understanding will somehow emerge from the materials themselves. It is a strange kind of phenomenological object-agency delusion that fails to recognize that artifacts don't have agency in the same way as people—they don't speak.

Figure 12.3: There is no one way for archaeological thinking.

The bead study became an opportunity to demonstrate how a number of archaeological ways of thinking could be used to construct a series of different ways of approaching a single artifact assemblage. Each set of questions evoked different archaeological ways of thinking, which in turn, required us to look at various aspects of the assemblage through distinctive kinds of analyses. What made any of the interpretive analyses possible were not the beads themselves—it was the way the beads were collected—in a way that paid attention to dimensions of time and space. This contextual information, the meat (or tofu for the vegans) of archaeological study, is what enabled this study. No one else can replicate this study without doing a comparable excavation of Mardi Gras. When we think back on the analyses of the bead assemblages created from these excavations, we should see that most of our analyses involved pulling out different sets of attributes of the beads to compare against one another. This is a very basic and straightforward kind of archaeological technique. Yet, even without relying on a bunch of fancy technology, the bead assemblage allowed us to explore a range of issues related to the throwing game: technological changes and the social changes they engendered, the struggle to juggle bead weight loads and growing consumer demand, changes in the symbolic economy, expressions of social identity, power struggles to achieve prestige, gender dynamics and sexuality, and changes in regional exchange systems and populations, and revitalization and environmental movements resulting from Hurricane Katrina. We were able to study each of these aspects of the throwing game not from ethnography, or documents, but by interrogating the archaeological materials.

Rarely are single archaeological assemblages studied through multiple theoretical lenses as the bead assemblage was here. A rare exception is an assemblage excavated by Adelaide and Ripley Bullen (1945). The site was a historical period house site associated with a free black woman named Lucy Foster, and was interpreted according to the standards of the cultural historical school, with the Bullens spending much of the site report explaining the chronology and artifacts recovered from the site. The site assemblage was reanalyzed first by Vernon Baker in 1980, as he attempted to look for evidence of African American ethnicity by analyzing plate-to-bowl ratios found at the site to see if there was a preference for stewed foods. Most recently, using a third-wave feminist perspective, Whitney Battle-Baptiste (2011) has presented a new interpretation of the materials and emphasized Foster's social relations with her community as evidenced through her material culture. None of the three studies is wrong, and each are actually very good examples of the theoretical frameworks in which they were constructed. Each has contributed in some way to the construction of archaeological knowledge. Is there an interpretation I prefer? Yes, most certainly. Usually, a reanalysis is presented, as Binford did with his Old Copper culture case study, or as Hodder did in his rethinking of Neolithic tombs and houses, to demonstrate a new and improved way of archaeological thinking. But reanalysis can be part of an additive process, where instead of replacing knowledge, we acknowledge that we are expanding it.

Archaeologists are not always as tolerant of other people's theoretical orientations as they could be. Part of this results from a funding culture that has limited resources and supports the notion that some research questions are inherently more valuable to ask than others. Kent Flannery (2006) in a *Annual Reviews in Anthropology* article lampooned the post-processual critique as a failure that was a faddish attempt to incorporate postmodern theory into archaeology, stating that archaeology was returning to its empirical, scientific roots. The tone of his article suggests he sees himself as gleefully dancing on the grave of post-processual archaeologies. Why his hostility? He cites a line from the third *Indian Jones* film, in which Indiana states that "archaeology is about facts, if you want truth, go to the philosophy department." Yet, Flannery is advocating not for facts, but a single kind of archaeological truth. Facts, or data, are not inherent in the artifacts, data are simply observations that an archaeologist has decided to systematically record based on what his/her theoretical orientation has dictated is important. We saw in a previous chapter how actor network theory, a new way of thinking about systems, developed since Flannery wrote his classic article on subsistence systems, actually solves the problem that Flannery encountered with his theory to account for how change occurred. The same empirical data that Flannery so prizes and used in his interpretation hasn't been altered, just the framework through which we understand that data. I do not mean to pick on Flannery, whose work I have always admired and whose insights I have found invaluable, but his stance provides a useful example of a particular attitude about theory. There is a particular kind of discourse in the academy that posits there must be winners and losers. This kind of attitude enforces theoretical homogeneity within a field and discourages diversity. Neither archaeology, nor the academy is alone in being plagued by these attitudes. The theoretical diversity of the field over the last 20 years has brought more women and people of color into the field—people who had formerly seen archaeology as not addressing issues they saw of relevance or interest.

Ultimately, I don't think this is an argument about theory in archaeology. I think it's ultimately about research questions that different archaeologists ask. Let's be honest, I think Flannery just doesn't find interesting the questions that have been asked by post-colonial, feminist, and other post-processual archaeologies. That's okay, I am disinterested in some topics that other archaeologists are passionate about, but appreciate what they do. Some theories are better fits for particular research questions than others, but there are not research questions that are better than others, just research questions that are more popularly asked than others. I'm sure any number of archaeologists would be appalled that I would spend as much time studying Mardi Gras beads as I have. Is a strand of beads really any different than a pot sherd or a projectile point? Is a regional distribution system a more anthropologically valid subject for study because it traded shell beads rather than plastic ones?

In looking at the Mardi Gras beads through different lenses, I believe we have learned more about the totality of the throwing game and how it is intermeshed in the social life of Louisianans than we could have from a single perspective. In addition, I hope you have seen that we did not simply swap out one interpretation for another, but that insights developed from one approach could be used to build upon in other forms of analysis. For instance, it was thinking about the assemblage as a human behavioral ecologist would that allowed me to recognize the importance of bead shape and size for optimal throwing, and the selection of beads through time for lighter materials. Only by recognizing that there had been a rational logic to bead selection in the past allowed me to then interrogate why the game took the seemingly irrational turn toward larger, longer, heavier beads. It was a different theoretical lens, actor network theory, however, that allowed me to derive an explanation for that phenomenon, and yet another perspective, this time, feminism, that provided a means of interpreting sexual dynamics that entered the throwing game as a specific practice that contributed to bead inflation. Imagine how richer archaeological interpretations could be at any site if our culture of funding and publication was not so geared at chest-pounding and dismissing of theoretical diversity. Okay, off the soapbox now.

Why on Earth Beads?

We have one last question to address before we leave one another, it is the question that first prompted this study, and has continued to fuel the research as I have watched in astonishment as Mardi Gras beads have spread to other contexts. The question was originally, why on earth are Louisianans wearing these plastic beads at Mardi Gras? Now the question has expanded to, why are Americans across this country wearing plastic beads as part of celebrations, sporting events, charity events, and even political conventions? My answer has several parts.

First, remember when I rhetorically asked about the gift of beads and pondered whether they were a free gift or a gift that carried a social obligation (chapter seven)? New Orleans, more than any other city in the country, enjoys the reputation as a welcoming and vivacious host whose guests leave feeling charmed. It is a city that embodies all of the best of American society—music, food, and art derived from a rich culturally and racially diverse society, a love of life and friendliness. It is a city whose personal motto is "*Laissez les bontemps rouler*" (Let the good times roll!). It is also a city that has embodied all the worst of our country: racial hatred, sexism, poverty, ignorance, political corruption, and violence.

And every year, the city welcomes everyone to join in a chaotic celebration of the good, bad, and ugly of being American. It was Americans, not the French, who created Mardi Gras as it is celebrated. It is a wonderful and all-inclusive Christian religious festival where Islamic prayer beads have been thrown from parades named after Greek and Roman Gods, and that has welcomed Jewish Americans as Carnival kings. It is a festival where a straight man will show his penis to a gay man to get a strand of plastic beads. In the dynamics of the throwing game and street festivities, issues of class, race, sexuality, and gender are rendered visible, debated, contested, and re-inscribed simultaneously. That honesty and embracing all the complications, beauty, and ugliness of being an American is New Orleans' true gift. The beads are the physical embodiment of that gift. Carnival provides a funhouse of mirrors in which Americans and foreigners alike can view a multitude of reflections of itself.

In return, New Orleans ultimately asks for the country's love. It is a city that wants tourists to love its architecture and atmosphere, to delight in their African-European-Native American regional cuisine, to sway to its music, and to celebrate in its streets. And when it looked like our country was going to lose New Orleans, the gift was repaid: citizens from across the country rearranged work schedules to volunteer in New Orleans;

they sent money and supplies to relief agencies; provided housing to refugees; adopted abandoned pets; and returned to a storm ravaged city to pump money back into the tourist economy. They left carrying more beads.

That could be the end of the story. But the beads have agency in the way of beads; and since the development of MOS bead technology, the beads have the ability to do some pretty interesting things. Through their size, they denote rank; and through their colors, they can denote affiliation; and through their shape, they can convey function. Humans have long used ornamentation as an extension of their bodies (Joyce 2009), and ornamentation or decoration of the face and neck are a particularly important part of the body. We look to faces to identify persons, as individuals, but also their gender, age, and sexuality—and ornaments worn on the face facilitate the communication of rank, affiliation, gender, stage of life, and any number of other statuses.

At a Cal football game, wearing strands of blue and gold football shaped beads conveys the same information as painting one's face blue and yellow would. The beads' limited number of manipulateable attributes makes them excellent modes of communicating information about oneself. The attributes of color, size, and shape are generic enough to be transportable from one context of meaning to another. There are any number of football teams that have blue and gold as their team colors, but the beads are used within contexts where their meanings will be clear to other participants. Green and gold beads worn at an Eagles game would be interpreted differently than the same beads worn at a St. Patrick's Day parade. It would be interesting to know if there is bead bleed between St. Patrick's Day parade beads and beads worn at Notre Dame games—do fans of the Fighting Irish wear leprechaun beads like those thrown in Baton Rouge and New Orleans? As you can have seen from our archaeological study of the beads within Mardi Gras, the possibilities for creative expression are endless.

I have taken advantage of beads as a means of communicating status. I was among the organizers for an archaeological theory conference held at Berkeley a few years ago. I purchased blue and gold beads to hang nametags from, and bought each of the organizers a fancy strand of beads with a Cal medallion on them. Conference participants were told if they needed one of the organizers, to look for people wearing the big beads. It worked out beautifully. The beads were easier to spot than names on tags.

Interestingly, the glass beads now being thrown at Mardi Gras do not possess the same characteristics as the MOS beads. If there is a shift back toward throwing glass beads, it will be interesting to see if they change to mimic the communicative powers of the MOS beads. Already, as I sit at my computer in the fall of 2012, I have seen examples of glass beads being sold online for next year's Mardi Gras celebrations that feature green, yellow, and purple beads, something never seen prior to MOS beads. Will glass beads come to take on attributes of MOS beads, allowing the throwing game to develop along the same trajectory? Or, will we see the throwing game change into a new form, while MOS beads endure in other settings? We will just have to keep our eyes on the beads and see what happens. Mardi Gras is an archaeological site that continues to be created each year.

Final Thoughts

Archaeology is a discipline that embraces a particular way of thinking about the relationships between humans, places, and things. No matter an archaeologist's theoretical orientation, they share the recognition that it is the spatial and temporal situatedness of things relative to other things that allows us to study human social life. Archaeology may mean "the study of old things," but an archaeological mindset can be a powerful tool for understanding not just ancient human lives, but the lives of contemporary people as well. All human-made objects are endowed by their creators with meaning; but, unlike language, material objects have an inherent ambiguity about them that allows people to use them in creative ways to express themselves. It is this attribute of human nature that is ultimately the basis of the archaeological endeavor and what drives us to carefully interrogate the material traces people leave behind, whether those traces are burned corncobs, flaked stone tools, or a strand of plastic beads.

My daughter and I are sitting on a grungy street curb. In the gutter by our feet is a mass of discarded crawfish shells, wadded-up napkins, stepped-on Louisiana hot links, candy wrappers, broken strands of beads, and who knows what else. Fortunately for us, the stale beer smell emanating from this clotted mass is currently stronger than the competing aromatic hint of piss. Alex is bored. And impatient. Always impatient. And complaining. Some things do not change.

"When will the parades get here?" She gripes.

"Really?" I ask her, "Really? You're going there? It hasn't even started yet. Go bother Ian, he's standing over there with Kat."

I'm feeling pretty good. I have a can of Abita beer in my hand, and we're standing in the no man's land on St. Charles Street across from our friend's family's apartment. That's right; we have access to that most precious Mardi Gras resource—a toilet that actually flushes! But most importantly, Alex and I are at Mardi Gras for the first time in four years.

The Mardi Gras moratorium is over. It is February 2013, and I've turned in my book manuscript on Mardi Gras. I had declared after the 2009 Carnival season, much to Alex's chagrin, that there would be no more Mardi Gras until the book was submitted. Since I had a few years until I had a sabbatical, she knew she was in for a long-Mardi Gras-less drought in her life. We were here to celebrate, not conduct research—or so I told myself. I mean, it was okay that I had a series of bags labeled by parade stowed in my backpack, right?

We had flown in that day to catch the Thursday and Friday night parades in New Orleans for the first time ever. We would see Muses and Krewe d'Etat, Morpheus, Hermes, and Chaos and then drive up to Baton Rouge to see Spanish Town on Saturday. It was a much-needed trip. I was ready to participate in Carnival as a tourist instead of a scientist. That was, until the throwing started. The first parade was Babylon, one of the three parades now considered by Mardi Gras historian Arthur Hardy, along with Hermes and Proteus, to be the last remaining old line krewes. Alex and I would be seeing two of the three old line krewes. Babylon was celebrating their 74th year. They had originally formed as the Jester Krewe and later came to parade as Babylon.

We saw the small, brightly decorated illuminated wagon-based floats lurch toward us, and I was filled with all of those old feelings of excitement and anticipation—what would we catch? What would we see? Mardi Gras evokes many of the same emotions that I experienced during the course of archeological field work; It is the challenge of seeing what would be recovered and thinking about how the new discoveries fit in with what I already thought I knew; it's just with Mardi Gras, the gratification is a little more instantaneous. The first floats passed, arms and voices raised in response. I tested a few different spots to beg from. We were not in our usual place (due to the bathroom access), and behind me was a thicket of ladder chairs with children perched atop them. Despite obvious distractions caused by these begging tots, I was soon able to grab a small plastic bag containing a bead strand out of the air. Alex quickly grabbed it from me (other things don't change either) and tore the bag open to examine the strand.

"Cool!" she said, "look mom!" She passed me a hand-strung plastic bead necklace, about 42″ in length I estimated (it was actually 40″, I was a bit rusty), with 12 mm purple metallic and pearl finished beads, interspersed with gold beads shaped like Jester heads that were embossed "Babylon" on the back. These were not heavy resin medallions like those previously thrown as part of hand-strung krewe beads. These hollow plastic krewe beads were integrated into the necklace and did not increase the weight of the strand dramatically as a medallion would have. Yet, the bead very successfully communicated the identity of the krewe for anyone who carried the strand away from the parade. Now this was something new!

We ended up catching four of these fancy hand-strung krewe beads along with three Babylon doubloons, two cups, and two jester hats embroidered, "Babylon". I gave one of the hats to a kid standing nearby and horrified Alex by wearing the other one. We only caught seven other strands of beads. Out of our haul from the parade, that suffered the same limitations on weight and space that Proteus did, we had caught 11 items that bore the krewe's name, and even the non-krewe beads were of a decent quality. As I thought about the implications of this, I pondered whether other old line krewes were making a similar decision about how to deal with throws. The use of the hand-strung krewe beads offered an opportunity to throw a quality bead that was probably still lighter than solid plastic medallions strung on MOS beads.

I was excitedly thinking about all of this as we awaited Muse's arrival. The parade began with Ruby Bridges, the African American woman who as a child had desegregated the New Orleans' school system. Waving in wide slow arcs to the crowd, she rolled by regally on a giant high-heeled shoe. Imagine literally helping to change the world and getting to ride on a Mardi Gras float as thanks! What a strange world Carnival creates. Pink-wigged women on roller skates zig-zagged across the road. They were holding pamphlets, the programs for the parade which explained each of the floats, including a pair of kissing cows both wearing bridal gowns. Muses clearly intended to include all women in their Carnival embrace. My daughter and I were filled with a warm feminist glow as the parade commenced—a glow that ignited into indignation and anger with the behavior of the crowd around us.

Two young girls from our group (both under the age of 10), perched atop chairs, were each being handed one of Muses' coveted shoe throws when a pair of drunk college men (I'm talking about you, jerks in the Tulane shirts) literally knocked into them and stole one of the girl's shoes from her hand and, in a particularly cowardly move, ran from the scene. The tears and upset that followed ruined the parade for the poor child.

Our friends left, and Alex and I walked along the parade route as we looked for a less volatile space to watch the parade. Alex has been to Mardi Gras all her life and never felt afraid. Surrounded by aggressive college men on St. Charles, for the first time, I saw my daughter unhappy and scared at a Mardi Gras parade. The men in the crowds at that part of the route were aggressive in jumping over people and pushing smaller folks out of the way. We eventually scouted out a spot in front of a street pole, which allowed us protection on one side and that had attracted a less dense crowd. From there we were able to negotiate for some throws (most of which never reached us) and watch the bad behavior. Alex was able to watch the parade, catch some neat throws, and enjoy the humor of the floats and dance troops.

The male attendees at Muses were the worst I have ever encountered at a Mardi Gras parade. Women maskers riding on the lower levels of the floats were pummeled by jumping men attempting to yank throws and drinks out of the women's hands. The items thrown by Muses suggested the women anticipated these actions and came prepared. The krewe threw an endless supply of plastic blue butterfly nets marked "Muses" to the crowds. As the parade progressed, women and children waving butterfly nets were able to reach the maskers to have stuffed vegetables, glowing hair pieces, and other unique throws placed in their nets. Alex was thrilled to receive a laser pointer that projected Muses' crest. The nets were also convenient for bonking unruly parade goers on the head as well, not that I would ever engage in such activities. As Muses rolled away, I pondered the violent onlookers and wondered if the idea of strong, economically powerful, socially inclusive women was so threatening to some of the spectators that they needed to assert their displeasure with such outward aggression. Mardi Gras continues to provide us with a sometimes uncomplimentary reflection of ourselves.

The theme of Muses' parade had been "Muses making groceries," and one of my favorite throws of the night had been stuffed plush peppers, onions, and tomatoes embroidered with "MUSES" that were thrown at the crowd. I thought about Iris, who caused such ire when her members first dared to parade on floats, and the crowds that threw rotten vegetables at them. Were Muses' intentionally referencing that part of women's Mardi Gras history in their parade performance? Based on the behavior of some of the male members of the crowds, I contemplated whether things had really changed for women at Carnival. I decided not to share these sadder thoughts with Alex. She hears enough of my feminist critiques outside of Carnival. I hugged her instead.

Following Muses came the Knights of Chaos. The procession was running late and featured a mid-parade breakdown resulting in a large gap. The crowds that had been so aggressive during Muses melted away and seeped into bars that dotted St. Charles near

Tulane. We caught little from the krewe: only seven artifacts. Interestingly, three of the objects caught were jelly-blinkie pendants suspended on nylon strings like the seahorses thrown by Proteus four years before. Clearly, jelly-blinkie medallions had spread from Proteus to other parades. The Knights of Chaos jellies included two forms: one of the crest, the other a knight. The maskers squished the blinkies before throwing them to ensure the lights were activated, thus making it possible to see them as they arced through the black night air.

We would catch blinkie throws from every night parade we attended in 2013, and at the end of both Thursday and Friday nights, we saw a cacophony of blinkie lights hanging on people's chests, illuminating their faces in yellows, blues, greens, purples, and reds. It was hard not to think about E.T.'s heart light as I watched parade goers mill around. Each of these objects is powered with two to three small watch-type batteries. The environmental electronic waste sure to be caused by these objects is astounding to consider. And this in a year when we caught bunches of beads wrapped with green wrappers proclaiming them to be recycled and environmentally friendly. As always, the contradictions of Carnival abound.

It didn't really matter that Chaos wasn't throwing much. We were exhausted from our re-entry into Mardi Gras. We barely made an effort as the last floats whizzed by us. In four years, things had changed in really interesting ways (Figure 13.1). If the Thursday night

Figure 13.1: Krewe d'Etat demonstrates the range of krewe throws found in 2013. Left to right: resin medallion blinkie; hand-strung medallion beads; and MOS medallion beads.

parades were an indication of the rest of Carnival, the old line Krewes had found a new way to use beads to enhance their prestige in a way compatible with the limitations of their floats. I would soon learn that Proteus had also switched to the hand-strung krewe beads, and that Krewe d'Etat, the krewe reported comprised of members from the defunct parading wings of Momus and Comus, were also throwing these beads (among others).

We would see that while old line krewes wooed spectators with quality, the super krewes and krewes that longed for super status, had embraced MOS krewe beads, and threw larger and larger numbers of krewe-specific beads. Beads overall were still the most abundant throw in Mardi Gras, but blinkie medallions, plush krewe-themed throws, lighted Frisbees, and a number of other new krewe-themed throws were more in evidence than ever before.

"Are beads on the way out?" I wondered aloud to Alex as we wandered from the parade route to find our rented Chevy Aveo; she groaned at me and indicated she was too tired to care. But I cared, and I couldn't help but think about the three carefully labeled bags of artifacts we were hauling back to our hotel room. In fact, before the first parade was finished, I texted my friend Mike, who was going to be in New Orleans the day after we left, and begged him to attend Proteus and Orpheus so I would have the opportunity to compare several parades that I had excavated in previous years with their 2013 incarnations.

So instead of a regular-person vacation, Alex and I had an archaeology-person vacation—analyzing beads in our hotel room and photographing them (Figure 13.2). All my intentions to not excavate the parades of 2013 went to hell. Once you see the world through archaeologically tinted glasses, you can never take them off; and I would not want to live my life any other way. Thanks for sharing this journey with me. See you at Mardi Gras!

Figure 13.2: Examples of archaeological assemblages from the 2013 season. Photograph by Alexandra Wilkie Farnsworth.

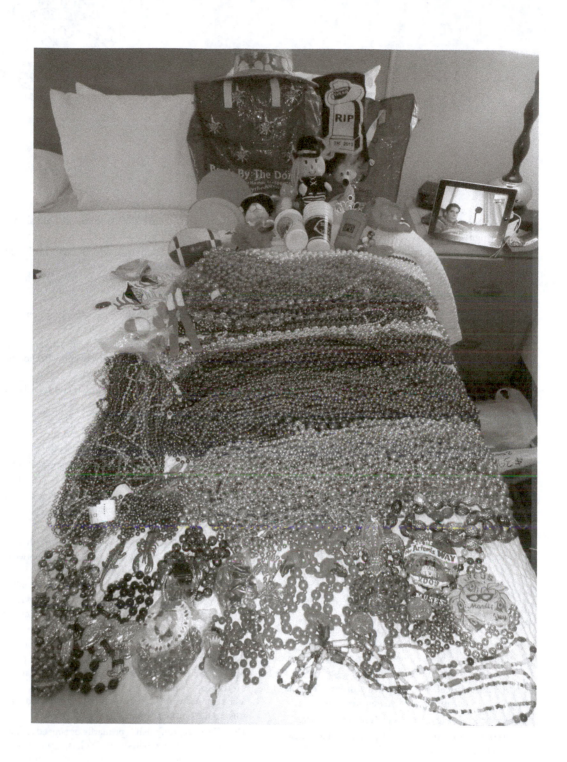

GLOSSARY OF ARCHAEOLOGICAL TERMS*

*Words that appear in italics in the glossary have their own separate entry.

Absolute Dating Techniques: Allows archaeologists to assign calendar dates to archaeological deposits. Examples include *dendrochronology, radiocarbon dating, thermoluminescence, and potassium argon dating.*

Accelerator mass spectrometry: An accelerator-based spectrometry unit counts all of the 14C atoms rather than just the decaying ones.

Achieved Status: Differences in social rank arising from a person's particular skills or personality.

Actor Network Theory: An archaeological school of thought that argues objects, just as people, have the ability to act (agency), in a way that makes them even (symmetrical) within a network.

Actors: See *agent.*

Agent: An individual human living within the structure of society who is conscious of her/his rules and their power to manipulate them and/or make choices.

Alienation: The process in which laborers make and create goods to which they do not have market access.

Archaeology: The study of the human past (and present) through the material traces people leave behind as they make their way through the world.

Archaeological Cultures: A shared set of normative material culture, which is a concept mostly developed by culture historians

Archaeological Record: The totality of the remains of the past that is preserved in the world.

Archaeological Landscape: Larger regions over which sites are distributed. A landscape view of a region takes into account how humans interact with and modify the natural space around them.

Archaeological Site: A spatially discrete complex of associated features, artifacts, and ecofacts.

Archaeozoology: See *zooarchaeology.*

Artifact: Any discrete and portable object made or modified by humans.

Artifact Biographies: The social history of an artifact usually focuses on exploring how an object's significance changes whether or not the object is physically modified.

Artifact Types: Clusters of attributes that are shared by all examples of a artifact form.

Ascribed Status: Status achieved through birthright rather than achievement.

Assemblage: The totality of artifacts and ecofacts recovered from a site.

Attribute: A distinguishable characteristic of an artifact recognized by an archaeologist.

Band: A small cohabitating group of families who live and work together cooperatively and with no one having structural power over another.

Barter: A form of exchange in which goods or labor perceived to be of similar value are traded at the same time.

Biological Anthropology: The study of the relationship between the human body and social life.

Biosphere: The portion of the earth that supports life.

Calibration Curve: A formula used in radiocarbon dating that corrects for temporal variations in the earth's atmospheric radiocarbon.

Cache: Intentional cluster of objects.

Central Place Theory: Developed by Christoph Waller, it examines the economic relationships between cities and surrounding rural areas. It asserts that larger cities develop as distribution centers to the smaller, rural towns surrounding them and that the widest array of goods are available nearest the center of the distribution.

Chaînes Opertoire: "Operational chain" is an approach developed by Leroi-Gourhan that examines the physical and cognitive series of actions that go into material production, from start (gathering materials) through labor of production (and by-products associated with this) to the finished object.

Chiefdom: A group that is primarily organized around kinship groups, has hereditary leaders, craft specialization, exchange, and social inequality consisting of at least two social classes (e.g., elites and commoners)

Cladistics: Typological tool used by selectionist archaeologists and drawn from biology. This system of classification is based on the proportion of measurable characteristics the study population has in common.

Classification: The process of sorting artifacts into types.

Cognitive Archaeology: Archaeological school of thought that specializes in the study of the cognitive steps of production.

Context: When or where a site, artifact, or feature is situated in the world.

Craft Specialization: When a society focuses on intensively producing one type of good over others, for instance, pottery or shell beads.

Cultural Change: The processes through which the practices and norms of a given group change through time. They can be internal or external to the society. Changes in environment would be an external change. The rise of a new set of practices originating in older traditions would be an internal example.

Culture: according to *culture historians*, the shared, normative set of practices and beliefs that held a community of people together. *Processualists* believe culture is an extrasomatic means of adaptation. *Post-processualists* mainly abandon the notion of culture as too essentializing and use the word "social" instead.

Culture Area: The region inhabited by a group, as identified by mapping of the groups normative, shared material culture.

Culture History: An archaeological paradigm wherein archaeologists sought to understand past peoples by reconstructing the changes in their cultural practices over time, within its historical context. Practitioners may be referred to as Culture Historians or Culture Historical archaeologists.

Cultural Type: Identified by Julian Steward as an artifact type that would represent a classification of whole cultures in terms of the functionally most important features.

Cultural Patrimony: A society's material and cultural heritage.

Data: The observations that we make about the world.

Dendrochronology: An absolute dating technique that calibrates a tree's growth rings from wood fragments to create a chronological sequence that other wood samples can be compared to. It is also often called tree-ring dating

Depositional Context: The circumstances through which the materials came to be deposited in the archaeological record.

Depositional History: The chronology of a site's stratigraphy.

Diffusion: The spread of a cultural practice, trait, artifact type, or style from one culture to another through contact.

Direct-historical Approach: An archaeological methodology first utilized during culture history. This approach involved starting with a known ethnographic group, locating historic period sites associated with that group, and then proceeding backward through the archaeological record, working from the ethnographically known to the unknown.

Distance Decay Model: See *down-the-line trade model*.

Down-the-line Trade Model: Trade models that demonstrate that in ancient societies, the further away something gets from its place of manufacture, the more rare it becomes (also known as the *distance decay model*).

Doxa: The set of taken-for-granted realities embraced within a society that learned as part of *habitus*, which serve to reinforce social hierarchies and structural inequalities within society by making those structures seem inevitable and natural.

Ecofacts: Naturally occurring aspects of the environment, such as animal bones and seeds, that are part of the human experience but are not made or modified by people.

Ecological Complementarity: The development of trade and exchange systems across environmental zones in order for each community to maintain the necessary resources for survival.

Egalitarian: A society that does not exhibit ascribed class stratification; instead all members have equal status.

Emancipatory Archaeology: Argues that a critical archaeological perspective can provide contemporary society with the tools necessary to dismantle the controlling structures of corporate capitalism (or at least that is the hope).

Embodiment: A person's daily, lived experience moving through the world.

Emic: An anthropological perspective that studies a culture from an insider's view.

Empirical Data: Data which have statistically verifiable results.

Emulation: Occurs when the fashion of one group is copied by another.

Ethnography: The research tool of anthropologists who learn about other societies through participant observation—or living within a group—and interviewing informants.

Ethnology: The study of modern societies.

Ethnoarchaeology: Branch of archaeological research that involves archaeologists doing particular kinds of ethnographic research with the explicit goal of understanding the archaeological record.

Ethnographic Analogy: Archaeological methodology that consists of using ethnographic information to interpret archaeological patterns.

Ethnogenesis: The formation of ethnic groups.

Etic: An anthropological perspective that studies a culture from an outsider's view.

Evolution: Adaptation through differential reproduction.

Evolutionary Archaeology: Views society as an organism with a genotype and phenotype. In this case, material culture serves as the phenotypic expression of human populations. It is also known as *selectionist archaeology.*

Excavation: The controlled removal of soil to reveal spatial and temporal relationships between artifacts and features.

Experimental Archaeology: Archaeological methodology that attempts to understand some past cultural or taphonomic processes through replicative experiments in the present.

Fashion: Prevailing style or mannerism at a given time and place.

Faunal Assemblage: The assemblage of bone from an archaeological site.

Feature: An immovable aspect of the environment that has been created or modified by humans.

Flotation: The process by which a soil sample from a feature expected to preserve plant remains is processed in a water tub (flotation tank). The micro and macro-botanicals (the *light fraction)* float to the surface and are removed for analysis. Larger materials (the *heavy fraction*), such as charred seeds and wood fragments, small animal bones, fish bones, scales, shell fragments, and even small artifacts like beads, can be recovered from a small wire mesh at the bottom of the tank.

Forensics: The application of scientific methods or technologies to reconstruct evidence that can be used in legal arguments.

Frequency Seriation: A type of seriation that orders the popularity of a particular (usually) aspect of an artifact class. These seriations usually appear as battleship curves.

Functional Type: Identified by Julian Steward as a type that is based on how an artifact was used.

General Covering Laws: Postulated by the processual movement. They explain large-scale, cross-cultural processes, such as cultural change.

General Systems Theory: A theoretical toolset used in understanding how parts of a society articulated and interacted with one another and how changes in one part of a system would lead to changes in the overall system.

Geographic Information Systems: Software that allows archaeologists to conduct locational analytics and create interactive maps and geodatabases. Very important tool used in site recording and archaeological analysis.

Ground Penetrating Radar: Remote sensing tool that allows for mapping of subsurface archaeological features by using radar pulses.

Habitus: The sense of cultural propriety and normative order that a person develops from childhood and through their everyday practices and experiences.

Half-life: The time it takes half an element to decay. For example, 14C (used in radiocarbon dating) has a half-life of 5,730 years.

Heavy Fraction: The archaeological remains in a *flotation* sample that sink and are recovered from the mesh at the bottom of the flotation tank.

Heteronormativity: The uncritically accepted idea that normal sex is heterosexual sex, and all other sex is somehow deviant.

Hermeneutic Reasoning: Utilizes dialogic thinking between parts and the whole; a scholar would be fitting pieces into an interpretive whole at the same time as constructing the whole out of the pieces. Thinking process advocated for post-processual archaeologists.

Historical Archaeology: Archaeological works that studies literate societies.

Historical-index Type: Identified by Julian Steward as an archaeological type defined by form that had chronological significance, not cultural significance.

Historical Particularism: School of anthropological thought founded by Franz Boas that argued cultures could not be compared against one another in artificially derived classifications but must be understood within their own historical contexts.

Human Behavioral Ecology (HBE): Archaeological school of thought that developed out of processualism and was influenced by evolutionary processes. It typically focuses on understanding strategies of resource acquisition and the social impacts that arise from those strategies.

Hypothesis: A possible, testable, reasonable answer to a research question.

Hypothetico-deductive Method: Means of conducting scientific research in which a researcher starts with a research question and then considers all the reasonable and testable possible answers to that question.

Ideology: A system of ideas and ideals that underpin a community's understanding of itself, be that community economic, political, religious, or social.

Ideo-technic Artifact: Artifacts that signified the ideological rational of the social system. For example, for Binford, figurines of gods were examples of ideo-technic artifacts.

Indigenous Archaeologies: Archaeological research that is designed and implemented by indigenous scholars that often uses post-colonial theorizing and indigenous ways of knowing to approach archaeological collaboration and interpretation. The subject of the scholarship need not be an indigenous site to be an indigenous archaeology.

Intensification: The process of getting more and more energy from the available environment.

Interface: In the archaeological record, the places where different sediments intersect.

Law of Superposition: Geological law proposed by Charles Lyell that states that the oldest layers of geological deposition will be the deepest, with the younger layers on top. Archaeologists use this concept to think about the age of different layers of the archaeological record.

Life History: An artifact's existence from manufacture to deposition in the archaeological record. Also known as an object biography.

Light Fraction: The macro and microbotanical remains in *flotation* that float to the top and are removed from the surface of the tank.

Linguistics: The study of languages.

Judgmental Sampling Strategy: See *nonprobablistic sampling strategy*.

Macrobotanical Remains: Archaeological plant remains that can be seen by the naked eye, like seeds, corncobs, and plant roots.

Macroscalar Analysis: Considers large populations over large periods of time.

Magnetometer: Remote sensing technique that measures differences in the earth's magnetism to create a map of subsurface features.

Marine Reservoir Effect: The difference in 14C present in organic matter caused by ocean waters exchanging radiocarbon at a different rate. As a result, marine animal bone, and shell can provide older dates (up to 400 years older) than charcoal from the same setting.

Masking Ideologies: A set of ideas that act as mechanisms of control which serve to structure (and thereby hide) inequality in society.

Matrix: The substance that surrounds artifacts, ecofacts, and features in the archaeological record. It is usu-

ally dirt, but in the case of underwater archaeology, it can be water.

Mental Models: A term taken from cognitive archaeology that describes an understanding of the sequences of production that had to be followed in order for the process to have the correct end result.

Microbotanical Remains: Archaeological plant remains that require the use of a microscope to be seen, like pollen, starches, phytoliths, and spores.

Microscalar Analysis: Considers small groups of people over short periods of time.

Microstratigraphic Analysis: The recovery of microscopic layers of dirt.

Middens: Trash deposits in the archaeological record.

Middle-range Research: See *middle range theory*.

Middle-range Theory: Defined by Lewis Binford as actualistic studies designed to control for the relationship between dynamic properties of the past and the present.

Morphological Type: Identified by Julian Steward as an archaeological type based on the physical or external properties of an artifact—it's style.

New Archaeology: See *processual archaeology*.

Nonprobabilistic Sampling Strategy: Utilizes only prior knowledge to select sampling areas. It is also known as *judgemental sampling*.

Normative: A society's unspoken expectations of behavior and practices.

Obsidian Hydration: A relative or absolute dating technique (depending on whether the obsidian has been sourced or not) developed within processual archaeology whereby the thickness of the hydration layer that forms on the outside of the obsidian artifact is measured and used to calculate a date.

Optimal Foraging Models: A range of theories based on an assumption that living creatures want to acquire as many calories as they can for the least amount of work, leaving as much time possible for reproduction. It was developed to explain how animals gather resources from their environment and mainly employed by human behavioral ecology archaeologists to understand hunter-gatherer lifeways.

Oral History: The process of interviewing people about their memories of the past.

Paleoethnobotany: The study of archaeological plant materials. It often focuses on human-plant relationships.

Palimpsest: An assemblage where chronological relationships are collapsed upon one another with no matrix between to keep materials from different periods of time separate.

Paramount Chiefdoms: A society that has a hierarchy of chiefs within the society and paramount chiefs at the top of the hierarchy.

Pollen: Plant reproductive products.

Provenience: The three-dimensional location of an artifact.

Pedestrian Survey: Also known as field walking. It is an archaeological recording method whereby archaeologists systematically walk over a bounded area, recording artifacts, features, and sites that are visible on the surface.

Phenomenological Archaeology: Branch of landscape archaeology that considers firsthand experience of phenomena in the world. It asserts that since all human understanding and experience of the world is three-dimensional and filtered through the senses of the body, it is the act of doing and experiencing that creates reality.

Phytoliths: Microscopic silicon structures found the cells of many plants.

Pompeii Effect: The idea that sites can be found frozen in time much like the Roman city of Pompeii after the eruption of Mount Vesuvius in AD 79.

Post-processual Archaeology: An umbrella term used to describe the theoretically and topically diverse range of archaeological studies that arose following Ian Hodder's critique of processual archaeology. These studies share an attention to the role of human agency and symbolic life.

Potassium-argon Dating: Radiometric dating technique that measures decay of radioactive potassium into argon gas. It is used mainly in archaeological settings to date hominid remains.

Prehistoric Archaeology: Area of archaeology that studies pre-literate societies.

Probabilistic Sampling Strategy: Also sometimes called a *random sampling strategy*. It avoids using prior knowledge to rank the selection of one sample over another. Instead, the site to be sampled is divided into a grid, and the areas to be sampled are randomly selected.

Processual Archaeology: Also known as the *new archaeology*. It is a school of archaeological thought that emphasizes the importance of the hypothetico-deductive method and scientific and anthropological rigor in archaeology.

Provenience: The three dimensional location of an *artifact, ecofact,* or *feature* in the *matrix*.

Racialization: Processes of imposing and creating racially designated categories.

Random Sampling Strategy: See also *probabilistic sampling strategy*; in a random sample, no statistical preference or weight is given to prior knowledge

Random Stratified Sampling Strategy: Uses probabilistic sampling strategies but may concentrate random samples more heavily in one section than another given prior knowledge.

Reciprocity: A form of exchange wherein a gift is expected to be returned in some way.

Reductive Technology: A method of tool making that entails subtraction from a larger raw material to make the finished product; flint knapping is an example of reductive technology.

Research Design: The plan for fieldwork and analysis that an archaeologist develops before beginning archaeological research.

Research Question: The guiding question or questions that shapes an archaeologist's research design at a particular site.

Relative Dating Techniques: Allows archaeologists to assign dates to deposits relative to one another—older or younger.

Remote Sensing: An archaeological survey technique that uses non-invasive technologies to discover subsurface anomalies. Examples of remote sensing techniques are *magnetometry*, electric or *soil resistivity*, and *ground-penetrating radar*.

Revitalization: When a society renews an older set of practices perceived to be more authentic or traditional. It usually corresponds to times of stress.

Sampling: The process of selecting a subset of a collection for study.

Sedentary: The practice of living in one settled area year-round.

Selectionist Archaeology: See *evolutionary archaeology*.

Seriation: A tool of archaeological dating and classification. The artifacts are put into a series based on a shared characteristic, such as style, appearance, or chronology.

Settlement Pattern Analysis: A different range of methods and analyses developed by processual archaeologists to study how humans occupied and used a landscape through time.

Site Cachement Analysis: An archaeological technique that examines the relative abundance of particular resources within a defined area around a site.

Site Formation Processes: The environmental effects and human behaviors that create a site and that effect it after its original deposition. This is also known as the *taphonomic* process.

Skeletal Element: The name of the bone in zooarchaeological analysis.

Social Evolution: Also known as "social Darwinism" or "unilinear evolution." It is a belief which that became widespread in the nineteenth century that a society's development could be charted as a trajectory with "primitive" societies at the bottom and "developed"

European societies at the top. This idea was used to justify forced assimilation and extermination of indigenous peoples throughout the world.

Social Complexity: Social development that includes, but is not limited to craft specialization, sedentism, subsistence resource intensification, and the development of social organizations to regulate the administrative challenges of coordinating labor, trade, and community living.

Sociobiology: Area of evolutionary biology that focuses on understanding how we can see evolutionary forces at play in present-day populations.

Socio-technic Artifact: Artifacts that served to connect people together in a culture—for example, artifacts related to kinship.

Spores: The reproductive products of fungi.

Starches: The energy storage of plants.

State Level Society: Forms of government that are highly centralized, entrenched, and maintained by a bureaucracy with a small number of elites at the top of society, the bureaucrats in the middle, and the masses at the bottom.

Stratigraphy: The study of geologic strata.

Structuralism: Idea that any culture has a set of mental templates that shape the way people in that society make and do things.

Structuration Theory: Set of ideas that consider the discursive relationship between agents and structures.

Style: Aspects of the aesthetic design of an object.

Stylistic Seriation: An artifact series organized by stylistic attributes.

Stylistic Variation: Drift and change in aesthetics of archaeological types through space and time.

Subjectivity: A person's physical and social role in the world. It is also known as "subject position."

Subsistence: What people eat and how they get it.

Superposition: The relationship between layers of sediments in the archaeological record.

Symmetrical Archaeology: An archaeological school of thought drawn from actor network theory that argues that the notion of symmetry does away with the objective/subjective divide that has characterized recent archaeological practice. It also argues that all components of a network should be recognized as having equal ability to act, be they human, material, or technological.

Systematic Sampling Strategy: A type of nonprobablistic sampling strategy that covers a set amount of the site. For example, taking a soil sample every five meters across the entire site would be a systematic sample.

Taphonomy: The study of processes that affect the decay and deposition of archaeological materials.

Task Differentiation: Different specialized craftsman working together to create one final product.

Technology: The sum of a society's shared knowledge regarding how to make things and extract resources.

Technomic Artifact: Artifacts whose form and nature arise most directly from the environment and are likely to be related to activities like subsistence.

Terminus Ante Quem: "Time before which"—meaning this is the latest possible end date for an archaeological deposit.

Terminus Post Quem: "Date after which"—meaning that this date indicates the earliest possible start date for an archaeological deposit.

Theissen Polygons: Generated from a set of sample points. Each polygon defines an area of influence around its sample point in such a way that any location in the polygon is closer to the center point than any other sample point.

Toolkit: The set of items associated with the labors of a particular person or group of people.

Trade: The exchange of goods and services.

Tradition: When a group of people evoke their understanding of their history to explain why things are done the way they are, and to justify those practices.

Typology: An organizational set that archaeologists use to classify artifacts. A particular typology is the result of whatever attributes the classification is focused on.

Unilinear Evolution: See social evolution

Vertical Archipelago: A mountainous area in which each ecological zone exists like an island surrounded on either side by different environments with different natural resources and different potentials for resource exploitation.

Wet-screening: The use of water to wash sediments through a small screen mesh, which leaves behind very small ecofacts and artifacts.

X-Ray Fluorescence [XRF]: A machine that uses x-rays to excite a material so it releases photons (fluorescing). Each element within the material responds in a way consistent with its atomic structure, which allows archaeologists to see the relative abundance of different elements within the material.

Zooarchaeology: Also known as *archaeozoology*. It is the study of animal remains from archaeological sites, and it often focuses on human-animal relationships.

REFERENCES CITED

Manuscript Collections

Gay, Andrew Hines and Family, Papers. Lower Louisiana and Mississippi Valley Collections, Hill Memorial Library, LSU.

Richardson, Henry Brown and Family Papers. Lower Louisiana and Mississippi Valley Collections, Hill Memorial Library, LSU

Savoy, Joseph and Family, Papers. Family Correspondence. 1861–1909. Lower Louisiana and Mississippi Valley Collections, Hill Memorial Library, LSU.

Thrasher, Arthur P. Correspondence 1895–1898. Lower Louisiana and Mississippi Valley Collections, Hill Memorial Library, LSU

Tower, L. F. Papers. Lower Louisiana and Mississippi Valley Collections, Hill Memorial Library, LSU.

United States Patent Office.

U.S. Patent 2,349,177. Applied for May 9, 1941, granted May 16, 1944. A Method of and for Making Blown Plastic Articles. Granted to William Kopitke.

U. S. Patent 2,392,459. Applied for April 4, 1942, granted January 8, 1946. A Method for Molding and cutting mechanically multiple plastic beads. Granted to J. Casalino.

U.S. Patent 3,196.064. Applied for December 14, 1962, granted July 20, 1965. Method and Apparatus for the Molding of Beads. Granted to Phillip Tell.

U. S. Patent 4,292,813. October 20, 1981. Apparatus for Molding Strand-mounted plastic members. Granted to Levine Irving.

Newspapers

Bangor Daily News

The Baton Rouge Morning Advocate

The New Orleans Times Picayune

The Dixie

The Los Angeles Times

Secondary Sources

Agarwal, Sabrina and Sam Stout (eds). 2003. *Bone Loss and Osteoporosis: An Anthropological Perspective*. Kluwer/Plenum Academics, New York

Agarwal, Sabrina, and Bonnie Glencross. 2010. "Examining Nutritional Aspects of Bone Loss and Fragility across the Life Course in Bioarchaeology." In T. Moffat and T. Prowse (eds.) *Human Diet and Nutrition in Biocultural Perspective: Past Meets present*. Berghahn Press, Oxford.

Altman, Dennis. 1982. *The Homosexualization of America, The Americanization of the Homosexual*. St. Martins Press, New York

Archaeological Institute of America. "Frequently Asked Questions." http://www.archaeological.org/sitepreservation/faqs

Arnold, C. J. 1997. *An Archaeology of the Early Anglo Saxon Kingdom*. Routledge, London

Arnold, Jean. 1995. Transportation, Innovation and Social Complexity Among Maritime Hunter-Gatherer Societies. *American Anthropology* 97(4): 733–747.

_____. 1987 *Craft Specialization in the Prehistoric Channel Islands, California*. University of California Press, Berkeley.

_____. 2007. "Credit Where Credit is Due: The History of the Chumash Oceangoing Plank Canoe." *American Antiquity* 72:196–209.

Ascher, Robert. 1961. "Analogy in Archaeological Interpretation." *Southwestern Journal of Anthropology* 16:317–325.

Ascher, Robert and Charles Fairbanks. 1971. "Excavation of a Slave Cabin: Georgia, U.S.A." *Historical Archaeology* 5:3–17.

Alva, Walter, and Christopher B. Donnan. 1993. *Royal Tombs of Sipan*. Fowler Museum of Cultural History, University of California at Los Angeles, Los Angeles.

Atalay, Sonya. 2012. *Community-Based Archaeology*. University of California Press, Berkeley.

Atwood, Roger. 2006. *Stealing History: Tomb Raiders, Smugglers, and the Looting of the Ancient World*. St. Martin's Griffin, New York.

Baadsguard, Aubrey, Alex T. Boutin, and Jane E. Buikstra (eds). 2012. *Breathing New Life into the Evidence of Death*. School for Advanced Research Press, Santa Fe, New Mexico.

Babuscio, Jack. 1993. "The Cinema of Camp (AKA Camp and the Gay Sensibility)." In: *Camp Grounds: Style, Homosexuality*, edited by D. Bergman. University of Massachusetts Press, Amherst.

Baker, Lee. 1998. *From Savage to Negro: Anthropology and the Construction of Race, 1896–1954*. University of California Press, Berkeley.

_____. 2010. *Anthropology and the racial politics of culture*. Duke University Press, Durham.

Baker, Vernon. 1980. "Archaeological Visibility of Afro-American Culture: An example from Black Lucy's Garden, Andover, Massachusetts." In Robert Schuyler (ed.). *Archaeological Perspectives on Ethnicity in America*. Baywood Publishing Company, Inc., Famingdale, New York.

Bar-Yosef, O. and P. Van Peer 2009. "The Chaîne Opératoire Approach in Middle Palaeolithic Archaeology." *Current Anthropology* 50:103–131.

Barnes, Ian and Mark G. Thomas. 2006. "Evaluating Bacterial Pathogen DNA Preservation in Museum Osteologicla Collections." *Proceedings: Biological Science* 275(1587):645–653.

Barrow, Clyde. 1993. *Critical Theories of the State: Marxist, Neomarxist, Postmarxist*. University of Wisconsin Press, Madison.

Barry, John M. 1997. *Rising Tide: The Great Mississippi Flood of 1927 and How it Changed America*. Simon and Shuster, New York.

Barth, Frederick. (ed.) 1969. *Ethnic Groups and Boundaries*. Little Brown, Boston.

Battle-Baptiste. Whitney. 2011. *Black Feminist Archaeology*. Left Coast Press, Walnut Creek.

Baynard, Kat. 2011. *The Equality Illusion: The Truth about Women and Men Today*. Faber and Faber, London.

Baxter, Jane Eva. 2005. *The Archaeology of Childhood*. Rowman, AltaMira, Walnut Creek.

Beck, Ronald D. 1980. *Plastic Product Design*. Van Nostrand Reihold Company Inc, New York.

Beaudry, Mary. 1993. "Personal Aesthetics versus Personal Experience: Worker Health and Well Being in Nineteenth Century Lowell Massachusetts." *Historical Archaeology* 27(2):90–105.

Beaudry, Mary, Lauren J. Cook, and Stephen A. Mrozowski. 1991. "Artifacts as Active Voices: Material Culture as Social Discourse." In *The Archaeology of Inequality*, Randall McGuire and Robert Paynter (eds), Blackwell Press, Oxford. Pp. 150–191.

Bender, Barbara, Sue Hamilton and Christopher Tilley. 2007. *Stone worlds: Narrative and reflexivity in landscape archaeology*. Left Coast Press, Walnut Creek.

Bentley, Gillian R. 1985. "Hunter-Gatherer Energetics and Fertility: A Reassessment of the !kung San." *Human Ecology* 13(1):79–109.

Bestofneworleans.com. 2012. "Unknown Pranksters Stick It to Krewe d'Etat." http://www.bestofneworleans.com/blogofneworleans/archives/2012/02/23/unknown-pranskters-stick-it-to-krewe-det at (webpage no longer accessible).

Big Bead Little Bead 2011. "A History of Czech Glass Bead Making." Available at http://www.bigbeadlittlebead.com/guides_and_information/history_of_czech_glass_beads.php

Binford, Lewis R. 1962. Archaeology as Anthropology. *American Antiquity* 28(2):217–225.

_____. 1967. Smudge Pits and Hide Smoking: The Uses of Analogy in Archaeological Reasoning. *American Antiquity* 32(1):1–12.

_____. (with contribution by George Quimby) 1972. *An archaeological perspective*. Seminar Press, New York.

_____. 1977. Forty-Seven trips. In *Stone Tools as Cultural Markers*, edited by RVS Wright, Austrailia Institute on Aboriginal Studies, Canberra, Australia, pp. 24–36.

_____. 1981. *Bones: Ancient Man and Modern Myths*. Academic Pres, Orlando.

Bird, Douglas W. and Rebecca Bliege Bird. 2000. The Ethnoarchaeology of Juvenile Foragers: Shellfishing strategies among Merriam Children. *Journal of Anthropological Archaeology* 19:461–476.

Blakey, Michael. 2001. Bioarchaeology of the African Diaspora n the America: Its Origins and Scope. Annual Review of Anthropology 30:387–477.

Bleed, Peter. 2011. "Loosening our Chaînes: Cognitive Insights for the Archaeological Application of Sequence Models." *PaleoAnthropology* 2011:297–304.

_____. 2001. "Trees or Chains, Links or Branches: Conceptual Alternatives for Consideration of Stone Tool Production and Other Sequential Activities." *Journal of Archaeological Method and Theory* 8(1):101–127.

Blinman, Eric. 2008. "2000 years of cultural adaptation to climate change in the southwestern U.S." Ambio, Special Report num. 14. Royal Colloquium: Past Climate Change: Human Survival Strategies pp. 489–497.

Bourdieu, Pierre. 1980. *Outline of a Theory of Practice*. Cambridge University Press, Cambridge.

_____. 1990. *The Logic of Practice*. Stanford University Press, Stanford.

_____. 1984. *Distinction: A Social Critique of the Judgment of Taste*. Harvard University Press, Cambridge.

Boyd, Robert and Peter J. Richerson. 1985. *Culture and the Evolutionary Process*. University of Chicago Press, Chicago.

Browman, David L. and Douglas R. Givens. 1996. Stratigraphic Excavation: The First "New Archaeology." *American Anthropologist, New Series*. 98(1):80–95.

Brown, Dee. 2001. *Bury My Heart at Wounded Knee: An Indian History of the American West*. New York: Holt Paperbacks, 2001.

Brück, Joanna. 2005. "Experiencing the Past? The development of a phenomenological archaeology in British Prehistory." *Archaeological Dialogues* 12(1):45–72.

Brumfiel, Elizabeth. 1991. "Weaving and Cooking: women's production in Aztec Mexico", in J. Gero and M. Conkey, Engendering Archaeology, pp. 224–251. Blackwell, Oxford.

Brumfiel, Elizabeth and Timothy K. Earle (eds). 1987. *Specialization, exchange and Complex Societies*. Cambridge University Press, Cambridge.

Bryant, Chad. 2002. Either German of Czech: Fixing Nationality in Bohemia and Moravia, 1939–1946. *Slavic Review* 61(4):683–706.

Buchli, Victor, and Gavin Lucas (eds.). 2001a. *Archaeologies of the Contemporary Past*. Routledge, London.

_____. 2001b. "The Archaeology of Alienation: A Late Twentieth-Century British Council House", In Buchli and Lucas (eds.) *Archaeologies of the Contemporary Past*. Routledge, London, pp. 158–67.

Buikstra, Jane. 1984. "The Lower Illinois River Region: A Prehistoric Context for the Study of Ancient Health and Diet." In Paleopathology at the Origins of Agriculture. Mark N. Cohen and George Armelagos, eds., Academic Press. pp. 215–234.

Bullen, Adelaide and Ripley P. Bullen. 1945. "Black Lucy's Garden." *Bulletin of the Massachusetts Archaeological Society* VI(2):17–28.

Butler, Judith. 1990. *Gender Trouble*. Routledge, New York.

_____. 1993. *Bodies that Matter*. Routledge, New York.

Capo, Lissa. 2011. Throw me something mister: The history of Carnival Throws in New Orleans. The UNO Thesis and Dissertation Paper 1294.

Casella, Eleanor Conlin. 2000. 'Doing Trade": A Sexual economy of nineteenth-century Australian Female Convict Prisons. *World Archaeology* 32(2): 209–229.

Catalhoyuk: Excavations of a Neolithic Anatolian Hoyuk. "History of the Excavations." http://www.catalhoyuk.com/history.html

Childe, V. Gordon. 1936. *Man Makes Himself*. Collin, London.

Clark, Bonnie J. 2011. *On the Edge of Purgatory: An Archaeology of Place in Hispanic Colorado*. University of Nebraska Press, Lincoln.

Clark, Bonnie and Laurie A. Wilkie. 2007. "Prism of Self: Gender and Personhood." In *Identity and Subsistence: Gender Strategies for Archaeology*, edited by Sarah Nelson. Alta Mira Press, Walnut Creek

Cleto, Fabio (ed.) 1999 *Camp: Queer Aesthetics and the Performing Subject—A Reader*. Ann Arbor: University of Michigan Press.

CNN.com. news.blogs.cnn.com/2012/02/20/strict-new-french-quarter-curfew-nets-almost-200-mardi-gras-arrests (Website no longer accessible).

Coles, John. 1979. *Experimental Archaeology*. Academic Press, London.

Collins, Patricia Hill. 2000. *Black Feminist Thought*. 2nd Edition. Routledge, New York.

Cordell, Liinda S. and Maxine E. McBrinn. 2012. *Archaeology of the Southwest*, 3rd edition. Left Coast Press, Walnut Creek, CA.

Conkey, Margaret and Janet Spector. 1984. "Archaeology and the Study of Gender." *Advances in Archaeological Method and Theory*. 7:285–310.

Costello, Julia. 2000. "Red Light Voices: An Archaeological Drama of Late Nineteenth-Century Prostitution." In R. A. Schmidt and B. Voss (eds.) *Archaeologies of Sexuality*. Routledge, London.

Cutler, Anne. Jan 9, 2012, Environmental Group takes on 25 million pounds of Trash", www.ABC26.com

D'Emilio, John and Estell B. Freeman. 1997. *Intimate Matters: A History of Sexuality in America*. (second edition). Unviersity of Chicago Press, Chicago. Part III toward a new sexual order, 1880–1900. pp. 171–238.

Damon, P. E. D. J. Donahue, B. H. Gore, A. L. Hathaway, A. J. T. Jull, T. W. Linick, P. J. Sercel, L. J. Toolin, C. R. Bronk, E. T. Hall, R. E. M. Hedges, R. Housley, I. A. Law, C. Perry, G. Bonani, S. Trumbore, W. Woelfli, J. C. Ambers, S.G. E. Bowman, M.N. Leese and M.S. Trite. 1989. Radiocarbon Dating of the Shroud of Turin. *Nature* 337:6208:-611–615.

Daniels, William and Peter Bright. 1996. *The World's Writing Systems*. Oxford University Press, Oxford, England.

Davis, Angela. 1983. *Women, Race and Class*. Vintage Books, New York.

Deagan, Kathleen. 1983. *Spanish St. Augustine: The Archaeology of a Colonial Creole Commmuity*. Academic Press, New York.

DeCunzo, LuAnn. 1995. "Reform, Respite and Ritual: The Archaeology of Institutions: The Magdalen Society of Philadelphia." *Historical Archaeology*. Special Issue 29(3).

Deetz, James. 1977. *In Small Things Forgotten*. Anchor, New York.

Dethelsen, Eric, and James Deetz. 1966. "Death's Heads, Cherubs and Willow Trees: Experimental Archaeology in Colonial America." *American Antiquity* 31(4): 502–520

Diamond, Jared. 2005. *Guns, Germs, and Steel: The Fates of Human Societies*. W. W. Norton, New York.

Dietler, Michael. 2006. "Alcohol: Anthropological/Archaeological Perspective." *Annual Review of Anthropology*, 35:229–249.

_____. 1990. "Driven by drink: the role of drinking in the political economy and the case of Early Iron Age France." *Journal of Anthropological Archaeology*, 9:352-406.

Dowson, Thomas. 2000. "Why Queer Archaeology? An Introduction." *World Archaeology* 32(2):161–165.

Early, Eleanor. 1947. *New Orleans Holiday*. Rinehart and Co., Inc. New York.

Evans, Oliver. 1959. *New Orleans*. The MacMillan Co., New York.

Farnsworth, Paul. 1992. "Missions, Indians, and Cultural Continuity." *Historical Archaeology* 26(1): 22–36.

Fausset,Richard. 2012. "Mardi Gras Beads Cause Environmental Hangover" *Los Angeles Times*, Feb. 15, 2012

Feathers, James K. 1997. "The Application of Luminescence Dating in American Archaeology." *Journal of Archaeological Method and Theory* 4(1):1–66.

Feder, Kenneth L. 2006. *Frauds, Myths, and Mysteries: science and Pseudoscience in Archaeology*. 5th edition. McGraw Hill, New York.

Federal Writers' Project. 1938. *The Federal Writers' Project of the Works Progress Administration for the City of New Orleans, New Orleans' City Guide*. Houghton-Mifflin, Boston.

Feitosa, Lourdes Conde. 2013. "The Archaeology of Gender, Love and Sexuality in Pompei." BAR International Series 2533. Archeopress, Oxford, England.

Flannery, Kent V. and Joyce Marcus. 2012. *The Creation of Inequality: How our Prehistoric Ancestors Set the Stage for Monarchy, Slavery and Empire*. Harvard University Press, Cambridge, MA.

Flannery, Kent. .2006. On the Resilience of Anthropological Archaeology. *Annual Review of Anthropology* 35:1–13.

_____. 1982. The Golden Marshalltown: A Parable for the Archeology of the 1980s. *American Anthropologist*, New Series, 84(2):265–278.

_____. 1968. Archeological Systems theory and early Mesoamerica. In B. J. Meggers, (ed.) *Anthropological Archeology in the Americas*. Pp. 67–87. Anthropological Society of Washington, Washington.

Ford, James. 1961. "In favor of simple typology." *American Antiquity* 27(1):113–114.

Ford, James A. 1954. Comment on A.C. Spaulding, "Statistical Techniques for the Discovery of Artifact Types." *American Antiquity* 19(3):282–285.

Ford, James A. and Julian Steward. 1954. "On the Concept of Types." *American Anthropologist*, New Series, 56(1):42–57.

Fowler, Chris. 2004. *The Archaeology of Personhood: An Anthropological Approach*. London: Routledge.

Fox-Genovese, Elizabeth. 1988. *Within the Plantation Household: Black and White Women of the Old Plantation South*. University of North Carolina Press, Chapel Hill.

Francis, Peter J. 1999. *Beads of the World*. Schiffer Books, Atglen, PA.

Franklin, Maria. 1997. "Power to the People: Sociopolitics and the Archaeology of Black Americans." *Historical Archaeology* 31(3): 36–50.

_____. 2001. "A Black feminist-inspired archaeology?" *Journal of Social Archaeology* 1(1):108–125.

Freedman, Estelle B. 2003. *No Turning Back: the History of Feminism and the Future of Women*. Ballantine Books, New York.

Gaudet, Marcia G. 2001. "Mardi Gras Chic-a-la-Pie": Reasserting Creole Identity through Festive Play. *Journal of American Folklore* 114:154–172.

Geller, Pamela. 2005. Skeletal Analysis and Theoretical Complications. *World Archaeology* 37(4):597–609.

Gero, Joan. 1996. *Archaeological Practice and Gendered encounters with Field Data*. University of Pennsylvania Press, Philadelphia.

Gero, Joan and Margaret Conkey (eds). 1991. *Engendering Archaeology*. Blackwell, Oxford.

Giddens, Anthony. 1984. *The Constitution of Society*. University of California Press, Berkeley.

Giddings, Paula. 1984. *When and Where I Enter: The Impact of Black Women on Race and Sex in America*. William Morrow, New York.

Gilchrist, Roberta. 1994. *Gender and Material Culture: The Archaeology of Religious Women*. Routledge, London.

Gill, James. 1997. *The Lords of Misrule: Mardi Gras and the Politics of Race in New Orleans*. University Press of Mississippi, Jackson.

Gillespie, Susan. 2000. Rethinking Ancient Maya Social Organization: Replacing "Lineage" with "House." *American Anthropologist* 102(3):467–484.

Gist, Karen. 2008. "In the Throes of Bead-Flation", *Times Picayune*, February 2, 2008

Glassie, Henry. 1975. *Folk Housing in Middle Virginia: A Structural Analysis of Historic Artifacts*. University of Tennessee Press, Knoxville.

González-Ruibal, Alfredo. 2008. "Time to Destroy: An Archaeology of Supermodernity." *Current Anthropology* 49(2):247–79.

Gorman, Robert A. 1982. *Neo-Marxism: The Meanings of Modern Radicalism*. Praeger, New York.

Gotham, Kevin Fox. 2005. "Theorizing Urban Spectacles: Festivals, tourism and the transformation of urban space." *City*, 9(2):225–246.

_____. 2007. *Authentic New Orleans: Tourism, Culture, and Race in the Big Easy*. New York University Press, New York.

Gould, L. 2007. *Disaster Archaeology*. University of Utah Press, Salt Lake City, UT.

Gray, Herman. 1995. "Black Masculinity and Visual Culture." *Callaloo* 18(2):401–405.

Graves-Brown, Paul (ed.). 2000. *Matter, Materiality and Modern Culture*. Routledge, London.

Greenfield, Haskell J. 1999. "The Origins of Metullurgy: Distinguishing Stone from Metal Cut Marks on Bones From Archaeological Sites." *Journal of Archaeological Science* 26:797–808.

Greenwood, Roberta. 1980. "The Chinese on Main Street. In Robert Schuyler" (ed.). *Archaeological Perspectives on Ethnicity in America*. Pp. 131–143. Baywood Publishing Company, Inc., Farmingdale, New York.

Johnsen, Harald and Bjørnar Olsen. 1992. "Hermeneutics and Archaeology: On the Philosophy of Contextual Archaeology." *American Antiquity* 57 (3), 419–436.

Hardy, Arthur. 1987. *Arthur Hardy's Mardi Gras Guide*. Arthur Hardy, New Orleans. 11th edition.

_____. 1988. *Arthur Hardy's Mardi Gras Guide*. Arthur Hardy, New Orleans. 12th edition.

_____. 1990. *Arthur Hardy's Mardi Gras Guide*. Arthur Hardy, New Orleans. 13th edition.

_____. 1991. *Arthur Hardy's Mardi Gras Guide*. Arthur Hardy, New Orleans. 14th edition.

_____. 1992. *Arthur Hardy's Mardi Gras Guide*. Arthur Hardy, New Orleans. 15th edition.

_____. 1993. *Arthur Hardy's Mardi Gras Guide*. Arthur Hardy, New Orleans. 16th edition.

_____. 1994. *Arthur Hardy's Mardi Gras Guide*. Arthur Hardy, New Orleans. 17th edition.

_____. 1995. *Arthur Hardy's Mardi Gras Guide*. Arthur Hardy, New Orleans. 18th edition.

_____. 1996. *Arthur Hardy's Mardi Gras Guide*. Arthur Hardy, New Orleans. 19th edition.

_____. 1997. *Arthur Hardy's Mardi Gras Guide*. Arthur Hardy, New Orleans. 20th edition.

_____. 1998. *Arthur Hardy's Mardi Gras Guide*. Arthur Hardy, New Orleans. 21st edition.

Harris, Edward C. 1979. *The Principles of Archaeological Stratigraphy*. Academic Press, New York.

Harris, Marvin. 1968. *The Rise of Anthropological Theory*. Harper Collins, New York.

Harrison, Rodney and John Schofield. 2010. *After Modernity: Archaeological Approaches to the Contemporary Past*. Oxford University Press, Oxford.

Harvey, Keith. 2002. "Camp Talk and Citationality: A Queer Take on 'Authentic' and 'Represented' Utterances." Journal of Pragmatics. 34:1145–1165.

Hassan, Fekri A. 1978. Demographic Archaeology. *Advances in Archaeological Method and Theory*, 1:49–103.

Hastorf, Christine and Virginia Popper. 1989. *Current Paleoethnobotany*. University of Chicago Press, Chicago.

Hauser, Kitty. 2008. *Bloody Old Britain: O.G.S Crawford and he Archaeology of Modern Life*. Granta Books, London

Hawkes, C. F. 1954. "Archeological Theory and method: some suggestions from the Old World." *American Anthropologist* 56:155–168.

Hegmon, Michelle. 2003. "Setting Theoretical Egoes Aside: Issues and theory in North American Archaeology." *American Antiquity*, 68(2):213–243.

-----.2005. "No More theory Wars: A Response to Moss." *American Antiquity* 70(3):588–590.

Heizer, Robert. (ed.) 1978. *Handbook of North American Indians, Volume 8. California.* Smithsonian Institution Press, Washington, D. C.

Helms, Mary. 1993. Craft and the Kingly Ideal: Art, Trade, and Power. University of Texas Press, Austin

Hempel, Carl G. 1942. "The Function of General Laws in History." *The journal of Philosophy* 39:35–48.

_____. 1966. *Aspects of Scientific explanation, and Other essays in the Philosophy of Science.* Free press: New York.

Hennessy, Rosemary. 1994–1995. "Queer Visibility in Commodity Culture." *Cultural Critique* 29 (Winter):31– 76.

Hill, James. 1978. "Individuals and their artifacts: An experimental Study in Archaeology." *American Antiquity* 43(2):245–257.

Hodder, Ian. 1997. 'Always Momentary, Fluid and Flexible': towards a reflexive excavation methodology. *Antiquity* 71(273):691–700.

_____. 1991. Interpretive Archaeology and Its role. *Ame-rican Antiquity* 56(1):7–18.

_____. 1989. *The Meaning of Things.* Unwin Hyman, London.

_____. 1986. *Reading the Past.* Cambridge University Press, Cambridge.

_____. 1985. Postprocessual Archaeology. *Advances in Archaeological Method and Theory* 8:1–26.

_____.1982. Theoretical Archaeology : A Reactionary View. In *Symbolic and Structure Archaeology,* Ian Hodder, editor. Cambridge University Press, Cambridge, pp. 4–16.

1979. Economic and Social Stress and Material Cultural Patterns. *American Antiquity* 44:446–454.

_____. 1972. "The Interpretation of Spatial Patterns in Archaelogy: Two Examples." *Area* 4(4): 223-229.

Holtorf, Cornelius. 2007. *Archaeology is a brand! The meaning of archeology in popular culture.* Archaeopress, Oxford.

_____. 2005. *From Stonehenge to Las Vegas: Archaeology as Popular Culture.* Alta Mira Press, Walnut Creek

Holtorf, Cornelius and O. Ortman. 2008. "Endangerment and Conservation Ethos in Natural and Culture Heritage: The Case of Zoos and Archaeological Sites." *International Journal of Heritage Studies* 14(1):74–90.

hooks, bell. 1992. *Black Looks.* South End Press, Boston.

_____. 1994. *Outlaw Culture.* Routledge, New York.

Howlett Hayes, Katherine. 2013. *Slavery Before Race: Europeans, Africans and Indians at Long Islands Sylvester Manor Plantation, 1651–1884.* New York University Press, New York.

Hubbard, George D. 1943. "An Economic Future for Japan." *Economic Geography* 19(4):380–387.

Ingold, Tim. 2007. "Materials versus Materialities." *Archaeological Dialogues* 14(1):1–16.

_____. 1993. "The Temporality of the Landscape." *World Archaeology* 25(2): 24–174.

Isherwood, Christopher. 1954. *The World in the Evening.* New York: Methuen Press

Jargstorf, Sibylle. 1997. *Baubles, Buttons and Beads: The Heritage of Bohemia.* Schiffer Publications, LTD, London.

Johnson, Matthew. 1995. *Archaeology of Capitalism.* Wiley-Blackwell, Oxford.

Jones, Peter R. 1980. "Experimental Butchery with Modern Stone Tools and Its Relevance for Palaeolithic Archaeology." *World Archaeology* 12(2): 153–165.

Jones, Sian. 1997. *The Archaeology of Ethnicity.* Routledge, London.

Joyce, Rosemary. 2009. *Ancient Bodies, Ancient Lives.* Thames and Hudson, New York.

Joyce, Rosemary and Susan Gillespie. (eds.) 2000. *Beyond Kinship.* University of Pennsylvania Press, Pennsylvania.

Joyce, Rosemary and Lynn Meskell. 2003. *Embodied Lives.* Routledge, London.

Joyce, Rosemary and John S. Henderson. 2007. "From Feasting to Cuisine: Implications of Archaeological Research in an early Honduran Village." *American Anthropologist* 109(4):642–653.

Joyce, Rosemary, Robert W. Preucel, Jeanne Lopiparo, Carolyn Guyer, and Michael Joyce. 2002. *The Languages of Archaeology.* Blackwell Publishers, Oxford, England.

Katz, Slyvia. 1984. *Plastics: Common Objects, Classic Designs.* Abrams Publishers, New York.

Kidd, Kenneth. 1978. "Glass Bead-making from the Middle Ages to the Early 19th century." *History and Archaeology* 30. Canadian Historic Sites, Ottawa, Canada.

Kidder, A. V. 1924. An Introduction to the study of Southwestern Archaeology. *Papers of the southwestern Expedition*, Phillips Academy no. 1, New Haven.

Kilborn, John Collins. 1992. *Riutalistic exchange at Mardi Gras: An Examination of a Contemporary Urban Bacchic Ritual*. Master's Thesis, Department of Sociology. Louisiana State University, Baton Rouge.

Kinser, Samuel. 1990. *Carnival American Style: Mardi Gras at New Orleans and Mobile*. University of Chicago Press, Chicago.

Kirch, Patrick V. 2007. *The growth and collapse of Pacific island societies: archaeological and demographic perspectives*. University of Hawai'I Press, Honolulu.

_____. 1990. "The Evolution of Social Culture Complexity in Prehistoric Hawaii." *Journal of World Prehistory*. 4(3):311–345.

_____. 2012. *A Shark Going Inland Is My Chief*. University of California Press, Berkeley.

Kirschbaum, Stanislov J. 2006. *History of Slovakia*. 2nd Edition revised. Palgrave, Macmillan.

Knappet, Karl and Irene Nikolakopoulou in press. "Inside Out? Materiality and Connectivity in the Aegean Archipelao." In: *Cambridge Handbook of the Mediterranean World in the Bronze-Iron Ages*. Edited by A. B. Knapp and P. Van Dommelen. (http://www.academia.edu/353429/Inside_Out_Materiality_and_Connectivity_in_the_Aegean_Archipelago) Accessed October 28.

Kohler, Timothy A. and Mark D. Varien, (eds.). 2012. *Emergence and Collapse of Early Villages, Models of Central Mesa Verde Archaeology*. University of California Press, Berkeley.

Kohler, Timothy A., Mark D. Varien, and Aaron M. Wright, (eds.). 2010. *Leaving Mesa Verde: Peril and Change in the Thirteenth-Century Southwest*. Amerind Studies in Archaeology, University of Arizona Press, Tucson.

Kopytoff, Igor. 1986. "The Cultural Biography of Things: Commoditization as Process." In *The Social Life of Things*, A. Appadurai, ed. Cambridge University Press, Cambridge.

Kovel, Ralph and Terry Kovel. 1986. *Kovels' New Dictionary of Marks*. Crown Publishers, New York.

Krewe of Zulu. www.kreweofzulu.com (accessed

Kristiansen, Kristian. 2008. "Should Archaeology be in the Service of 'popular culture'? A theoretical and political critique of Cornelius Holtorf's Vision of Archaeology." *Antiquity* 82:488–492.

Kuhn, S. L. 1995. *Mousterian Lithic Technology: An Ecological Perspective*. Princeton University Press, Princeton.

Kuijt, Ian and Nigel Goring-Morris. 2002. "Foraging, Farming, and Social Complexity in the Pre Pottery Neolithic of the Southern Levant: A Review and Synthesis." *Journal of World Prehistory* 164:361–440.

Kulka, Tomes. 1966. *Kitsch and Art*. College Station: Penn State University Press.

Laidlaw, James. 2000. "A Free Gift Makes No Friends." *The Journal of the Royal Anthropological Institute* 6(4):617–634.

Lanford, William A. 1977. "Glass Hydration: A Method of Dating Glass Objects." *Science*, New Series, vol 196(4293):975–976.

LaRoche, Cheryl and Michael Blakey. 1997. "Seizing Intellectual Power: The Dialogue at the New York African Burial Ground." *Historical Archaeology* 31(3):84–106.

Latour, Bruno. 2005. *Reassembling the Social: An Introduction to Actor Network Theory*. Oxford University press, Oxford

Lazzari, Marisa. 2010. "Landscapes of Circulation in Northwest Argentina: The Workings of Osidian and Ceramics During the First Millennium AD." In: *Social Archaeologies of Trade and Exchange*, edited by Alexander A. Bauer and Anna S. Agbe-Davies, pp. 49–68. Left Coast Press, Walnut Creek.

Lee, Richard B. 1972. "!Kung Spatial Organization: An Ecological and Historical Perspective." *Human Ecology* 1(2):125–147.

Leonard, Robert D. 2001. "Evolutionary Archaeology." In: *Archaeological Theory Today*, Ian Hodder (ed.). Polity Press, Cambridge, pp. 65–97.

Leone, Mark 1977. "The New Mormon Temple in Washington, D. C." In: *Historical Archaeology and the Importance of Material Things*, ed. By Leland Ferguson. *Historical Archaeology*, special publication 2:43–61.

_____. 1982. "Some opinions about recovering mind." *American Antiquity* 47(4):742-760.

_____. 2005. *The Archaeology of Liberty in an American Capital*. University of California Press, Berkeley.

_____. 2010. *Critical Historical Archaeology*. Left Coast Press, Walnut Creek.

Lightfoot, Kent, Antoinette Martinez, and Ann M. Schiff. 1998. "Daily Practice and Material Culture in Pluralistic Social Settings: An Archaeological Study of Culture Change and Persistence from Fort Ross, California." *American Antiquity* 63(2): 199–222.

Lucas, Gavin. 2005. *The Archaeology of Time*. Taylor and Francis, London.

Lyman, R. Lee and Michael J. O'Brien. 1998. "The Goals of evolutionary Archaeology: History and Explanation." *Current Anthropology* 39:615–662.

Longacre, William and Michael W. Graves. 1976. "Probability Sampling Applied to an Early Multi-Component Surface Site in East-Central Arizona." *Kiva* 41(3/4):277–287.

Mardigrasneworleans.com. "Info: Proteus" http://www.mardigrasneworleans.com/schedule/parade-info/parades-proteus.html

_____. "Info: Elks Trucks" www.mardigrasneworleans.com /schedule/parade-ifno/parades-elk-orleans .html

McCash, Doug. February 10, 2012. "Catch and Release Trailer brings Instant Mardi Gras Beads Recycling." www.nola.com/mardigras/index.ssf/2012/02/catch_and_release_trailer_brin.html

McClung de Tapia, E. 1992. "The Origins of Agriculture in Mesoamerica and Central America." In: *The Origins of Agriculture: An International Perspective*, edited by C. W. Cowan, and P. J. Watson, pp. 143–171. Smithsonian Institution Press, Washington, D.C.

McGuire, Randall. 1982. "The Study of Ethnicity in Historical Archaeology." *The Journal of Anthropological Archaeology* 1(2):159–178.

_____. 2008. *Archaeology as Political Action*. University of California Press, Berkeley.

Marquardt, William H. 1978. "Advances in Archaeological Seriation." *Advances in Archaeological Method and Theory*, 1:257-314.

Martin, Naomi. 2012. "Baton Rouge Parades Get Shorter: City Limits Number of Floats." *Baton Rouge Morning Advocate*. February 14,2012.

Mauss, Marcel. 2011 [reprint of 1954 edition] *The Gift: Forms and Functions of Exchange in Archaic Societies*. Martino Fine books, New York.

McMains, Frank. 2010. We Did it Our Way. Baton Rouge 225. January 31, 2010.

Meskell, Lynn. 1999. *Archaeologies of Social Life*. Blackwell, Oxford.

Meyer, Moe. 2010. *An Archaeology of Posing: Essays on Camp, Drag and Sexuality*. Madison, WI: Macater Press.

Mildenberg, David. 2011. "Census finds post Katrina new Orleans Richer, Whiter, Emptier." *Bloomberg Reports, February 3, 2011.

Miller, George. 1980. "Classification and economic Scaling of Nineteenth-Century Ceramics." *Historical Archaeology* 14:1–42.

Miller, George. 1991. "A Revised Set of CC Index Values for Classification and Economic Scaling of English Ceramics from 1787 to 1880." *Historical Archaeology* 25(1):1–25.

Mindsmedia. 2002. "New Orleans Mardi Gras 1947 in color." Posted Youtube. January 11, 2008.

Mitchell, Reid. 1995. *All on a Mardi Gras Day*. Harvard University Press, Cambridge,MA.

Morris, Ian. 1986. "Gift and Commodity in Archaic Greece." *Man* 21(1):1–17.

Mullins, Paul. 1999. *Race and Affluence: An Archaeology of African America and Consumer Culture*. Kluwer Academic/Plenum, New York.

Munsey, Cecil. 1970. *The Illustrated Guide to Collecting Bottles*. Hawthorn Books, Inc. Publishers, New York.

Mytum, Harold. 2003/2004. "Artefact Biography as an Approach to Material Culture: Irish Gravestones as a material form of Genealogy." *Journal of Irish Archaeology*. 12/13:111–127.

Nance, Jack D. 1981. "Statistical Fact and Archaeological Faith: Two Models in Small-Sites sampling." *Journal of Field Archaeology* 8(2):151–165.

Narayan, Uma. 1997. *Dislocating Cultures: Identities, Traditions, and Third-World Feminism*. Routledge, New York.

Nash, Stephen E. Archaeological Tree-Ring Dating at the Millenium. *Journal of Archaeological Research* 10(3):243–275).

National Science Foundation. "Timeline of NSF History." http://www.nsf.gov/news/special_reports/history-nsf/timeline/index.jsp (accessed date here)

Nečas, Jaromir. 1937. "Economic and Social Problems in German-Bohemia." *The Slavonic and East European Review*, 15(45):599–611.

Neff, Hector. 1993. "Theory, Sampling, and Analytical Techniques in the Archaeological Study of Prehistoric Ceramics." *American Antiquity* 58(1):22–44.

Newman, T. Stell. 1970. "A Dating Key for Post-Eighteenth Century Bottles." *Historical Archaeology* 4:70–75.

Nicholas, George (ed.). 2010. *Being and Becoming Indigenous Archaeologists*. Left Coast Press, Walnut Creek.

NoAids Task Force. "History." www.noaidstaskforce.org /history

Noel-Hume, Ivor. 1969. *Guide to Artifacts of Colonial America*. Alfred A. Knopf, New York.

Nolan, Bruce. 2012. "Bitter Mardi Gras Debate of Race, Class evolves 20 years later into a diverse celebration." *New Orleans Times Picayune*, February 12, 2012.

Oanda.com. "Historical Exchange Rates" (http://www .oanda.com/currency/historical-rates/)

O'Brien, Michael J. and R. Lee Lyman. 2000. *Applying Evolutionary Archaeology: A Systematic Approach.* Plenum Press, New York.

O'Brien, Michael J., R. Lee Lyman and John Darwent. 2000. "Time, Space, and Marker Types: James A. Ford's 1936 Chronology for the Lower Mississippi Valley." *Southeastern Archaeology* 19(1):46–62.

The Onion. "Mardi Gras 2006?." October 21, 2005, Issue 41–42. www.theonion.com/articles/mardi-gras-20 06,14851

Olsen, Bjørnar, Michael Shanks, Timothy Webmoor, and Christopher Witmore. 2012. *Archaeology: The Discipline of Things.* University of California Press, Berkeley.

Oneal, Marion Sherrard. 1965. "New Orleans Scenes." *Louisiana History: The Journal of the Louisiana Historical Association* 6(2):189–209.

Orser, Charles E., Jr, 2007. *The Archaeology of Race and Racialization.* University Press of Florida, Gainesville.

———. 2002a. Terminus Post Quem. In Charles E. Orser, Jr. (ed.). *Encyclopedia of Historical Archaeology*, Rout-ledge, New York, p. 541.

———. 2002b Terminus Ante Quem . In *Encyclopedia of Historical Archaeology*, Charles E.

Orser, Jr. (ed.). Routledge, New York, p. 540.

———. 2001. (ed.). *Race and the Archaeology of Identity.* University of Utah Press, Salt Lake City.

Patterson, Thom. 2006. "Let the Good Times Roll (but not too much)", February 27, 2006, CNN. (articles. cnn.com/2006-02-24/us/differentmardi-gras-guide-zulu-social-aid?_s=PM:US)

Pauketat, Timothy R. 2009. *Cahokia: Ancient America' Great City on the Mississippi.* Viking, New York.

———. 2007. *Chiefdoms and other archaeological delusions.* Alta Mira press, Lanham.

-----. 2001 (ed.) *The Archaeology of Traditions.* University Press of Florida, Gainesville.

Pauketat, T., Lucretia S. Kelly, Gayle J. Fritz Neal H. Lopinot, Scott Elias and Eve Hargrave.

2002. "The Residues of Feasting and Public Ritual at early Cahokia." *American Antiquity* 67:257–279.

Penner, D'Ann R. and Keith C. Ferdinand (eds.) 2009. *Overcoming Katrina: African American Voices from the Crescent City and Beyond.* Palgrave, Mamillan, New York.

Perlin, Susan A., Ken Sexton, and David S. Wong. 1999. "An Examination of Race and Poverty for Populations living near industrial sources of air pollution." *Journal of Exposure Analysis and Environmental Epidemiology* 9:29–48.

Picard, John and Ruth Picard. 1995. *Prosser Beads Revisited.* Bead Collector Network. http://www.bead collector.net/picards/

Piperno, Dolores R. 2009. "Identifying crop Plants with Phytoliths (and starch grains) in Central and South America: A review and update on the Evidence." *Quarternary International* 113(1–2):146–159.

Plog, Stephen. 1978. "Sampling in Archaeological Surveys: A Critique." *American Antiquity* 43(2):280–285.

Pluckhahn, T. J., J. Compton, J. Matthew, and M.T. Bohage-Freund. 2006. "Evidence of Small-Scale Feasting from the Woodland Period Site of Kolomoki, Georgia." *Journal of Field Archaeology* 31(3):-263–284.

Popper, Karl. 1959. *The Logic of Scientific Discovery.* Basic Books: New York.

Price, Douglas T., Jmaes H. Burton, Andrea Cucina, Pilar Zabala, Robert Frei, Robert Ykot and Vera Tiesler. 2012. "Isotopic Studies of Human Skeletal Remains from a Sixteenth to Seventeenth Century AD Churchyard in Campeche, Mexcio: Diet, Place of Origin and Age." *Current Anthropology* 53(4): 396–433.

Raab, L. Mark and Albert C. Goodyear. 1984. "Middle Range Theory In Archaeology : A Critical Review of Origins and Applications." *American Antiquity* 49(2):255–268.

Radcliffe-Browne, 1952. *Structure and Function on Primitive Society.* Cohen and West, London.

Ralph, Julian. 1893. New Orleans, Our Southern Capital. *Harper's New Monthly Magazine* 0086(513, Feb 1893) : 364–386.

Ransley, Jesse. 2005. "Boats are for Boys: Queering Maritime Archaeology." *World Archaeology* 37(4): 621–629.

Rathje, William. 1979. "Modern Material culture Studies." *Advances in Archaeological Method and Theory* 2:1–37.

Rathje, William and C. Murphy. 2001. *Rubbish! The Archaeology of Garbage.* Harper Collins, New York.

Rawls, Alex. 2012. "Krewe of Muses Mardi Gras Throws."

Redman, Charles. 1973. "Multistage Fieldwork and Analytical Techniques." *American Antiquity* 38(1):61–79.

Redman, Charles. 1987. "Surface Collection, sampling, and Research Design: A Retrospective." *American Antiquity* 52(2):249–265.

Redmon, David. 2005. *Mardi Gras: Made in China*. Documentary film, Carnivalesque Studios.

Rego, J. L. and C. Li. 2009. "On the Receding of Storm Surge along Louisiana's Low Lying Coast." *Journal of Coastal Research, Special Issue 56. Proceedings of the 10th International Coast Symposium* ICS 2009. Volume II (2009). Pp. 1045–1049.

Renfrew, Colin and Paul Bahn. 1996. *Archaeology: Theories, Methods and Practice*. Second Edition. Thames and Hudson, London.

Rex official website, "Tradition." http://www.rexorganization.com/Tradition

Roach, Joseph. 1993. "Carnival and the Law in New Orleans." *TDR* 37(3):42–75.

Roberts, Dorothy. 1997. *Killing the Black Body*. Pantheon Books, New York

Robinson, M.J. 2000. "The Poetics of Camp in the Films of Alfred Hitchcock." *Rocky Mountain Review of Language and Literature* 54(1):53–65.

Rodger, Gillian. 2004. "Drag, Camp and Gender Subversion in the Music and Videos of Annie Lennox." *Popular Music* 23(1):17–29.

Rollo, Franco Massimo Ubaldi, Luca Ermin and Isolina Marota. 2002. "Otzi's Last Meals: DNA Analysis of the Intestinal Content of the Neolithic Glacier Mummy from the Alps." *Proceedings of the National Academy of Sciences of the United States of America* 99(20):12594–12599.

Rose, Al. 1978. *Storyville, New Orleans: Being an Authentic, Illustrated Account of the Notorious Red Light District*. University of Alabama Press, Tuscaloosa.

Rowe, John H. 1961. "Stratigraphy and Seriation." *American Antiquity* 26(3):324–330.

Rutland, Lucile. 1927. *Jacques Rides in a Lotus Flower: Reminiscence of A New Orleans Mardi Gras*. Kentell Shop, Covington, LA.

Rubertone, Patricia. 2001. *Grave Undertakings: An Archaeology of Roger Williams and the Narragansett Indians*. Smithsonian Institution Press, Washington, DC and London.

Sabloff, J. A. and G. R. Willey. 1967. "The collapse of Maya civilization in the southern lowlands: A consideration of history and process." *Southwestern Journal of Anthropology* 23:311–36.

Sahlins, Marshall D., and Elman Service. 1960. *Evolution and Culture*. University of Michigan Press, Ann Arbor, Michigan

Saitta, Dean. 1997. "Power, Labor and Change in the Chacoan Political Economy." *American Antiquity* 62:7–26.

_____. 2007. *The Archaeology of Collective Action*. University Press of Florida, Gainesville.

Salmon, Merillee 1978. "What Can Systems Theory Do for Archaeology?" *American Antiquity*, Vol. 43, No. 2, Contributions to Archaeological Method and Theory (Apr., 1978), pp. 174–183

Saunders, Rebecca. 2002. "Tell the Truth: The Archaeology of Human Rights Abuses in Guatemala and the Former Yugoslavia." In: Schofield, Johnson, and Beck, (Eds.) *Matérial Culture: The Archaeology of Twentieth Century Conflict*. Routledge, London, pp.103–114.

Saxon, Lyle. 1928. *Fabulous New Orleans*. Pelican Press, New Orleans [1989 reprint].

Saxon, Lyle, Edward Dreyer and Robert Tallant. 1989. *Gumbo Ya Ya*. Pelican Books, New York.

Sciama, Lidia and Joanne Eicher (eds). 1998. *Beads and Beadmakers* Berg Publishers, London.

Schiffer, Michael. 1987. Formation Processes of the Archaeological Record. University of New Mexico Press, Albuquerque.

Schiffer, Michael B., James M. Skibo, J.F. Griffitts, K.L. Hollenbeck, William Longacre. 2001. "Behavioral Archaeology and the Study of Technology." *American Antiquity* 66(4):729–738.

Schiffer, Michael B., James M. Skibo, tamara C. Boelke, Mark A. Neupert, Meredith Aronson. 1994. "New Perspectives on Experimental Archaeology: Surface Treatments and Thermal response of the Clay Cooking Pot." *American Antiquity* 59(2):197–217.

Schindler, Henri. 1997. *Mardi Gras, New Orleans*. Flammarion Press,

Schuyler, Michael T. 2004. "Camp for Camp's Sake: Absolutely Fabulous, Self-Consciousness and the Mae West Debate." *Journal of Film and Video* 56 (4): 3–20.

Schuyler, Robert (ed.). 1980. *Archaeological Perspective on Ethnicity in America: Afro-American and Asian American Culture History*. Baywood Publishing Company, Farmingdale, N.Y.

Sclanger, N. 1996. "Understanding Levallois: Lithic Technology and Cognitive Archaeology." *Cambridge Archaeological Journal* 6(2):231–254.

Scott, Linda M. 2004. *Fresh Lipstick: Redressing Fashion and Feminism*. Palgrave Macmillan, New York.

Scott, Liz. 1979. *The Reach and Screech Manual: Or How to Survive Mardi Gras*. Long Measure Press, New Orleans, LA.

Sedgewick, Eve Kosofsk. 1990. *Epistemology of the Closet*. Berkeley: University of California Press.

Seifert, Donna. (ed.) "Gender in Historical Archaeology." *Historical Arcaheology* 25(4). Special Issue.

Seifert, Donna. (ed.) 2005. Sin City. *Historical Archaeology* 39:1. Special Issue.

Searight, Sarah. 1973. *New Orleans*. Stein and Day Publishers, New York.

Semaw, Sileshi. 2000. "The World's Oldest Stone Artefacts from Gona, Ethiopia: Their Implications for Understanding Stone Technology and Patterns of Human Evolution between 2.6 to 1.5 Million Years Ago." *Journal of Archaeological Science* 27: 1197–1214.

Shackel, Paul. 1996. *Culture Change and the New Technology: An Archaeology of the Early American Industrial Era*. Plenum, New York.

Shackley, M. Steven. 2005. *Obsidian: Geology and Arch aeology in North American Archaeology*. University of Arizona Press, Tucson.

Shanks, Michael. 2007. "Symmetrical Archaeology." *World Archaeology* 39(4):589–596.

_____. 1991. *Experiencing the Past*. Routledge, London.

Shanks, Michael and Christopher Tilley. 1987. *Social Theory and Archaeology*. University of New Mexico Press, Albuquerque.

Shapiro, Beth and Michael Hofreiter (eds) 2012. *Ancient DNA: Methods and Protocals*. Humana Press, New York.

Shott, Michael J. 1987. "Feature Discovery and the Sampling Requirements of Archaeological evaluations." *Journal of Field Archaeology* 14(3):359–371.

Sillar, Bill. 1994. "Playing with God : Cultural perceptions of children, play and miniatures in the Andes." *Archaelogical Review from Cambridge* vol. 13, no2, pp. 47–63

Silliman, Stephen. 2004. *Lost Laborers in Colonial California: Native American and the Archaeology of Rancho Petaluma*. University of Arizon Press, Tucson.

Sofaer-Derevenski, Joanne. 1994. "Where are the Children?: Accessing Children in the Past." *Archaeological Review from Cambridge* 13(2):7–12.

_____. (ed.) 2000. *Children and Material Culture*. Routledge, New York.

Sontag, Susan. 1966 "Notes on Camp." In: *Against Interpretation*. New York: Picador Press.

South, Stanley. 1977. *Method and Theory in Historical Archaeology*. Academic Press, New York.

Spaulding, Albert C. 1953. "Statistical Techniques for the Discovery of Artifact Types." *American Antiquity* 18(4):305–313.

Spelman, E. V. 1988. *Inessential Woman*. Beacon Press, Boston.

Spencer-Wood, Suzanne. (ed.) 1987. *Consumer Choice in Historical Archaeology*. Plenum, New York.

Sprague, Roderick. 2002. "China or Prosser Buttons: Identification and Dating." *Historical Archaeology* 35(2):111–127.

Stanonis, Anthony. 2001. "Always in Costume and Mask": Lyle Saxon and New Orleans Tourism. *Louisiana History: The Journal of the Louisiana Historical Association*. 42(1):31–57.

Steele, C. 2008. "Archaeology and the Forensic Investigation of Recent mass Graves: Ethical Issues for a New Practice of Archaeology." *Archaeologies* 4(3):414–28.

Steward, Julian. 1942. "The Direct Historical Approach and Archaeology." *American Antiquity* 7(4):337–343.

_____. 1951. "Levels of Sociocultural Integration: An Operational Concept." *Southwestern Journal of Anthropoloogy* 7(4):374–390.

_____. 1956. "Cultural Evolution." *Scientific American* 194:69–80.

Steward, Julian and Frank Setzler. 1938. "Function and Configuration in Archaeology." *American Antiquity* 4:4–10.

Steward, Jane, and Robert C. Murphy (eds). 1977. *Evolution and Ecology: Julian Steward Essays on Social Transformation*. University of Illinois Press, Urbana.

Stěpánek, Bedrich. 1922. "Economic and Financial Reconstruction of Czechoslovakia." *Annals of the American Academy of Political and Social Science*. Vol. 102 America and the Rehabilitation of Europe. July 1922, pp. 1–13.

Stocking, George W., Jr. (ed.) 1974. *A Franz Boas Reader: The Shaping of American Anthropology, 1883–1911*. University of Chicago Press, Chicago.

_____. 1987. *Victorian Anthropology*. The Free Press, New York.

Storm Warning IV. http://www.stormwarning4.com/ (website no longer accessible)

Strathern, Marilyn. 1988. *The Gender of the Gift*. University of California Press, Berkeley.

Sutton, Mark. 2010. *Paleonutrition*. University of Arizona Press, Tucson.

Tallant, Robert. 1948. *Mardi Gras*. Pelican Press, New Orleans [1989 reprint].

Taylor, Walter. 1948. "A Study of Archaeology." *American Anthropological Association Memoir*, no 69. Southern Illinois University Press, Carbondale.

Thomas, Julian. 2004. *Archaeology and Modernity*. Routledge, London.

Thomas, Julian. 1996. *Time, Culture and Identity*. Routledge, London.

The Times Picayune. 1924. *The Tourist's Guide to New Orleans*. 14th Edition. Times Picayune, New Orleans.

Tinker, Edward Larocque. 1953. *The Creole City: Its Past and Its People*. Longmans, Green and co., New York.

Tinkcom, Mathew. 1996. "Working like a homosexual: Camp Visual Codes and the Labor of Gay Subjects in the MGM Freed Unit." *Cinema Journal* 35(2):24–42.

Tilley, Christopher. 1997. *A Phenomenology of Landscape*. Berg, London.

Tokofsky, Peter. 1999. "Masking Gender: A German Carnival Custom in Its Social Context." *Western Folklore*. Vol. 58(3/4:299–318).

Trigger, Bruce. 1989. *A History of Archaeological Thought*. Cambridge University Press, Cambridge.

Trilussa. 2008. "Mardi Gras 1957, High Quality." Posted November 14, 2008 on www.youtube.com.

Turner, B. L. and Jeremy Sabloff. 2012. "Classic Period Collapse of the Central Maya Lowlands: Insights about human-environment relationships for sustainability." *Proceedings of the National Academy of Sciences*, August 21, 2012.

Turnbough, William. "Calumet Ceremonialism as a Nativistic Response." *American Antiquity*, Vol. 44, No. 4 (Oct., 1979), pp. 685–691

Tv.boingboing.net. n.d. 1956 Footage of Krewe of Midcity Parade.

Vita Finzi, C and Higgs, E S. 1970. "Prehistoric Economy in the Mount Carmel Area of Palestine; Site Catchment Analysis." *Proceedings of the Prehistoric Society*, XXXVI, 1–37

Voss, Barbara. 2008. "Sexuality Studies in Archaeology." *Annual Review of Anthropology* 37(1):317–336.

---- 2000. "Feminisms, Queer Theories and the Archaeological Study of Past Sexuality." *World Archaeology* 32(2):180–192.

Voss, Barbara and Elenor Conlin Casella, eds. 2012. *The Archaeology of Colonialism: Intimate Encounters and Sexual Effects*. Cambridge University Press, Cambridge.

Voss, Barbara and Robert Schmidt. (eds.) 2001. *Archaeologies of Sexuality*. Routledge, London and New York.

Walker, Evan. "Canine Case Closed?." *Archaeology Archive*. July 14 2004. http://archive.archaeology.org/online/features/dogs

Walker, P. L. and Sandra E. Holliman. 1989. "Changes in Osteoarthritis associated with the development of a maritime economy among southern California Indians." *International Journal of Anthropology* 4(3):171–183.

Wall, Diane di Zerga. 1994. *The Archaeology of Gender: Separating the Spheres in Urban America*. Plenum, New York.

Walters, Margaret. 2005. *Feminism: A Very short Introduction*. Oxford University Press, Oxford.

Watts, Annette. February 23, 2006. blog.nola.com/bourbon/2006/02/mardi_gras_were_sving_what_we .html (webpage no longer accessible)

Watson, Patty Jo, Steven A. LeBlanc, and Charles L. Redman. 1984. *Archaeological Explanation: The Scientific Method in Archeology*. Columbia University Press, New York.

Ware, Carolyn E. 2007. *Cajun Women and Mardi Gras: Reading the Rules Backward*. University of Illinois Press, Urbana.

Warrick, Gary. 2005. "European Infectious Disease and Depopulation of the Wendat Tionotate (Huron-Petun)." *World Archaeology* 35(2):258–275.

Watkins, Joe Edward. 2001. *Indigenous Archaeology: American Indian values and Scientific Practice*. Alta Mira Press, Walnut Creek.

_____. 2006. *Sacred sites and Repatriation*. Chelsea House Publishers, Philadelphia.

Whelan, Mary. 1991. "Gender and Historical Archaeology: East Dakota Patterns in the Nineteenth Century." *Historical Archaeology* 25(4):17-32.

Whoopwaah. 2009. "Mardi Gras in the 1960s." Posted August 14, 2009 on www.youtube.com.

White, Leslie. 1959. *The Evolution of Culture: The Development of Civilization to the Fall of Rome*. McGraw-Hill, New York.

Wilk, Richard. 1988. "Maya Household Organization." In: *Household and Community in the Mesoamerican Past*, edited by R. Wilk and W. Ashmore. University of New Mexico Press, Albuquerque, pp. 135–169.

Wilkie, Laurie A. 2010 *The Lost Boys of Zeta Psi*. University of California Press, Berkeley.

_____. 2003. *The Archaeology of Mothering: An African-American Midwife's Tale*. Routledge, New York.

_____. 2000. *Creating Freedom: Material Culture and African-American Identity at Oakley Plantation, Louisiana, 1845-1950*. Louisiana State University Press, Baton Rouge.

Wilkie, Laurie A. 1998. Beads and Breasts: the Negotiation of Gender Roles and Power at New Orleans *Mardi Gras*. In *Beads and Beadmakers* edited by Lidia Sciama and Joanne Eicher, Berg Publishers, London, pp. 193–211.

———. 1996. "Glass-knapping at a Louisiana plantation: African-American tools?" *Historical Archaeology 30(4):37–49*

Wilkie, Laurie A. and Paul Farnsworth. 2005. *Sampling Many Pots*. University Press of Florida, Gainesville.

Wilkie, Laurie A. and George W. Shorter, Jr. 2001. "Lucrecia's Well: An Archaeological Glimpse of an African-American Midwife's Household." University of South Alabama Center for Archaeological Studies Mobile, Alabama.

Willey, G. R. and J. A. Sabloff. 1974. *A history of American Archaeology*. Thames and Hudson, London.

Wilson, E.O. 1975. *Sociobiology: The New Synthesis*. Harvard University Press, Cambridge, MA.

Winkler-Schmit, David. 2007. "Mardi Gras Sisterhood: All-female krewes are redefining Carnival with a Woman's Touch." *Gambit*. Februrary 13, 2007.

Winterhaulder, Bruce and Eric Alden Smith (eds) 1981. *Hunter-Gather Foraging Strategies: Ethnographic and Archeological Analyses*. University of Chicago Press, Chicago.

Wisconsin Historical Society. "Preservation of Wisconsin Archaeological Sites." https://www.wisconsinhistory.org/archaeology/preserve/

Witmore, Christopher. 2007. "Symmetrical Archaeology: Excerpts of a manifesto." *World archaeology* 39(4):546–562.

Wolfiered1. 2007. "Mardi Gras Exposed: 1954." Posted October 13, 2007 on www.youtube.com.

Xie, C.Z., C. X. Li, Y. Qu. Cui, Q. C. Zhang, Y. Q. Fu, H. Zhu and H. Zhou. 2007. "Evidence of Ancient DNA evidence for first European Lineage in Iron Age Central Chine." Proceedings: *Biological Science* vol. 274(1618):1597–1601.

Young, Perry. 1939. *Carnival and Mardi Gras in New Orleans*. Harmanson's, New Orleans.

Zimmerman, Larry and Jessica Welch. 2011. "Displaced and Barely Visible: Archaeology and the Material Culture of Homelessness." *Historical Archaeology* 45(1): 67–85.

Zimmerman, Larry J., J. D. McDonald, W. Tall Bull, and T. Rising Sun. 1991. "The Cheyenne Outbreak of 1879: Using Archaeology to Document Northern Cheyenne Oral History." In R. Paynter and R. McGuire (eds.), *The Archaeology of Inequality*. Oxford: Basil Blackwell. pp. 64–78.

http://www.arcgno.org

http://goneneworleans.about.com/od/mardigras/p/Proteus.html

http://thesga.org/2005/04/loss-of-georgias-archaeological-heritage-detailed/).

INDEX

N

ABOUT THE AUTHOR

Laurie Wilkie completed her undergraduate work in Anthropology at Syracuse University and her MA and PhD in the Archaeology Program at UCLA. While completing her doctoral work, she conducted research and taught in southern Louisiana, where she first became acquainted with Mardi Gras celebrations in the area. She joined the faculty at the University of California, Berkeley in 1995, and has been there ever since. Wilkie has conducted archaeological field research in the Caribbean, American South, Texas, and California. She is the author of *Creating Freedom* (LSU Press: 2000), *The Archaeology of Mothering* (Routledge: 2003), *Sampling Many Pots* (with Paul Farnsworth, University of Florida Press: 2005), and *The Lost Boys of Zeta Psi* (University of California Press: 2010). In her spare time, Wilkie herds cats and her teenager, and chases her husband up rock walls.